PREHISTORY AND HUMAN ECOLOGY
OF THE VALLEY OF OAXACA

Kent V. Flannery and Joyce Marcus
General Editors

Related Volumes

Flannery, Kent V.
1986   *Guilá Naquitz: Archaic Foraging and Early Agriculture in Oaxaca, Mexico*. New York: Academic Press.

Flannery, Kent V., and Joyce Marcus
2003   *The Cloud People: Divergent Evolution of the Zapotec and Mixtec Civilizations*. Clinton Corners, NY: Percheron Press.

Marcus, Joyce, and Kent V. Flannery
1996   *Zapotec Civilization: How Urban Society Evolved in Mexico's Oaxaca Valley*. London: Thames and Hudson.

Frontispiece. Village life in the Valley of Oaxaca began on this piedmont spur overlooking the Atoyac River. Settlement took hold in Area C, spread to Area B, then Area A, and eventually moved beyond the right-hand margin of the photograph. The site's Main Plaza (between Mounds 1 and 8) was laid out during Monte Albán II. (Aerial photo by C. L. Moser.)

Museum of Anthropology, University of Michigan
Memoirs, Number 40

PREHISTORY AND HUMAN ECOLOGY
OF THE VALLEY OF OAXACA

Kent V. Flannery and Joyce Marcus
General Editors
Volume 13

Excavations at San José Mogote 1
The Household Archaeology

by Kent V. Flannery and Joyce Marcus

with a multidimensional scaling of houses
by Robert G. Reynolds

ANN ARBOR
2005

Printed in the United States of America
ISBN 0-915703-59-9

Cover design by Katherine Clahassey

The University of Michigan Museum of Anthropology currently publishes two monograph series: Anthropological Papers and Memoirs, as well as an electronic series in CD-ROM form. For a complete catalog, write to Museum of Anthropology Publications, 4009 Museums Building, Ann Arbor, MI 48109-1079.

Library of Congress Cataloging-in-Publication Data

Flannery, Kent V.
  Excavations at San José Mogote 1 : the household archaeology / by Kent V. Flannery and Joyce Marcus ; with a multidimensional scaling of houses by Robert G. Reynolds.
     p. cm. -- (Memoirs ; no. 40) (Prehistory and human ecology of the Valley of Oaxaca ; v. 13)
  Includes bibliographical references and index.
  ISBN 0-915703-59-9 (alk. paper)
  1. Indians of Mexico--Mexico--San José Mogote--Antiquities. 2. Indian pottery--Mexico--San José Mogote. 3. Excavations (Archaeology)--Mexico--San José Mogote. 4. San José Mogote (Mexico)--Antiquities. I. Title: Excavations at San José Mogote one. II. Marcus, Joyce. III. University of Michigan. Museum of Anthropology. IV. Title. V. Series. VI. Memoirs of the Museum of Anthropology, University of Michigan ; no. 40.
  GN2.M52 no. 40
  [F1219.1.S215]
  306--dc22

                                2005002562

*dedicated to the memory
of three founding members
of the Oaxaca Project*

Eligio Martínez, 1935-1989

William O. Payne, 1918-2002

C. Earle Smith, Jr., 1922-1987

Contents

Tables

Illustrations

Acknowledgments

Excavations began at San José Mogote, Oaxaca in 1966 and continued until 1980. The analysis of our data on household archaeology took another twenty years, from 1981 to 2001. Our analyses of public buildings, cognitive archaeology, and burials are ongoing at this writing. We have not finished with San José Mogote, and would be working there today were it not for our obligation to report fully on what we have already done. The road to perdition is paved with archaeologists who dug for so many years that they died without publishing.

When a project lasts for more than thirty years, there are so many people to thank that one hardly knows where to start. Let us begin with the officers of Mexico's Instituto Nacional de Antropología e Historia who gave us permission to work in Oaxaca. The late Ignacio Bernal, José Luis Lorenzo, and Guillermo Bonfil showed confidence in us by issuing some of our first permits; we wish that they had lived to receive a copy of this report. Enrique Florescano, Angel García Cook, Joaquín García-Bárcena, and Eduardo Matos Moctezuma oversaw our later permits. From the Consejo de Arqueología, and especially Linda Manzanilla, we received great support and encouragement. Because Linda does household archaeology herself, she knew what we were trying to accomplish.

Before the creation of the INAH Regional Center in Oaxaca, we were greatly helped by INAH representative Lorenzo Gamio. The first Director of the Centro Regional de Oaxaca, Manuel Esparza, took such an active interest in our work that we literally could not fail. Other members of the Centro Regional – María de los Angeles Romero Frizzi, Nelly Robles, Roberto Zárate, Raúl Matadamas, Ernesto González Licón, Arturo Oliveros, and others – provided invaluable support.

The first grant we received was from the Smithsonian Institution. It supported the 1966 excavation of Area A at San José Mogote (in addition to work at Guilá Naquitz Cave, Cueva Blanca, and the Martínez Rockshelter). Our next four grants came from the National Science Foundation, as follows: GS-1616 (1967), GS-2121 (1968), GS-42568 (1974), and BNS-7805829 (1978). Thank you, John Yellen (and all your predecessors)! More recently, we have received grants for additional radiocarbon dating from the Office of the Vice President for Research, University of Michigan (2003) and from the Foundation for the Advancement of Mesoamerican Studies Inc. (2004). We acknowledge their generous support, as well as special advice from Darden Hood at Beta Analytic Inc.

Because grants to our Oaxaca Project were used for many tasks at many sites, it is not easy to calculate exactly how much was allocated to Formative houses at San José Mogote. Our best estimate is that the household archaeology reported in this volume resulted from $200,000 worth of research. That sounds like a lot of money, but spread out over 15 years of field work, it averages out to less than $14,000 per field season.

The people of San José Mogote and Guadalupe Etla embraced our project from the beginning. So many *vecinos* of both villages worked for us that it is impossible to list them all. The family of Heliodoro and Delfina Jiménez virtually allowed us to turn their home into a field station. We are grateful to them and to their sons, Armando and Isaac Jiménez, who not only worked in the excavation but also labeled thousands of potsherds. Heliodoro's brother, Carlos Jiménez, became such a knowledgeable excavator that the INAH Regional Center appointed him Archaeological Inspector for the Etla District. Carlos's son Israel was just a toddler in 1966; he entertained us by helping to search for pieces of magnetite on the surface of Area A. By 1980, the former toddler had grown to be one of our best workmen. How do you thank all the people who invited us into their homes and let us watch their children grow up, marry, and have children of their own?

We arrived at San José Mogote in 1966 with a group of six workmen from Mitla, all veterans of the excavations at Guilá Naquitz and Cueva Blanca. It was their job to help teach neophyte workmen at San José Mogote our method of excavation. In a different village, the Mitleños might have been resented. At San José Mogote they were accepted immediately. By the end of the first week, an intervillage trade system had been established: kilos of San José Mogote's mozzarella-like cheese (*quesillo*) were exchanged for bottles of Mitla's *mezcal de gusano*.

We are grateful to the six Mitleños who accompanied us on so many excavations. Two of them – Ernesto Martínez and Pablo García – have since been appointed INAH custodians of the ruins of Mitla. We are sad to report that our gifted dig foreman and Zapotec interpreter, Eligio Martínez, eventually found work in the United States, where he became one more victim of senseless handgun violence.

We are grateful to the many scholars who joined in our research at San José Mogote. The late C. Earle Smith, Jr. identified the bulk of the carbonized plants from the site. The late William O. Payne performed technical analyses on our Formative pottery. From 1966 to 1974, Chris L. Moser took thousands of photographs for us and developed them under Spartan conditions. (From 1975 through 1981, when Marcus was taking most of our photographs, Foto Zárate in Oaxaca City developed them.) At various times we were joined in the field by Henry T. Wright, Richard I. Ford, Ronald Spores, Dudley Varner, James Schoenwetter, Joseph W. Hopkins, and Robert and Judith Zeitlin.

Among the students who helped us dig Formative houses and middens were Richard J. Orlandini, Suzanne K. Fish, Kathryn Blair Vaughn, John W. Rick, and Andrew Nickelhoff. Many went on to direct their own projects in later years. Jacqueline Winter analyzed fragments of burned daub, while Sue-Ann Florin determined the Munsell color range of the whitewashed surfaces. Still other students, who helped in the excavation of palaces and public buildings, will be acknowledged in future volumes.

The list of colleagues who analyzed portions of our data set is very long. William J. Parry, Frank Hole, and John Rick studied our chipped stone. Jane Pires-Ferreira, A.A. Gordus, and Robert Zeitlin sourced our obsidian. Pires-Ferreira and B. J. Evans sourced iron ores. Pires-Ferreira, Gary Feinman, and Linda Nicholas identified marine shell. Judith Smith, Suzanne Harris, and Virginia Popper identified some of our carbonized plants. In addition to Flannery, archaeozoologists Katherine M. Moore, Jane C. Wheeler, Karen Mudar, Sonia Guillén, and Eloise Baker identified faunal remains. James Schoenwetter analyzed our Formative pollen samples and discovered that, rather than documenting climatic change, they mainly showed that San José Mogote was surrounded by fallow cornfields, full of chenopods, amaranths, and Compositae. Students who assisted us in pottery analysis have already been thanked in Flannery and Marcus (1994), but the crucial design element studies carried out by Stephen Plog and Nanette Pyne deserve special mention.

Art work is a crucial part of any site report, and we relied on a number of talented artists. John Klausmeyer created the digitized collages that combine line drawings, coquille board drawings, and photographs (e.g., Figs. 9.17-9.20). He also did all the piece-plotting maps (e.g., Figs. 18.22-18.29). Kay Clahassey created settlement pattern maps like Figs. 1.6 and 1.7. She also did all the charts and diagrams in Chapters 25 and 26. David West Reynolds did architectural reconstructions like Figs. 9.7 and 18.2. Most chipped stone drawings (e.g., Fig. 9.9) are the work of Nancy Hansen; the remainder (e.g., Fig. 18.15) are by William J. Parry. Hundreds of artifact photos were printed by Charles M. Hastings, John Clark, S. O. Kim, Eric Rupley, and David Mackres. We thank them all and apologize to anyone we left out.

In the realm of moral support and encouragement, there are many colleagues to acknowledge. The late Ignacio Bernal, John Paddock, and Richard S. MacNeish were the godfathers of our Oaxaca project, and we regret not being able to present them with this report. During the early years of the project, the late Alfonso Caso wrote Flannery repeatedly, having heard from Bernal about "Tlatilco-like material being found in Etla," which made him "hope to visit soon." Declining health denied him the opportunity.

Over the years we were visited, or otherwise encouraged, by fellow Mesoamericanists including David Grove, Susan Gillespie, Christine Niederberger, Gareth W. Lowe, Tom Lee, Pierre Agrinier, Ann Cyphers, Richard Diehl, Paul Tolstoy, Louise Paradis, Claude Baudez, Charlotte Arnauld, Robert Sharer, Loa Traxler, Arthur Miller, Ronald Spores, Robert and Judith Zeitlin, William J. Folan, Lynda Folan, Geoffrey Braswell, Vernon Scarborough, Stephen Plog, Susana Ekholm, Jason Yaeger, Linda Manzanilla, Lorenzo Ochoa, Alfredo López Austin, Leonardo López Luján, Ernesto González Licón, Lourdes Márquez Morfín, Arturo Oliveros, MariCarmen Serra Puche, Teresa Rojas Rabiela, and Jeremy Sabloff. They kept us going by asking how this report was progressing. And of course, information was continuously exchanged with our colleagues on the Oaxaca Settlement Pattern Project, Richard Blanton, Gary Feinman, Laura Finsten, Stephen Kowalewski, and Linda Nicholas. We also obtained crucial data and support from other excavators in Oaxaca, including Robert D. Drennan, Michael Whalen, Charles Spencer, Elsa Redmond, Andrew Balkansky, Christina Elson, Alan Covey, Jason Sherman, Laura Villamil, and Luca Casparis. Enrique Fernández of the INAH Centro Regional de Oaxaca carried out additional excavations on Mound 1 at San José Mogote and shared his findings with us. And very special thanks go to Leonardo López Luján, Jorge Silva and Sonia Guillén.

Finally, we raise our steins to the late "Señor Biche," proprietor of the *comedor familiar* Los Globos on the Etla-Oaxaca highway. No day at San José Mogote —whatever the theoretical or culture-historical implications of our discoveries— was officially over until the carryall had rolled into Los Globos, finding a dozen frozen schooners of Dos Equis waiting for our hot and dusty crew. And as if that weren't enough, behind the schooners were platters of *tasajo, cecina, morcilla, flautas, memelas,* and *caldo de gato. "Agua de las buenas matas/ Tú me tumbas, tú me matas/ Tú me haces andar a gatas."*

I

Chapter 1

The Anthropological Problem and the Archaeological Site

It was late spring, 1966. The University of Michigan project, "Prehistory and Human Ecology of the Valley of Oaxaca," had been in the field since January. We had been working on the first question the project was designed to answer: To what extent had Oaxaca participated in Mesoamerica's agricultural revolution?

Excavations at Guilá Naquitz Cave, Cueva Blanca, and the Martínez Rockshelter showed that Oaxaca had indeed participated in that revolution (Flannery [ed.] 1986; Marcus and Flannery 1996: Chapters 4-5). Guilá Naquitz produced domestic gourds, domestic squash, "phenotypically wild" runner beans, and primitive, two-rowed maize cobs. Our 1966 radiocarbon dates suggested that the earliest cultivated squash went back to 8000 B.C. (Later AMS dates obtained by B. Smith [1997], Kaplan and Lynch [1999], and Piperno and Flannery [2001] would give us the oldest gourds, squash, runner beans, and maize so far directly dated.)

Excavations at Cueva Blanca suggested that by 3000 B.C., the Indians of the eastern Valley of Oaxaca had made the transition from "foraging" to "collecting." Small foraging groups, involving both men and women, seemed to have created the earliest Archaic living floors at Cueva Blanca. Level C, however, appeared to be an all-male deer-hunting camp, perhaps created by a small group of men sent out from a base camp to obtain venison. With agriculture now added to hunting and wild plant collecting, late Archaic bands seemed to be traveling less, spending more time in base camps, and sending smaller task groups out to collect specific resources (Marcus and Flannery 1996:61). In still later Archaic levels at the Martínez Rockshelter, our project had found fragments of stone bowls—regarded by some as the precursor to pottery.

As work on the caves of the eastern Valley of Oaxaca drew to a close, we were able to focus on a second research question posed by our project: What would the earliest agricultural villages in the Valley of Oaxaca have been like?

This simple-sounding question glossed over a genuine mystery. Despite the fact that there had been archaeological work in the valley since the 1800s (our colleague Ignacio Bernal had already recorded 280 sites with one or more mounds), as of 1966 not a single Early Formative occupation had been identified. So puzzling was this "Formative hiatus" that some believed the valley had been filled with a giant lake prior to Monte Albán's founding.

Arguing against the lake theory was a collection of figurines in the Frissell Museum of Zapotec Art in Mitla. By any typological criterion, these figurines had to be Formative. Some, in fact, looked like Type D figurines from Vaillant's excavations in the Basin of Mexico (Vaillant 1935a, 1935b). The figurines were not attributed to any specific site; the provenience card simply read "brought from San Sebastián Etla by Hipólito."

And so, in the late spring of 1966, a small team of archaeologists from the University of Michigan project set out to walk the lands of San Sebastián Etla, searching for the source of the figurines. We were accompanied on that day by the late Richard S. "Scotty" MacNeish, who was taking a busman's holiday.

Our survey began the politically correct way. With our government permit letter in hand, we paid a visit to the mayor of San Sebastián Etla. We told him that we would pay a citizen of his village, to be designated by him, a day's wages to guide us over San Sebastián's lands and explain to each farmer what we were doing. As expected, he assigned one of his relatives to accompany us.

The Valley of Oaxaca is shaped like a three-pointed star, with northern, eastern, and southern arms (see Chapter 2). San Sebastián lay in the eastern piedmont of the northern, or Etla, arm. We began in the middle piedmont near the village, spread out, and began walking downhill toward the center of the valley. There were sherds on the surface from various periods of the Monte Albán sequence, but nothing that looked Early Formative. We continued west across the Panamerican Highway and climbed to the top of a piedmont ridge. There was an artificial mound on the top of the ridge, and backdirt from a couple of looters' holes contained Monte Albán II pottery.

"How much farther does San Sebastián's land extend?" we asked our guide.

"To the *ferrocarril*," he said, indicating the tracks of the Oaxaca-Mexico City railroad at the base of the ridge below. We were running out of land and had yet to find what we were looking for.

"Boy, look at those pyramids down there," said Scotty Mac-Neish. We looked. Almost a kilometer to the west and below us, on the last piedmont spur before the Atoyac River, lay an impressive ceremonial plaza. We could see half a dozen pyramidal mounds, one of them at least 15 m high. The conical ruins of temples poked up from the plaza in the manner of Buildings G, H, I, and J at Monte Albán. We thought we could see a ballcourt as big as Monte Albán's.

"It must be a Classic site," Flannery remembers saying. "No Formative site could have mounds that big."

"Remember Chiapa de Corzo," MacNeish reminded us. "It's huge, but it has Early Formative underneath it. Let's look for gullies and ravines where the early levels might be exposed."

"What's the name of that place down there with all the big mounds?" we asked our guide from San Sebastián.

"It's called San José Mogote," he told us. "It belongs to the *municipio* of Guadalupe Etla. I have no authority to take you there."

"Take us as close as you can," we said.

As we started down the piedmont ridge toward the railroad tracks, we climbed into every ravine and scratched the vegetation off the lowest stratum of earth. Predictably, it was MacNeish who found the first white-slipped sherd with two parallel lines incised on the rim. "Here's Canoas White," he said, referring to a Middle Formative pottery type defined during the course of his Tehuacán Project (MacNeish, Peterson, and Flannery 1970).

"And here's a figurine head," said Eligio Martínez from Mitla, who had been our dig foreman at Guilá Naquitz and Cueva Blanca.

Our guide from San Sebastián looked at the figurine. "The children of San José Mogote will try to sell you dozens of those," he laughed. "They find them in the *milpas* every time they're plowed."

At the limits of San Sebastián's land, we paid our guide and thanked him for his help. From here on, our success would depend on whether the people of San José Mogote were hospitable or wary of strangers.

Just below the ceremonial plaza with its towering artificial mounds, we saw an elderly man drawing water from a well. He was dressed in the traditional white, pajamalike *traje típico* of the hacienda era. Behind him, overgrown with vegetation, was a dry arroyo that descended from the ceremonial plaza to the plain below.

We introduced ourselves and explained our mission. He said he was Santiago Méndez, owner of that particular parcel of land. Could we look in his arroyo for potsherds? we asked politely. "Of course," he said with equal politeness. "Just be careful, because. . . ," he apologized, ". . . people sometimes use the arroyo as an outhouse."

We scrambled into the fragrant arroyo and looked for sherds eroding from the profile. Some were coarse and nondescript, belonging to utilitarian wares we had never seen. None, however, looked like types from the Monte Albán sequence.

"Is this anything?" asked Eligio. It was a piece of white-slipped, red-rimmed *tecomate* with zoned rocker stamping.

"Bingo," said MacNeish.

That was the last we heard of the claim that the Valley of Oaxaca had once been filled with a giant lake. It was also the last time we heard anyone say that Monte Albán had "no antecedents in the Valley of Oaxaca." Once we knew what to look for—ceramics combining early Tlatilco with Chiapa de Corzo I—we began finding Early Formative sites all over the valley. None, however, turned out to be as large as San José Mogote, the Formative site so monumental we presumed it would be Classic (Fig. 1.1).

Armed once again with a permit from the Mexican government, we returned to ask the authorities of San José Mogote if we could conduct a stratigraphic test in the arroyo. It turned out that San José was only an *agencia* below Guadalupe Etla, and the position of *agente* rotated annually. The occupants of the village, roughly 400 strong, were mainly the descendants of workers on a turn-of-the-century hacienda. With the fall of the hacienda its lands had been divided into *pequeñas propiedades*, small individually owned parcels like the one belonging to Santiago Méndez. The governance of San José Mogote was egalitarian and consensus-based; Guadalupe Etla rarely interfered in San José's affairs. Yes, if Santiago Méndez gave us permission to dig on his land, it was all right with the *agente*, so long as we paid don Santiago for any damage to his crops.

The other things we learned were almost too good to be true. San José Mogote was a village without crime, where people walked in safety and left their doors unlocked. Their hospitality was legendary. Egalitarianism was maintained by a system of relentless joking relationships, making it impossible to put on airs. You would be teased mercilessly if you became *presumido*, and no matter how great the teasing you dared not lose your temper; to do so would brand you an *enojón* or "sorehead," the worst thing anyone could be called.

So tranquil and bucolic was life in San José Mogote that no one expressed an interest in moving to Oaxaca City. It was considered a dangerous, sinful place, where one might run across

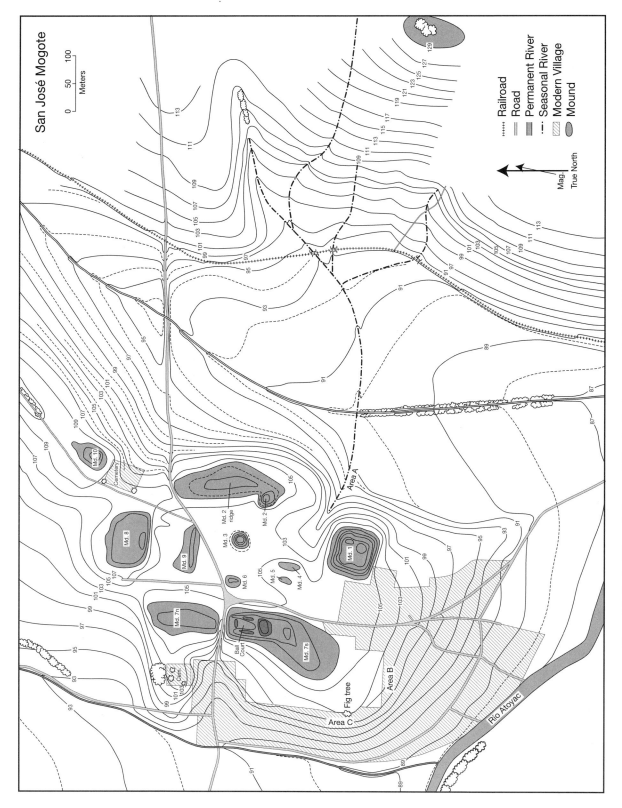

Figure. 1.1. San José Mogote in the central Etla subvalley (contour map by M. J. Kirkby).

"bad people . . . not like the people here, good people, neighbors you can trust." We went to San José Mogote hoping to dig a stratigraphic test, and wound up excavating for 15 years. Fifteen years that virtually spoiled us for any other place. Fifteen years of unflagging hospitality, generosity, friendship, hard work, and unconditional love.

Our workmen at San José Mogote were all related by blood or marriage: fathers, sons, uncles, nephews, brothers, brothers-in-law. Almost all went by nicknames—sometimes female soubriquets like La Chiva or La María, sometimes descriptive terms like El Obediente or El Panadero. Was your head round? You became La Mandarina ("the Mandarin orange"). Spend too much time on your hair? You became El Champú. Not particularly handsome? You became El Tribilín (Walt Disney's "Goofy"). An elderly workman with white hair on his forearms became El Oso Polar. A young man with long arms became La Tarántula. A workman famous for rarely bathing became El Ahumado, his dark color attributed to his having spent time in a smokehouse.

Only a few men, held in tremendous respect by their peers, had never been given a nickname. Included were don Leandro Méndez, gentlemanly brother of Santiago, for whom we eventually named a pottery type; our talented mason, maestro Genaro Luis; and Carlos Jiménez, a born labor organizer, who learned archaeology so well that he became the Mexican government's inspector for the sites of the Etla region.

The Anthropological Problem

When we began work at San José Mogote in 1966, no one was using the term "household archaeology." Formative archaeology at that time was all about setting up sequences of chronological phases based on changing pottery types. We wanted to do more than that. We wanted to know how the semi-nomadic life of the agricultural revolution had given way to sedentary life in farming villages. What had been the units of residence? Did people live in individual houses or multifamily long houses? What were men's tasks, and what were women's? How were crafts organized? Did every family possess all the necessary skills, or was there specialization? What form did leadership take, and would it be recognizable in the archaeological record? What social and political changes had led to the founding of Monte Albán, a city on a mountaintop, around 500 B.C.?

It did not take long to learn that San José Mogote was the appropriate archaeological site at which to investigate this anthropological problem. Within days of beginning work at Santiago Méndez's arroyo—now assigned to Area A—we could see that Formative houses were indeed preserved, and that they were the small kind used by nuclear families. We also went on to find smaller units, such as activity areas, and larger units, such as residential wards. In Chapter 3 we describe how the household units were excavated.

There are phrases and numbers to describe what we found at San José Mogote, but really no words to describe how much fun we had finding it. At first, we were unaware that we were providing our workmen with the only chance they would ever have to work together in a large group for months on end. Only later, when some of them described our project as "the best years of their lives," did we realize that they considered working with us to have been one continuous party. Thirty men, sometimes working together for six to eight months at a stretch, each good for at least two practical jokes a day.

The most skilled workmen gravitated quickly to the trowels, ice picks, and paintbrushes. Those with sharp eyes took over the screens. Others found trowel work too *fastidioso*, and preferred swinging a pick or moving large rocks—the bigger the better. "*Para mí no pesa nada*" was heard often as a boulder was moved. "*Por supuesto*," came the response from a trowelman, "*como eres buey.*"

Workmen took turns pushing wheelbarrow loads of earth to the backdirt pile, a role that earned them the title *choferes*. Unfortunately, with both hands gripping the handles of the barrow, *choferes* were at the mercy of anyone with a small dirt clod. During the last half hour of work each day, the hail of dirt clods launched at the wheelbarrow men was so great that it became known as *granizo negro*.

Such "black hail," however, set the launcher up for retribution. One day a *chofer* leaned over the excavation to fill his barrow, only to have a brightly wrapped ball of a popular hard candy fall from his shirt pocket. "*Gracias, compadre*," laughed the trowelman, opportunistically popping the hard candy out of its wrapper and into his mouth. The *chofer* had fled by the time the trowelman realized that what he was sucking was a ball of backdirt disguised as hard candy.

Some men worked in inexpensive plastic shoes, taking them off and leaving them by the side of the excavation when the earth was wet from rain. One day the workman known as El Chato emerged from the excavation to take a *pozole* break. His shoes had vanished. Being careful not to sound like an *enojón*, he asked which son of a toothless slattern had hidden his shoes. Blank stares and innocent faces all around. Some 20 meters away, two workmen were burning brush cleared from the site. Finally, La Chiva sneezed loudly and remarked, "I guess I'm allergic to burning plastic." El Chato barely had time to retrieve his shoes from the pile of burning brush before they had curled up like an elf's slippers.

Next day, of course, it was El Chato's turn for revenge. To this day, no one knows how he raised La Chiva's sandals to the top of a six-meter-tall columnar cactus. All we know is that they could not be retrieved without felling the cactus.

Our workmen did not simply laugh when these events took place. They laughed every time they were recounted, which was so many times that we lost track. Every practical joke became a rerun in syndication.

By 1980, we had collected so many data from San José Mogote that we faced an agonizing reality. Unless we stopped excavating for a while, allowing ourselves to analyze and publish what we had already found, our backlog would be unmanageable. We recalled Scotty MacNeish's warning that "if you never write it up, it's as if the excavation never took place" and we didn't want that to happen to us.

With great sadness, we informed our workmen that we needed a pause to catch up on analysis and publication. "Think of it as halftime at a basketball game," we told them. "We'll play the second half after enough of the reports have been published."

"But how do we know you'll come back?" they asked.

"Because we're leaving all the wheelbarrows, picks, shovels, screens, trowels, and paintbrushes in our storeroom here at the site." And so we did, little knowing how long the halftime would be.

Of course there was a sendoff for us, a party for which they supplied the *barbacoa* and we supplied a ten-gallon *garrafón* of mezcal from San Lorenzo Albarradas. Mezcal so good that Rick Bayless even serves it in his prize-winning Chicago restaurant, Frontera Grill. A good time was had by all, so good in fact that El Obediente was carried home in a wheelbarrow. "For the first time in his life," said the workman called La Bucha, "he was *Desobediente*."

The Formative before Monte Albán

No prison stretch can compare with having to analyze and write up your data, when all you can think about is getting back to the field. We consoled ourselves with the fact that while there might be more to do, we had at least defined five new chronological phases, all of which preceded the founding of Monte Albán. Subsequent work at sites like Tierras Largas, Fábrica San José, Tomaltepec, and Barrio del Rosario Huitzo expanded our understanding of the pre-Monte Albán sequence. Eventually, the Settlement Pattern Project found evidence of our new phases at scores of additional sites throughout the valley (Kowalewski et al. 1989).

Diagnostic pottery from the first three periods has been described and illustrated in an earlier monograph in this series (Flannery and Marcus 1994). The diagnostic pottery of the fourth and fifth periods, while not yet given book-length treatment, has been capably introduced by Drennan (1976a, 1976b) and is summarized in Appendix A. Today we take these five Formative phases for granted, sometimes forgetting that when our project began in 1966, the oldest ceramics known for the Valley of Oaxaca were still those of Monte Albán I (Paddock 1966).

In the sections that follow, we provide a sociopolitical context for San José Mogote's Formative residences by summarizing what is known of the site's regional role during each of its five earliest phases. We are able to keep these summaries brief, since the reader who wants more detail can refer to earlier descriptions of the way of life for each period (Marcus and Flannery 1996).

The Espiridión Complex

Date: Estimated to fall somewhere between 1800 and 1500 b.c. (uncalibrated).[1] We have no Espiridión radiocarbon dates,

but our oldest uncalibrated Tierras Largas phase date (on a burnt post from House 19, Area C) is 1540 b.c. (see Chapter 7).

Ceramics: Undecorated buff wares (Flannery and Marcus 1994: Chapter 7), mostly resembling the Purrón Complex of the Tehuacán Valley (MacNeish, Peterson, and Flannery 1970).

Society: Little is known of Espiridión society, since we have recovered evidence for only one nuclear-family house (House 20; see Chapter 7). We presume that San José Mogote was at that time a small, egalitarian, politically autonomous hamlet whose economy was a mixture of humid bottomland farming, wild plant collecting, and hunting.

Demography: The data are too limited to provide a size estimate for the population of San José Mogote at this time period. We expect that a few other hamlets of the Espiridión Complex will be found through excavation one day, but cannot predict where or how many. The drab nature of Espiridión Complex pottery makes it very difficult to recognize on the surface. Until more data are available, we prefer to treat it as an archaeological complex rather than a full-fledged "phase." This is how MacNeish treated the Purrón Complex.

The Tierras Largas Phase

Date: 1500-1150 b.c.

Ceramics: The Tierras Largas phase was the first period with pottery sufficiently decorated to be recognizable on surface survey. Types such as Avelina Red-on-buff, Matadamas Red, and Matadamas Orange were among the diagnostics (Flannery and Marcus 1994: Chapter 8). The red-on-buff pottery, in particular, assigns the Valley of Oaxaca to an early style province incorporating the Basin of Mexico, Puebla, Morelos, Tehuacán, Nochixtlán, and Tehuantepec (Clark 1991: Fig. 8; Flannery and Marcus 2000:9-11).

Society: In a previous synthesis (Marcus and Flannery 1996:76-88), we reconstructed the Tierras Largas phase as a time of egalitarian or "autonomous village" society (Carneiro 1981, 1991). In such societies individuals do not inherit prestige, but can acquire it through advanced age and experience, personal accomplishment, entrepreneurial skills, or the accumulation of valued items. No Tierras Largas phase burials have so far produced convincing sumptuary goods.

However, three middle-aged men (one from the site of Tierras Largas and two from San José Mogote) were buried in a distinctive seated position, so tightly flexed as to suggest that they were placed in bundles. Their position differs from that of other burials of the period, which were horizontal and fully extended. We believe the seated males to be men of high achieved status, fully initiated individuals who had passed through all the ritual levels typical of societies of this type. Some of them were buried near small public buildings, which we believe were Men's Houses.

---

[1] In this volume, uncalibrated dates are given as "b.c.," and dendrocalibrated dates as "B.C." (see Chapter 26, Radiocarbon Dating; see also last two paragraphs of this chapter).

These ritual buildings, which will be discussed in a later volume, were one-room structures plastered inside and out with lime and oriented 8° north of true east—roughly the point where the sun rises on the equinox.

We believe that each residential ward (whatever that might mean in terms of social divisions) maintained its own Men's House. Those found in Area C of San José Mogote were confined to a small area. Because each was surrounded by a plaster apron (Flannery and Marcus 1994: Fig. 4.7), it was possible to determine stratigraphically that they had been built in sequence. In several cases, a later Men's House was built almost directly over an earlier one. Even when the later one was built off to one side, traces of its plaster apron were likely to overlie traces of an earlier Men's House apron. By analogy with autonomous village societies in the ethnographic record, we suspect that these ritual structures were built by self-selected leaders who were able to organize labor for public construction. There is no evidence at this time that the influence of Tierras Largas phase leaders extended to neighboring communities.

The combination of Men's Houses, a defensive palisade in Area C (Chapter 5), and burials showing only modest differences in acquired status all suggest that the Tierras Largas phase was a time of segmentary society (sometimes referred to as "tribal"). The figurines suggest that young women of marriageable age wore elaborate hairdos with expert braiding and colored ribbons (Marcus 1998a: Chapter 6). As explained in Chapter 4, it would seem that initiated men owned small loop-handled metates that could be stored at home but carried to the Men's House for rituals. There they were perhaps used to grind wild tobacco, mixing it with the powdered lime stored in a pit in the ritual structure. Among other things, this mixture was believed to impart the courage needed for intervillage raids (Marcus and Flannery 1996:87).

Demography: The Settlement Pattern Project (Kowalewski et al. 1989) located 19 permanent Tierras Largas phase settlements in the Valley of Oaxaca (Fig. 1.2). Nine of these settlements, or nearly half, were in the northern or Etla subvalley, and most of the localities chosen were the tips of piedmont spurs overlooking highly productive land. It was typical of Tierras Largas phase hamlets on the east side of the Atoyac River to be spaced at least 4-5 km apart (Fig. 1.3).

As one of us observed in a previous study, the regularity of settlement spacing on the upper Atoyac makes it

> tempting to see this spacing as the result of a need for each village to maintain exclusive rights to an inner circle of 2.5-km radius. This temptation must be resisted. As shown in [a maize productivity study], such a circle was far larger than all but the largest of the villages needed; had agricultural factors alone determined the spacing, sites could have been much closer together than they actually were. [Flannery 1976a:111]

When the paragraph above was written, it was already clear to us that villages in Oaxaca were leaving more space between themselves and their neighbors than their agricultural needs required. Their view of the world evidently included some notion of just how close their neighbors ought to live. This principle of social spacing probably helped to keep peace between settlements. What we did not know at that time was that some postholes we were finding at San José Mogote would turn out to be part of a Tierras Largas phase palisade (Chapter 7). With the wisdom of hindsight, we now realize that there were even more reasons for keeping your neighbors at a distance than we had originally imagined.

According to the Settlement Pattern Project (Kowalewski et al. 1989), all but one of the 19 permanent Tierras Largas phase settlements were hamlets of less than 3 ha. Most, in fact, had surface scatters of Tierras Largas phase sherds covering less than a hectare. The lone exception was San José Mogote, whose surface scatter of Tierras Largas phase sherds was made up of discontinuous patches totaling at least 7 ha.

How large, precisely, was San José Mogote during the Tierras Largas phase? The most honest answer is, no one really knows. It is extremely difficult to estimate the size of a deeply buried component at a large multicomponent site. Later occupants at the site might bury the earliest component under pyramids and earthen platforms. Alternatively, they might build those pyramids using basketloads of fill dug up from earlier components, transporting early sherds to parts of the site where there never had been an early occupation. By the time the later occupants are finished, it can be nearly impossible to figure out the size and shape of the original community without excavating it completely.

San José Mogote is just such a site. For some periods, one can derive very different estimates of the size and shape of the site, depending on whether one uses (1) the estimates of the Settlement Pattern Project, which are based on sherds picked up on the surface, or (2) the estimates of the excavators, which are based on what was revealed when they dug to bedrock.

It is inevitable that a comprehensive surface pickup will cover a much larger area than can be excavated. However, we frequently found that (1) areas where there were Tierras Largas phase sherds on the surface sometimes had no *in situ* Tierras Largas phase occupation below the surface; or alternatively, that (2) areas where *in situ* Tierras Largas occupation was deeply buried sometimes had no Tierras Largas phase sherds on the surface.

The lack of fit between surface and subsurface remains at San José Mogote is sufficiently great that we will postpone its discussion until a future volume. In this chapter, we simply use the same population estimates given in Marcus and Flannery (1996:78).

The Settlement Pattern Project estimates San José Mogote to have had between 71 and 186 persons; their estimate for the entire Valley of Oaxaca during the Tierras Largas phase is 185 to 463 persons, with a mean of 325. Our estimates for the site of San José Mogote, based on excavation, would be 170-340 persons; our estimate for the entire Tierras Largas phase population of the Valley of Oaxaca would be 463 to 925 persons, with a mean of 693. There is no way to know, at present, whether either of those estimates is accurate.

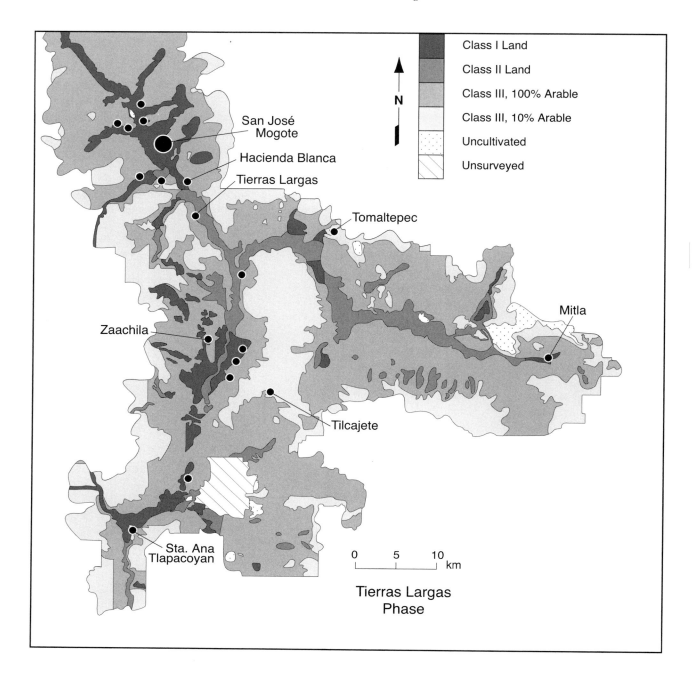

Figure 1.2. The Settlement Pattern Project discovered 19 villages of the Tierras Largas phase in the Valley of Oaxaca. On this map, they are plotted on the arable land classes discussed in Chapter 2.

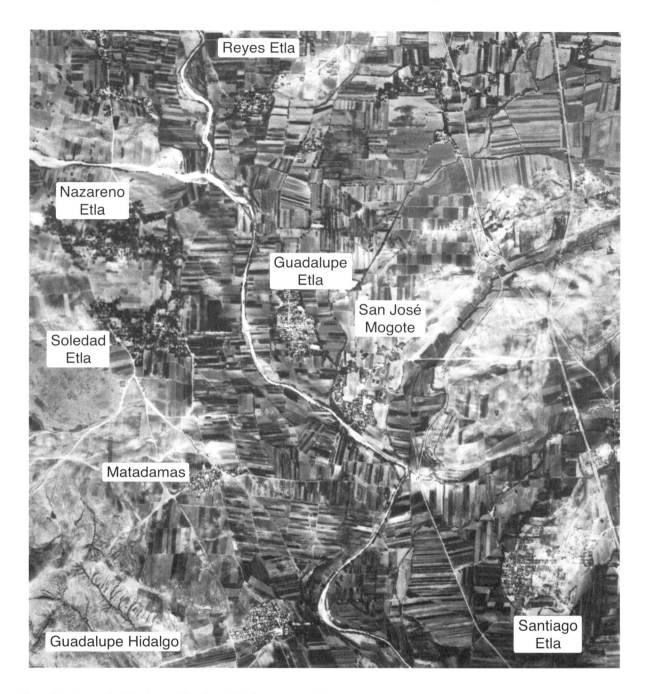

Figure 1.3. Aerial photograph of the Atoyac River floodplain, from Reyes Etla in the north to Guadalupe Hidalgo in the south. The alluvial plain appears as a dark patchwork of maize and alfalfa fields. The whitish ridges are the spurs of piedmont on which most Early Formative villages were founded. The spacing between Tierras Largas phase sites at Reyes Etla and San José Mogote could be considered typical for villages on the east side of the Atoyac. The early site at Nazareno Etla did not violate this social distance, since it was founded on the opposite side of the river.

The San José Phase

Date: 1150-850 b.c.

Ceramics: The San José phase witnessed an explosion of vessel shapes, surface colors, and plastic decoration (Flannery and Marcus 1994: Chapter 12). Leandro Gray, Atoyac Yellow-white, and Fidencio Coarse were among the most common types. Plastic decoration included carved or carved/incised representations of Sky/Lightning and Earth/Earthquake (Fig. 1.4). Eighteen of the most common freestanding motifs have been defined and numbered by Pyne (1976); they are shown in their entirety in Flannery and Marcus (1994: Figs. 12.5-12.16). Certain residential wards at San José Mogote were associated with Sky motifs, while others were associated with Earth motifs (Marcus 1989, 1999). The implications of this dichotomy will be pursued in a later volume.

A simplified version of Pyne's Motifs 12 and 13, known as the "double-line-break," was incised on Atoyac Yellow-white bowls (Flannery and Marcus 1994: Figs. 12.17-12.18). There was considerable variation in the way individual double-line-breaks were done (see Fig. 1.5 for the derivation of the double-line-break from Pyne's Motif 13). Plog (1976 and n.d.) defined 139 versions of the double-line-break in the Valley of Oaxaca; they are shown in their entirety in Flannery and Marcus (1994: Figs. 12.19-12.21).

In this volume, we will refer to both Pyne's freestanding motifs and Plog's double-line-breaks by number, but will not illustrate them because they are all published in our 1994 volume on the Early Formative pottery of the Valley of Oaxaca.

Stylistically, the pottery of the San José phase was most like the coeval pottery of the Basin of Mexico, and other highland areas like Morelos and Puebla. All those areas shared black or gray pottery with freestanding "pan-Mesoamerican" motifs, and white-slipped pottery with double-line-breaks (Flannery and Marcus 2000). San José phase pottery was much less similar to the San Lorenzo phase pottery of the Gulf Coast, which lacked most of the freestanding Earth/Earthquake motifs and had no white-slipped pottery with double-line-breaks at all (ibid.).

That does not mean, however, that San José Mogote did not receive gifts of pottery from areas to the south and east. As Chapter 4 makes clear, some families at San José Mogote received gifts of Xochiltepec White, La Mina White, or Calzadas Carved pottery from Veracruz, while others received Guamuchal Brushed from Chiapas (or farther south). To be sure, San José Mogote also received Paloma Negative and Cesto White from the Basin of Mexico (Flannery and Marcus 1994).

Society: One of the most dramatic developments of the San José phase was an enormous increase in the size of San José Mogote itself: it grew to an estimated 70 ha. Accompanying this growth were signs that society now featured differences in both achieved and inherited status. These differences were reflected in many parts of the archaeological record, including burial treatment, house construction, sumptuary goods, access to products from different regions, and specialization in trade and craft activity (Marcus and Flannery 1996: Chapter 8).

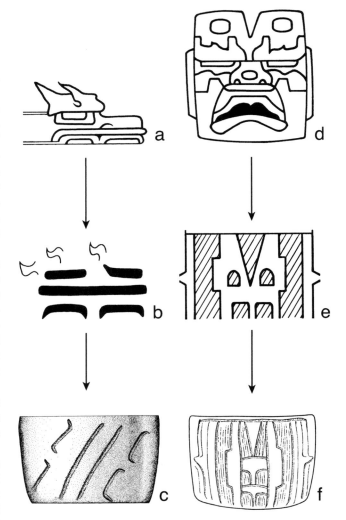

Figure 1.4. Two of the major classes of freestanding San José phase pottery motifs were Sky/Lightning (*a-c*) and Earth/Earthquake (*d-f*). *a* depicts Lightning as a serpent of fire; *d* depicts Earthquake as a snarling earth monster. *b* and *e* are more stylized versions of *a* and *d*, respectively (after Flannery and Marcus 1994: Fig. 12.2).

The archaeological evidence suggests that rank differences at San José Mogote formed a continuum from high to low, without divisions into social classes. Given what is known about groups speaking Otomanguean languages, we suspect that kinship was bilateral, perhaps resembling the Hawaiian type, which allows for gradations in rank in both men and women (Spores and Flannery 1983).

We believe that certain children inherited the right to have their skulls deformed in tabular erect style, and that certain male children inherited the right to be buried with vessels bearing Earth or Sky motifs (Marcus and Flannery 1996:106). Goods reserved for individuals of high status may have included mirrors

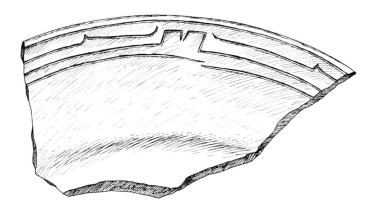

Figure 1.5. An Atoyac Yellow-white sherd from San José Mogote, showing the derivation of the "double-line-break" from Pyne's freestanding Motif 13. The incising includes stylized versions of Earth's cleft head and associated "music brackets" (after Flannery and Marcus 1994: Fig. 12.17).

of magnetite and ilmenite, earspools of jadeite(?), and genuine stingray spines (op. cit.:101-6).

Many other exotic goods circulated in San José phase society, but we cannot show a dichotomy between those who could, or could not, use them. Mollusk shell is an example. Thousands of Gulf Coast mussels, Pacific pearl and spiny oysters, and Pacific estuary snails reached San José Mogote (Chapter 5). While some may have been considered sumptuary goods, others may have been used as bride wealth, or had their value as trade goods enhanced by being converted into ornaments. We also suspect that materials like mother of pearl, mica, armadillo shell, and exotic feathers were used as decoration on ritual masks and costumes.

In addition to showing a continuum in access to venison, shell, and mica, the houses of the San José phase displayed a continuum from well-made and whitewashed to simple and clay-plastered.

A San José phase cemetery at the site of Tomaltepec (Whalen 1981) suggested that men of high rank might have been polygamous. Almost all primary burials were fully extended and prone. In contrast to the Tierras Largas phase, when most burials were solitary, the Tomaltepec cemetery had paired burials of adult men and women, presumably husband and wife. Six adult men stood out as different: buried in a kneeling position, so tightly flexed as to have been tied or bundled. These six men, while constituting only 12.7% of the cemetery, were accompanied by 50% of the vessels carved with motifs of Sky/Lightning, 88% of the jadeite(?) beads, 66% of the stone slab grave coverings, and the lion's share of the accompanying secondary burials. While not all secondary burials were female, at least a few might have been multiple wives.

The figurines of the period show the same positions of authority and obeisance seen in the burials, and seem to wear many of the same ornaments (Marcus 1998a: Chapters 10-15). The contexts in which these figurines occur suggest that they were part of women's ritual and are presumably venues to which the spirits of recent ancestors could return (see the setting of Feature 63, House 16, in Chapter 18).

Much more is known about the organization of San José Mogote during this period than in the preceding Tierras Largas phase. The enormous growth of the village resulted in new barrios or residential wards being founded on natural rises, separated from other barrios by natural gullies or ravines. Each of these wards engaged in its own range of craft activities; each featured either Sky/Lightning or Earth/Earthquake on its pottery, but not both (Flannery and Marcus 1994).

Early in the phase, each barrio appears to have built its own lime-plastered Men's House. By the Late San José phase, we also begin to see large temple platforms built of planoconvex adobes and earthen fill, with sloping walls of drylaid stone masonry. In the case of Structures 1 and 2 of Area A (Marcus and Flannery 1996:108-10), many of the stones used were limestones and travertines from areas 5 km distant. The implication is that the authority of the leaders of San José Mogote now extended to a network of smaller villages who could be called upon to bring raw materials and help build temples of regional significance. This loss of autonomy by satellite villages is part of the definition of a chiefdom (Carneiro 1991).

Demography: Problems of lack of fit between surface and subsurface evidence persist into the San José phase. There is, nevertheless, general agreement on the size of San José Mogote at this time (Marcus and Flannery 1996:106). The Settlement Pattern Project found three large areas of San José phase sherds on the surface, totaling 79 ha; from that, they have estimated a population of 791-1976 persons. The excavators see San José Mogote as consisting of a main village with numerous outlying barrios. The main village (which included Areas A, B, and C) covered at least 20 ha. If all outlying barrios were truly part of one sprawling community, we estimate its total size as 60-70 ha and its population at around 1000. Once again, we cannot prove that either estimate is accurate.

Why was San José Mogote so large? Two of the main reasons may have been (1) a deliberate attempt to become large enough so that a defensive palisade would no longer be necessary, and (2) an effort by the emerging elite of the village to attract as many additional followers as possible. The growth of San José Mogote after 1200 b.c. is simply too extreme to be accounted for by normal population increase; deliberate immigration must also have been involved. Inducements to immigration may have included (1) protection from raiding; (2) redistribution of imported luxuries like pearl oyster, *Spondylus*, pearly mussel, obsidian, and other exotica imported by the leaders of San José Mogote; (3) chiefly patronage of any craft specialties possessed by the newcomers; (4) religious leadership, provided by the builders of the valley's largest temples and the ritual specialists who served them; and (5) a chance to share in political domination of the surrounding area.

Analyses by the Settlement Pattern Project (Kowalewski et al. 1989) show just how dominant San José Mogote was at this time. There were at least 40 communities in the Valley of Oaxaca, with an estimated total population of 2000 (Fig. 1.6). This means that half the population of the valley might have lived at San José Mogote. It had no rivals; most villages are believed to have had populations of 100 persons or fewer. The northern or Etla subvalley was by far the most densely populated, partly because San José Mogote was surrounded by 12-14 satellite villages. These smaller communities chose to remain within 8 km of San José Mogote even though vast stretches of unoccupied farmland existed elsewhere in the valley. Obviously there were sociopolitical and economic incentives that overrode the desire for prime land.

The Guadalupe Phase

Date: 850-700 b.c.

Ceramics: The pottery of the Guadalupe phase shows continuity from the San José phase. Atoyac Yellow-white reached its peak in popularity, and Fidencio Coarse remained the most common cooking ware. These continuities present difficulties for anyone attempting to distinguish San José and Guadalupe occupations based on surface sherds alone. One new pottery type, Josefina Fine Gray, was highly diagnostic of the Guadalupe phase, but occurred in low frequency. Two other pottery types, Socorro Fine Gray and Guadalupe Burnished Brown, occurred with higher frequency but continued into the Rosario phase (Drennan 1976a, 1976b).

One other aspect of the Guadalupe phase should be mentioned. Its ceramic diagnostics were first recognized in the *municipio* of Guadalupe Etla and are most abundant in the Etla subvalley. The farther one moves south and east from the Etla region, the less one encounters these diagnostics. At Abasolo in the eastern subvalley, for example, the ceramics of 850-700 b.c. could just as easily be called "epi-San José" as "Guadalupe." They differ appreciably from the Guadalupe phase ceramics of the Etla subvalley. As we stated before (Marcus and Flannery 1996:111): "this regional diversity tells us that dynamic changes were underway, with competing centers arising in different areas of the valley."

Society: On the one hand, differences between high-status and low-status families were escalating. On the other hand, San José Mogote was having trouble retaining control of its network of satellite hamlets, since rival centers were arising not far away (Marcus and Flannery 1996: Chapter 9).

One of those rival centers was Barrio del Rosario Huitzo, a village 16 km upriver, roughly twice as far from San José Mogote as most of the latter's satellite villages. While smaller than San José Mogote, Huitzo built its own temple on a 1.3-m-high adobe platform, set atop a 2-m-high pyramid. Huitzo appears to have done a good deal of "networking" with emerging chiefly centers in the Nochixtlán Valley, some 50 km to the north. For example,

its yellow-white ceramics share more motifs with Nochixtlán (and fewer with San José Mogote) than would be expected based on the intervening distances (Plog 1976). Such alliance-building is typical of villages who want to retain their political autonomy from aggressive nearby centers.

For its own part, San José Mogote strengthened alliances with its nearest neighbors. The richest Guadalupe phase burials at Fábrica San José, a salt-producing hamlet only 5 km from San José Mogote, were those of women (Drennan 1976a; Marcus and Flannery 1996:114-15). We suspect that these were hypogamous brides, elite women sent from San José Mogote to marry the male leaders of Fábrica San José. Some were buried with elegant white drinking vessels made outside the valley—imported, we suspect, by chiefly families at San José Mogote, since they seem to have had more of them than anyone else (Flannery and Marcus 1994:277-82).

San José Mogote, of course, built its share of impressive temples during the Guadalupe phase. The best known is Structure 8 in Area C, which had an outer wall of fieldstone and an inner construction of planoconvex adobes and fill (Marcus and Flannery 1996: Fig. 117). The fact that Guadalupe phase public construction extended eastward all the way to Area B (Chapter 15) suggests that Structure 8 may have been only one of a series of temples. Unfortunately, at least from the standpoint of household archaeology, this program of public construction reduced our sample of Guadalupe phase residences by turning Areas C and B into a ceremonial precinct. (Area A had already been covered with temples by Late San José times.)

The figurines of the Guadalupe phase (Marcus 1998a:50-53) reflected the escalation of status paraphernalia. A great deal of time was spent giving female figurines elaborate turbans, necklaces, ear ornaments, and very detailed sandals. The intent was clearly to show that women of high rank were distinguished both by sumptuary goods and by the fact that, in contrast to lower-status women, their feet never directly touched the ground.

Demography: It is so difficult to measure Guadalupe phase occupations using surface sherds alone that we take all Guadalupe population estimates with a grain of salt. Our best guess is that there were 2000-2500 persons in the valley, perhaps distributed through 45 communities. We believe that in each subvalley there was at least one village (and perhaps more) whose chiefly family felt it was in a position to challenge San José Mogote's preeminence. In spite of these challenges, San José Mogote retained its grip on the 16 smaller settlements lying within 8 km.

The Settlement Pattern Project (Kowalewski et al. 1989) estimates that San José Mogote was now a village of 791-1976 persons distributed over 60-70 ha. Our impression, based on a lack of Guadalupe phase residences in Areas A and C, is that San José Mogote actually may have lost population during the Guadalupe phase. We are not sure to what extent this reflects (1) the siphoning off of followers by rival centers, (2) the conversion of former residential wards to areas of public buildings, or (3) the fact that Guadalupe was a relatively short phase, leaving fewer traces (Chapter 26).

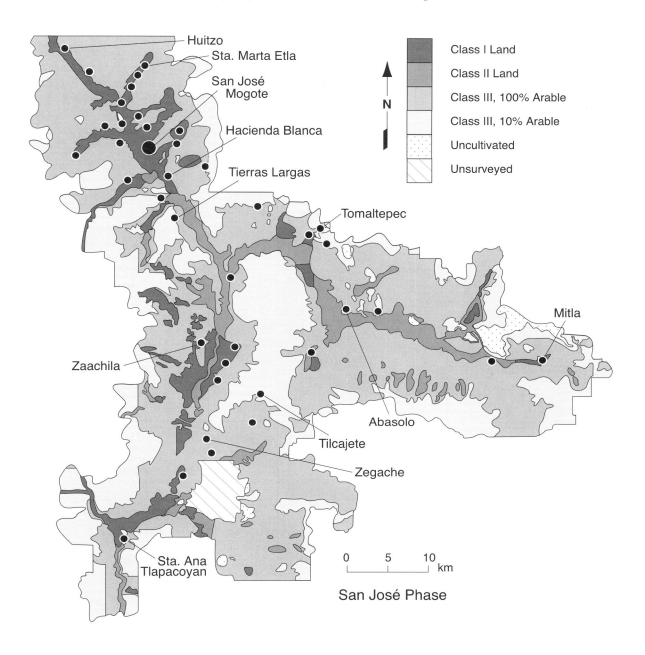

Figure 1.6. Villages of the San José phase, superimposed on a map of the Valley of Oaxaca that shows classes of arable land.

Wright (1984) and Anderson (1994) have pointed to a widespread process in the history of chiefdoms called "cycling." Such are the dynamics of chiefdoms that few remain stable in size and political influence for their full lifespans. For a variety of reasons—not the least of which are internal factionalism and external rivalries—most chiefly centers rise, shrink, then sometimes rise again under reinvigorated leadership. We believe that the Guadalupe phase was a period of "cycling down" for San José Mogote, one from which it would rebound at 700 b.c.

The Rosario Phase

Date: 700-500 b.c.

Ceramics: Many pottery types of the Guadalupe phase—Socorro Fine Gray, Guadalupe Burnished Brown, and Fidencio Coarse—continued into the Rosario phase (see Appendix A and Drennan 1976a, 1976b). The pottery assemblage had, however, become increasingly divided into (1) utilitarian vessels, which were used by households at every level of the social hierarchy, and (2) more elegant vessels, which occurred mainly in high-status residences and around public buildings.

While everyone used Fidencio Coarse and Guadalupe Burnished Brown for cooking and storage, elite families used elegantly decorated vessels of Socorro Fine Gray to serve themselves and their guests. Bowls and beakers might have white-on-gray "negative" or "resist" motifs, created by protecting parts of the vessel surface with resin or clay so that they would not turn gray in a reduce-firing kiln. Bowls might be given eccentric everted rims, decorated with incising. San José Mogote had many such vessels. Even at satellite communities like Fábrica San José, the residences of community leaders yielded more fine gray serving dishes than did those of lower-status families (Drennan 1976a, Marcus and Flannery 1996:121-22).

Society: We have previously reconstructed Rosario phase society as a "maximal" or "complex" chiefdom, one with a hierarchy of three administrative levels (Marcus and Flannery 1996: Chapter 10). Settlement pattern data (see "Demography" below) make it clear that there were several such chiefdoms in the valley at this time, separated by an 80 km² buffer zone with little or no settlement (Fig. 1.7). That relations among the three principal chiefly centers (San José Mogote in the north, Tilcajete in the south, and Yegüih in the east) were competitive is visible even on the surface. Chunks of burnt daub, presumably from houses burned in raids, occur on the surface of Rosario phase sites with seven times the frequency seen at typical Valley of Oaxaca sites (Kowalewski et al. 1989:70).

Once one gets below the surface, there is even more evidence for raiding. The main Rosario temple at San José Mogote, Structure 28 on Mound 1, was reduced to vitrified cinders by a fire so intense it can only have been set deliberately (Marcus and Flannery 1996:128). A carbonized roof beam has dated this fire to 600 b.c. (Flannery and Marcus 2003). For their part, the leaders of San José Mogote seem to have removed the heart of a prominent enemy and recorded the event on a stone monument. That carved stone, designated Monument 3, was found stratigraphically below two hearths with radiocarbon dates of 630 and 560 b.c. (ibid.).

Not surprisingly, Rosario phase houses reflect a lengthening continuum of rank between chiefly families and those of lower status. In Chapter 23 we describe the most elaborate Rosario residence so far known, Structure 25/26/30 of Mound 1 at San José Mogote. Built of rectangular adobes, it had an interior patio and a stone masonry tomb.

Fábrica San José, possibly a second-tier village in the hierarchy below San José Mogote, had large wattle-and-daub houses with fieldstone foundations. Some of them had been burned, perhaps in raids. The pattern of hypogamous marriages between local subchiefs and elite women from San José Mogote seems to have continued, with Burial 54 of Fábrica San José being particularly richly furnished (Drennan 1976a: Appendix XI). That young woman displayed tabular skull deformation similar to that of high-status women buried at San José Mogote (Marcus and Flannery 1996: Fig. 142).

Demography: The Rosario phase saw an increase in population. There were now between 70 and 85 communities in the valley, and we estimate that they held a minimum of 3500 persons, possibly more (Marcus and Flannery 1996:124). The fact that the most diagnostic pottery of the Rosario phase was elite gray ware, however, posed a problem for the Settlement Pattern Project. Simply put, areas of low-status Rosario residences are difficult to distinguish from those of the subsequent phase because of their shared utilitarian brown and buff wares.

The chiefdom centered at San José Mogote might have numbered 2000 persons. Of these, we estimate that 1000 lived at San José Mogote itself, which sprawled over 60-65 ha. As in previous periods, this large village consisted of a "downtown" area of public buildings and elite residences surrounded by lower-status residential wards. San José Mogote lay at the top of a hierarchy of 18-23 villages (Marcus and Flannery 1996:125).

The other Rosario chiefdoms were not as large. In the southern subvalley, San Martín Tilcajete (Spencer and Redmond 2003) was the 25-ha paramount center of a polity we have estimated at 700-1000 persons. In the eastern subvalley, Yegüih was the chiefly center for a polity similar in size to Tilcajete's. More distant villages seem to have monitored the major entrances to the Valley of Oaxaca: Huitzo on the north, Mitla and Xaagá on the east, Mazaltepec on the west, Santa Ana Tlapacoyan on the south (Marcus and Flannery 1996:126).

The Founding of Monte Albán

At roughly 500 b.c., San José Mogote and many of its satellite villages were completely or partially abandoned. Since this abandonment was contemporaneous with the founding of Monte Albán—on a mountaintop in the former buffer zone—San José Mogote and its allies are strongly implicated in that founding. Monte Albán provided a defensible stronghold from which former occupants of the Etla region could begin to subdue their rivals in other parts of the valley (Marcus and Flannery 1996: Chapter 11). However, excavations by Spencer and Redmond (2003) at San Martín Tilcajete in the southern arm of the valley suggest that it took Monte Albán until roughly 20 b.c. to finish off its main rival.

No Monte Albán I residences are reported in this volume, since none were discovered during fifteen years of research at San José Mogote. This fact underscores the extent of the abandonment that took place at the end of the Rosario phase (Chapter 24).

How the Data Will Be Presented

We stress that this volume should not be considered "the site report on San José Mogote." The data collected from that site will eventually fill several volumes, of which this is only one. Below we'll briefly review how this material is covered in this volume and previously published volumes, as well as those planned for the future.

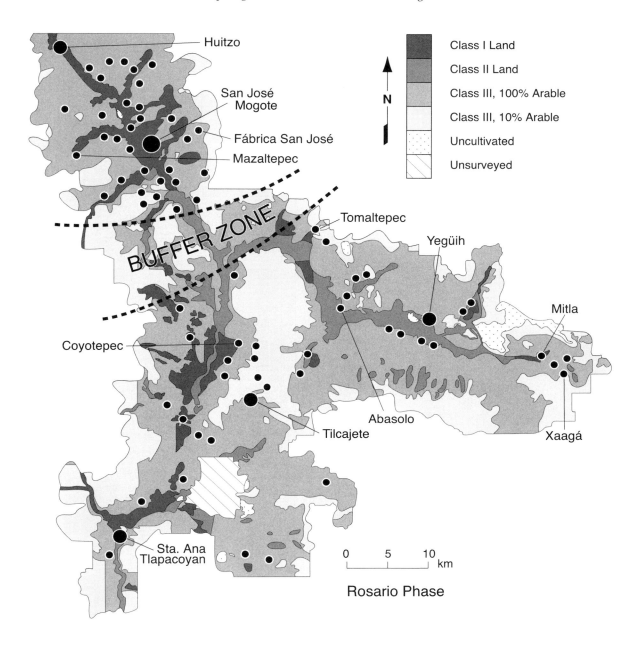

Figure 1.7. Villages of the Rosario phase, superimposed on a map of the Valley of Oaxaca that shows classes of arable land. Note the buffer zone separating the chiefdoms headed by San José Mogote, Yegüih, and San Martín Tilcajete.

- The pottery of the Espiridión Complex, the Tierras Largas phase, and the San José phase has already been published (Flannery and Marcus 1994). Since that volume lists every sherd from the houses of those periods at San José Mogote, it will be unnecessary to repeat those data here. We may, however, refer to restorable vessels from time to time.

- The pottery of the Guadalupe and Rosario phases will be published in a future volume on Middle Formative ceramics. Since that volume is not yet available, we list all sherds from

the Rosario phase residences described here. We also discuss Middle Formative pottery types in Appendix A.

- The chipped stone tools from most Formative houses at San José Mogote have already been published (Parry 1987). As a result, although we will list all chipped stone from each of the houses discussed below, we will not repeat Parry's type descriptions. We will, however, refer to potentially informative patterns discovered by piece-plotting.

- The figurines from all Formative houses at San José Mogote have already been published (Marcus 1998a). Since that volume lists every figurine from every house, it will be unnecessary to repeat those data here. We will, however, refer to potentially informative patterns recovered by piece-plotting.

- Obsidian, iron ores, and mollusk shells recovered during the first half of the University of Michigan Project have been published in a previous volume (Pires-Ferreira 1975). However, many more data from later field seasons are now available. The items listed for each house described here reflect a synthesis of data from all field seasons to date.

- The present volume describes every Early and Middle Formative residence so far excavated at San José Mogote. It also describes the dooryards associated with some houses, and every midden, storage pit, hearth, earth oven, or other feature relevant to the activities of a household. Accompanying the description of each house is *a complete inventory of every item associated with that house*. Included are not only artifacts and raw materials, but also all animal bones and carbonized plant remains.

- No public buildings will be described in this volume. They will be discussed in detail in a future volume, *Excavations at San José Mogote 2: The Cognitive Archaeology*. That work will cover cosmology, religion, ideology, and iconography.

- No burials will be described in this volume, with the exception of a few found inside or in close proximity to a residence. Burials will be discussed in detail in a future volume, *Excavations at San José Mogote 3: The Mortuary Archaeology*.

- Most Formative site reports have chapters devoted to pottery, chipped stone, ground stone, bone tools, and so on. No such chapters will be found in this volume, in view of our decision to focus on residences. Inevitably, of course, it became necessary for us to define the terms we used throughout the book for various artifact categories. Those terms are explained in Chapters 4 and 5, where we discuss *activities engaged in by the households of Formative San José Mogote*.

- We asked our colleague Robert G. Reynolds to undertake a multidimensional scaling of twenty key items (artifacts or commodities) associated with our best eighteen proveniences (houses or dooryards). The results told us which houses were most similar in content, and which groups of items co-occurred (Chapter 25). This in turn left us better prepared to suggest some of San José Mogote's potential contributions to anthropological theory (Chapter 27).

- Finally, we should explain our somewhat unorthodox use of lower case "b.c." for some radiocarbon dates. In this volume, we give ^{14}C dates three ways. "B.P." refers to conventional radiocarbon years before the present. "B.C." refers to the two-sigma range of each date when converted to calendar years B.C. by dendrocalibration. Lower case "b.c." refers to conventional radiocarbon years B.C., derived by the 50-year-old tradition of subtracting 1950 from the B.P. date.

- We continue to use "b.c." dates because Mexico's Formative chronology is still heavily based on dates derived by subtracting 1950 from the B.P. date. Many Formative sequences were established before dendrocalibration existed, and we do not want to confuse things by interspersing new calibrated dates with old uncalibrated dates, without indicating which are which. Perhaps one day someone will dendrocalibrate all the dates from decades past. At the moment, however, the conversion formula is still being upgraded.

Chapter 2

The Environmental Setting

In a region of rugged mountains like Mexico's Mesa del Sur, any patch of level land with humid alluvium had the potential to lure Archaic farmers out of nomadism. And the greatest expanse of level land was Oaxaca's Central Valley System, originally shaped by a downfaulted trench some 95 km long and 25 km wide.

Geographers recognize at least five valleys in this system. Three of them, created by the Atoyac River and its tributary the Río Salado, interconnect to form the 2000 km² Valley of Oaxaca. On the northwest is the Etla subvalley, narrowest of the three. On the east is the Tlacolula subvalley, broader but drier. On the south is the still broader Valle Grande, where the Atoyac is swelled by additional water from the Río Salado (Fig. 1.2).

In this volume we focus on the Etla subvalley, which—despite being the narrowest, highest, and coolest of the three—seems to be where village life began, population grew most rapidly, and complex society first arose in the Central Valley System. At least some of the reasons may be environmental. The Etla subvalley has the greatest number of useful tributary streams and the lowest potential evapotranspiration (A. Kirkby 1973:Table 2). Virtually every type of agriculture practiced in the valley, including well irrigation, canal irrigation, and high-water-table farming, is possible in the Etla region. In addition, the subvalley's very narrowness puts the resources of the mountains, piedmont, and river floodplain within easy walking distance of each other.

We should stress, however, some likely social reasons for Etla's priority. Its position on the Atoyac River put it near routes to trading partners in other valleys, such as Nochixtlán and Tehuacán. In addition, early sociopolitical evolution in the Etla subvalley seems to have encouraged satellite villages to cluster near San José Mogote. Part of that clustering was undoubtedly

the result of actions by human agents whose names we will never know.

Bedrock Geology and Mineral Resources

A trip across the Valley of Oaxaca reveals three basic physiographic zones: (1) a flat alluvial valley floor with an average elevation of 1550 m above sea level; (2) a zone of rolling piedmont from 1700 to 2000 m elevation; and (3) a zone of mountains rising to 3000 m (A. Kirkby 1973:7-15). Below the surface of these basic zones, to be sure, lies a long and dynamic geological history (Lorenzo 1960; Michael J. Kirkby, unpublished studies, 1966-1968; Payne 1994).

The oldest bedrock consists of Precambrian metamorphic rocks, predominantly gneiss and schist. Such rocks are so altered that one cannot usually tell what their geological makeup was before their metamorphosis. As Payne (1994:7) points out, however,

> Oaxaca's basal complex gives every evidence of having been igneous material of the granite-granodiorite-diorite group. Not only are there dikes of pegmatite, granite, and diorite still to be found in the area, but also the minerals in the Precambrian gneiss are ones that are common to crystalline rocks like granite and diorite.

In terms of useful minerals, Precambrian gneiss is one of the richest and most widespread rock formations. It was the source of the magnetite and ilmeno-magnetite used by Early Formative people in their crafts, in addition to black, brown, gold, and white mica. Its minerals included veins of hematite and limonite for red pigment, as well as crystalline hematite for making specular red

Figure 2.1. Aerial oblique of the Etla subvalley near Hacienda Blanca. Site 1-1-16 of the Settlement Pattern Project occupies the tip of a piedmont spur, surrounded on three sides by high alluvium. This was a prototypic settlement choice for Early Formative villages.

paint. Pods of *barro colorado* in the Precambrian gneiss could be used for making the red wash common on utilitarian pottery (Payne 1994: Fig. 2.1). Precambrian schist was also useful, with chlorite schist convertible into fine-grained celts.

The second oldest rocks in the region are Cretaceous limestones, exposed primarily in the western part of the valley. They outcrop at places like San Lázaro Etla and Rancho Matadamas, not far from San José Mogote. There they served multiple uses. Silicified veins of chert and chalcedony in the limestone provided raw material for chipped stone tools (Whalen 1986). Limestone could be baked to produce powdered lime, either for whitewash or plaster, or to mix with water in order to soak maize before grinding. By Middle Formative times, rectangular blocks of limestone were being quarried for the walls of public buildings.

A third stage in the geological history of the valley was the deposition of Miocene ignimbrites. These were massive flows of molten volcanic ash which, like the ignimbrites of Alaska's "Valley of Ten Thousand Smokes," must have smoldered for years before cooling (Williams and Heizer 1965). Such ignimbrites are especially extensive in the Tlacolula subvalley, but outcrop in the Etla region as well. Bedrock below the site of San José Mogote is Miocene volcanic tuff, although today it is largely hidden from view by the archaeological deposits. Ignimbrite is a soft, easily cut stone, widely used for metates and manos or for the rubble fill in public buildings.

By the Pleistocene era, faulting had created the general outline of the Valley of Oaxaca. It remained for the Atoyac River and its tributaries to create the valley's present shape. The piedmont

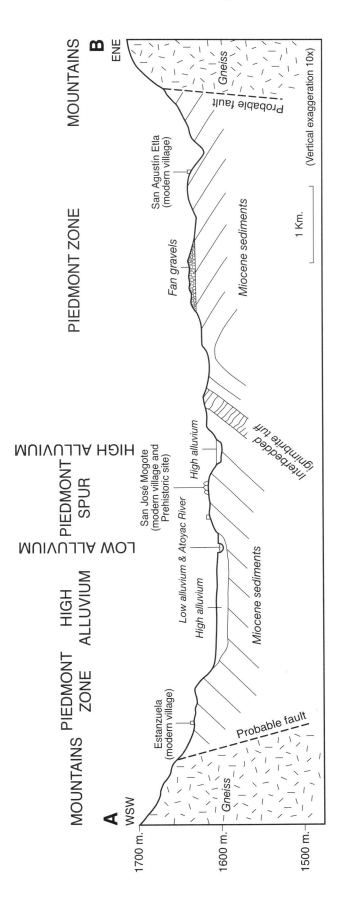

Figure 2.2. Geological cross-section of the Etla subvalley, showing the basic soil and bedrock formations within a day's walk of San José Mogote.

zone originally formed "as a series of coalescing fans which have since been dissected into a line of ridges and valleys delimiting the outer edge of the valley floor" (A. Kirkby 1973:11). Dissection of the piedmont is greater in the narrow Etla subvalley than elsewhere. The result is that all along the course of the upper Atoyac, the river is flanked by spurs of piedmont that project out into the floodplain like narrow peninsulas. Because these spurs are close to the river but too high to be flooded, their tips became favored locations for early villages (Fig. 2.1). San José Mogote is on just such a spur of piedmont, surrounded on three sides by alluvial bottomland.

During the Pleistocene and Holocene, the Atoyac River and its tributaries laid down the level plain called the "high alluvium" by A. Kirkby (1973:11-13). This alluviation—accompanied by floods, changes in river course, and periods of downcutting—"reworked the erosion products of all earlier rock formations and altered the grain size" (Payne 1994:8). Some of the transported and reworked clays of the high alluvium were used for pottery making, and the fact that they include the erosion products of "all earlier rock formations" is significant. The Valley of Oaxaca's combination of Precambrian gneiss, pegmatite dikes, Cretaceous limestone, and Miocene volcanic tuff is unique. When one finds all those ingredients in the same piece of pottery, one is almost certainly dealing with a vessel made in Oaxaca (Chapter 4).

According to A. Kirkby (1973:11), the high alluvium forms the main part of the valley floor "and is the most important zone for agriculture both in quantity and quality." It varies in width from one kilometer in the Etla subvalley to 17 km in the southern Valle Grande. As discussed below, variations in rainfall and depth to water table affect the productivity of the alluvium in each of the subvalleys.

In some parts of the valley the Atoyac and Río Salado have incised their way 6 to 7 m below the high alluvium, and a new floodplain, called the "low alluvium," is forming. We need not concern ourselves with the low alluvium in this volume; the incisions leading to its formation did not begin until after A.D. 1500 in the Valle Grande "and as late as A.D. 1800 upstream in the Etla Valley near Huitzo" (A. Kirkby 1973:15). For the whole of the Formative and Classic eras, in other words, the relevant floodplain would have been the current high alluvium.

Figure 2.2 is a geological cross-section of the Etla subvalley, showing the basic soil and bedrock formations within a day's walk of San José Mogote. Note that the piedmont spur covered by the archaeological site is sandwiched between two expanses of high alluvium. From the Late San José phase through the Rosario phase, occupation extended east-northeast to the hill shown in the cross-section as interbedded ignimbrite tuff.

Soil, Water, and Agricultural Productivity

With 2000 km² from which to choose, why did so many of the earliest villagers in the Valley of Oaxaca choose to settle in the Etla subvalley? There is no simple answer, though we looked at

a few reasons in an earlier paragraph. Now we look at several other reasons.

The high alluvium is the best soil for agriculture, yet Etla has the narrowest expanse of it. The Valle Grande, which has the widest expanse of alluvium, also has the lowest probability of frost. In the Valle Grande, air frosts occur less than once every 20-40 years; in Etla, it is once every three years (A. Kirkby 1973:13). Rainfall increases (and evapotranspiration decreases) with altitude; thus the alluvial plain gets less rain (500-600 mm) than the high mountains (>1000 mm). On the other hand, the stony mountain soils have poorer water retention. Finding the best agricultural land, therefore, is not a matter of optimizing any one of the above variables, but of finding the right combination.

As we see in Figure 2.3, there are two main sources of variation in the valley's rainfall. One is predictable; the other is not. *Seasonal* variation is predictable: all farmers know that the November-March period will be dry, and the May-September period will be wet. They know, moreover, that June and September are likely to be the rainiest months, while July-August is likely to be a less rainy period called the *canícula*.

Oaxaca also, however, has annual variation in rainfall that is completely unpredictable. Tlacolula gets an average of 550 mm per year, but as the 40-year record in Figure 2.3*B* shows, there were years when rainfall was as high as 1100 mm, and years when it was as low as 300 mm. The local farmers know that November-March will be dry, but they cannot predict whether June-September will reflect an average year, a drought year, or a year of torrential rains. Because of this uncertainty, many of today's Zapotec farmers divide their fields among the valley floor, piedmont, and mountains (Schmieder 1930).

Here is where ground water comes in. Along the main rivers in the valley there runs a strip of land where the water table is so close to the surface that it creates a zone of permanently humid alluvium. When maize is planted in this zone—called *yuh kohp* in Zapotec (Messer 1978:94)—the roots of the plants can extract water continuously by capillary action, helping them to survive when rain is insufficient. *Yuh kohp* occurs on less than 10% of the valley floor, but virtually all the villages of the Tierras Largas phase lie adjacent to this type of humid bottomland. San José Mogote would have been flanked by it on three sides.

Apparently, therefore, the decision made by the earliest villagers in the Valley of Oaxaca was this: "We will settle near the best available stretches of *yuh kohp*, relying on a combination of rainfall and high water table to grow our crops. We will put up with occasional frosts and ignore the higher rainfall of the mountains and upper piedmont because the high alluvium is finer soil." The fact that Etla was the narrowest subvalley did not pose a problem, since there were only a few hundred people in the valley when village life began.

In 1973, Anne Kirkby divided all farmland in the Valley of Oaxaca into six categories, based on the way it was used (A. Kirkby 1973). The categories were as follows:

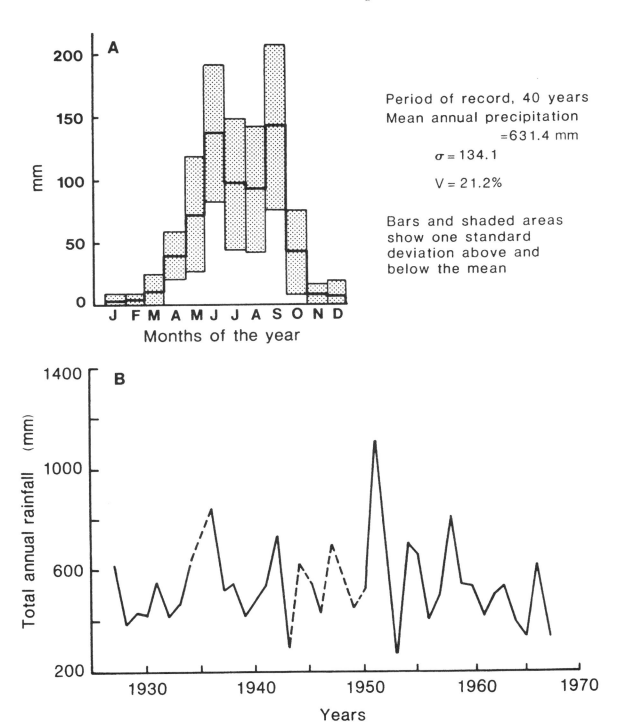

Period of record, 40 years
Mean annual precipitation
=631.4 mm

$\sigma = 134.1$

$V = 21.2\%$

Bars and shaded areas
show one standard
deviation above and
below the mean

Figure 2.3. Rainfall in the Valley of Oaxaca, based on data collected by A. Kirkby (1973: Figs. 6 and 58). *A*, mean monthly precipitation at Oaxaca City over a 40-year period. *B*, annual precipitation at Tlacolula between 1926 and 1968. The seasonal variation, shown in *A*, is relatively predictable. The annual variation, shown in *B*, is unpredictable.

1. Water table farming
2. Marginal water table farming
3. Canal irrigation
4. Good floodwater farming
5. Poor floodwater farming
6. Dry farming

Sixteen years later, as part of the Oaxaca Settlement Pattern Project's final report, Linda Nicholas (1989) consolidated Kirkby's categories into three agricultural land classes, based on twentieth-century maize yields. These classes were as follows.

Class I land consisted of "water table" and "canal irrigated" land, which produces more than 2 metric tons of maize per hectare with today's races of maize.

Class II land consisted of "marginal water table" and "good floodwater farming" land, which produces 1.2-2.0 metric tons per hectare with today's races of maize.

Class III land consisted of "poor floodwater farming" and "dry farming" land, which usually produces less than 1.2 metric tons per hectare with today's races of maize.

For valley-wide plotting of archaeological sites on land types, Nicholas' land use areas are more convenient because they are larger and less mosaic than Kirkby's. For early periods like the Tierras Largas phase, however, one must sometimes use Kirkby's more fine-grained classification. For example, it separates water table farming (which was important by 1300 b.c.[1]) from canal irrigation (which may have evolved later) and floodwater farming (used mainly in areas where neither water table nor canal farming are possible).

One should also bear in mind that Formative maize would not have produced the same yields as modern maize. A. Kirkby (1973: Fig. 48) estimates that the maize of 1000 b.c. may have produced only 0.3-0.4 metric tons per hectare. The lower yields of Formative maize, resulting from its smaller cob size, made it all the more crucial for early villages to settle near the best permanently humid *yuh kohp*. Here is where Nicholas' 1989 study helps to explain the higher density of early villages in the Etla region. Of the estimated 12,740 ha of Class I land in the Valley of Oaxaca, 5117 ha (about 40%) can be found in the Etla subvalley. Another 3345 ha occur in the northern Valle Grande, the region with the second largest number of Tierras Largas phase communities (Nicholas 1989).

Thus Etla, the smallest, narrowest, highest, and coolest of all the subvalleys, got a headstart on its neighbors for agricultural reasons. It also maintained its demographic advantage right up to the moment that Monte Albán was founded. We believe, however, that maintaining that advantage was as much the result of sociopolitical strategy as agricultural potential. San José Mogote performed many acts to draw populations within its sphere of influence: fomenting crafts, ritual, and public construction, and monopolizing some kinds of long-distance exchange.

The Regime of the Río Atoyac

One of the great resources available to San José Mogote was the Atoyac River, which flows close to the site (Fig. 2.1). It would have been the villagers' major source of water for drinking, cooking, washing, bathing, making daub and adobes, and mixing clay mortar and lime plaster. It was also their source of sand and gravel for construction.

It should be stressed that today's Atoyac is a pale shadow of the river that would have coursed down the Etla subvalley in Formative times. In those days there would have been no dams, no diversions, no gasoline-driven pumps, and no large towns reducing its flow. When A. Kirkby studied the Atoyac in the late 1960s, it was dry for most of the year; seasonal rains temporarily raised its flow to 200 cubic meters per second (A. Kirkby 1973:21).

Elderly informants at San José Mogote described to us a very different river. Before the revolution of 1910, they said, there was almost always water in the river. In the dry season it was reduced to a few channels, occupying a fraction of its bed. Once the rains had begun in its 2470 km² drainage area, it was a rushing, yellowish brown ribbon.

Most striking were the elderly informants' descriptions of how *forested* the river was then: it was lined with giant baldcypress (*Taxodium mucronatum*). Known to Nahuatl speakers as *ahuehuemeh* and to Spanish speakers as *tules* or *sabinos*, these trees could live to be thousands of years old. We are sure that they grew along the river at San José Mogote because their trunks were used as columns in Structure 36, one of our Monte Albán II temples (Marcus and Flannery 1994:66). "It was so dark in the shadow of the *sabinos*," octogenarian Leandro Méndez told us, "that as boys we were afraid to go down to the Atoyac at night."

Sadly, those magnificent trees have all but vanished from the course of the river, withering as their limbs were relentlessly cut off for firewood. By the 1960s it was only in a few places, one of which is shown in Figure 2.4, that we could still find stretches of the Atoyac (or its tributaries) where huge baldcypresses grew with their roots penetrating the bed of the river. In such areas, the river could be crossed on informal bridges made by suspending wooden planks from tree to tree (Fig. 2.5).

At Santa Inés Yatzeche, still a nearly monolingual Zapotec-speaking town in the 1960s, old villagers rhapsodized about the Atoyac of their youth. It had been cool in the riparian forest, one told us. "You could wade in the water and collect basketloads of minnows. And there were birds—ducks, coots, and doves—so many that you could always get one with your blowgun." We didn't doubt him, since he was carrying a blowgun (*quèteyàga* in Zapotec) and a bag of dead birds even as he spoke.

In 1969 we had a glimpse of just how much water the Atoyac could carry in a rainy year. More than 500 mm of rain fell in August alone, a month that averages 90 mm. The result was the

---

[1]In this volume, uncalibrated dates are given as "b.c.," and dendrocalibrated dates as "B.C." (see Chapter 26, Radiocarbon Dating).

Figure 2.4. In ancient times the Atoyac River would have been shaded by giant baldcypress trees, some of them thousands of years old. Few of those trees remain today. This stretch of river near Cuilapan in the southern subvalley was, at least until the 1960s, one of the few places where the original riparian forest could be found.

rushing, chocolate-colored flood shown in Figure 2.6. The Atoyac overflowed its banks, inundating maize and alfalfa fields (Fig. 2.7), depositing new layers of alluvium, and changing its course in places. Willow trees were uprooted, bridges washed out, and many roads were impassable.

At the height of the flood, a taxi from Oaxaca tried to make it to Soledad Etla by fording the Atoyac. The driver was transporting a bride and groom in full wedding dress, and his motor stalled when his tailpipe went under water. Abandoning the taxi, the wedding party waded the hip-deep Atoyac. In all the excite-

ment, the driver forgot to roll up his windows; when he returned with a team of oxen, he found that the still-rising Atoyac had filled his taxi to the roof with wet sand. We are not sure what a taxi full of wet sand weighs, but it was more than a team of oxen could move.

From their vantage point on the piedmont spur in San José Mogote's Area C, our workmen watched the whole drama unfold. They knew that the taxi would be there until the flood receded and the sand could be shoveled out. "How long has that taxi been there?" asked a visitor to the site. "Four days," he was told.

Figure 2.5. How do you cross a rushing stream lined with baldcypress trees? On a plank bridge suspended between trees. This stream is the Río de las Grutas, a tributary of the Atoyac River.

"*¿Y los pasajeros?*" he asked.

"*Lástima,*" one workman said gravely. "*La novia se mojó antes de su tiempo.*"

The "Original" Flora of the Etla Subvalley

Seen from the air today, the Etla subvalley is a mosaic of maize and alfalfa fields "divided by boundary lines which are the only areas in which [wild] plants grow undisturbed over a long period of time" (C. E. Smith 1978:13). Ten thousand years of agriculture, 500 years of livestock grazing, and millennia of firewood-cutting have greatly changed the vegetation of the Atoyac River valley. It would once have been almost completely forested.

During the course of the Oaxaca Project, botanist C. Earle Smith, Jr., attempted to reconstruct the "original" Post-Pleistocene flora of the valley, the native vegetation that would have been in place when San José Mogote was founded (C. E. Smith 1978). The data at Smith's disposal were (1) remnants of the original vegetation, still surviving today; (2) principles of plant growth as they apply to the physiographic, soil, and rainfall features of the valley; (3) Smith's knowledge of vegetation in similar environments in neighboring valleys; and (4) plant remains recovered from Archaic and Formative archaeological sites.

Smith's reconstruction of primary vegetation zones in the ancient Valley of Oaxaca is given in Map 2 of his 1978 monograph. In Figure 2.8 of this chapter, we show how those vegetation zones would apply to a cross-section of the Etla subvalley, the same cross-section shown in Figure 2.2.

Along the Atoyac River, wherever the water table was within 3 m of the surface, there would have been mesophytic riverine forest. Baldcypress (*Taxodium mucronatum*), willow (*Salix bonplandia*), and alder (*Alnus* sp.) would have been common, but there may also have been *Anona purpurea, Cedrela oaxacensis,* fig trees (*Ficus* sp.) like the big one growing in Area C of the site today, and even *Persea americana,* the wild ancestor of the domestic avocado. Attenuated versions of this riverine forest would have grown along permanently humid *barrancas* in the piedmont.

On the high alluvium, wherever the water table was 3-6 m below the surface, there would have been mesquite forest (Fig. 2.9*b*). Dominant species here would have included mesquite (*Prosopis juliflora*), huizache (*Acacia farnesiana*), and members of the Burseraceae, Malvaceae, and Euphorbiaceae family (C. E. Smith 1978).

As one moves up to the piedmont, the vegetation would gradually have changed to thorn-scrub-cactus forest. Mesquite began to thin out, huizache increased and was joined by a whole series of thorny legume trees called guajes; included in the latter category are *Conzatia* sp., *Cassia* sp., and *Leucaena* spp. Prickly pear cactus (*Opuntia* spp.), organ cactus (*Lemaireocereus treleasi* and *Myrtillocactus schenkii*), and barrel cactus (*Mammillaria* sp.) still grow among these legume trees. Other genera of the thorn forest include *Croton, Lantana, Jatropha,* and *Bunchosia.* A wide range of agaves, several of them used for food or fiber,

occur in this vegetation zone.

As the upper piedmont grades into steeper mountains, rainfall increases and cooler temperatures create lower evaporation rates. The mountains would originally have supported oak-pine forest (Fig. 2.9*a*), now greatly reduced by woodcutting and charcoal burning. According to C. E. Smith (1978:25), "the original oak-pine forest undoubtedly consisted of much larger trees spaced much farther apart."

There were once many species of oaks, of which *Quercus impressa* survives. There were once many species of pines, of which *Pinus michoacana* survives. Other trees of the oak-pine forest include manzanilla (*Arctostaphylos polifolia*) and madroño (*Amelanchier denticulata*). Black walnut (*Juglans* sp.), wild black zapote (*Diospyros* sp.), guamuchil (*Pithecolobium dulce*), and copal (*Bursera* sp.) can still be found in this zone.

For more extensive discussion of the native Holocene vegetation of the Valley of Oaxaca, we refer the reader to C. E. Smith (1978), Messer (1978), and M. J. Kirkby, Whyte, and Flannery (1986).

The "Original" Fauna of the Etla Subvalley

Just as C. E. Smith (1978) was able to reconstruct the Archaic and Formative vegetation of the Valley of Oaxaca, we can reconstruct the original complex of animals. One of our major sources of information is the archaeological fauna from San José Mogote (this volume), Fábrica San José (Drennan 1976a), and Guilá Naquitz Cave (Flannery and Wheeler 1986a). In addition, the University of Michigan Museum of Zoology has extensive collections of recent fauna from Oaxaca, much of it brought back by the late Emmet T. Hooper. Flannery and Wheeler (1986b) were able to collect additional specimens of the valley's fauna, including rodents from more than 500 owl pellets.

The complete list of animals recovered from San José Mogote is given in Chapter 4. In this chapter we discuss only the most common species eaten, those that appear to have been staples.

The most important large animal in the diet was the white-tailed deer, *Odocoileus virginianus,* which would have inhabited the entire valley. Even when agricultural land clearance had reduced its habitat on the high alluvium, it would have been abundant in the oak-pine forests of the nearby sierra (Fig. 2.10). Collared peccary (*Dicotyles tajacu*) was taken much less frequently.

Rabbits, because of their great abundance in spite of land clearance, were clearly a dietary staple. The small eastern cottontail, *Sylvilagus floridanus connectens,* popped out of the underbrush whenever we cleared a new excavation area on the site. Almost as common was its larger relative, the *tepetoztle* or Mexican cottontail, *Sylvilagus cunicularius,* which lives in drier habitats. Third in frequency was the jackrabbit, *Lepus mexicanus,* a large hare that does well in still drier and more open habitats.

Another staple was the pocket gopher, *Orthogeomys grandis,* whose remains were common in Formative houses and middens. As discussed in Chapter 4, this gopher seems to have disappeared

Figure 2.6. The Atoyac River at full flood, August 1969. In this view, looking south from the Guadalupe Etla bridge, the hilltop ruins of Atzompa can be seen in the background.

from the valley. We find this puzzling, since *O. grandis* loves to live in maize fields and is still considered a delicacy in other parts of its range (Coe and Flannery 1967:15).

Other small animals, such as opossums (*Didelphis marsupialis*) and raccoons (*Procyon lotor*), were eaten on occasion, but none as regularly as rabbits and gophers.

Among the reptiles, only one reached the level of a staple: the mud turtle, *Kinosternon integrum*, which could easily have been collected from pools or mudholes along the Atoyac and its tributaries. Bird life in Oaxaca is rich and varied, but only a handful of species appear to have been staples. Included were the band-tailed pigeon (*Columba fasciata*), the mourning dove

(*Zenaidura macroura*), the bobwhite quail (*Colinus virginianus*), and the Montezuma quail (*Cyrtonyx montezumae*). Other birds like hawks and chachalacas were occasionally taken, but so rarely that we are not sure whether they were killed for their meat or their plumage.

One last dietary staple of San José Mogote was the dog (*Canis familiaris*). Dogs were not part of the original fauna, but a domestic animal introduced to the valley and raised as food. In addition to providing a reliable source of meat, dogs seem to have played a role in feasting, analogous to the role played by domestic pigs in highland New Guinea (Chapter 4).

Figure 2.7. Two views of the Atoyac River floods, 1969. When the water receded from the maize and alfalfa fields, it was discovered that the river had changed its course in places.

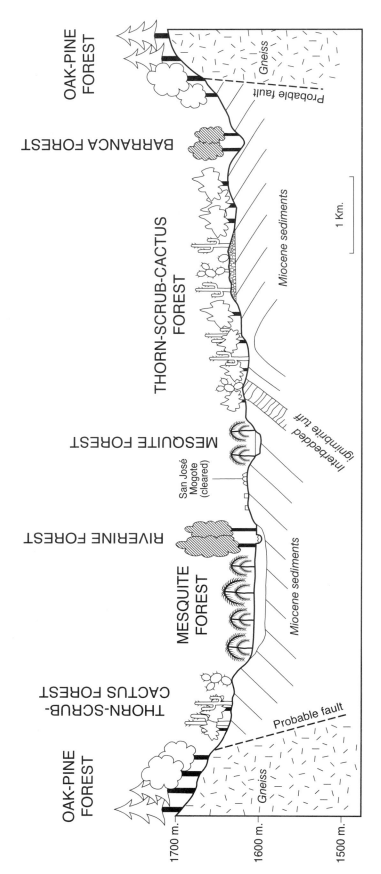

Figure 2.8. The same cross-section of the Etla subvalley given in Figure 2.2, showing the basic plant communities present on each type of geological formation.

Figure 2.9. Within a day's walk of San José Mogote, strikingly different plant communities were available at different altitudes. *a*, dense pine forest at 2500 m elevation on a mountain ridge. *b*, groves of mesquite at 1650 m elevation on an alluvial floodplain. The mountains in the background, now denuded, would once have supported oaks and pines.

Figure 2.10. Remnants of the original Holocene vegetation have survived centuries of land clearance, grazing, and woodcutting. In the foreground, mesquite, acacia, and prickly pear—all components of the piedmont thorn forest—can still be found in Area A of San José Mogote. In the background, oaks and pines still grow on the mountains above Fábrica San José. Those mountains, some 8-10 km distant, would have been a source of pine posts and venison for San José Mogote.

Chapter 3

Excavating Formative Household Units

We began work at San José Mogote determined to make the residence, rather than the pit or trench, our unit of analysis. Standing in our way was the fact that we were not sure what Early Formative houses in Oaxaca would look like. We knew that MacNeish had found four postmolds from a Middle Formative house at Pánuco, Veracruz (MacNeish 1954), so houses were potentially recoverable—at least, for someone trained in the Midwestern United States by Fay-Cooper Cole.

Without a guidebook, we set out to learn by trial and error, using primarily Midwest field techniques. It took two field seasons and a bit of luck to figure out the "forensics" of a collapsed wattle-and-daub house. The bit of luck was the fact that Early Formative houses looked a lot like the wattle-and-daub houses still being used in traditional Oaxaca villages. That meant that we could use the latter as our guide, just as Wauchope (1938) had used traditional houses in the Maya region.

Traditional Houses

In the 1960s a number of hamlets and small villages in Oaxaca still featured wattle-and-daub houses, either as residences or outbuildings (Fig. 3.1a). These houses were 3 × 5 m to 5 × 7 m in area, and if the family needed more space, they built a second house adjacent to the first.

Figure 3.1b shows the frame or substructure from such a house. Six large upright posts have been driven into the ground to outline the floor. Pine is the preferred wood when available because its resin repels termites; it also grows straight. The crooked post in Figure 3.1b indicates that pine was not available in the case of this house.

Typically the roof is laid out as shown in the drawing. While some of the key materials may be slender wooden poles, the bulk of the framing is done with strong canes such as *Phragmites* sp. (carrizo). In the most traditional construction, all canes and timbers are secured with rope rather than nails. Agave or yucca fiber was the basic Formative source for rope. Note in Figure 3.1b that the roof is laid out to extend well beyond the walls of the house, and is steeply peaked to shed rain. Reed mats would next be stitched over the frame, forming a continuous surface over which the thatch would be laid. The thatch itself would consist of thick layers of a monocot like *Phalaris* sp. (reed canary grass). This material might have to be renewed after a few rainy seasons.

Next come the wattle walls, composed of bundles of reeds or canes lashed together with rope. These are tied to the weight-bearing posts, usually on the outside. Over the wattle goes a layer of daub, or clay, often the same kind used for pottery. On the houses of some families, like those shown in Figure 3.1a, this daub is the final coat, and may develop a crazed surface as it dries. The houses of more well-to-do families, however, may get a layer of even finer clay mixed with lime whitewash. This layer may be burnished, producing a smooth, uncrazed surface that sheds rain and looks more attractive. Care may be taken to make sure that the corners of these better-made houses are nicely squared, rather than rounded.

As Figure 3.1a shows, houses typically have a door on one of the long sides and perhaps windows, framed with poles, just below the roof. The doorways may be archaeologically recoverable, especially since some have a sill of stones to keep out the mud. Indeed, some houses may have complete fieldstone foun-

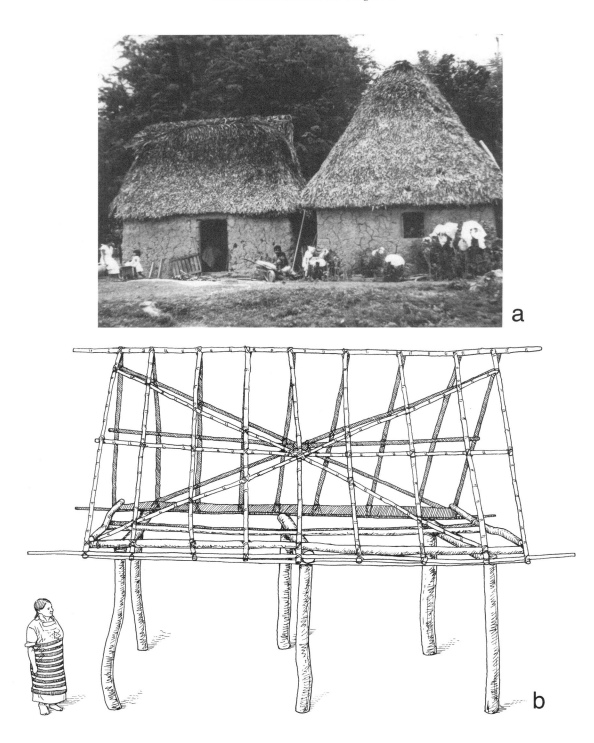

Figure 3.1. Traditional thatched-roof, wattle-and-daub houses of the Oaxaca region. *a*, two-structure household unit near Valdeflores in the Valle Grande or southern subvalley. *b*, pole and carrizo frame for a wattle-and-daub house at Ojitlán, Oaxaca (drawn by J. Klausmeyer from a photograph by W. Reuter, Archives of the Governor of Oaxaca).

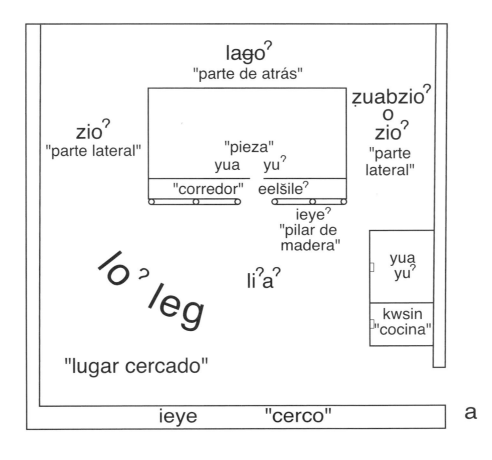

lago?
"parte de atrás"

zio?
"parte lateral"

ẕuabzio?
o
zio?
"parte lateral"

"pieza"
yua   yu?

"corredor"   eelšile?

ieye?
"pilar de
madera"

lo?leg

li?a?

yua
yu?

kwsin
"cocina"

"lugar cercado"

ieye   "cerco"

a

b

Figure 3.2. The dooryards of traditional Oaxaca houses. *a*, the *lo'leg* or dooryard of a house in Yalálag, Oaxaca, 1937-1941 (redrawn from de la Fuente 1949: Fig. 1). *b*, artist's reconstruction of Household Unit LTL-1 at the site of Tierras Largas, showing ten storage pits in the dooryard. The pit at the far right still had its stone lid.

dations below their wattle-and-daub walls, making the outline of a collapsed house easier to follow. The windows would not be archaeologically recoverable, since they occur too far up on the wall.

When houses were built on slopes, it was occasionally necessary to dig into the earth on the uphill side in order to produce a level floor. Twentieth-century Zapotec often took advantage of the resulting cut bank by using it to reinforce the rear wall of the house (de la Fuente 1949:35). Many wattle-and-daub houses have simple floors of stamped earth, or what Southwest U.S. archaeologists call "puddled adobe." At Formative San José Mogote, floors were often more formal than this. An actual layer of clay was laid down on the floor and smoothed; over this went a layer of clean river sand, presumably to keep the floor dry when family members were coming and going on a rainy day. Another way of keeping the floor dry was to dig rain runoff canals upslope of the house.

The custom of coating floors with clay and sand made it possible to determine whether a floor had been resurfaced during the lifetime of a house. Some Formative houses had as many as three superimposed floors, each consisting of a layer of fine sand over smoothed clay.

The Dooryard

Every Formative wattle-and-daub house (or pair of adjoining houses) was part of a "household unit" of perhaps 300-400 m², consisting of the buildings themselves and a "dooryard" or outdoor work area. This dooryard, which surrounded the residence, sometimes had sheds, ramadas, lean-tos, storage pits, wells, hearths, earth ovens, craft activity areas, and household middens associated with it. It might, or might not, be a venue for burials.

The dooryard was so much larger than the house that any given excavation square had a better chance of hitting dooryard than house. This was not, however, all bad. It turns out that a great deal of the family's activity took place in the dooryard, and that certain work areas and features could *only* be found there. In fact, after 15 years of digging at San José Mogote, we can honestly say that unless you excavate the dooryard of an Early Formative residence, you will probably recover less than half the story.

For example: during the San José and Guadalupe phases, a lot of cooking was done over portable ceramic charcoal braziers. Houses occupied during these phases, therefore, tended not to have hearths. In the dooryard, where there was much more room (and no roof overhead to prevent the smoke from escaping), there might be very substantial earth ovens, or large hearths filled with fire-cracked rocks.

Furthermore, because dooryards were so much larger than houses, there was less pressure on the family to keep them swept. This meant that artifacts associated with activity areas in dooryards had a greater chance of being left near the spot where they had been used.

In dooryards, we often found both "drop zones" and "toss zones" in the terminology of Binford (1983: Fig. 89). Drop zones were places where tools or raw materials had been left within reach of an individual performing a task. Toss zones were more distant areas, where items no longer wanted by that individual might be thrown to get them out of the way. It was harder to find drop zones and toss zones on house floors, since floor areas were limited to 15 to 35 m², and their debris was periodically swept out.

In Spanish-speaking villages today the dooryard is known by the term *solar*, "an area exposed to the sun." Zapotec speakers actually have separate terms for the different parts of the dooryard. Fortunately for us, some of those terms were collected in the late 1930s by Julio de la Fuente (1949) when he studied Yalálag, a Zapotec town in the mountains north of the Tlacolula subvalley.

Wattle-and-daub houses were in the process of being replaced by adobe structures in 1937, but the Zapotec words for the dooryard were still in use. The general term for a dooryard was *lo'leg*, "*lugar cercado*" or "an area enclosed by a fence." Many dooryards were in fact surrounded by a barrier of canes, living cactus plants, or informal fieldstone walls (de la Fuente 1949:35). Household units tended to be set back from major roads, since the latter were "traveled by sorcerers and evil spirits" (ibid). This fact reminds us that Zapotec communities had strategies for house placement that might not be deduced even as a result of the most careful archaeological research. It is possible that Early Formative dooryards were also fenced off with perishable materials, but we have no way of knowing.

Figure 3.2a shows a Yalálag household unit mapped and labeled by de la Fuente (1949: Fig. 1). The *yu'*, or house proper (from the sixteenth-century Zapotec *yoho* or *yo'o*), was entered via a porch whose roof was supported by wooden posts. There were two outbuildings in the dooryard, one a cook shack known by the loan word *kwsin* ("*cocina*"). The dooryard in front of the house was *li'a'*; the dooryard behind the house was *lago'*, "*la parte de atrás*." To either side were the lateral dooryards, both called *zio'*. In the case of the House 16/17 Complex of San José Mogote (Chapters 18-19), we were fortunate enough to find the *lago'* and both *zio'*. In the case of Household Unit LTL-1 at the site of Tierras Largas (Fig. 3.2b), Winter (1972) was fortunate enough to find ten storage features in the *lo'leg*.

Excavating Wattle-and-Daub Houses

We came across Early Formative houses in our excavations in two ways: from above or from the side. In Areas B and C of San José Mogote we could see house floors from the side, in cross-section, after shaving the vertical profiles left by modern adobe makers (Fig. 3.3). After removing the overlying deposits, we could then trace the remaining floor from square to square, recording those artifacts that lay *in situ* upon it.

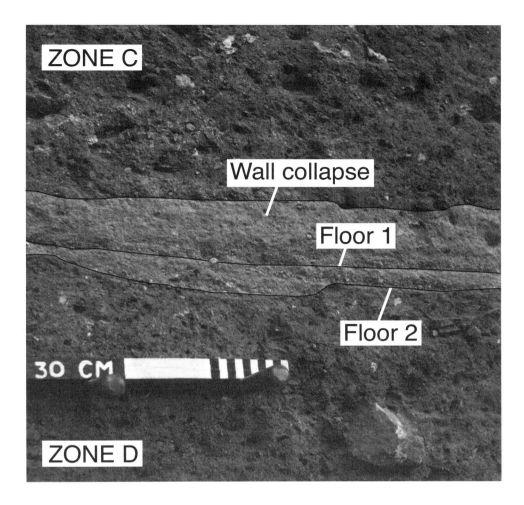

Figure 3.3. This stratigraphic profile from Area C, San José Mogote, shows how house floors appear in cross-section. Zone C is a midden layer overlying the house. "Wall collapse" is a layer of rain-melted daub from the collapse of House 14. "Floor 1" is the upper of the house's two superimposed sand floors (i.e., a "floor resurfacing"). "Floor 2" is the lower of the two sand floors (i.e., the "original floor"). Zone D is a midden underlying the house. (Total length of wooden scale, 30 cm.)

In shallow sites like Tierras Largas, where sterile soil often lay only 20 cm below the surface, it proved possible to strip off the plow zone over a wide area and discover houses from above (Fig. 3.4). At Tierras Largas we learned how far apart Early Formative houses might be spaced—20 to 40 meters—and how important it was to excavate the dooryard along with the house.

Houses in Area A of San José Mogote were discovered both ways. Many dooryard surfaces, which consisted simply of stamped earth, and were therefore less readily detectable than house floors, were visible in the original profile we shaved. Many of the house floors in Area A, however, were discovered from above while we were digging down to the level of a known dooryard surface.

However a house may be discovered, one is likely to find chunks of cane-impressed daub from the walls lying on or near the house floor. Even a house that has not been deliberately burned is likely to produce a few chunks of daub that were baked hard enough to survive the post-abandonment rains. Figures 3.5 and 3.6 show examples of the daub chunks that can aid in reconstructing a house. Included are house corners, impressions of cane bundles and rope, and whitewashed surfaces whose color can be matched to chips in the Munsell Soil Color Charts (Munsell Color Company 1954).

We dug house floors slowly, piece-plotting all those artifacts considered significant (Fig. 3.7). We did not attempt to plot abundant, marginally diagnostic items such as chert debitage or undecorated body sherds; they were, however, recorded by 1 × 1 m square. Inevitably, some artifacts hidden in small dirt clods were not found *in situ* by a trowelman and wound up in the screen. The screen operator called these items to our attention so that they could at least be recorded by square, perhaps even to the area of the square from which the last bucket of dirt had come.

We should say a word about the results of our artifact plotting. We never assumed that artifacts would be lying on the house floor just where they had last been used. We knew that if a typical wattle-and-daub house lasted 10-20 years, its floor would be swept hundreds of times. The only artifacts that stood any chance of remaining *in situ* were those used just before the house was abandoned. We expected, however, that some artifacts would inevitably be trodden into the sand of the floor, or swept into a dark corner of the house and forgotten. In other words, we expected to learn a lot even from discard behavior, and we were not disappointed. Most of all, we hoped to excavate so large a sample of houses that we would see repetitive patterns—items repeatedly discarded together because they were typically used

Figure 3.4. Area A of the site of Tierras Largas, with the plow zone removed. The unexcavated floor of House LSJ-1 appears as a dark rectangle of organic debris surrounded by orange, gneiss-derived sterile soil.

Figure 3.5. Clay daub from Formative houses at Tierras Largas. *a*, chunk of daub showing impressions of both the cane bundles and the rope used to lash them together. *b*, fragment of house surface, showing whitewashed clay. *c*, cross-section of daub, showing the gap between cane bundles. *d*, cross-section of *b*, showing superimposed layers of wall plaster left by resurfacing. (Dimensions of *a*, 8 × 7.5 cm.)

together, regardless of whether or not they remained near the spot where they were used.

We also hoped to find evidence for sexual division of labor by locating men's and women's work areas. We had in mind Vogt's study of highland Maya houses (Fig. 3.8), which were "conceptually divided" into different living spaces: (1) the house and associated objects owned and used by women, (2) the house altar and associated objects owned and used by men, and (3) places where men's and women's objects might co-occur as the result of shared activities (Vogt 1969:83-84). What we discovered is that gender-related activity areas were easier to identify in the dooryard, since its greater size reduced its need to be swept.

As the record for each household will show, we learned a great deal from our artifact plotting, even when it was not what we had expected to learn. Some houses had been swept just prior to abandonment, leaving only discard behavior to observe. Other houses had witnessed one last episode of craft activity just before abandonment, yielding relatively pristine "drop zones" with conjoinable items. Some dooryard features were surrounded by the artifacts likely to have been used there.

Figure 3.6. Clay daub from Formative houses at Tierras Largas. *a*, fragment of square corner from residence (or Men's House?), showing clay plaster and lime whitewash. *b*, fragment of clay daub, showing impressions of two different bundles of canes; a small stone was included in the clay. (Dimensions of *b*, 17 × 15.5 cm.)

Some items presumed to have been used together—for example, pearl oyster shells and the chert perforators/gravers with which they were cut and drilled—were repeatedly discarded together (Chapter 25). Culinary hearths, presumed to have been made and used by women, were sometimes surrounded by charcoal braziers, cooking pots, maize grinding stones, sewing needles, and hand-made figurines, just as one might predict. To be sure, some craft activities could not be clearly linked to one gender or the other, despite our hope of doing so.

On balance, we were glad we had taken the time to piece-plot. Even when we did not learn what we had hoped, we learned something: evidence for feasts involving as many as five domestic dogs; evidence that sewing might have required more outdoor light than basket making; evidence that two chert knappers in the same household might have employed different techniques for primary flake production.

Once all the artifacts from a household had been recorded and lifted, the sand overlying the floor was removed, and the search for postmolds began (Fig. 3.9). Using a crop sprayer, we moistened both the house floor and the dooryard surface with a fine mist of water. This procedure enhanced any color differences between the floor and the postmolds. Eventually, each potential postmold would be cross-sectioned to make sure it was not a rodent burrow.

All ash deposits, whether inside or outside the house, were saved to see if they contained carbonized plant remains. The ash was allowed to dry slowly in the shade for days, so that the seed coats of any carbonized seeds would not dry rapidly and shatter. Finally, the dried ash was added to a basin filled with water and sodium silicate. Any carbon that floated to the surface was poured off into a carburetor-mesh screen (Fig. 3.10). When dry, the screen could be perused for carbonized plants.

The Middle Formative Period and the Early Adobe House

All Early Formative houses excavated so far at San José Mogote, Tierras Largas (Winter 1972), and Tomaltepec (Whalen 1981) had walls of wattle-and-daub. Late in the San José phase, however, both adobe and stone masonry made their first appearance in our sequence. The earliest adobes were oval to circular in plan, and planoconvex in cross-section; we found evidence that the lower halves of broken jars were used as molds for these "bun-shaped" adobes.

The earliest stone masonry buildings had sloping walls of irregular stones, fitted together without mortar. Both adobes and drylaid masonry were first used for public buildings like Structures 1 and 2 of San José Mogote (Flannery and Marcus 1994:365-71). We have yet to find them used in residences of the San José phase.

The pattern seen in Late San José continued during the Middle Formative Guadalupe phase. All Guadalupe phase houses found so far at San José Mogote, Tierras Largas, and Fábrica San José (Drennan 1976a) were constructed of wattle-and-daub. The only stones associated with them were occasional wall foundations,

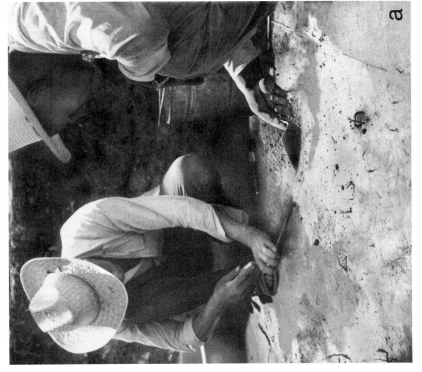

Figure 3.7. Once a house floor was reached, the process of recovering artifacts *in situ* began. In *a*, workmen carefully uncover the floor surface of a house in Area C. In *b*, Eligio Martínez takes the coordinates of a figurine head (white arrow) in Area A, while Irán Matadamas loosens the debris on the house floor with a sharpened screwdriver.

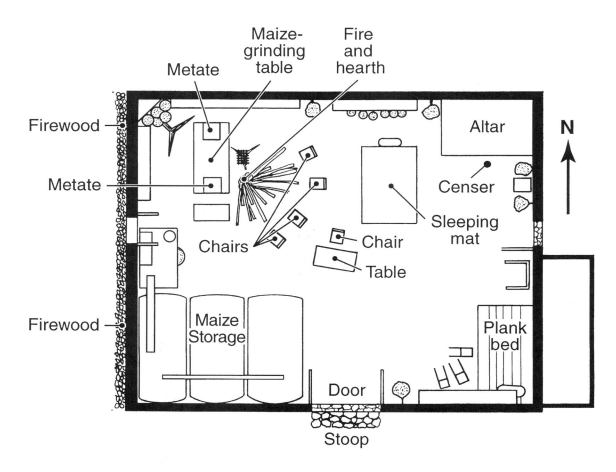

Figure 3.8. Plan of an idealized highland Maya house from Zinacantán, Chiapas (redrawn from Vogt 1969: Fig. 32).

like those in the earlier San José phase houses. On the other hand, the platforms for Guadalupe phase public buildings like Structure 8 at San José Mogote and Structure 3 at Huitzo featured drylaid stone masonry exteriors, with the interior fill strengthened by retaining walls of planoconvex adobes (Marcus and Flannery 1996:112-13).

Thus, several centuries after adobe making and stone masonry had come into existence, those construction techniques had apparently still not spread to residences—not even to the houses of relatively high-status families. It may be that while planoconvex adobes were deemed suitable for retaining walls within masses of earthen fill, they were not considered appropriate for stand-alone vertical walls. (We should stress, however, that the houses of the most highly ranked Guadalupe phase families have yet to be found.)

This situation changed in the Rosario phase with the introduction of rectangular adobes. From that point on community leaders, like the occupants of Structure 25/26/30 at San José Mogote (Fig. 3.11), lived in houses with adobe walls. Such walls, usually two adobes wide, were often set on fieldstone foundations.

The appearance of adobe houses changed our excavation techniques from "Midwest U.S." to "Near Eastern." That is, we set aside our crop sprayer and had our workmen expose the adobe walls with ice picks and sharpened trowels, much as Near Eastern workmen expose mud brick walls with lightweight picks (Hole, Flannery, and Neely 1969:23-24). And while we continued to piece-plot artifacts, we found that the hard clay floors of adobe houses yielded much less debris than those of wattle-and-daub houses, perhaps because they were easier to sweep clean.

Figure 3.9. Searching for postmolds in Area A house floors, San José Mogote. In *a*, Richard Orlandini uses a crop sprayer to moisten a San José phase house floor from which the artifacts have been removed. The fine mist of water enhances the color difference between the floor itself and the postmold, which appears as a dark circle half a meter in front of Orlandini. In *b*, the postmold poses for its portrait.

Figure 3.10. Flotation of ash deposits at San Sebastián Abasolo, Oaxaca. Felix and Rodolfo Sosa pour a solution of ash, water, and sodium silicate into a very fine mesh screen. Later, the screen will be searched for carbonized maize kernels, bean cotyledons, squash seeds, and other plant remains.

Figure 3.11. Elite families of the Rosario phase lived in houses made of rectangular adobes. This is Room 1 of Structure 26 (see Chapter 23).

Not every Rosario phase family, of course, was entitled to an adobe house; less highly ranked families continued to live in wattle-and-daub houses, like those excavated by Winter (1972) at Tierras Largas. Drennan's relatively large sample from Fábrica San José (at least eight Rosario phase houses) showed us a bit of the architectural variety present at that time. The house associated with Household Unit R-2 (Drennan 1976a:116-21) was 2.5 m wide and more than 11 m long; its walls had impressive fieldstone foundations, two courses high in places. This long narrow house may have been divided into smaller rooms by wattle walls. Other Rosario phase houses were more modest in size, and had no fieldstone foundations for their wattle-and-daub walls.

Whalen (1981) found at least one multistructure Rosario phase household at Tomaltepec. Houses 5 and 7 formed an L-shaped unit, occupying two sides of a patiolike space within the dooryard. Each house had roughly 10.5 m² of floor area and was built of rectangular adobes over a stone foundation. This unit may represent the residence of an extended family.

In sum, the Rosario phase was one in which there was a wide range of house types, perhaps reflecting the wide range of social statuses present at that time. The most highly ranked families lived in large adobe residences with interior patios (Chapter 23); the lowliest lived in one-room wattle-and-daub houses. In between lay a variety of single and multistructure households with flexible combinations of adobe or wattle walls.

Chapter 4

Household Activities, Part 1

Every traditional site report has a series of chapters describing classes of artifacts. One's colleagues depend on such chapters when comparing their artifacts to yours, and comparisons are difficult without explicit typologies.

Because of our determination to analyze San José Mogote *as a village*, however, our data will not be presented in the form of chapters on artifact categories. In Chapters 4 and 5 we synthesize our data as an old-time ethnographer might, into *a series of household activities*. We begin with subsistence activities like farming, plant collecting, and hunting, proceed to household activities like pottery and basketry making, and then to more esoteric crafts like the working of mother-of-pearl, mica, and magnetite. We try to make the *activity* our focus, while still including the typological information our colleagues want. Perhaps in the future, this will become a more common format for site reports.

Chapters 4 and 5 cover most village activities, but do not deal with *house-to-house variation*. The all-important issue of variation will be considered in Chapters 7-23, where we give the full inventory of every residence, and in Chapter 25, where Robert Reynolds subjects 18 of our San José phase residential units to multidimensional scaling.

Farming

The principal source of agricultural information in Formative houses consisted of carbonized plant remains (Figs. 4.1, 4.2). The process of flotation by which these remains were recovered is described in Chapter 3. The bulk of the plants were identified by the late C. Earle Smith, Jr. Additional identifications were done by students in the Laboratory of Ethnobotany, University

of Michigan Museum of Anthropology, under the direction of Richard I. Ford. Chief among these students were Judith Smith, Suzanne Harris, and Virginia Popper.

Cultivated plants identified from San José Mogote were as follows:

Domestic Plants
    maize (*Zea mays*)
    teosinte (*Zea mexicana*)
    bottle gourd (*Lagenaria* sp.)
    squash (*Cucurbita* sp.)
    chile pepper (*Capsicum* cf. *annuum*)
    avocado (*Persea americana*)
    beans (*Phaseolus* sp.)
        Comment: The carbonized beans from San José Mogote could not be identified to species. There are several possibilities. Tepary beans (*P. acutifolius*) were identified from Early Formative levels at Tomaltepec (J. E. Smith 1981). Common beans (*P. vulgaris*) were identified from Formative levels at both Tomaltepec (ibid.) and Fábrica San José (Ford 1976).

Plants That Might Be Either Wild or Domestic
    maguey (*Agave* spp.)
    prickly pear (*Opuntia* spp.)

Plants Conspicuous by Their Absence
    cotton (of any type)
    tomato (of any type)

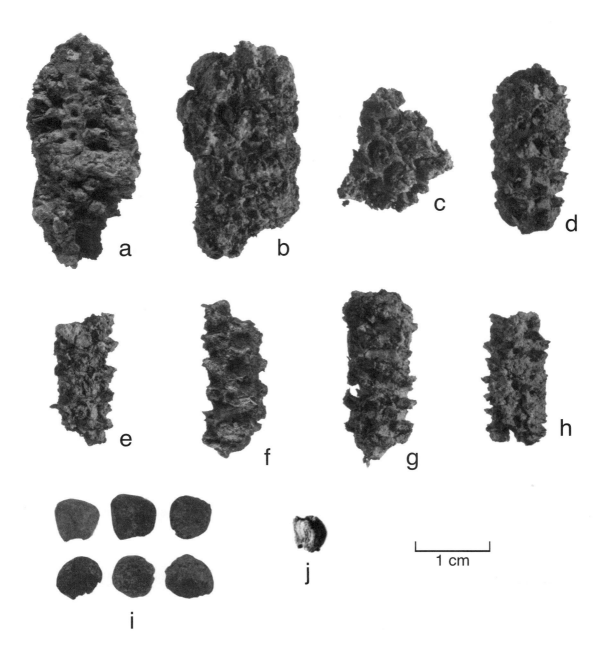

Figure 4.1. Carbonized maize and teosinte from Formative sites in the Valley of Oaxaca (shown twice actual size). *a*, Late Tierras Largas phase cob from Zone F, Area C, San José Mogote. *b, c*, San José phase cobs from Feature 3, Abasolo. *d*, Rosario phase cob from Feature 8, Abasolo. Cobs *e-h* all have indurated glumes showing teosinte introgression. *e, g*, from Feature 3, Abasolo (San José phase). *f*, from Vessel 2, House 2, Area C, San José Mogote (San José phase). *h*, from Feature 8, Abasolo (Rosario phase). *i*, Guadalupe phase kernels from Huitzo. *j*, teosinte caryopsis from Feature 32, Area C, San José Mogote (San José phase).

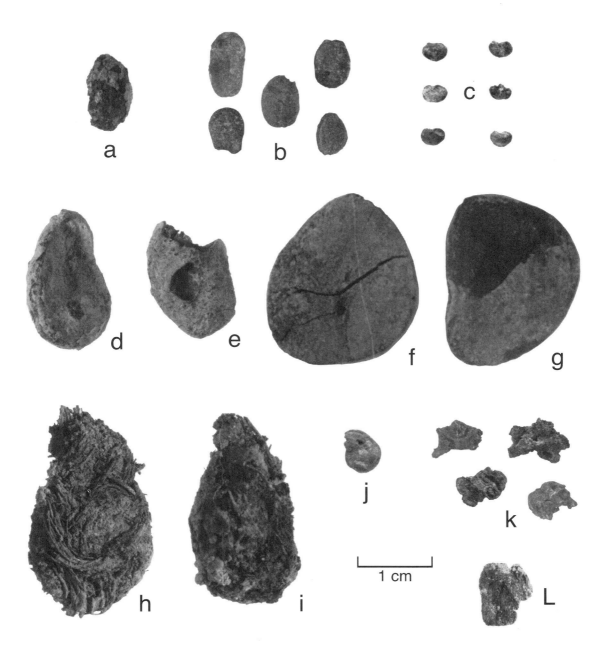

Figure 4.2. Carbonized plants from Formative sites in the Valley of Oaxaca (shown twice actual size). *a-g* are domestic. *a*, San José phase squash seed from House 2 Midden, Area C, San José Mogote. *b*, Guadalupe phase beans (*Phaseolus* sp.) from Huitzo. *c*, San José phase chile pepper seeds from Feature 6, Abasolo. *d, e*, small avocado seeds from Feature 8, Abasolo (Rosario phase). *f, g*, large avocado seeds from Huitzo (Guadalupe phase). *h-j* could be either wild or cultivated. *h, i*, agave quids from Feature 8, Abasolo (Rosario phase). *j*, prickly pear seed from Feature 22, Area C, San José Mogote (Tierras Largas phase). *k*, seeds of West Indian cherry from Huitzo (Guadalupe phase). *L*, fragment of carrizo (*Phragmites* sp.) from Vessel 2, House 2, Area C, San José Mogote (San José phase).

Figure 4.3. Low-level aerial oblique of the San José Mogote/Guadalupe Etla region. In this view from the east, the principal mounds and main ceremonial plaza of San José Mogote are clearly visible in the foreground. All the alluvial land in the lower two-thirds of the photo would have been available to the farmers of San José Mogote. Their nearest Early Formative neighbors would have been at Nazareno Etla. (Aerial photo by C. L. Moser.)

Farming Techniques

As Figure 4.3 indicates, San José Mogote had a great deal of farmland available, relative to its estimated population. We have previously calculated that within a radius of 2.5 km of the village, San José Mogote would have had more than 1400 ha of good alluvium available (Flannery 1976a:107). Such an area could have produced more than 400 metric tons of the maize known from 1000 b.c.[1] (ibid.). This in turn would have been enough to supply every family in the village with more than a metric ton of maize per year. By the time of the Rosario phase, of course, maize cobs would have been larger. In addition, by that time San José Mogote might have received additional foodstuffs in tribute from its satellite communities.

Several different types of agriculture could have been practiced within walking distance of San José Mogote. The simplest would have been planting in the *yuh kohp,* or permanently humid river bottomland, described in Chapter 2. A more labor-intensive, but highly productive second type of agriculture would have been well irrigation (sometimes called "pot irrigation"), which is shown in Figure 4.4. In this technique, usually practiced where the water table lies within 3 m of the surface, water is drawn from shallow wells using large jars and poured directly on the plants. Wells suitable for this type of irrigation are known from the San José phase (Flannery 1983:325-26).

In the piedmont flanking the Atoyac floodplain, simple canal irrigation would have been possible using tributary streams. Figure 4.5 shows small-scale canals used today for such irrigation. Brush-and-boulder dams are used to divert water from mountain streams; the water is then brought to lower piedmont fields in narrow, gravity-flow canals. Many of San José Mogote's satellite communities could have practiced this type of water control; the technology may have evolved from the rain-runoff canals that existed at least as early as the San José phase (Chapter 17).

Piedmont streams could also be used for floodwater farming, as shown in Figure 4.6*a*. In this technique, impromptu stone or brush dams are thrown across the mouths of normally dry arroyos, so that the water from summer cloudbursts will be spread out over a wide area and penetrate the soil, rather than simply running off. This type of farming is common in the Tlacolula subvalley, where it is associated with Middle and Late Formative sites (Fig. 4.6*b*). We are not sure to what extent it would have been practiced near San José Mogote, where so many other techniques were available, but it would have been possible on the strip of alluvium just east of Area A.

Wild Plant Collecting

Our flotation samples from San José Mogote revealed that wild plant collecting went on alongside agriculture (Fig. 4.2). Arboreal fruits and nuts, canes and grasses for weaving and construction,

and second-growth weeds from fallow agricultural fields were all used by Formative villagers. The full assemblage identified so far is as follows:

Wild Fruits, Nuts, and Seeds
nanche or West Indian cherry (*Malpighia* sp.)
guaje (*Conzatia multiflora, Leucaena* spp., others)
black walnut (*Juglans* cf. *major*)
barrel cactus fruit (*Mammillaria* sp.)
biznaga (*Echinocactus* sp.)

Fruits Conspicuous by Their Absence
hackberry (*Celtis* sp.), common in the area and eaten at Guilá Naquitz Cave

Second-Growth Weeds Used as Herbs and Seasonings (Messer 1978: Fig. 21)
chipil (*Crotalaria* cf. *pumila*)
quintonil (*Amaranthus* cf. *hybridus*)
epazote (*Chenopodium* sp.)

Plants Used for Construction, Matting, and Basketry
carrizo (*Phragmites* cf. *australis*), used for wattle walls
balloon vine (*Cardiospermum* sp.), whose fruits were probably used as jar stoppers, as they are elsewhere in Mexico (Felger and Moser 1985:361)
reed canary grass (*Phalaris* sp.), used as roof thatch
pine posts (*Pinus* sp.), used for houses and palisades

Plants Used as Fuels
pine (*Pinus* spp.)
oak (*Quercus* spp.)
tree legumes (*Prosopis* sp., *Acacia* sp.)
baldcypress (*Taxodium* sp.)

Other Plants Found at Neighboring Formative Sites
verdolaga (*Portulaca* sp.), another second-growth weed used as an herb or seasoning, was identified at Tomaltepec by J. E. Smith (1981)
Dalea sp., a legume collected during the Archaic, also showed up at Tomaltepec (ibid.)
manzanita (*Arctostaphylos* sp.), a mountain tree whose wood can be used as fuel, was identified at Tomaltepec (ibid.)
Comment: Sampling error probably accounts for the absence of these plants in our samples from San José Mogote.

Dog Raising

Like most villages in Formative Mexico, San José Mogote raised dogs (*Canis familiaris*) for food. Dogs were the only domestic animal present in the Valley of Oaxaca at that time, and for many families they may have represented the most reli-

Figure 4.4. Well irrigation in the Valley of Oaxaca. In *a*, a farmer at San Sebastián Abasolo in the Tlacolula subvalley draws water from a small well to irrigate a series of rectangular seed beds. The water table in this area is only 3 m below the surface. In *b*, Pablo García points to the cross-section of a Monte Albán I well, discovered in an old bank of the Río Salado in the town of Mitla.

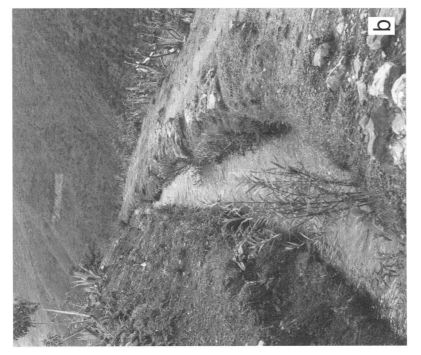

Figure 4.5. Canal irrigation in the Valley of Oaxaca. *a*, a simple brush-and-boulder dam used to divert a piedmont stream for irrigation near Tlalixtac de Cabrera, in the Tlacolula subvalley. *b*, a narrow, hand-dug canal in the piedmont near San Agustín Etla, northeast of San José Mogote. (Both photos from Lees 1973.)

Figure 4.6. Floodwater farming in the Valley of Oaxaca. *a,* floodwater being diverted into the furrows of a field near Macuilxochitl in the Tlacolula subvalley (photo from A. Kirkby 1973). *b,* aerial view of the mounds of Yegüih (Site 4-4-14 of the Settlement Pattern Survey) in the Tlacolula subvalley. Traces of an old floodwater farming channel can be seen in the lower left corner of the photograph. (Aerial photo by C. L. Moser.)

able source of meat. The nature of the bone fragments and the meager evidence for burning suggest that most dog meat was used in soups and stews, rather than being cooked directly over the fire (see "Cooking," below). We do have evidence, however, for occasional feasts at which multiple dogs were eaten; in such cases, the animals were likely cooked in an earth oven or outdoor roasting pit. There are hints that portions of meat were distributed according to predetermined rules.

Early Evidence for Domestication

We do not know exactly when the domestic dog reached the southern Mexican highlands. No dog remains were found in Archaic levels at Guilá Naquitz (Flannery and Wheeler 1986a) or Cueva Blanca (Flannery and Wheeler n.d.). The oldest hints of dog in the caves of the Tehuacán Valley date to the Late Archaic Abejas phase (Flannery 1967:150). The earliest remains, from Zone X of Coxcatlán Cave (ca. 3200 b.c.) and Zone L of Purrón Cave (ca. 2500 b.c.), consist of teeth which appear to belong to dog rather than coyote or wolf.

One of the changes following the domestication of the dog was a crowding together of teeth in the mandible, a trait not found in its wolf ancestors. This crowding was almost certainly the result of a shortening of the muzzle under the relaxed selection pressure of domestication. Abejas phase dogs also appear to have been smaller than coyotes (Flannery 1967:162).

Once sedentary life in villages had begun, the frequency of dog remains increased steadily. Dogs represented 17 percent of the animals eaten in Tehuacán's Early Formative Ajalpan phase, and rose to 23 percent in the Middle Formative Santa María phase (Flannery 1967:168). There was a considerable size range in Middle Formative dogs, which could be as small as a cocker spaniel or as large as a collie. Our sample from Tehuacán, unfortunately, is too small to show whether discrete breeds of dog existed at that time.

One Santa María phase specimen from Zone H of Purrón Cave, however, showed an intriguing genetic anomaly. This complete right mandible, 103 mm long, had no first premolar, lacking even the alveolus (or "socket") for that tooth (Flannery 1967:165). In 1967, that missing tooth seemed no more than an isolated genetic defect. Since then, in the process of analyzing Early and Middle Formative collections from the Basin of Mexico and the Valley of Oaxaca, Flannery has found more and more examples of dogs congenitally lacking the first premolar, and we have learned that such tooth loss was also characteristic of the fattened, voiceless, hairless dog the Aztec called *xoloitzcuintli* (N. Wright 1960; Schwartz 1997:139). To be sure, we are not suggesting that this Postclassic breed of dog, discussed below, was fully formed at this time.

The Xoloitzcuintli *or* Pecoxolo

When the Spaniards arrived in Mexico, they found herds of small, fattened, hairless, almost voiceless dogs being raised for food by the Aztec. The Zapotec had a similar breed of dog which they called *pecoxolo*. The latter is almost certainly a partial loan word, drawing on the Zapotec term for dog, *peco*, and the Aztec word *xolotl*.

The term *xoloitzcuintli* is still applied to a modern Mexican breed, the *perro pelón* or "Mexican hairless" (N. Wright 1960). According to N. Wright (op. cit.), this small dog is almost totally hairless, has a raspy voice that is seldom used, maintains a high body temperature, and generally lacks several or all premolars. Owing to its hairless condition, the *xoloitzcuintli* visibly perspires, something for which most dogs are not noted (except during hard exercise). We return to the *xoloitzcuintli* later in this chapter.

The Use of Dogs in Feasts

We have previously suggested that periodic feasts were a strategy for alliance-building in the Formative (Marcus and Flannery 1996:115-16). It is not always easy to get archaeological data for feasting, but there are hints of dog feasts at both Tierras Largas and San José Mogote. Let us begin with the following description from Marcus and Flannery (1996:116):

> At some point in the Guadalupe phase, Tierras Largas was the scene of a feast at which a number of domestic dogs were eaten. Feature 99, a pit used for refuse, contained the remains of at least five dogs (and probably more), all systematically butchered. A number of forelegs were found together, a number of hind legs were found together, and a number of skull elements were found together, as if someone had made a systematic division of the meat in order to provide certain people with specific parts of the animal. All the shoulder blades had been similarly smashed in order to free the humerus and the rest of the forelimb, as if a single chef had done all the butchering.
>
> We do not know whether this feast involved guests from a neighboring community, or only the residents of Tierras Largas itself. Evidence for systematic butchering, cooking, and eating of large quantities of dog meat—at least 50 kg in this case—is rare in the Guadalupe phase, suggesting that Feature 99 records a special event of some kind.

Less direct evidence for an even earlier dog feast comes from House 4, Area C, San José Mogote (Chapter 9). This San José phase evidence does not involve the post-feasting discard of bones from the *edible* parts of the carcass, as we saw in Feature 99 of Tierras Largas. Instead, what we seem to see in House 4 are the *inedible* elements systematically trimmed off a group of dogs and swept into one corner. The edible parts of the carcass had evidently been transported to the place of cooking.

The grouping of identical elements in Feature 99 of Tierras Largas, plus the hints that one chef did all the butchering, remind us of passages in M. R. Gilmore's classic article, "The Arikara Method of Preparing a Dog for a Feast" (Gilmore 1934). Gilmore witnessed the killing, dressing, and cooking of a dog for a feast of the Arikara Buffalo Society in 1926. The first stage of cooking involved turning the dog's carcass slowly over an open fire until all the hair was singed off. This was done because "the skin is too rich to lose" (Gilmore 1934:38).

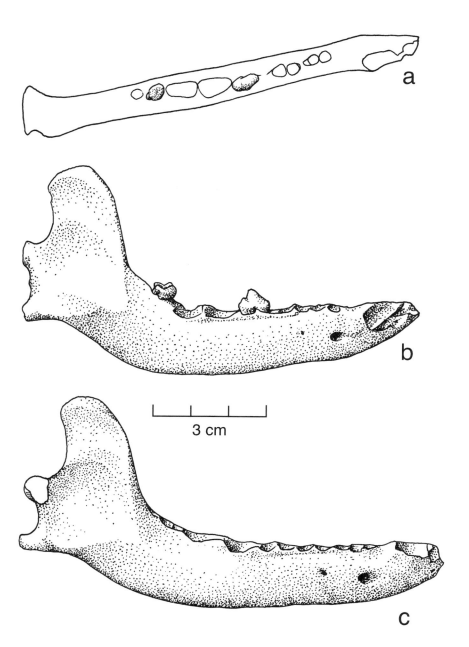

3 cm

Figure 4.7. Dog mandibles from Paul Tolstoy's excavations at Atoto, Basin of Mexico. *a, b*, mandible from A59 which congenitally lacks the first premolar. *c*, mandible from A83, which has sockets for a full complement of premolars. Both specimens are Totolica subphase, equivalent in time to the Rosario phase in the Valley of Oaxaca.

Once the now-hairless dog had been eviscerated, the carcass, still bearing its skin

> was divided into portions in accordance with a well-established tradition. These portions are the two forequarters, the two hindquarters, the two sets of ribs, the cervical and dorsal vertebrae with adjacent bones and muscles between the shoulders, and the lumbar vertebrae with the bones and muscles which form the pelvic girdle. [Gilmore 1934:38]

We are struck by the fact that if five dogs were divided this way, and the forequarters, hindquarters, and pelvic girdles later discarded as uniform groups, the results would resemble what was found in Feature 99 of Tierras Largas. While we doubt that Zapotec and Arikara ways of preparing dogs were identical, it is clear that both cultures had traditional or ritual ways of apportioning the body parts.

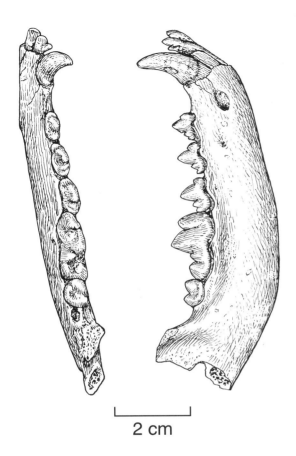

2 cm

Figure 4.8. Right mandible of a dog, congenitally missing the first premolar. Found on the floor of San José Mogote's House 16, Area B (Square N3E6, northeast quadrant). San José phase.

Congenital Tooth Loss in Formative Dogs

As mentioned above, faunal studies since the Tehuacán Project have turned up additional Formative dogs with congenital premolar loss. For example, such dogs were found in the faunal remains recovered by Tolstoy in his work at Tlatilco (and nearby Atoto) in the Basin of Mexico (Tolstoy and Guénette 1965; Tolstoy and Paradis 1970). Tolstoy's Totolica subphase for Tlatilco runs from 800 to 500 b.c., broadly coeval with the Late Guadalupe and Rosario phases in the Valley of Oaxaca.

Figure 4.7 shows two right mandibles from dogs of the Totolica subphase. The mandible shown in *c* has sockets for the full complement of four premolars. The mandible shown in *a-b* is shorter, and lacks even an alveolus for the first premolar. Thus, villagers in the Tlatilco-Atoto region raised a mixture of normal dogs and dogs with congenital tooth loss.

Far to the south, on the Pacific Coast of Chiapas, another Formative dog with congenital tooth loss turned up in the excavations of the New World Archaeological Foundation. The provenience was Pit 4A, Level 11, at the Formative site of Chilo. Based on

data provided by Blake et al. (1995: Table 1), this level should be broadly coeval with the Tierras Largas phase.

Congenital Tooth Loss in Formative Oaxacan Dogs

At San José Mogote, one of our clearest examples of congenital tooth loss comes from House 16 in Area B. Figure 4.8 shows the broken right mandible of a dog, piece-plotted in Square N3E6 on the floor of that San José phase lean-to (see Chapter 18). This dog lacks even the alveolus for a first premolar. Other dogs from this same household, however, have their normal complement of teeth.

One other dog with congenital tooth loss, redeposited in the fill of Structure 1, Area A, can date to no later than the San José phase, since that is the age of the structure as determined by ceramic stratigraphy (Flannery and Marcus 1994:367-71).

Now let us return to Feature 99 at Tierras Largas and the remains of the Guadalupe phase dog feast discussed above. Figure 4.9 compares two dog mandibles from that feast. A normal dog with its full complement of teeth is shown in *a*; *b*, on the other hand, shows a dog whose first premolar was congenitally absent. Because of the broken condition of many of the mandibles in Feature 99, it is difficult to estimate exactly how many of these Guadalupe phase dogs had congenital tooth loss. If forced to guess, we would estimate that about one in four had the condition.

Dog mandibles with congenitally missing first premolars also show up in later phases of the Formative. Structure 23 at San José Mogote was a Monte Albán Ia altar, built on the highest point of the site after the latter had been essentially abandoned. A mandible congenitally missing its first premolar was found nearby. A still-later dog mandible with congenital tooth loss was discovered in Monte Albán Ic debris during Whalen's (1981) excavations at Santo Domingo Tomaltepec (unpublished faunal study by Flannery).

We stress that none of these Formative dogs was small enough to be a true *xoloitzcuintli* or *pecoxolo*. We find it significant, however, that one of the traits of the later fattened, voiceless, hairless dog—congenital tooth loss—was already widespread in the Formative.

The Stunting of Limbs

Tooth loss was not the only distinctive character of the small dogs raised for food in ancient Mexico. Some breeds also displayed stunted limbs. Some ceramic effigy vessels from ancient Colima, in fact, depict dogs so squat that they seem bowlegged (Fig. 4.10).

There are hints that this bowleggedness may not have been an artistic exaggeration. Once again, some of the best evidence comes from Tolstoy and Paradis's (1970) work in the Basin of Mexico. One of their Middle Formative sites was El Arbolillo East, near the north shore of a bay of Lake Texcoco. The two earliest subphases there, El Arbolillo and La Pastora, span the

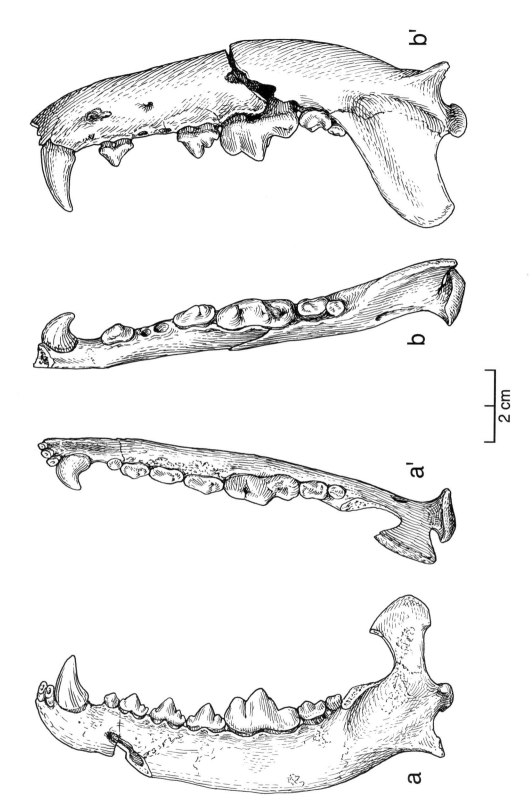

Figure 4.9. Two dog mandibles from Feature 99 at the site of Tierras Largas. *a, a'*, left mandible from dog with all four premolars present. *b, b'*, right mandible from dog with the first premolar congenitally missing. Guadalupe phase.

period 850-500 b.c. and are therefore coeval with Guadalupe and Rosario in the Valley of Oaxaca.

Figure 4.11 shows three complete radii from Tolstoy and Paradis's excavation. Normal radii are shown in *a* and *b*, one from each of the two subphases mentioned above. Shown in *c* is a radius from the El Arbolillo subphase that is not only stunted but also slightly bowed. To be sure, we would not argue that the little bowlegged breed depicted in the Colima effigies already existed in the Middle Formative. We only suggest that some of the genetic changes leading to that breed had begun to appear.

These changes appeared in the Valley of Oaxaca as well. During his excavations at Fábrica San José, Drennan (1976a:120) found a deposit of disarticulated dog bones which he designated Feature 60. This feature was associated with Household Unit R-2, a residence of the Rosario phase. The dog involved had no congenital tooth loss, but displayed the same kind of stunted radius and ulna seen in the specimen from El Arbolillo East.

Selection for the Xoloitzcuintli: *A Puzzle for the Future*

Occasional discoveries of stunted limbs and missing teeth in Formative dogs suggest that traits of the "Colima dogs" and Aztec *xoloitzcuintli* existed before those breeds were formalized. Such finds do not, however, answer the question of why anyone would want to produce a hairless, nearly voiceless, squat little dog with less than the normal complement of teeth. For which trait were these dogs' creators selecting?

While doing research on dogs in the mid-1970s, zooarchaeologist Karen Mudar (n.d.) learned of a human disorder called *hereditary ectodermal dysplasia* (Lowry et al. 1966). Apparently caused by an accidental mutation, this genetic disease produces traits in humans that resemble those of the *xoloitzcuintli*. Included are hairlessness; a decrease in pigmentation; papular changes in the face; partial to complete toothlessness; a hoarse or raspy voice; and a high body temperature (D. W. Smith 1970).

Because ectodermal dysplasia is caused by a mutation in the ectoderm—the embryonic layer from which the entire epidermis will ultimately develop—it simultaneously affects the skin, sweat glands, hair, teeth, and lining of the mouth and voice box. One form of this dysplasia is believed to be transmitted from one generation to another by a recessive gene on the X, or female, chromosome (Lowry et al. 1966).

Mudar reminds us that the literature on this genetic disorder concerns humans, not dogs. What struck her as interesting was the evidence that hairlessness, tooth loss, and hoarseness were all linked. Thus, to select for one of the traits would be to select for the others. This might explain how all the traits could show up as a package.

We find it unlikely that prehistoric dog raisers cared about the number of premolars a dog had, or its degree of voicelessness. Hairlessness, on the other hand, might have been seen as desirable. Recall that the Arikara singed the hair off their dogs because "the skin is too rich to lose." Breeding a hairless dog would remove one whole step in food preparation. And if an

Figure 4.10 Large hollow dog effigy in redware from Colima. Height, 13 cm. (Drawn from a photo in Weaver 1972: Plate 4h.)

ectodermal mutation were involved, selecting for hairlessness might also give you tooth loss, near voicelessness, and sweating as part of the genetic package.

Neither we, nor anyone else, as yet knows whether this is how the little fattened, hairless, almost voiceless dogs of sixteenth-century Mexico were created, but the stunted limbs and missing premolars of the Formative suggest that the "Mudar model" is at least worth thinking about.

Hunting and Trapping

In addition to domestic sources of protein—beans, squash seeds, and dogs—the villagers of San José Mogote ate substantial quantities of wild game (Fig. 4.12). Perhaps their most prized quarry was the white-tailed deer, which provided an average of 20 kg of usable meat per individual (Flannery 1986b: Table 24.6). Collared peccary, which provides an average of 14 kg per individual, was apparently killed less frequently.

Both deer and peccary would have been available within a 10 km radius of the village. Since both are known to eat acorns, they should have been particularly common in the oak woodland of the mountains and upper piedmont. There is some question about *how* they were hunted, since chipped stone atlatl points were rare to absent in the Valley of Oaxaca during the Tierras Largas, San José, and Guadalupe phases (see our discussion of chert tools later in the chapter). This scarcity of stone points was unexpected, given how common they had been in the Archaic period (Hole 1986). Clearly, a change in hunting strategy had taken place during the transition from Archaic to Formative. What was it?

A possible answer to this question comes from the Central Depression of Chiapas, another region where chipped stone atlatl points were rare during the Formative. The sixteenth-century

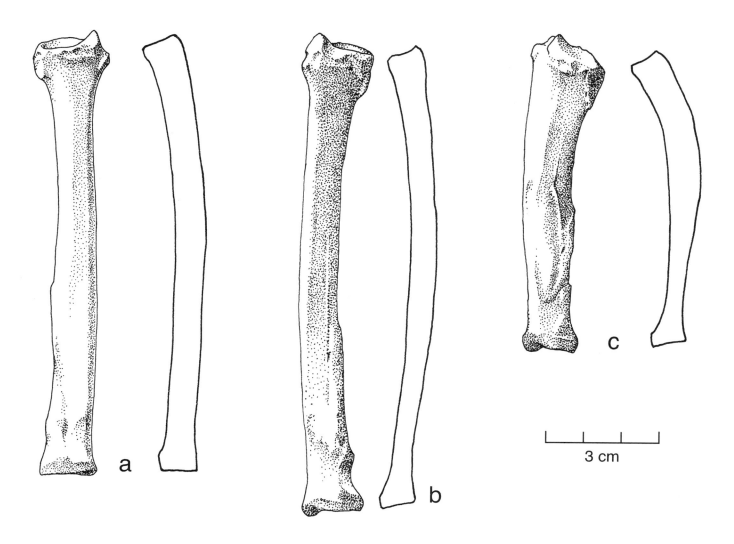

Figure 4.11. Dog radii from Paul Tolstoy's excavations at El Arbolillo East, Basin of Mexico. *a*, normal radius from L51 (El Arbolillo subphase). *b*, normal radius from L59 (La Pastora subphase). *c*, stunted and bent radius from L63 (El Arbolillo subphase), suggesting genetic change in the direction of a dog with short, stubby legs. All specimens are Middle Formative, equivalent in time to Guadalupe and Rosario.

Chiapanec who occupied that region

are described as being great hunters, with deer the principal game. They had as weapons wooden spears with fire-hardened tips, the bow and arrow, and slings "larger than those of the Spanish." Deer were also hunted with nets. [Lowe 1959:7]

If we eliminate the bow and arrow (for which there is no evidence in the Formative), what the passage above suggests is *communal hunting*. Instead of individual hunters stalking deer with atlatls, which evidently characterized the Archaic, the Chiapanec took advantage of the larger human population created by successful agriculture. In communal hunting, one group could stretch a large tennis-style net across a barranca, while another group drove the deer herd into it by beating the brush.

Once impeded by the net, the deer could be dispatched at close range with slings and fire-hardened wooden spears. Such hunts might yield large numbers of deer, yet leave little archaeological evidence, owing to poor preservation of wood and netting. The strategic change between the Archaic and the Early Formative might thus have been a shift of emphasis from (1) hunting in small groups with atlatls to (2) communal hunting with nets and wooden spears.

During the Rosario phase the frequency of projectile points began to rise, but as discussed below under "The Procurement and Working of Chert," we believe that to be the result of increased raiding, not a change in hunting techniques.

As the population of the Valley of Oaxaca grew, the point was eventually reached when there was not enough deer meat for all. By the sixteenth century, venison was reserved for Za-

Figure 4.12. Wild animals hunted by the occupants of San José Mogote included white-tailed deer (*a*), collared peccary (*e*), jackrabbits (*b*), Mexican cottontails (*c*), eastern cottontails (*d*), the common bobwhite (*f*), Montezuma quail (*g*), and mud turtles (*h*).

potec nobles, while the commoners contented themselves with rabbits, lizards, wood rats, and other small game. We will never know the exact moment when these restrictions on venison were instituted. Faunal remains suggest that as early as the San José phase, greater consumption of deer was typical of more highly ranked families.

Use of Small Game

Every family seems to have had access to jackrabbits, cottontails, pocket gophers, and an occasional opossum or raccoon. Many small mammals were probably caught with traps or snares. Such devices were not preserved at San José Mogote, but probable snare fragments were identified by MacNeish, Nelken-Terner, and Johnson (1967:153) in the dry caves of Tehuacán.

A word should be said about the pocket gopher, *Orthogeomys grandis*, which was one of the most common small mammals eaten at San José Mogote. Its preferred habitat should have been the maize fields of the alluvial valley floor, which likely surrounded the village on three sides. Farmers should have been able to trap gophers right in the *milpa*, and indeed, their bones appear in most residential debris. To our surprise, this pocket gopher seems to be no longer present in the Valley of Oaxaca. We failed to collect a single modern specimen, and no one we questioned could remember having seen one. We do not know why *Orthogeomys* disappeared, but we suspect it may be related to human activity.

Other small game included birds such as doves, pigeons, and quail. These may have been taken in snares or nets, but could also have been killed with blowguns, which some Zapotec-speaking villages were still using in the 1960s. Quail were also important as animals for sacrifice because the Zapotec, having observed them drinking dewdrops, considered them ritually pure creatures who reject dirty water (Marcus and Flannery 1994:60). Small songbirds such as finches, orioles, and tanagers appear in the debris, but were more likely captured for their brightly colored feathers than for food.

During certain seasons of the year the Atoyac River provided coots and migratory ducks, and in pools and puddles along its banks it would have been easy to collect mud turtles. Like the abundant racerunner lizards that frequent the site today, mud turtles could have been procured even by children.

The Faunal Remains

Fragments of animal bone were abundant at San José Mogote, especially in middens and dooryards. In addition to Flannery himself, a number of students in the Laboratory of Zooarchaeology, University of Michigan Museum of Anthropology, carried out the identification of faunal remains. Chief among these were Katherine M. Moore, Jane C. Wheeler, Karen Mudar, Sonia Guillén, and Eloise Baker. Because there are now so many ways of quantifying faunal remains—MNI, MNE, NISP, etc.—and such

passionate advocates for each, in this volume we do not take sides; we simply list every bone in every house. That way each reader can apply his or her favorite method of quantification.

Wild animals identified at San José Mogote were as follows:

Large Mammals
> white-tailed deer (*Odocoileus virginianus*)
> collared peccary (*Tayassu tajacu*)

Small Mammals
> opossum (*Didelphis marsupialis*)
> jackrabbit (*Lepus mexicanus*)
> eastern cottontail (*Sylvilagus floridanus connectens*)
> Mexican cottontail (*Sylvilagus cunicularius*)
> pocket gopher (*Orthogeomys grandis*)
> raccoon (*Procyon lotor*)
> ring-tailed cat (*Bassariscus astutus*)
> weasel (*Mustela frenata*)

Birds
> mourning dove (*Zenaidura macroura*)
> band-tailed pigeon (*Columba fasciata*)
> bobwhite quail (*Colinus virginianus*)
> Montezuma quail (*Cyrtonyx montezumae*)
> coot (*Fulica americana*)
> lesser scaup (*Aythya affinis*)
> other ducks (unidentified)
> crow (*Corvus corax*)
> crested guan (*Penelope purpurascens*)
> small songbirds (finches, tanagers, and others), possibly killed for their feathers rather than food

Reptiles
> mud turtles (*Kinosternon integrum*)
> lizards (including *Sceloporus* sp.), some of which may have been intrusive burrowers, rather than food

Small Wild Mice, Perhaps Intrusive Rather Than Food
> spiny mouse (*Liomys irroratus*)
> white-footed mouse (*Peromyscus* sp.)
> other mice (unidentified)

Amphibians, Probably Intrusive
> toad (*Bufo marinus*)

Land Snails, Probably Intrusive
> *Euglandina* sp. (and others)

Aquatic Snails, Unidentified
> found only in waterlogged features

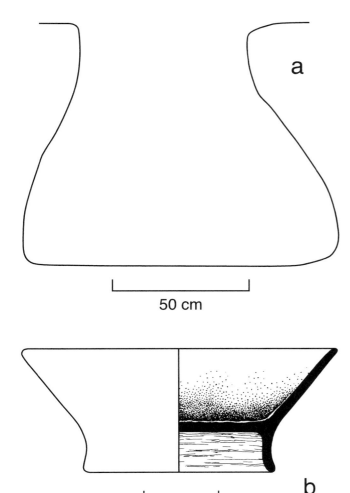

50 cm

10 cm

a

b

Figure 4.13. Facilities for cooking and storage. *a*, cross-section of typical Formative bell-shaped pit. *b*, Lupita Heavy Plain charcoal brazier/potstand.

Other Animals Found at Nearby Fábrica San José (Drennan 1976a:221). Sampling error is the most probable reason the following animals did not show up in our samples from San José Mogote. The three birds were probably killed for their feathers, and the skunk for its pelt.

gray squirrel (*Sciurus poliopus*)
coatimundi (*Nasua narica*)
skunk (*Mephitis* sp.)
gray fox (*Urocyon cinereoargenteus*)
red-tailed hawk (*Buteo jamaicensis*)
great horned owl (*Bubo virginianus*)
sparrow hawk (*Falco sparverius*)

Storage

One of the most common ways Formative villagers stored their crops was in subterranean pits. Such pits, typically bottle-shaped or bell-shaped, were excavated into the earth (or soft bedrock) of the dooryard (Fig. 4.13*a*). Most were too large to have been placed in the house.

The bottlelike shape of the pit resulted from the fact that its mouth and neck were typically narrower than the large chamber at the bottom. We suspect that this was done in order to provide a small mouth that could be sealed shut, keeping out rodents and insect pests. Some bell-shaped pits still had collars of mud or clay around their mouths, and few were found with stone slab lids still in association. Sealing a pit with a stone lid in an airtight clay collar makes it likely that any insects reaching the interior will ultimately suffocate (Hall et al. 1956).

Our best preserved pits showed traces of having been given an inner lining of clay or grass, presumably to keep the contents clean. Nevertheless, over time any pit would begin to deteriorate as the result of use, opening and reopening, and the effects of rain penetration. When a pit became unusable, it was often filled with domestic trash and a new pit excavated. One wattle-and-daub house at the site of Tierras Largas, belonging to Household Unit LTL-1, had at least 10 bell-shaped pits in its dooryard. It is unlikely that all these pits were in use at one time; they probably represent a sequence of storage features. One pit, Feature 75, still had its stone lid (Fig. 3.2*b*, Chapter 3).

We assume that maize was one of the main commodities stored in bell-shaped pits, but we do not know whether it was stored on the cob or as shelled kernels. In the case of today's maize cobs, a lot more maize would fit in the pit if the cobs were shelled. Given how small Early Formative cobs were, however, it might not have made a lot of difference.

The smallest outdoor bell-shaped pits at San José Mogote would have had a volume of 0.15-0.24 m³. The largest had volumes of 0.72-1.08 m³. Collectively, the pits associated with some residences could have held a metric ton of shelled maize, about what a family of four would use over the course of a year (A. Kirkby 1973). To be sure, it is not always clear how many pits were in use at one time.

We did find occasional *small* bell-shaped pits inside houses, like Feature 38 in House 9, Area C (Chapter 9). Such in-house pits seemed too small for maize storage; they were more likely for storing raw materials for craft activities. Feature 38, for example, had a capacity of only 0.08 m³ and was filled with the kind of fine wood ash used in press-molding ceramics.

We do not know when large bell-shaped pits were phased out as storage facilities. Their use by lower-status families continued at least into the Protoclassic. By the Rosario phase, however, high-status families living in adobe-walled houses had begun to designate specific rooms as storage units (Chapter 23).

Cooking

Cooking at San José Mogote involved several techniques, some of which had been used since the hunting-gathering era. For example, a small basin-shaped hearth filled with gray ash was found in Zone D of Guilá Naquitz Cave, a living floor dated to 8750-7840 b.c. (Flannery, Moser, and Maranca 1986: Fig. 5.22). In Zone B1 of the same cave, dated to 6670 b.c., we found a hearth lined with five stones (op. cit.: Fig. 5.26). By that time, in other words, Archaic foragers had found that cooking could be enhanced by allowing stones to absorb, store, and slowly release heat.

This discovery made possible a second Archaic cooking facility, the earth oven, baking pit, or roasting pit. In this case, a larger subterranean pit was lined with stones, then heated with a slow-burning wood like oak, manzanita, or mesquite until the stones were intensely hot. Food was then baked for an extended period by sealing it in the pit with the heated stones. One of the first uses of such an earth oven was for baking maguey hearts to render them edible. Baked maguey appeared at Guilá Naquitz Cave by 8750 b.c. Probable Late Archaic earth ovens are known from Yuzanú in the Mixteca (Lorenzo 1958) and Site Ts-381 in the Tehuacán Valley (MacNeish et al. 1972).

The use of basin-shaped hearths and rock-filled earth ovens continued at San José Mogote, but such features were usually found in the dooryard rather than in the house itself. Feature 6, found in the dooryard of Household Unit C3, Area A, is an example of a stone-lined, basin-shaped culinary hearth (Chapter 14). Feature 5, found in the dooryard of Household Unit C4 in the same area, is an example of a larger pit where food was cooked over heated rocks. Occasionally, a bell-shaped pit that had fallen into disuse might be reused as an earth oven. Such was the case with Feature 2, found in the dooryard of Household C3.

One reason why so much cooking was done outdoors is that thatch-roofed houses with no chimneys can become unpleasantly smoky when hearths are lit indoors. Botanist C. Earle Smith, Jr., assured us that this would be particularly true once villagers had begun using prepared pine charcoal, which is very resinous. As anyone who has barbecued with charcoal briquettes knows, one advantage of prepared charcoal is that it is lighter and easier to transport than firewood. This advantage had been recognized by the San José phase, when villagers evidently began burning pine logs in the mountains and bringing the charcoal back to their homes.

The use of prepared charcoal led to the creation of a new pottery vessel—the portable charcoal brazier, which could be carried from place to place, stored in a corner of the house, and taken outside to cook. Such charcoal braziers, made of Lupita Heavy Plain pottery, made their first appearance in the Early San José phase (Flannery and Marcus 1994: Table 13.1) and lasted into Early Rosario times. Each consisted of a ceramic basin set on an annular base, frequently displaying burning on the interior of the basin (Fig. 4.13b). The charcoal found in association with these braziers was most often pine, but occasionally oak, manzanita, or mesquite. Mesquite would have been the most readily

accessible of these fuels, of course; but mesquite wood is hard, so difficult to cut with a stone axe that we suspect the villagers burned only those mesquite trees felled in the course of clearing the alluvium for agriculture.

Finally, it seems likely that gender-related differences in cooking can be detected at San José Mogote. Based on the associated artifacts, we suspect that most cooking done over charcoal braziers or basin-shaped hearths was boiling, and done by women. We believe that large outdoor roasting pits, on the other hand, were features used by men on special occasions, such as preparing large dog or deer feasts for guests. In this regard, our conclusions are similar to those of Speth (2000) at the Henderson site, a pueblo in New Mexico. Based on a combination of taphonomic data and ethnographic analogy, Speth concluded that routine domestic food preparation—especially boiling—was generally performed by women. Roasting or baking could be done by either sex, depending on the social context; however, men were more likely to be the cooks when meat was being prepared for "large-scale extradomestic feasts or ceremonials" (Speth 2000:102). We believe that these conclusions fit San José Mogote as well.

Pottery Making

Sometime between the abandonment of the Martínez Rockshelter (Flannery and Spores 1983:25) and the building of House 20 at San José Mogote (Chapter 7), the craft of pottery making was introduced into the Valley of Oaxaca. The first pottery vessels were shaped like the gourd containers that had preceded them (Marcus 1983a, Flannery and Marcus 1994:47-50); they may even have been press-molded over gourds. Press-molding remained one of the main vessel-forming techniques during the Early Formative.

While pottery making was one of the most common household activities at San José Mogote, our discussion of that craft will be brief, since we have already published a monograph on the Early Formative pottery of the Valley of Oaxaca (Flannery and Marcus 1994). We refer the reader to that report for definitions of pottery types, illustrations of vessels, inventories of design motifs, and total counts of all sherds from the households discussed in this volume.

Included in the pottery monograph is a chapter by the late William O. Payne (1994), himself a potter as well as a geologist and ceramic technologist. Payne traced the clays, engobes (slips), paints, stains, and other materials to their geological sources, and was able to recognize "foreign" pottery because he knew the geology of the Valley of Oaxaca so well. We will mention Payne's discoveries from time to time, but refer the reader to his 1994 study for details.

The Ceramics of a Typical Residence

Any description of the "typical ceramic assemblage" of a residence must take into account stylistic change over time.

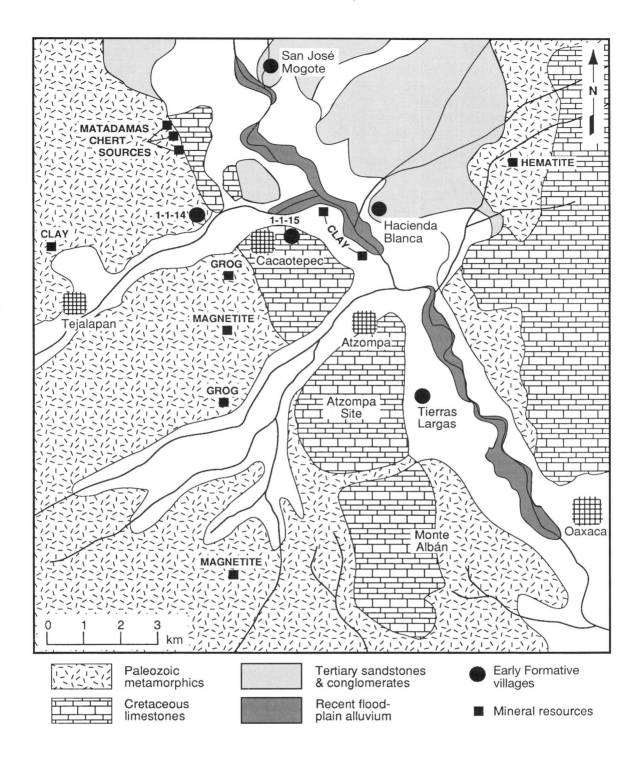

Figure 4.14. Geological map of the Etla subvalley between San José Mogote and Oaxaca City, showing mineral resources such as *barro liso* (clay), *barro áspero* (grog), hematite, magnetite, and chert.

From 1150 to 500 b.c., San José Mogote was the largest chiefly center in the valley, and had a greater variety of ceramics than any other village. It received more gifts of "foreign" pottery, probably gave away more pottery in return, and had artisans who could produce vessels finer than those made at smaller villages. Every family could make Fidencio Coarse jars and Lupita Heavy Plain braziers. Not every family could make Delfina Fine Gray (Flannery and Marcus 1994).

Tierras Largas phase houses had necked jars for boiling or storing liquids; *tecomates* or neckless jars for wet or dry storage; hemispherical bowls for individual servings; and bottles for special liquids. During the San José phase, hemispherical bowls gave way to flat-based bowls that could be deep (and cylindrical) or shallow (with outleaned walls). Necked jars and tecomates got larger as storage needs grew and pottery making improved.

Some new vessel forms of the San José phase were portable braziers for cooking with prepared pine charcoal (see "Cooking," above); spouted trays for pouring pigment; and large tubs that could have been for washing or dyeing. Burnished white beakers, perhaps for use with fermented beverages, appeared late in the phase.

The Guadalupe phase saw bowls with outcurved or flaring walls—and composite silhouette bowls—increase at the expense of cylinders and outleaned-wall bowls. By the time of the Rosario phase, one could see clear differences between the ceramic assemblages of low-status families and elite families. Low-status families had more jars relative to individual serving bowls, and their assemblages were dominated by wares that tended to be buff with a red wash or monochrome brown (Drennan 1976a). High-status families had more fine gray bowls relative to jars, and the former were often decorated with "negative" or "resist" white-on-gray decoration (Appendix A).

Clay Sources Used

Finding potter's clay was not a problem for San José Mogote, or for that matter, for any village in the Valley of Oaxaca (Payne 1994). For 70 km along the western margin of the valley, the piedmont was composed of Precambrian metamorphics such as gneiss and schist. As the gneiss weathers, *residual clays* suitable for ceramics form above bedrock. Many meters of suitable clay appear in the stream-cut sides of barrancas. No temper needs to be added to this clay; the non-plastic mineral content is so high that one need only screen out the larger particles and leave the finer ones. These particles include quartz, feldspar, hornblende, mica, and occasionally diorite, hematite, and magnetite.

In the eastern parts of the valley, the Miocene ignimbrites, or volcanic tuffs, break down into montmorillonite clay. Where there are hot springs in the ignimbrites, the clay may even be white to off-white kaolinite. The Oaxaca ignimbrites are geologically very distinctive; the ancient volcanic ash flows contain glass and pumice particles which remain in the clay, and have been used to identify exported Oaxaca vessels (Flannery and Marcus 1994:259-63).

Eventually, streams and rivers carry clays from both the Precambrian gneiss and the Miocene volcanic tuff out into the alluvial floor of the valley, where they are blended. Such *transported clays* are finer than residual clays, owing to their reworking by the watercourses that carried them. In some parts of the valley they may contain a third component, calcareous clay derived from Cretaceous limestone. This limestone is exposed at places like the Matadamas and San Lázaro Etla chert quarries (see "Working of Chert" below), and even at Monte Albán. It should be stressed that this combination of Precambrian gneiss, Cretaceous limestone, and Miocene volcanic tuff is so unusual that it has enabled geologists to identify Oaxaca pottery when it shows up in places like the Basin of Mexico or the Olmec region, where the bedrock geology is different (see "Exchanging Ceramics with Other Regions" below).

Some of today's traditional potters combine clays from several sources in order to get the exact texture they want. For example, the potters of Atzompa today mine *barro liso*, or "smooth clay," from a buried Pleistocene alluvial layer near the Atoyac River, east of Cacaotepec (Fig. 4.14). They then combine that clay with *barro áspero*, or "rough clay," which comes from decomposing Precambrian gneiss in the piedmont to the west of Atzompa (Payne 1994: Fig. 2.2; Stolmaker 1973). It appeared to Payne that many of our Formative wares had similar mixtures of clays, with the percentage of *barro áspero* determined by the fineness or coarseness. Significantly, *barro áspero* has to be pounded in a mortar, like some of those found at San José Mogote, before mixing with *barro liso*.

Colorants

The pottery of San José Mogote was decorated either by plastic alteration of the surface, by the application of colored slips or washes, or both. Plastic decoration included incising (possibly with agave spines), excising (possibly with a slat of cane), and rocker stamping.

Payne (1994) has identified the major colorants used. The weak red wash used on Fidencio Coarse, for example, was made from *barro colorado*, an iron-oxide-filled clay occurring in "pods" in the Precambrian gneiss. The red paint or slip used on Avelina Red-on-Buff or San José Red-on-White came from veins of limonite or red ochre, lumps of which were found in House 9 of Area C (Chapter 9). Specular hematite paint or slip was made with crushed and ground crystalline hematite (see "The Crushing and Grinding of Hematite," Chapter 5).

The slip used to make Atoyac Yellow-white, on the other hand, needed to be virtually iron-free in order to turn white when fired. Payne found local sources of kaolin at ancient hot springs in the ignimbrite, or in feldspar dikes near hydrothermal vents. Traces of red or white engobes in spouted trays of the San José phase (see above) showed that these surface colorings were poured on the vessel.

San José phase potters also made gray, black, or white-rimmed black vessels. These darker colors were the result of firing in a reduc-

Figure 4.15. Use of a potter's bat to form a vessel at San José Mogote (reconstruction drawing by John Klausmeyer based on a photo by Shepard 1963: Frontispiece). The potter forms a new vessel on the bat, rotating the latter slowly on an inverted jar.

ing atmosphere. The differential firing of San José Black-and-White may also have been enhanced by burying the part to be darkened in smudging material (such as corn cobs) during firing.

Vessel Forming

As mentioned above, some Early Formative bowls appear to have been press-molded over gourds (or over previously made vessels). In some cases, actual molds appeared in village debris. A Tierras Largas phase mold for forming hemispherical bowls with pinched-in sides was found in the Zone F Midden of Area C (Chapter 7). A San José phase mold for making flat-based cylindrical bowls was found in House 16 of Area B (Chapter 18). In the case of jar necks and shoulders, forming seems to have been done by laying concentric rings one above another, an alternative to coiling (Payne 1994:9-11).

During the San José phase, potter's bats were introduced for the first time. These saucerlike artifacts, examples of which were found in houses at San José Mogote, could be used to rotate the vessel slowly during forming and decoration (Fig. 4.15).

Burnishing

Burnishing was done with a quartz, chert, or chalcedony pebble, faceted examples of which were abundant at the site. Burnishing one time closed the pores in the vessel and made it waterproof. Burnishing a second time, just before firing, gave the vessel a high gloss. During the Rosario phase, Socorro Fine Gray bowls were sometimes decorated by a technique called "zoned toning," in which a matte band was left between twice-burnished areas.

Firing

We found no indisputable pottery kilns at San José Mogote. We presume that this is because most firing was done above ground, with the fuel simply piled on top of the pottery. This type of firing is still done at San Marcos Tlapazola in the Tlacolula subvalley (Payne 1994: Figs. 2.10, 2.11).

> When the firing is over, the pots are carefully removed; we observed a firing in San Marcos during which not one single vessel broke. What remains from such firing is nothing but a layer of fine ash; no archaeologist would ever be able to prove that pottery had been made in that dooryard. [Flannery and Marcus 1994:21]

By Monte Albán Ic (a period for which we have found no evidence at San José Mogote), two-chambered subterranean kilns for reduced firing had been developed. At Santo Domingo Tomaltepec in the Tlacolula subvalley, Whalen (1981: Figs. 27, 28) discovered a number of these kilns in association with Late Monte Albán I residences. We are not sure what method was used to reduce-fire pottery before subterranean kilns came into use.

Exchanging Pottery with Other Regions

In addition to making its own pottery, San José Mogote received gifts of pottery from other regions and sent them some of its pottery in return. We suspect that some of this exchanged pottery was passed along by intermediary villages. In many cases the contents of the vessel may have been the gift, rather than the vessel itself.

It would be good to have detailed data on the extensive network of pottery circulating in Formative Mesoamerica. The problem is that tracing pottery to its source is not as straightforward as sourcing obsidian. In the case of obsidian, there were probably only a dozen or so sources relevant to Formative exchange; in contrast, there were hundreds of Formative villages making pottery, and only a handful of them have been excavated. Second, all obsidian is volcanic glass; pottery clay, on the other hand, can originate from many parent rock materials. Third, even in the case of obsidian, there are problems with some of our current analytical techniques. In a later section, "The Importation and Use of Obsidian," we will see that neutron activation and optical emission spectroscopy often yield different results on the same pieces of obsidian. One can only imagine how different the results with pottery clay might be.

We have the utmost respect for the practitioners of the aforementioned techniques. However, we believe that nothing beats a mineralogical analysis (whether by thin section or trituration) that traces the clay to the parent rock material from which it was derived. Let us give one example.

Alluvial clay in the Valley of Oaxaca derives mostly from Precambrian gneiss on the western side of the valley, sillar-type Miocene tuffs (ignimbrites) on the eastern side, and some Cretaceous limestone. The ignimbrites, in particular, are so distinctive, with their characteristic glass and pumice inclusions, that geologists like Howel Williams and Wayne Lambert felt they could recognize them in "foreign-looking" gray sherds at Tlapacoya in the Basin of Mexico (Weaver 1967:30; Lambert 1972:3).

In 1972 Nanette Pyne, a member of our Oaxaca Project, had an opportunity to examine sherds of carved gray pottery from San Lorenzo in the Olmec region. Pyne noted that while most of the sherds were similar to each other, eight struck her as "Oaxaca-like" because they had Sky/Lightning motifs applied to the vessel at a 45° angle (Flannery and Marcus 2000: Fig. 21). She was allowed to take pieces off these sherds so that our ceramicist/geologist William O. Payne could perform a mineralogical analysis on them. According to Payne (Flannery and Marcus 1994:262-63), at least five of these sherds could be matched to the parent rock formations (gneiss, ignimbrite, limestone) from which our types Leandro Gray and Delfina Fine Gray were made.

This is significant, because that combination of rock formations does not occur in the San Lorenzo area. The geology of that region is dominated by sandstone and lutite (mudstone, a sedimentary rock that settles out of swamps or oceanic mud environments). The sandstone probably broke down into the "fine, quartzite sand" with which Coe and Diehl (1980a:162) describe their carved gray pottery as having been tempered. Regardless of the trace elements detectable through neutron activation or optical emission spectroscopy, no sherd whose clay was derived from a combination of gneiss, ignimbrite, and limestone could possibly be from San Lorenzo.

San José Mogote, of course, received its share of pottery from distant regions. Perhaps the most distinctive was Xochiltepec White, a widely traded monochrome white ware. Payne's mineralogical analyses showed that our samples of Xochiltepec White were coming from at least two sources (Flannery and Marcus 1994:256). Most were made from kaolinized sedimentary clay and, we believe, came from San Lorenzo or some other site in the Olmec region. Other vessels, however, were made from a kaolinized feldspar, probably from a vein or pegmatite dike like those which supplied the white slip for Atoyac Yellow-white.

Those white monochrome vessels may have been local imitations of Xochiltepec White.

While its presence in Oaxaca is interesting, Xochiltepec White never approached so much as half a percent of the sherds in any house. And because it was undecorated, it cannot have influenced the art or iconography of San José Mogote. Sites in the Basin of Mexico, among them Tlapacoya and Tlatilco, had a greater stylistic impact on Oaxaca because their pottery had a more extensive design repertoire than San Lorenzo's. For example, Tlapacoya had six pottery types bearing "pan-Mesoamerican" motifs; San José Mogote had four such types; San Lorenzo had only one (Flannery and Marcus 2000:27).

We wish that all the "foreign" pottery at San José Mogote could be traced to its bedrock geological sources. Unfortunately, the expense involved would be too great. From time to time in this volume, we will mention foreign sherds for which we have been given tentative sources, based on neutron activation. While we are happy to have these analyses, we suspect that in some cases optical emission spectroscopy or a complete mineralogical workup would yield different results. We also realize that San José Mogote must have received gifts of pottery from villages that no one has ever excavated.

A rudimentary model of San José Mogote's ceramic exchange might include the following:

1. San José Mogote received Paloma Negative and Cesto White from the Basin of Mexico.
2. San José Mogote received Xochiltepec White and Calzadas Carved vessels from the Gulf Coast.
3. San José Mogote received Guamuchal Brushed vessels from the Isthmus/Chiapas.
4. San José Mogote sent Delfina Fine Gray and Leandro Gray vessels to all the regions mentioned in 1, 2, and 3.

The Procurement and Working of Chert

Chipped stone tools were relatively abundant in residences at San José Mogote. The most common raw material was chert or chalcedony, which usually constituted 70-85% of the assemblage. Obsidian, which had to be imported from hundreds of kilometers away, was understandably less frequent. Still rarer were tools of poor quality raw materials like quartz or ignimbrite.

Chert Sources

In the early 1970s Michael Whalen (1986) undertook a survey of chert sources in the Valley of Oaxaca, to which the reader is referred for details. Here we will only summarize his findings.

1. The Matadamas Quarries (see Fig. 4.14)

The source nearest to San José Mogote is also the highest in quality. Only 3 km to the southwest, on the opposite side of the Atoyac River, a limestone ridge overlooks the hamlet of Rancho Matadamas. The limestone breaks off in blocks which, during the Rosario phase, were transported to San José Mogote for the construction of stone masonry platforms. Running through the limestone are veins of waxy chert and chaldecony, mostly white, off-white, or reddish in color. So desirable is this source that it was visited even by the Archaic foragers encamped in caves near Mitla, some 50 km away (Whalen 1986: Table 7.1). It was widely used at San José Mogote, especially by the biface makers of the House 16/17 Complex in Area B (Chapters 18-19).

2. The Loma del Trapiche Source

Only slightly farther away was a limestone ridge near Loma del Trapiche, 4 km to the south and across the Atoyac River. This ridge produces chert that can be white to bluish white, grayish white, brownish white, or mottled. It was widely used.

3. The Rancho Alemán Source

In the piedmont near Rancho Alemán, 5-6 km northwest of San José Mogote and on the opposite side of the Atoyac River, was a source of black or very dark brown flint, occurring as veins in limestone. It stands out among the lighter-colored cherts.

4. The San Lázaro Etla Source

Another source of white (or off-white) waxy chert and chalcedony can be found on a limestone hill across the Atoyac River from San Lázaro Etla, 6-7 km northwest of San José Mogote. Artifacts on the surface of the hill suggest that this source was visited as far back as the Archaic period.

5. The Rojas de Cuauhtémoc Source

Lower quality chert can be found near Rojas de Cuauhtémoc in the western Tlacolula subvalley, 25-30 km southwest of San José Mogote. The color is brownish white or occasionally black to dark gray. In spite of its distance from San José Mogote and its lower quality, some chert from this source reached households in Area C (see below).

6. Sources of Silicified Tuff

Finally, at the eastern extreme of the Tlacolula subvalley, there are veins of silicified material in the Miocene ignimbrites (volcanic tuffs) of the Mitla region. These cherts were widely used by the Archaic foragers of the Mitla area, and continued to be used occasionally at San José Mogote, in spite of the 50-60 km journey required to obtain them.

Household Variation in the Use of Chert Sources

Parry (1987:27) found statistically significant variation among San José phase residential wards in their use of chert sources. Houses in Area B had the highest percentage of white and red chert from the Matadamas/Loma del Trapiche sources, and the lowest frequencies of gray and brown chalcedonies and silicified tuffs. Houses in Area C had the highest percentage of gray and brown chalcedonies and silicified tuffs, the latter from the Tlacolula-Mitla region; Matadamas chert made up only a third of

the material from Area C. Area A residences were intermediate between Areas B and C in their use of sources.

Significantly, Parry found less variation *among residences within each ward* than he did between wards. These findings led Parry (1987:27) to the following conclusion:

> This pattern suggests that residences within an area did cooperate in procurement or exchange of local raw materials, but did not cooperate with households in different residential wards, a pattern consistent with the suggestion that each area was occupied by a different corporate group.

The Uses of Chert Tools

We are grateful to several chipped stone analysts, including Frank Hole and John Rick, who examined various subsets of the San José Mogote assemblage over the years. The terminology used in this report, however, was established by William J. Parry, who examined the largest number of tools and published the definitive monograph (Parry 1987). The reader is referred to that publication for details.

Parry characterizes the San José Mogote chert assemblage as an "expedient flake tool industry." Chert arrived at the site primarily in the form of nodules, some of which became hammerstones and others of which were made into flake cores. Deer antler hammers and pressure flakers (discussed in Chapter 5) were used to produce scrapers, drills, bifaces, and other tools from flakes. The main categories of items found in houses and middens were as follows:

    nodules
    hammerstones
    ordinary (usually multidirectional) flake cores
    bipolar flake cores
    discoidal cores
    core choppers
    core scrapers
    core perforators
    lanceolate bifaces
    biface preforms or roughouts
    projectile points (rare)
    flake spokeshaves
    flake perforators/gravers
    gravers
    drills
    burins
    denticulate scrapers
    denticulate flakes
    choppers
    choppers/scrapers
    scrapers
    sidescrapers
    sidescrapers/knives
    endscrapers
    spurred scrapers

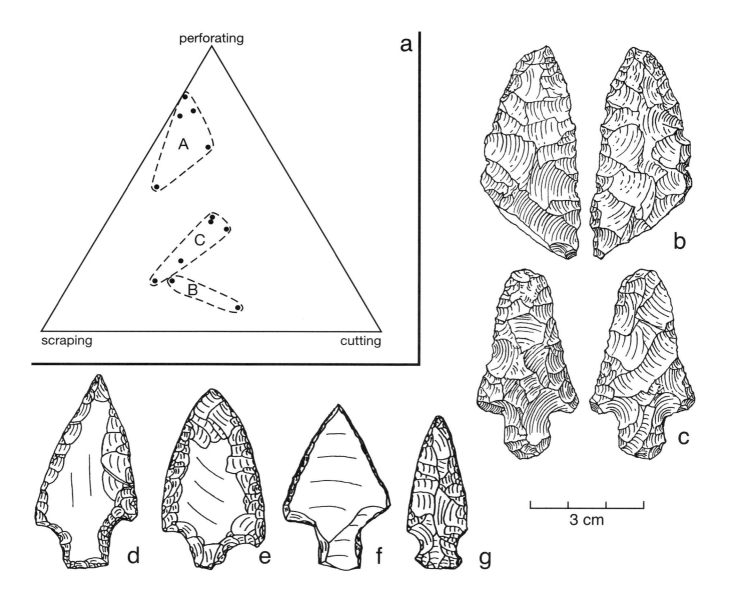

Figure 4.16. Chert tools from San José Mogote. *a*, diagram of the relative proportions of tools for cutting, scraping, and perforating in Areas A, B, and C (after Parry 1987: Fig. 42). *b, c*, projectile points redeposited in the fill of Structure 1, a Late San José phase public building. *d-g*, projectile points from secondary deposits (mostly Rosario phase), Mound 1 (Parry 1987: Fig. 12).

wedges
retouched flakes
utilized flakes
flakes, not utilized
angular fragments

Just as the use of chert sources varied among residential wards, so did the mix of tool types. In Figure 4.16 we reproduce a diagram from Parry (1987: Fig. 42), which compares the frequencies of scraping tools, cutting tools, and perforating tools in different wards. Area A had by far the highest percentage of flake perforators/gravers and drills, almost certainly because the families of that ward were heavily involved in shell working. Area B had many fewer perforating tools, but showed the highest frequencies of bifaces, biface roughouts, and biface thinning flakes (Parry 1987:41-53). House 16/17 in Area B seems to have been heavily involved in producing lanceolate bifaces from heat-treated Matadamas chert.

Our evidence suggests that many crafts tended to center in one residential ward or another. However, the finished products of those localized artisans—whether biface workers (House 16/17, Area B) or pearl oyster ornament makers (House 4, Area C)—somehow got distributed to families in neighboring residential wards. Thus there are two different variables to consider: *production* and *access.* Many families apparently had *access* to craft products which they did not *produce* for themselves. An unanswered question is: Did they receive these craft goods directly from the families that produced them, or were such goods accumulated and redistributed by families of high rank? That question can tentatively be answered in the case of obsidian (below).

On the Scarcity of Projectile Points

As we indicated under "Hunting and Trapping," projectile points became rare during the Tierras Largas, San José, and Guadalupe phases, presumably as the result of a change in hunting strategy. In Figure 4.16 we illustrate our meager collection of chert atlatl points. All seem to have been stemmed or corner-notched, and resemble Palmillas or Salado points from the Tehuacán Valley (MacNeish, Nelken-Terner, and Johnson 1967: Figs. 56, 57).

During the Rosario phase, projectile points seem to have increased in frequency, although they never became common. We do not believe that this increase signals a return to the hunting techniques of the Archaic. The Rosario phase was a period of increased raiding, which may have resulted in greater use of the atlatl in combat. One Rosario phase tomb even featured an offering of eleven obsidian atlatl points (Chapter 23).

The Importation and Use of Obsidian

Roughly 15-25% of the chipped stone in Formative households at San José Mogote was obsidian. Since there are no obsidian sources in the Valley of Oaxaca, all this volcanic glass had to be imported from elsewhere.

Obsidian reached Formative residences in two main forms: (1) as small nodules or chunks, and (2) as prismatic blades. Oaxaca families regularly made flake cores from the nodules or chunks; there is no evidence, however, that they knew how to make prismatic blades (Parry 1987:37). We cannot be sure how the fragile blades were transported from their sources, but MacNeish (pers. comm., 1963) has provided a clue. In one of his dry Tehuacán caves he found that obsidian blades had been laid out on a strip of cloth, which was then rolled up so as to produce a cylindrical package in which no blade touched another.

Obsidian Tools

There can be little doubt that obsidian was sought because its cutting edges are much sharper than chert's. For any task involving fine cutting (including ritual bloodletting), obsidian would have been superior. As a result, obsidian tools at San José Mogote were used for long periods and often show signs of reworking.

The categories used for obsidian tools in this volume follow the work of Parry (1987) and are as follows:

> raw nodules
> flake cores
> prismatic blades, utilized
> prismatic blades, no sign of use
> projectile points (rare, presumably imported)
> scrapers
> spurred scrapers
> wedges
> scaled flakes
> utilized flakes
> flakes, not utilized

Pires-Ferreira's Research, 1967-1973

In the late 1960s, Jane Pires-Ferreira began a study of the obsidian used by Formative villages in Oaxaca and neighboring regions (Pires-Ferreira 1975:11-35). The tracing of archaeological obsidian to its sources was then in its infancy (see Renfrew et al. 1966). Pires-Ferreira teamed up with A. A. Gordus of the University of Michigan, whose preferred method of trace element analysis was neutron activation (Gordus et al. 1967). Pires-Ferreira visited 20 obsidian sources, from Jalisco in the north to Guatemala in the south, collecting 600 control samples. She then drew a sample of 422 archaeological specimens of obsidian from Formative sites. The reader is referred to Pires-Ferreira's 1975 monograph for details.

In the case of the Valley of Oaxaca, Pires-Ferreira sampled obsidian from 19 house floors or dooryard surfaces, eight at Tierras Largas and eleven at San José Mogote (Pires-Ferreira 1975: Table 6). The total number of samples run from these households was 151. (We would like to have analyzed every piece of Formative obsidian, but the cost of doing so would have far exceeded our available funds.)

Pires-Ferreira was only able to sample Areas A and C at San José Mogote. By the time we excavated Area B, both she and Gordus had moved on to other research projects. House 16/17 therefore remains unsampled.

Parry's Research, 1981-1983

William J. Parry provided the typology we use in this volume, complementing the earlier work of Pires-Ferreira (Parry 1987). As in the case of any two studies that overlap, we can report both good news and bad news. The good news is that Pires-Ferreira had provided a tentative source for 151 of our obsidian pieces. The bad news was that any piece she had removed for neutron activation was unavailable for Parry's study. We have done our best to synthesize the two studies.

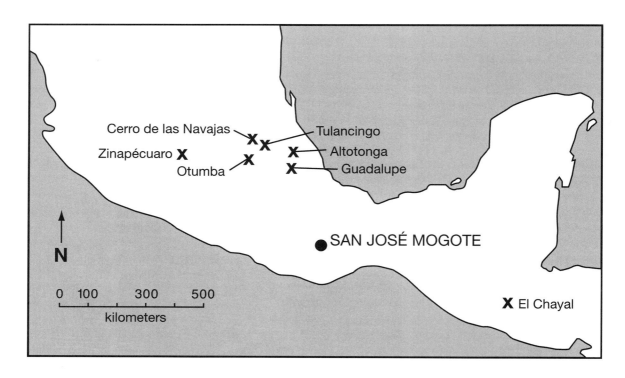

Figure 4.17. Map of Mexico, showing sources (X) from which obsidian reached San José Mogote (modified from Pires-Ferreira 1973: Fig. 3).

Trace element analysis, of course, continued to evolve during the decade between Pires-Ferreira's work and Parry's. During the course of writing his monograph, Parry learned that Spence et al. (1984:100) had discovered at least four new, chemically distinct varieties of green obsidian in the area of Pachuca, Hidalgo. He was therefore able to suggest that one of Pires-Ferreira's most common "unknown" sources might lie in the Pachuca region, rather than in the state of Oaxaca as we suspected in the 1970s (Parry 1987:17).

A Cautionary Note about Neutron Activation

The method of source identification used by Gordus and Pires-Ferreira involved calculating the percentages of sodium (Na) and manganese (Mn) in each obsidian sample. They established a .95 confidence ellipse for each source, and considered archaeological samples to be "identified" only if they fell within the ellipse.

While based on good science, neutron activation does not always yield the same results as optical emission spectroscopy, which is based on equally good science. For an example of how different the results can be, look at Table 5 of Pires-Ferreira (1975): *when the same eight obsidian samples from Oaxaca were analyzed by both methods, the results were identical in only three cases.*

How reliable is any source-identification method that relies on one or two trace elements? We would like to think that use of one or two elements is reasonable for obsidian sources, *which consist only of volcanic glass*, but the results mentioned above make us wonder. We give our neutron activation results in Chapters 7-14, but remain cautious about them. As for trace element analysis of pottery clays, which can have complex and variable geological origins, we remain even more deeply cautious. One problem is that the same trace elements can occur in many different types of bedrock.

The Sources of Obsidian Used at San José Mogote

Pires-Ferreira found that the obsidian sources used at Tierras Largas and San José Mogote had changed over time. One of the reasons was an increased desire for prismatic blades. Unfortunately, some of the sources nearest to the Etla subvalley were unsuitable for blade making. Figure 4.17 shows the sources from which Pires-Ferreira believes that most of the obsidian used at San José Mogote originated.

1. Guadalupe Victoria, Puebla

The Guadalupe Victoria source was the nearest to Etla (245 km), but does not lend itself to blade making. The obsidian, semi-transparent to cloudy gray, occurs mainly as stream-laid cobbles and boulders. This was one of the earliest sources used (e.g., in Espiridión and Tierras Largas times), probably because it was the closest. Its importance faded during the Middle Formative as better sources for blade making arose.

2. *Otumba, Basin of Mexico*

This source, some 390 km from Etla, was one of the first to supply prismatic blades to Oaxaca (e.g., in the Tierras Largas and Early San José phases). The Otumba source features flows of gray obsidian "ideally suited for controlled pressure flaking and blade production" (Pires-Ferreira 1975:26).

3. *Zinapécuaro, Michoacán*

The Zinapécuaro source provides cloudy gray obsidian of high quality for blade making. However, because it was farther away than Otumba (525 km), it was only the second largest supplier of prismatic blades to Tierras Largas and Early San José phase sites. (It should be noted that some samples identified by neutron activation as coming from Zinapécuaro have been identified by optical emission spectroscopy as coming from Otumba; see Pires-Ferreira 1975: Table 28).

4. *Altotonga, Veracruz*

The source at Altotonga, some 315 km from Etla, was a minor provider of obsidian to Tierras Largas and San José phase households.

5. *El Chayal, Guatemala*

The high-quality gray obsidian source of El Chayal, near Guatemala City, lay an impressive 725 km from the Etla region. One wonders how obsidian from this far away ever reached Tierras Largas and San José phase households. Pires-Ferreira (1975:26) suggests that it may have reached Oaxaca indirectly, passed along by villages on the Pacific Coast of Chiapas. In that coastal region, where there are no local chert sources available, many villages had no choice but to import highland Guatemalan obsidian.

6. *Tulancingo and Cerro de las Navajas, Hidalgo*

Two sources in Hidalgo, both suitable for prismatic blade making, provided increasing amounts of obsidian to the Etla region during the Guadalupe and Rosario phases. These were the Tulancingo source (385 km distant) and the Cerro de las Navajas source, near Pachuca (420 km distant). Cerro de las Navajas had massive flows of green obsidian from which large blades, suitable for autosacrifice in formal temples, could be made. (Note that if Parry is correct in suspecting that our former "unknown Oaxacan" green obsidian comes from the Pachuca region, Hidalgo's contribution to Etla's Middle Formative obsidian supply was even greater than originally suspected.)

Interfamily Variation in Obsidian Sources Used

It appears that every Early Formative family had access to obsidian. By itself, obsidian was not a commodity whose possession conferred prestige or reflected high rank at that time. The distribution of obsidian from various sources may, however, indirectly reflect some of the changes that accompanied the emergence of ascribed status around 1150 b.c.

According to Pires-Ferreira (1975:31), the obsidian samples she drew from three household units of the Late Tierras phase at the hamlet of Tierras Largas showed "considerable variation from house to house." For example, in Unit LTL-1, 21 of 25 samples came from the Guadalupe Victoria source. In Unit LTL-3, seven of ten samples came from the Otumba source. These differences suggest that individual families were negotiating for their own obsidian, and may even have had different trading partners in regions outside the Valley of Oaxaca.

Tierras Largas was still only a hamlet during the subsequent San José phase, and variation in obsidian sources continued during that period. In Household Unit LSJ-1, 12 of 19 samples came from Zinapécuaro. In Unit LSJ-2, 9 of 11 samples were either from Otumba or Guadalupe Victoria, with Zinapécuaro a distant third (Pires-Ferreira 1975: Table 6).

San José Mogote, a 60-70 ha chiefly center of the San José phase, told a different story. For example, four household units in Area A (Chapter 14) displayed obsidian percentages from various sources that were "unexpectedly uniform from house to house" (Pires-Ferreira 1975:31). Of four samples drawn from Household Unit C4, half were from Zinapécuaro and half were from Otumba. Of eight samples from Unit C3, three were from Zinapécuaro and three were from Otumba. Of six samples from Unit C2, half were from Zinapécuaro and half from Otumba. Of seven samples from Unit C1, two were from Zinapécuaro and two from Otumba. Such uniformity suggested to Pires-Ferreira (1975:31) that "some form of centralized pooling, which resulted in a mixture of the incoming obsidian prior to its distribution, might have been taking place."

This suggestion needs to be confirmed by further sampling and source identification. There are two reasons, however, why it seems plausible. First, other lines of evidence suggest the presence of elite families at San José Mogote during the San José phase. The second reason is that prismatic blades were becoming an increasingly sought-after commodity, one whose importation and distribution those elite families might have wanted to monopolize. As Pires-Ferreira (1975:35) puts it:

> the pooling of imported obsidian should probably be seen as a gradual process, beginning in the Early Formative among important families at the largest sites and spreading as the demand for high quality obsidian and prismatic blades grew. By Middle Formative times, elite families probably controlled, pooled, and [distributed] obsidian to their affines even at small hamlets.

Grinding Corn (and Other Materials)

Limey crusts on jar sherds indicate that families at San José Mogote softened their maize kernels in lime water before grinding with a metate and mano. Grinding went far beyond cornmeal preparation, however. The variety of metates and manos we found suggests that families were involved in many different grinding activities, more than we will ever be able to identify. As many as five or six different types of manos, each implying a different

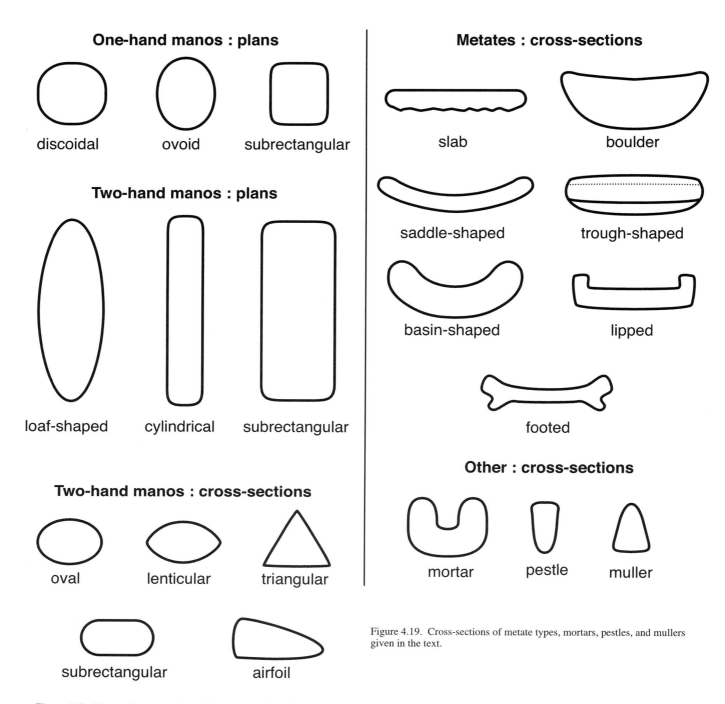

One-hand manos : plans

discoidal   ovoid   subrectangular

Two-hand manos : plans

loaf-shaped   cylindrical   subrectangular

Two-hand manos : cross-sections

oval   lenticular   triangular

subrectangular   airfoil

Figure 4.18. Plans and cross-sections of mano types given in the text.

Metates : cross-sections

slab   boulder

saddle-shaped   trough-shaped

basin-shaped   lipped

footed

Other : cross-sections

mortar   pestle   muller

Figure 4.19. Cross-sections of metate types, mortars, pestles, and mullers given in the text.

One-Hand Manos

motion, might be present in a single residential area. The raw material was equally varied. Ignimbrite, or volcanic tuff, was of course available right on the piedmont spur below the village. But many grinding stones were of limestone, sandstone, granite, fine-grained metamorphic rock, or even vesicular basalt. The last must have been gifts from elsewhere, since we know of no basalt source within the Valley of Oaxaca.

Manos small enough to hold in one hand are very old tools in Oaxaca, having been used to grind acorns at Guilá Naquitz Cave before 7000 b.c. (Flannery 1986a: Fig. 8.1). Often, such manos began as stream cobbles that already had a convenient size and shape. After use, their final shape was typically (1) *discoidal*, (2) *ovoid*, or (3) *subrectangular*, depending on how the grinding had been done (Fig. 4.18). Some subrectangular one-hand manos appeared to have been used both for grinding (on the sides) and as pounders (on the ends).

We suspect that one-hand manos were as likely to have been used by men as by women. For example, the grinding of tobacco, powdered lime, and/or red pigment in Men's Houses was done on metates too small to have been used with anything larger than a one-hand mano (Marcus 1998a: Figs. 9.12 and 9.13).

Two-Hand Manos

Manos so elongated as to require holding with both hands were a different case. This category included the familiar maize-grinding mano, which is normally used by Zapotec women in the kneeling position. The variety of shapes seen in two-hand manos, however, clearly indicated that we were dealing with more than one basic activity. As with metates (below), we believe that the final shape was the result of the grinding motion used, and that the range of motion went far beyond the typical grinding of maize into cornmeal.

In overall shape, two-hand manos were likely to be (1) *loaf-shaped* (we have in mind here a loaf of French bread), (2) *cylindrical*, or (3) *subrectangular* (Fig. 4.18). The variety of cross-sections was even greater, including (1) *oval*, (2) *lenticular*, (3) *triangular*, (4) *subrectangular*, and (5) *airfoil* (Fig. 4.18).

Consider the variety of wrist actions suggested by all these cross-sections. To get an airfoil cross-section, the fingers have to rest on the broad front edge while the mano slides back and forth. To get an oval cross-section, the mano has to be rotated while grinding. The lenticular cross-section implies a rocking motion, with the mano flipped over from time to time so that both grinding surfaces develop the same convexity. The triangular cross-section implies a relatively flat sliding motion, but one in which three different sides or facets get used over time. Subrectangular cross-sections could only develop on a flat surface like that of a slab metate.

Metates

In the case of metates, it seems clear to us that the final shape was more the result of use than design. We believe that most metates began as boulders or slabs of bedrock, and were gradually worn into saddles or basins as their use progressed. Most of the metates we recovered (especially in middens) were only fragments, or exhausted metates that had been discarded. Often, therefore, we were seeing these artifacts at a very late stage of the use cycle.

The terms used in this report are as follows. (1) *Slab metates* or (2) *boulder metates* were probably implements that had not been used very long. (3) *Saddle-shaped metates* were elongated, worn down further at the midpoint than at either end. (4) *Trough-shaped metates* were similar to the saddle-shaped type, but had a long narrow concavity. (5) *Basin-shaped metates* were circular or oval rather than elongated, and had a concavity worn in the center. (6) *Lipped metates* were ones whose grinding had been so

Figure 4.20. Two boxlike, loop-handled ritual metates. *a*, from Feature 65, Area A, San José Mogote. *b*, from Tlaltizapan, Morelos (based on a photo in Serra Puche 1993:108). Width of *a*, 14 cm; no scale given for *b*.

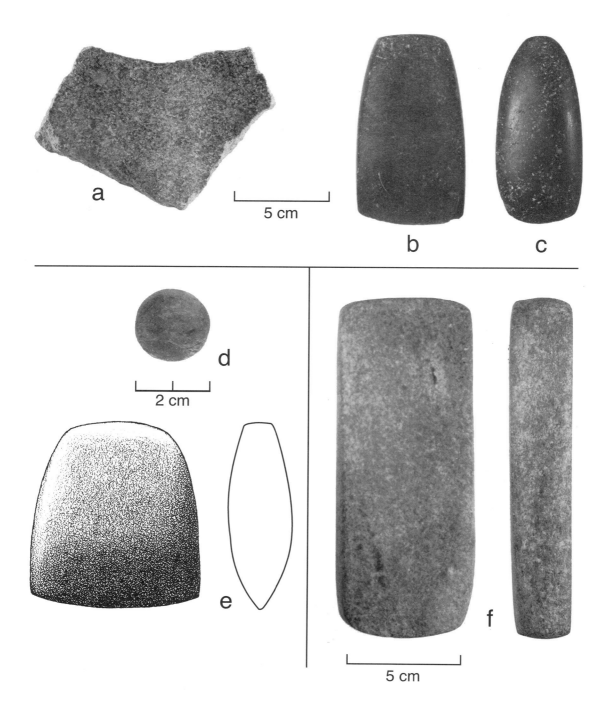

Figure 4.21. Ground stone tools. *a*, fragment of stone bowl, Zone D Midden, Area A. *b*, square-polled celt, Zone E Midden, Area C. *c*, round-polled celt, Zone D Midden, Area C. *d, canica,* Zone D Midden, Area A. *e*, small celt made by resharpening a broken large celt, Area B profile. *f*, possible woodworking tool stored below the floor of House 17, Area B.

carefully restricted to the interior surface that the margin stood up like a narrow ridge or lip. Finally, (7) *footed metates* were ones that had deliberately been given nubbin feet, presumably to raise one end or to keep the stone from moving during grinding. All these metate varieties (Fig. 4.19) were present from Tierras Largas times onward.

Possible Ritual Metates

One unusual type of metate, made during the Tierras Largas and Early San José phases, deserves special mention. These metates were small (about 25 cm long and 15 cm wide) and portable; one end had, in fact, been carved into a loop handle which made the metate easy to carry. The metate itself was shaped like a rectangular box, whose vertical sides prevented the contents from spilling (Fig. 4.20).

It appears to us that this metate was designed to be carried back and forth between one's home and a ritual venue like a Men's House, where it was used to grind (and keep from spilling) some important ritual substance. Given the powdered lime stored in the Tierras Largas phase Men's Houses, one possibility for that substance is tobacco, since we know that powdered tobacco was mixed with lime by the ancient Zapotec and ingested during certain rituals (Marcus and Flannery 1996:87).

Since these loop-handled metates were found with some residences but not others, our suspicion is that they were owned only by those men fully initiated into Men's House ritual.

It is worth noting that loop-handled, boxlike ritual metates were not unique to Oaxaca. Serra Puche (1993:108) illustrates a metate from Tlaltizapan, Morelos, that differs from ours only in that its loop handle is attached to one of the long sides, rather than the narrow end (Fig. 4.20).

Mortars, Pestles, and Mullers

Compared to back-and-forth grinding on metates, up-and-down pounding was a less common activity in Formative houses. Implements for such trituration included (1) mortars, (2) pestles, and (3) mullers, but none of these were particularly common (Fig. 4.19). Nor can we be sure what material the villagers were pounding. On the Archaic cave floors of the Mitla region, it would have been acorns. However, by Early Formative times we suspect that *barro áspero* and the other coarse clays used in pottery making were also being pounded in mortars (Payne 1994).

Finally, some particularly smooth and well-made fragments seem to be from actual stone bowls rather than mortars (Fig. 4.21*a*). In both Tehuacán and Oaxaca, such stone bowls preceded pottery (e.g., MacNeish, Nelken-Terner, and Johnson 1967:114-17).

Canicas

Among the more enigmatic artifacts in Formative houses and middens were small pecked and ground stone balls, referred to by our workmen as *canicas* or "marbles" (Fig. 4.21*d*). Usually only a centimeter or two in diameter, these perfect little stone spheres required considerable grinding and polishing. Many were made of travertine from nearby Fábrica San José—a calcareous material that does, in fact, resemble marble. Others were made from Matadamas limestone or chalcedony. We have no idea why the villagers of San José wanted so many of these little curiosities, the making of which required a lot of grinding.

Tree Felling and Woodworking

Before the alluvium near San José Mogote could be planted, it had to be cleared of mesquite. Before a house could be built, pines had to be felled, trimmed, and brought down from the mountains. Such tree felling required stone axe heads hafted to wooden handles. The type of axe head found at San José Mogote is referred to as a *celt*, since it was given no groove to facilitate hafting.

Celts at San José Mogote were made in two styles, *square polled* and *round polled* (Fig. 4.21*b, c*). The preferred raw material was chlorite schist, a fine-grained black to dark green stone. This extremely hard raw material can be found in the metamorphic zone of the piedmont, west of San José Mogote.

Making a celt was very labor intensive. The axe head was roughed out, then worked into shape with an abrasive stone, and finally had its bit sharpened by polishing with a large quartz pebble. Very few houses provided evidence for celt making; it was one of those crafts that may have been restricted to one or two families per residential ward. The Zone E Midden in Area C produced a cluster of celt-making items that had apparently been discarded together (Chapter 8).

Hafted celts could be used to fell trees, hew logs into roof beams or other artifacts, perhaps even to produce wooden boxes or storage chests. To put the final touches on a wooden artifact, however, the artisan needed sanding and smoothing tools like those found stored beneath the floor of House 17 in Area B (Chapter 18). These probable woodworking tools, like our celts, were made of chlorite schist (Fig. 4.21*f*).

Hafted celts might also be used to hack through soft volcanic tuff bedrock, either to produce storage pits or to convert a gentle slope into a series of occupational terraces. Such use (for example, in Area B) left the celts so blunted and battered that they eventually had to be discarded (Chapter 17). On occasion, it appeared that broken celts had been reworked into smaller but still useful versions (Fig. 4.21*e*).

Chapter 5

Household Activities, Part 2

In Chapter 4 we discussed activities related to subsistence. In this chapter we make the transition from subsistence to craft activity, household ritual, and intervillage conflict.

Basket Making

Basket making is ancient in the Valley of Oaxaca. Coiled baskets made from grass bundles, stitched together with strips of yucca or agave leaf, were used by the occupants of Guilá Naquitz Cave at 6670 b.c. (King 1986:159-60). Unfortunately, basketry was not preserved at San José Mogote, so we have to rely on basket-making tools for our evidence.

We recovered two types of bone artifacts that were likely employed in basket making. The first was an awl made from a deer metapodial, examples of which are shown in Figure 5.1c, d. We should note that most of the awls we recovered had been used for so long that the point was worn down.

Deer metapodial awls identical to ours were used by the Seri of Baja California to make coiled baskets. Felger and Moser (1985:182-87 and Fig. 15.7) describe awls made from the proximal end of a mule deer metapodial, which were usually roughed out by a man and given their final shape by a woman. These awls were roughly 25 cm long when first used, had to be resharpened as they wore down, and were discarded after they had been reduced to about 10 cm in length.

The Seri used awls first to split and trim the stitching splints to exact widths, and then to make a hole between the stitches of a previous coil, so that a stitching splint could be pulled through the perforation to attach a new coil (Felger and Moser 1985: Figs.

15.10, 15.11). For this purpose, the awl "was held between the index and middle fingers with the [condyle] seated in the palm of the hand" (Felger and Moser 1985:186). Figure 5.1a and b illustrate this procedure.

Older residents of San José Mogote could remember baskets being made that way by their grandparents. They also pointed out that when the awl had worn down to about 10 cm in length, it could still be used for other tasks. It could, for example, be used to slit open corn husks, then shell the cob by forcing the blunt point of the awl between two rows of kernels. When used for this purpose, the awl was sometimes referred to as a *piscador* (Fig. 5.1c, d). Because of their possible multiple functions, we have classified our worn metapodial tools as "awls/*piscadores*."

A second tool we believe was used in basket making was a very large needle, up to 10-13 cm in length, with an eye at one end (Fig. 5.2a). Such needles were made from deer bone splinters, and seem too large for ordinary sewing. They would have been ideal for pulling the stitching strips through the coils of a basket, especially since many were oval rather than circular in cross-section.

Sewing

Small bone needles, of a size appropriate for sewing, appeared in a number of residences (Fig. 5.2b, c). Most were no more than 5 cm in length and circular in cross-section, unlike our presumed basketry needles, whose cross-sections were oval. Our complete specimens usually had eyes to receive thread.

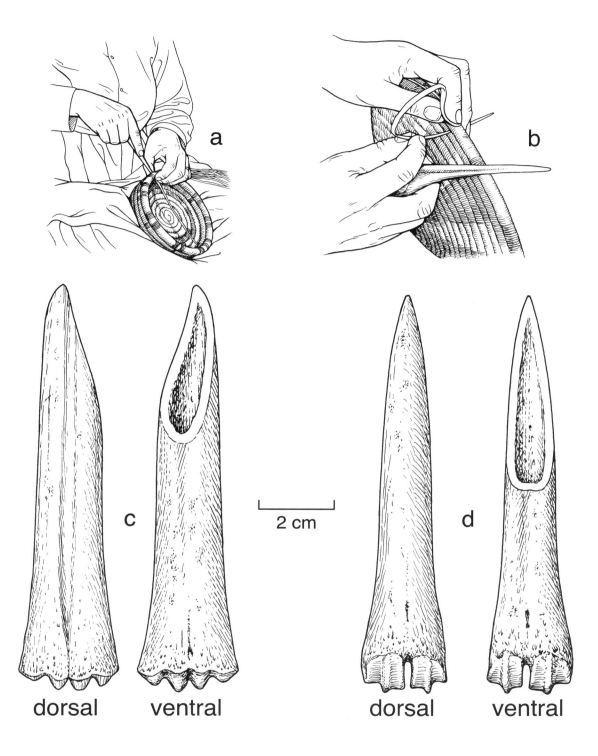

dorsal ventral   dorsal ventral

Figure 5.1. Basket-making tools. *a,* Seri woman pushing a deer metapodial awl between the coils of a basket. *b,* stitching through a hole made with the awl. *c, d,* dorsal and ventral views of *piscadores* (worn-down awls, still useful as corn shellers) from House LSJ-1 at the Tierras Largas site. (*a, b,* drawn from photos in Felger and Moser 1985: Figs. 15.10 and 15.11.)

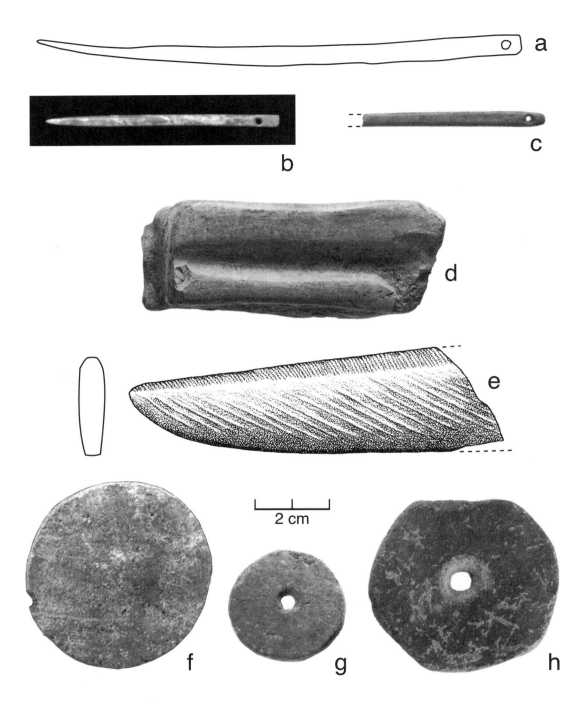

Figure 5.2. Artifacts from San José Mogote. *a*, reconstruction drawing of presumed basketry needle, based on broken specimens. *b*, *c*, sewing needles. *d*, grooved rubbing stone, probably for sharpening bone awls and needles. *e*, slate "cutting board" or "whetstone," covered with fine cut marks. *f*, unperforated sherd disk. *g*, *h*, biconically drilled sherd disks.

The Sharpening of Awls and Needles

We believe that bone awls and needles were sharpened through abrasion with a grooved rubbing stone, like the one shown in Figure 5.2*d*.

"Cutting Boards" or "Whetstones"

In addition to grooved rubbing stones, we also found pieces of stone (often slate) that were covered with fine cut marks (Fig. 5.2*e*). Some of these may have been for sharpening tools; others may simply have provided a hard surface on which some other material (like shell or mica) could be cut (see Chapter 25).

Soft Hammering

The lower end of a shed deer antler was sometimes converted into a hammer for gentle percussion (see Fig. 9.19*a*, Chapter 19).

Pressure Flaking

Fire-hardened tines of deer antler were suitable for the kind of gentle pressure flaking used to make lanceolate bifaces, projectile points, and some drills and perforators. We found a number of antler tines that showed signs of fire-hardening and use-related chipping (see Figs. 9.36*e-g*, Chapter 9).

The Manufacture of Sherd Disks

The villagers of San José Mogote occasionally selected sherds to be chipped and ground into the shape of a disk. Some of these disks were also perforated, probably by drilling through from both sides with a chert drill (Fig. 5.2*f-h*).

While the functions of these disks were not always clear, we suspect that most were homemade lids, or temporary covers, for vessels like jars and bottles. In the 1960s, we observed Zapotec women using worked sherds in this way. Cords were attached to the perforated disks to facilitate lifting them off jars of heated liquid. The cords were attached to the lid simply by tying two knots larger than the perforation, one on either side of the disk.

The Weaving of Mats

The weaving of reeds and rushes into *petates*, or mats, is undoubtedly as old as basket making, but such mats are usually not preserved in open-air village sites. A piece of clay from an Early Formative provenience in the Tehuacán Valley bore what seemed to be the impression of a twilled mat (MacNeish, Nelken-Terner, and Johnson 1967:167). We found the silica exoskeleton of a mat on the floor of one of our San José phase houses, House 2 in Area C (Chapter 9).

During the Guadalupe phase, the floors of Lupita Heavy Plain charcoal braziers often retained impressions of reed mats, basketry, or coarse textiles, made while the clay was still wet (Flannery and Marcus 1994:243-50). In Figure 5.3*a* we illustrate the plasticine impression of such a mat.

Net Making

The making of nets from the fiber of agave, yucca, or some other plant is a very old craft in Oaxaca. Knotted netting was preserved in Zone B3 of Guilá Naquitz Cave (King 1986: Fig. 9.1). The date of this specimen should be in the neighborhood of 6910 b.c. ± 180[1], based on a date from Zone B2 + 3 (GX-0784). While we have no doubt that the villagers of San José Mogote used nets as bags for carrying things, none were preserved at the site.

Textile Weaving

Simple weft-twined textiles are known from Archaic levels in the dry caves of Tehuacán (MacNeish, Nelken-Terner, and Johnson 1967:197). Exactly when the transition from twining to loom weaving took place is not known. We suspect that this shift took place after permanent villages arose, but since open-air sites usually have poor preservation, we have no conclusive proof. There are enough impressions of textiles on ceramics—made while the clay was still wet—to confirm that the villagers of San José Mogote made textiles. An unanswered question is what fibers were used. We have plenty of evidence for carbonized maguey fiber, but no evidence for cotton.

Cotton is not grown commercially in the Valley of Oaxaca today. The sixteenth-century *Relación de Tlacolula y Mitla* (Canseco 1580) states that the people of Tlacolula imported their cotton from the Isthmus of Tehuantepec, while the people of Mitla grew their own. The latter statement is supported by the fact that preserved bolls of cotton were discovered in Zone A of Guilá Naquitz Cave, a living floor dated to A.D. 620-740 (Flannery and Smith 1983:206). This cave lies only 5 km from Mitla. Today, however, the only cotton one can find growing in Mitla are a few plants in the house lots of families who believe that cottonseed oil has medicinal properties.

We doubt that cotton was grown in the higher and cooler parts of the Valley of Oaxaca during the Formative, but we simply do not know. Four warmer regions from which San José Mogote might have imported cotton are the Valley of Morelos, the Gulf Coast, the Cuicatlán Cañada/southern Tehuacán Valley, and the Isthmus of Tehuantepec. The source of Formative cotton is an important topic for future research.

Salt Making

In the piedmont 5 km east of San José Mogote lie the springs of Fábrica San José, whose waters contain both sodium chloride

---

[1] In this volume, uncalibrated dates are given as "b.c.," and dendrocalibrated dates as "B.C." (see Chapter 26, Radiocarbon Dating).

Figure 5.3. Evidence for Formative mat weaving and salt making. *a,* plasticine impression of a Lupita Heavy Plain brazier sherd, showing the imprint of a reed mat (Flannery and Marcus 1994: Fig. 12.129). *b,* sherd from Household Unit R-2 at Fábrica San José, showing the white carbonate crust that formed on vessels used for salt making (Drennan 1976a: Fig. 90a).

and calcium carbonate. Left to evaporate, the calcium carbonate precipitates out in the form of travertine, a marble-like rock that was made into artifacts at San José Mogote. If the spring water is collected and boiled, it can produce 82 grams of sodium chloride, or table salt, per 5 liters of water (Drennan 1976a:257).

As early as the Tierras Largas phase, someone carrying Tierras Largas Burnished Plain jars and *tecomates* visited the area of the springs. Some of the broken vessels left behind have carbonate crusts on the interior surface. The most likely explanation is that villagers from nearby San José Mogote visited the area to make salt (Drennan 1976a:74).

During the Middle Formative Guadalupe and Rosario phases, Fábrica San José became a satellite village within the chiefdom headed by San José Mogote. Excavations by Drennan (1976a) reveal that salt making was one of Fábrica San José's activities during that period, with some coarse jars developing mineral crusts on the interior surface up to 1 cm thick (Fig. 5.3*b*). What had begun in the Early Formative as an activity requiring a 10 km round trip, therefore, eventually turned into an economic relationship—perhaps even a tributary relationship—during the Middle Formative, when Fábrica San José was presumably San José Mogote's major supplier of salt.

The Importation and Working of Mollusk Shell

It goes without saying that not all household activities were related to subsistence. In fact, we believe that an impressive amount of the debris in the houses we excavated was related to the manufacture of ritual paraphernalia, the creation of masks and costumes, the making of personal ornamentation, or the accumulation of goods that conferred prestige. Some of these goods had come from regions hundreds of kilometers distant. Mollusk shells were among the most common.

During an earlier stage of the Oaxaca Project, Pires-Ferreira (1975) identified a large sample of mollusk shell from San José Mogote, Huitzo, Tierras Largas, and Abasolo. Based mainly on the collections of the Smithsonian Institution, but also with help from Gary Feinman and Linda Nicholas, we have identified the mollusks recovered during the later stages of the project.

Pires-Ferreira found that our Formative villagers were receiving mollusks of many genera, and that the structural properties of each genus dictated the way it could be worked. Two of the most impressive mollusks were the Pacific pearl oyster (*Pinctada mazatlanica*) and the Pacific spiny oyster (*Spondylus calcifer*). Both have shells which are not only large, but so thick that they can be cut into the desired shape without shattering. Of the pearl oyster, Pires-Ferreira (1975:74) says:

> The shells of an adult animal are sufficiently thick and durable to permit cutting, grinding, and drilling into elaborate forms. The shape of these shells provides a relatively large flattish working surface, with waste limited to the marginal valve area. These characteristics differ from those exhibited by the fragile Atlantic freshwater shells, which could be drilled but not cut or ground into decorative forms. [unpublished experimental data]

Other Pacific coast bivalves, like the clams *Polymesoda* sp. and *Chione* (=*Anomalocardia*) sp., were evidently considered too small to be cut up; they were usually just perforated for suspension. The same was true of the numerous small Pacific gastropods found in household debris. Particularly popular were the horn shells *Cerithium stercusmuscarum* and *Cerithidea mazatlanica*, both of which could be drilled at one end for suspension on a necklace.

Two Pacific gastropods large enough to be extensively worked were the conch shell, *Strombus galeatus*, and the cask shell, *Malea ringens*. *Strombus* shells were made into ritual trumpets, often enhanced with carved symbols. In the 1960s, there were still Zapotec communities where the conch shell trumpet was blown to assemble villagers for rituals or corvée labor. Such use of trumpets was widespread in Central and South America. For example, among the Cubeo of the northwest Amazon, flutes and trumpets were considered the embodiment of the ancestors, and thus the sounds they produced were believed to be "the voice of the ancestors" (Goldman 1963:190-96).

In addition to the mass of marine and estuarine genera from the Pacific Coast, we recovered a series of pearly freshwater mussels from the rivers of Mexico's Atlantic watershed. Chief among these was *Barynaias* spp., including *Barynaias* cf. *pigerrimus*. This mussel is native to large river systems of the Gulf Coast, from Tampico in the north to Tabasco in the south (Pires-Ferreira 1975:75). It has occasionally been lumped with *Quadrula* sp., the prototypic freshwater bivalve of mussel shoals in the southeastern U.S.

While these mussels have a pearly, attractive surface like that of the Pacific pearl oyster, their shells are too fragile to allow as much drilling, cutting, and grinding into complex shapes (Pires-Ferreira 1975:75). We found some evidence that they might have been trimmed to serve as inlays in masks and costumes, much the way mica was used. Substantial amounts of the pearly freshwater mussel debris appeared to be from shells that had shattered while being modified.

Chronological Change in Shell Working

Long-distance circulation of shell has a long history in the Valley of Oaxaca. One Pacific olive shell, *Agaronia testacea*, reached Cueva Blanca (near Mitla) in the Late Archaic (Marcus and Flannery 1996: Fig. 50). The Pacific gastropod *Busicon* cf. *columella* reached Tierras Largas during the Early Tierras Largas phase, perhaps for use as a trumpet (Pires-Ferreira 1975: Table 19). Pearl oysters, horn shells, and pearly freshwater mussels all reached San José Mogote prior to 1200 b.c. Shell ornaments, therefore, played a role even during those periods when prestige was acquired rather than inherited.

At the transition from the Tierras Largas phase to the San José phase, however, the quantity of shell being imported into the Valley of Oaxaca increased dramatically. While this explosion in shell working probably had something to do with the emergence of ascribed status during the San José phase, we are reluctant to provide a simplistic model for the way this worked. What we see is a continuum featuring residences with abundant shell, residences with modest amounts of shell, and residences with little shell.

There was, however, interesting information in the variation from house to house. Some houses had finished ornaments, but little debris from shell working; others had shell debris, but few finished products. Pearl oyster ornaments seemed to be more abundant in the houses that we think (on the basis of other criteria) belonged to higher-status families. Lower-status families seem to have settled for pearly freshwater mussels, from which less complex ornaments could be made. Some families were so involved in shellwork that they discarded chert perforators/gravers at a dramatic rate. Others were less involved, and the chipped stone assemblage reflected that.

Perhaps the safest way to put it is this: the higher your status, the greater the likelihood that archaeologists will recover pearl oyster and *Spondylus* ornaments in your house or midden. The issue is complicated, however, by the fact that some lower-status clients may have worked shell for higher-status patrons.

Common Mollusks at San José Mogote

In the lists that follow, we have grouped the most common mollusks found at San José Mogote into three broad categories: (1) pearly freshwater mussels from rivers of the Gulf Coast; (2) Pacific marine (or estuarine) bivalves; and (3) Pacific marine univalves (gastropods). Latin names, common names, and habitat preferences of the Pacific genera are taken from Keen (1958).

1. Pearly Freshwater Mussels (Fig. 5.4a)

All these mussels belong to the family Unionidae, but their taxonomy is not universally agreed upon. The following generic names were supplied to Pires-Ferreira by the Smithsonian. While we presume that most mussels at San José Mogote originated on the Mexican Gulf Coast, they belong to genera well known from Texas and Louisiana as well.

Actinonaias spp. Called a "mucket" in the Mississippi drainage, this genus lives in water less than 3 feet deep, in gravel, sand, or mud-bottomed rivers.

Anodonta cf. *globosa*. A typical mussel of the lakes, bayous, and large rivers of Texas and Louisiana, *Anodonta* is usually found in several feet of water, or among water plants.

Barynaias (= *Quadrula*) sp.; some are *Barynaias* cf. *pigerrimus* (Pires-Ferreira 1975:75). This Mexican genus is related to *Quadrula,* the prototypic freshwater bivalve of mussel shoals in large to medium-sized rivers in the southeastern U.S.

Nephronaias spp. Another mussel of Gulf Coast rivers.

2. Pacific Marine Bivalves

Anadara spp. Ark shells, found from Baja California to Peru on sandy or muddy bottoms or in mangrove swamps.

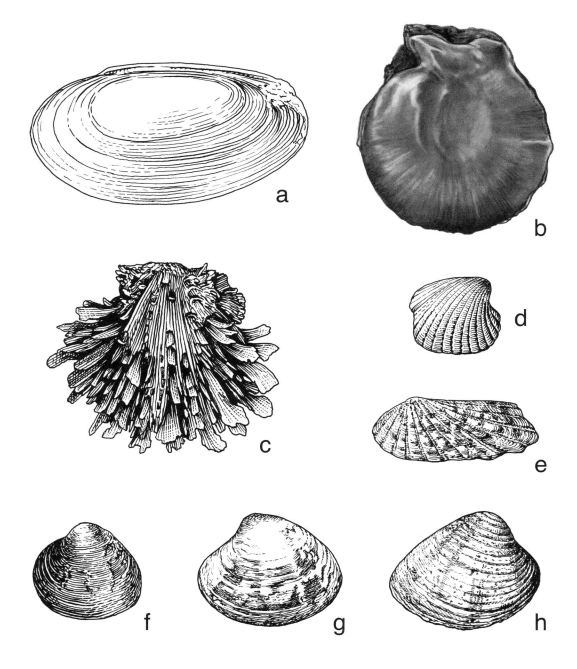

Figure 5.4. Some of the bivalves imported by San José Mogote. *a*, pearly freshwater mussel (*Barynaias* sp.). *b*, pearl oyster (*Pinctada mazatlanica*). *c*, spiny oyster (*Spondylus calcifer*). *d, e*, different species of heart shell (*Cardita* spp.). *f*, marsh clam (*Polymesoda* [=*Neocyrena*] sp.). *g*, Venus clam (*Pitar* sp.). *h*, Venus clam (*Chione* [=*Anomalocardia*] *subrugosa*).

Anadara perlabiata. An ark shell found on sand bars at low tide on the west coast of Mexico.

Pinctada mazatlanica. The Pacific pearl oyster, found in moderately shallow water from Baja California to Peru (Fig. 5.4*b*).

Ostrea corteziensis. An oyster found clinging to mangroves or rocks, from Baja California to Panama.

Spondylus calcifer. The Pacific spiny oyster, found from Baja California to Ecuador (Fig. 5.4*c*).

Spondylus cf. *princeps.* Another spiny oyster, found from Baja California to Peru, attached to corals and rocks in moderately deep water.

Cardita spp. The heart shell, a shallow water mollusk attaching under rocks in quieter bays along the Pacific coast (Fig. 5.4*d, e*).

Polymesoda (= *Neocyrena*) spp. A clam found in brackish to fresh water along the Pacific coast (Fig. 5.4*f*).

Tivela byronensis. A Venus clam found on sand bars and sandy beaches from Baja California to Ecuador; can be locally abundant.

Pitar spp. A Venus clam found mostly offshore, often at depths of 40 m, from Baja California to Panama; the species *P. sanguineus* is native to the Oaxaca coast. This shell was probably recovered when it washed up on the beach (Fig. 5.4*g*).

Chione (= *Anomalocardia*) *subrugosa.* This Venus clam was eaten in abundance at Formative sites of the Guatemalan coast (Coe and Flannery 1967) (Fig. 5.4*h*).

Strigilla spp. Small clams found in sandy bays from Baja California to Ecuador.

Amphichaena kindermanni. A small coquina clam of sandy beaches and bays from Mazatlán to Guatemala; where abundant (as near Ocós, Guatemala), it was eaten.

3. Pacific Marine Univalves (Gastropods)

Ancistromesus mexicanus. The largest of all living limpets, found on surf-beaten rocks at the low-water line from Mazatlán to northern Peru. Growing to 150 mm in length, it was carved into elegant vessels during the Rosario phase (Marcus and Flannery 1996: Color Plate XIII).

Neritina spp. Called nerites, these mollusks live in tide pools and running streams at river mouths from Acapulco to Ecuador (Fig. 5.5*b, c*).

Neritina cf. *latissima* (= *cassiculum*). One of the nerites reaching the Oaxaca coast.

Turritella spp. Turret shells are gregarious mollusks, tending to form large colonies that live just under the surface of the sea floor. Many species live along the Pacific Coast.

Modulus catenulatus. This button shell lives on mud flats from Baja California to Ecuador.

Cerithium stercusmuscarum. This horn shell lives in sand flats, estuaries, and mangroves from Baja California to Peru (Fig. 5.5*d*).

Cerithidea mazatlanica. Another horn shell, distributed from Baja California to Panama. On tide flats in favorable localities, *Cerithidea* can occur in astronomical numbers, making it possible to obtain many specimens for stringing on necklaces (Fig. 5.5*e, f*).

Strombus galeatus. This large conch can be found in intertidal areas or below the low tide zone, from Baja California to Ecuador. In the Gulf of California it was widely eaten; in Oaxaca it was used as a conch shell trumpet (Fig. 5.5*a*).

Strombus spp. There are hints of other conchs in Formative Oaxaca, all fragmentary.

Cypraea spp. Cowries occur in warm, shallow water, including coral reef areas. There are many species, so once they have been modified, identification is difficult.

Malea ringens. Often called a "cask shell," this mollusk was probably treated as a type of conch. It is found under ledges of rock at extreme tides (e.g. at Mazatlán), from Mexico to Peru.

Thais biserialis. This dogwinkle can be found on rocky substrate from Baja California to Chile.

Columbella (= *Pyrene*) *major.* This dove shell grazes on algae and can be found under rocks between tides, from Baja California to Peru (Fig. 5.5*g*).

Anachis spp. Another dove shell living intertidally under rocks. There are many species distributed from Mazatlán to Panama.

Nassarina spp. Too many species are possible to allow us a firm identification.

Nassarius spp. Called a basket shell or dog whelk, this is a scavenger on sea floors or tidal mud flats. Once again, too many species are present along the Pacific Coast to make the identification of modified shells possible.

Oliva spp. Olive shells of many species occur along the Pacific Coast.

Agaronia testacea. This is one of the most widely found and traded of the olive shells, since it lives higher on the beach than most members of its family; it ranges from Baja California to Peru. *Agaronia* was traded to the Valley of Oaxaca as far back as the Late Archaic (Marcus and Flannery 1996: Fig. 50) (Fig. 5.5*h*).

Olivella spp. This genus of small olive shell is also represented by many species along the Pacific Coast of Mexico.

Polishing Iron Ore Mirrors

One of the most interesting, yet locally restricted, activities of certain San José phase families was the grinding and polishing of small iron ore mirrors. It appears to have been virtually monopolized by one residential ward at San José Mogote: Area A (Chapter 14). Our surface surveys revealed a unique, one-hectare scatter of 500 iron ore chunks on that part of the site. That amounts to 99% of all the archaeological iron ore found so far in the Valley of Oaxaca (Fig. 5.6).

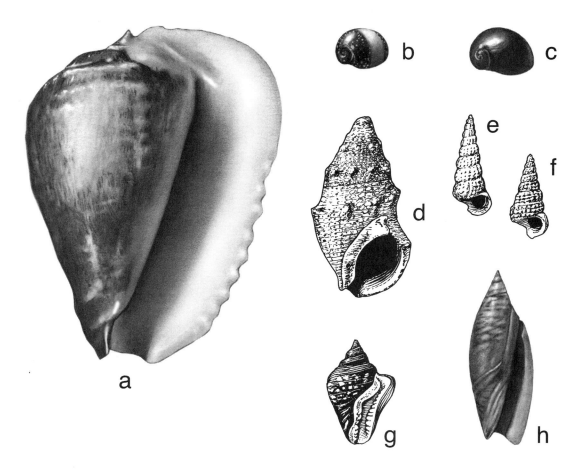

Figure 5.5. Some of the gastropods imported by San José Mogote. *a*, conch (*Strombus galeatus*). *b*, *c*, nerites (*Neritina* spp.). *d*, horn shell (*Cerithium stercusmuscarum*). *e*, *f*, horn shells (*Cerithidea mazatlanica*). *g*, dove shell (*Columbella* [=*Pyrene*] *major*). *h*, olive shell (*Agaronia testacea*).

When we excavated Area A, we found that four generations of families, spanning most of the Middle San José phase, had been involved in the production of small, flat mirrors of magnetite (Fe_3O_4), ilmenite ($FeTiO_3$), or a mixed ore called ilmeno-magnetite. These mirrors, examples of which are shown in Figure 5.7*a* and *b*, had been roughed out using very hard metamorphic stones; they were then given a mirror-like finish with multifaceted polishers of hematite (Fe_2O_3), using hematite powder as the abrasive (Fig. 5.6). While isolated iron ore lumps or small mirror fragments can occasionally be found in other residential wards (or even at other San José phase sites), no other set of household units yet found shows the dedication to mirror production we saw in Area A.

Iron ore mirrors do not show the continuum of access described above for mollusk shell. Their use seems so restricted that we believe they can be considered true sumptuary goods, indicators of hereditary rank. The fact that other residential wards

excavated at San José Mogote show no evidence of magnetite or ilmeno-magnetite working suggests that mirror polishing may have been under the strict control of one group of related families in Area A, perhaps clients of an elite patron.

Most mirrors seem to have been destined for highly ranked individuals, either within the Valley of Oaxaca or in other regions of Mexico. One woman at the site of Santo Domingo Tomaltepec was buried with an iron ore mirror in the shape of a Lightning motif (Whalen 1981: Plate 25), but there was no evidence of mirror working at that site. Trace element studies by Pires-Ferreira (1975) and Evans (1975) show that iron ore mirrors made in Oaxaca reached sites as distant as Etlatongo in the Mixteca Alta and San Lorenzo in Veracruz. A piece of high quality magnetite from Oaxaca reached the Early Formative village of San Pablo in Morelos. All four of these sites—Tomaltepec, Etlatongo, San Lorenzo, and San Pablo—are places where other lines of evidence suggest the presence of a hereditary elite. We

Figure 5.6. Iron ore mirror production at San José Mogote. *Above*: a sample of unused lumps of magnetite, ilmenite, and ilmeno-magnetite found on the surface of Area A. The photo includes a multifaceted hematite polisher. *Below*: mirrors unfinished, or broken in the process of manufacture, found on the surface of Area A or nearby Mound 1.

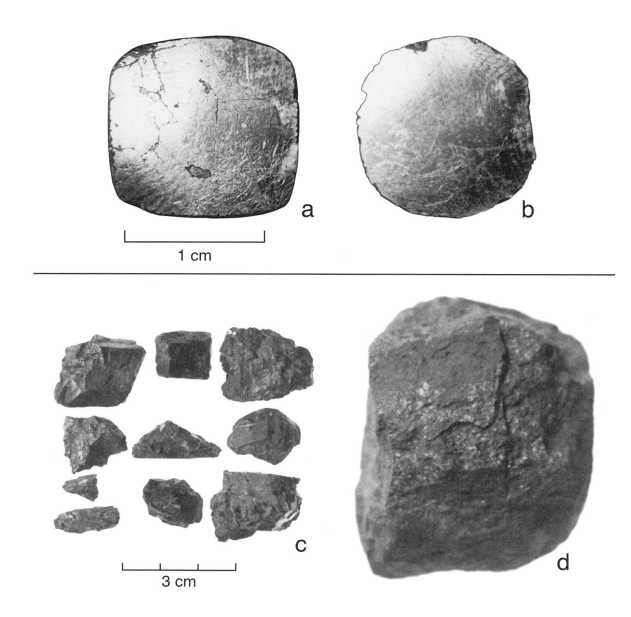

Figure 5.7. Evidence for iron ore mirror and pigment production at San José Mogote. *a*, rectangular mirror redeposited in stratigraphic Zone B, Area A. *b*, circular mirror from Household Unit C3, Area A (*a, b* shown larger than actual size). *c*, unused ore lumps redeposited in Middle Formative fill on Mound 1, near Area A. *d,* large chunk of crystalline hematite found in slopewash on Mound 1. This is the type of ore from which specular hematite pigment could be made.

suspect, therefore, that the reason mirror production at San José Mogote was restricted to one ward (and probably placed under elite supervision) was because many mirrors were destined to be gifts to the leaders of other communities, both inside and outside the valley.

Mössbauer Spectroscopy

For five years, beginning in 1967, archaeologist Jane Pires-Ferreira and chemist B. J. Evans (1975) teamed up to identify the sources of the magnetite and ilmenite used in Formative Mexico. For details, the reader is directed to Pires-Ferreira's 1975 monograph.

Pires-Ferreira first tried neutron activation, which had seemed to work well on obsidian. It did not work well on iron ores, whose iron content was so high that it masked every other element. Evans suggested nuclear gamma-ray resonance spectroscopy, also known as Mössbauer spectroscopy, which had been successful at distinguishing iron sources.

A survey by Pires-Ferreira revealed 36 surface exposures of iron ore in the Valley of Oaxaca, most of them in the Precambrian gneiss which dominates the valley's western piedmont (Fig. 5.8). Pires-Ferreira and Evans then analyzed a sample of archaeological specimens, drawn not only from San José Mogote but also from other villages with which it might have had exchange relations. In the end, it appeared that only four of the Valley of Oaxaca sources had been extensively used, presumably because the ore characteristics at those sources made them appropriate for mirror making.

It is possible that the analysis of a larger sample would have revealed that other sources were used. The time and expense involved in Mössbauer spectroscopy, however, precluded analyzing as many samples as we would have liked.

Our earliest lumps of magnetite turned up in the Zone D Midden of Area A, an Early San José phase provenience. The bulk of the finished, unfinished, and fragmentary mirrors were found in Middle or Late San José phase contexts. Perhaps the safest way to characterize this distribution is to say that while procurement of ore lumps for mirror making had begun by Early San José times, the production of mirrors escalated in the second half of that phase. By the Guadalupe phase the production of mirrors had waned, although redeposited mirrors and ore lumps were occasionally found in the fill of Middle Formative public buildings (Fig. 5.7c).

The Four Main Iron Sources

The four main sources found to be used at San José Mogote were as follows (Pires-Ferreira 1975: Tables 9, 11, 12, 16, 17).

Group I-A (11 specimens)
Pure magnetite from Loma de la Cañada Totomosle (a corruption of the Nahuatl *totomochtli*, "dried corn husks"), near

Santiago Tenango, 27 km northwest of San José Mogote. This is a surface scatter of roughly 350 × 200 m, consisting of very high quality ore eroding out of gneiss. The following archaeological samples from San José Mogote proved to be from Group I-A:

Zone D3 Midden (Area A): one lump of ore
Zone D1 Midden (Area A): one lump of ore
Household Unit C3 (Area A): two lumps of ore
Household Unit C2 (Area A): one unfinished mirror
Household Unit C1 (Area A): one lump of ore
redeposited in fill of Structures 1 and 2 (Area A): two lumps of ore
found on surface of Structures 1 and 2 (Area A): one unfinished mirror
House 2 (Area C): one lump of ore

In addition, one lump of Group I-A magnetite ore was recovered at San Pablo in the Valley of Morelos by David Grove (Pires-Ferreira 1975: Table 11).

Group I-B (7 specimens)
Pure magnetite from Loma los Sabinos, near Zimatlán, 33 km south of San José Mogote. This source covers roughly one square kilometer. The ore is eroding out of a gneiss-quartz formation, deeply cut by arroyos. Pires-Ferreira describes the ore as high quality, ranging from small lumps up to cobbles as large as 30 × 20 cm. The following archaeological samples from San José Mogote proved to be from Group I-B:

Zone D2 Midden (Area A): one lump of ore
Zone D1 Midden (Area A): one lump of ore
Household Unit C4 (Area A): one lump of ore
redeposited in the fill of Structures 1 and 2 (Area A): two lumps of ore

In addition, one lump of Group I-B ore was found on the surface of a Formative site at San Bartolo Coyotepec (between San José Mogote and Loma los Sabinos); and a finished mirror of Group I-B magnetite was found by Ronald Spores in the stream-cut profile of a major Formative site at Etlatongo in the Nochixtlán Valley (Pires-Ferreira 1975: Table 12).

Group IV-A (4 specimens)
A mixed magnetite-ilmenite ore from Loma del Arroyo Terrero, near Arrazola, 14 km south of San José Mogote. This is a small surface scatter of ore lumps, eroding out of decomposing gneiss. The following archaeological samples from San José Mogote proved to be from Group IV-A:

Household Unit C2 (Area A): one lump of ore
Feature 2, Unit C2 (Area A): one lump of ore
Household Unit C1 (Area A): one lump of ore

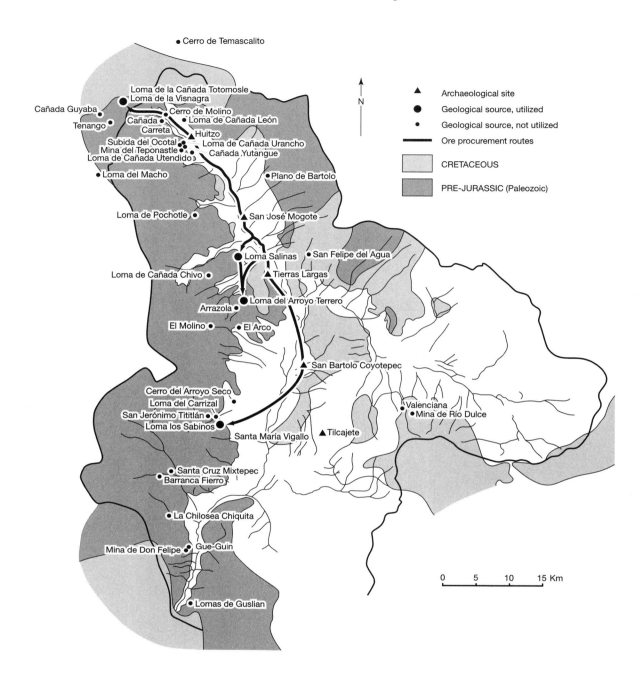

Figure 5.8. Map of the western Valley of Oaxaca, showing iron ore sources and some of the suspected routes by which the ore might have reached San José Mogote (modified from Pires-Ferreira 1975: Fig. 17).

In addition, one lump of Group IV-A ore was found on the surface of Tierras Largas (between San José Mogote and Loma del Arroyo Terrero).

Group IV-B (3 specimens)

A mixed magnetite-ilmenite ore from Loma Salinas, near San Lorenzo Cacaotepec, only 6 km south-southwest of San José Mogote. This source lies very near an arroyo where the modern potters of Santa María Atzompa go to mine pottery clay. Small pieces of ilmeno-magnetite sparkle on the surface of the hill, and there are pockets of ore exposed in gneiss bedrock where it is cut by arroyos. The area is also a source of mica. One of the specimens from San José Mogote sampled by Pires-Ferreira proved to belong to Group IV-B, as follows:

Household Unit C4 (Area A), one lump of ore

In addition, two small flat ilmeno-magnetite mirrors found at San Lorenzo, Veracruz, proved to be made from Group IV-B ore (Pires-Ferreira 1975: Table 18). According to Michael Coe (pers. comm. to Pires-Ferreira, 1970), both of these mirrors had been redeposited in later fill but "probably" date to the Nacaste phase, believed to run from 900 to 750 b.c. Pires-Ferreira (1975:61) believes that the peak period for widespread exchanges of small, flat mirrors was 1000-800 b.c.

The Limits of San José Mogote's Control over Iron Ore Sources

Pires-Ferreira (1975) makes the point that all four of the main iron ore localities used during the Early Formative provided resources of other kinds. Loma de Cañada Totomosle was high enough in the hills to have been surrounded by pine trees useful for house construction, palisade building, and culinary charcoal. Loma Salinas had pottery clay of the type used for several San José phase wares. Loma los Sabinos was near biotite mica sources. Trips to these localities might thus have been multi-purpose.

San José Mogote's apparent monopoly on iron ore mirror making also raises interesting questions about the geographic limits of its control over restricted resources. It would appear that during the San José phase, the craftsmen of Area A had unimpeded access to magnetite sources 27 km to the north and 33 km to the south. It is significant that thirty kilometers is roughly a day's travel on foot; most models for simple chiefdoms consider a day's travel to be the typical distance between a chief's residence and the limits of the territory he controls (Spencer 1990).

Future research, however, is needed to decide between these two alternatives: (1) Did the mirror workers of San José Mogote travel to Loma de la Cañada Totomosle and Loma los Sabinos themselves? (2) Or do the ore lumps found on the surface of the Tierras Largas and San Bartolo Coyotepec sites indicate that iron ore was collected and passed along to San José Mogote by subordinate villages, perhaps in the form of tribute?

Whatever the route taken by the iron ore lumps, the heyday of mirror making seems to have been the San José phase. During the Guadalupe phase, the craft was rapidly abandoned. There are several possible explanations for this decline. The simplest, of course, is that iron ore mirrors had gone out of favor as sumptuary goods. This seems doubtful, given the fact that 850-700 b.c. was a period of peak production of large concave iron ore mirrors in areas to the east (Drucker, Heizer, and Squier 1959).

A more intriguing possibility is that during the Guadalupe phase, San José Mogote's access to the iron ore sources at Loma de la Cañada Totomosle and Loma los Sabinos was thwarted by emerging rival chiefdoms. We have already mentioned (in Chapter 1) that the Guadalupe phase was a time of retrenchment or "cycling down" for San José Mogote. The chiefly center of Huitzo, to the north, stood between San José Mogote and Loma de la Cañada Totomosle. San Martín Tilcajete, to the south, lay only 15 km from Loma los Sabinos. While neither of these emerging rivals engaged in mirror making, their growing strength may have presented obstacles to San José Mogote.

The Crushing and Grinding of Hematite

As mentioned earlier, the red washes, stains, and slips used on Tierras Largas and San José phase pottery were made from iron-rich limonites and *barro colorado*. House 9 of Area C had ground stone tools coated with such red pigment (Chapter 9). In addition, metallic hematite (Fe_2O_3) and crystalline hematite were collected and used. Metallic hematite was evidently used to make mirror polishers like the one seen in Figure 5.6. Crystalline hematite, on the other hand, could be crushed and ground into the pigment known as "specular hematite," in which tiny crystal fragments sparkle throughout the red powder. Specular hematite could be used to make pottery slips, to rub into the excisions on carved pottery, to coat ritual items, or to paint the human body. A very large chunk of crystalline hematite is shown in Figure 5.7*d*. Sizable quantities of this material were locally available, a fact that could have made San José Mogote an exporter to other regions.

The tools used to crush and grind crystalline hematite were most often sandstone pigment palettes (as in House 2 of Area C), slab metates, or small basin-shaped metates (as in House 18 of Area C). Often the manos or pestles used were of quartz or chalcedony, which are harder and have a less vesicular surface than volcanic rock. Rarely was crystalline hematite crushed on what appeared to be a corn-grinding metate.

The Cutting and Trimming of Mica

San José phase craftsmen cut mica sheets into geometric shapes, trimming it much the way they did pearly freshwater mussels, and probably with the same chert gravers. We suspect that much of their mica working produced shiny inlays that were applied to the costumes and wooden masks used in rituals.

Micas are aluminosilicates that occur naturally in what are called "books"—crystalline blocks that derive their name from the fact that they split readily into thin sheets resembling the pages of a book. Micas are abundant in the Precambrian metamorphic rocks that run for 70 km along the west side of the Valley of Oaxaca. They occur mainly in schists and pegmatites. Pieces of mica schist, found discarded on the floors of Early Formative houses, suggest that mica was sometimes procured from those formations.

Three varieties of mica used at San José Mogote were *muscovite*, which is colorless, white, or pearly; *phlogopite*, which is golden or amber; and *biotite*, which is brown to black in color (Fig. 5.9). Geologist Michael Kirkby identified samples of these for us, but he did not have time to examine every archaeological specimen we found. Thus, when we refer to the waste from mica working simply as "white," "gold," or "brown," it is because we do not presume to act as our own geologists.

We found considerable variation among residences in terms of how much or how little mica they worked. We often wished that wood (and other perishable materials) had been preserved at the site, so that we could see the designs created by the geometric inlays.

Mica working in Oaxaca was, of course, not restricted to the Formative. During the Classic period, large quantities were worked on the North Platform at Monte Albán. Occasional Teotihuacán-style Thin Orange pottery and cylindrical tripod vessels with hollow slab feet have also been found on the North Platform, inevitably leading to speculation about whether Valley of Oaxaca mica made its way to Teotihuacán (Marcus and Flannery 1996:233-34). Some Classic palaces at Teotihuacán do, in fact, have floors made of mica. Whether the mica is from Oaxaca, or from a source nearer to Teotihuacán, can only be determined by trace element analysis.

Figure 5.9. Mica of three different colors from San José Mogote.

Ancestor Ritual

During the last century, agricultural village societies analogous to those of Formative Oaxaca have been studied worldwide. The ethnographic literature on such societies stresses the continuing involvement of families with their ancestors (see Marcus 1998a:17-23 for references). The Zapotec were no exception. For them, the ancestors were *binigulazaa* or "old people of the clouds," and were thought to remain actively involved in the ongoing affairs of the family (Marcus 1998a:11-15). The ritual relationship was reciprocal: the descendants' role was to invoke the ancestors' names and make offerings to them, while the ancestors' role was to advise, guide, and intercede on their descendants' behalf with powerful supernaturals like Lightning and Earthquake.

In many parts of Africa, Asia, and the New World, small solid figurines were seen as an appropriate venue to which the spirits of recent ancestors could return. In figurine form, the ancestors could be contacted through a ritual called *geneonymy*, the "call-

ing of an ancestor by name." This was thought to animate the figurine. At such times, ancestors could also be ritually "fed," a task that usually fell to the women of the household. In many village societies worldwide, women were expected to feed, communicate with, and maintain links to near ancestors, "leaving more remote ancestors to men or even to ritual specialists" (Marcus 1998a:17).

Literally hundreds of small figurines appropriate for such ritual have been found in Oaxaca's Early and Middle Formative villages. A large sample from San José Mogote, Tierras Largas, Huitzo, Abasolo, Fábrica San José, and Tomaltepec has been studied by Marcus (1998a), to whom the reader is referred for more complete information. Here we will summarize Marcus' basic conclusions.

1. When found in primary archaeological context, small solid figurines occur only in and around residences, never in Men's Houses or temples. Often, in fact, they appear in localities we believe (on the basis of various lines of evidence) to be women's work areas. Special household contexts include (a) a complete "dedicatory" figurine buried under a house foundation stone, and (b) an arranged "scene" of four figurines buried beneath the floor of a woman's work area. As a result, we suspect that small solid figurines were artifacts made by women, for use in household ritual involving the ancestors (Fig. 5.10).

Figure 5.10. Zapotec woman engaged in ancestor ritual. She has constructed a scene using figurines, which provide a venue for the spirits of recent ancestors. (Drawing by John Klausmeyer.)

2. In most of the societies in Marcus' ethnographic sample, death brings about loss of individuality. Ancestors belong to a generic category analogous to elders: "the behavior of ancestors reflects not their individual personalities but rather a particular legal status" (Kopytoff 1971:129). Ancestors are "faceless" (Newell 1976:22), and thus do not need to be depicted as old. Not only are deceased relatives of all ages considered ancestors, even those dying at an advanced age are likely to be remembered as the active and vigorous people they were when their descendants were young (Ahern 1973:216-18). This probably explains why Formative figurines have stereotyped rather than individualized faces, and are rarely shown as old (Marcus 1998a:21-22).

3. While little effort was put into giving faces any distinguishing characteristics, there seem to have been attempts to convey information about marital status, social *persona*, and rank. Some female figurines have elaborate hairdos, like those given to marriageable Zapotec daughters by their mothers. Others have the conservative hairdos of married Zapotec women. High status may be reflected in carefully depicted sandals, ear and nose ornaments, necklaces and pendants. Some men have completely shaved heads, resembling tonsured warriors or stern-eyed chiefs. Other

men wear animal costumes, small masks, or ballplayer's gear. This suggests that depicting the various social roles or statuses of an ancestor were more important than accurately depicting his or her face.

Social Changes Reflected in Figurines

The attributes of small solid figurines changed during the course of the Formative. Some of those changes—especially the ways the eyes were made—were stylistic, and can be used for chronological purposes. Other changes seemed to reflect the shift from a society based on achieved status to a society based on ascribed status. The stylistic/chronological attributes are summarized in Chapter 8 of Marcus (1998a), to which the reader is referred for details. Here we discuss only those variables conveying social information.

The Tierras Largas phase was a time of modest differences in achieved status. We have the impression that figurine makers were concerned mainly with showing an ancestor's social *persona*. Men and women were distinguished by body shape (Fig. 5.11*a, b*), hairdo, and head covering. Some females display elaborate hairdos which we suspect were given to young women reaching marriageable age (Fig. 5.11*c*). Some hairdos were even perforated in such a way that colored yarns or ribbons could be added. "Married" vs. "single" may therefore have been considered important aspects of the *persona*.

The San José phase was a time of emerging differences in hereditary rank, and this seems to be reflected in body position. Some male figurines sit crosslegged in what appears to be a position of authority (Fig. 5.12*a*), while others stand with their arms folded across their chest in a posture of obeisance (Fig. 5.12*b*). Some females wear their hair with a central part and two braids, just as married Zapotec women wore it when first contacted by Europeans, and continue to wear it today (Fig. 5.12*c*). Some males (dubbed "tonsured caciques") display shaved heads and stern faces (Fig. 5.12*d*); others have headgear and an elite demeanor (Fig. 5.12*e*). Still others seem to show the artificially deformed skull associated with high hereditary rank (Fig. 5.12*f*).

By the Guadalupe phase, figurine makers took great pains to depict some women wearing elaborate ear ornaments, necklaces or pendants, pectorals, and sandals. These were presumably highly ranked women, whose footgear prevented their feet from touching the ground directly, and who wore jadeite and mother-of-pearl in abundance (Fig. 5.13*a*). During the Rosario phase, when San José Mogote was the paramount village of a complex chiefdom, elite women were depicted with coffee-bean eyes and a range of hairdos so great that there seem to be no two exactly alike (Fig. 5.13*b-e*).

Large Hollow White-Slipped "Dolls"

Finally, we should say a word about large hollow "baby dolls," slipped with local Atoyac Yellow-white engobe, fragments of

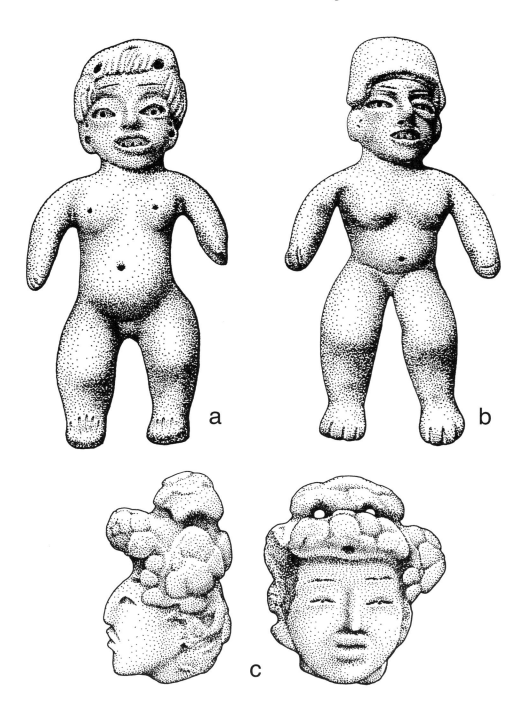

Figure 5.11. Formative figurines. *a*, female figurine of the Tierras Largas phase. *b*, male figurine of the Tierras Largas phase. *c*, front and side views of a Tierras Largas phase woman's head with an elaborate hairdo produced by braiding. Her hair has been perforated in three places, so that colored ribbons or yarn could be added to the hairdo. *a, b*, from Hacienda Blanca (Ramírez Urrea 1993); *c*, from San José Mogote (after Marcus 1998a).

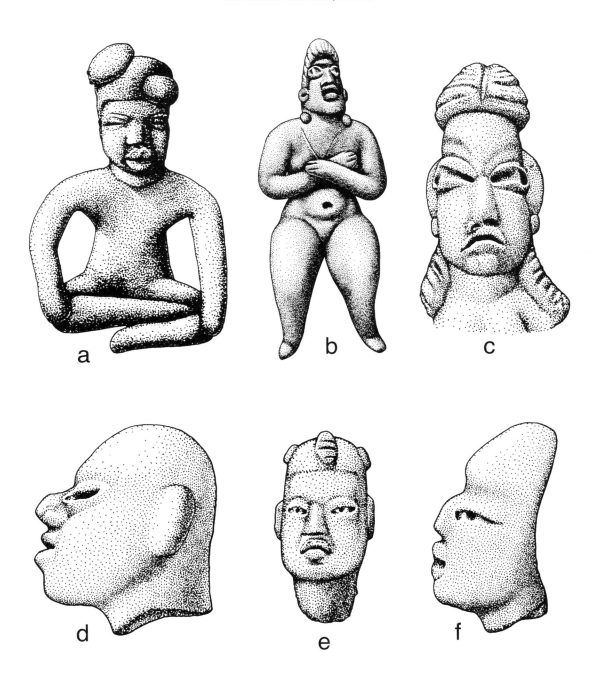

Figure 5.12. Formative figurines. *a*, man seated in position of authority. *b*, figure with arms crossed in "obeisance posture." *c*, "married woman's hairdo": parted in the center and plaited into two braids. *d*, tonsured male. *e*, white-slipped head of elite male with decorated headgear. *f*, man with tabular erect skull deformation. *a*, from Tomaltepec; *b-f*, from San José Mogote (after Marcus 1998a).

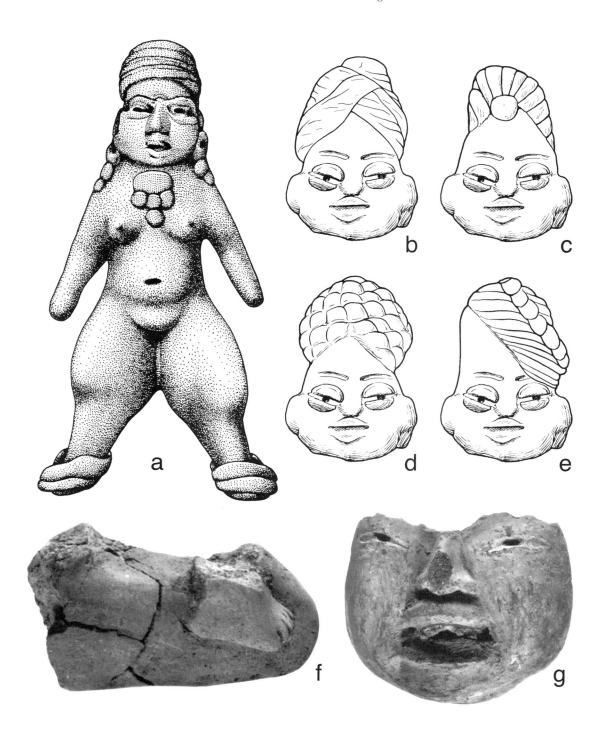

Figure 5.13. Formative figurines. *a*, artist's reconstruction of a prototypic female figurine of the Guadalupe phase, with turban, ear ornaments, pectoral, and sandals. *b-e*, four examples of Rosario phase women with elaborate hairdos or headwraps. *f*, *g*, fragments of hollow white "baby dolls" of the San José phase. *a*, based on specimens from Huitzo. *b-g*, from San José Mogote (after Marcus 1998a).

which occurred frequently in San José and Guadalupe phase debris (Fig. 5.13*f, g*). Such dolls were widespread in highland Mexico at that time, especially in the Basin of Mexico and Morelos, regions where (as in Oaxaca) white slips were popular (Flannery and Marcus 2000:16-19).

Large hollow white dolls do not belong in the same category as small solid figurines, and we do not consider them to represent *recent* ancestors. Judging by whole or restored specimens, the large hollow dolls appear either male or sexless. In our opinion,

> We should consider the possibility that such hollow dolls depict more remote male ancestors of some special type, portrayed at an infantile stage for cosmological reasons which we do not fully understand. . . . They may depict primordial ancestors so mythologized that their biological sex is of less concern than their infantile life stage. [Marcus 1998a:29]

We further suspect that these large, mythological babies were associated with elite families, and were created by individuals with skills beyond those of the ordinary potter.

Dancing in Masks and Costumes

By analogy with similar societies worldwide, we suspect that one of the most important ritual activities at San José Mogote would have been dancing. We further suspect that some dancers wore masks and costumes. Archaeological evidence for dancing is indirect and often based on representations in art (e.g. Garfinkel 2003), so let us look at some of the clues.

1. Dancing may be very ancient in Oaxaca. At the Archaic open-air site of Gheo-Shih, near Mitla, Frank Hole discovered a 20 m × 7 m boulder-lined area that could have been a cleared dance ground (Marcus and Flannery 1996:58-59).
2. Dancers in Zapotec villages often wear masks, and one of the earliest pieces of ceramic art in Oaxaca is a miniature mask from House 20 at San José Mogote (see Chapter 7). This mask, the right size to be worn by a figurine, dates to the Espiridión complex.
3. Fragments from at least three ceramic masks were found in and around Structure 6 of San José Mogote, a Tierras Largas phase Men's House (Marcus 1998a: Fig. 9.11).
4. A complete, grotesque miniature mask was found in the Zone G Midden, Area C, San José Mogote, a Tierras Largas phase provenience (see Chapter 7).
5. More fragments of pottery masks were found in San José phase proveniences at San José Mogote, including two from "Plácido's Midden" in Area C (Marcus 1998a: Fig. 10.26).
6. Figurines from Tlapacoya in the Basin of Mexico show individuals wearing masks that cover only the lower half of the face (Marcus 1998a: Fig. 8.28). Masks this small would be appropriate in Mesoamerica because the mask would be covering the nose and mouth, the venue from which the vital force—"wind," "breath," and "life"—is-

sued. Hence the wearer would be transformed even though his or her eyes were uncovered, making it easier to dance. A complete mask of the right size was found in Household Unit LSJ-1 at the site of Tierras Largas, a San José phase provenience (Fig. 5.14*a*).

7. Some figurines from the Basin of Mexico and Morelos clearly depict dancers. One example is the dancing woman found with Burial 7 at Nexpa, Morelos (Grove 1974: Fig. 11*j*). A dancing woman in a skirt similar to the Nexpa dancer's was found in Household Unit LSJ-1 at the site of Tierras Largas (Fig. 5.14*b*).
8. Many figurines of the San José phase show individuals in costumes or body paint, suggesting rituals that may have included dance. For example, one figurine from the Zone E Midden, Area C, San José Mogote, depicts an individual painted red with hematite like a harlequin (Marcus 1998a: Fig. 11.20). Another figurine, from Household Unit LSJ-1 at the Tierras Largas site, shows a man in animal costume (Marcus 1998a: Fig. 5.14*b*).
9. By the Late San José phase there were ceramic roller stamps that could have been used to transfer painted designs to the body, including the faces and bodies of dancers. One such stamp was found in the Zone C Midden, Area C, San José Mogote (see Chapter 10).
10. Some ceramic mask fragments have holes drilled near the edges, so that they could be attached with cords. A few larger pieces seem to have come from masks that would have covered the entire face. Since such full-sized masks would have been quite heavy, we suspect that most were made of lighter-weight material, such as wood. Judging by the costumed figurines and raw materials we found in Formative households, we believe that masks and costumes were decorated with mica, mollusk shell, animal fur or hide, paint, plant material, and other substances.

Singing and Chanting

If there was dancing at San José Mogote, there should also have been music, perhaps including singing or chanting. The evidence is circumstantial, and involves figurines that seem to show individuals caught in the act of vocalizing. Several such figurines are illustrated by Marcus (1998a), and we reproduce one here as Fig. 5.14*d*.

Divination

Ethnohistory tells us that divination was practiced by most Mesoamerican societies. It is difficult, however, to find archaeological evidence for specific forms of divination. In the case of the Zapotec, sixteenth-century sources indicate that divination could involve water, fire, air, birds, and the sacrifice of animals or humans (Córdova 1578). At the time of the Conquest, much of this was carried out in temples by male priests.

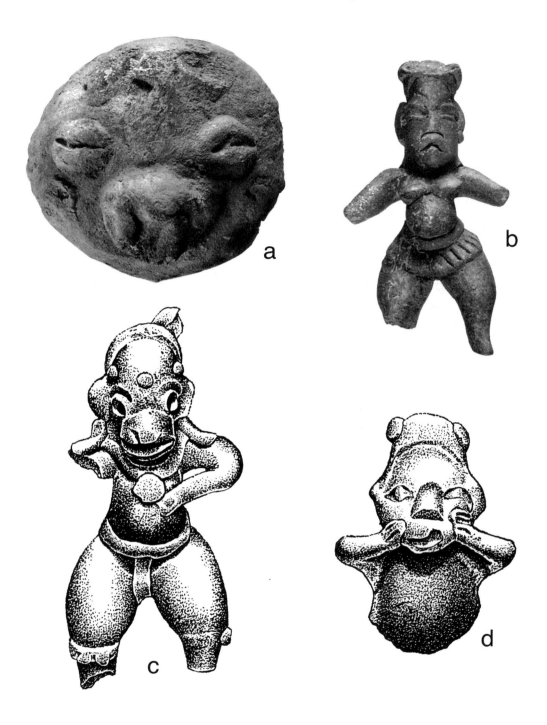

Figure 5.14. Evidence for masks, costumes, dancing, and singing or chanting during the San José phase. *a*, complete ceramic mask. *b*, woman dancing in grass(?) skirt. *c*, dancer in animal mask, loincloth, and anklets with shell(?) tinklers. *d*, man singing or chanting. *a-c*, from Household Unit LSJ-1 at the site of Tierras Largas; *d*, from San José Mogote (after Marcus 1998a).

Figure 5.15. Zapotec woman practicing *tiniyaaya niça*, or water divination, by tossing maize kernels into a water-filled basin in the dooryard of her house.

In contrast, much of women's ritual was carried out in the context of the house (Marcus 1998a:11-15). Household divination was aimed at finding the cause of an illness affecting a family member, predicting the outcome of a pregnancy or marriage, or determining whether a given day was auspicious for a family activity.

In Household Unit C3 of Area A at San José Mogote we discovered several features that could have been used for a type of divination the Zapotec called *tiniyaaya niça* (see Chapter 14). This ritual, carried out by women, involved kneeling on a mat while casting maize kernels onto the surface of a water-filled basin (Fig. 5.15). The woman then noted the number of kernels that remained floating, including whether it was an odd or even number. Some women divined by observing whether the kernels floated in groups of three, five, or thirteen.

In the dooryard of Unit C3 were two shallow basins, Features 3 and 8. Feature 3 was circular, 1.2 m in diameter, and recessed 5 cm into the dooryard. It had been mud-plastered, waterproofed with a coasting of lime plaster, then painted red with specular hematite. Feature 8 was similar, but painted yellow (Fig. 14.1, Chapter 14).

Each of these basins would have retained water long enough to allow for the ritual of *tiniyaaya niça*. At the same time, our im-

pression is that neither was a permanent feature of the dooryard. We suspect that both basins were constructed for the performance of a short-term ritual, and had been preserved only because they were covered up by soft wattle-and-daub debris not long after their use. We found it significant that both features were painted with one of the colors associated with the four "world directions" of the ancient Zapotec.

Ritual Bloodletting

Autosacrifice was a widespread form of personal ritual in ancient Mesoamerica. One of the most common types of auto-sacrifice was the offering of one's own blood by perforating one's tongue, earlobes, fingers, or other parts of the body. This could be done with a sharp obsidian lancet, an agave spine, or an exotic perforator such as a stingray spine.

Spines of the stingray (family Dasyatidae), with their stiletto-like shape and serrated edges, were evidently prized. In addition to receiving genuine stingray spines from the coast, villagers in Formative Oaxaca imitated them in both bone and obsidian. Highly ranked families, like the one occupying House 16/17 in Area B of San José Mogote, had access to the genuine article (Fig. 5.16*a*). Families of lower rank whittled imitation stingray

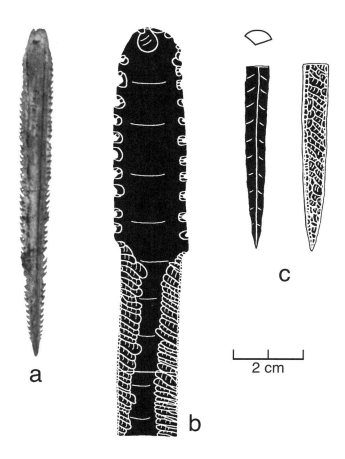

a

b

c

|__|__|__|
2 cm

Figure 5.16. Bloodletting tools. *a,* stingray spine from the House 16/17 Complex, Area B. *b,* large obsidian blade chipped to resemble a stingray spine (point broken off), Structure 28, Mound 1. *c,* both sides and the cross-section of a stiletto point chipped from an obsidian blade, Zone B Residence, Mound 1. The missing point of *b* may have resembled *c.* (*a,* San José phase; *b, c,* Rosario phase.)

Among the cranial parts that did show up were otoliths of drum (Fig. 5.17*c, d*). These shiny calcifications may have been kept as charms or amulets of some kind.

Finally, we found occasional teeth from sharks (Carcharhinidae) in the household refuse. These were sharp enough to be used for bloodletting, and as revealed by Borhegyi (1961), have an indirect connection with stingray spines. Because some sharks eat stingrays, Borhegyi points out, fishermen often recover stingray spines stuck between the teeth of captured sharks.

Ritual Use of Exotic Birds, Mammals, and Reptiles

In addition to fish parts from coastal regions, families at San José Mogote received bird, mammal, and reptile parts from other Mexican environments. We believe that these exotic animal parts were incorporated into Formative ritual life as musical instruments, costume parts, and offerings.

Musical Instruments

Shells of lowland river turtles were converted into drums (Fig. 5.17*a*). Especially favored was the large *tortuga aplanada* (*Dermatemys mawii*), a species native to the large river systems of the Gulf Coast (an environment it shares with pearly freshwater mussels, like those worked at San José Mogote). Fragments of *Dermatemys* shell have been found at both San José Mogote and Tierras Largas. In some Zapotec villages, turtle shell drums are still played with deer antler drumsticks (Covarrubias 1946: Plate 87).

Shells of the nine-banded armadillo (*Dasypus novemcinctus*), a native of the Isthmus of Tehuantepec, are still used as rattles by the Zapotec (Fig. 5.17*e*). They might also have been used as containers or, broken down into their small individual plates, added to masks and costumes as ornaments.

Sources of Feathers

Like most Mesoamerican peoples, Formative Oaxaca's villagers made extensive use of feathers in costumes and ritual items. Local finches, tanagers, grosbeaks, and orioles were of course used, but so were birds from other regions. Two large birds whose remains showed up at Tierras Largas and San José Mogote were the military macaw (*Ara militaris*) and the wild turkey (*Meleagris gallopavo*). The macaw, native to the mountains between the Valley of Oaxaca and the Pacific coast, was sought for its blue-green feathers. The wild turkey, a native of the oak-forested highlands to the north, had large feathers that were barred brown and black (Fig. 5.17*b*). The Basin of Mexico is perhaps the region nearest to Oaxaca where turkeys are known to have occurred in the wild. Both macaws and turkeys were represented by skeletal elements, which suggests that they arrived in the form of complete eviscerated and dried birds, not simply wings or loose feathers.

spines from splinters of deer bone, like the one from the site of Tierras Largas shown in Figure 11.7 of Flannery (1976b). Important Rosario phase individuals using the Structure 28 temple on Mound 1 drew blood with imitation stingray spines chipped from large imported obsidian blades (Fig. 5.16*b, c*).

In addition to stingray spines, households at San José Mogote imported the spines of other genera of fish. The evidence consists mainly of needlelike vertebral spines, and sometimes the vertebrae to which they had once been attached. To be sure, there is no evidence that all these spines were used for bloodletting; some, in fact, could have been used for fine perforating. We believe that the most common parts imported were vertebrae with the spines attached, rather than whole dried fish. There simply were too few cranial bones present in the refuse to suggest that San José Mogote received many complete fish. The most commonly identified families of fish were (1) drums or croakers (Sciaenidae), (2) grunts (Pomadasyidae), and (3) snappers (Lutjanidae).

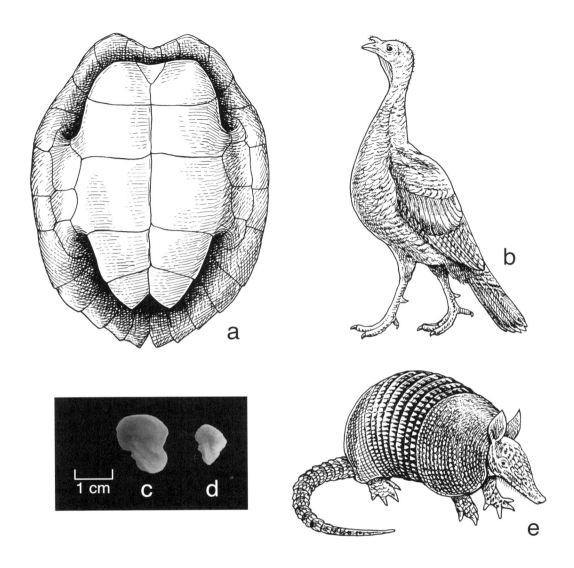

Figure 5.17. Some of the exotic fish, reptiles, birds, and mammals imported by San José Mogote. *a*, drum made from the shell of a lowland river turtle. *b*, wild turkeys, probably imported as dried specimens for their feathers. *c, d*, otoliths from fish of the family Sciaenidae (drums), whose spines were also imported. *e*, nine-banded armadillo, whose shells were probably used as containers, rattles, and costume parts.

By Monte Albán II (100 b.c.-A.D. 200) the domesticated turkey had arrived in Oaxaca, making it unnecessary to import wild specimens of that particular species.

Ritual Offerings

In Stratigraphic Zone F below Structure 19 on Mound 1 at San José Mogote, we found the skull of a young spider monkey (*Ateles geoffroyi*) buried as an offering below a San José phase Men's House (Marcus 1998a: Fig. 8.37). This monkey could have been brought from the tropical forests of the Isthmus of Tehuantepec.

Personal Ornamentation

As far back as the era of hunting, gathering, and incipient agriculture, the people of Oaxaca had taken time to make personal ornaments. At the open-air camp site of Gheo-Shih, Archaic food collectors collected thin stream pebbles and drilled them into pendants (Marcus and Flannery 1996: Fig. 44). On a Late Archaic living floor at Cueva Blanca, they left a Pacific sea shell perforated for suspension (op. cit: Fig. 50).

Personal ornamentation increased during the Formative, probably because the villagers wanted to convey both social *persona* (male, female, single, married) and social status (whether

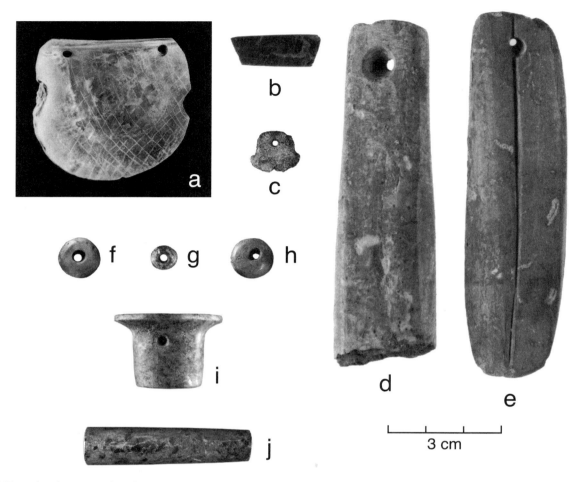

Figure 5.18. Examples of ornaments from San José Mogote. *a*, pearl oyster pendant, Zone D Midden, Area C. *b*, iron ore mirror (possibly an inlay), Area B-C Connecting Trench. *c*, "bifid tongue" bead, malachite, Burial 16, Area C. *d, e*, plummet-shaped stone pendants from middens, Area C. *f, h*, disk beads of jadeite(?), Burial 18, Area B. *g*, small disk bead of jadeite(?), Burial 16, Area C. *i*, earspool of jadeite(?), House 16, Area B. *j*, tubular bead of mottled jadeite(?), found near Structure 8, a Guadalupe phase temple platform, Area C.

achieved or inherited). Unfortunately, in the case of most ornaments, we have no foolproof way of deducing what was being
conveyed.

During the Tierras Largas phase, a period with no convincing
evidence for inherited rank, both pearl oysters and pearly freshwater mussels were made into ornaments. The villagers also accumulated dog canines, a readily available resource, to perforate
for suspension on necklaces. During the transition from Tierras
Largas to San José times, the importation of shell escalated, with
horn shells and marsh clams joining oysters and mussels.

San José phase ornamentation was complex and varied, with
dozens of marine and freshwater mollusk species imported (e.g.,
Fig. 5.18*a*). The strengths and limitations of various shells have
been discussed in an earlier section. Along with dog canines, the
villagers occasionally perforated peccary tusks to be worn on
necklaces. They also cut hollow bone shafts into tubular beads.

Stone ornaments increased in number and variety during the San
José phase. The simplest were small disk beads for bracelets and

necklaces. Some of the heaviest were plummetlike pendants, ground
into shape, polished, and perforated for suspension (Fig. 5.18*d, e*).

One commodity that may have been restricted to families
of high rank was the iron ore mirror (Fig. 5.18*b*). As discussed
earlier ("Polishing Iron Ore Mirrors," above), access to magnetite
and ilmenite seems to have been restricted.

Another commodity that may reflect emerging rank was jadeite, which made its first appearance around 1150 b.c. Because we
were unable to have every artifact of fine green stone examined by
a geologist to see whether it was authentic jadeite, or serpentine,
or a related mineral, in this report we simply refer to such items
as "jadeite(?)," employing a question mark.

It would appear that many, perhaps most, villagers at San
José Mogote had access to small disk beads of this material (Fig.
5.18*f-h*). A large number of San José phase burials had at least
one jadeite(?) bead in the mouth. Not every burial, however, had
a set of jadeite(?) earspools like those found with Burial 18, Area
B (Chapter 18). And few houses produced large, flaring jadeite(?)

earspools like the one from House 16 (Fig. 5.18*i*). We suspect that only families of high rank had access to that much jadeite.

One question concerning ornamentation remains unresolved. Scores of figurines of the San José, Guadalupe, and Rosario phases are shown wearing earspools. Of what material were those earspools made? Most were probably not made of jadeite, since we found relatively few earspools of that material. Nor can they have been burnished pottery earspools, like those found in other regions of Mesoamerica, for we recovered only a few of those at San José Mogote. Our guess is that most earspools must have been made of some perishable material—wood, perhaps—onto which decorative material like mica or mother-of-pearl could be glued.

Raiding

We began our work at San José Mogote expecting to uncover the houses of peaceful farmers. Today we realize that intervillage raiding had begun almost as soon as there were neighbors to raid. Our oldest known Tierras Largas phase residence, House 19, had been burned to the ground at 1540 b.c. Within a few centuries, the occupants of San José Mogote had built several versions of a defensive palisade (Zapotec *leeyaga*) along the western periphery of the village (Chapter 7). By 1310-1210 b.c., part of one palisade had been burned.

We now suspect that one reason for San José Mogote's enormous growth during the Tierras Largas/San José transition was a deliberate attempt to become a community too large to be raided. To be sure, the community's leaders were also "able to organize labor for public construction, attract large numbers of followers, organize trade, and stimulate craft production" (Marcus and Flannery 1996:91). It would be an oversimplification, however, to attribute all of the community's growth to "chiefly aggrandizement." Security was probably an additional factor, and would remain so for the entire Formative sequence.

During the 1960s, unfortunately, we were still under the effect of "the pacification of the past." This is how Keeley (1996), in *War before Civilization*, describes the widespread Rousseauian view that pre-state peoples were essentially peaceful. Nothing could be farther from the truth, as studies by Carneiro (1991), Redmond (1994), Kelly (2000), and LeBlanc (2003) have now shown us: tribal and chiefly societies had high frequencies of raiding, high mortality rates, and no end of terror tactics like torture, mutilation, cannibalism, and trophy head-taking.

We found Feature 21, our first stretch of Tierras Largas phase palisade, in 1969, but were hesitant to call it more than a "double line of staggered posts" or "an enclosure . . . set apart from the residential areas" (Flannery and Marcus 1976a:208). During the 1970s we continued to find more sections of this palisade, tracing it 30-40 m until it disappeared into a modern cattle pen without turning a corner. During the course of these later field seasons, we also discovered that what we had originally considered an "open area (perhaps 7 m wide from west to east)" (ibid.) was simply a gap between earlier and later versions of the palisade. We even found a stone-and-posthole structure, Feature 66, that

may be a "baffle entrance" for one of the early versions (Fig. 7.6, Chapter 7).

A Maori Analogy

Because of the fragmentary nature of Features 21 and 66, we cannot single out a palisade in the ethnographic literature that exactly matches ours. We are struck, however, by the extent and variety of defensive works built by the Maori of New Zealand. In Figure 5.19, we compare one of our double lines of palisade posts to the fortifications used by the Maori at the village of Paeroa Pa in 1772 (Fox 1976; Davidson 1987). Paeroa Pa sat on a long ridge, not unlike the piedmont spur of San José Mogote. The outer tip of the ridge was undefended, while the opposite end had a defensive ditch. Running along either side of the ridge were double lines of posts. Entrance to the village was by small gaps that provided an indirect route through stretches where the space between post lines widened; enemies would have been forced to enter these gaps single file, leaving them vulnerable.

Interpreting Burned Houses

In addition to palisades of wooden posts, some badly burned houses strengthen our evidence for raiding in Formative Oaxaca. We realize, of course, that houses might catch fire for reasons other than deliberate burning by enemies, so we have developed a few "rules of thumb" for interpreting conflagrations.

The upright posts in Formative houses were generally of pine, procured by means of a strenuous round trip to the mountains. Today's Zapotec say that if fire breaks out accidentally in a wattle-and-daub house, they rush to put it out, and attempt to salvage as much of the construction wood as they can. Because Formative villagers tended not to have hearths inside their houses, almost the only accidental source of fire would have been a spilled charcoal brazier, and that should have been relatively easy to extinguish.

Our rule of thumb, therefore, is not to consider small amounts of burned daub to be evidence for a deliberate fire, especially if no posts were burned. On the other hand, if all the upright posts in a house have been burned, the roof beams have fallen in, there are many kilograms of burned daub on the floor, and some of the daub has literally vitrified, there is a strong likelihood that the fire was deliberate. For example, Drennan (1976a) found that three of his Guadalupe phase houses at Fábrica San José—Units LG-1, LG-3, and LG-5—had been heavily burned, with carbonized roof beams and impressive quantities of burned daub. San José Mogote's main Rosario phase temple was burned in a fire so intense that the clay in its walls turned to vitrified cinders (Marcus and Flannery 1996:128).

The Mounting Evidence for Warfare

Burned houses were, of course, not our only evidence for raiding and warfare. During the Rosario phase, a stone monument

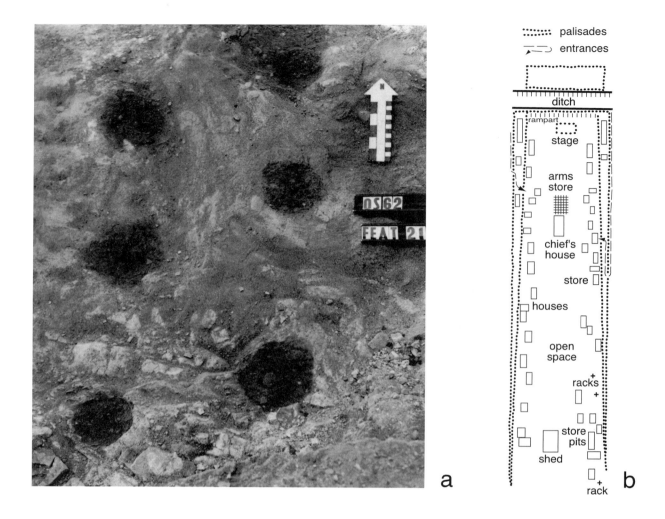

Figure 5.19. Palisades from San José Mogote, Mexico, and Paeroa Pa, New Zealand. *a*, six burned postholes in bedrock from Feature 21, a section of Tierras Largas phase palisade featuring a double line of posts. *b*, partial plan of the fortified Maori village of Paeroa Pa in 1772 (redrawn from Davidson 1987: Fig. 106). Paeroa Pa was defended on two sides by double lines of posts.

was carved at San José Mogote depicting an elite rival who had had his heart removed. Designated Monument 3, it was set up as the threshold of a corridor between two temples (Marcus and Flannery 1996:128-30; Flannery and Marcus 2003:11802-804). The victim's hieroglyphic name, "One Earthquake," was carved between his feet. The fact that his name was given may provide another analogy with Maori warfare. Ethnographer Peter Buck, himself a Maori, reveals that Maori warriors "gained prestige from the quality of the men they killed and not from the quantity. . . . No matter how great the casualty list after an engagement, . . . [i]f there was no chiefly name to connect the engagement with a tribal genealogy, the battle was without a name" (Buck 1949:399-400).

Warfare continued into Monte Albán I. Early in the history of Monte Albán itself, the occupants built three kilometers of defensive walls (Blanton 1978). Dozens of other Monte Albán I sites sought defensive locations (Kowalewski et al. 1989).

The effects of escalating warfare on settlement patterns become clear in a "decision tree" analysis of Valley of Oaxaca data undertaken by Reynolds (2000). Reynolds drew on the scores of variables recorded by the settlement pattern survey for every archaeological site in the Etla subvalley (Kowalewski et al. 1989). Using techniques of "machine learning" (a subfield of artificial intelligence), Reynolds created "decision trees" in which the decisions determining settlement choices were ranked in order of priority. For all periods up to and including the Rosario phase,

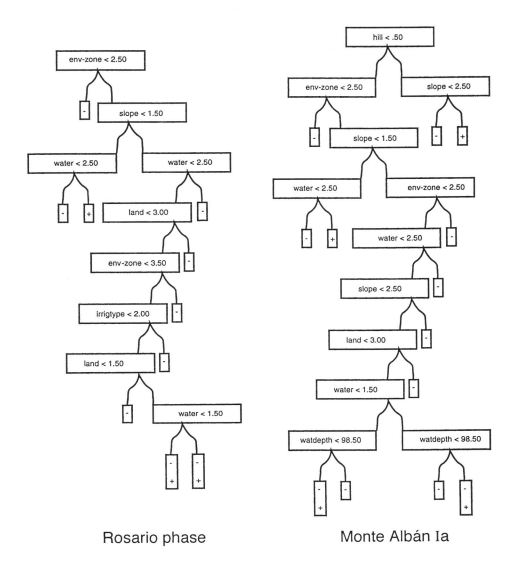

Figure 5.20. Decision tree diagrams for the locations of villages with evidence of raiding in the Etla subvalley. During the Rosario phase (*n* = 36 sites), "environmental zone" was still the dominant variable influencing settlement choice. By Monte Albán Ia (*n* = 77 sites), "hilltop location" had moved above both environmental zone and water source as a key variable, reflecting the need for defensible locations during a time of increased raiding. (Tree diagrams taken from Reynolds 2000: Figs. 5 and 6.)

"environmental zone" was the key variable at the top of the tree (Fig. 5.20, *left*). In Monte Albán Ia (500-300 b.c.), for the first time, "hill" became the key variable. In other words, the need for a defensible location was now as important as, if not more important than, a site's environmental zone (Fig. 5.20, *right*).

In sum, the accumulated evidence for raiding (and eventually, full-scale warfare) in Formative Oaxaca overcame any doubts we might have had about our early palisades. The final straw came when Carneiro (2003:210) reprimanded Flannery for omitting "war leader" from his list of a chief's roles (Flannery 1972:402-3), and Flannery had no choice but to smile and agree. It is an omission he will not make again.

The Origin of War: Kelly's Model

In a recent cross-cultural study of pre-state societies, Kelly (2000) investigated the question of why some were "warless" and others not. His sample included (1) ethnographically known hunter-gatherers who, like the Andaman Islanders, were already involved in raiding when first contacted, and (2) archaeologically known hunter-gatherers who, like the massacred victims of Jebel Sahaba (Wendorf 1968), were involved in raiding before either agriculture or complex society had arisen. This preempted any claim that group violence was the result of contamination by more complex "warlike" cultures.

Kelly found that the highest incidence of warlessness was among unsegmented societies like the !Kung and Mbuti of Africa. These hunter-gatherers had no level of organization beyond the local group, and little tendency to form segments like lineages and clans; even their extended family structure was relatively impermanent. Such foragers did have individual homicides, and might respond to them with capital punishment, reaching a consensus to kill the offender. They did not, however, display much in the way of group-vs.-group violence.

Once societies had developed to the point where they became divided into equivalent segments—for example, patrilineal, matrilineal, or ancestor-based cognatic descent groups, which combined into progressively more inclusive units—the story became different. Such segmentary societies (which are usually agricultural, but can include foragers like the Andaman Islanders) display a principle Kelly calls *social substitutability*. If someone from another segment kills a member of your segment, it is not necessary to track him down and kill him. Killing *any* member (or members) of his segment is sufficient to even the score.

The importance of this principle is that it treats raiding as a form of social action. Group violence is not simply a "pathology" that occurs when innately "peaceful" societies go astray, as those who seek to pacify the past would have us believe. Raiding is so common a part of segmentary societies' behavior that one wonders why any archaeologist (including ourselves) would leave it out of a reconstruction of the Formative period.

Like Carneiro (1987) before him, Kelly observes that raiding often begins not in the most resource-poor environments, but in the richest. In marginal environments, conditions of scarcity encourage sharing and cooperation among neighbors for survival. Only in rich environments can societies "afford to have enemies for neighbors" (Kelly 2000:135). Stored agricultural surplus helps make raiding affordable, as does population growth, which provides more warriors for raiding while making one's own village easier to defend. The motivation for most raids, according to Kelly, is not to steal resources, but to avenge a homicide or some real or imagined insult.

Three of the preconditions mentioned by Kelly as increasing the likelihood of raiding are present at Early Formative San José Mogote. The site is located in one of the richest environments of the Atoyac River floodplain. It has bell-shaped storage pits

capable of holding a metric ton of maize per household. The iconography of the San José phase strongly suggests that there were ancestor-based cognatic descent groups, focused on Sky/Lightning and Earth/Earthquake. In fact, it is likely that social segments were present as early as the Tierras Largas phase, when San José Mogote had begun to build Men's Houses (Marcus and Flannery 1996:87-88). By the Early San José phase, residential wards A and C appear to have maintained separate Men's Houses, suggesting multiple societal segments (Chapter 22).

Palisades, Men's Houses, Powdered Tobacco, and Lime

Because we could not trace them for their entire length, we do not know whether the Area C palisades defended the entire Tierras Largas phase site, or only one sector. It may be significant that some of our Men's Houses lay just inside the lines of posts. Based on his fieldwork among the Etoro of New Guinea, Kelly (pers. comm., 2000) reports that Men's Houses were often located near the palisade entrance, because the fully initiated men occupying those ritual buildings were the village's first line of defense.

It was usually in the Men's House, of course, that raids on other New Guinea villages were planned (Barth 1987). The sixteenth-century Zapotec chewed a powdered mixture of strong wild tobacco and lime before battles, believing that it increased their physical strength (Espíndola 1580:130; Whitecotton 1977:137). Several Tierras Largas phase Men's Houses contained pits full of powdered lime which we suspect was prepared for that purpose (Marcus and Flannery 1996:87). In Chapter 4 we have already described portable, boxlike metates that we believe were used to grind tobacco or other ritual plants into powder.

The small-scale raiding reflected in our Tierras Largas phase palisades was, of course, only the beginning. With the conversion of San José Mogote into a 60-70 ha chiefly center during San José, Guadalupe, and Rosario times, elite competition only escalated. Other chiefly centers—Huitzo in the Guadalupe phase, Tilcajete and Yegüih in the Rosario phase—became potential rivals. As Carneiro (1991:180-81) has observed, "chiefdoms were born out of war, were powerfully shaped by war, and continued to be heavily involved in war as they evolved."

II

Chapter 6

Introduction to Area C

Permanent settlement at San José Mogote began, so far as can be determined, on the extreme western tip of the piedmont spur. The first residences there were established on a low rise overlooking the Atoyac River. From these initial houses, settlement gradually spread east past the natural hill which forms the core of Mound 1 (see Frontispiece).

This western residential ward has been designated Area C, and today it falls within a barrio of Guadalupe Etla. When we decided to investigate it in 1969, its three major landmarks were: (1) a long, north-south cut bank left by modern adobe makers prior to our arrival; (2) a large fig tree whose roots had penetrated an area of roughly 6 × 7 m; and (3) a brick threshing floor built during the era of the hacienda.

Since the stratigraphy of Area C has been described in detail in our Early Formative pottery volume (Flannery and Marcus 1994), we will present here only enough information to place the Area C houses in context.

We began our work in Area C by shaving the north-south cut bank until it was a true vertical profile whose stratigraphy could be read (Fig. 6.1, *left*). The first section we shaved was a 37.5 m stretch that happened (by sheer luck) to run almost due magnetic north-south. The stratigraphy of these deposits proved so interesting that our colleague James Schoenwetter took a second crew of workmen and extended our profile-cutting northward for another 36 m. At this point bedrock was encountered at a higher level, and some of the earliest deposits (e.g., Tierras Largas phase) were no longer present in the profile, so we ended our shaving. A third crew, working with Flannery, extended the profile an additional 19.5 m to the south. At this point it intersected the east-west cut bank of Area B, discussed in Chapter 15.

What resulted from all this shaving was a 93-m cross-section, designated the Area C Master Profile. While the entire 93 meters were informative, some sections were more interesting than others. The long profile revealed that bedrock in Area C was irregular, featuring high ridges alternating with low gullies. Most of the houses had been built on the ridges, while the gullies had been used as places to dump midden. It turned out that the original 37.5 m section of profile appeared the most interesting, so we designated it a Control Section. That meant that it would be excavated by small teams of experienced workers, all deposits would be screened, and all artifacts, plants, and animal bones would be saved, no matter how small. When houses were encountered, an effort would be made to piece-plot all significant items.

Our next step was to establish a grid of 1 × 1 m squares for the excavation of the Control Section. Fortunately, our profile shaving had uncovered a *mojonera*, or deeply buried stone property marker, which divided the lands of two neighbors, Sr. Espiridión Hernández and Sr. Plácido Hernández. Such *mojoneras*, which have been used since the Colonial period, are never supposed to be moved once they have been buried. The stone marker was therefore the perfect landmark to serve as a datum point.

With the *mojonera* serving as zero north/zero east, we set stakes made from steel reinforcing rods along the profile at one-meter intervals to establish the first column of 1 × 1 m squares. These squares were to be labeled South 1 to South 38 (abbreviated S1-S38), with S1 running from 0.0 to 1.0 m south of the *mojonera* and S38 running from 37.0 to 38.0 m south. We considered the earth we had removed while cutting the profile to have come from this initial set of squares, making the shaved profile itself the east wall of Squares S1-S38 (Fig. 6.3). This al-

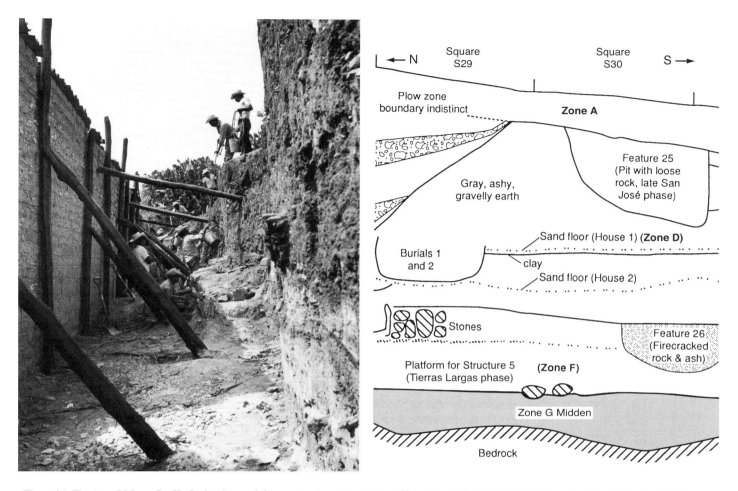

Figure 6.1. The Area C Master Profile. In the photo at left, some workmen shave the profile to a state of verticality, while others use posts to buttress a nearby adobe wall that was leaning badly. The drawing at right shows how Houses 1 and 2 and Burials 1 and 2 appeared in the east profile of Squares S29 and S30.

lowed us to establish the grid shown in Figure 6.2, one in which numbers ran north and south and letters of the alphabet east and west. In other words, as we began systematic excavation beyond the shaved profile, we would be cutting into Squares S1A–S38A. In those cases where house floors were already visible during the preliminary shaving, we recorded everything we found on those patches of floor so that it could be added to the drawings of the houses later.

The entire Master Profile was drawn before excavation began. Numbers were assigned to every house, feature, public building, and burial that could be seen in the profile. For example, the first two houses and the first two burials appeared in the east profile of Squares S29 and S30 (Fig. 6.1, *right*). To be sure, the fact that a house floor could be seen in cross-section meant that its western portion had already been removed by recent adobe makers. The large number of floors visible in the Control Section, however, led us to expect a good sample of residences.

Figure 6.2 shows our principal excavation in Area C. In order not to disturb the large fig tree (whose fall would have

caused great destruction), we gave its root system a wide berth. Whenever we were at a safe distance from the tree, we expanded eastward as necessary to complete the excavation of houses or public buildings. The public buildings will be discussed in a future volume.

The Threshing Floor Sector

The excavation block framed by Squares S13G, S13-O, S24G, and S24-O was designated the Threshing Floor Sector. It is here that the oldest houses at the site came to light.

During the 1969 field season, Kathryn Blair Vaughn made a deep sounding, designated Test 1, in Squares S17M and S17N of the Threshing Floor Sector. When the sherds from this test were washed and analyzed, they appeared to include the earliest Formative material we had found so far. During the 1974 season, Marcus reopened Vaughn's excavation and expanded into Squares S17H–S17N and S18H–S18N. Her discovery of House

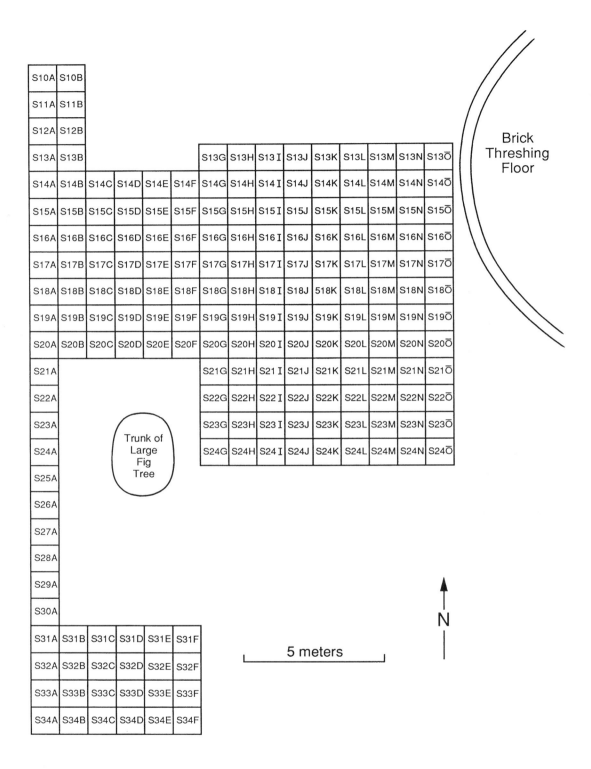

Figure 6.2. Part of the Master Grid of 1 × 1 m squares established for Area C. The Control Section of the Master Profile runs along the western border of the N-S column of squares marked S10A-S34A.

20, our earliest, and Feature 66, the possible "baffle entrance" to a palisade, led to our excavation of a larger area.

The Stratigraphy of Area C

The stratigraphy of the Control Section was complex, including houses, middens, bell-shaped pits, collapsed public buildings, and other features. At the same time, the stratigraphy was very readable, with changes in soil color and texture making it easy to follow the disconformities between one stratigraphic unit and the next (Flannery and Marcus 1994:103-7, 287-96).

What complicated matters was that as we excavated eastward into the Threshing Floor Sector, we encountered strata older than the lowest levels of the Control Section—completely new levels and buildings that had to be interdigitated with those of the Master Profile. As a result, there was no single profile we could draw that would display all houses, features, and middens in chronological order.

British archaeologist Edward C. Harris (1975, 1979) solved this problem by creating the matrix that bears his name. In a Harris Matrix, every conceivable bit of stratigraphic information is used to interdigitate the levels and features of every part of the excavation, allowing strata from widely separated trenches to be placed in chronological order. What we did in 1969 was to cobble together our own version of a Harris Matrix. One difference is that we will give the results verbally, rather than in a complicated diagram.

House 20 in stratigraphic Zone H of the Threshing Floor Sector, dating to the Espiridión Complex, was our oldest house. Above that came House 19 in Zone G and House 18 in Zone F, both dating to the Tierras Largas phase. Fortunately, Zones G and F of the Threshing Floor Sector could be matched up with Zones G and F of the Master Profile. To be sure, the content of each zone changed slowly from house debris to midden and back to house debris over a distance of 15 meters, but the change was so gradual that there was no difficulty following each level.

In the Master Profile, stratigraphic Zone E (overlying Zone F) was an Early San José phase midden.

Stratigraphically above Zone E was Zone D, a very thick stratum resulting from the collapse of a series of Middle San José phase houses. First came House 6, at a depth of about 2 m below the surface, just north of the *mojonera* used as a datum point. House 5 (140 cm depth) and House 2 (130-140 cm depth) were broadly contemporaneous. House 3, the next in order, was never excavated. House 11 (127-139 cm depth) followed House 3. Then came House 9 (roughly 125 cm depth), followed by House 1 at 110 cm. Next came House 10 (70-80 cm depth). House 4 (roughly 60 cm depth) was the uppermost in Zone D.

Above Zone D came stratigraphic Zone C, which produced two Late San José phase houses. The first was House 7 (only 40 cm depth). Stratigraphically more recent was House 14. Ironically, although House 14 was later than House 7, it was buried 140-150 cm below the surface, since a large Guadalupe phase public building had later been built above it.

The preceding summary, of course, simplifies the situation and omits any discussion of associated dooryards, features, and multiple refloorings. Those details will be added as we describe each of the Area C residences.

A Note on Chronology

In our volume on Early Formative ceramics (Flannery and Marcus 1994), we divided the Tierras Largas and San José phases into "Early" and "Late" subphases, based on stratigraphy and changes in the frequencies of pottery types. In this volume, we consider many more proveniences; as a result, we are able to expand our chronology somewhat. We now believe we can divide both the Tierras Largas phase and the San José phase into "Early," "Middle," and "Late" subphases, and those terms will be used throughout this report. Such subphases, we should emphasize, are based on stylistic change in ceramics. Our radiocarbon dates are not precise enough to contribute to their definition (Chapter 26).

Chapter 7

Area C: Houses of Espiridión and Tierras Largas Times

The Espiridión Complex

House 20

During the field season of 1974, while expanding a deep sounding in the Threshing Floor Sector of Area C, we came across the remains of a small wattle-and-daub residence with the earliest ceramics so far discovered in Oaxaca. The base of House 20 had been dug down into the sterile greenish-black clay that forms naturally above volcanic tuff bedrock. Postholes from the house had penetrated the bedrock itself. To create a level surface for the floor, the builders had also filled some natural hollows in the bedrock with sand.

Stratigraphically, House 20 belonged to Zone H (Figs. 7.1-7.2). Its remains filled excavation squares S18K-S18N, and extended part way into S19K-S19N and S17K-S17L. Unfortunately we could not recover the entire house, since it had been truncated by construction and pit-digging during the subsequent Tierras Largas phase.

Ceramics

Some 262 sherds were found in association with House 20; they have been described by Flannery and Marcus (1994:45-54, and Figs. 7.5-7.9). This collection of sherds has been assigned to the Espiridión Complex, which we originally dated to the period 1600-1500 b.c. (Flannery and Marcus 1994:374-75).[1] Espiridión's closest ceramic crossties are to the Purrón Complex of the Tehuacán Valley (MacNeish, Peterson, and Flannery 1970);

the two complexes share the pottery type Purrón Plain. Vessel shapes suggest that gourd vessels may have been the prototypes for many Espiridión Complex vessels (Flannery and Marcus 1994: Figs. 7.2-7.3).

New dates for the Early Tierras Largas phase hint that Espiridión might be earlier than we once thought (see House 19, below). However, since we have no Espiridión dates, the exact age of the complex remains unknown.

Chipped Stone
Chert (86%)
 ordinary flake core: 1 (Fig. 7.3*a*)
 bipolar flake core fragment: 1 (Fig. 7.3*b*)
 flake perforator/graver: 1 (Fig. 7.3*c*)
 flakes, not utilized: 3 (Fig. 7.3*d*)
Obsidian (14%)
 utilized flake: 1 (Fig. 7.3*e*)
Unused Raw Material
 one weathered polyhedral chert nodule
 one fire-cracked nodule of silicified ignimbrite
Comment: While the chipped stone sample from House 20 is small, its similarity to samples from the later Tierras Largas and San José phases is worth noting. It would appear that both of the common chert core types of the Early Formative were already present in House 20, as was the flake perforator/graver commonly used to work shell and mica. In addition, our discovery of a fire-cracked nodule of silicified ignimbrite suggests that the heat-treating of raw material was already practiced in Espiridión times. William J. Parry, who studied the House 20 collection, has kindly provided us with the following comment:

---

[1] In this volume, uncalibrated dates are given as "b.c.," and dendrocalibrated dates as "B.C." (see Chapter 26, Radiocarbon Dating).

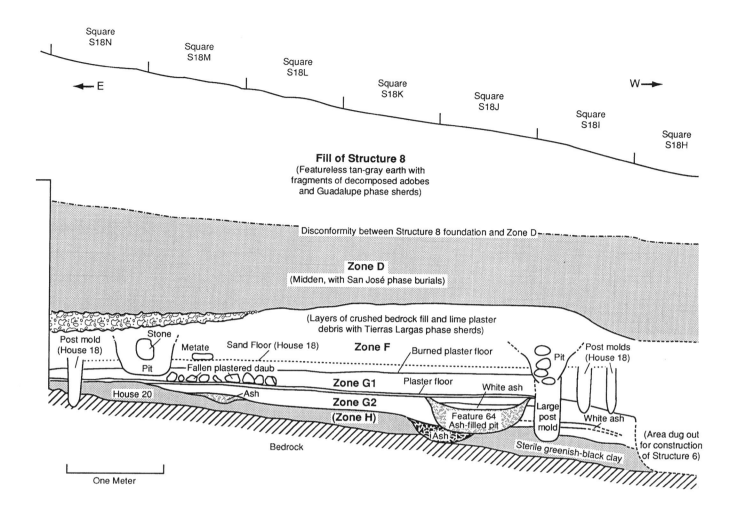

Figure 7.1. The south profile of Squares S18H-S18N of the Threshing Floor Sector, Area C. Visible in the profile are House 20 (Zone H); stratigraphic Zone G, here divided into building collapse (G1) and midden (G2) facies; and House 18 in Zone F. For a closeup of Square S18L, see Figure 7.2.

Figure 7.2. The south profile of Square S18L of the Threshing Floor Sector, Area C. At the bottom we see stratigraphic Zone H, the ashy, chocolate brown fill of House 20 (Espiridión Complex). Above that is Zone G2, a layer of ashy midden from the Tierras Largas phase. Separating Zones G1 and G2 is a plaster floor of the type usually found as an "apron" around Men's Houses. Zone G1 contains debris from the destruction of such a Men's House. Separating Zones G1 and F is another plaster floor, this one burned black from a conflagration. The lower part of Zone F is dark debris from the burning of a Men's House, possibly during a raid. Just above the card marked "F," we see a disconformity between this dark debris and an overlying whiter layer. That disconformity is the sand floor of House 18, a Tierras Largas phase residence.

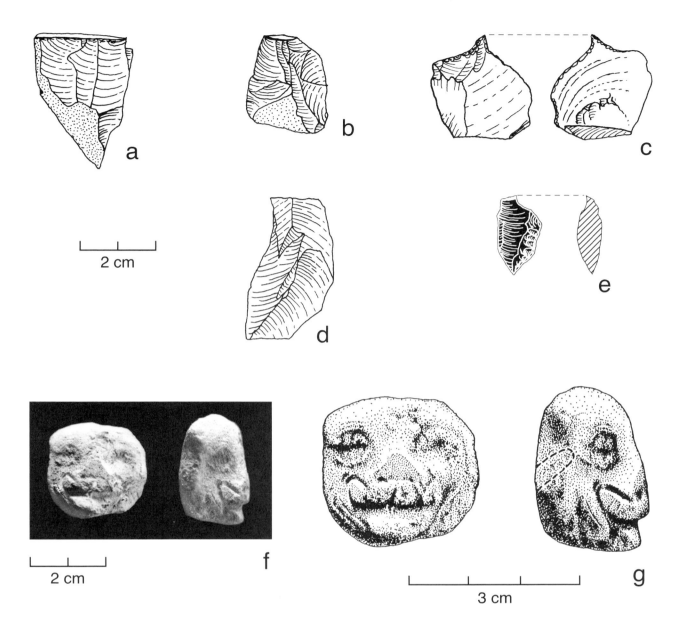

Figure 7.3. Objects from House 20. *a*, ordinary chert flake (Sq. S18M). *b*, fragment of bipolar chert core (Sq. S18K). *c*, chert perforator/graver (Sq. S17N). *d*, chert flake, not utilized (from screen). *e*, utilized obsidian flake from Guadalupe Victoria source (from screen). *f*, front and side views of feline head or miniature mask, lightly fired buff clay. *g*, artist's enlarged rendering of *f*. The dashed line shows an area perforated from behind, as if a peg had been inserted.

Very little can be said concerning the Espiridión lithic assemblage, owing to the extremely small size of the excavated sample. Only 7 artifacts—one obsidian and six chert—have been recovered from Espiridión Complex deposits. The single obsidian artifact is a small utilized flake of gray obsidian, identified by Robert Zeitlin (personal communication to Kent Flannery, 1975) as coming from the Guadalupe Victoria source. The proportion of obsidian in the assemblage (1 of 7 pieces; 14%) is comparable to that of later Tierras Largas and San José phase contexts at San José Mogote.

The Espiridión Complex chert artifacts include one perforator—a flake with two small pointed bits, used for drilling or graving—which is similar in appearance to the chert perforators that are so abundant in San José phase households at San José Mogote. The remaining chert specimens are flake cores, flakes, and fragments. None of these artifacts would be out of place in a San José phase context, and this small collection is indistinguishable from any Tierras Largas or San José phase lithic assemblage of similar size.

Ground Stone

1 fragment of mano, ignimbrite, 4 × 3 × 2.5 cm

Figurine

House 20 produced what appears to be a small feline head, or perhaps a miniature feline mask used to cover the face of a figurine. It has been described by Marcus (1998a:39-41), and we illustrate it again here because it is, at the moment, the oldest figurine fragment from the Valley of Oaxaca (Fig. 7.3f-g).

The object is a small disk of lightly fired clay, modeled to depict the face of a puma or jaguar. On the back of the head it bears a small perforation, made before firing, which would allow it to be mounted on a small wooden or bone peg. In later phases of the Formative, miniature masks this size were provided for the faces of figurines in ritual costumes. The fact that a puma or jaguar is depicted at this early period reinforces our suspicion that long before the rise of the Gulf Coast Olmec, feline motifs were part of a widespread, long-established cosmology among Mesoamerican village cultures.

The Early Tierras Largas Phase

House 19

House 19, one of our earliest Tierras Largas phase houses, came to light in the Threshing Floor Sector. It was represented by nine postmolds in Squares S16I, S16J, S17J, S17K, and S18L (Fig. 7.4). Three postmolds first appeared at the disconformity between stratigraphic Zones F and G, and extended down into lower Zone G, which in that part of the Threshing Floor Sector was designated Zone G2 (Fig. 7.1).

It would appear from the arrangement of the postmolds that our excavation caught the northeast corner of a residence which was oriented northwest-southeast. The single postmold in Square S17J seems not to have been part of the outer wall. Two of the postmolds in Square S16J lie so close together that we suspect one might have been added later, to provide additional support to the corner of the house.

No artifacts could be securely associated with the house because postoccupational disturbance at the Zone G/Zone F boundary had damaged the floor. Since both Zones G and F dated to the Tierras Largas phase, we had no reservation about assigning the house to that period. The radiocarbon date, in fact, places it early in the Tierras Largas phase (see below).

One of the most interesting aspects of House 19 was the fact that it had clearly been burned, right down to its wooden posts. Seven of the postmolds were filled with blackened earth and pieces of pine charcoal, while two others were filled with ash. The earth around the posts was reddened in places.

Although we realized in 1974 that we had found a burned house, its full significance eluded us at first. In those days, few of us suspected that intervillage raiding might go back to the beginnings of village life. It was only with the subsequent discovery of more burned houses, and defensive palisades, and burned temples, and depictions of slain enemies in art, that we began to realize that raiding was an integral part of Formative life (Flannery and Marcus 2003; Spencer 2003).

Radiocarbon Date

Charcoal from the burned post in Square S18L dated to 3490 ± 80 B.P. in conventional radiocarbon years, or roughly 1540 b.c. (Beta-173807). The calibrated two-sigma range would be 2020 to 1620 B.C.

This date is significant for several reasons. First, it suggests that the Early Tierras Largas phase began longer ago than we had originally estimated. Second, it means that the Espiridión Complex must be earlier still.

House 19 . Square designations

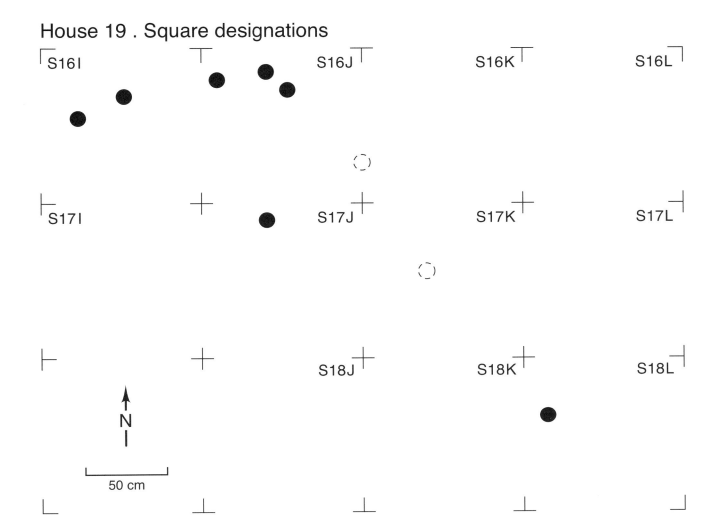

Figure 7.4. Plan view of the House 19 area, showing square designations and postholes in bedrock. Black circles indicate postholes that still had traces of carbonized post in them. Dashed-line circles indicate postholes that were shallower, owing to a dropoff in bedrock.

The Middle Tierras Largas Phase

Feature 21: A Tierras Largas Phase Palisade

Once the Area C Master Profile had been shaved to bedrock, we put a crew to work sweeping the exposed bedrock surface and examining it carefully for pits and postholes. As it turned out, bedrock had indeed been penetrated in many places.

One of the first discoveries made as a result of this sweeping was Feature 21, the double line of postholes shown in Figure 7.5. As can be seen in the photograph, the two lines of posts were parallel, but staggered in such a way that the posts in the second row lined up with the gaps between posts in the first row. It was clearly a barrier of some kind. The postholes first came to light near the western edge of Squares S12-S13 and ran for at least 4 m in a generally south-to-north direction. We reconstruct Feature 21 as having originally included 26-28 postholes, some of which have been lost owing to depressions in bedrock. Not surprisingly, the postholes were clearest and best preserved where bedrock was high, and faintest where it dipped down. A number of the postholes, including the six southernmost, still had the tips of burned pine posts in them.

The deepest postholes penetrated roughly 11-12 cm into bedrock; their diameters were about 9-12 cm. The spaces between posts in each of the lines were about 20 cm, and the second line of posts lay about 15 cm from the first.

While this feature looked like a section of palisade to us, our first report of it was very cautiously worded (Flannery and Marcus 1976a:208). We referred to it simply as "a double line of staggered posts," "an enclosure," or "an open area . . . set apart from the residential areas." Our caution stemmed from the fact that, as mentioned earlier, we had simply not expected that defensive features would be present in such an early village. We did not want to say anything we would have to take back.

Subsequent work, however, showed us that we were dealing with more than an "enclosure." By carefully scraping and sweeping the bedrock west of the Master Profile, we eventually discovered that Feature 21 was only one section of a much longer palisade that evidently defended the western periphery of San José Mogote. The problem was that its postholes could only be detected where bedrock was firm and level; wherever bedrock dipped down or became soft and crumbly, the postholes had been lost.

We were able to trace the postholes intermittently for about 30-40 m. They emerged from below the Master Profile somewhere around Squares S16 or S17, then disappeared for awhile, appearing again in Feature 21. From there they could be traced north intermittently until they passed below the modern adobe wall shown on the left in Figure 6.1, reappearing on the other side of the wall in an area of dairy cattle pens. There they became untraceable, because the constant shoveling of cow manure had damaged the surface of bedrock. As a result, we do not know whether this palisade protected the whole village or only one part.

An unresolved question was, from which level had these posts been inserted into the ground? Only the tips had penetrated bedrock, but by examining the Master Profile we concluded that even had the posts been sunk a full meter through the overlying earth, the palisade would have been at least as early as Zone F of Area C. That fact suggested that the posts dated to the Tierras Largas phase, and at the least might have protected the area of Men's Houses on the western side of the piedmont spur.

In preparation for writing this volume, we obtained a new grant to run a series of radiocarbon dates on charcoal from the postholes in Feature 21. The results are as follows.

Radiocarbon Dates

1. Post 3 produced a date of 3160 ± 130 B.P. in conventional radiocarbon years, or roughly 1210 b.c. (Beta-175895). The calibrated two-sigma range would be 1720-1060 B.C.

2. Post 4 produced a date of 3250 ± 80 B.P., or roughly 1300 b.c. (Beta-175896). The calibrated two-sigma range would be 1700-1390 B.C.

3. Post 5 produced a date of 3260 ± 60 B.P., or roughly 1310 b.c. (Beta-177623). The calibrated two-sigma range would be 1680-1410 B.C.

Comment: Given the close agreement between the Post 4 and Post 5 dates, as well as their small standard deviations, we consider 1300-1310 b.c. to be a good general date for Feature 21. The calibrated two-sigma range would be from 1680/1700 B.C. to 1390/1410 B.C. The Post 3 date has a much larger standard deviation, and is therefore less precise.

Another Possible Section of Palisade in Squares S28 and S29

Fourteen meters south of Feature 21, in Squares S28 and S29, we found six postholes in bedrock from what may be a second palisade (Fig. 7.6a). This double line of posts ran southwest-northeast, a very different orientation from Feature 21. The postholes averaged 13-16 cm in diameter and had penetrated 6-20 cm into the undulating bedrock. None of the postholes showed any sign of burning, making it impossible to obtain a radiocarbon sample.

This small section of palisade was drawn but not assigned a feature number, since it was not clear at first whether or not it was another stretch of the Feature 21 palisade. We now believe it to be part of a second palisade, but whether it was built earlier or later than the Feature 21 palisade cannot be determined.

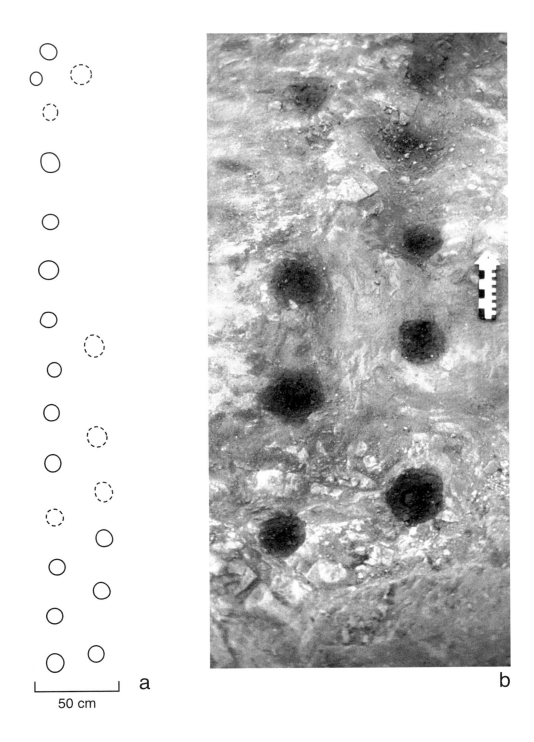

50 cm

a

b

Figure 7.5. Drawing and photograph of Feature 21, a 4-m stretch of palisade consisting of a double line of pine posts. In the drawing (*a*), deep postholes are shown as solid circles, shallow postholes as dashed circles (five postholes were missing, owing to dropoffs or depressions in bedrock).

Feature 66

In Squares S18H-S18I of the Threshing Floor Sector, we found an unusual feature that could be part of the "baffle entrance" to yet another palisade (Fig. 7.6b). Designated Feature 66, the evidence consisted of a double line of postholes like those of Feature 21, flanked on the west by a series of flat stone slabs set vertically. As the slab-and-posthole line crossed into Square S17H, it made a right-angle turn to the east, as if framing an entrance.

In Chapter 5, we compared our palisades to those used by the historic Maori at sites like Paeroa Pa (see Fig. 5.19). Like other societies occupying fortified villages, the Maori used mazelike "baffle entrances" to make entry through the wall of posts more difficult. The stones used to reinforce the Feature 66 post line, some 7-8 m east of the Feature 21 posts, may have been part of such an entrance.

It is probably significant that no Early Tierras Largas phase residences or Men's Houses have been found beyond (i.e., to the west of) Feature 21. By the San José phase, on the other hand, the village had grown so large that it probably had no need of defensive works. San José phase settlement expanded westward past Feature 21 and down the slope toward the river.

Comment: Given our mounting evidence for raiding, the burning of houses and temples, and the sacrifice of captives in Formative Oaxaca, we should no longer be surprised to find defensive works at Early Formative villages (Flannery and Marcus 2003). Indeed, we now suspect that the only reason palisades have not previously been found at sites this early is that they were constructed near (or just beyond) the limits of the village. The only reason we found Feature 21 was because the cut bank left by adobe makers ran along the west margin of the Tierras Largas phase village. Most excavators of Early Formative sites do not usually excavate that far out from the center of the site. In the future it might be interesting for them to run a trench out beyond the supposed limits of the village, just to see if a palisade or defensive ditch shows up.

Domestic Middle Tierras Largas Phase Features

It appears that during the Middle Tierras Largas phase, the area just east of the Control Section had been used primarily as a series of dooryards. Outdoor pits such as Features 22, 23, 42, and 48 were excavated into bedrock in that area. We believe that most of the houses with which these dooryards were associated lay upslope, to the east. Further evidence that the Control Section lay downslope from the nearest houses is the fact that it also became the dumping ground for a barrio midden, included in stratigraphic Zone G (see below). Such middens were usually created downslope.

Our presumed date for the Middle Tierras Largas phase is 1400-1250 b.c. This presumption is supported by the radiocarbon date of 1330 b.c. from Feature 23 (see below). It is also supported by a series of four dates from Tierras Largas phase

Men's Houses (see Chapter 26). These dates range from 1400 to 1320 b.c. (Chapter 26).

Feature 22

Feature 22 was a Tierras Largas phase pit found in Squares S15-S16 while we were cutting the Master Profile. The rim of the pit was gone, but the base was preserved because it had penetrated 28 cm into bedrock. The pit was oval, 88 cm in diameter east-west, and 66 cm north-south (Fig. 7.7). The fill of the lowermost 28 cm was soft gray ash with carbonized plants and Tierras Largas phase sherds.

Ceramics

The sherds from Feature 22 were studied by Flannery and Marcus (1994: Table 13.1). In our expanded chronology (see Chapter 6), we assign this pit to the Middle Tierras Largas phase.

Carbonized Plants

14 kernels of maize (*Zea mays*)
1 stem fragment of maize
1 seed of teosinte(?), *Zea mexicana*
1 seed of prickly pear fruit (*Opuntia* sp.) (Fig. 4.2j, Chapter 4)
1 cotyledon of avocado (*Persea americana*), showing cut marks

Feature 23

Feature 23 was a Tierras Largas phase pit in Squares S24 and S25. Only the lower 30 cm were preserved, as a result of having penetrated bedrock; the pit's diameter was 80 cm (Fig. 7.8). The fill in the lower 30 cm consisted of alternating layers of white ash, black ash, and gray ash, as well as a mano fragment, carbonized plants, fire-cracked rocks, and 89 sherds.

Radiocarbon Date

Charcoal from Feature 23 produced a radiocarbon date of 3280 B.P. ± 180 in conventional radiocarbon years, or roughly 1330 b.c. (M-2330). The calibrated two-sigma range would be 2010-1110 B.C.

Ceramics

The 89 sherds from Feature 23 were studied by Flannery and Marcus (1994: Table 13.1). The entire sample consisted of Tierras Largas phase types.

Ground Stone

One fragment of mano, metamorphic rock, still covered with the red pigment it had been used to grind; 7 × 7 × 7 cm.

Carbonized Plants

11 kernels of maize
many cupules from disintegrated maize cob fragments
3 fragments of carrizo (*Phragmites australis*)

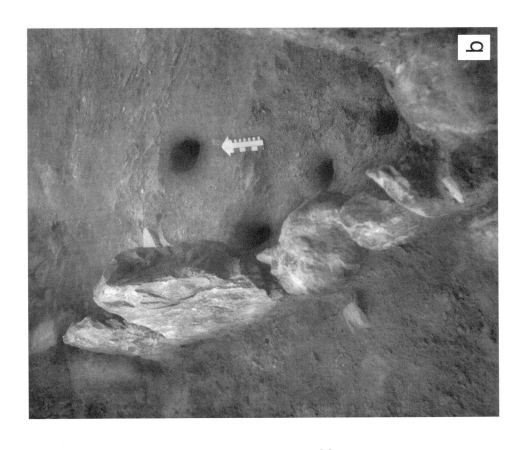

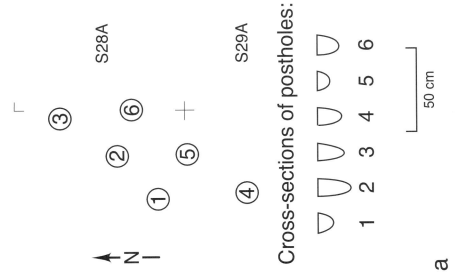

Figure 7.6. Other traces of palisades in Area C. *Left*, six postholes in bedrock in Squares S28 and S29. *Right*, Feature 66, the possible remains of a "baffle entrance" combining a double line of posts with a row of upright stone slabs.

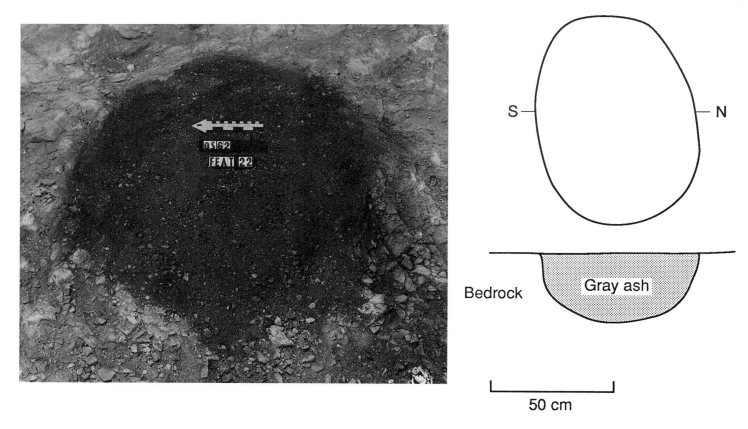

Figure 7.7. Photograph and drawing of Feature 22, a Tierras Largas phase pit excavated into bedrock.

Feature 42

Feature 42 was a Tierras Largas phase bell-shaped pit in Squares S27-S28. Its basal diameter was 64 cm, but its other dimensions are unknown because the upper portion had been disturbed by modern adobe makers. As will be clear from the photograph (Fig. 7.9), the only well-preserved portion of the pit was the basal 20-25 cm, which had penetrated bedrock. Less than three meters away, in Square S25, we found three postholes in bedrock that might have belonged to the Tierras Largas phase house with which Feature 42 was associated. While the base of Feature 42 was filled with ash, no identifiable plant remains emerged during flotation.

Feature 48

Feature 48 was a large circular pit cut into bedrock in Square S31C. On its south side, it merged with a natural bedrock depression. Superficially, it looked like an attempt to convert a preexisting natural depression into a bedrock cistern or water storage facility, like the one found in Area B (Chapter 17).

Feature 48 had been cut 50 cm into bedrock, but its diameter could not be determined because it extended into Square S30C, which was never excavated. We estimate that the pit was greater than 1 m in diameter, and might have exceeded 2 m.

Filled with ash and hearth sweepings after it fell into disuse, Feature 48 produced a small sample of carbonized plants.

Carbonized Plants
    2 kernels of maize (*Zea mays*)
    2 cob fragments of maize
    1 unidentified grass seed

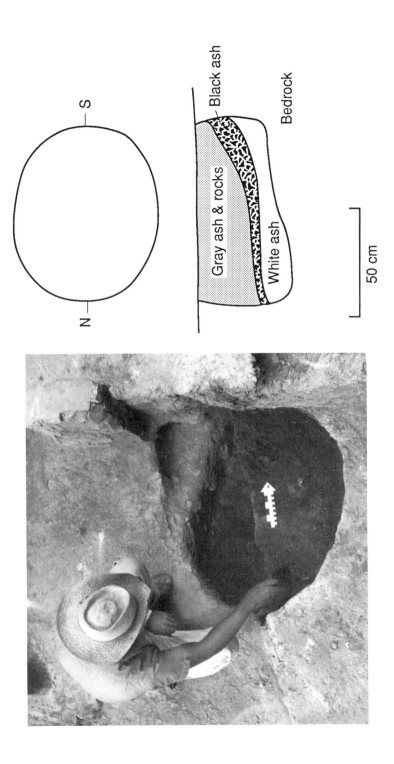

Figure 7.8. Photograph and drawing of Feature 23, a Tierras Largas phase pit dug into bedrock. Radiocarbon date: 1330 b.c.

Figure 7.9. Photograph and drawing of Feature 42, a Tierras Largas phase pit dug into bedrock.

The Zone G Midden

Stratigraphic Zone G of Area C was a complex level, with many different facies. In the Threshing Floor Sector, Zone G was divided into G1 and G2 layers by an intervening plaster floor of the kind serving as an "apron" around some Tierras Largas phase Men's Houses (see Fig. 7.2, this volume, and Chapter 4 of Flannery and Marcus 1994). Zone G2, the lower portion, was an ashy midden layer. Zone G1, the upper portion, was a layer of midden and construction debris, including plastered daub fragments that appeared to have fallen from the walls of a Men's House. It would thus appear that both public buildings and ordinary residences were present in the Threshing Floor Sector during the deposition of Zone G. Some 458 sherds from Zone G2, and 173 sherds from Zone G1, are described in Table 9.1 of Flannery and Marcus 1994.

In the Control Section of the Master Profile, Zone G seemed to be a pretty straightforward neighborhood midden. Its contents were ash; greenish clay; bedrock fragments, which probably resulted from the digging of pits into bedrock; sherds; artifacts; animal bones; and other domestic refuse, probably dumped there by households upslope (to the east). The artifact sample discussed below came from the Master Profile Sector.

Daub

Reinforcing our view that there must have been residences not far east of the Master Profile was the discovery in Squares S29A and S30A of five chunks of daub with whitewash 1 mm thick. In the Munsell system, the surface color of the plaster would have been "pinkish white" (7.5 YR 8/2).

Ceramics

Some 1909 sherds from Zone G have been reported previously by Flannery and Marcus (1994: Table 13.1). Of these, 96% were of types that peaked in frequency during the Tierras Largas phase; only 2% were of types that went on to reach their peak in the San José phase. In our expanded chronology, Zone G of the Master Profile is considered equivalent to Zone G1 of the Threshing Floor Sector, and assigned to the Middle Tierras Largas phase.

Imported Ceramics

Included among the ceramics from the Zone G Midden were four conjoining sherds from the shoulder of the carinated, pure white bottle shown in Figure 7.10a. This bottle is not of local origin. It is indisputably Xochiltepec White, a kaolin ware, substantial amounts of which were produced by the potters of San Lorenzo, Veracruz (Coe and Diehl 1980a:152).

Our mineralogical analyses suggest that later Xochiltepec Whites, of the period 1150-850 b.c., probably had multiple sources (Flannery and Marcus 1994:254). However, we believe that this early white bottle was likely produced at Chicharras phase San Lorenzo. Dating to perhaps 1400-1300 b.c., it is our earliest known imported vessel from southern Veracruz.

Chipped Stone
Chert (90%)
    ordinary flake cores: 7
    bipolar flake cores: 3
    core scraper: 1
    flake perforator/graver: 1
    denticulate scraper: 1
    chopper/scraper: 1 (Fig. 7.10b)
    scraper: 1
    retouched flake: 1
    utilized flakes: 13 (Fig. 7.10c, d)
    flakes, not utilized: 85
    angular fragments: 9
Obsidian (5%)
    prismatic blade fragment, utilized: 1
    utilized flakes: 2 (Fig. 7.10e)
    flakes, not utilized: 4
Other (5%)
    quartz flake: 1
    volcanic core: 1
    utilized volcanic flake: 1
    volcanic flakes, not utilized: 4

Ground Stone
Two pieces from the same slightly lipped basin-shaped metate, vesicular basalt (Fig. 7.10f). One piece is 17 × 14 cm and averages 3.5 cm thick; the second piece is 12 × 8 cm and averages 4 cm thick.

Fragment of small basin-shaped metate, sandstone, 9 × 5 cm in area and 7.5 cm thick.

Pounder/hammerstone made from a chalcedony cobble 8 cm in diameter (Fig. 7.11a). We were uncertain whether to include this with chert items (chipped stone) or put it in the "ground stone" category. We decided on the latter because it appears to have been subjected to some grinding, which gives it a more spherical shape.

Pounder/hammerstone 6 cm in diameter, made of poor-quality ignimbrite (Fig. 7.11b).

Bone Tools
Disintegrating tine of deer antler, possibly fire-hardened for use as a pressure flaker.

Fragment of a large bone needle made on a deer(?) bone splinter; length of fragment, 31 mm; thickness, 4 mm. This artifact, oval in cross-section and slightly curved at the tip, was probably a basketry needle.

Shell
Ornament
    One complete, beachworn *Pilosabia trigona*, perforated for suspension. Diameter, 14 mm.
Pearly Freshwater Mussels
    One fragment of mussel, possibly *Barynaias* sp., drilled, possibly manufacturing waste; 22 × 14 × 1 mm.

One small fragment of mussel, cf. *Anadonta* sp., possibly
    manufacturing waste.
Pacific Marine Bivalves
    Triangular fragment of pearl oyster (*Pinctada mazatlani-
        ca*), 40 × 30 mm, 3 mm thick (Fig. 7.12*a*). We cannot
        tell whether this is a broken piece of ornament, or a shell
        that broke in the process of being worked.
    One fragment of pearl oyster, 40 × 20 × 3 mm.
Unidentified
    One fragment of beachworn shell with a natural worm hole
        in it, 29 × 16 × 2 mm.
    One fragment of shell, 10 × 7 × 1 mm.

Figurines

Some 19 pieces of small solid figurines from the Zone G
midden have been reported previously by Marcus (1998a:82-
84). Details included Mohawk haircuts, perforated hairdos to
which colored ribbons could be added (Fig. 7.12*c*), and a clear
depiction of a sandal (Marcus 1998a: Fig. 9.4).

Miniature Masks

Included with the figurine fragments were two miniature terracotta masks, appropriately sized to have been worn by figurines.
These objects represent our earliest evidence for the use of ritual
masks. Both are grotesque; one is shown in Figure 7.12*d*. These
would seem to be figurine-sized versions of larger pottery masks,
fragments of which have been found in and around Structure 6, a
Tierras Largas phase Men's House (Marcus 1998a: Fig. 9.11).

> Clearly, some "beings" depicted on Tierras Largas phase masks
> were malevolent, and if human dancers of that period wore larger

versions of such masks, their intent must have been to frighten.
[Marcus 1998a:83]

Unusual Pottery Artifact

Zone G produced an unusual rosette, made from the same
    kind of fired clay used for figurines. It has 10 petals and is
    3.5 cm in diameter (Fig. 7.12*b*).

Carbonized Plants
    64 kernels of maize (*Zea mays*)
    many fragments of maize cobs
    2 cotyledons of beans (*Phaseolus* sp.), not identifiable to
        species
    6 cotyledons of avocado (*Persea americana*)

Animal Bones
    Large Mammals
        collared peccary (*Dicotyles tajacu*)
            1 R. proximal scapula
    Small Mammals
        eastern cottontail (*Sylvilagus floridanus*)
            1 L. innominate
            1 L. femur
        Mexican cottontail (*Sylvilagus cunicularius*)
            1 L. femur
            1 R. femur
        unidentified cottontail (*Sylvilagus* sp.)
            1 R. femur
    Unidentified
        1 splinter

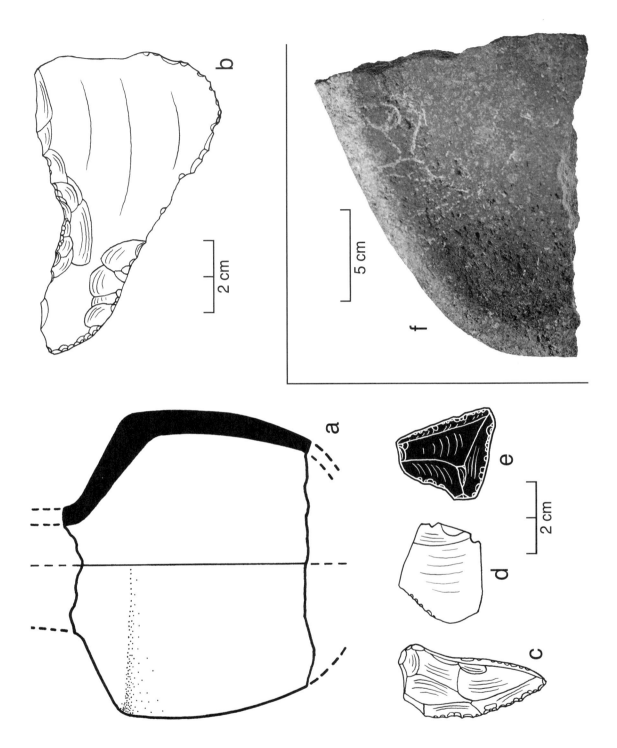

Figure 7.10. Artifacts from the Zone G Midden. *a*, Xochiltepec White bottle. *b*, chert chopper/scraper (ventral aspect). *c*, *d*, utilized chert flakes. *e*, utilized obsidian flake. *f*, fragment of slightly lipped metate, vesicular basalt. Tierras Largas phase.

Figure 7.11. Hammerstones from the Zone G Midden. *a*, spherical hammerstone, Matadamas chalcedony. *b*, asymmetrical hammerstone, ignimbrite. Diameter of *a*, 8 cm. Tierras Largas phase.

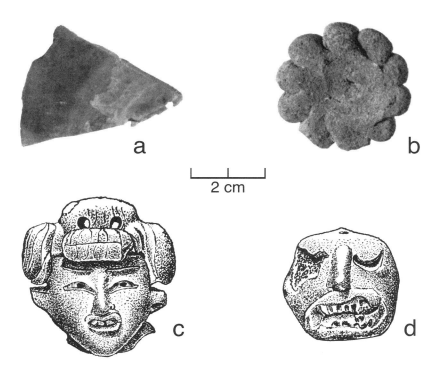

Figure 7.12. Objects from the Zone G Midden. *a*, triangular fragment of pearl oyster. *b*, unusual pottery rosette. *c*, small solid figurine head, female, with holes pushed through its hairdo so that ribbons could be added. *d*, grotesque miniature ceramic mask, sized for a figurine. Tierras Largas phase.

The Late Tierras Largas Phase

House 18

House 18 was found deeply buried in the Threshing Floor Sector of Area C. It could not be fully exposed, because to do so would have required removing tons of later overburden. The house appears in the south profile of Squares S18H through S18N as a sand-covered floor accompanied by three postmolds (Fig. 7.1). To the north of the profile, 8-10 of the remaining posts from House 18 could be traced down to bedrock (Fig. 7.13). A metate fragment can be seen resting on the floor in Square S18M of the profile drawing (Fig. 7.1). Three more pieces of ground stone occurred elsewhere in the house.

House 18 seems to have been an ordinary wattle-and-daub residence of the Tierras Largas phase, completely contained within stratigraphic Zone F. It overlay a 10-cm-thick area of burned debris in lower Zone F of the Threshing Floor Sector; above House 18 lay the crushed bedrock fill and lime plaster debris of upper Zone F (Flannery and Marcus 1994:107).

Ceramics

Some 54 sherds were associated with House 18; they have been described by Flannery and Marcus (1994:Table 9.1). All were of common Tierras Largas phase types.

Chipped Stone

No chipped stone tools were found in our limited exposure of House 18.

Ground Stone

Nearly complete oval mano with airfoil cross-section, metamorphic rock. Length, 17 cm; width, 12 cm; average thickness, 4.5 cm (Fig. 7.14*a*).

Half of a loaf-shaped two-hand mano with airfoil cross-section, sandstone(?). Length, 15+ cm (broken); width, 10 cm; thickness, 5.5 cm (Fig. 7.14*b*).

Roughly half of a rectangular slab metate of fine-grained metamorphic rock. This metate had clearly been used to grind red pigment, with which it was still covered. Original length, probably at least 18 cm (broken); width, 13.5 cm; thickness, 3.2 cm (Fig. 7.14*c*).

Fragment of basin-shaped metate, pink granite. This metate had clearly been used to grind red pigment, with which it was still covered. The original dimensions are unknown; the fragment is 15 × 9 × 4.5 cm (Fig. 7.14*d*).

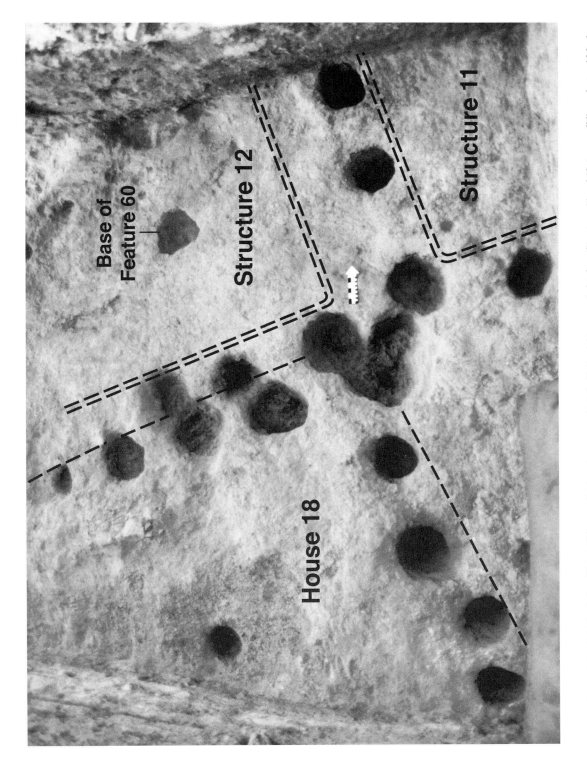

Figure 7.13. Postholes in bedrock from House 18 form an L-shaped corner on the left. To the right are postholes from Structures 11 and 12, two small lime-plastered Men's Houses. (Structures 11 and 12 were built at different times, after the abandonment of House 18, and were nearly superimposed one upon another.) Feature 60 was a lime-filled pit in Structure 12.

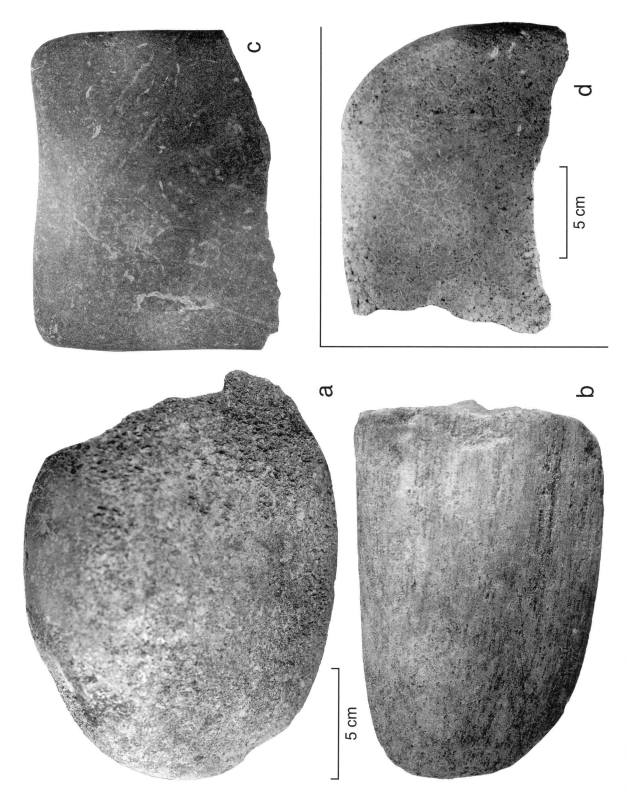

Figure 7.14. Ground stone tools from House 18. *a,* oval mano with airfoil cross-section (Sq. S17L). *b,* fragment of loaf-shaped mano with airfoil cross-section (Sq. S17L). *c,* fragment of slab metate used to grind red pigment (Sq. S17L). *d,* fragment of basin-shaped metate used to grind red pigment (Sq. S18M).

The Zone F Midden

Stratigraphic Zone F, like Zone G, was a complex level with many different facies. In the Control Section of the Master Profile, much of Zone F was taken up by the remains of Tierras Largas phase Men's Houses like Structures 3 and 6 (Flannery and Marcus 1994: Figs. 13.1-13.4). However, in the Threshing Floor Sector (Fig. 7.2), Zone F included traces of both ordinary Tierras Largas phase houses and midden debris. In that sector, we believe that Zone F accumulated over a period greater than the lifetime of any one building, and had detectable breaks in it like the one provided by the House 18 floor.

Ceramics

A sample of 512 sherds from the Zone F Midden has been reported previously by Flannery and Marcus (1994: Table 13.1). Roughly 92% were Tierras Largas phase diagnostics, while 4% were of types that went on to reach their peaks in the San José phase. Two sherds were Xochiltepec White, a possible import from San Lorenzo on the Gulf Coast. In our expanded chronology, Zone F remains in the Late Tierras Largas phase.

Chipped Stone

The chipped stone sample from the Zone F Midden consisted of 96 pieces. Notable for their absence were prismatic obsidian blades and chert perforators/gravers, two tool types present in both earlier and later proveniences.

Chert (85%)
    ordinary flake cores: 4
    bipolar flake cores: 2
    denticulate scrapers: 2
    scrapers: 3
    retouched flake: 1
    utilized flakes: 7
    flakes, not utilized: 58
    angular fragments: 5
Obsidian (9%)
    scaled flake: 1
    utilized flake: 1
    flakes, not utilized: 7
Other (5%)
    quartz flake: 1
    volcanic flakes, not utilized: 4

Ground Stone

One fragment of mano made from fine-grained ignimbrite, 4 × 8 × 7 cm.
One fragment of mano, rectangular in cross-section, granite. The fragment is 6 cm long, 6.2 cm wide, and 5 cm thick (Fig. 7.15a).
Fragment of basin-shaped metate with nubbin foot, basalt. The fragment is roughly 10 cm × 10 cm, and averages 3 cm thick (Fig. 7.15b).

A nearly complete basin-shaped metate of fine-grained ignimbrite. Length, 19 cm; width, 16.5 cm; thickness, 7.5 cm (Fig. 7.15c). This small metate, made of pink ignimbrite, may have been used with a one-hand mano. It resembles a similar pink ignimbrite metate found in a Tierras Largas phase Men's House (Structure 5; see Marcus 1998a: Fig. 9.12). That metate is believed to have been used for grinding lime to be mixed with powdered tobacco, a combination chewed during certain rituals.

Bone Tool

Fragment of antler tine from white-tailed deer, possibly hardened for use as a pressure flaker. Length of fragment, 42 mm; maximum diameter, 12 mm (Fig. 7.16a).

Worked Sherds

Partially worked sherd, oval, 8 × 6.5 cm.
Worked disk made from Matadamas Red body sherd, 3.9 cm in diameter.
Broken disk made from Tierras Largas Burnished Plain sherd, 4 cm in diameter.
Broken sherd rectangle, worked on three edges, 6.4 cm long and 2.5 cm wide on average.

Shell

Portions of two pearly freshwater mussel valves, one 32 × 21 × 1 mm, the other 36 × 20 × 1 mm (Fig. 7.16b, c)

Figurines

Fifteen pieces of small solid figurines from the Zone F Midden have been reported previously by Marcus (1998a:84-86). They include features such as hairdos perforated to receive ribbons, elaborate chignon hair styles, earspools, clear representations of sandals, and at least one bird head.

Carbonized Plants

3 cobs of maize (*Zea mays*) with Nal Tel/Chapalote attributes (Fig. 4.1a, Chapter 4)
many cupules from maize cobs showing teosinte introgression
7 kernels of maize
1 cotyledon of avocado (*Persea americana*)

Animal Bones

Mexican cottontail (*Sylvilagus cunicularius*)
    1 L. innominate
    1 complete sacrum

The Tierras Largas Phase/San José Phase Transition

While the transition from the Tierras Largas phase to the San José phase cannot be fixed precisely in time, it may have begun as early as 1200 b.c. and was essentially complete by 1150 b.c.

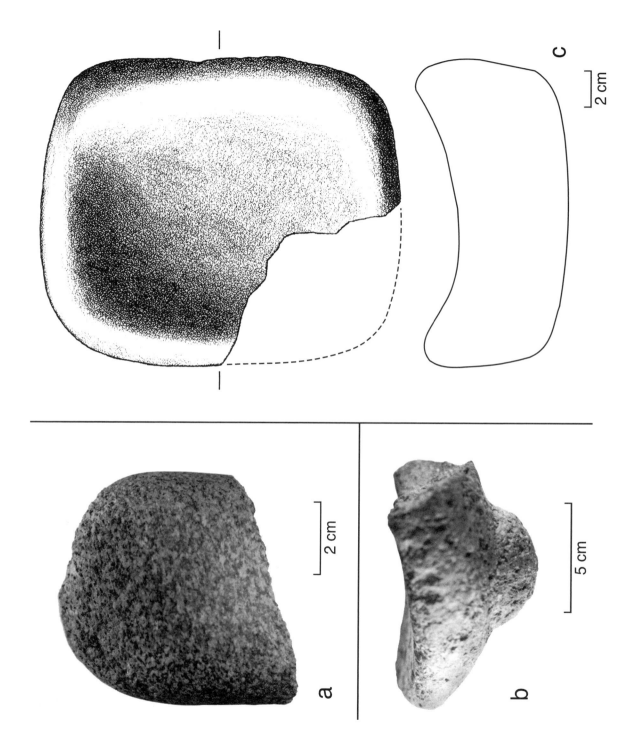

Figure 7.15. Ground stone tools from the Zone F Midden. *a*, fragment of granite mano, rectangular in cross-section. *b*, fragment of basin-shaped metate with nubbin foot, basalt. *c*, basin-shaped metate of fine-grained pink ignimbrite. Tierras Largas phase.

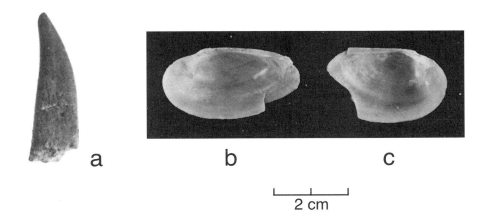

Figure 7.16. Objects from the Zone F Midden. *a*, antler tine, possibly hardened to serve as a pressure flaker. *b, c*, portions of pearly freshwater mussel valves. Tierras Largas phase.

Radiocarbon Date

We did obtain one radiocarbon date, M-2331, which falls near our presumed Tierras Largas/San José transition. The date is 3120 B.P. ± 150 in conventional radiocarbon years, or about 1170 b.c. The calibrated two-sigma range would be 1720-970 B.C.

The charcoal for M-2331 came from Zone G of Square S33A. However, as the stratigraphic profile of the adjacent Square S33 shows (see Fig. 10.1, Chapter 10), Zone F shrinks as it runs south in that area of the site. The disappearance of Zone F leaves Zone G in contact with the overlying San José deposits. Thus, M-2331 comes from very close to the interface between Tierras Largas and San José.

Cluster of Discarded Shells

Just above the ruins of Structure 15, a Men's House of the Late Tierras Largas phase, we found a cluster of discarded marine shells and possible shell ornaments. These shells lay right at the disconformity between Upper Zone F (which dated to Late Tierras Largas) and Lower Zone E (which dated to the Early San José phase). Owing to their stratigraphic position, the shells could not be confidently attributed to either zone, so we have assigned them to the Tierras Largas/San José transition.

This cluster of shell is particularly rich and varied compared to most Tierras Largas phase samples. It reinforces our impression that there was an escalated importation of exotic goods at the start of the San José phase. The shells were as follows:

Pacific Marine Bivalves
    1 small fragment of oyster (*Ostrea* sp.)
    4 valves of marsh clam, *Neocyrena* (= *Polymesoda*) *radiata*
    1 valve of Venus clam, *Chione* (= *Anomalocardia*) *subrugosa*
    2 worked bivalve fragments
Pacific Marine Univalves
    11 horn shells (*Cerithium stercusmuscarum*), clustered as if from a necklace
    7 horn shells (*Cerithidea mazatlanica*), clustered as if from a necklace
    1 dog whelk (*Nassarius* sp.)
Unidentified
    5 small fragments of shell debris weighing less than 1 g

Chapter 8
Area C: Houses of the Early San José Phase

During the Early San José phase, the Master Profile Sector of Area C was used mainly for outdoor features, like those typically found in residential dooryards. Off to the east, however, in the area encompassed by our Squares S31B-S33F, the villagers were still building lime-plastered Men's Houses like those of the Tierras Largas phase (Flannery and Marcus 1994:357-62). Our earliest San José phase ordinary residence was actually found in a test pit to the east of the threshing floor.

House 15

House 15 was found at a depth of 3.40 to 3.56 m below the surface in Test Pit 2, an exploratory 2 × 2 m excavation east of the threshing floor (Fig. 8.1). The family occupying House 15 had excavated one end of the house into sloping bedrock in such a way that the floor would be level. In this part of the site, Tierras Largas phase sherds lay directly on bedrock, so House 15 was probably the first house of the San José phase built on that spot.

We were only able to expose about 1.5 m² of the house, since most of it lay to the west and north of Test 2. Exposing more of it would have required us to remove 3.4 m of overburden, including the crushed-bedrock platform for a Late San José phase public building. We decided to leave this task for the future.

Unfortunately, House 15 lay too far from the other Area C excavations to be tied into our version of a Harris Matrix. Based on its ceramic assemblage and the fact that it was built in all probability on (or just above) exposed bedrock, however, we consider it to be our oldest San José phase house.

Daub

Ten or twelve small chunks of daub were visible in the west profile of Test Pit 2, immediately overlying the sand floor of House 15. None preserved the outer surface of the house, making it impossible to assess the thickness and color of any clay plaster or whitewash.

Ceramics

A small collection of sherds, consisting of types typical of the Late Tierras Largas and Early San José phases, was found in association with the floor. It most resembled the sherd sample from House 6.

Shell

A few small pieces of unidentified mollusk shell were found, each smaller than 10 × 10 mm.

Stone Ornament

One small fragment of jadeite(?) was found, cut in such a way as to suggest that it may once have been part of an inlay for a mosaic of some kind. Its original size is unknown. Assuming that it is actual jadeite, this would be our oldest known specimen of that material.

Feature 27

Feature 27 was found in Squares S20-S25 and S20A-S25A of the Master Profile. It was a shallow intrusive pit, more than 5 m long north-south and irregular in shape, dug down from Zone E

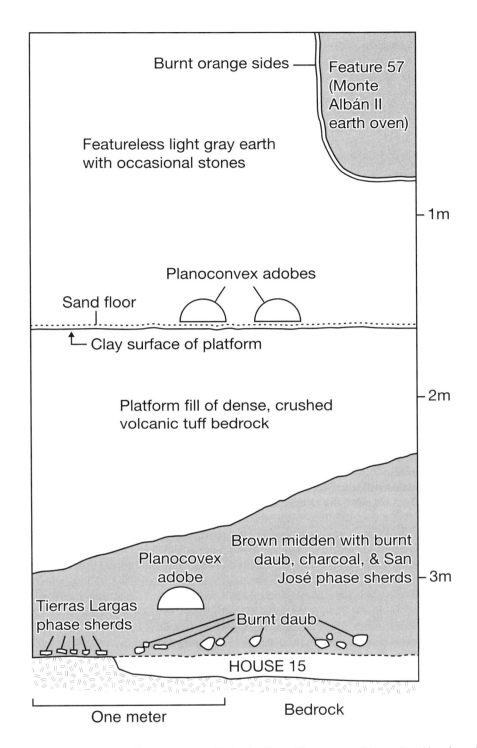

Figure 8.1. West profile of Test Pit 2, Threshing Floor Sector, Area C, showing House 15 at the base of the stratigraphic column. Early San José phase.

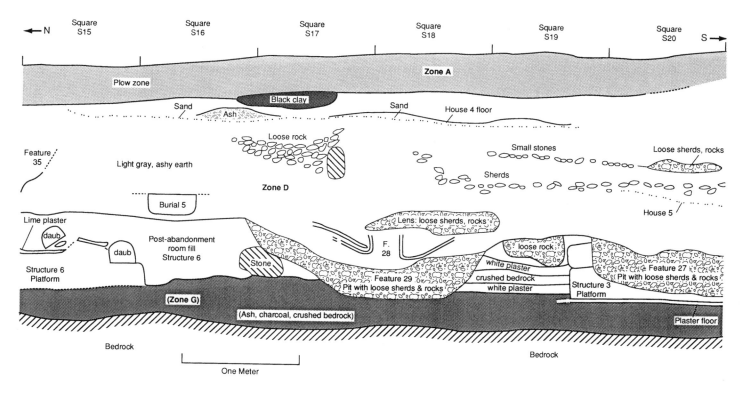

Figure 8.2. East profile of Squares S15-S20 of the Control Section, Area C Master Profile. This profile illustrates the stratigraphic relationships of House 4, House 5, Features 27 and 29, and the Zone G Midden.

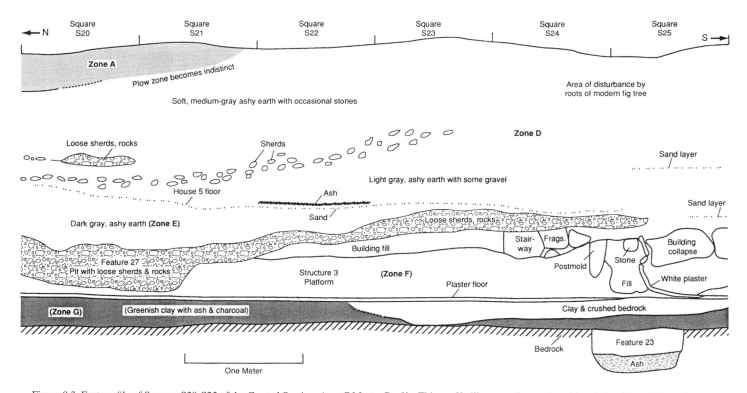

Figure 8.3. East profile of Squares S20-S25 of the Control Section, Area C Master Profile. This profile illustrates the stratigraphic relationships of House 5, Feature 27, the Zone G Midden, and Feature 23.

into the top of Structure 3 after it was abandoned (Figs. 8.2-8.3). Its contents included Early San José phase sherds, loose rock, shells, and fish otoliths.

Ceramics

The sherds from Feature 27 have been discussed by Flannery and Marcus (1994:292-93). The collection seems to belong to the early part of the San José phase. At least three sherds were of types foreign to the Valley of Oaxaca. Two were Coatepec White-rimmed Black. We believe that this type, originally defined in the Tehuacán Valley (MacNeish, Peterson, and Flannery 1970:108), is also present in Ann Cyphers' collections from San Lorenzo, Veracruz.

The third foreign sherd appears to be a *tecomate* rim of Guamuchal Brushed, an important type of the Pac phase of central Chiapas (Agrinier 1989) and the Cuadros phase of the Pacific Coast of Guatemala (Coe and Flannery 1967: Plates 6-9).

Shell

Shell consisted of two valves of pearly freshwater mussels, possibly *Barynaias*. One had been deliberately cut and the other merely broken. Also, one fragment of unidentifiable marine shell was found.

Imported Marine Fish Parts

Two otoliths of drum (family Sciaenidae) were found. One measures 20 × 10 mm, the other 12 × 8 mm. These otoliths constitute our earliest evidence for the importation of marine fish parts into the Valley of Oaxaca.

Feature 29

Like Feature 27, Feature 29 was a large irregular pit dug down from Zone E and intruding into Zones F and G (Fig. 8.2). It was more than 2 m long north-south, occupying parts of Squares S17-S18 and S17A-S18A. Its fill consisted of Early San José phase sherds, loose rock, and quantities of ash from which we were able to float carbonized plants.

Ceramics

The ceramics from Feature 29 have been discussed by Flannery and Marcus (1994:293). A second *tecomate* rim of Guamuchal Brushed, presumably from Chiapas or the Pacific Coast of Guatemala, appeared among the Feature 29 sherds. In fact, Guamuchal Brushed sherds showed up sporadically in the Area C sequence, beginning with Features 27 and 29 of the Early San José phase and ending with Feature 41 of Zone D, a Middle San José phase provenience (Chapter 9).

Carbonized Plants

91 kernels of maize (*Zea mays*)
a few maize cob fragments, some showing highly indurated glumes (probably as a result of back-crossing with teosinte)

3 fragments of carrizo (*Phragmites australis*), a cane used in house building and the manufacture of large baskets

Feature 37

Feature 37 was a typical San José phase bell-shaped pit, 56 cm in diameter at the top, 85 cm in diameter at the bottom, and 65 cm deep. It originated in Zone E and was intrusive into the ruins of Structure 5, occupying parts of Squares S28A and S29A (Fig. 8.4).

This pit had to have been deliberately filled in before House 2 could be built above it (Flannery and Marcus 1994:317). Its debris included sherds dating to the Early San José phase; a small solid white-slipped figurine head; charcoal; fire-cracked rock; and the deer and peccary bones described below.

Please note that while the description of Feature 37 on page 317 of Flannery and Marcus (1994) is accurate, the statement on page 313 relating Feature 37 to House 9 is a typographical error that we wish to correct here. Features 38, 40, 40-east, and 41 were all related in some way to House 9, but Feature 37 was not. It originated in Zone E.

Animal Bones

Complete radius of white-tailed deer (*Odocoileus virginianus*).
Left mandible of young collared peccary (*Dicotyles tajacu*).

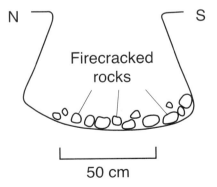

Figure 8.4. Cross-section of Feature 37, a bell-shaped pit of the Early San José phase.

The Zone E Midden

Zone E of the Master Profile was a diffuse layer of sherds and refuse that overlay the razed Men's Houses of Zone F. In part it seemed to reflect a period of leveling and filling, prior to the construction of ordinary wattle-and-daub residences of the San José phase. The fill itself appeared to represent refuse from relatively low-status families. In 1994, the material in Zone E seemed assignable to the first half of the San José phase (1150-1000 b.c.), though perhaps not to the very beginning of the phase (Flannery and Marcus 1994:292-93). In our expanded chronology, it is assigned to Early San José.

Ceramics

A sample of 712 sherds from Zone E, drawn only from squares that had no intrusive features, was studied by Flannery and Marcus (1994: Table 13.1). Some 217 of the sherds were from Fidencio Coarse cooking and storage vessels. More elegant wares like Delfina Fine Gray and San José Black-and-White were absent, contributing to our impression of low-status domestic refuse.

Chipped Stone

The sample of chipped stone from Zone E, limited in size by having been drawn only from squares with no intrusive features, was too small to be treated statistically.

Ground Stone

Most of an incipient basin-shaped metate, ignimbrite; it was only slightly used and undoubtedly would have become more basin-shaped had it been used for a greater length of time (Fig. 8.5). Length was >33 cm (broken); width, 25 cm; thickness, 10 cm.

One fragment of slab metate, vesicular basalt (Fig. 8.6b). The fragment is 6 × 6.5 × 3 cm.

One fragment of lipped metate, highly crystalline metamorphic rock (Fig. 8.6a). This metate had last been used for grinding iron ore pigment, and the lip probably served to keep the red powder from escaping. The fragment measures 15.5 × 12.5 cm. The thickness near the center of the metate is 5 cm, while the rim is 8 cm high, 1.5 cm of which was the lip itself.

One fragment of vesicular basalt pestle, greater than 6 cm long, 5.5 cm in diameter (Fig. 8.6c).

One combination pounder/abrader, subrectangular (Fig. 8.7d). Length, 12 cm; width, 6 cm.

Roughly half of a flat schist pebble, very worn from use in sanding and abrading (perhaps for sharpening bone tools?).

Two *canicas*, or pecked and ground stone balls, of Fábrica San José travertine; one 1.2 cm in diameter (Fig. 8.7g), the other 1.8 cm in diameter.

One pottery burnishing stone made from a discarded chert core, 4 × 3 × 2.5 cm.

Evidence for Celt Making

In Square S28A of the Master Profile we found two celts and a possible celt polisher, all discarded as a group in the Zone E Midden. They were as follows:

1 unfinished celt, 16 cm long, averaging 8 cm wide (Fig. 8.7a)

1 finished celt, 10.4 cm long, averaging 5.6 cm wide (Fig. 8.7b)

1 quartz pebble 8.4 cm long, 3 cm wide, with a flat facet probably used to put the final polish on a celt bit (Fig. 8.7c)

This interesting discovery suggests that during the Early San José phase at least one family in Area C was engaged in making celts from dark, greenish black metamorphic rock (possibly chlorite schist), pecking and grinding them into shape, then sharpening the bit with a large quartz or travertine pebble.

Bone Tools

One bone awl or *piscador* made on the unfused distal metapodial of an immature white-tailed deer; 9.3 cm long (Fig. 8.7e).

One bone awl or *piscador* made on the fused distal metapodial of an adult white-tailed deer, 7.5 cm long (Fig.8.7f).

Shell Ornaments

Circular plaque of pearl oyster(?), 20 mm in diameter and 2.5-3 mm thick, with a hole roughly 1 mm in diameter drilled for suspension (Fig. 8.7h).

Small claw made of pearl oyster(?), 12 mm long, 4 mm wide, 1 mm thick, with a hole 2 mm in diameter, drilled for suspension (Fig. 8.7i).

Small oval of pearl oyster(?), 10 mm long, 6 mm wide, 1 mm thick (Fig. 8.7j).

One fragment of what may be a "shell tinkler," made from an unidentified limpet.

Pearly Freshwater Mussels

one broken valve of mussel, possibly *Barynaias*, 36 × 16 × 1 mm (Fig. 8.7k).

Carbonized Plants

Ash Deposit in Square S15C

3 fragments of maize cobs (*Zea mays*)

Ash Deposit in Square S26A

55 kernels of maize

1 peduncle of maize

many cob fragments of maize

1 teosinte caryopsis

1 prickly pear seed (*Opuntia* sp.)

Animal Bones (Fig. 8.8)
    Large Mammals
        white-tailed deer (*Odocoileus virginianus*)
            1 shed antler, possibly saved to make artifacts
            1 fragment of maxilla
            2 L. mandibles
            1 R. mandible
            1 distal humerus
            1 third phalanx
        collared peccary (*Dicotyles tajacu*)
            1 R. mandible
            1 L. mandible
    Small Mammals
        domestic dog (*Canis familiaris*)
            1 R. mandible
            2 L. mandibles

The Zone E/Zone D Contact

In Squares S18G-S18H, we found a group of discarded animal bones right at the disconformity between Zones E and D. While we are not sure to which zone they should be assigned, these bones can at least be dated to the first half of the San José phase.

Animal Bones
    Large Mammals
        white-tailed deer (*Odocoileus virginianus*)
            1 L. innominate
            1 rib fragment
            1 phalanx, possibly from a fawn
    Small Mammals
        pocket gopher (*Orthogeomys grandis*)
            1 R. distal tibia
        eastern cottontail (*Sylvilagus floridanus*)
            1 L. humerus
        Mexican cottontail (*Sylvilagus cunicularius*)
            1 R. femur
            1 L. calcaneum
        unidentified cottontails (*Sylvilagus* spp.)
            1 fragment of mandible
            1 fragment of innominate
    Reptiles
        mud turtle (*Kinosternon integrum*)
            4 carapace scutes

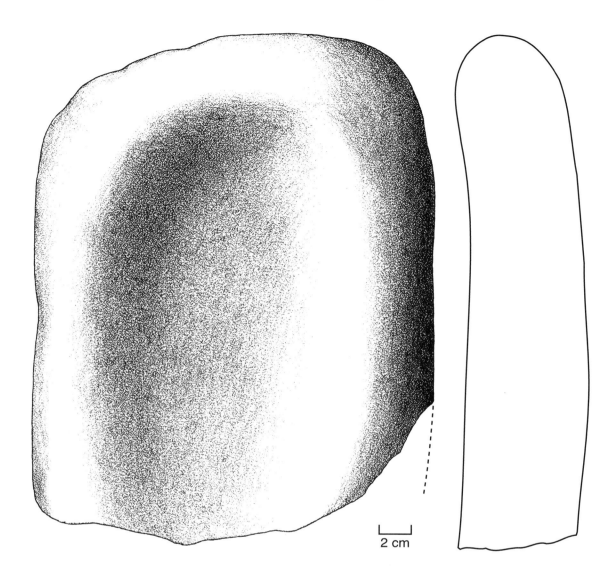

Figure 8.5. Broken metate, slightly basin-shaped, from the Zone E Midden. The raw material was a thick slab of volcanic tuff bedrock.

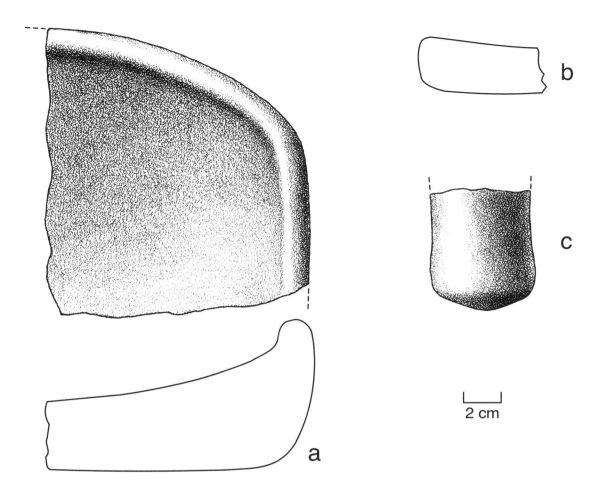

Figure 8.6. Ground stone tools from the Zone E Midden. *a,* fragment of lipped metate, metamorphic rock. *b,* cross-section of slab metate fragment, vesicular basalt. *c,* broken pestle, vesicular basalt.

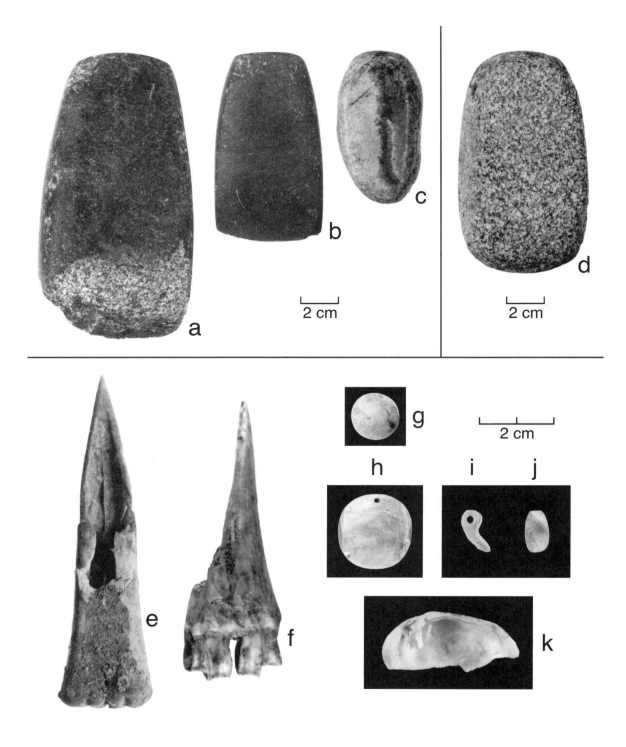

Figure 8.7. Objects from the Zone E Midden. *a-c* were all discarded as a group in Square S28A: *a*, unfinished celt; *b*, finished celt; *c*, quartz cobble with flat facet, presumably a celt polisher. *d*, combination pounder/abrader. *e, f*, deer metapodial awls. *g*, travertine *canica* or pecked and ground stone ball. *h*, circular shell plaque; *i*, shell claw; *j*, small shell oval (*h-j* are believed to be made from pearl oyster). *k*, one broken valve of mussel, possibly *Barynaias*.

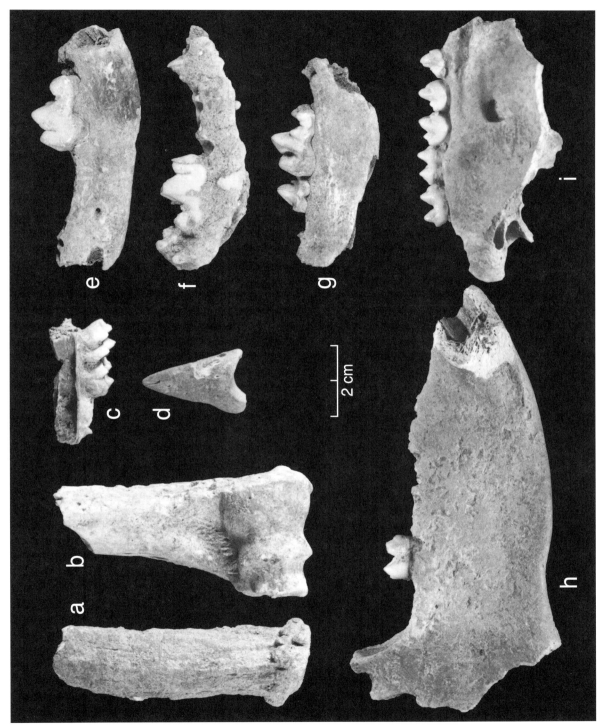

Figure 8.8. Animal bones from the Zone E Midden. *a,* shed deer antler. *b,* distal humerus, deer. *c,* fragment of deer maxilla. *d,* third phalanx, deer. *e-g,* mandibles of domestic dog. *h-i,* peccary mandibles.

Chapter 9

Area C: Houses of the
Middle San José Phase

Zone D of the Control Section

In the Control Section of the Master Profile, stratigraphic Zone D was a uniform stratum of buff debris from the decomposition of dozens of whitewashed wattle-and-daub houses. It was up to 1.5 m thick in places, but offered no color or texture differences that would have allowed us to subdivide it.

The sole exception to this uniformity was provided by a series of sand-coated clay floors from houses of the San José phase, which were visible in the profile as soon as it had been cut (Fig. 6.1, Chapter 6). For a century or more, the area of the Master Profile was the scene of repeated house construction.

We identified more than a dozen probable house floors in the profile, and numbered ten of them before excavation. Selecting a block of 1 × 1 m squares that incorporated a given house, we worked down carefully through the overlying deposits until we were 15 cm above the house floor. From that point down, work proceeded even more slowly, using trowel, ice pick, paint brush, and whisk broom. All the houses had been partially truncated by modern adobe-makers, but we excavated as many squares as we could in an effort to complete the surviving part of the house floor.

Time constraints prevented us from excavating more than nine of the potential floors. One of these ("House 8") turned out not to be a residence; it was merely the sand foundation from an eroded plaster "apron" adjoining a Men's House (Flannery and Marcus 1994:357). House 3 was numbered but never excavated.

The houses of Zone D were numbered in the order in which they were discovered. That was not, however, the order in which they had been built. According to our version of a Harris Matrix, the earliest was House 6; then came House 5 and House 2; then

the never-excavated House 3; next, in chronological order, House 11, House 9, House 1, and House 10, and finally House 4, the latest. We will present them in that order.

Since the houses of Zone D were sandwiched stratigraphically between Zones E and C, for the purposes of this volume we have assigned them all to the Middle San José phase.

House 6

House 6, the earliest and northernmost of the Zone D houses, occupied parts of Squares N1A-N1B, S1A-S1B, and S2A-S2B (Fig. 9.1). In this area Zone D rested on bedrock, with no underlying Zones E-G. Feature 32, a large bell-shaped pit dug into bedrock a short distance to the north, was probably in the dooryard of House 6 (see below).

The artifacts cached below the floor of House 6 were as interesting as those found lying on it. Unfortunately, only a small remnant of the floor remained intact.

Ceramics

Some 196 sherds were found on the surviving remnant of the House 6 floor. They have been studied by Flannery and Marcus (1994: Table 14.2).

Vessels Cached below the Floor

A Lupita Heavy Plain potter's bat and a Leandro Gray pigment dish, two vessels used by potters, were found cached beneath the floor (Fig. 9.2g, h). The pigment dish had been used for both kaolin white slip and red hematite pigment, remains of which were still visible on it.

Chipped Stone Lying on the Floor
Chert (76%)
flake cores: 4 (Fig. 9.2*a*)
sidescraper: 1 (Fig. 9.2*b*)
utilized flakes: 2
flakes, not utilized: 6
Obsidian (24%)
prismatic blade fragments, utilized: 3 (Fig. 9.2*c*)
flake, not utilized: 1 (Pires-Ferreira 1975 claimed an Otumba source)

Chipped Stone Found Just below the Floor
One flake core of brownish-white chert was found.

Ground Stone Tool Lying on the Floor
A small fragment from what may have been a mano was found.

Ground Stone Tool Cached below the Floor
One flat schist pebble was found, apparently used as a "cutting board." It was covered with fine scratches that give it the appearance of a whetstone. The original pebble was roughly 6 × 3.8 cm (Fig. 9.2*f*).

Bone Tool
Middle section from a possible sewing needle. Length of fragment, 37 mm; diameter, 3 mm (Fig. 9.2*d*).

Shell Found Just below the Floor
Two pieces of pearl oyster (*Pinctada mazatlanica*): (1) rectangular, cut on all four edges, 31 × 14 × 3 mm; (2) uncut, 30 × 12 × 2 mm.

Figurines
Six figurine fragments (4 heads, 2 limb fragments) were found in association with House 6; three of the figurine heads were stylistically similar enough to have been made by the same woman, although each had a different hairdo. These figurines have been described and illustrated by Marcus (1998a:109 and Figs. 11.1-11.2), and the locations of the four heads are given in Figure 9.1 of this volume.

In a midden not far from House 6 we found a complete seated figure, not unlike the "house dedication" figurine found under one of the doorway stones of House 2 (see below). That figurine is shown in Marcus (1998a: Fig. 10.23) and is republished in Figure 9.2*e* of this volume because of its proximity to the House 6 remnant.

Mask Found Just below the Floor
One fragment of a badly broken mask, showing the nose and left cheek of a human face, was found just below the floor. It has been illustrated by Marcus (1998a: Fig. 11.1, Specimen 5), and its location is shown in Figure 9.1 of this volume.

Animal Bones
Large Mammals
white-tailed deer (*Odocoileus virginianus*)
1 L. proximal tibia
Small Mammals
domestic dog (*Canis familiaris*)
1 lower L. canine tooth
1 L. innominate
pocket gopher (*Orthogeomys grandis*)
1 R. upper incisor
1 L. lower incisor
Mexican cottontail (*Sylvilagus cunicularius*)
1 R. distal humerus
Comment: this fragment appears pitted, as if it had passed through the digestive tract of a mammal, possibly a dog
raccoon (*Procyon lotor*)
1 lower L. 1st molar
1 R. proximal ulna
Reptiles
1 costal plate of unidentified turtle
Unidentified
7 splinters of deer or dog limb bones

Feature 32

Feature 32 was a large bell-shaped pit dug into bedrock in Square N7A — on the same level with, and probably in the dooryard of, House 6 (Fig. 9.3*a*). It contained sherds of a pigment dish and a potter's bat, like those found cached below the floor of House 6. This strengthened our evidence that one of the activities of the House 6/Feature 32 family was pottery making.

Ceramics
The trash swept into Feature 32 included quantities of Tierras Largas Burnished Plain and Avelina Red-on-Buff, as well as San José Red-on-White sherds with rocker stamping.

Chipped Stone
A hammerstone of Matadamas chalcedony was found, 8 × 5 × 4 cm (Fig. 9.4*c*).

Ground Stone
Fragment of loaf-shaped two-hand mano with oval cross-section, crystalline metamorphic rock. Length of fragment, 7.5 cm; width, 9.2 cm; thickness, 4.7 cm.
Fragment of loaf-shaped two-hand mano with elliptical cross-section, badly battered; 10 × 6.5 × 3.5 cm.
Fragment of loaf-shaped two-hand mano with airfoil cross-section, crystalline metamorphic rock. Fragment is 13 × 9 cm (thickness unknown).
Nondescript fragment of mano, metamorphic rock; 7 × 4 × 3 cm.

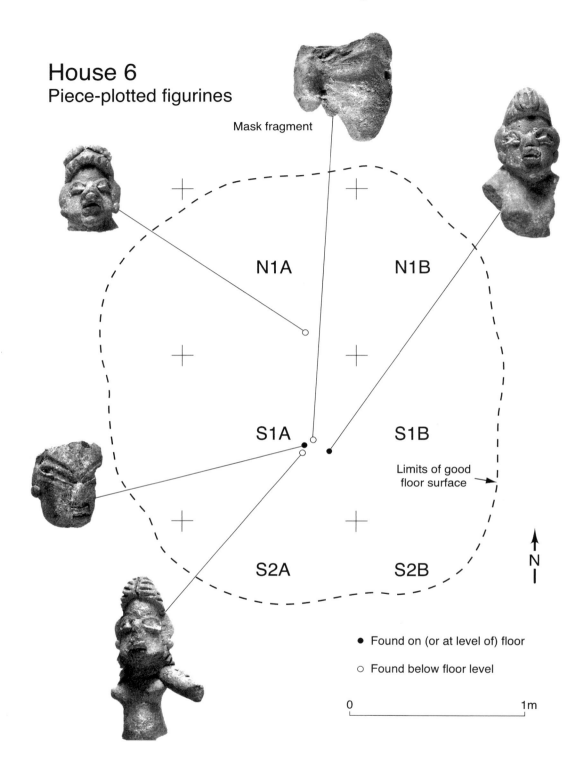

Figure 9.1. Remnant of House 6 floor, showing square designations and piece-plotted figurines. San José phase.

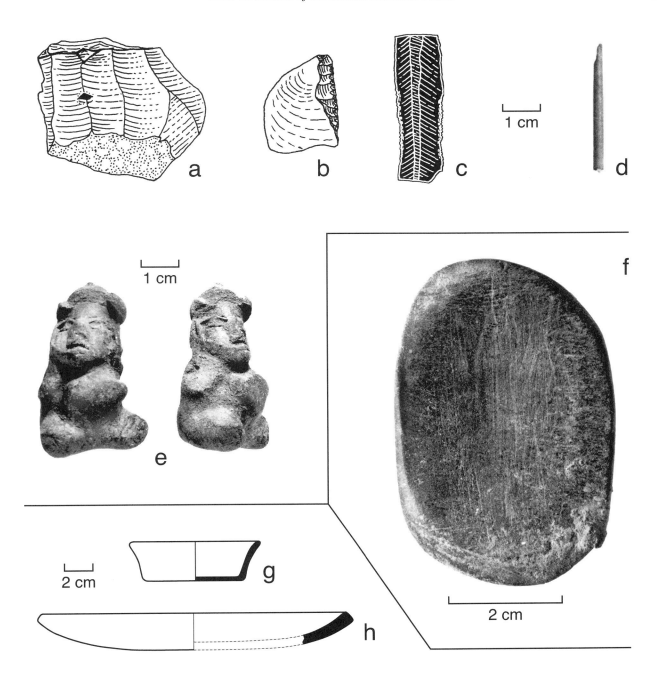

Figure 9.2. Artifacts found on, below, or near the floor of House 6 (note different scales). *a*, chert flake core. *b*, chert sidescraper. *c*, utilized obsidian blade. *d*, fragment of bone needle. *e*, possible "house dedication" figurine. *f*, flat schist pebble, apparently used as a "cutting board" (note fine scratches). *g*, Leandro Gray pigment dish bearing both kaolin white slip and red hematite pigment. *h*, Lupita Heavy Plain *tournette* or potter's bat, crushed by overburden. *a-d* and *f* on house floor; *g-h* cached below floor; *e* found in a midden nearby.

Figure 9.3. Feature 32, a bell-shaped pit presumed to be in the dooryard of House 6, and some of its contents. *a*, Sergio Cruz cleans out the lower portion of the pit, the part cut into bedrock (the bell-shaped upper portion, which was cut through soil, had been removed at this point). *b*, nearly complete bone sewing needle. *c*, chipped disk made from a body sherd of Fidencio Coarse pottery. (Length of *b*, 29 mm.)

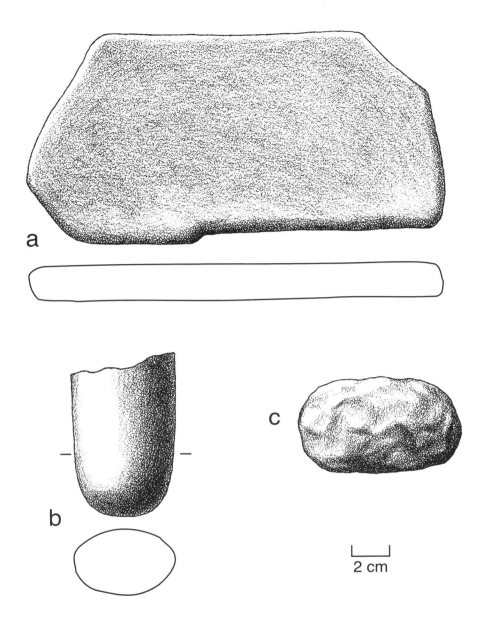

Figure 9.4. Stone tools found in the fill of Feature 32. *a*, pigment palette made on a sandstone slab. *b*, lower part of a cylindrical pestle with oval cross-section, metamorphic rock. *c*, hammerstone made of Matadamas chalcedony.

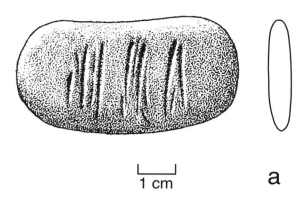

└─ 1 cm ─┘   **a**

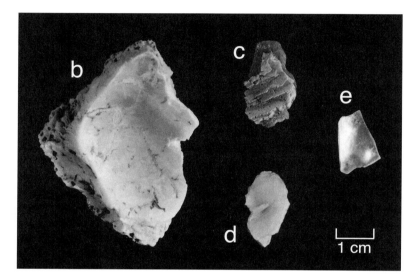

└─ 1 cm ─┘

Figure 9.5. Objects from House 5. *a*, thin pebble used as a "cutting board." *b*, large piece of *Spondylus* shell. *c*, *d*, fragments of unidentified marine shell. *e*, small piece of pearl oyster.

Lower part of cylindrical pestle with oval cross-section, metamorphic rock. Length of fragment, 9 cm; width, 5.5 cm; thickness, 3.5 cm (Fig. 9.4*b*).

Fragment of basin-shaped metate, badly broken; 8.5 × 4.5 × 4 cm.

Intact pigment palette made on a sandstone slab, 22 cm long, 11.5 cm wide, and 1.8 cm thick (Fig. 9.4*a*).

Pot burnisher made on a chert pebble, 3 × 2 × 1.6 cm.

One *canica,* or pecked and ground ball of fine-grained ignimbrite, 1.7 cm in diameter.

Bone Tool

Nearly complete sewing needle with eye, made on a splinter of deer(?) bone. Length, 29 mm (tip broken); maximum diameter, 3 mm; diameter of eye, 1 mm (Fig. 9.3*b*).

Worked Sherd

One complete chipped sherd disk, 5.7 cm in diameter, made from a body sherd of Fidencio Coarse (Fig. 9.3*c*).

Figurines

Some 13 discarded figurine fragments, clearly in secondary context, had been swept into Feature 32. Included were fragments of large hollow figurines, some white-slipped (Marcus 1998a:109-10).

Carbonized Plants

numerous fragments of maize cobs (*Zea mays*)

7 kernels of maize (*Zea mays*)

1 caryopsis of teosinte (*Zea mexicana*) (Fig. 4.1*j*, Chapter 4)

1 seed of tree legume, possibly *Conzatia multiflora*

1 seed of balloon vine (*Cardiospermum* sp.)

1 unidentified seed

Bone

One complete human mandible, possibly from an elderly male.

House 5

The floor of House 5 was found at a depth of approximately 1.4 m in Squares S20A through S24A; we consider it to be roughly contemporary with House 2. Only about a third of the house was recovered, which accounts for the small sample of artifacts.

Ceramics

Some 147 sherds were found in association with House 5. They are listed in Flannery and Marcus (1994: Table 14.2).

Chipped Stone
Chert (76%)
    flake core: 1
    utilized flakes: 4
    flakes, not utilized: 11
Obsidian (24%)
    prismatic blade fragment, utilized: 1
    prismatic blade fragment, no sign of use: 1
    flakes, not used: 2
    flake with cortex: 1
    Comment: Pires-Ferreira (1975) determined one obsidian blade to be from Zinapécuaro, and one obsidian flake to be from Otumba.

Ground Stone
One small flake, possibly from a mano.
One thin pebble, evidently used as a "cutting board"; one face has a number of cuts on it, running perpendicular to the long axis. Length, 5.8 cm; width, 3.2 cm; thickness, 0.5 cm (Fig. 9.5*a*).

Bone Tool
One worked bone fragment, burned and broken, 17 × 5 × 3 mm.

Shell
One piece of pearl oyster (*Pinctada mazatlanica*), apparently manufacturing waste, 15 × 10 × 3 mm (Fig. 9.5*e*).
One piece of *Spondylus* shell, apparently manufacturing waste, 55 × 40 × 10 mm (Fig. 9.5*b*).
Two pieces of unidentified marine shell, one 25 × 13 mm, the other 21 × 11 mm (Fig. 9.5*c, d*).

Figurines
Four figurine fragments were found in association with House 5. Three of these were on the house floor, and the fourth was found in the wall collapse. They have been described and illustrated by Marcus (1998a:110 and Figs. 11.3-11.4).

Animal Bones
There were at least two dogs represented in the remains from House 5, one adult and one puppy. Deer, if present, were represented only by splinters.

Small Mammals
    domestic dog (*Canis familiaris*)
        1 fragment of adult canine tooth
        1 fragment of premolar
        1 fragment of R. mandible
        1 unidentified cheek tooth
        1 deciduous canine tooth (juvenile)
        1 deciduous incisor (juvenile)
        1 unerupted permanent incisor
    pocket gopher (*Orthogeomys grandis*)
        1 burned, chewed distal humerus
    jackrabbit (*Lepus* sp.)
        1 L. maxilla
Reptiles
    mud turtle (*Kinosternon integrum*)
        1 fragment of burned costal plate
Unidentified
    20 mammal bone splinters, possibly including deer

House 2

We were only able to excavate the eastern third of House 2, since its western portion had been removed by modern adobe makers (Fig. 9.6). The architectural evidence consisted of two clear postmolds from weight-bearing corner posts, and a series of wall foundation stones that extended for almost the full length of the east wall (Fig. 9.7). The only break in the wall stones came in Square S27A, where there appears to have been a doorway. There was a small gray ash midden in the dooryard south of the house. One of the most interesting discoveries made in House 2 was the silica "ghost" or exoskeleton of a reed mat, found on the floor in the northeast corner of the house. This may have been the remains of a sleeping mat (Fig. 9.8).

There were enough fire-cracked rocks on the floor of the house to suggest that there may once have been an earth oven not far away. A few of the fire-cracked rocks were discarded manos (or fragments thereof). A bell-shaped pit immediately to the east of House 2, designated Feature 105, was almost certainly in the dooryard of the residence, and provided us with an extensive inventory of carbonized plants (see below).

Radiocarbon Date[1]
Charcoal in the ash spilled from Vessel 2, a charcoal brazier in Square S27A (see "Ceramics," below), yielded a date of 2850 ± 40 B.P., or roughly 900 b.c. (Beta–179082). The calibrated two-sigma range of this date would be 1120-910 B.C.

Daub
Half a dozen fragments of daub were found on the floor of House 2, most of them in and around the stone wall foundations. Two of the fragments still bore whitewashed plaster from

---

[1]In this volume, uncalibrated dates are given as "b.c.," and dendrocalibrated dates as "B.C." (see Chapter 26, Radiocarbon Dating).

Figure 9.6. Don Juan Martínez completes his careful uncovering of the House 2 floor.

Figure 9.7. Artist's reconstruction of House 2 (view from the west). Note that the weight-bearing posts are near the interior side of the wattle wall, rather than incorporated within it.

the surface of the wall. In the Munsell system, the color of the plaster would be "pink" (7.5 YR 7/4).

Ceramics

Some 275 sherds were found on the floor of House 2; they have been described by Flannery and Marcus (1994: Table 14.2). In addition, we found three restorable vessels on the floor (Fig. 9.8). Vessel 1, an Atoyac Yellow-white cylinder, was found among the wall foundation stones at the boundary of Squares S28A and S29A. Vessel 2, a Lupita Heavy Plain charcoal brazier, was found broken in S27A, with its gray ashy contents spilled east into the doorway of the house. Vessel 3, a Leandro Gray outleaned-wall bowl, lay near the wall foundation stones in S26A.

Chipped Stone
Chert (82%)
    ordinary flake cores: 11 (Fig. 9.9a)
    bipolar flake cores: 3
    core chopper: 1 (Fig. 9.9b)
    flake perforators/gravers: 10 (Fig. 9.9c-e)
    burin: 1
    denticulate scraper: 1 (Fig. 9.9g)

denticulate flakes: 3 (Fig. 9.9h)
    end scraper: 1 (Fig. 9.9f)
    scraper fragment: 1
    retouched flake: 1
    utilized flakes: 40 (Fig. 9.9i-m)
    flakes, not utilized: 180
Obsidian (13%)
    prismatic blade fragments, utilized: 9 (Fig. 9.10a)
    prismatic blade fragments, no sign of use: 2
    drill: 1
    utilized flakes: 15 (Fig. 9.10b, c)
    flakes, not utilized: 13 (Fig. 9.10d)
Other (5%)
    quartz flake: 1
    ignimbrite cores: 4
    igneous flakes: 10
Comment: One obsidian flake was determined by Pires-Ferreira (1975) to be from the Otumba source.

Unused Nodules of Chert
4 nodules

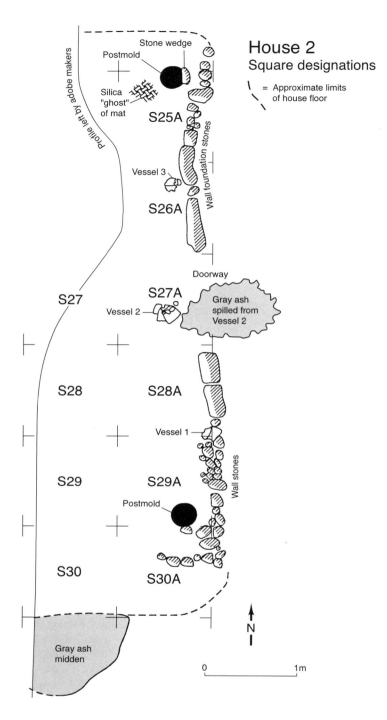

Figure 9.8. Plan of the House 2 floor, showing square designations, wall foundation stones, postmolds, restorable vessels, and other landmarks.

Ground Stone

Fragment of loaf-shaped two-hand mano with oval cross-section, two convex grinding surfaces, fine-grained ignimbrite. Fragment is 6 cm long (broken), 8 cm wide, and 4 cm thick (Fig. 9.10*e*).

Nondescript mano fragment, ignimbrite, 9 × 8 × 5 cm.

Fragment of pigment palette, sandstone, 5 × 4 × 2 cm, used to grind specular hematite.

Broken fragment of stream cobble, possibly used as a hammerstone. Diameter, 9 cm; thickness, 5 cm.

Elongated cobble, sandstone, one end broken through use as a hammer. Length, 8.5 cm; width, 3.5 cm; thickness, 4 cm.

Burnishing pebble of Matadamas chalcedony, covered with red specular hematite pigment. Length, 4 cm; width, 4 cm; thickness, 1.5 cm (Fig. 9.10*f*).

Several other pebbles on the floor, mostly of quartz or crystalline metamorphic rock, may have been saved for pot burnishing, but most do not show appreciable wear from that activity.

Former chert scraper reused as a burnisher.

Ten fire-cracked rocks, possibly from an earth oven, were found on the house floor; three or four of them may once have been parts of manos, but are now badly burned.

Bone Artifact

Bone tube, 1 cm long and 3 mm in diameter (Fig. 9.10*g*), possibly a bead.

Shell

Ornaments

In Square S28A we found 6 pieces cut from valves of pearl oyster, lying together as if the maker had been engaged in preparing a multi-piece ornament of some kind. They are illustrated in Figure 9.10*i-n*, and are as follows:

triangular ornament drilled at one end, 16 × 6 × 1 mm

subrectangular ornament drilled at one end, 19 × 11 × 1 mm

broken subrectangular ornament drilled at one end, 26 × 10 × 1 mm

ornament shaped like a human hand, 15 × 9 × 1 mm

triangular ornament, 26 × 10 × 1 mm

subrectangular ornament, 23 × 8 × 1 mm

Elsewhere, we found an unfinished triangular ornament that broke either during manufacture or drilling; it is 14 × 6 × 1 mm.

Pearly Freshwater Mussel

fragment, cf. *Barynaias*, 16 × 5 × 1 mm

fragment, cf. *Barynaias*, 30 × 15 × 1 mm

fragment, cf. *Barynaias*, 17 × 8 × 1 mm

fragment, cf. *Barynaias*, cut on several edges, 34 × 20 × 1 mm

fragment, cf. *Barynaias,* 20 × 6 × 1 mm

fragment, cf. *Barynaias,* 10 × 10 × 1 mm

fragment, cf. *Anodonta,* 10 × 10 × 1 mm

fragment of unidentified mussel, 10 × 8 × 1 mm

Pacific Marine Bivalves

piece of pearl oyster(?) refuse, 22 × 10 × 2.5 mm

triangular piece cut on at least two edges, possibly pearl oyster, 14 × 10 × 2 mm

fragment of pearl oyster(?), 25 × 16 × 2 mm

fragment of Venus clam, *Chione* (= *Anomalocardia*) *subrugosa*, 15 × 10 × 1 mm

Pacific Marine Univalves

2 complete horn shells (*Cerithidea* cf. *hegewischi*), one 24 mm long and the other 20 mm long

Iron Ore Specimens

Lump of magnetite ore from Group I-A, near Tenango. Pires-Ferreira (1975: Table 11) describes this group as one of the most commonly used sources; it was also used by the families in Area A (Chapter 14) and traded as far as Morelos.

Small fragment of crystalline hematite, potential raw material for grinding up into specular hematite pigment, 7 × 5 × 2 mm.

Mica Specimens

Lump of mica schist, 18 × 15 × 4 mm, found on the floor of the house (Fig. 9.10*h*). The presence of this raw material suggests that this family obtained its mica from schist deposits in the western piedmont of the valley.

Three small pieces of mica, scattered over the south half of the floor.

Figurines

Some 28 figurines or fragments thereof were found in association with House 2. They have been described and illustrated by Marcus (1998a:110-12 and Figs. 11.5-11.6). Perhaps the most interesting is the figurine shown in Figure 9.14 of this volume. It is a complete seated figurine, possibly male (or sexless), with its arms folded across its abdomen. It was found buried beneath a wall foundation stone to the north of the doorway. This figurine may have been part of a house dedicatory ritual, like those performed with terracotta figurines in some prehistoric Mali households (McIntosh and McIntosh 1979). It resembles another seated figurine from near House 6 (see above). One white-slipped figurine leg fragment was found in the gray ash midden banked up against the outside surface of the south wall of House 2.

Carbonized Plants

On the House Floor Itself

1 maize cob (*Zea mays*)

Still inside Vessel 2 (Lupita Heavy Plain Charcoal Brazier)

1 maize cob (Fig. 4.1*f*, Chapter 4)

1 fragment of carrizo (*Phragmites* cf. *australis*) (Fig. 4.2*L*, Chapter 4)

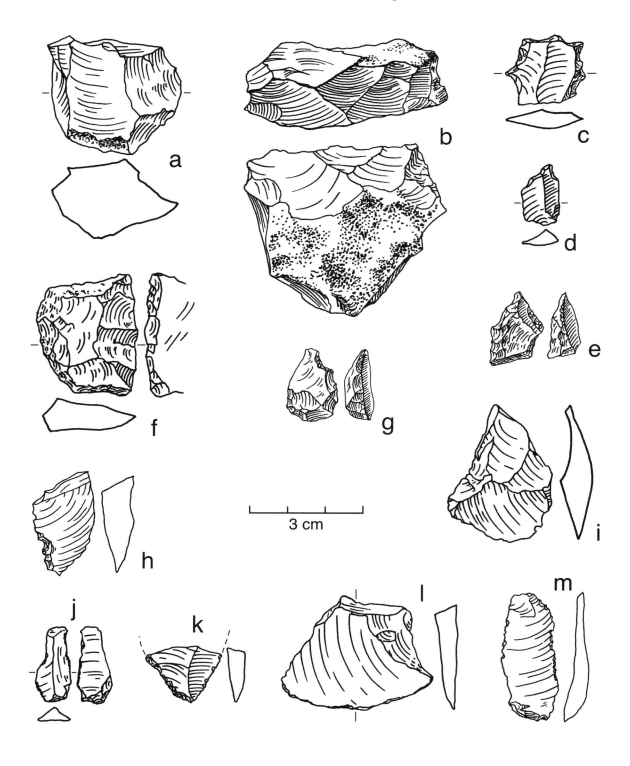

Figure 9.9. Chert tools from House 2. *a*, chert flake core. *b*, core chopper. *c*, flake with multiple perforator/graver nipples. *d, e*, worn perforators/gravers. *f*, endscraper. *g*, denticulate scraper. *h*, denticulate flake. *i-m*, utilized flakes.

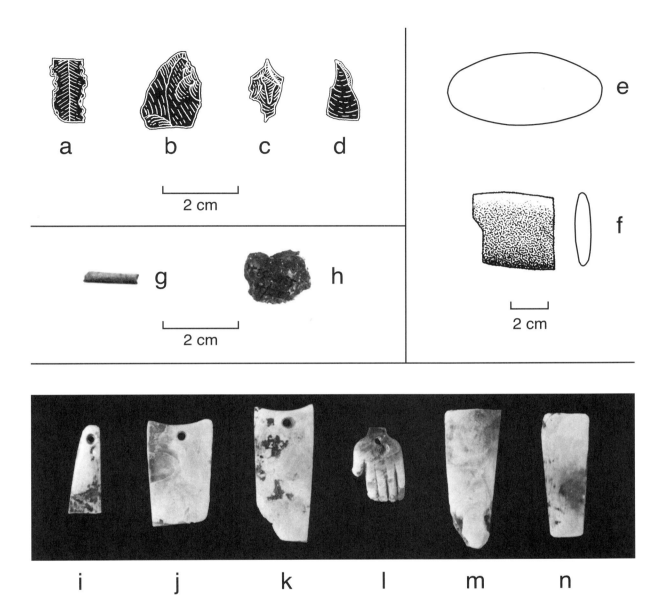

Figure 9.10. Objects from House 2. *a*, prismatic obsidian blade, utilized. *b, c*, utilized obsidian flakes. *d*, obsidian flake, not utilized. *e*, oval cross-section of loaf-shaped mano. *f*, burnishing pebble covered with specular hematite pigment. *g*, tubular bone bead. *h*, lump of mica schist. *i-n*, six ornaments from valves of pearl oyster, all found together in Square S28A. Length of *n*, 23 mm (photo is larger than actual size).

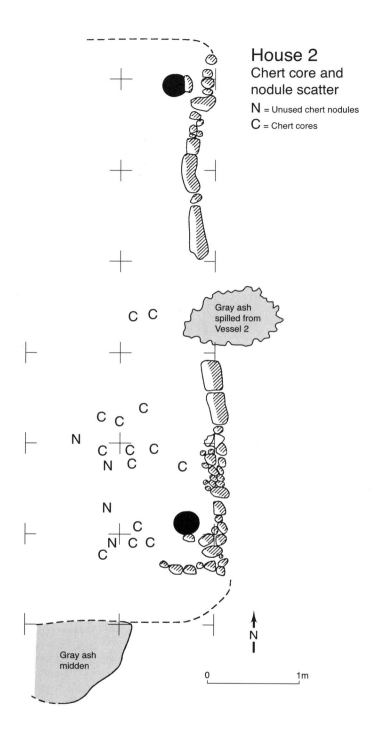

Figure 9.11. Plan of House 2, showing the distribution of chert cores and nodules.

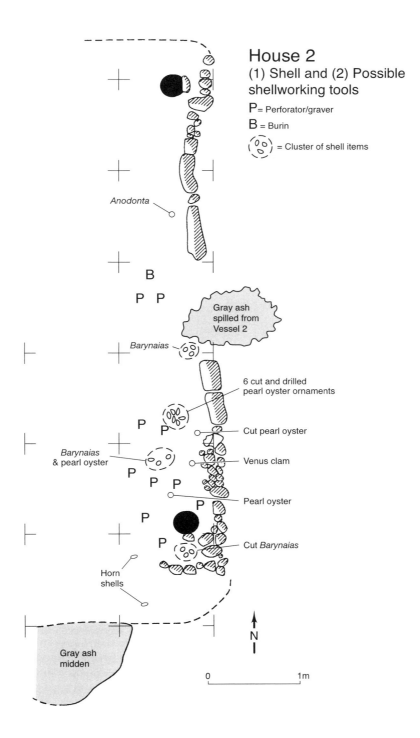

Figure 9.12. Plan of House 2, showing the distribution of shell fragments and possible shell-working tools.

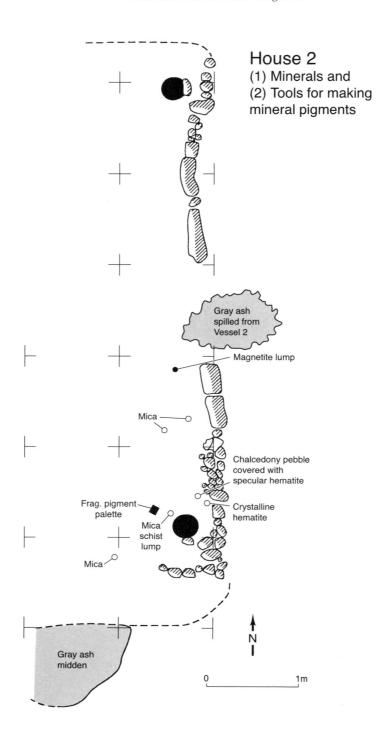

Figure 9.13. Plan of House 2, showing the distribution of mineral specimens and tools for making mineral pigments.

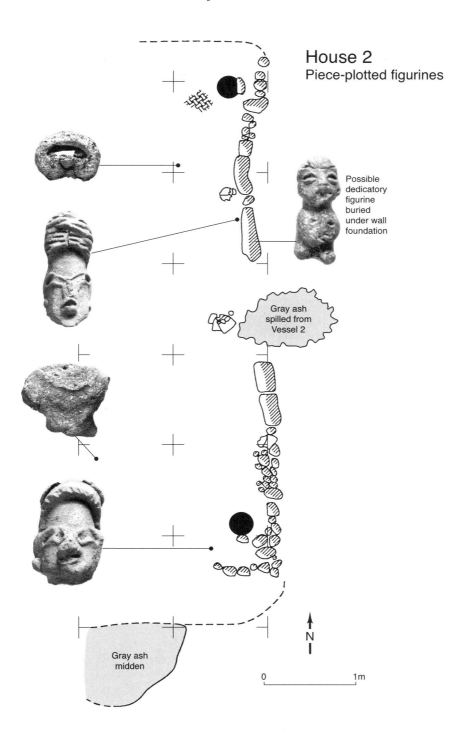

House 2
Piece-plotted figurines

Possible dedicatory figurine buried under wall foundation

Gray ash spilled from Vessel 2

Gray ash midden

N

0   1m

Figure 9.14. Plan of House 2, showing notable piece-plotted figurines or figurine fragments.

Figure 9.15. Leandro Gray bowl found with Burial 5. This vessel is excised with Pyne's Motif 1, depicting Lightning as a "fire-serpent," with sine curves as eyebrow flames and inverted U's as the serpent's gums. Rim diameter, 22 cm. (Chalk has been rubbed into the excising so that the motif will show up in the photograph.)

In the Ash Spilled from Vessel 2
    6 kernels of maize
    many fragments of maize cobs showing teosinte intro-
        gression
    2 prickly pear seeds (*Opuntia* sp.)
    1 fragment of carrizo
In the Gray Ash Midden Just South of the House
    17 kernels of maize
    many fragments of maize cobs
    1 squash seed (*Cucurbita* sp.) (Fig. 4.2*a*, Chapter 4)
    3 chile pepper seeds (*Capsicum* sp.)

Animal Bones
Animal bones were not particularly abundant in House 2, suggesting that our excavations missed the major area of bone discard. The most common remains in our sample were those of pocket gopher, represented by at least two individuals.
    Large Mammals
        white-tailed deer (*Odocoileus virginianus*)
            1 possible limb bone splinter
    Small Mammals
        domestic dog (*Canis familiaris*)
            1 lower incisor
            1 fragment of canine tooth
            1 L. temporal bone from skull

    pocket gopher (*Orthogeomys grandis*)
        1 complete L. mandible with incisor
        1 L. lower incisor from a second gopher
        1 R. upper incisor
        1 fragment from a second upper incisor
        1 broken cheek tooth
        1 R. lower incisor
        1 fragment from a second lower incisor
        1 R. distal humerus
        1 L. distal tibia
    jackrabbit (*Lepus mexicanus*)
        1 lower incisor
    eastern cottontail (*Sylvilagus floridanus*)
        1 lower incisor
        1 R. distal humerus
    unidentified cottontail (*Sylvilagus* sp.)
        1 fragment of proximal ulna
    raccoon?
        1 phalanx
    unidentified
        31 small fragments, one of them burned
Human
    1 tooth
    1 possible skull fragment

Feature 105

Feature 105 was a bell-shaped pit, dug just to the east of House 2 and undoubtedly associated with it. The pit was filled with fine ash, perhaps hearth sweepings but more likely the ash from charcoal braziers. We could not excavate the pit fully, since most of it extended into the profile. We did, however, manage to take a large flotation sample from it. The sample yielded both carbonized food remains and pieces of the charcoal used as fuel.

One of the most interesting revelations of Feature 105 was that many herbs growing on fallow agricultural land—herbs widely used by today's Zapotec as seasonings and condiments (Messer 1978)—were already being gathered in the San José phase. Included among these herbs were *Crotalaria, Chenopodium,* and *Amaranthus.*

Carbonized Plants

193 cupules from disintegrated maize cobs (*Zea mays*)
2 chile pepper seeds (*Capsicum* cf. *annuum*)
1 seed of barrel cactus fruit (*Mammillaria* sp.)
1 seed of chipil (*Crotalaria* cf. *pumila*)
1 seed of quintonil (*Amaranthus* cf. *hybridus*)
69 seeds of epazote (*Chenopodium* sp.)
3 seeds of small-seeded herbaceous legumes
12 unidentified seeds
33 fragments of pine charcoal (*Pinus* sp.)
22 fragments of oak charcoal (*Quercus* sp.)
1 fragment of conifer charcoal (possibly *Taxodium*)
1 fragment of tree legume charcoal
3 charcoal fragments from unknown trees

Insights from Artifact Plotting

Figures 9.11-9.14 show the distributions of chert nodules and cores, perforators/gravers, burins, shell, mica, mineral pigments, and figurines on the floor of House 2. What emerges from these drawings is a strong suggestion that the southeast quadrant of the house was an area for craft activity, especially shell working. The family in House 2 evidently produced both pearl oyster and freshwater mussel ornaments, and all stages in shell working appeared to be present in this quadrant of the house. We found both unused chert nodules, and nodules that had been turned into flake cores (Fig. 9.11). More than 200 flakes had been struck from these cores, and at least ten of these had been made into perforators/gravers, presumably for shell working (Fig. 9.12). Included among the shell items were parts for an elaborate multipiece pearl oyster ornament (Fig. 9.10*i-n*), and several geometric elements cut from pearly freshwater mussel. Also in the southeast quadrant debris we found crystalline hematite, some of which had evidently been ground into pigment on a sandstone palette (Fig. 9.13).

In contrast, the northeast quadrant of House 2 was relatively free of nodules, cores, perforators, shells, mica, and pigments. We

can think of several possibilities to account for this difference. Possibly the area north of the doorway, whose floor produced the silica "ghost" of a reed mat (Fig. 9.8), was a sleeping area, kept free of craft debris.

Another possibility is that the northeast and southeast corners of the house were work spaces for two different individuals. They may even have been gender-specific work spaces. Had we recovered more of the floor (including a larger sample of tools specifically associated with women), we would be in a better position to say more about this. Unfortunately, gender-related artifacts such as two-hand manos and sewing needles were neither abundant nor clustered.

Figurine fragments (Fig. 9.14) provided little help, as they were scattered fairly widely across the eastern third of the house. Only the dedicatory figurine buried below the door stone appeared to be *in situ.*

House 3

House 3, discovered in the east profile of Square S33, had an obvious sand floor topped with fallen chunks of daub. Unfortunately, we ran out of time before we could expand to the south and excavate it.

House 11

The adobe makers had left very little of House 11 for us to excavate. We did recover the foundation stones from one wall, running from Square S16C to S18C. In a midden just outside the house, we recovered three burials that may have been associated with it. Burial 5, an adult male, was accompanied by a Leandro Gray bowl with an excised Lightning motif (Fig. 9.15). Burials 10 and 11 were infants; one was accompanied by a mano, a miniature jar, a bead, and a drilled shell. The other was accompanied by a small cylindrical bowl, a hemispherical bowl, and the sherds of a large storage jar.

Nine lumps of daub were found among the wall foundation stones of House 11. Unfortunately, no artifacts could be associated securely with the remaining patch of floor.

Daub

Of the nine lumps of daub associated with House 11, one bore cane impressions, and eight had traces of whitewashed plaster still remaining. In the Munsell system, the color of the plaster would be "pink" (7.5 YR 8/4) to "very light brown" (10 YR 8/3).

House 9

We recovered perhaps 25% of House 9 in Squares S14A through S18B (Fig. 9.16, left). Associated with the house were a number of features, the most significant of which was Feature 38, an in-floor pit filled with fine wood ash. Other pits nearby

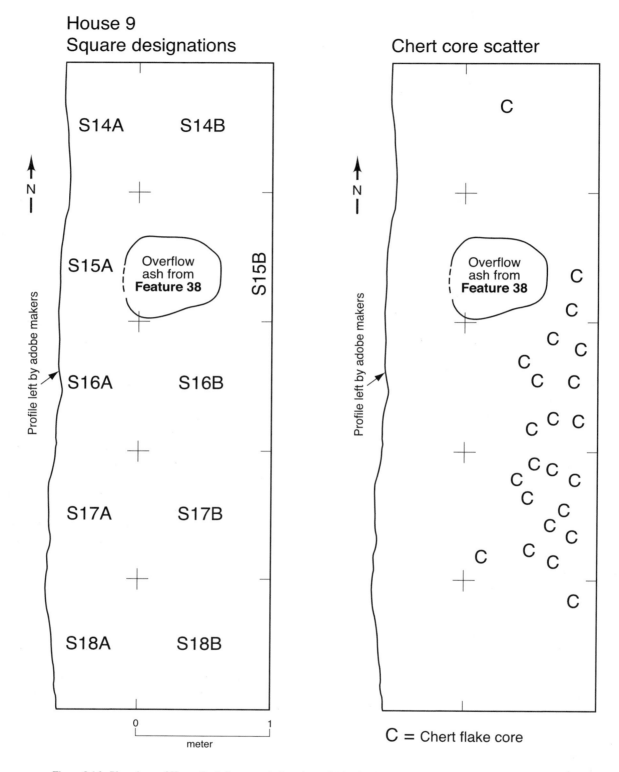

Figure 9.16. Plan views of House 9. *Left*, square designations. *Right*, the distribution of chert cores on the house floor.

were Features 40, 40-east, and 41, several of which antedated House 9 and had to be filled in before the floor could be laid (see below).

Radiocarbon Date

See Feature 38, below.

Daub

Three medium-sized pieces of daub were found on the house floor. They included a corner fragment which, while too damaged to provide useful measurements, showed that the house had had square corners. The other two lumps showed that in the gaps between cane bundles, the daub had varied between 2.8 and 3.8 cm in thickness. Where canes were present, the distance between the surface of the daub and the nearest cane impression was 2.5 cm.

Ceramics

Some 536 sherds were found on the surviving remnant of the floor. They have been described by Flannery and Marcus (1994: Table 14.2).

Chipped Stone

House 9 produced an unusually high number of chert cores and unused flakes, combined with a low number of retouched tools. Among other things, the sample contained none of the flake perforators/gravers so common in other houses. (One chert perforator/graver, one chert flake, and one igneous flake were found in a shallow pit or disturbed area below the house floor, but these could not be securely associated with the house.) We also found no prismatic obsidian blades in House 9. Pires-Ferreira (1975) sampled five of the obsidian flakes and determined that two were from Zinapécuaro, two from Guadalupe Victoria, and one from Altotonga.

Chert (76%)
  flake cores: 23 (Fig. 9.17*a*)
  scraper: 1
  spurred scraper: 1 (Fig. 9.17*b*)
  burin: 1 (Fig. 9.17*c*)
  utilized flakes: 12
  flake, utilized as a chopper: 1 (Fig. 9.17*d*)
  flakes, not utilized: 179
Obsidian (18%)
  utilized flakes: 22
  flakes, not utilized: 30
Other (6%)
  quartz flakes: 2
  igneous flakes: 14

Ground Stone

Battered end of a loaf-shaped two-hand mano with oval cross-section, two convex grinding surfaces, ignimbrite; used as a pounder after it broke. The surviving piece is 13 cm long, 10.5 cm wide, and 6 cm thick (Fig. 9.17*e*).

Fragment of two-hand mano, elliptical in cross-section, ignimbrite. The fragment is 7.5 × 5 × 4.8 cm (Fig. 9.18*b*).

Small mano fragment, ignimbrite.

Spall that may be from a mano, possibly reused as a rock in an earth oven.

Fragment of a slab metate or large palette, sandstone. The fragment is 8.5 × 4.5 × 2.5 cm (Fig. 9.18*e*).

Subcuboid pounder, limestone, 5-6 cm in diameter (Fig. 9.18*c*).

Barely used subcuboid pounder, limestone, 5-6 cm in diameter (Fig. 9.18*d*).

Ovoid pounder or hammerstone, ignimbrite, used to crush hematite and still covered with red pigment. Roughly 6.5 × 6 × 4 cm (Fig. 9.17*g*). This hematite grinding tool may have been used with the pigment palette described below.

Broken slab metate/pigment palette made from a flat stream pebble of metamorphic rock. The surviving fragment is 7 × 6 cm and 9 mm thick (Fig. 9.17*f*). This palette is covered with the same red hematite pigment covering the pounder/hammerstone described above, and may have been used with it. It is significant that House 9 produced three lumps of raw hematite suitable for grinding up into pigment, perhaps for pottery slips (see below).

Two spalls from celts made of metamorphic rock.

Large piece of dark fine-grained metamorphic rock, the very raw material of which celts were usually made at San José Mogote. One surface of this rock has been worn flat from being used as a polisher, perhaps in the course of sharpening the bits of celts made from the same raw material. Dimensions 10 × 8.5 × 4 cm (Fig. 9.18*a*).

At least four fire-cracked rocks (and half a dozen spalls from other fire-cracked rocks) were found on the floor of House 9, suggesting there may have been an earth oven or agave-roasting pit in use nearby. Some of the fire-cracked rocks appear to be discarded manos.

Bone Tools

Hammer made from the base of a shed deer antler, broken. The antler was 1.8 cm in diameter, and the surviving hammer fragment is 2.1 cm long (Fig. 9.19*a*).

Tips from two deer metapodial awls, or *piscadores*. One fragment is 2.3 cm long, the other 1.7 cm.

Pointed end of what was probably a bone sewing needle, 2.8 cm long and 3 mm in diameter, with an oval cross-section (Fig. 9.19*b*).

Almost complete basketry needle with eye. The needle would have been about 12.5 cm long before it broke, and its average diameter is 4 mm. The needle has been flattened by grinding on opposite surfaces, presumably so that it would fit between the coils of the basket (Fig. 9.19*c*).

Evidence for Fire Making

A carbonized stick that looks very much like the broken-off end of a fire drill was found on the floor (Fig. 9.19*d*). The fragment is 4 cm long and 8 mm in diameter, similar in size to the fire drills found at Guilá Naquitz cave (Flannery 1986c:163-64). One end shows the characteristic trimming and wear.

Evidence for Pottery Making

Two pats of unfired clay body for pottery making were found on the floor (Fig. 9.19*h*, *i*). One pat is a simple unused disk of clay; the other had been punched into a concave shape to serve as the base for a small jar or bowl. From their small size, it would appear that these pats were for miniature vessels, perhaps burial offerings (it is interesting in this regard that two infant burials were found in the midden just outside the house). The clay itself is the kind of residual piedmont clay used for Fidencio Coarse (Payne 1994:13).

Three lumps of red ochre or nonspecular hematite were found on the floor. All appeared to be suitable for grinding into pigment, either to be mixed with pottery engobe or to be rubbed into pottery excisions in the form of dry powder. Their rough dimensions were: (1) 18 × 16 × 6 mm; (2) 15 × 10 × 5 mm; (3) 7 × 7 × 4 mm (Fig. 9.19*e-g*).

Shell

The occupants of House 9 left behind manufacturing waste suggesting that they did some working of freshwater mussels, but not necessarily marine shell. All items in the house that were made from marine bivalves seemed to be finished ornaments or fragments thereof, and we found no marine gastropods at all. The lack of evidence for marine shell working could account for the absence of chert perforators.

A land snail tentatively identified as *Drymaeus* sp. was found in a shallow pit or disturbed area below House 9, but cannot be securely associated with the house (Fig. 9.20*d*).

Ornaments

Complete pearl oyster(?) ornament, slightly broken (Fig. 9.20*a*). Length, 35 mm; width, 10 mm; thickness, 2 mm. This artifact has been deeply carved with a variant of what was once called the "paw-wing" motif, now generally regarded as the foot of a crocodile (Grove 1984:126; Marcus 1999: Fig. 7).

Fragment of a broken pearl oyster(?) ornament, 15 × 10 × 2 mm.

Parallelogram-shaped ornament, too modified to allow the raw material to be identified, 20 × 7 × 1 mm (Fig. 9.20*b*).

Complete ornament resembling a disk bisected by a groove (Fig. 9.20*c*). This artifact (which resembles an aspirin tablet) is too modified to allow the raw material to be identified. Diameter, 12 mm; groove, 2 mm wide.

Pearly Freshwater Mussels

half of a *Barynaias* valve, 22 × 20 × 1.5 mm
fragment, possibly *Barynaias,* 11 × 8 × 1 mm
fragment, possibly *Barynaias,* 11 × 6 × 1 mm
fragment, possibly *Barynaias,* 9 × 8 × 1 mm
fragment of pearly mussel, 7 × 6 × 1 mm

shattered fragments of pearly mussel, 8 × 8 × 1 mm
fragment of pearly mussel, 8 × 8 × 1 mm
fragment of pearly mussel, 7 × 7 × 1 mm
fragment of unidentified mussel, badly burned, 24 × 14 × 1 mm
fragment of pearly mussel tentatively identified as *Strigilla* sp., 11 × 9 × 1 mm
fragment of pearly mussel, 6 × 6 × 1 mm

Mica

Four badly disintegrated fragments of mica were piece-plotted during the excavation of House 9, but their original dimensions could not be determined accurately.

Figurines

Some 21 figurine fragments were found on the floor of House 9. They have been described and illustrated by Marcus (1998a: 112 and Figs. 11.7-11.8). Nineteen fragments were from small solid figurines; two were from large hollow white-slipped dolls.

Stone Ornaments

Tubular bead of dark jadeite(?), broken longitudinally. Length, 16.6 mm; diameter, 8.6 mm; hole, 3.3 mm in diameter and biconically drilled (Fig. 9.20*e*).

Complete disk bead of light green jadeite(?). Diameter, 8 mm; hole, 2.7 mm in diameter and biconically drilled (Fig. 9.20*f*).

Damaged disk bead of dark jadeite(?). Diameter, 8 mm; hole, 2.3 mm in diameter, biconically drilled, and slightly off-center (Fig. 9.20*g*).

Imported Reptile and Mammal Products

Costal scute from a large lowland river turtle, possibly *Dermatemys;* such turtle shells were imported from the Gulf Coast to be made into drums (Fig. 9.20*i*).

Second, smaller fragment of nonlocal turtle carapace, also possibly part of a turtle shell drum.

Two pieces of shell from a nine-banded armadillo (*Dasypus novemcinctus*). Complete shells of armadillo could be used as containers or rattles, while individual pieces could be used in the making of masks or costumes (Fig. 9.20*h*).

Imported Marine Fish

Fragment of unidentified marine fish vertebra (Fig. 9.20*j*).

Two vertebral spines of unidentified marine fish (Figs. 9.20*k*, *l*). Teleost fish spines, like stingray spines, were probably imported for ritual bloodletting. However, based on signs of wear, one of these spines might have been used as a needle.

Carbonized Plants

A patch of ash on the floor was floated, and produced the following collection of carbonized plants:

2 kernels of maize (*Zea mays*)

2 cobs of maize with highly indurated glumes, showing teosinte introgression

1 cotyledon of avocado (*Persea americana*)

1 fragment of reed canary grass (*Phalaris* sp.), a species often used as roof thatch

Animal Bones

House 9 produced the smallest number of dog bones of any extensively excavated house. The most common mammal in the sample was pocket gopher, represented by at least three individuals. Katherine Moore, who analyzed the faunal remains from this house, noted that some bones in Squares S14A and S14B had a pitted appearance which suggested that they might have passed through an animal's digestive system before they were deposited on the house floor. This raises the possibility that some of the bones might be from dog feces or owl pellets deposited in the house after abandonment. This possibility is strengthened by the fact that the "digested" remains include species of wild rodents, songbirds, and lizards not usually found in San José phase refuse.

Large Mammals

    white-tailed deer (*Odocoileus virginianus*)

        1 burned antler fragment, probably kept to be fire-hardened as an artifact

        1 small piece of limb bone with a butchering cut 1 cm from the articular surface

Small Mammals

    domestic dog (*Canis familiaris*)

        1 incisor

        1 premolar

        1 fragment of upper molar

        1 lower L. first molar

    pocket gopher (*Orthogeomys grandis*)

        2 L. upper incisors from two different gophers

        2 R. upper incisors from two different gophers

        1 fragment of another upper incisor from a third gopher

        1 fragment of lower incisor

        6 cheek teeth from several gophers

        1 axis vertebra

        1 burned R. scapula

        2 R. distal humeri from two different gophers

        1 L. distal radius

    eastern cottontail (*Sylvilagus floridanus*)

        1 lower incisor

        1 R. distal humerus

        1 L. distal humerus

        1 R. proximal radius

        1 metacarpal

        1 fragment of L. innominate

        1 R. proximal femur

        1 L. distal tibia

        1 L. calcaneum

        1 R. calcaneum

    Mexican cottontail (*Sylvilagus cunicularius*)

        1 R. upper incisor

        1 L. mandible

        1 L. innominate

        (1 distal femur of *S. cunicularius* was found in a shallow pit or disturbance below the floor of House 9, but cannot be securely associated with the house)

    unspecified cottontails (*Sylvilagus* spp.)

        1 lower incisor

        1 metacarpal

        1 L. distal tibia

Small Wild Rodents

    1 ascending ramus of mandible

    1 L. innominate

    1 L. femur

    1 fragment of tibia

Reptiles

    mud turtle (*Kinosternon integrum*)

        2 carapace fragments

        1 marginal scute

        2 costal scutes

        1 plastron fragment

    unidentified lizard

        2 vertebrae

Birds

    mourning dove (*Zenaidura macroura*)

        2 tarsometatarsi

    unidentified quail

        1 tarsometatarsus

    unidentified finch

        1 beak

    unidentified large bird

        1 long bone fragment

    unidentified songbirds

        1 thoracic vertebra

        1 carpometacarpus

        1 tarsometatarsus

        1 long bone fragment

        1 phalanx

Human

    1 skull fragment

    1 juvenile humerus

Unidentified

    139 fragments, mostly mammal; only one or two are burned

Features Associated with House 9

Feature 38

Feature 38 was a small bell-shaped pit in the floor of House 9 (Fig. 9.21). The pit was 32 cm deep and expanded from 52 cm to 64 cm in diameter as it descended. A ring-shaped indentation in the floor indicated that while it was not being used, Feature

38 was kept covered with a lid of some kind, either to protect the contents or prevent anyone from stepping in it. The pit was filled with fine white wood ash, some of which had overflowed onto the floor.

Among the Zapotec, fine wood ash is used in a variety of craft activities, much the way modern craftsmen use talcum, chalk dust, or powdered graphite. For example, in the press-molding of ceramics, Oaxaca potters often use a coating of wood ash to prevent the clay of the new vessel from adhering to the mold (Payne 1994:11). Discovering fine wood ash stored in the house in a pit with a lid should thus not be surprising; it is a clue to craft activity (see below).

Radiocarbon Date

A small piece of charcoal from Feature 38 yielded an AMS date of 2950 ± 40 B.P., or roughly 1000 b.c. (Beta-179081). The calibrated two-sigma range for this date would be 1290-1020 B.C.

Feature 41

Feature 41 was a bell-shaped pit in Square S28, north of and probably in the dooryard of House 9 (Fig. 9.21). Its rim diameter was 52 cm and its basal diameter 80 cm. Included in the contents of Feature 41 were sherds, fragments of chert, and pieces of charcoal (probably house floor sweepings). The small sample of sherds suggests a date somewhere in the middle of the San José phase.

Perhaps the pit's most interesting contents were two *tecomate* rims of Guamuchal Brushed, a pottery type reported from central Chiapas and the Guatemalan Pacific coast. This evidence for contact with the tropical lowlands is interesting in light of the fact that House 9 also contained spines of marine fish, fragments of armadillo shell, and pieces of a large lowland turtle (see above).

Feature 40 (Below House 9)

Features 40 and 40-east were oval pits that had to be deliberately filled in before House 9 could be built over them. Feature 40-east was larger and less symmetrical, while Feature 40 was smaller and lay *within* 40-east—a kind of "pit within a pit" (Fig. 9.21). Feature 40 contained Leandro Gray cylinders with excised Lightning motifs; Leandro Gray bolstered-rim bowls; Lupita Heavy Plain braziers/potstands and rocker-stamped *tecomates*; Tierras Largas Burnished Plain jars and hemispherical bowls; and Avelina Red-on-Buff hemispherical bowls.

Feature 40-East (Below House 9)

Feature 40-east was a large straight-sided pit, irregularly oval in plan view. It was 43 cm deep and 85 × 40 cm in width at both top and bottom (Fig. 9.21). The fill consisted of sand, gravel, ash lenses, sherds, loose stone, and shell. The inclusion of sand and gravel suggests that the pit may have been deliberately filled with surplus construction material.

Ceramics. The sherds from Feature 40-east have been described by Flannery and Marcus (1994:317). In our expanded chronology, they would be considered Middle San José phase.

Shell. Four fragments from a broken pearly freshwater mussel were found, possibly Barynaias.

Figurines. Some six fragments from small solid figurines were found in Feature 40-east. One was the head of a "tonsured cacique" with cranial deformation, illustrated by Marcus (1998a: Fig. 11.9).

Insights from Artifact Plotting

Figures 9.16 (*right*) and 9.22-9.25 show the distributions of chert cores, mano and celt fragments, pounders, artifacts for pigment grinding and pottery making, figurines, mussel shell, basketry awls and needles, and exotic animal parts found on the House 9 floor. Our exposure of this house amounts to a long, narrow transect which touched no walls or corners, giving us few landmarks to work with. Some categories of material show patterning; many do not.

Twenty-two of the 23 chert flake cores were scattered along the eastern edge of the transect, leading us to suspect that they were tossed (or swept) toward a wall just east of Squares S15B-S17B (Fig. 9.16, *right*). It is difficult to consider this pattern the result of anything beyond housecleaning behavior. The distribution of cores simply does not match the pattern of any other material on the floor.

Several other artifact categories, however, seem to have been discarded in a line curving partly around Feature 38, suggesting that the ash-filled pit may have been part of an activity area. We have already mentioned that fine wood ash was used in a number of Zapotec crafts. One of those activities was the press-molding of pottery, and Figure 9.22 (*right*) shows that all the items potentially associated with pigment grinding and pottery making could be considered to lie in a "drop zone" around Feature 38. Included were an unfired miniature vessel, a lump of unused pottery clay, three lumps of red pigment, and two pigment palettes. Both the clay and the red pigment would be appropriate for making Fidencio Coarse, a common cooking ware.

Since we suspect that women produced most or all of the household's utilitarian pottery, we were naturally curious to see if any other artifact distributions suggested that Squares S15A-S15B lay in the center of a woman's work area. All three of the largest House 9 figurine fragments were found near Feature 38 (Fig. 9.23), but that is not much of a sample. Mano fragments and pounders were lying on roughly the same parts of the floor as the pigment lumps (Fig. 9.22, *left*). Unfortunately, most mano fragments were so small that they would have been useful mainly as pounders, rather than maize grinders.

Our suspicion that Feature 38 lay in a woman's work area does receive some support from the distribution of sewing needles, basketry needles, and potential basketry-making awls (Fig. 9.24, *left*). These artifacts, too, seem to lie in a "drop zone" near the ash-filled pit. So does an apparent carbonized fire drill, which might have been used to light cooking fires in Lupita Heavy Plain braziers.

Whoever worked in Squares S15A-S15B may also have been involved in cutting inlays from freshwater mussel shell (Fig. 9.24, *right*). A number of other materials that we suspect were used to decorate masks, costumes, or ritual artifacts were also discarded in our suspected "drop zone." Included were fragments of exotic lowland species like armadillo and river turtle. As mentioned above, however, House 9 produced no evidence for the drilling of marine shell.

In sum, our transect of House 9 leads us to suspect that Feature 38, a deposit of carefully stored wood ash, lay at the center of an activity area where pottery vessels were formed, pigment ground and applied, baskets made, sewing done, and items decorated with materials such as mussel shell inlays. We believe that this may have been a woman's work area. Two activities that seem *not* to have been carried out near Feature 38 were (1) the drilling of pearl oyster and *Spondylus* (for which there were none of the familiar perforators/gravers) and (2) the striking of primary flakes from cores. Indeed, exhausted flake cores had a discard pattern all their own.

Here is a case where, had modern adobe makers not destroyed so much of the house, we might well have been able to identify several gender-specific activity areas.

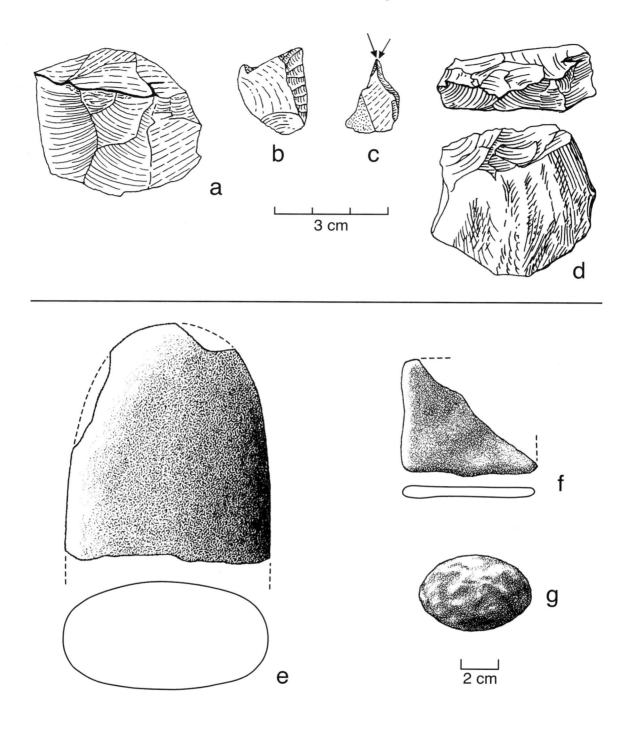

Figure 9.17. Artifacts from House 9. *a*, chert flake core. *b*, spurred scraper. *c*, burin. *d*, thick flake used as a chopper. *e*, battered end of loaf-shaped mano with oval cross-section, used as a pounder after it broke. *f*, broken slab metate/palette covered with hematite pigment; possibly used with *g*, an ovoid pounder/hammerstone used to crush hematite.

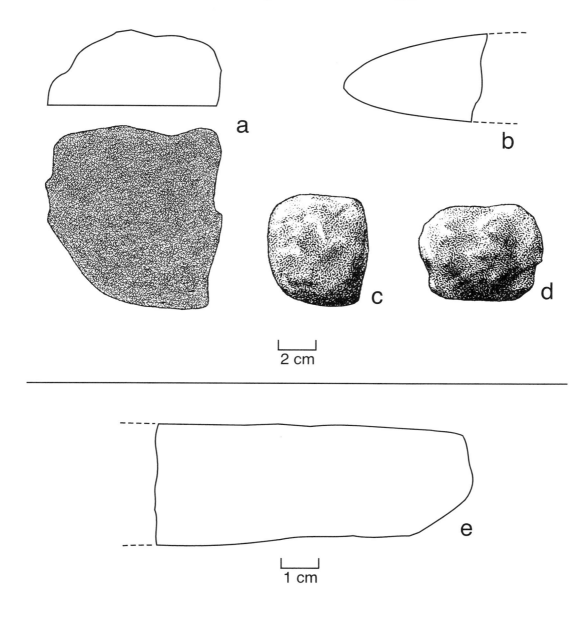

Figure 9.18. Ground stone objects from House 9. *a*, possible celt polisher of dark metamorphic rock. *b*, cross-section of broken mano, elliptical in cross-section. *c, d,* subcuboid pounders, limestone. *e*, fragment of slab metate or large palette, sandstone.

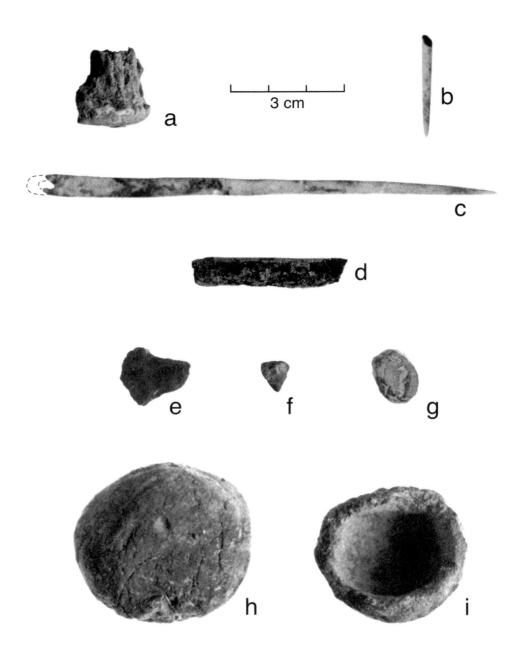

Figure 9.19. Objects from House 9, including items for sewing, basketry, fire making, and pottery making. *a*, deer antler hammer. *b*, fragment of bone sewing needle. *c*, nearly complete basketry needle with eye. *d*, carbonized fragment of wooden fire drill? *e-g*, three lumps of red ochre suitable for making pottery pigment. *h*, unused pat of pottery clay. *i*, small pat of pottery clay, punched into a concave shape to serve as the base for a small jar or bowl. This may be an unfired miniature vessel.

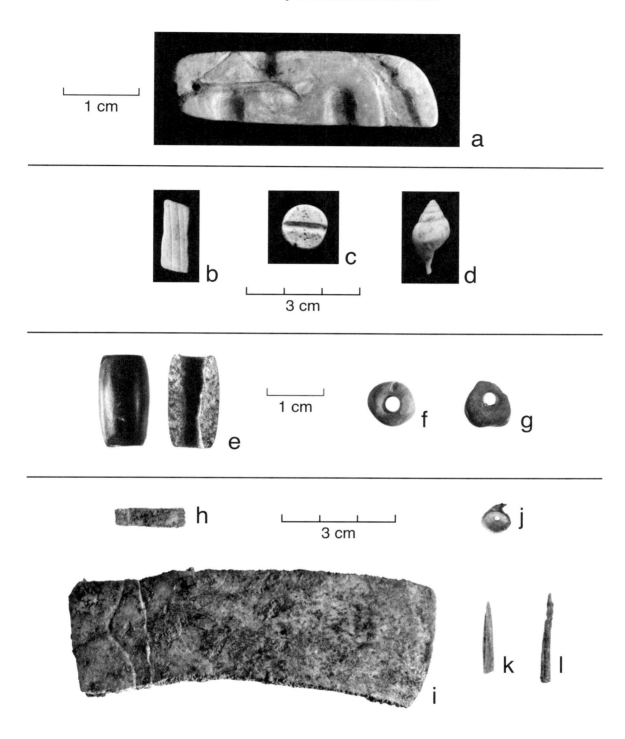

Figure 9.20. Objects from House 9. *a*, complete pearl oyster(?) ornament, carved with the "crocodile's foot" motif, which broke when drilled near the far left end. Length, 35 mm (shown larger than actual size). *b*, parallelogram-shaped shell ornament. *c*, shell disk bisected by a groove. *d*, land snail found in a shallow pit below the house floor. *e*, two views of broken tubular bead, jadeite(?). *f*, light green disk bead. *g*, damaged disk bead. *h*, plate from armadillo shell. *i*, costal scute from lowland turtle, possibly part of a drum. *j*, marine fish vertebra. *k, l*, vertebral spines of marine fish.

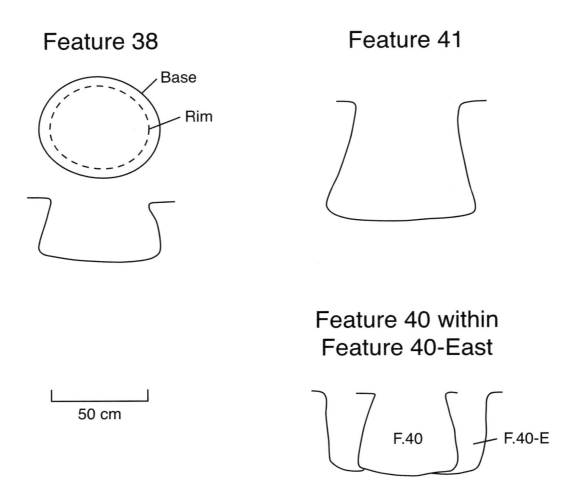

Figure 9.21. Features associated with House 9.

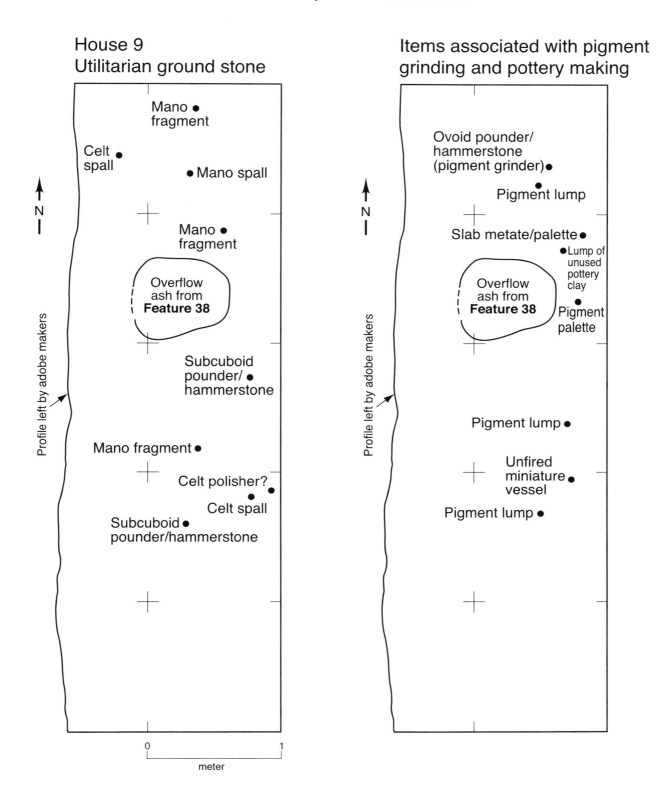

Figure 9.22. Plan views of House 9. *Left*, distribution of utilitarian ground stone tools. *Right*, items associated with pigment grinding and pottery making.

House 9
piece-plotted figurine frags.

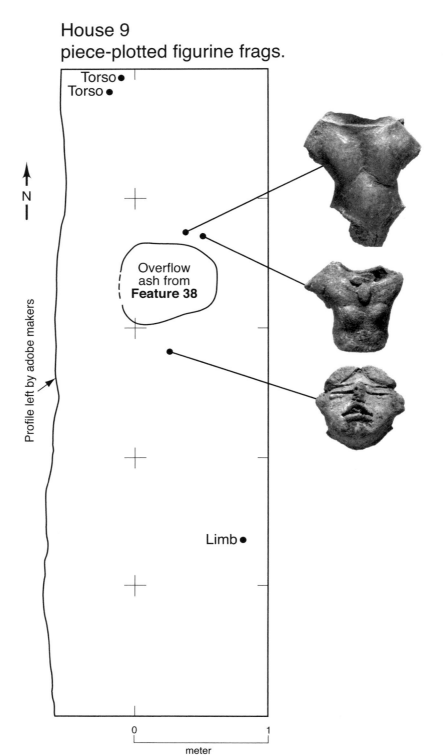

Figure 9.23. Figurine fragments piece-plotted on the floor of House 9.

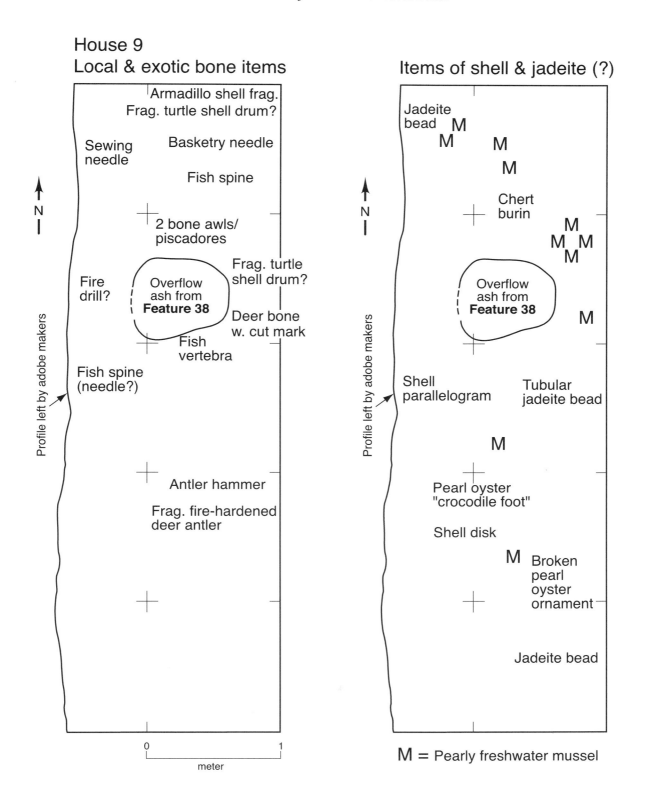

Figure 9.24. Plan views of House 9. *Left*, distribution of local and exotic bone items. *Right*, items of shell and jadeite(?).

House 1

Our excavations uncovered part of the southern half of House 1, including the southeast corner (Fig. 9.25). The western part of the house had been removed by modern adobe makers prior to our arrival. It also proved impossible to trace the floor north into Square S28A, since that area had been disturbed by an erosion channel in ancient times.

A series of other disturbances had removed parts of the original house floor. For example, Burials 1 and 2 were intrusive through it, and an intrusive pit from a higher level had just grazed it. In spite of all these problems, the intact parts of the floor yielded very interesting material, including one of our most complex San José phase pearl oyster ornaments.

Just beyond the south wall of House 1, we found a shallow midden with ash and charcoal flecks. This midden rested against the house, and seemed to represent a place where the ash from hearths or charcoal braziers had been dumped over a period of time. This is one of several instances in which the area immediately to the south of a house was chosen as the place to dump hearth ash; House 2 had a similar dump. We presume that this pattern had something to do with the prevailing wind on the west side of the piedmont spur.

Daub

Just to the south of Burial 1, we found a mass of small stones and burned daub fragments. Unfortunately, it was not always clear which lumps went with House 1 and which had been left by an intrusive pit from above the house. Where whitewashed plaster survived on the daub, it would have been classified in the Munsell system as "pink" (7.5 YR 7/4).

The scatter of daub included what seemed to be a fragment of mud-plastered stairway. Owing to its proximity to the intrusive pit mentioned above, we cannot be sure that it was associated with House 1.

Ceramics

Some 182 sherds were recovered from the House 1 floor. They have been described by Flannery and Marcus (1994: Table 14.2).

Chipped Stone

The chipped stone sample from House 1 consisted of 90 fragments, and in most aspects it resembled chipped stone from other houses in Area C. One unique item, however, was the obsidian biface shown in Figure 9.26a and b, which may be the tip of a projectile point. Projectile points were rare in the San José phase, and obsidian points almost unheard of. It is very likely, therefore, that this point was an exchange item from outside the Valley of Oaxaca.

Regions where we know obsidian points were common in the Early Formative include the Basin of Mexico, the Valley of Puebla, and the Valley of Tehuacán. According to Pires-Ferreira (1975), the prismatic obsidian blade fragment in House 1 came from the Otumba source in the Basin of Mexico. The point might well have come from that same source, but has not been analyzed.

Chert (86%)
  flake cores: 5
  flake perforators/gravers: 3
  drill: 1
  denticulate flakes: 2
  side scraper: 1
  retouched flake: 1
  utilized flakes: 9
  flakes, not utilized: 55
Obsidian (13%)
  biface tip, possibly from a projectile point: 1 (Fig. 9.26a, b)
  prismatic blade fragment: 1
  utilized flakes: 4
  flakes, not utilized: 6
Other (1%)
  quartz fragment: 1

Ground Stone

Fragment of subrectangular two-hand mano with airfoil cross-section, coarse limestone. The fragment is 8.5 cm long, 9.5 cm wide, and averages 5 cm thick. Because it was found near an intrusive pit, its association with House 1 is not totally secure (Fig. 9.26l). Typologically, of course, it would not be out of place in the San José phase.

Agate(?) stream pebble, apparently used as a pottery burnishing stone.

Shell

Ornaments
  Fragments of a complex circular pendant made from pearl oyster. Originally between 4.5 or 5 cm in diameter, this ornament has been reconstructed by our artist (Fig. 9.26c) on the basis of fragments found on the floor in Squares S31B and S32B (Fig. 9.26d, e). We suggest that the shell worker began by cutting a circular disk from an oyster valve, then removed small oval areas near the edge, and finally a larger four-pointed area near the center. There is no evidence in the form of manufacturing waste to suggest that this ornament was made in House 1.

  Two local land snails (*Euglandina* sp.), modified for suspension (Fig. 9.25f, g).
Pearly Freshwater Mussels
  none
Pacific Marine Bivalves
  Fragment of Venus clam (*Chione* [= *Anomalocardia*] *subrugosa*), 16 × 11 mm.
Pacific Marine Univalves
  Beachworn shell of an unidentified gastropod, 15 × 10 mm (Fig. 9.26h).

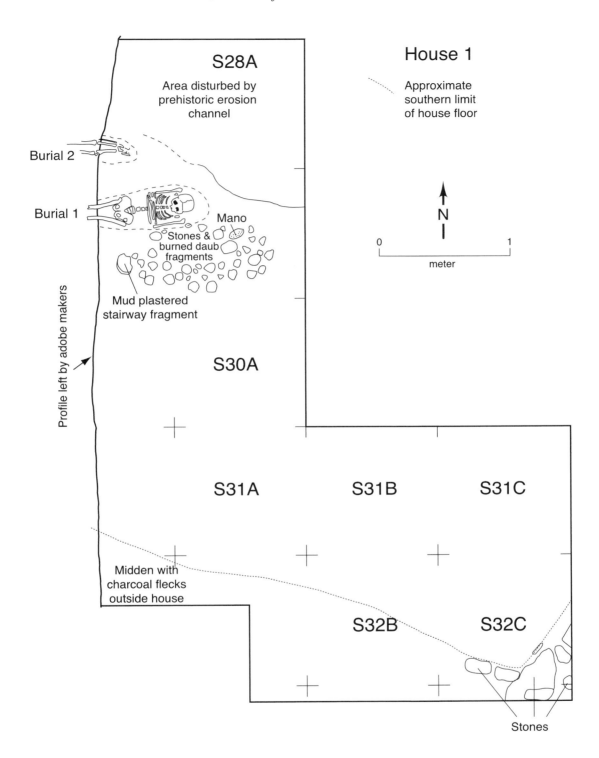

Figure 9.25. Plan of House 1, showing square designations, intrusive burials, and disturbed areas.

Mica

Lump of mica schist, 2.2 × 2.0 × 1.0 cm (Fig. 9.26*i*). This piece of raw material may have been brought back when villagers traveled to the western piedmont to get mica.

Two disintegrating pieces of mica, each weighing less than 0.5 g.

Figurines

Some 12 fragments of small solid figurines were associated with House 1. They have been described, and their locations on the floor indicated, by Marcus (1998a:115 and Fig. 11.10).

Imported Marine Fish

Large pectoral spine of marine catfish, too broken for species identification (Fig. 9.26*j*).

Worked and polished vertebral spine of unidentified teleost, possibly for bloodletting (Fig. 9.26*k*).

Animal Bones

Large Mammals

white-tailed deer (*Odocoileus virginianus*)

1 R. distal radius

1 distal tibia?

Small Mammals

domestic dog (*Canis familiaris*)

1 fragment of canine tooth

1 cervical vertebra

eastern cottontail (*Sylvilagus floridanus*)

1 L. maxilla

1 L. proximal tibia

Mexican cottontail (*Sylvilagus cunicularius*)

1 R. innominate

unidentified cottontail (*Sylvilagus* sp.)

2 metatarsals

Reptiles

mud turtle (*Kinosternon integrum*)

2 costal scutes

Birds

unidentified bird, roughly the size of a coot

1 distal femur

Human

1 phalanx

Unidentified

30 small fragments, two of them burned

Insights from Artifact Plotting

The good news about House 1 was that we found the southeast corner of the residence, giving us a landmark with which to work (and a good idea of the house's orientation). The bad news was that that was about all we found in the way of landmarks.

Figures 9.27-9.29 give the locations of perforators/gravers, drills, worked shell, figurine fragments, mica, animal bones, and a possible obsidian projectile point on the house floor. The distribution of piece-plotted figurine parts (Fig. 9.28) is about what one would expect if the floor debris had been swept toward the south wall whenever the house was cleaned.

While shell working had clearly taken place in the house, the distribution of perforators/gravers and shell (Fig. 9.27) also looked like debris swept into the southeast corner. The faunal remains simply appeared to have been swept toward the south wall (Fig. 9.29). We suspect that we would have learned more about this house, had its north half not been disturbed by an erosion channel.

Burials 1 and 2

Burials 1 and 2 were interred in a pit intrusive through the floor of House 1 (Fig. 6.1, Chapter 6). They clearly postdated the abandonment of the house, but perhaps not by many years, since the pit seemed to be fully contained within stratigraphic Zone D.

Not much can be said about Burial 2, a 6-8 year old child, since modern adobe makers had removed all but its lower legs (Fig. 9.29). Burial 1, however, was complete from head to thighs. This was the skeleton of a young woman who had died between the age of 15 and 20 years (Hodges 1989:87). Both her burial position and cranial deformation were rare, perhaps even unique, for the San José phase (Fig. 9.30).

Most women of the San José phase were buried prone and fully extended. Burial 1 was fully extended and supine, with her arms folded across her chest and her head propped up. While some women of the San José, Guadalupe, and Rosario phases did show cranial deformation—presumably a sign of rank—that deformation was almost always of the tabular erect type (see, for example, Fig. 23.17*a* of Chapter 23). Burial 1, on the other hand, had deformation of the annular type, created by tying a band of some type around her head.

Our suspicion is that Burial 1 may have been a bride from another region, one where annular deformation and supine burial were more common. Such exchanges of brides, especially among important families, were typical of chiefly societies in the ethnographic record. At the time we excavated Burial 1, there were no techniques available to test this possibility. Now there are two: (1) DNA analysis, and (2) bone chemistry analysis, specifically the type now being used to determine whether Maya lords spent their youth in a region different from the one in which they later ruled (White et al. 2000). Perhaps in the future we will know where Burial 1 came from.

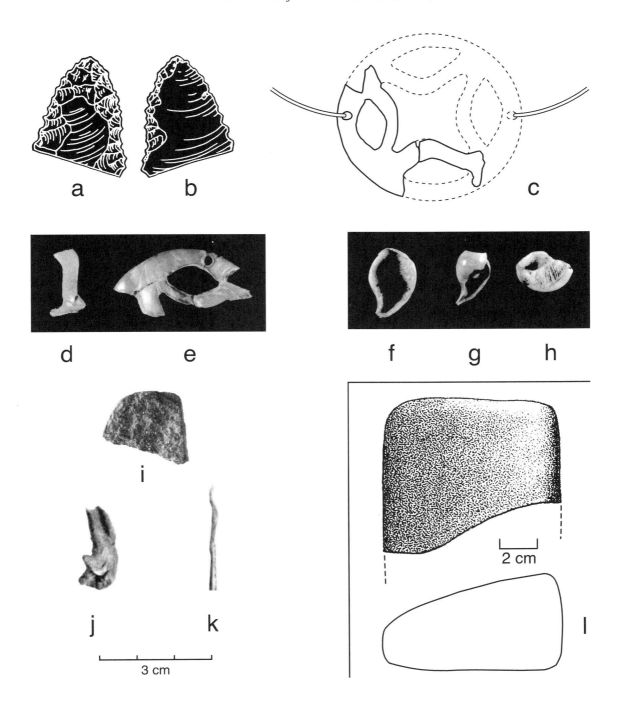

Figure 9.26. Objects from House 1. *a, b,* two sides of an obsidian biface, possibly the tip of a projectile point. *c,* artist's reconstruction of complex pearl oyster(?) pendant from Squares S31B and S32B. *d, e,* fragments of pendant shown in *c. f, g,* land snails modified for suspension. *h,* beachworn gastropod. *i,* lump of mica schist. *j,* broken pectoral spine of marine catfish. *k,* polished vertebral spine of unidentified teleost. *l,* fragment of mano with airfoil cross-section (note that scale differs from that of all other objects).

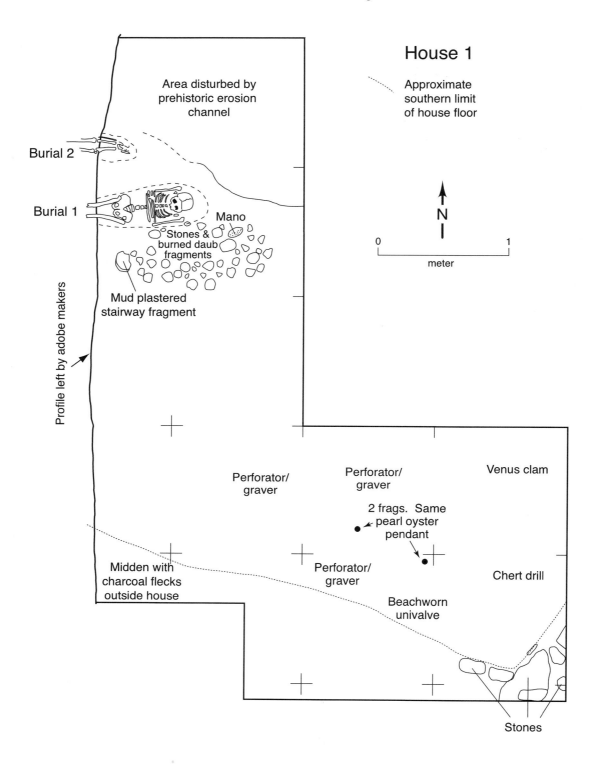

Figure 9.27. Plan of House 1, showing the distribution of items possibly associated with shell working.

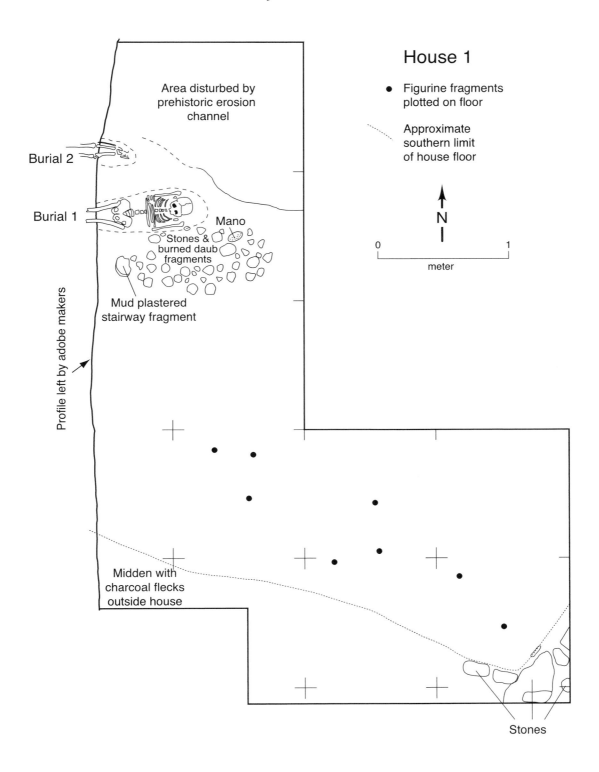

Figure 9.28. Plan of House 1, showing the locations of piece-plotted figurine fragments.

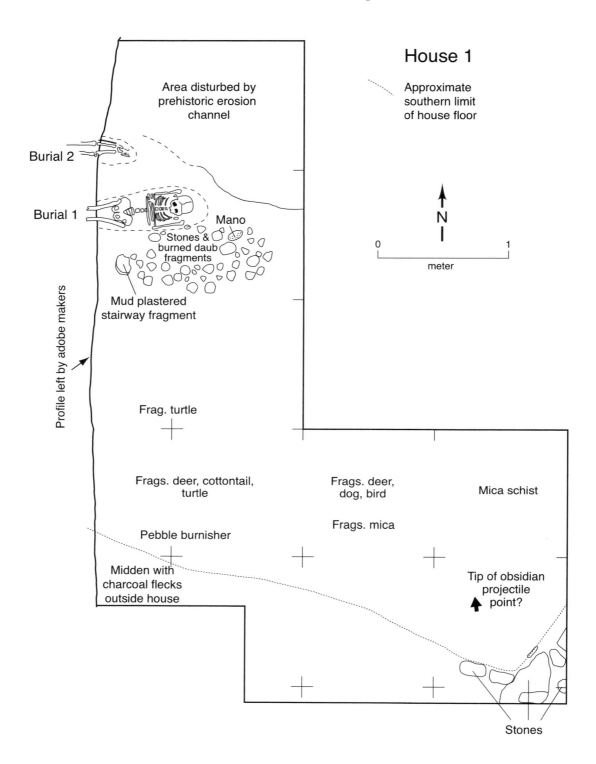

Figure 9.29. Plan of House 1, showing the distribution of miscellaneous items of obsidian, mica, stone, and bone.

Figure 9.30. Burial 1 of San José Mogote, intrusive through the floor of House 1, Area C. The skeleton is that of a young woman who died between 15 and 20 years of age. Both her burial position (supine, with arms folded and head propped up) and her annular skull deformation are atypical for San José phase burials. She could be a bride from another region or ethnic group.

House 10

The floor of House 10 was first detected in the profile of Squares S12A-S13A and later traced into Squares S10B through S13B. We suspect that House 10's original orientation was north-south, but cannot be sure. It was a frustrating house to work on, since parts of it had been disturbed by intrusive features.

Daub

Square S13B produced four lumps of daub, three with cane impressions and one with a layer of whitewashed plaster 1 mm thick. In the Munsell system, the color of the plaster would have been "light grayish brown" (10 YR 6/2). Elsewhere on the house floor we found three more lumps of daub, two with whitewashed plaster classifiable as "pink" (7.5 YR 7/4).

Ceramics

Some 93 sherds were recovered from House 10. They have been described by Flannery and Marcus (1994: Table 14.2).

Chipped Stone

Chert (67%)
    flake cores: 4 (Fig. 9.31*a*)
    flake perforator/graver: 1 (Fig. 9.31*b*)

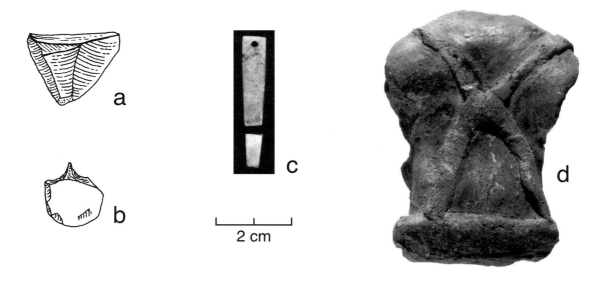

Figure 9.31. Artifacts from House 10. *a*, small chert flake core. *b*, flake perforator/graver. *c*, elongated, tapering ornament of pearl oyster(?), perforated for suspension. *d*, torso of figurine, male, wearing a heavy belt and suspenders that may represent ballplaying gear.

retouched flake: 1
utilized flakes: 2
flakes, not utilized: 12
Obsidian (27%)
    prismatic blade fragment, utilized: 1
    prismatic blade fragment, no sign of use: 1
    utilized flakes: 4
    flakes, not utilized: 2
Other (7%)
    quartz fragments: 1
    igneous flakes: 1

Comment: Pires-Ferreira (1975) has determined that both prismatic obsidian blades came from the source near Otumba, Basin of Mexico.

Shell

Ornament

    Elongated, tapering ornament of pearl oyster(?), perforated for suspension; broken into two pieces, tip missing. The ornament would originally have been slightly more than 34 mm long, 6 mm wide at its upper end, and 1 mm thick. The hole is 1 mm in diameter and drilled from one side only (Fig. 9.31*c*).

Figurines

Three fragments of small solid figurines were found on the House 10 floor. They have been described and illustrated by Marcus (1998a:115 and Fig. 11.11). The most interesting is a fragment of male torso, wearing heavy suspenders of the type sometimes used to hold up ballplaying gear (Fig. 9.31*d*).

Animal Bones

Two unidentified fragments, small to medium-sized mammal.

House 4

House 4 turned out to have three superimposed floors. These floors were first detected in the Master Profile between Squares S15 and S19. Examination of the profile showed that at some point, the lower two floors had been cut through by an irregular pit which we designated Feature 35 (see below). The original purpose of Feature 35 may have been to provide space for caching objects of some kind below the floor. It had to be filled in before the final floor of House 4 could be laid down.

We ended up exposing more of this house than any other in Area C. We found the northern and southern limits, which suggested that the house was roughly 7 m long north-south (Fig. 9.32). By expanding into the S14 row of squares, we also reached the eastern limit of the house in S14D-S14E. The west side of the house had been removed by modern adobe makers prior to our arrival, but we estimate that the house had been at least 4 m wide east-west. To the north of the house, we exposed roughly six square meters of its dooryard by opening up Squares S10A-S10B, S11A-S11B, S12A-S12B, and S13A-S13B.

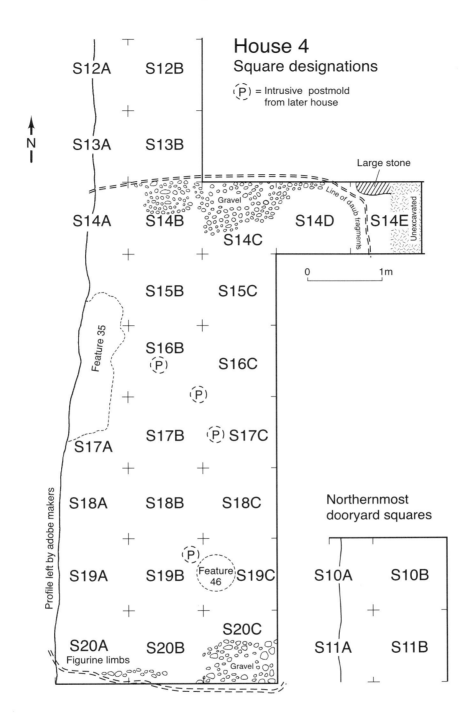

Figure 9.32. Plan of House 4, showing square designations, lines of daub, and intrusive postmolds and features.

Each of House 4's floors consisted of a packed clay layer with the usual coating of river sand. Along the northern and southern limits of the most recent floor, we found fallen daub fragments and substantial quantities of gravel; it is possible that this gravel had been used to fill hollows worn in the previous floor, leveling it for the next surfacing. In two places, one or more of the superimposed floors had been disturbed by intrusive features (see below), but these were clear enough so that we could work around them. We only piece-plotted artifacts on the uppermost or final floor, since the earlier floors seem to have been swept before the new layer of clay was laid down.

There were hints that the family occupying House 4 was of relatively high rank. Among these hints were the house's larger-than-average size; its high access to pearl oyster for ornaments; its higher-than-average access to obsidian nodules; and evidence that it may have hosted a feast at which at least five dogs were eaten (see "Animal Bones," below).

In addition to the figurine fragments in the house, we recovered a miniature four-legged stool (see "Figurines"). Scaled down to a size appropriate for a seated figurine, this stool may be a tiny symbol of rank. Sixteenth-century chiefs in parts of Central America had their personal stools carried wherever they went (see, for example, Lothrop 1937). In addition, Formative sites in Chiapas have produced figurines of costumed individuals seated on similar stools (Lesure 1999). It could be that some highly ranked ancestors of the House 4 family, when represented by figurines, required such stools.

In the process of excavating the final floor of House 4, we had to work carefully around four postmolds and a truncated conical pit, Feature 46, which were intrusive from a later house (Fig. 9.32). We never found the house from which the pit and postmolds came. This experience reinforced our suspicion that the houses we found in each area were never more than a fraction of those built.

Radiocarbon Date

Carbonized reeds from the floor of House 4 yielded a date of 2950 ± 40 B.P., or roughly 1000 b.c. (Beta-179080). The calibrated two-sigma range for this date would be 1290-1020 B.C.

Daub

The lumps of daub along the north wall of the house included two with cane impressions and three with surviving whitewashed plaster. In the Munsell system, the color of the plaster ranged from "pink" (7.5YR 7/4) to "very pale brown" (10 YR 7/3 to 10 YR 8/3).

The sample of daub from the south wall of the house was even larger, and included one fragment bearing the impression of a bundle of canes and the rope with which it was tied. The canes ranged in diameter from 0.7 to 1.0 cm. Daub tended to be 2.5 cm thick next to the bundles of canes, and 3.7 cm thick at the gaps between bundles. One sample of daub had whitewashed plaster 1 mm thick, in the "pink" color range (7.5 YR 8/4). Ten more lumps (several of them with cane impressions) bore two superimposed layers of plaster, totaling 2.5 mm in thickness; this plaster was "dark brown" (7.5 YR 3/2), suggesting that it had been slightly burned. The bulk of the evidence, however, did not suggest that House 4 had been destroyed by fire.

Ceramics

Some 770 sherds were found in association with the final floor of House 4. They have been described by Flannery and Marcus (1994: Table 14.2).

Chipped Stone

The collection of chipped stone from the final floor of House 4 totaled 527 pieces. Several items are worthy of mention. The collection included a large chert biface with a concave base, almost identical to those produced in quantity in House 16/17 of Area B (see Chapter 18). We found no evidence of actual biface-working in House 4, however. This strengthened our suspicion that such bifaces were created only by certain families, and the finished products distributed to their neighbors. House 4 also yielded the midsection of a projectile point, a rare artifact in the San José phase.

Finally, House 4 produced 11 small obsidian-nodule flake cores or fragments thereof. Such nodules were suitable for flake production, but not for making prismatic blades. It would be interesting to know from which obsidian source the nodules came, but unfortunately Pires-Ferreira's time and funding ran out before she could obtain the necessary neutron activation data. By superficial inspection, the nodules resemble those from the Guadalupe Victoria source near the Puebla-Veracruz border. Those nodules are generally too small to be chipped into prismatic blades (Pires-Ferreira 1975).

We collected additional chipped stone from the dooryard north of House 4. This chipped stone, and other artifacts from the dooryard, have not been included in our counts from the house, since it was not clear with which of the three superimposed floors they might have been associated.

Chert (74%)
  flake cores: 23 (Fig. 9.33a)
  core scrapers: 4
  core perforator: 1 (Fig. 9.33c)
  large lanceolate biface, concave base: 1 (Fig. 9.33i)
  projectile point midsection: 1 (Fig. 9.33b)
  flake spokeshaves: 2
  flake perforators/gravers: 18 (Fig. 9.33d-h)
  burins: 2
  denticulate scraper: 1
  scrapers: 3
  spurred scraper: 1
  wedge: 1
  retouched flakes: 12 (Fig. 9.33j)
  utilized flakes: 59
  flakes, not utilized: 259

Obsidian (23%)

Comment: some 120 pieces of obsidian were found in House 4. This is an unusually large amount, and undoubtedly results from the fact that, as mentioned above, this household was able to obtain quite a few nodules for flake making. The obsidian from House 4 was removed for study by Pires-Ferreira, whose counts are given below.

nodule flake cores, or fragments thereof: 11

prismatic blade fragments, utilized: 31

prismatic blade fragments, no sign of use: 5

utilized flakes: 34

flakes, not utilized: 39

Other (4%)

quartz flake: 1

quartz fragments: 2

retouched igneous flake: 1

igneous flakes, utilized: 2

igneous flakes, not utilized: 13

Ground Stone

Small fragment of discoidal one-hand mano, ignimbrite.

Small fragment of loaf-shaped two-hand mano with airfoil cross-section, recrystallized rock.

Midsection of two-hand mano with lenticular cross-section, fine-grained ignimbrite. The fragment is 13 cm long, 9.5 cm wide, and 4.2 cm thick (Fig. 9.34*a*).

Fragment of slab metate, vesicular basalt, 5 × 4 × 2.5 cm.

Fragment of slab metate, fine-grained ignimbrite, 5 × 4 × 2.8 cm.

One-third of a basin-shaped metate, metamorphic rock, 27 × 22 × 5 cm (Fig. 9.35).

Fragment of lipped metate, vesicular basalt, 7.5 × 6.5 × 3 cm (Fig. 9.34*b*).

Nondescript metate fragment, metamorphic rock, 7 × 3.5 × 4.5 cm.

Fragment of cobble mortar, metamorphic rock, 5 × 6 × 4.5 cm (Fig. 9.36*a*). This cobble had a circular hole, 2.5 cm in diameter, pecked into the upper surface to provide a grinding socket. A similar hole was started, but not completed, on the under surface.

Grooved rubbing stone, fine-grained pink sedimentary rock, 6 × 5 × 2.5 cm (Fig. 9.34*c*; Fig. 9.36*b*). This squarish stone has a groove on one edge which is 1 cm wide in the middle, but narrows at both ends. It looks like the type of tool that could be used to sharpen bone awls and needles; it is lightweight and fits easily in the hand.

Flake broken off a celt of fine-grained, dark green metamorphic rock.

Spherical pounder or hammerstone of Matadamas limestone, 7.5-8 cm in diameter (Fig. 9.34*d*).

Spherical pounder or hammerstone, broken in half, with the flat surface then used for polishing; original diameter 6-7 cm (Fig. 9.34*e*).

Small pounder or hammerstone of sedimentary rock, 3 cm in diameter (Fig. 9.36*c*).

Pottery-burnishing pebble, quartz, 4 cm long, 2.5 cm in diameter (Fig. 9.36*d*).

Small fragment of pottery-burnishing pebble.

(Additional ground stone items were found in the dooryard north of House 4, but are not included in our house counts because it was not clear with which of the three floors they might have been associated.)

Bone Tools

Deer antler tool, possibly an awl or pressure flaker, 9 cm long (Fig. 9.36*e*).

Fragment of antler tine tool, possibly an awl or pressure flaker, 3 cm long (Fig. 9.36*f*).

Fragment of antler tine tool, fire-hardened, chipped in such a way as to suggest it may have been a pressure flaker, 2.4 cm long (Fig. 9.36*g*).

Fragment of deer bone awl or *piscador*, 2.5 cm long. This is exactly the kind of bone tool that might have been sharpened with the grooved rubbing stone described above (see "Ground Stone").

Sliver of worked deer ulna, 7.5 cm long.

Sewing needle, incomplete, 4 cm long, lozenge-shaped (3 × 1 mm) in cross-section (Fig. 9.36*h*). Because one end is missing, we cannot determine whether or not it had an eye.

Possible basketry needle fragment, 1 cm long.

Deer antler bead, 15 mm long, 7 mm in diameter; this might have been a tubular element for a necklace (Fig. 9.36*i*).

Shell

Ornaments

Fragment of broken ornament, pearl oyster(?), 20 × 17 × 1 mm. The ornament appears to have been rectangular originally, and has two parallel grooves crossing it (Fig. 9.37*a*).

Fragment of circular ornament, pearl oyster(?), 16 × 7 × 1 mm (Fig. 9.37*b*).

Slightly beachworn ark shell, *Anadara incongrua,* found just below the floor in Square S20A. It has a hole cut into it for suspension; the edges of the hole have been ground smooth (Fig. 9.37*c*).

Pearly Freshwater Mussels

Fragment of mussel, possibly *Actinonaias* sp., 13 × 9 × 1 mm.

Fragment of mussel, possibly *Barynaias* sp., 16 × 7 × 1 mm.

Fragment of mussel, possibly *Barynaias* sp., 10 × 9 × 1.5 mm.

Pacific Marine Bivalves

Hinge section from valve of pearl oyster, *Pinctada mazatlanica,* 45 × 15 × 10 mm; manufacturing waste (Fig. 9.37*d*).

Piece of pearl oyster, broken into three fragments: (1) 15
× 15 × 1 mm; (2) 10 × 7 × 1 mm; (3) 14 × 6 × 1 mm;
manufacturing waste (Fig. 9.37*e*, *f*).

Seventeen fragments of shell-working debris, all from the
same pearl oyster valve; they can be refitted to form a
piece 55 × 15 × 10 mm, evidently manufacturing waste
(Fig. 9.37*h-l*).

Fragment of pearl oyster, 10 × 10 × 2 mm.

Two pieces of pearl oyster: (1) 25 × 19 × 3 mm, and cut on
three edges (Fig. 9.37*g*); (2) 15 × 15 × 1 mm.

Two pieces of pearl oyster, both cut on 1-2 edges: (1) 19
× 16 × 2 mm; (2) 13 × 16 × 2 mm.

Three pieces of pearl oyster, possibly from the same valve:
(1) 27 × 11 × 3 mm; (2) 19 × 10 × 3 mm; (3) 19 × 12
× 3 mm; manufacturing waste.

Piece of pearl oyster, 18 × 13 × 2 mm.

Piece of pearl oyster, 12 × 9 × 1 mm.

Valve of pearl oyster broken into three pieces, the largest
of which is 15 × 8 × 1 mm.

Fragment of pearl oyster, 10 × 8 × 1 mm.

Pacific Marine Univalves

Worn nerite (*Neritina latissima* [= *cassiculum*]), diameter
8 mm (Fig. 9.37*q*).

Complete horn shell (*Cerithium stercusmuscarum*), length
22 mm (Fig. 9.37*n*).

Two complete horn shells (*Cerithidea* cf. *hegewischii*), one
17 cm long, and the other 15 cm long (Fig. 9.37*o*).

Piece cut from the shell of a conch, possibly *Strombus
galeatus*, 38 × 15 × 2.5 mm (Fig. 9.37*m*). Conch shell
trumpets were sometimes carved with decorative motifs before being put into use; this fragment may have
resulted from such carving.

Dove shell, *Anachis* sp., perforated for suspension, diameter 8 mm (Fig. 9.37*p*).

Mica

fragment of white mica, weighing less than 1 g
fragment of mica, cut on two edges, less than 1 g
2 small fragments, less than 1 g total
small piece of mica schist
(1 other small piece of mica found in the dooryard east of
the house)

Figurines

Some 76 figurine fragments were found in association with
House 4; 41 of these were piece-plotted *in situ*. Most of the un-
plotted fragments came from a pile of debris swept up against
the south wall of the house. All figurine fragments have been
described and illustrated by Marcus (1998a:115-17 and Figs.
11.12-11.16). The collection of figurines from House 4 was one
of the most extensive and varied from any house in Area C. In
addition to the figurines, we found the miniature four-legged
stool already described above (Fig. 9.36*j*).

Stone Ornaments

Disk bead of jadeite(?) 8 mm in diameter, with a hole 3 mm
in diameter drilled through the center (Fig. 9.38*b*).

Irregular stone bead of unknown raw material, diameter 12
mm, with a hole 2.5 mm in diameter drilled through the
center; possibly unfinished (Fig. 9.38*a*).

Fragment from broken stone bead, unknown raw material, 15
× 16 × 6 mm (Fig. 9.38*c*).

Imported Bird and Reptile Products

Distal tibiotarsus and second phalanx from a wild turkey
(*Meleagris gallopavo*). Since wild turkey has never been
reported from the Valley of Oaxaca, these fragments
may have come from a dried bird, imported from Central
Mexico for its feathers.

Carapace fragment from a large river turtle, possibly *Dermatemys* sp.; perhaps a piece of a turtle shell drum imported
from the Gulf Coast.

Imported Marine Fish

thoracic vertebra of the snapper family, Lutjanidae (Fig.
9.38*d*)
fragment of vertebra, unidentified fish (Fig. 9.38*e*)
polished dorsal spine of unidentified fish (Fig. 9.38*f*)
tip of polished dorsal spine, unidentified fish (Fig. 9.38*g*)
tip of fish vertebral spine (Fig. 9.38*h*)

Imported Marine Invertebrate?

A possible cranial fragment was found.

Animal Bones

An unusually large sample of animal bones was found in
House 4, so many that we doubt that the house was swept prior
to abandonment. To be sure, a great deal of the material consisted
of small elements like teeth, which would not have taken up a
lot of room. Much of the bone debris came from four squares
near the southern limit of the house (S19B, S19C, S20B, S20C).
Included in House 4 were the remains of at least five dogs, three
gophers, and six cottontails. Perhaps most interesting was the
evidence, discussed below, that the five dogs might have been
butchered for a feast of some kind.

Large Mammals
white-tailed deer (*Odocoileus virginianus*)
1 burned and broken antler tine
2 fragments of teeth
1 fragment of thoracic vertebra
1 vertebral epiphysis
1 fragment of L. scapula, burned
1 distal humerus
1 fragment of L. ulna, burned
1 L. distal tibia epiphysis, unfused
1 distal epiphysis of metapodial
Small Mammals
domestic dog (*Canis familiaris*)*

1 fragment of sagittal crest from skull
1 fragment of temporal bone from skull
1 petrous bone
1 fragment of basioccipital from skull
1 R. and 1 L. occipital condyles
1 R. premaxilla
1 distal R. mandible fragment (with the alveolus for the
    first premolar present)
8 loose incisors
1 deciduous incisor
2 canine teeth
2 upper R. third premolars
1 upper L. fourth premolar
1 worn upper R. first molar
1 upper L. first molar
1 unerupted upper R. first molar
1 upper L. second molar
1 unerupted lower R. fourth premolar
1 lower R. deciduous premolar
2 lower L. deciduous premolars
1 lower L. first molar
1 unerupted lower L. first molar
1 lower R. deciduous molar
1 unerupted lower R. second molar
1 fragment of premolar
1 fragment of molar
1 fragment of cheek tooth
3 atlas vertebrae
1 fragment of L. radius
1 R. and 1 L. calcaneum
1 R. ulnar carpal
3 R. fourth metcarpals
1 L. third metacarpal
2 L. fourth metatarsals
1 distal metapodial fragment
1 first phalanx
2 second phalanges
2 third phalanges
2 phalanx fragments
pocket gopher (*Orthogeomys grandis*)
    5 upper incisors from three different gophers
    2 lower R. and 1 lower L. incisors
    4 loose cheek teeth

1 fragment of maxilla and palate
1 L. and 1 R. humerus
1 unfused L. radius
jackrabbit (*Lepus mexicanus*)
    1 L. zygomatic arch and part of maxilla
    1 loose cheek tooth
    1 L. ulna
    1 metapodial
eastern cottontail (*Sylvilagus floridanus*)
    1 R. glenoid
    1 R. mandible
    1 lower incisor
    1 L. proximal scapula
    1 R. and 1 L. proximal femur
    2 L. proximal tibiae from two cottontails
    1 L. metatarsal
    1 R. calcaneum
    1 R. astragalus
Mexican cottontail (*Sylvilagus cunicularius*)
    1 L. mandible
    1 loose cheek tooth
    1 atlas vertebra
    1 R. proximal scapula
    1 L. radius
    1 R. distal radius
    2 R. ulnae (one burned) from two cottontails
    1 L. innominate
    1 distal femur
    1 L. proximal tibia
    1 L. fifth metatarsal
    1 R. calcaneum
unidentified cottontails (*Sylvilagus spp.*)
    1 zygomatic arch
    1 petrous
    1 R. premaxilla
    1 upper incisor
    4 loose cheek teeth
    1 R. mandible fragment
    1 L. proximal scapula
    1 R. ulna
    1 lumbar vertebra
    2 L. proximal tibiae from two cottontails
    1 R. calcaneum

Comment: House 4 produced the remains of at least five individual dogs, three adults and two juveniles. The elements left behind on the floor were almost entirely restricted to skull fragments, teeth, and feet, with virtually no major limb bones present. The evidence indicated that the dogs had been killed by having their skulls cracked; next the heads and feet had been removed, after which all the major edible parts of the carcass had been transported elsewhere.

The remains we found suggested that the occupants of House 4 might have hosted a large meal, removing the heads and feet in the house and taking most of the carcass outside, perhaps to be cooked in a dooryard earth oven. The data from House 4 remind us that Feature 99 at the site of Tierras Largas—a Guadalupe phase bell-shaped pit—contained the remains from a feast at which more than 50 kg of dog meat were served (Marcus and Flannery 1996:116). The amount of dog meat represented by the House 4 remains would be comparable. The dogs were relatively large, and none showed the congenital premolar loss discussed in Chapter 4. While both samples included some cranial elements, House 4 seemed mainly to have the less-desirable body parts, trimmed from the dogs *before* cooking, while Feature 99 contained meat-bearing bones discarded *after* the feast (Fig. 9.39).

ring-tailed cat (*Bassariscus astutus*)
  1 lower R. premolar
Reptiles
 mud turtle (*Kinosternon integrum*)
  1 fragment of costal plate
  1 fragment of plastron
 small lizards
  2 broken dentaries
Amphibians
 toad (*Bufo sp.*)
  1 vertebra
  1 pelvic girdle
  1 long bone fragment
Birds
 band-tailed pigeon, *Columba fasciata*(?)
  1 fragment of tibiotarsus
 unidentified quail
  1 fragment of tibiotarsus
 unidentified medium-sized bird
  1 fragment of humerus
 unidentified songbird, possibly Thraupid or Emberizid
  1 tibiotarsus (this small bird may have been killed for its feathers)
Human
 18 small skull fragments
 3 proximal metatarsals
 1 talus
Unidentified
 427 small fragments which could be from deer, dog, rabbit, or human; 24 are burned
 Comment: most fragments are concentrated in the south end of the house

Feature 35

Feature 35 was a shallow, irregular pit, intrusive through the first two floors of House 4, but covered by the third and final floor. It is not clear why the pit was made (possibly to cache something?). Eventually, it had to be filled in order to level the area for the laying down of the final floor (Fig. 9.38*i*).

Ceramics

The sherds from Feature 35 have been described by Flannery and Marcus (1994:317). In our expanded chronology, they are assigned to Middle San José.

Shell

The fill of Feature 35 produced one fragment of pearl oyster(?) ornament, 12 × 10 × 1 mm, with two holes drilled in it for suspension; it evidently broke during the drilling of the second hole (Fig. 9.38*j*). There was also a fragment of pearl oyster raw material measuring 14 × 5 × 1 mm, as well as an unidentified marine univalve (Fig. 9.38*k*). The broken ornament and the manufacturing waste suggest that the working of pearl oyster in

House 4 was a long-standing activity, one that had been going on before the laying down of the final house floor.

Mica

1 disintegrating flake of brown mica, 15 × 5 mm
1 flake of white mica weighing less than 0.1 g, 15 × 10 mm

Figurine

One solid unslipped figurine limb.

Imported Marine Fish

One fragment of unidentified fish vertebra (Fig. 9.40*a*).

Animal Bones (Fig. 9.40 b-i)

Large Mammals
 white-tailed deer (*Odocoileus virginianus*)
  1 astragalus
Small Mammals
 domestic dog (*Canis familiaris*)
  1 large fragment of L. maxilla and premaxilla
  1 L. upper molar (from a second dog)
  1 carbonized metapodial
 jackrabbit (*Lepus mexicanus*)
  1 proximal radius
 eastern cottontail (*Sylvilagus floridanus*)
  proximal and distal fragments of 1 L. humerus
 Mexican cottontail (*Sylvilagus cunicularius*)
  1 calcaneum
 opossum (*Didelphis marsupialis*)
  1 complete R. mandible
Reptiles
 mud turtle (*Kinosternon integrum*)
  6 scutes from carapace, including a marginal scute

Feature 46

Feature 46 was a pit from a later house, intrusive through the floor of House 4 (Fig. 9.38*L*). Judging by its shape, this pit was dug to accommodate a large outleaned-wall bowl, perhaps sunk into the ground to serve as a permanent basin. Feature 46 was 50 cm in diameter at the rim and tapered to 38 cm in diameter at the base; its depth was 25 cm. Eventually, the vessel had been removed and the cavity filled with sand.

Feature 39

Feature 39 was a basin-shaped pit in Squares S13A and S13B, stratigraphically below House 4 but possibly related to its original floor. The pit was 35 cm deep, 79 cm in diameter at the rim, and 50-55 cm in diameter at the base (Fig. 9.38*L*). Its contents were mostly sand and crushed bedrock, suggesting that the pit may have been filled in with leftover construction material. Included in Feature 39 was a Leandro Gray body sherd bearing the impression of a corncob.

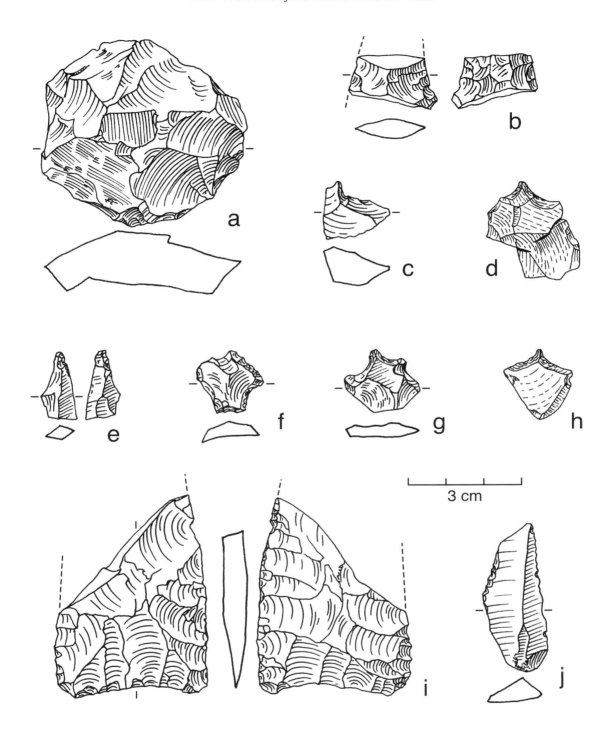

Figure 9.33 Chert tools from House 4. *a*, flake core. *b*, projectile point midsection (two views). *c*, core perforator. *d-h*, flake perforators/gravers (*g* has multiple nipples). *i*, large lanceolate biface with concave base (two views). *j*, retouched flake.

Insights from Artifact Plotting

Figures 9.41-9.47 show the distributions of chert cores and core scrapers, ground stone tools, bone awls and needles, flake perforators/gravers, shell, figurines, spokeshaves, ornaments, imported fauna, and other materials on the uppermost floor of House 4.

Some artifact categories were widely scattered across the house floor. Chert flake cores and core scrapers (Fig. 9.41) were two such categories. About all one can conclude is that their densities seem to increase as the scatter approaches the southeast corner of the house. This pattern could result from bulkier chert debris having been tossed toward the corner. Piece-plotted figurine fragments (Fig. 9.45) were also widely scattered, although a cluster of limbs had accumulated against the south wall of the house.

Fragments of manos, metates, and mortars (Fig. 9.42) were widely scattered as well, but in contrast to cores, their numbers do not increase as one approaches the southeast corner of the house. Many of the ground stone tool fragments were so small

that they could only have had a secondary use: as an expedient pounder, for example.

In the case of animal bones and bone tools (Figs. 9.43 and 9.47), the tendency for debris to accumulate in the southeast corner of the house is very clear. While exotic animal parts, such as wild turkey bones and marine fish spines, tended to be spread around the floor, the extensive debris from the butchering of the five dogs was concentrated in Squares S19 B-C and S20 B-C. Bone needles and antler awls/pressure flakers also had come to rest in the southeast corner. So did the grooved rubbing stone on which some bone tools had likely been sharpened.

Shell-working debris (Fig. 9.44) was particularly widespread on the House 4 floor. One could argue, in fact, that several episodes of shell working had taken place late in the history of the house, and that the debris had not been swept out before the house was abandoned. Reinforcing this argument is the fact that several clusters of pearl oyster debris (up to 17 items in one case) appeared to be relatively undisturbed, and featured numerous conjoining shell fragments (Fig. 9.37). Further strengthening

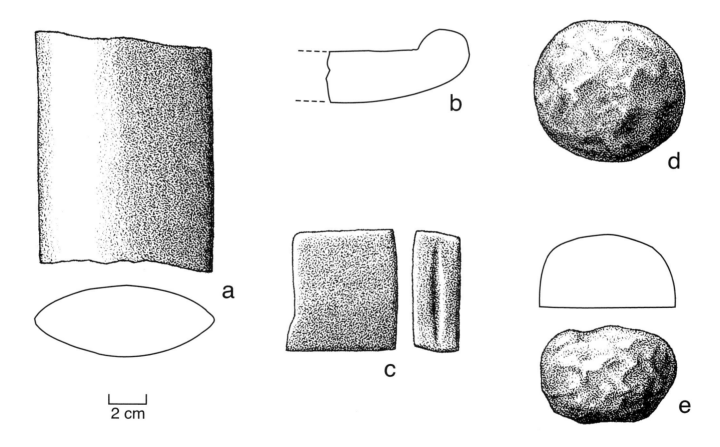

2 cm

Figure 9.34. Ground stone tools from House 4. *a*, midsection of mano with lenticular cross-section. *b*, cross-section of lipped metate fragment. *c*, side and front views of grooved rubbing stone. *d*, spherical pounder or hammerstone, limestone. *e*, spherical pounder or hammerstone, broken in half, with the flat surface used for polishing (top and side views).

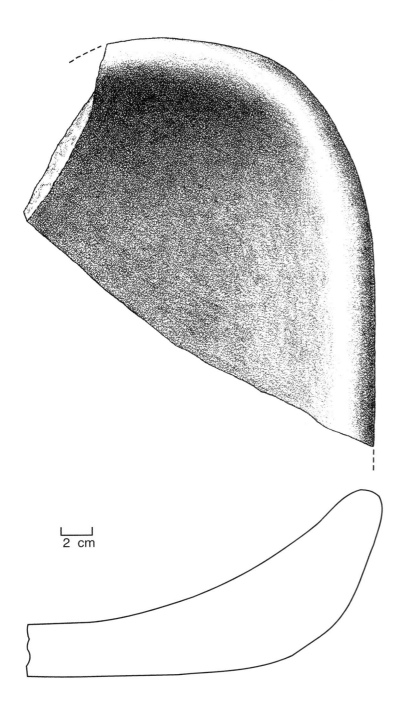

Figure 9.35. One-third of a basin-shaped metate from House 4, Square S14D.

2 cm

the argument was the fact that not a single perforator/graver or shell fragment showed up in the dooryard; that is, all evidence for shell working was confined to the house itself. That would almost certainly not have been the case had the house been swept before abandonment.

Several of the households we excavated taught us that even "final" artifact scatters are the end products of multiple episodes of activity. House 4 was one of those. Its awls and needles, dating to earlier episodes, had been tossed or swept into the southeast corner. Its perforators/gravers and shell fragments, dating to later episodes, appeared never to have been swept from the central floor. Without artifact plotting, we would never have been able to reconstruct this sequence of events.

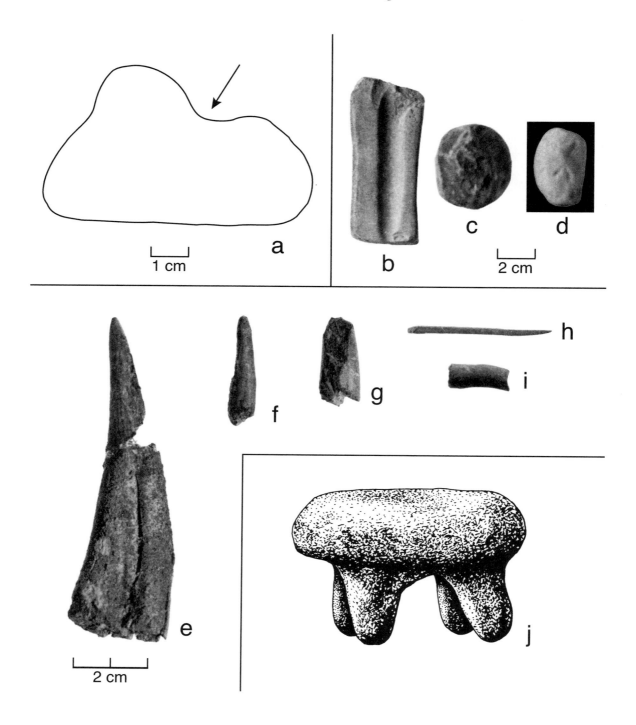

Figure 9.36. Objects from House 4. *a*, cross-section of cobble mortar (arrow indicates circular hole pecked into upper surface). *b*, grooved rubbing stone. *c*, small pounder or hammerstone. *d*, quartz pottery-burnishing pebble. *e*, deer antler awl or pressure flake. *f*, antler tine fragment, possibly part of an awl or pressure flaker. *g*, fragment of fire-hardened antler tine, possibly part of pressure flaker. *h*, incomplete bone sewing needle. *i*, tubular bead of deer antler. *j*, miniature pottery stool, 3 cm in diameter (drawn larger than actual size).

Figure 9.37. Shell from House 4. *a*, broken pearl oyster(?) ornament with two parallel grooves. *b*, fragment of circular pearl oyster(?) ornament. *c*, ark shell with cut and ground hole (found just below floor). *d*, hinge section from valve of pearl oyster. *e, f*, pearl oyster manufacturing waste. *g*, piece of pearl oyster cut on three edges. *h-l*, five pieces from the same large pearl oyster valve. *m*, piece cut from conch shell. *n*, horn shell (*C. stercusmuscarum*). *o*, horn shell (*C. hegewischii*). *p*, dove shell (*Anachis* sp.). *q*, worn nerite (*N. latissima*).

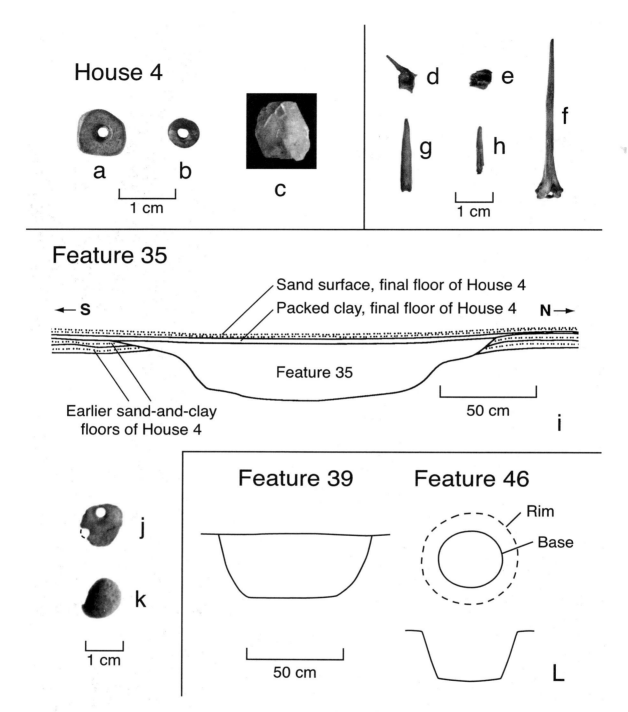

Figure 9.38. Objects from House 4 (*a-h*) and associated features (*i-k*). *a*, irregular stone bead, possibly unfinished. *b*, small disk bead of jadeite(?). *c*, fragment from broken stone bead. *d*, thoracic vertebra of snapper. *e*, vertebra fragment, unidentified fish. *f*, polished dorsal spine, unidentified fish. *g*, tip of polished dorsal spine, unidentified fish. *h*, tip of vertebral spine, unidentified fish. *i*, Feature 35. *j*, small pearl oyster(?) ornament which broke during the drilling of a second hole. *k*, unidentified marine univalve. *L*, cross-section of Feature 39; plan and cross-section of Feature 46.

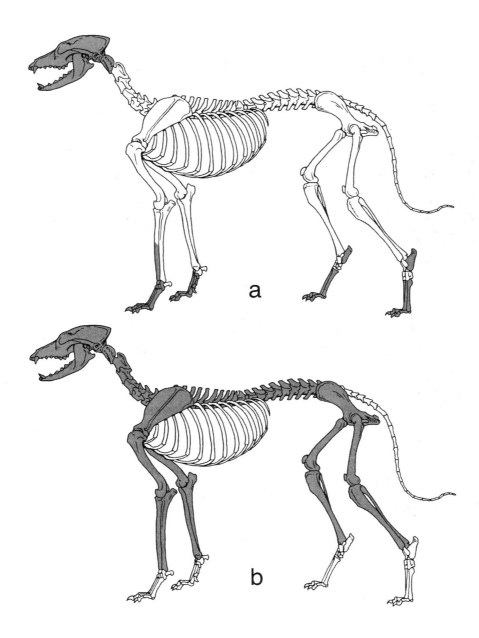

Figure 9.39. A comparison of the dog remains from House 4 of San José Mogote (*a*) and Feature 99 of the Tierras Largas site (*b*). The remains in House 4 came from at least five dogs, but consisted almost entirely of bones from the extremities (shaded). The remains in Feature 99 came from at least five dogs, and featured major meat-bearing bones (shaded). These two collections may reflect the "before" and "after" stages of feasting. Before cooking, the head and feet were trimmed off and left behind (*a*); after the meal, the meat-bearing bones were discarded in a pit (*b*).

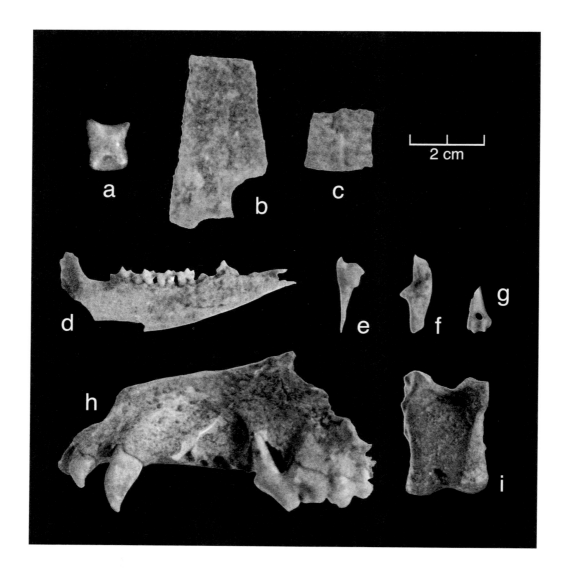

Figure 9.40. Faunal remains from Feature 35. *a*, fragment of marine fish vertebra. *b, c*, fragments of mud turtle carapace. *d*, mandible of opossum. *e*, distal tibia of jackrabbit. *f*, calcaneum of Mexican cottontail. *g*, distal humerus of eastern cottontail. *h*, skull fragment of domestic dog. *i*, astragalus of white-tailed deer.

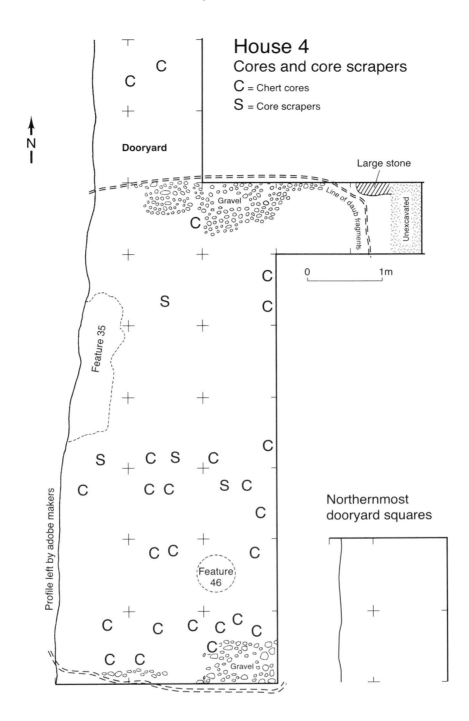

Figure 9.41. Plan of House 4, showing the distribution of chert cores and core scrapers.

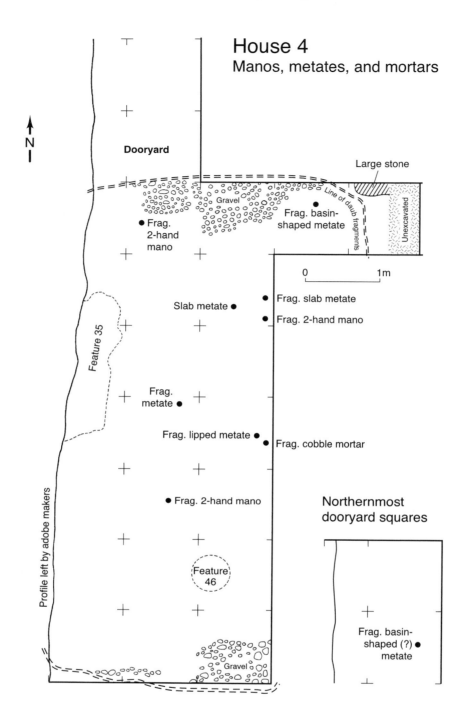

Figure 9.42. Plan of House 4, showing the location of utilitarian ground stone tools.

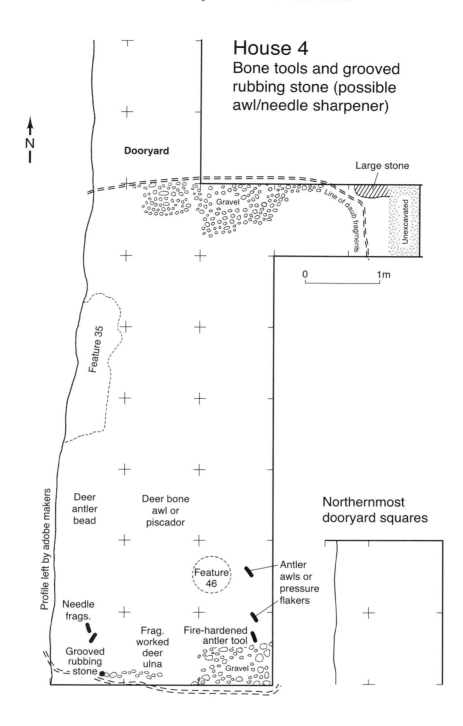

Figure 9.43. Plan of House 4, showing the distribution of bone tools (and a grooved rubbing stone possibly used to sharpen some of them).

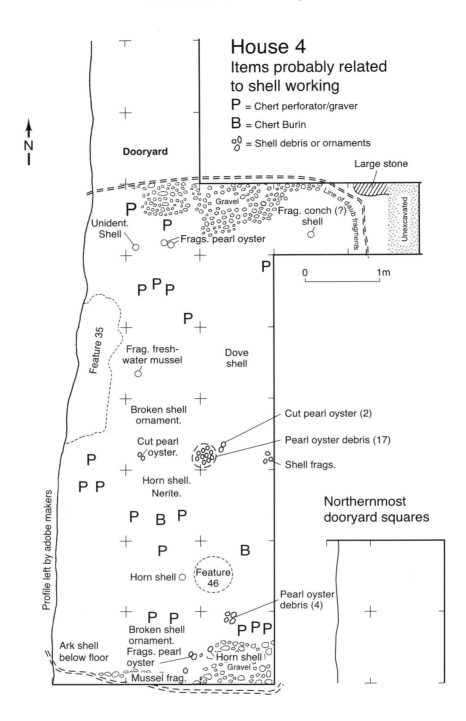

House 4
Items probably related
to shell working

P = Chert perforator/graver

B = Chert Burin

⚬ᵒ = Shell debris or ornaments

Dooryard

Large stone

Gravel

Line of daub fragments

Frag. conch (?) shell

Unexcavated

P

P

Unident. Shell

Frags. pearl oyster

P

0   1m

P P P

P

Feature 35

Frag. fresh-water mussel

Dove shell

Cut pearl oyster (2)

Broken shell ornament.

Pearl oyster debris (17)

Cut pearl oyster.

Shell frags.

P

Horn shell. Nerite.

P P

P B P

Northernmost dooryard squares

P

B

Horn shell

Feature 46

Pearl oyster debris (4)

P P

P P

Broken shell ornament.

Ark shell below floor

Frags. pearl oyster

Horn shell

Gravel

Mussel frag.

Profile left by adobe makers

Figure 9.44. Plan of House 4, showing the distribution of items probably related to shell working.

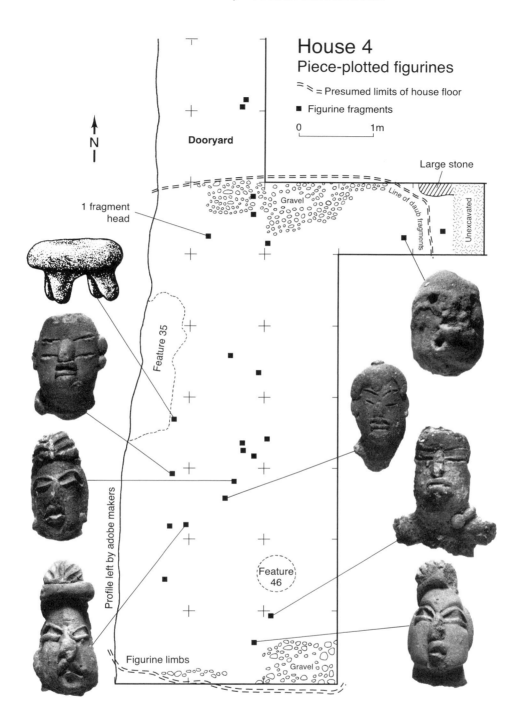

Figure 9.45. Plan of House 4, showing the locations of piece-plotted figurine fragments. Included is a miniature four-legged stool.

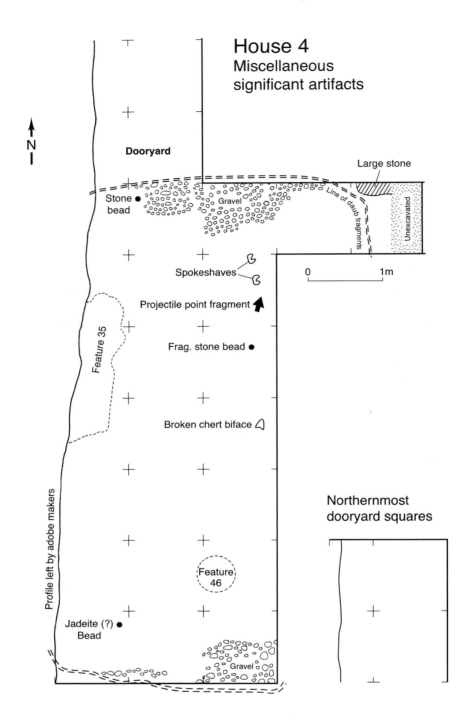

Figure 9.46. Plan of House 4, showing the locations of miscellaneous significant artifacts.

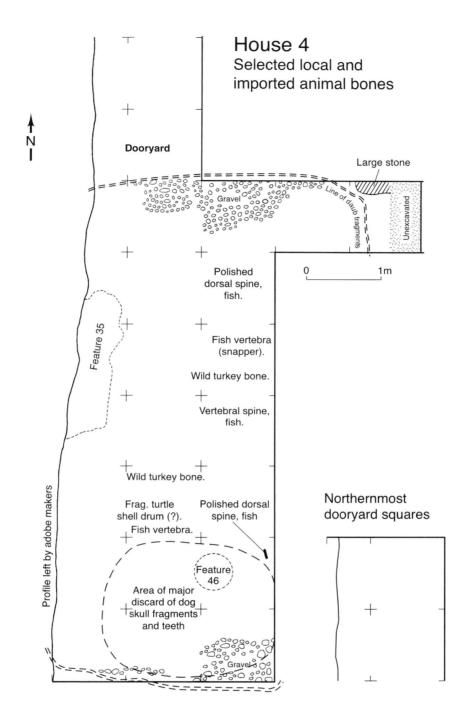

N

House 4
Selected local and
imported animal bones

Dooryard

Large stone

Gravel

Line of daub fragments

Unexcavated

0   1m

Polished
dorsal spine,
fish.

Feature 35

Fish vertebra
(snapper).

Wild turkey bone.

Vertebral spine,
fish.

Profile left by adobe makers

Wild turkey bone.

Frag. turtle
shell drum (?).
Fish vertebra.

Polished dorsal
spine, fish

Feature
46

Area of major
discard of dog
skull fragments
and teeth

Gravel

**Northernmost
dooryard squares**

Figure 9.47. Plan of House 4, showing the distribution of selected local and imported animal bones.

The Zone D2 Midden

As mentioned earlier, most of stratigraphic Zone D consisted of wattle-and-daub houses and the products of their decomposition. Below the floor of House 6, however, we found a facies of Zone D that appeared to be "midden debris from relatively low-status households" (Flannery and Marcus 1994:293). In our expanded chronology this midden facies, called Zone D2 because it lay in the lower part of its stratigraphic unit, would be assigned to the Middle San José phase.

Ceramics

Some 605 diagnostic sherds from Zone D2 have been described previously by Flannery and Marcus (1994: Table 13.1). Of these, 82% are San José phase diagnostics, and 14% belong to Tierras Largas types that lasted into San José times.

Chipped Stone

The small collection of chipped stone from Zone D2 was not considered worth including in Parry's detailed analysis.

Ground Stone

Fragment of loaf-shaped two-hand mano with planoconvex cross-section, vesicular basalt. Length of fragment, 11 cm; width, 9 cm; maximum thickness, 4.2 cm (Fig. 9.48*a*).

Fragment of loaf-shaped two-hand mano with airfoil cross-section. Length of fragment, 10 cm; width, 8.5 cm; average thickness, 4 cm (Fig. 9.48*b*).

Fragment of basin-shaped metate, fine-grained ignimbrite, 9 × 12 × 6.5 cm (Fig. 9.48*c*).

Complete muller, basalt. Length, 8.5; width, 4.5 cm; thickness, 3.2 cm (Fig. 9.49*a*).

Fragment of possible pestle, fine-grained metamorphic rock. Diameter, 4.1 cm.

Complete round-polled celt, dark chlorite schist. Length, 10.4 cm; average width, 4.6 cm (Fig. 9.49*b*).

Fragment of badly battered celt, fine-grained metamorphic rock. Length of fragment, 7 cm; width, 6 cm; thickness, 2.2 cm (Fig. 9.48*d*).

Possible celt polisher, planoconvex, with oval grinding surface; fine-grained metamorphic rock. Length, 7 cm; width, 3.5 cm; thickness, 4 cm (Fig. 9.48*e*).

Possible celt polisher, planoconvex, with irregularly shaped grinding surface, made from a chlorite schist(?) cobble. Grinding surface, 9 × 9 cm; thickness, 1.5 cm (Fig. 9.48*f*).

Possible stone reamer, tip broken. Length, 37 mm; diameter, 7 mm (Fig. 9.49*c*).

Possible stone reamer (or pendant), tip broken. Length, 55 mm; diameter, 6 mm (Fig. 9.49*d*).

Comment: This artifact is somewhat puzzling because it has a hole drilled partly through its upper end, as if for suspension; this suggests an attempt to facilitate wearing it around one's neck. However, the way the tip was broken suggests use as a working tool. We are undecided as to whether the unfinished perforation was an attempt to attach a string to a tool, or to convert it into a pendant.

Pottery burnishing stone, limestone or chert, 6 × 3 × 2 cm.

Pottery burnisher made on a chert pebble, 6 × 3 × 2.5 cm (Fig. 9.49*e*).

Pottery burnisher made on a chert pebble, 3 × 2.5 × 1.5 cm.

Bone Tools

Broken antler tine artifact, possibly a pressure flaker. Length of fragment, 5 cm (Fig. 9.49*f*).

Broken tip from a bone awl or *piscador*, probably of deer metapodial. Length of fragment, 3.9 cm (Fig. 9.49*g*).

Broken tip of spatula, probably made from deer long bone. Dimensions of fragment, 13 × 10 mm (Fig. 9.49*h*).

Shell

Ornaments

Pendant made from a valve of pearl oyster, shaped like the tongue of a shoe, with a notch on either side and two perforations for suspension near its upper edge; it has been crosshatched with a chert or obsidian graver (Fig. 9.49*i*). Its dimensions are 42 × 39 mm, and each perforation is 2 mm in diameter.

Rectangular plaque cut from a pearl oyster valve, 20 × 20 mm and 2 mm thick (Fig. 9.49*j*). Such a plaque could have been glued to a mask or composite ornament.

Elongated pendant made on an unidentified beachworn shell. Length, 33 mm; width, 13 mm; thickness, 4 mm. Perforation at upper end for suspension, 2 mm in diameter (Fig. 9.49*k*).

Plaque in the shape of a truncated triangle, pearl oyster, 33 × 20 mm (Fig. 9.50*a*).

Fragment of a ring-shaped pearl oyster ornament, possibly the holder for a circular magnetite mirror or some other object; the space allowed for the circular object would have been about 14 mm in diameter.

Fragment of narrow, rectangular pearl oyster pendant, 21 × 7 × 1 mm; perforation for suspension, 2 mm in diameter (Fig. 9.50*b*).

Rectangular plaque with rounded corners, appearing to be *Spondylus* shell, 16 × 17 × 3 mm (Fig. 9.50*c*).

Complete valve of marsh clam, *Neocyrena* (=*Polymesoda*) *radiata*, perforated for suspension (Fig. 9.50*d*).

Pearly Freshwater Mussels

Large piece of *Barynaias* valve, 37 × 20 × 1 mm (Fig. 9.50*e*).

Fragments of disintegrated *Barynaias* valve, unmeasurable.

Fragment from the hinge area of *Barynaias* valve, 20 × 18 × 1 mm.

Two fragments of freshwater mussel: (1) 16 × 18 × 1 mm; (2) 18 × 15 × 1 mm.

Pacific Marine Bivalves
Fragment of pearl oyster (*Pinctada mazatlanica*), manufacturing waste, 32 × 20 × 5 mm.
Hinge area of pearl oyster valve, manufacturing waste, 30 × 25 × 5 mm.
Entire hinge area of *Spondylus* valve, trimmed off during ornament manufacture, 50 × 30 mm (Fig. 9.50*h, i*).
Pacific Marine Univalves
Unmodified cowrie shell (*Cypraea* sp.), 25 mm long (Fig. 9.50*f*).
Unmodified turret shell (*Turritella* cf. *jewetti*), 35 mm long (Fig. 9.50*g*).

Iron Ore Specimens
Triangular fragment from a circular or oval magnetite mirror, 10 × 14 mm (Fig. 9.50*j*).
Lump of magnetite ore, 20 × 23 × 10 mm (Fig. 9.50*k*).
Lump of hematite ore, raw material for red pigment, 30 × 20 × 15 mm.

Stone Ornament
Odontoform pendant of green metamorphic rock that broke while being drilled. Length, 54 mm; diameter, 6 mm.

Carbonized Plants
17 kernels of maize (*Zea mays*)
many cupules from shattered maize cobs
3 stems of chile pepper (*Capsicum* sp.)

Animal Bones
Small Mammals
domestic dog (*Canis familiaris*)
1 L. zygomatic arch
1 L. maxilla
1 fragment of premaxilla
2 R. mandibles from adult dogs
1 mandible with unerupted teeth from a puppy
1 L. lower first molar
1 atlas
1 metapodial
pocket gopher (*Orthogeomys grandis*)
1 L. mandible (Fig. 9.50*L*)
spotted skunk (*Spilogale augustifrons*)
1 L. mandible
Human
1 skull fragment
Unidentified
5 splinters of mammal long bone

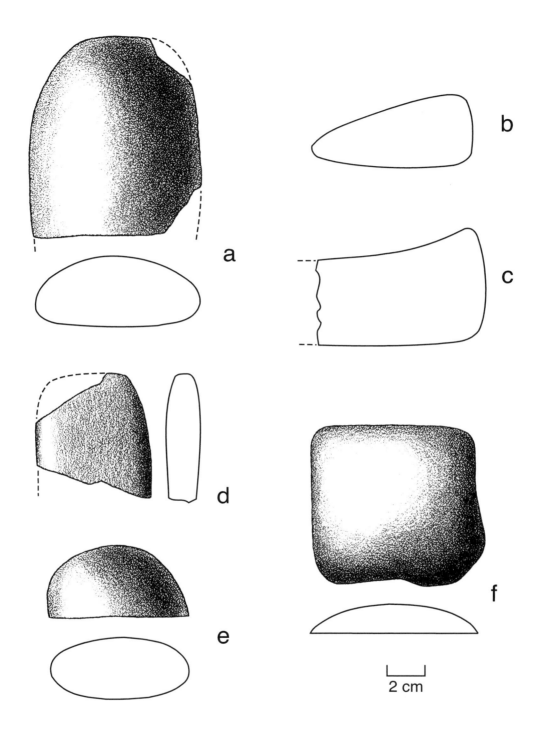

Figure 9.48. Ground stone tools from the Zone D2 Midden. *a*, fragment of loaf-shaped two-hand mano with planoconvex cross-section. *b*, airfoil cross-section of loaf-shaped two-hand mano. *c*, cross-section of basin-shaped metate fragment. *d*, fragment of battered celt. *e*, possible celt polisher, oval in plan. *f*, possible celt polisher, planoconvex in section.

Figure 9.49. Artifacts from the Zone D2 Midden. *a*, basalt muller. *b*, round-polled celt. *c*, possible stone reamer. *d*, possible stone reamer, drilled for suspension. *e*, pottery burnisher made on a chert pebble. *f*, possible antler tine pressure flaker. *g*, tip of bone awl. *h*, tip of bone spatula. *i*, crosshatched pendant made from valve of pearl oyster. *j*, rectangular pearl oyster plaque. *k*, elongated pendant made on beachworn shell. (Artifacts *i-k* are shown larger than actual size; dimensions of *j*, 20 × 20 mm.)

Figure 9.50. Objects from the Zone D2 Midden. *a*, truncated triangular plaque, pearl oyster. *b*, narrow rectangular pearl oyster pendant. *c*, rectangular *Spondylus* plaque with rounded corners. *d*, marsh clam perforated for suspension. *e*, valve of pearly freshwater mussel. *f*, cowrie shell. *g*, turret shell. *h, i*, two views of hinge area from *Spondylus* valve. *j*, fragment from circular or oval magnetite mirror. *k*, lump of magnetite ore. *L*, left mandible of pocket gopher.

Isolated Middle San José Phase Features

Feature 49

Feature 49 was a cylindrical pit, 96 cm in diameter and 1.0 m deep, originating in Zone D. It intruded through Zone E and into Zone F. The pit, whose original function is unknown, occupied parts of Squares S20B and S20C. It eventually had been filled in with San José phase sherds and middenlike debris. Its most impressive artifact was a giant mortar, made on a rectangular block of ignimbrite that appeared to have been quarried from bedrock. This mortar, shown in Figure 9.51, strains the definition of "portable."

Feature 54

Feature 54 was a pit 95 cm in diameter and 65 cm deep, filled with gray and tan ash, animal bones, and sherds of the San José phase (Fig. 9.52). It originated in Zone D and was intrusive through Zone E into Zone F, occupying parts of Squares S17G and S18G.

Animal Bones
　　white-tailed deer (*Odocoileus virginianus*)
　　　　1 complete occiput and parts of the parietal bones, adult
　　　　　　individual
　　domestic dog (*Canis familiaris*)
　　　　1 L. mandible

Feature 31

In order to connect the Master Profiles of Areas B and C, we excavated a stratigraphic trench from the south end of the Area C profile to the west end of the Area B profile. In the process we encountered Feature 31, a prototypic bell-shaped pit, 60 cm in diameter at the rim and 120 cm in diameter at the base (Fig. 9.53). Feature 31 originated in Zone D of Area C, and had been dug down into soft ignimbrite bedrock. Immediately to the south of this pit, we found what appeared to be the backdirt resulting from its excavation—a series of alternating layers of brown earth and fragmented bedrock. Included in the contents of Feature 31 were charcoal-flecked midden material, a large boulder, and a complete two-hand mano. This bell-shaped pit was undoubtedly part of a San José phase household unit, but we failed to locate the associated house.

Ground Stone
　　Complete two-hand mano made of metamorphic rock, shaped like a loaf of French bread. The mano has an oval cross-section and two convex grinding surfaces. Length, 30 cm; width at center, 9.5 cm; thickness, 4.5 cm (Fig. 9.53, *below*).

Other Artifacts Found near Feature 31
　　A few other artifacts were found near Feature 31, and are included here because they may once have been associated with the same household unit as the bell-shaped pit.
　　Bone Tool
　　　　Deer metapodial awl, 8.5 cm long (Fig. 9.54a).
　　Iron Ore Specimen
　　　　Quadrilateral mirror, weighing 1.7 g; 24 × 8 mm in area; 1.5-2.0 mm in thickness (Fig. 9.54b). This artifact suggests that some iron ore mirrors were made to be geometric inlays within a larger item, such as a mask or a complex pectoral. It is larger than the usual circular or rectangular mirror found at San José Mogote.

Figure 9.51. A workman from Guadalupe Etla cleans the giant mortar, made on a slab of ignimbrite bedrock, found in Feature 49. Middle San José phase.

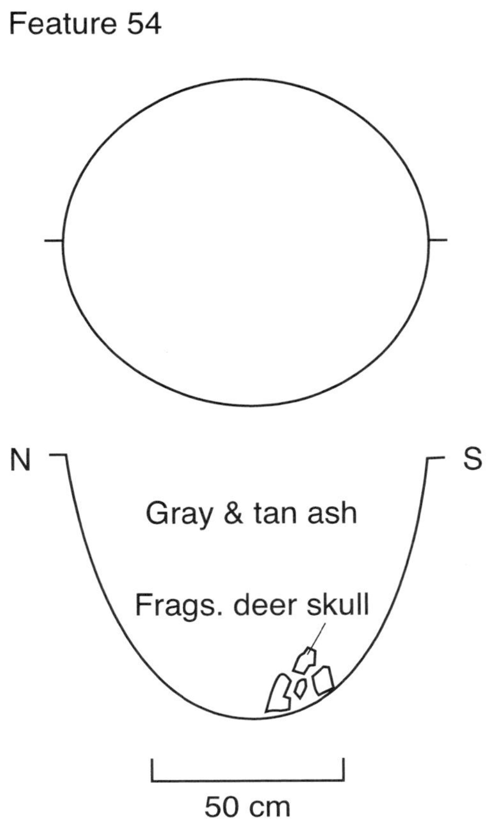

Feature 54

Figure 9.52. Plan and cross-section of Feature 54, a pit originating in Zone D.

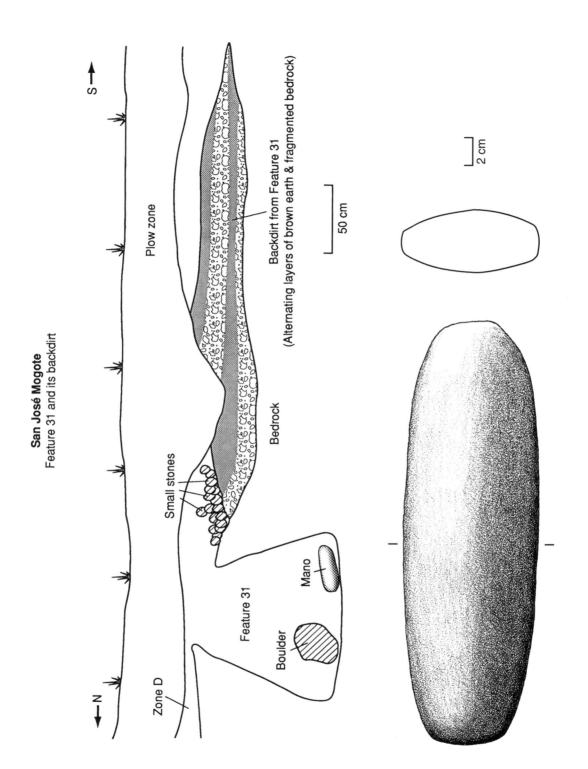

Figure 9.53. Highlights of Feature 31. *Above*, stratigraphic cross-section of the Area C–Area B connecting trench, showing both the bell-shaped pit and the backdirt that resulted when it was created. *Below*, the plan view and cross-section of a complete two-hand mano found in the pit.

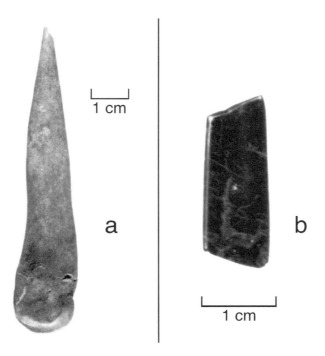

Figure 9.54. Artifacts found near Feature 31, in the Area A-Area B connecting trench. *a*, deer metapodial awl. *b*, quadrilateral iron ore mirror, shown larger than natural size. Middle San José phase.

Chapter 10

Area C: Houses of the Late San José Phase

Zone C of the Control Section

House 7

During the shaving of the Master Profile, we noticed a lens of brown earth in stratigraphic Zone C of Squares S31 and S32 (Fig. 10.1). Originally designated Zone C2, this lens turned out to be the collapsed remains of a San José phase house. Little remained of the house, since most of it had been removed by modern adobe makers prior to our arrival. The surviving portion had been further reduced by Feature 25, an intrusive pit. We did, however, recover artifacts from the house floor when we excavated Squares S31A and S32A. The lens was therefore renamed House 7.

Daub

Three lumps of daub, one with its whitewashed surface still remaining, were found on the floor of House 7. In the Munsell system, the color of the surface was "very pale brown" (10 YR 7/3).

Ceramics

The sample of sherds from House 7 was small, but indicated a Late San José phase date. This date was reinforced by House 7's stratigraphic position, some 20 cm above House 4 and in a later stratigraphic level.

Chipped Stone
Chert (93%)
flake cores: 2

core scraper?: 1
utilized flake: 1
flakes, not utilized: 9
Obsidian (7%)
prismatic blade fragment, utilized: 1 (Fig. 10.2a)

Ground Stone
Roughly half of a very battered celt was found, made of fine-grained metamorphic rock (Fig. 10.2b, c). The fragment is 6 cm wide, 6.5 cm long, and a maximum of 2 cm thick. It had clearly been used on very resistant material; in fact, it reminds us of some of the battered celts from Area B, which had been used to contour bedrock (Chapter 17).

Shell
Ornament
Broken pearl oyster(?) ornament, 10 × 8 × 1 mm (incomplete). It appears that the ornament would have been a long narrow rectangle when whole (Fig. 10.2d).
Pacific Marine Bivalves
Complete valve of marsh clam identified as *Neocyrena* (= *Polymesoda*) sp., 30 × 22 mm; probably unused raw material (Fig. 10.2e).

Mica
A substantial piece from a sheet of black mica was found, 7 × 5 cm in size and more than 2 mm thick in places (Fig. 10.2f). We have seen biotite of this type from the piedmont west of Zimatlán.

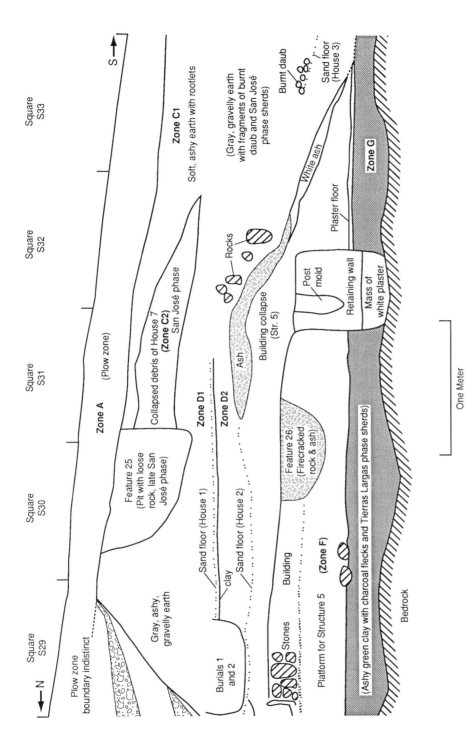

Figure 10.1. East profile of Squares S29–S33 of the Control Section, Area C Master Profile, showing the location of House 7 and Feature 25.

Figure 10.2. Objects from House 7. *a*, prismatic obsidian blade fragment, utilized. *b, c*, front and side views of the lower half of a battered celt. *d*, rectangular pearl oyster(?) ornament, broken. *e*, valve of marsh clam *Neocyrena* (= *Polymesoda*) sp. *f*, 7 × 5 cm sheet of black mica. *g*, dog canine, perforated for suspension.

Figurines

Only four fragments of small solid figurines were associated with House 7. They have been described and illustrated by Marcus (1998a:117-19 and Fig. 11.17).

Bone Ornament

A complete dog canine tooth was found, 33 mm long, perforated for suspension; the drill hole is 2 mm in diameter (Fig. 10.2*g*).

House 14

House 14 was found in Squares S18F-S20F and S18G-S20G, some 6-8 m east of the Master Profile. Like House 7, it lay in stratigraphic Zone C, which we have assigned to the Late San José phase. In those squares, however, Zone C was buried beneath Structure 8, the platform for a public building of the Guadalupe phase. The foundations for that platform had destroyed the western part of the house.

House 14 had two superimposed floors—the original floor, and the second a careful resurfacing done at a later stage in the life of the house. Our plan drawing (Fig. 10.3) was done at the level of the upper, or second floor. We found three postmolds along the east side of the house, as well as traces of a second building nearby that may have been an associated lean-to or ramada. To the east of House 14, we found a dooryard with an ashy gray midden banked up against the east side of the house. This midden actually produced most of the artifacts associated with House 14, since the upper house floor had been swept relatively clean.

The House 14 Upper Floor

Ceramics

The sherd sample from the House 14 floor was insignificant compared to the sample from the dooryard midden (see below).

Chipped Stone
Chert (80%)
    flake cores: 3
    utilized flakes: 2
    flakes, not utilized: 7
Obsidian (20%)
    prismatic blade fragment, utilized: 1
    utilized flake: 1
    flake, not utilized: 1

Ground Stone
Fragment of loaf-shaped mano with oval cross-section, two convex grinding surfaces, fine-grained ignimbrite; 7 cm long, 8 cm wide, 5 cm thick.

Bone Tool

Section of sewing needle, broken right at the eye; 42 mm long, 2 mm in diameter (Fig. 10.4*b*).

Shell
Ornament
    Nearly complete pearl oyster(?) pendant (possibly a holder for a magnetite mirror), originally ca. 37 × 32 mm in size and 1 mm thick (Fig. 10.4*c*). This ornament resembles a diamond-shaped frame, originally with four lobes, each drilled for suspension with a hole 2 mm in diameter. If it were indeed designed to hold an object of some other material, that object would have been 14 mm on a side. One lobe had been broken off.
Pacific Marine Bivalve
    Fragment of pearl oyster valve (*Pinctada mazatlanica*), 20 × 20 × 1.5 mm, probably manufacturing waste.

Animal Bones
    white-tailed deer (*Odocoileus virginianus*)
        1 L. distal femur
    domestic dog (*Canis familiaris*)
        1 L. maxilla
        1 R. ulna
    pocket gopher (*Orthogeomys grandis*)
        1 upper incisor
        1 fragment of premaxilla
    jackrabbit (*Lepus mexicanus*)
        1 R. zygomatic arch
    mud turtle (*Kinosternon integrum*)
        1 carapace scute
    unidentified
        10 fragments of mammal long bone

The Dooryard Midden

Ceramics
Some 157 sherds were found in the dooryard midden of House 14; they have been described by Flannery and Marcus (1994: 325-26). The Late San José phase date of this household is confirmed by ceramic features such as (1) a Leandro Gray bowl with an outcurved, rather than outleaned, rim; (2) a series of Atoyac Yellow-white cylinders incised with Motifs 50, 58, and 68 in Plog's inventory (Flannery and Marcus 1994: Fig. 12.20); and (3) a nonlocal brick-red composite silhouette bowl. These shapes and attributes went on to be more common during the subsequent Guadalupe phase.

Chipped Stone
Chert (95%)
    flake cores: 3
    scraper(?) fragment: 1

House 14
Square designations

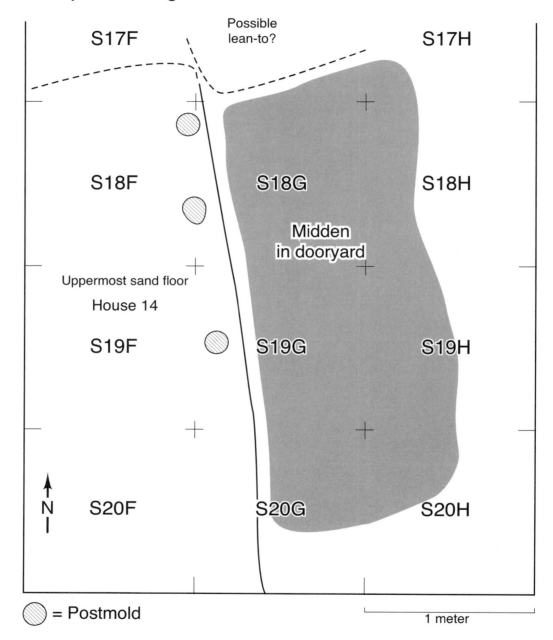

Figure 10.3. Plan of House 14 and its associated dooryard midden, with square designations indicated.

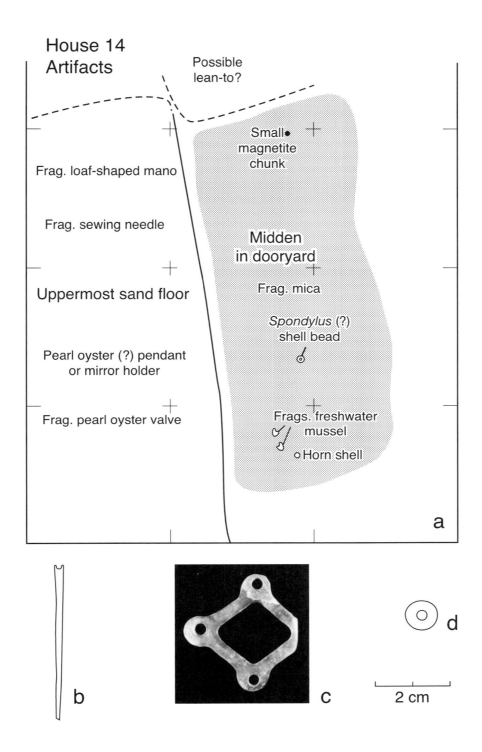

Figure 10.4. Objects from House 14 and the midden in its dooryard. *a*, plan of the house and midden, showing artifact locations. *b*, section of bone sewing needle. *c*, nearly complete pearl oyster(?) pendant. *d*, complete disk bead of *Spondylus*(?) shell. (*b* and *c* are from the house floor; *d* is from the midden.)

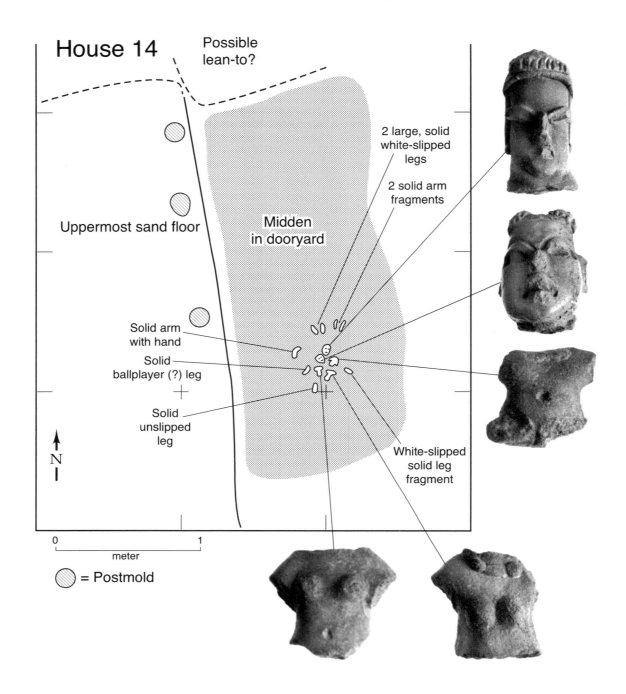

Figure 10.5. Plan of House 14 and its dooryard midden, showing the location of piece-plotted figurine fragments.

utilized blade: 1
utilized flakes: 5
flakes, not utilized: 10
Obsidian (5%)
flake, not utilized: 1

Shell
Ornament
Complete disk bead made from *Spondylus*(?), 8 mm in diameter and 4 mm thick, with a hole 1.5 mm in diameter drilled in the center (Fig. 10.4*d*).
Pearly Freshwater Mussels
Two fragments of unidentified mussel: (1) 16 × 10 × 1 mm; (2) 8 × 10 × 1 mm.
Pacific Marine Univalve
Fragment of unidentified horn shell, 14 mm in diameter.

Iron Ore Specimen
Piece of magnetite ore weighing less than 1 g.

Mica
Piece of gold mica, cut on at least two edges, 20 × 20 × 1 mm.

Figurines
Some 13 fragments of small solid figurines were piece-plotted in the dooryard midden (Fig. 10.5). They have been described and illustrated by Marcus (1998a:119 and Figs. 11.18-11.19).

Animal Bones
domestic dog (*Canis familiaris*)
1 L. maxilla (from a second individual; see "The House 14 Upper Floor," above)
1 L. mandible
3 fragments of vertebrae
1 fragment of metapodial
unidentified rabbit
1 third phalanx
mud turtle (*Kinosternon integrum*)
1 carapace scute
unidentified
11 fragments of mammal long bone

Feature 24

Feature 24, a pit dug into bedrock, was found just south of the Area C Master Profile. It lay near a stratigraphic trench that we created in order to connect Area C to Area B. More than likely, it had once been a feature in a Late San José phase dooryard (Fig. 10.6).

Feature 24 was an irregular, basin-shaped pit, largely destroyed by modern adobe makers prior to our arrival. Its lower 35 cm were preserved as a result of having penetrated bedrock.

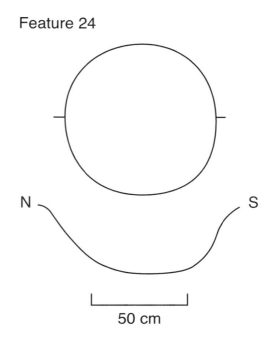

Figure 10.6. Plan and cross-section of Feature 24, a pit excavated into bedrock. This feature provided a good sample of Late San José phase carbonized plants and a radiocarbon date of 890 ± 150 b.c.

The diameter of the preserved portion was about 80 cm. Contents of the pit included ash, San José phase sherds, and carbonized plants.

Radiocarbon Date[1]
Carbonized plant material from Feature 24 yielded a date of 2840 ± 150 B.P., or about 890 b.c. (M-2354). The calibrated two-sigma range would be 1410-780 B.C.

Carbonized Plants
51 kernels of maize (*Zea mays*), many showing Nal-Tel/Chapalote characteristics
1 cob fragment of maize
1 fruit case of teosinte (*Zea mexicana*)
1 cluster of seeds from biznaga (*Echinocactus* sp.)
1 seed of balloon vine (*Cardiospermum* sp.)
4 unidentified seeds, possibly hackberry (*Celtis* sp.)

Ashy Hollow in Bedrock

A hollow in bedrock one meter north of Feature 24 produced San José phase sherds, marine shell, and carbonized plants.

---

[1]In this volume, uncalibrated dates are given as "b.c.," and dendrocalibrated dates as "B.C." (see Chapter 26, Radiocarbon Dating).

Shell

A very small unmodified marsh clam, presumably raw material for shell working, was found.

Carbonized Plants

5 kernels of maize (*Zea mays*)
many cupules of disintegrated maize cobs
1 fruit of nanche or West Indian cherry (*Malpighia* sp.)

The Zone C Midden

Zone C of the Master Profile was a layer of soft earth that overlay Zone D in places. In some squares, it had two facies: (1) Zone C1, the largest facies, which consisted of soft ashy midden, and (2) Zone C2, the lens of brown earth that turned out to be the collapsed remains of House 7 (see above).

The midden facies of Zone C did not produce large samples of pottery and chipped stone. Its most notable contributions were several artifacts that would not have been out of place in the Basin of Mexico. Included were a Tlatilco-style roller stamp and a *yuguito* or "miniature yoke" in polished black stone (see below).

Ceramics

The small sample of sherds from Zone C was Late San José phase in date, like the sherds from House 14.

Chipped Stone

The small, nondescript collection of chipped stone from Zone C was not considered worth including in Parry's analysis.

Ground Stone

Almost complete saddle-shaped metate with centrally placed mortar socket (Fig. 10.7). Made from greenish ignimbrite, this metate may have been used to process some material that required two stages of grinding: first with a two-hand mano, after which it would have been collected in the mortar socket and pounded, either with a pestle or with one end of the mano. The metate is 38 cm long, 24 cm wide, and 10-11 cm thick; the mortar socket is 10 cm in diameter and about 4.8 cm deep.

Fragment of basin-shaped metate, 10 × 7.5 cm; 5.5 cm thick at the lip, but only 2.5 cm thick near the center of the basin (Fig. 10.8*a*).

Complete muller or pestle of volcanic rock. Length, 6 cm; diameter, 4 cm (Fig. 10.8*b*).

Yuguito

Square S2 of the Master Profile produced a complete *yuguito* or "miniature yoke" in polished black stone, roughly 15 cm across (Fig. 10.9*a*). Such *yuguitos* are thought by some scholars to be stone representations of ballplayers' equipment or artifacts associated with the ballgame, but their actual function has not

been determined. We suspect that this artifact may be an import from some area like the Basin of Mexico, where they are more common (Porter 1953: Plate 13H).

Ceramic Roller Stamp

Square S20C of the Master Profile yielded a broken, Tlatilco-style cylindrical roller stamp (Fig. 10.9*b*). The stamp, which was 3.5 cm in diameter, produces a "crocodile's foot" design when rolled on a slab of plasticine (Fig. 10.9*c*). This motif was formerly called the "paw-wing" motif, but it is now clear that it depicts the foot of a crocodile and is a *pars pro toto* allusion to Earth (Grove 1984:126; Flannery and Marcus 1994:295; Marcus 1999:77). Many Mesoamerican groups conceived of the surface of the Earth as the back of a giant crocodile floating in a primordial body of water.

Shell

Ornaments

Broken pearl oyster(?) ornament, 15 mm long, 10 mm wide, 1 mm thick, and drilled at one end.

Broken pearl oyster(?) ornament, 32 mm long, 16 mm wide, 2 mm thick, and drilled at one end.

Pacific Marine Bivalves

Fragment of pearl oyster valve, 10 × 10 × 1 mm.

Disintegrating fragments of a pearl oyster valve that appears to have shattered while being drilled, the result being that the perforation remains unfinished. Unmeasurable.

Pacific Marine Univalves

Fragment of possible perforated limpet?

Unidentified

Margin of unidentified shell, 45 × 10 × 3 mm.

Stone Ornament

Pendant of dark metamorphic rock, 10 cm long and 2.6 cm wide, with a deep groove incised along its midline (Fig. 10.8*c*). The upper end has been biconically drilled for suspension, with the hole 5 mm wide at the surface and narrowing to 2 mm in diameter.

Carbonized Plants

2 fragments of maize cobs (*Zea mays*)
fragment of carrizo (*Phragmites australis*)

Animal Bones

Large Mammals

white-tailed deer (*Odocoileus virginianus*)
1 R. scapula
1 L. scapula
1 R. radius
1 L. proximal tibia
1 L. distal tibia
3 L. calcanea (one of them unfused)
1 distal metapodial

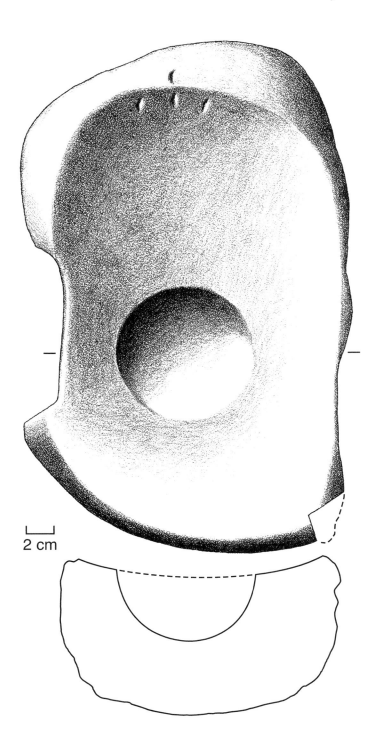

2 cm

Figure 10.7. Combination saddle-shaped metate and mortar from the Zone C Midden. The cross-section (below) shows the depth of the mortar socket. The four pockmarks near the upper edge of the metate appear to be scars left from the roughing-out process. The stone is green ignimbrite.

Small Mammals
    domestic dog (*Canis familiaris*)
        1 upper premolar
        2 R. mandibles
        1 axis
        1 L. ulna
        1 metapodial

pocket gopher (*Orthogeomys grandis*)
    1 R. mandible
Mexican cottontail (*Sylvilagus cunicularius*)
    1 R. innominate
Reptiles
    mud turtle (*Kinosternon integrum*)
        half of a plastron

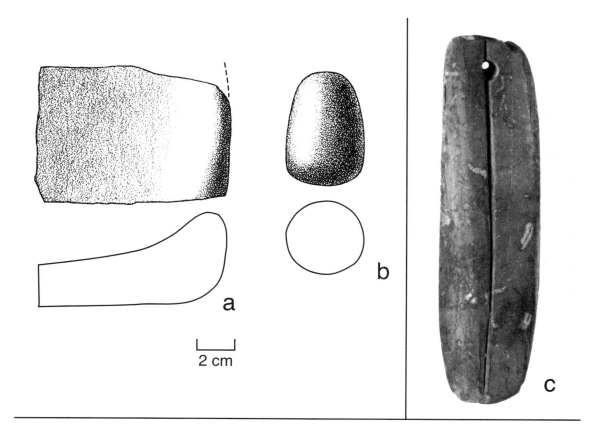

Figure 10.8. Artifacts from the Zone C Midden. *a*, fragment of basin-shaped metate. *b*, muller or pestle of volcanic rock. *c*, pendant of dark metamorphic rock.

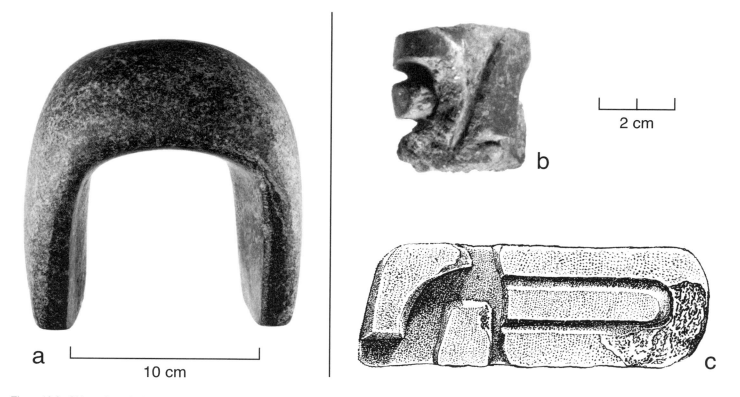

Figure 10.9. Objects from the Zone C Midden that would not be out of place at Tlatilco in the Basin of Mexico. *a*, *yuguito* or "miniature yoke" of highly polished black stone. *b*, pottery roller stamp. *c*, artist's rendering of rolled-out design on *b* (drawing by Rubén Méndez).

Chapter 11
Area C: Epilogue

The abandonment of Houses 7 and 14 was followed by further change in the use of Area C. The ground surface was leveled, and Structure 8—the platform for a Guadalupe phase public building—was erected just east of the Master Profile (Marcus and Flannery 1996:112 and Fig. 117). These activities obliterated the Terminal San José phase deposits over much of the area.

Feature 25

Feature 25, a pit intrusive through Zone C and House 7 of the Master Profile, occupied parts of Squares S30-S31 and S30A-S31A (Fig. 10.1, Chapter 10). Circular in plan but irregular in cross-section, the pit had a maximum diameter of about 1.0 m. Included in its contents were loose rock, Late San José phase sherds, discarded metate and mano fragments, and shell. Feature 25 would have to have been filled in before Structure 8 could be built. Given its stratigraphic position, it could date either to the Terminal San José phase or the San José/Guadalupe transition.

Ground Stone
Fragment of loaf-shaped two-hand mano with oval cross-section, fine-grained crystalline metamorphic rock. The surviving fragment is 13 cm long, 8 cm wide, and 5 cm thick (Fig. 11.1a).
Fragment of two-hand mano with airfoil cross-section. The surviving fragment is 7 cm long, 8 cm wide, and 4 cm thick at the midpoint (Fig. 11.1b).
Fragment of apparent saddle-shaped metate, ignimbrite. The surviving fragment is 16 × 8 × 4.5 cm (Fig. 11.1c).

Shell
Fragment of pearly freshwater mussel, 16 × 13 × 1 mm.
Fragment of unidentified shell, 15 × 10 × 1 mm.

Animal Bones from the San José/Guadalupe Interface

One of the few places where a plausible San José phase/Guadalupe phase interface had survived was in Squares S17J-S17K-S17L. A scatter of animal bones lay at the disconformity between deposits of the two phases, as follows:
Large Mammals
white-tailed deer (*Odocoileus virginianus*)
1 L. ulna
collared peccary (*Dicotyles tajacu*)
1 L. premaxilla, large male
Small Mammals
domestic dog (*Canis familiaris*)
2 canine teeth
Birds
crow (*Corvus corax*)
1 R. femur

Evidence for Rosario Phase Cannibalism: Feature 47

During the excavation of Squares S20N, S21N, S20-O, and S21-O of the Threshing Floor Sector, we came upon an interesting Rosario phase feature. As Figure 11.2 shows, it originated very near the surface.

Feature 47 was a circular roasting pit or earth oven, 1.31 m in diameter. Its original depth is unknown because its upper portion had been plowed away, but its lower 30 cm were still intact. The pit was filled with fire-cracked rocks and ash, and its walls had been burned so intensely that they survived as a 10-15 cm thick, brick-hard reddish ring encircling the entire feature. This hard ring had actually been truncated by plowing, so it is possible that it once continued upward to form a dome over the oven.

Feature 47 could be dated to the Rosario phase by a series of sherds from Socorro Fine Gray composite silhouette bowls, bearing the typical resist white-on-gray decoration of Rosario times. Equally diagnostic were sherds of Socorro Fine Gray bowls with everted rims like those featured in Drennan's (1976a) multidimensional scaling. Two sherds of Guadalupe Burnished Brown and two sherds of Atoyac Yellow-white were also present.

The most intriguing discovery in Feature 47 was a series of roasted human bones, including part of a cranium. Someone had evidently been cooked in this earth oven, located on what would have been the western outskirts of the village during the Rosario phase.

Several possibilities come to mind. For one thing, we know that the Rosario phase was a time of intense intervillage raiding, during which San José Mogote's main temple was burned, and a sacrificed captive was depicted on a stone monument (Flannery and Marcus 2003:11802). One possibility, therefore, is that the individual roasted in Feature 47 was a captive from a rival polity. On the other hand, a sixteenth-century document from the Etla subvalley (Zárate 1581) states that the Zapotec punished some crimes, like adultery, by execution, followed by ritual eating of the offender. The evidence from Feature 47 is insufficient to allow us to decide between these alternatives.

Radiocarbon Date[1]

A piece of charcoal from Feature 47 dated to 2640 ± 40 B.P., or roughly 690 b.c. (Beta-179878). The calibrated two-sigma range would be 840-790 B.C.

---

[1]In this volume, uncalibrated dates are given as "b.c.," and dendrocalibrated dates as "B.C." (see Chapter 26, Radiocarbon Dating).

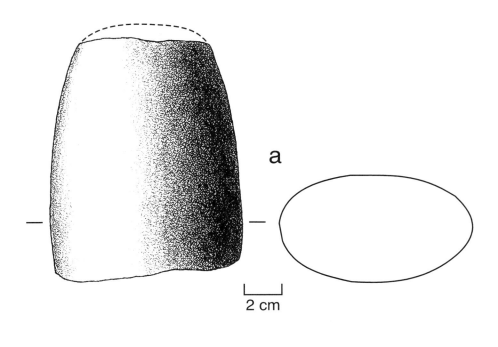

a

b

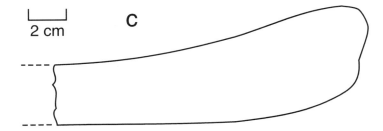

c

Figure 11.1. Ground stone tools from Feature 25. *a*, fragment of loaf-shaped two-hand mano with oval cross-section. *b*, airfoil cross-section of a two-hand mano fragment. *c*, cross-section of broken metate, apparently saddle-shaped.

Figure 11.2. Feature 47, a Rosario phase roasting pit or earth oven with evidence of ritual cannibalism. *Above*, workmen clean carefully around the fire-cracked rocks. *Below*, the cleaned oven, showing the brick-red collar of burned earth surrounding it.

III

Chapter 12

An Introduction to Area A

Area A, on the extreme eastern edge of the piedmont spur, was the venue for our first excavation at San José Mogote. It was the first place in the Valley of Oaxaca where Early Formative ceramics were discovered *in situ*, and the first to yield Early Formative houses (Chapter 1).

Since the stratigraphy of Area A has been described in detail in our volume on Early Formative pottery (Flannery and Marcus 1994:301-5), we will present here only enough data to put the Area A residences in context.

During the Tierras Largas phase, Area A had not yet been occupied. It was settled sometime during the first half of the San José phase, as occupation spread eastward to cover the entire 400-m-wide piedmont spur. The first houses in Area A were built either on exposed bedrock, or on bedrock covered only by the thinnest layer of sterile soil. Immediately to the east of Area A, the piedmont spur slopes down to a strip of dark black alluvial soil that is continuously under cultivation today.

One of the major landmarks of Area A is a small arroyo that descends from the southeast corner of the site's Main Plaza to the alluvial bottomland. That arroyo was not yet present in the Early Formative. It is largely a product of massive construction during Monte Albán II, when the heights of Mound 1, the Mound 2 Ridge, and the Main Plaza were all increased. This construction so steepened the gradient between the plaza and the alluvial bottomland that sometime after the site was abandoned, rain runoff from the mounds and plaza created a small arroyo running west-to-east through Area A. Over the centuries, this arroyo downcut to bedrock through all the accumulated strata of Area A.

While we lamented the destruction caused by the arroyo, its south bank provided a stratigraphic cross-section of the Area A deposits. We decided to take advantage of this window into the stratigraphy of the area. At a point roughly 60 m east of the northeast corner of Mound 1, we shaved the south side of the arroyo into a vertical face (Fig. 12.1*a*). As we had hoped, several clay floors could be seen in cross-section. Even before excavation began, we could see that the arroyo had cut through a large midden just above bedrock; a series of superimposed houses and dooryards; and a thick layer of artificial fill, which we later learned was the interior of Structure 1, a Late San José phase public building (Flannery and Marcus 1994: Figs. 18.7-18.11).

The Stratigraphy of Area A

We laid out an area 3 × 4 m in extent, oriented magnetic north-south and divided into twelve 1 × 1 m squares, running south from the vertical profile. Excavation of alternate squares began at the arroyo profile so that each cultural stratum seen in the profile could be traced southward, leaving the unexcavated squares as temporary baulks to increase exposure of the stratigraphy. As work proceeded, the intervening squares were excavated as well (Figs. 12.1*b*, 12.2).

At this point in the project, we had yet to excavate an Early Formative house in Oaxaca and did not know what to expect. We worked very slowly and carefully, piece-plotting everything found *in situ* and drawing every stratum of every square. Eventually, of course, we decided that it was not worthwhile to piece-plot everything in (1) midden deposits or (2) public building fill. We never regretted, however, being overly careful at this early stage of the project.

Area A was excavated entirely by "cultural" or "natural" stratigraphy. Certain natural strata, however, were so thick that we subdivided them into arbitrary 20 cm levels.

When we had finished all twelve of the original squares (plus a thirteenth square, H13, which we added in order to complete the excavation of certain features), we drew the profile of the south and west walls (Fig. 12.3). From earliest to latest, the stratigraphy was as follows.

Bedrock

We reached bedrock at a depth of 2.2 to 2.4 m below the surface. It was soft white volcanic tuff (ignimbrite), and had been penetrated by postholes (Fig. 12.4*a*), pits, and even a hearth. The house associated with the hearth and at least eleven of the postholes had been essentially destroyed, but we designated it Household Unit E.

Zone D

Zone D was a dark brown midden with charcoal flecks, so thick and extensive that we believe it to have been a neighborhood midden for houses upslope (to the west). It dated to the first half of the San José phase (Flannery and Marcus 1994:303).

Zone C

Zone C was a thick stratum of tan wattle-and-daub debris, resulting from the collapse of four superimposed San José phase household units. These units were designated C1, C2, C3, and C4; all dated to the Middle San José phase.

Zone B

Zone B was a thick layer of construction fill associated with Structure 1, the stone masonry platform for a Late San José phase public building. The fill for this platform appeared to have been provided by at least two different work gangs, one bringing dark grayish brown clay from the nearby alluvial bottomland while the other brought tan earth with many small white rock chips from the ridge east of the bottomland (Flannery and Marcus 1994:305). Figure 12.2 shows two of the boulder retaining walls found within the platform. Structure 1 will be described more fully in a later volume on public buildings.

It should also be noted that a lime-plastered public building—probably a Men's House—was built atop Mound 1 during the San José phase (Chapter 22). This Men's House may well have been built by the residents of Area A, who lived only a short distance from Mound 1.

Zone A

Zone A, a layer of brown earth with rootlets, was the plow zone. Its contents were badly eroded sherds washed down from nearby mounds, mixed with redeposited San José phase materials brought to the surface by platform construction and plowing. Once we realized this we stripped off Zone A rapidly, and did not waste time screening it through 6 mm mesh as we did with the households, features, and middens.

Backfilling

When our work ended in Area A, we found that because we had removed the arroyo bank, there was no way to backfill our excavation. We solved this problem by constructing an adobe wall where the south wall of the arroyo had been (Fig. 12.4*b*).

Figure 12.1. Excavations in Area A. In *a*, workmen convert the south bank of the arroyo to a vertical profile, giving us a preview of the stratigraphy. In *b*, working south from the arroyo bank profile, workmen begin to excavate by alternate 1 × 1 m squares.

Figure 12.2. Looking south over the Area A excavation. Squares H11 and H10-K10 have been excavated to bedrock, and three postholes from an early house have appeared. In the distance one can see Monte Albán, the defensible mountaintop to which the occupants of San José Mogote moved at the end of the Rosario phase.

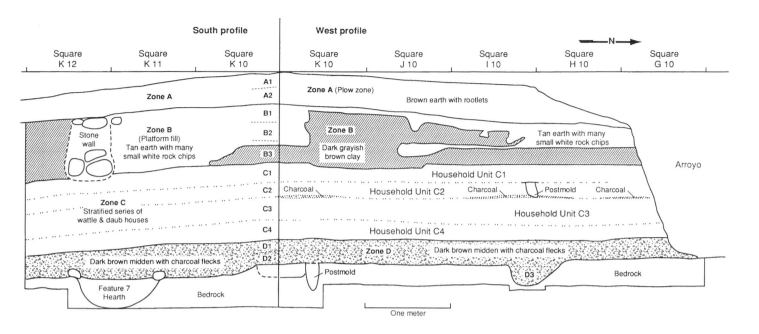

Figure 12.3. South and west profiles of Area A, showing the stratigraphic relationships of Feature 7 from Household Unit E; the Zone D Midden; and Household Units C4-C1.

Figure 12.4. Scenes from Area A. *a*, postmold in cross-section, Square K10 (see Fig. 12.3). *b*, Heliodoro Jiménez and Irán Matadamas construct an adobe wall where the arroyo bank had been, allowing us to backfill Area A. This in turn allowed landowner Santiago Méndez (*background*) to plant maize once again.

Chapter 13
Colonization of Area A

Postholes and Features in Bedrock

We reached bedrock in Area A at a depth of 2.2-2.4 m below the surface. The rock was soft ignimbrite, so white that if any post had penetrated it, the posthole stood out as a brown to greenish-black disk.

We discovered thirteen postholes from houses built before the deposition of the Zone D Midden (Figs. 13.1, 13.2). Unfortunately, no house floors had survived intact. This was disappointing, since we were curious to know exactly when this part of the piedmont spur had been colonized. All available evidence, including the sherds from the Zone D Midden just above bedrock, suggested a date in the first half of the San José phase (Flannery and Marcus 1994:303). It would have been nice to have at least one good house floor sample antedating the Zone D Midden.

Household Unit E

Eleven of the postholes in bedrock seemed to belong to a house with an attached lean-to or roofed work area, like the House 16/17 Complex of Area B (Chapter 18). We designated this residence Household Unit E, to emphasize its stratigraphic position below the Zone D Midden. Our excavation seems to have caught the southeast quadrant of the house and part of the dooryard to the east and south (Fig. 13.2). Feature 7, an outdoor roasting pit similar to one found in Household Unit C4 (Chapter 14), lay less than a meter south of the house.

The postholes we assigned to Household Unit E were not uniform in size. It should be remembered, however, that we were not dealing with the diameters of the posts themselves, but the diameters of the holes dug into bedrock to accommodate them. Soft ignimbrite is crumbly, and some holes might have ended up with diameters significantly greater than the posts inside them. A few of the smaller postholes were slanted rather than vertical, and might have been for "leaners," added to stabilize a nearby post that had become loose.

Finally, the two postholes in Squares H12 and I12 seemed unrelated to the Unit E house, and might be associated with a second structure built to the northeast.

Feature 7

Feature 7 was a large, irregular roasting pit or outdoor hearth, filled with fire-cracked rocks and ash. It occupied parts of Squares K11 and K12 and continued beyond them into the south profile (Figs. 13.1, 13.2). Roughly a meter in diameter and 36 cm deep, it combined a deliberately excavated pit and an adjacent natural depression in bedrock. Both the pit and the bedrock depression were heavily burned. While we do not know what the villagers were cooking over heated stones, large hearths like this seem to have been fairly common features in San José phase dooryards.

As for the fire-cracked rocks in Feature 7, many were fragments of broken metates and manos. The five largest are described below.

Ground Stone

Fragment of subrectangular one-hand mano with triangular cross-section, sandstone; its two working surfaces are slightly concave (Fig. 13.3*b*). Because of its size and the nature of its working surfaces, we suspect that this mano

Figure 13.1. Two views of bedrock in Area A, showing postholes and features of Household Unit E. *Above*, view from the south, showing postholes from the house and its possible lean-to. *Below*, view from the west, showing Feature 7 (and an adjacent depression) to the south of the lean-to. At this stage of the excavation, the south walls of Squares K11-K12 had been shaved back far enough to allow Feature 7 to be excavated completely. The white arrow points north.

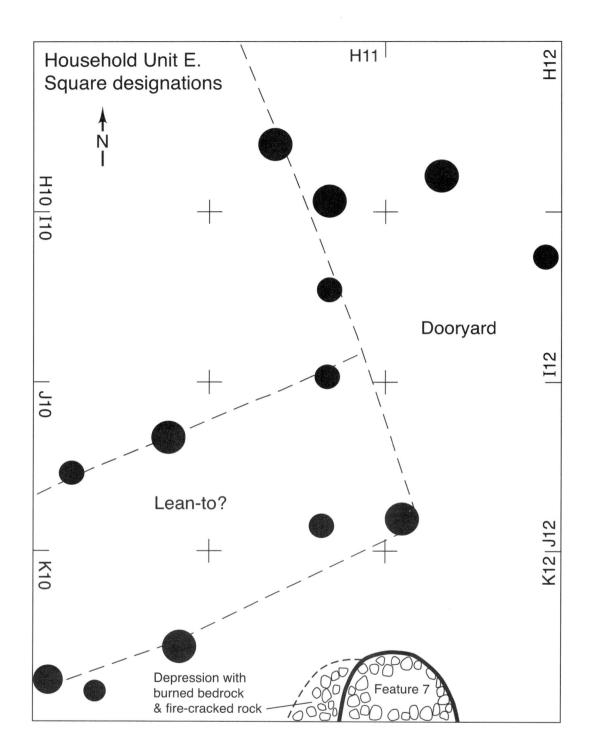

Figure 13.2. Plan of Household Unit E, showing square designations and postholes in bedrock.

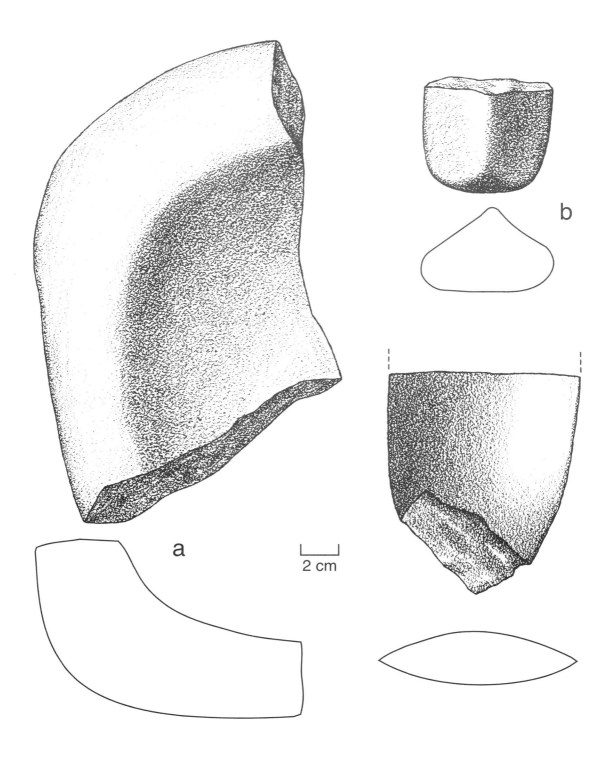

Figure 13.3. Ground stone tools found among the fire-cracked rocks of Feature 7. *a*, fragment of basin-shaped metate. *b*, fragment of one-hand mano with triangular cross-section. *c*, fragment of two-hand mano with two convex grinding surfaces, lenticular in cross-section.

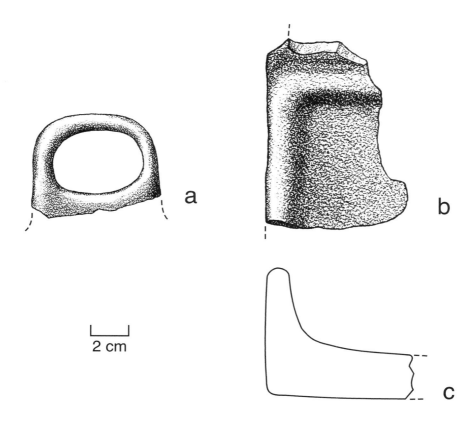

Figure 13.4. Two fragments of a small, portable, rectangular lipped metate with a loop handle, found among the fire-cracked rocks of Feature 7. *a*, handle. *b, c*, plan and section of the corner to which the handle was attached. This metate is similar to one found in Feature 65, Area B, and may have been used for grinding tobacco.

might have been used with the rectangular lipped metate whose fragments were also found in Feature 7 (see Fig. 13.4). Maximum width, 7.5 cm; maximum thickness, 4.7 cm.

Fragment of two-hand mano with two convex grinding surfaces, gneiss; lenticular cross-section (Fig. 13.3*c*). Length, 12+ cm (broken); maximum width, 10.6 cm; maximum thickness, 3.4 cm.

Fragment of basin-shaped metate, ignimbrite (Fig. 13.3*a*). What may be another fragment of this same metate was found redeposited in Zone D3 of the midden above. Rim-to-base height, 4 cm; distance from rim to grinding surface, 2 cm.

Fragment of basin-shaped metate, 4.5 cm thick near the center of the basin.

Two fragments of rectangular lipped metate with loop handle, ignimbrite (Fig. 13.4). This metate resembles the more complete one found in Feature 65 of Area B (Chapter 16), and like the latter, may have been a portable metate for the grinding of tobacco or some other ritually important plant. Rim-to-base height, 6.5 cm; distance from rim to grinding surface, 4 cm. These boxlike portable metates appear to have peaked in popularity during the Late Tierras Largas and Early San José phases.

The Zone D Midden

Bedrock in Area A was covered by a chocolate brown midden more than half a meter thick in places (Fig. 12.3, Chapter 12). This deposit appeared to be a neighborhood midden, the product of long-term dumping of refuse by San José phase houses located just upslope of our excavation. The artifacts in the Zone D Midden left no doubt that the residences from which they came were involved in the same kinds of shell and magnetite working as Household Units C4-C1 (Chapter 14).

Although there were no clear stratigraphic breaks in the midden, we were reluctant to remove such a thick deposit as one unit (Fig. 13.5). We therefore divided the midden into arbitrary 20-cm units which we called Zone D1 (uppermost), Zone D2, and Zone D3 (lowest). We will present the Zone D artifacts by these units, even though no significant change through time was readily apparent. In fact, sherds from the same restorable vessel were sometimes scattered through adjacent arbitrary units (Fig. 13.6).

A word should be said about the chipped stone tools recovered from the Zone D Midden. This collection was studied first by Frank Hole and then by William J. Parry, during different field seasons. While their typologies were similar, there were slight differences for which we have designed compromises. For example, some discarded chert cores had been reused as hammerstones; it appears that Parry grouped them with the cores, while Hole grouped them with the hammerstones. While both Hole and Parry made a distinction between "cores" and "core fragments," Hole further divided the latter into "core faces," "core tablets," and "core platform edges."

In the case of obsidian at San José Mogote, Hole's "debitage" category was usually divided by Parry into "angular fragments" and "flakes, not utilized." However, Parry was unable to restudy the obsidian from the Zone D Midden, since it had been removed by Pires-Ferreira (1975) for neutron activation analysis. We have therefore followed Hole's typology for the Zone D obsidian.

Daub

Fragments of daub from house walls occurred throughout the Zone D Midden, but most were very small, as might be expected in the case of transported refuse. The range of colors seen on the whitewashed surface of these fragments was quite variable, suggesting that they had come from a number of different houses. In the Munsell system, the range of colors was as follows:

"pink" (actually cream or creamy pink to our eyes), 5 YR 7/4 to 7.5 YR 8/4

"pinkish gray," 7.5YR 7/2

"light reddish brown," 2.5 YR 6/4

Zone D3

Ceramics
Some 990 sherds were recovered from Zone D3. They have been described by Flannery and Marcus (1994: Table 14.1).

Chipped Stone (see Fig. 13.7 for examples)
Chert (82%)
    hammerstone: 1
    ordinary flake cores: 2
    core faces: 3
    core platform edge: 1
    bipolar flake cores: 2
    flake perforators/gravers: 7
    denticulate scraper: 1
    utilized flakes: 3
    flakes, not utilized: 26
    angular fragments: 3
Obsidian (17%)
    prismatic blade fragment: 1
    notched blade: 1
    scaled flakes: 2
    debitage: 6
Other (1%)
    volcanic angular fragment: 1

Bone Tool
Fragment of probable basketry needle, 3.2 mm in diameter, original length unknown.

Shell
Fragment of unidentified shell, possibly *Spondylus,* 21 × 8 × 7 mm.

Broken disk of unidentified shell, 14 mm in diameter and 2-3 mm thick.

Iron Ore Specimen
Lump of magnetite ore, Group I-A, from near Tenango. Pires-Ferreira (1975: Table 11) considers this the most common source used at San José Mogote.

Mica
Shattered piece of black mica weighing 0.2 g, cut on at least one edge; 20 × 15 × 1 mm.

Figurines
Four figurine fragments were recovered from Zone D3; they have been described and illustrated by Marcus (1998a:152 and Fig. 12.15). Three of the fragments were from small solid figurines, while the fourth came from the head of a large hollow doll.

Figure 13.5. Excavation of the Zone D Midden, Area A. *Above*, dig foreman Eligio Martínez uncovers a mass of partially restorable vessels in Zone D1. *Below*, portions of a Delfina Fine Gray bowl with incised "mat motifs" in cartouches.

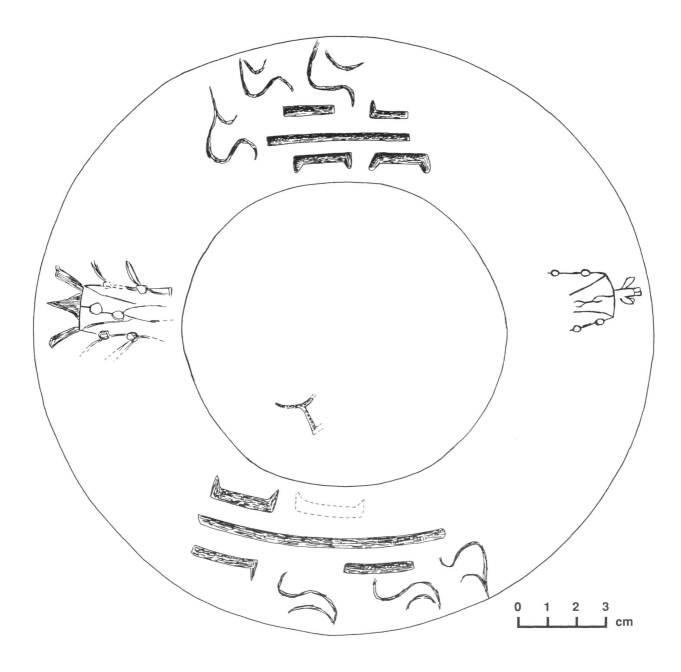

Figure 13.6. Top view of a reconstructed Leandro Gray bowl from the Zone D Midden. The vessel features excised Sky (Lightning) motifs made prior to firing, as well as stick figures of costumed humans done with a sharp instrument after firing.

Animal Bones
    Small Mammals
        domestic dog (*Canis familiaris*)
            1 R. distal humerus
            1 L. proximal ulna
            1 R. distal femur
            2 metapodials
        pocket gopher (*Orthogeomys grandis*)
            1 L. distal humerus
    Unidentified
        23 mammal fragments

Zone D2

Radiocarbon Date[1]
    Our expected date for Zone D2 (based on dates from Zone D1) would be roughly 1000 b.c. One 1960s-era conventional date came out 2810 ± 120 B.P., or roughly 860 b.c. (SI-467). Adding one sigma would get it close to our expected date. The calibrated two-sigma range would be 1310-790 B.C.

Ceramics
    Some 3456 sherds were recovered from Zone D2. They have been described by Flannery and Marcus (1994: Table 14.1).

Chipped Stone
    Chert (71%)
        hammerstones: 4
        ordinary flake cores: 4
        core faces: 2
        core tablet: 1
        core platform edges: 2
        bipolar flake cores: 4
        flake perforators/gravers: 24
        retouched flakes: 3
        utilized flakes: 14
        flakes, not utilized: 104
        angular fragments: 10
    Obsidian (25%)
        prismatic blade fragments: 3
        scaled flakes: 4
        debitage: 54
    Other (3%)
        quartz flake: 1
        volcanic flakes: 5
        volcanic angular fragments: 2

Ground Stone
    Broken subrectangular one-hand mano with subrectangular cross-section, metamorphic rock (Fig. 13.8*a*). Length, 10 cm; width, 4+ cm (broken); thickness, 6 cm.

Fragment of subrectangular two-hand mano with airfoil cross-section, andesite(?). Too small and broken to be worth measuring.
    Large polishing stone with one flat facet, ignimbrite (Fig. 13.8*d*). Length, 10.2 cm; width, 8.4 cm; thickness, 5.4 cm.
    One *canica* or pecked and ground stone ball, 20 mm in diameter.
    Two stone "cutting boards," found near each other and possibly discarded together (Fig. 13.9*e, f*). Both were made on elongated pieces of black metamorphic rock, smoothed by grinding, and covered by hundreds of small cut marks which give the superficial appearance of a whetstone. One, from Square I10, is 8.2 cm long and 2 cm in diameter. The second, from Square I11, is only 2.4 cm long and 1 cm in diameter. The latter has a triangular cross-section, caused by the fact that it had been given three very smooth facets as the result of prolonged grinding. It is unclear what was being cut on these unusual tools, but we note that Reynolds' multidimensional scaling (Chapter 25) associates them with shell.

Bone Tools
    Two fragments of probable sewing needles, both 2.5 mm in diameter (Fig. 13.9*h, i*). One fragment is 26 mm long, the other 21 mm long; the original lengths of the needles are unknown.

Worked Sherds
    One complete perforated sherd disk, 4 cm in diameter, with its edges roughly chipped and ground. A hole 5 mm in diameter has been biconically drilled through the center (Fig. 13.9*j*).
    Broken fragment representing about one-third of a perforated sherd disk; it may originally have been 6-7 cm in diameter. The edges have been roughly chipped and ground, and a hole was biconically drilled through the center (Fig. 13.9*k*).

Shell
    Ornament
        Fragment of ring-shaped ornament with drill holes, probably pearl oyster (Fig. 13.10*a*). Original dimensions are unknown; the surviving fragment is 30 × 4 × 2 mm.
    Pearly Freshwater Mussels
        Worn valve, cf. *Barynaias*, 40 × 35 × 1 mm (Fig. 13.10*d*).
        Valve of *Barynaias*, broken, 35 × 24 × 1 mm (Fig. 13.10*e*).
        Fragment trimmed from the margin of an unidentified pearly mussel, obviously manufacturing waste; 43 × 8 × 1 mm.
    Pacific Marine Bivalves
        Fragment of pearl oyster (*Pinctada mazatlanica*), 20 × 10 × 3 mm.

---

[1]In this volume, uncalibrated dates are given as "b.c.," and dendrocalibrated dates as "B.C." (see Chapter 26, Radiocarbon Dating).

Triangular fragment of shell, probably pearl oyster, 19 × 13 × 3 mm.

Two fragments of pearl oyster, one 31 × 20 × 3 mm, the other 20 × 19 × 5 mm.

Two fragments of *Spondylus* shell.

Broken valve of *Chione* (= *Anomalocardia*) *subrugosa*, 24 × 15 × 7 mm.

Pacific Marine Univalves

Two complete horn shells (*Cerithidia mazatlanica*), one 17 mm long, the other 16 mm long.

Beachworn dogwinkle (*Thais* sp.), 15 × 12 × 3 mm (Fig. 13.10*m*).

Unidentified

Fragment of beachworn shell, 24 × 19 × 3 mm.

Fragment of unidentified shell, 20 × 17 × 3 mm.

Iron Ore Specimens

Lump of magnetite ore, Group I-B, from Loma Los Sabinos near Zimatlán. Ore from this same source was also found in Household Unit C4 (Chapter 14) and on the surface of a site near Coyotepec in the southern arm of the Valley of Oaxaca.

Piece of metallic hematite ore, 29 × 17 × 15 mm (Fig. 13.10*n*). This is the type of ore which, when ground to a powder, can be used in making specular hematite pottery slip. As a dry powder, it was also frequently rubbed into the excisions on white or gray pottery.

Mica

Piece of black mica, cut on one edge, 28 × 18 × 1 mm (Fig. 13.10*q*).

Figurines

Thirty fragments of small solid figurines were recovered from Zone D2. They have been described and illustrated by Marcus (1998a:153-54 and Figs. 12.16-12.19). Included are at least five fragments depicting men seated crosslegged in what may be a position of authority, plus the upper portion of a grotesquely masked figure (perhaps a costumed dancer).

Imported Bird Products

Fragment of sternum from a wild turkey (*Meleagris gallopavo*). Since wild turkeys are not native to the Valley of Oaxaca, this fragment may be from a dried specimen imported for its feathers.

Imported Marine Fish Products

Rear tooth of a shark, family Carcharhinidae (Fig. 13.10*t*). Unidentified cranial element, marine fish.

Animal Bones

The animal bones in the Zone D Midden probably came from several different houses, making it difficult to draw firm conclusions from their spatial association in the refuse. In Zone D2, however, bones from a number of animals that frequent riverine habitats were found in the same excavation square. These were the raccoon, which visits the Atoyac River to wash its food; the mud turtle, which seeks out backwaters and shallow pools along the margin of the river; and the band-tailed pigeon, which during the dry season is known to gather daily in the morning at water sources like the Atoyac, where it can be ambushed (Leopold 1959:295). (Another bird that could have been found along the Atoyac is the coot, whose remains were found in Zone D1; see below.)

Large Mammals

white-tailed deer (*Odocoileus virginianus*)

2 cheek teeth

1 L. proximal ulna

5 long bone splinters

Small Mammals

domestic dog (*Canis familiaris*)

1 fragment petrous bone

1 upper R. second molar

5 canine teeth, from at least 2 different dogs

1 proximal R. femur

1 proximal L. femur

2 fused metapodials

1 unfused metapodial

1 first phalanx

1 second phalanx

pocket gopher (*Orthogeomys grandis*)

1 upper incisor

1 lower incisor

unidentified cottontail (*Sylvilagus* sp.)

1 smashed maxilla

raccoon (*Procyon lotor*)

1 skull fragment

Reptiles

mud turtle (*Kinosternon integrum*)

3 carapace scutes

1 plastron scute

Birds

band-tailed pigeon (*Columba fasciata*)

1 humerus fragment

Unidentified

8 splinters

Zone D1

Radiocarbon Dates

We submitted two pieces of charcoal from Zone D1 for conventional radiocarbon dating. One came out 2990 ± 120 B.P., or roughly 1040 b.c. (SI-466). The calibrated two-sigma range would be 1500-900 B.C. The other piece came out 2925 ± 85 B.P., or roughly 975 b.c. (Gx-0785). The calibrated two-sigma range would be 1390-900 B.C.

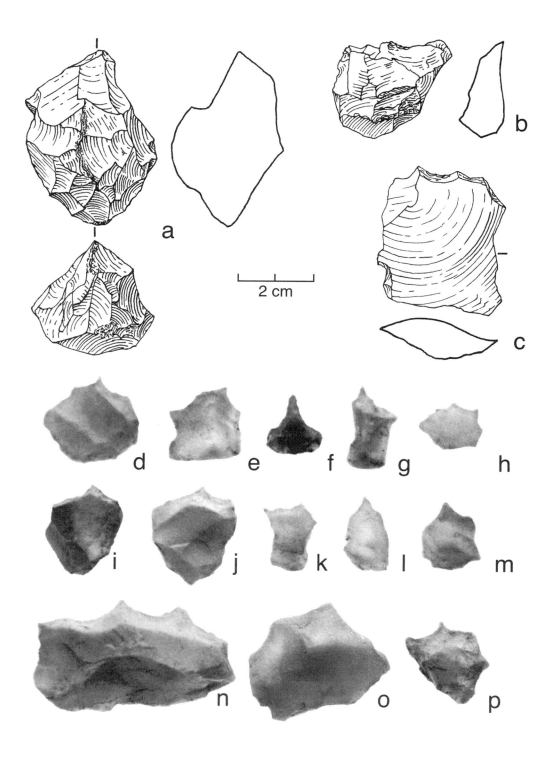

Figure 13.7. Examples of chert artifacts from the Zone D Midden. *a*, hammerstone. *b*, core tablet. *c*, utilized flake. *d-p*, flake perforators/gravers.

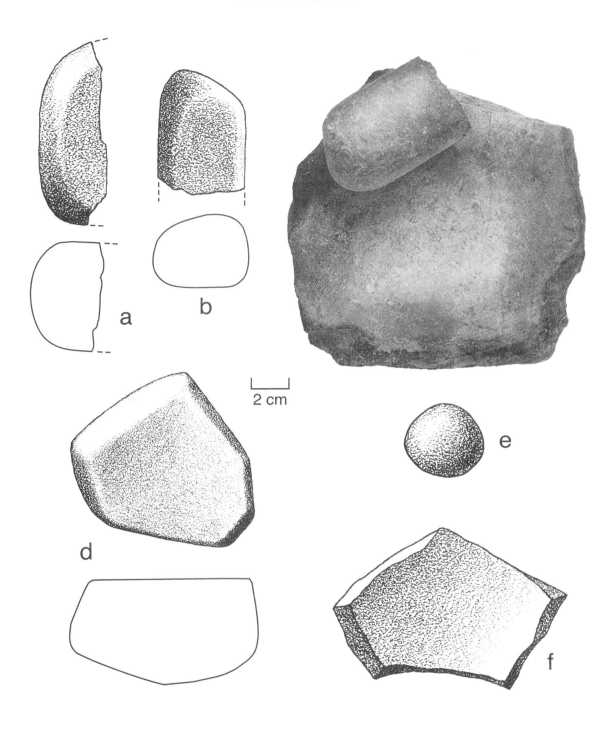

Figure 13.8. Ground stone artifacts from the Zone D Midden. *a*, broken one-hand mano. *b*, combination one-hand mano/pounder, broken. *c*, photograph of the same mano/pounder shown in *b*, together with the basin-shaped metate with which it was discarded; both were covered with red pigment. *d*, polishing stone with one flat facet. *e*, spherical polishing pebble. *f*, fragment of stone bowl, diorite.

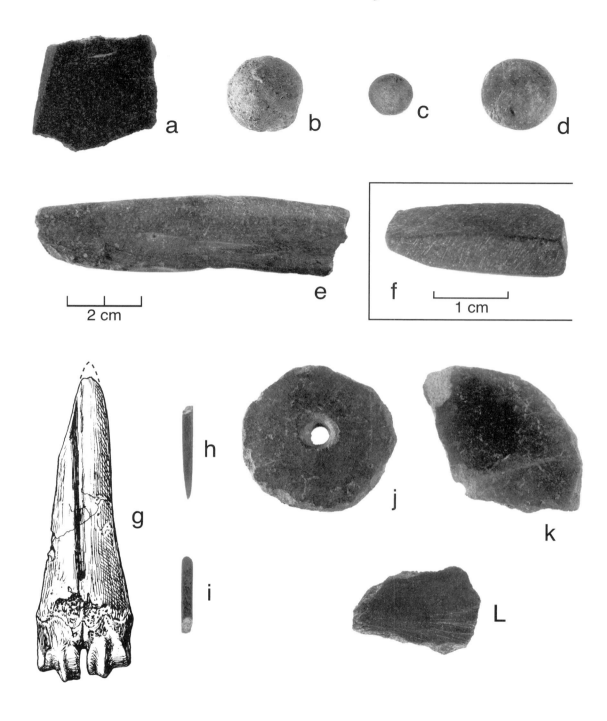

Figure 13.9. Artifacts from the Zone D Midden. *a*, fragment from broken celt. *b-d*, *canicas* or pecked and ground stone balls. *e, f*, stone "cutting boards," discarded together. *g*, deer metapodial awl or *piscador*. *h, i*, fragments of sewing needles. *j*, perforated sherd disk. *k*, one-third of a perforated sherd disk. *L*, worked sherd, apparently used as a cutting board.

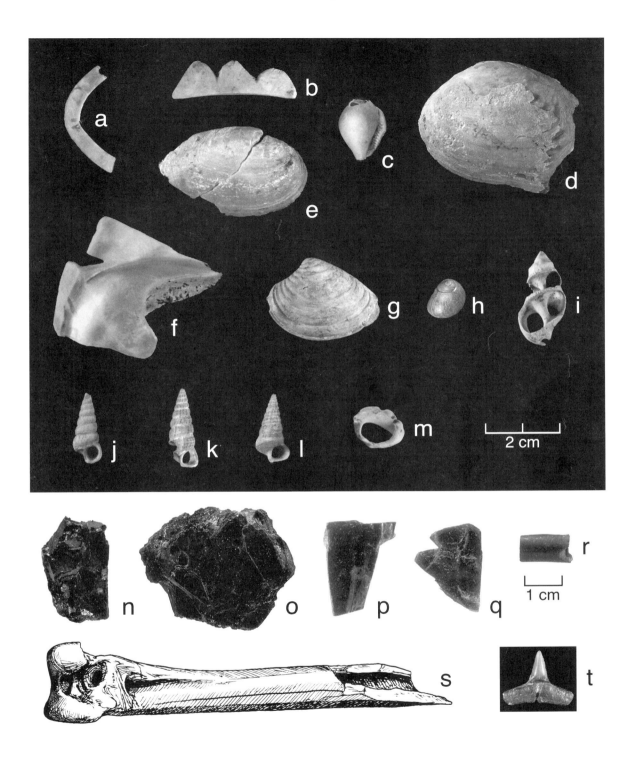

Figure 13.10. Objects from the Zone D Midden. *a*, fragment of ring-shaped pearl oyster(?) ornament with drill hole. *b*, trilobed ornament of *Spondylus* shell. *c*, *Columbella* [= *Pyrene*] shell, perforated for suspension. *d, e*, mussels, cf. *Barynaias*. *f*, piece trimmed from pearl oyster valve. *g*, *Chione* [= *Anomalocardia*] valve. *h*, *Neritina*. *i*, worn horn shell (*Cerithium*). *j-l*, horn shells (*Cerithidea*). *m*, beachworn dogwinkle (*Thais*). *n*, metallic hematite ore. *o-q*, black mica. *r*, tubular stone bead. *s*, tibiotarsus of wild turkey. *t*, shark tooth.

Ceramics

Some 7197 sherds were recovered from Zone D1. They have been described by Flannery and Marcus (1994: Table 14.1). Included is one sherd believed on the basis of neutron activation to be Calzadas Carved from San Lorenzo, Veracruz (Hector Neff, pers. comm.). In addition, Zone D1 produced 7 sherds of Xochiltepec White and 25 sherds of La Mina White, other possible imports from the Gulf Coast. While we consider these 33 sherds to reflect some sort of exchange relationship with Veracruz, it should be pointed out that they constitute only 0.005 of the Zone D1 sherd sample.

A significant discovery made in Zone D1 was part of the Delfina Fine Gray bowl shown in Figure 13.5 (another part of the same vessel was found in Zone D2). This low cylindrical bowl with a slightly bolstered rim had been deeply incised on the outside with two horizontal rows of cartouches inside rectangles. In each cartouche appears the "mat" symbol. While this motif is found at San José Mogote on both Leandro Gray and Delfina Fine Gray vessels, it does not appear in the Calzadas Carved sample from San Lorenzo illustrated by Coe and Diehl (1980a). The significance of the "mat" motif is that it goes on to become a widespread symbol of elite authority in both the Zapotec and Maya regions (Marcus 1992: Fig. 10.1). Its appearance on San José phase pottery may reflect the emergence of chiefly symbolism (Marcus and Flannery 1996:96).

Chipped Stone

Chert (84%)
    hammerstones: 4 (Fig. 13.7*a*)
    ordinary flake cores: 8
    core face: 1
    core tablets: 2
    core platform edge: 1
    bipolar flake cores: 5
    flake perforators/gravers: 52 (Fig. 13.7*d-p*)
    denticulate scrapers: 4
    retouched flakes: 2
    utilized flakes: 19
    flakes, not utilized: 154
    angular fragments: 8
Obsidian (12%)
    prismatic blade fragments: 4
    burin/graver: 1
    scaled flakes: 2
    utilized flake: 1
    debitage: 30
Other (4%)
    quartz angular fragment: 1
    volcanic flakes: 9
    volcanic angular fragment: 1

Ground Stone

Found Together
    Combination one-hand mano and pounder, broken, covered with red pigment; and one slightly basin-shaped metate made from metamorphosed Cretaceous mudstone(?), also covered with red pigment. The metate's length was 7+ cm (broken); maximum width, 4.7 cm; thickness, 4.1 cm (see Fig. 13.8*b, c*).
Found Separately
    Fragment of hemispherical stone bowl, diorite, measuring 12.6 × 8 cm, thickness 2.5-3.6 cm (Fig. 13.8*f*). This stone bowl resembles those used in the Late Archaic of the Tehuacán Valley (MacNeish, Nelken-Terner, and Johnson 1967:117-18) and at the Martínez Rockshelter near Mitla (Flannery and Spores 1983:25).
    Fragment from a broken celt, dark greenish-black metamorphic rock, roughly 3 × 3 cm (Fig. 13.9*a*).
    Three *canicas* or pecked and ground stone balls; one 38 mm in diameter, one 20 mm in diameter, and one 11 mm in diameter (Fig. 13.9*b-d*).
    Spherical polishing pebble, fine sandstone, diameter irregular but between 3.1 and 4.2 cm (Fig. 13.8*e*).

Bone Tools

Awl or *piscador* made from the distal metapodial of a deer. The tip is broken off; the object was originally more than 8.3 cm long (Fig. 13.9*g*).
Broken artifact of unknown function, made of deer long bone.

Worked Sherd

Irregular worked sherd, 3.2 × 2.3 cm, apparently used as some kind of cutting board; one surface is covered with small blade marks (Fig. 13.9*L*).

Shell

Ornaments
    Part of a *Spondylus* ornament with three lobes, covered with red pigment; 32 × 10 × 3 mm (Fig. 13.10*b*).
    Dove shell, *Columbella* (= *Pyrene*) cf. *major*, top perforated for suspension; 17 mm long (Fig. 13.10*c*).
Pearly Freshwater Mussels
    Fragment of cut mussel shell, 30 × 20 × 1.5 mm.
    Fragment of cut mussel shell, 20 × 15 × 1.5 mm.
    Fragment, possibly *Barynaias,* 15 × 11 × 1 mm.
    Fragment, possibly *Barynaias,* 29 × 13 × 1.5 mm.
    Fragment, possibly *Barynaias,* 30 × 22 × 1 mm.
Pacific Marine Bivalves
    Big piece from the hinge area of a pearl oyster (*Pinctada mazatlanica*), cut irregularly, clearly manufacturing waste; roughly 42 × 40 mm (Fig. 13.10*f*).
    Fragment of pearl oyster, manufacturing waste, 21 × 14 × 2 mm.
    Fragment of pearl oyster, 25 × 25 × 3 mm.

Fragment from the hinge area of a pearl oyster, 24 × 17 × 7 mm, manufacturing waste.

Fragment of pearl oyster, rectangular, cut on three edges, 15 × 13 × 3 mm.

Fragment from the hinge of a very large spiny oyster (*Spondylus calcifer*), 64 × 50 × 3 mm, evidently manufacturing waste.

Two valves of Venus clam, *Chione* (= *Anomalocardia*) *subrugosa*, one complete (30 × 24 × 1 mm), the other broken (20 × 19 × 1 mm) (Fig. 13.10*g*).

Pacific Marine Univalves

Complete nerite (*Neritina* cf. *usnea*), 18 mm long (Fig. 13.10*h*).

Horn shell (*Cerithium stercusmuscarum*), worn, 26 mm long (Fig. 13.10*i*).

Complete horn shell (*Cerithidea* sp.), 19 mm long (Fig. 13.10*j*).

Two complete horn shells (*Cerithidea* cf. *pliculosa*): one 22 mm long; the other 19 mm long (Fig. 13.10*k, l*).

Unidentified Shells

Shell fragment, burned, 22 × 10 × 1 mm.

Shell fragment, 20 × 14 × 2 mm.

Iron Ore Specimens

Lump of magnetite ore, Group I-A, from near Tenango. Pires-Ferreira (1975: Table 11) considers this one of the most common sources used at San José Mogote.

Lump of magnetite ore, Group I-B, from Loma los Sabinos near Zimatlán. According to Pires-Ferreira (1975: Table 12), examples from this source were also found in Household Unit C4 (Chapter 14) and on the surface of a site near Coyotepec in the southern subvalley.

Mica

Piece of black mica weighing 10.5 g, trimmed on several edges, 35 × 35 × 5 mm (Fig. 13.10*o*).

Piece of black mica weighing 1.0 g, irregular in shape, cut on at least three edges, 26 × 17 × 2 mm (Fig. 13.10*p*).

Piece of gold mica weighing 0.3 g, 17 × 17 × 1 mm.

Shattered piece of gold mica weighing 0.2 g., possibly cut on one edge, 20 × 16 × 1 mm.

Figurines

Some 25 fragments of figurines were recovered from Zone D1; they have been described and illustrated by Marcus (1998a: 154-56 and Figs. 12.20-12.22). While most are fragments of small solid figurines, four are pieces of large hollow white-slipped dolls. The slip on the hollow dolls appears to be the same used for Atoyac Yellow-white, which indicates that they are of local manufacture.

Stone Ornament

Tubular stone bead, unfinished or broken during manufacture, made of fine metamorphic rock; 7 mm in diameter and roughly 14 mm long (Fig. 13.10*r*).

Imported Bird Products

Distal tibiotarsus of wild turkey (*Meleagris gallopavo*), with many blade marks on its ventral surface (Fig. 13.10*s*). Since wild turkeys have not been reported from the Valley of Oaxaca, this fragment may be from a dried specimen imported for its feathers.

Carbonized Plants

Several chunks of wood charcoal from Zone D1, probably the remains of fuel used in hearths or charcoal braziers, were large enough to be identified to genus by Suzanne Harris of the University of Michigan Ethnobotany Lab. The wood proved to be pine (*Pinus* sp.) and mesquite (*Prosopis* sp.).

Animal Bones

Large Mammals

white-tailed deer (*Odocoileus virginianus*)

1 cheek tooth

1 complete atlas vertebra

1 R. proximal radius

Small Mammals

domestic dog (*Canis familiaris*)

1 incisor

1 R. lower third premolar

1 R. lower first molar

1 R. lower third molar

1 R. proximal radius

1 second phalanx

pocket gopher (*Orthogeomys grandis*)

upper left incisors from two different gophers

eastern cottontail (*Sylvilagus floridanus*)

1 R. and 1 L. innominate

1 R. calcaneum

Mexican cottontail (*Sylvilagus cunicularius*)

1 L. and 1 R. mandible

1 R. proximal radius

unidentified cottontail

1 unfused radius

1 L. calcaneum

Unidentified Mammal

1 tibia shaft fragment

1 rib

Birds

coot (*Fulica americana*)

1 humerus

unidentified bird

1 humerus

Chapter 14

Area A: Houses of the Middle San José Phase

Zone C of Area A was an 80-cm-thick stratum of buff debris from the decomposition of wattle-and-daub houses. Once we began to excavate it, we discovered that it comprised a series of four superimposed household units which we labeled (from top to bottom) C1, C2, C3, and C4.

As luck would have it, we were unable to expose any of the houses completely. In most cases, what we recovered was part of a house plus part of its adjacent dooryard. This was not all bad, since we learned more about the use of dooryards in Area A than we did in Area C. Often there were features in the dooryard that rarely, if ever, occurred inside a house: bell-shaped pits, earth ovens, outdoor hearths, and even (in the case of Unit C3) ritual basins. By combining data from Areas A and C, one can develop a sense of the distribution of activities throughout a household unit.

One of the interesting lessons learned from Area A was that specific craft activities, once established in a residential ward, could persist for many generations. Every residence in Zone C had been involved in (1) the grinding of iron ore lumps into small mirrors, and (2) the conversion of mollusk shells into ornaments or costume parts. If we include the evidence for those same activities in the Zone D Midden (Chapter 13), it means that perhaps five generations of families were involved.

Judging by their pottery, all the households we excavated were ones whose iconography featured Sky/Lightning motifs on gray, black, or white-rimmed black vessels (Flannery and Marcus 1994:303). In our expanded chronology, Zone C would be considered Middle San José phase.

Household Unit C4

Our excavation of Unit C4, the earliest of the four households, exposed part of the dooryard (Fig. 14.1). Based on the areas of wattle-and-daub wall collapse we found, the house itself must have been just west of Squares H10-K10. The major discovery in the dooryard was Feature 5, a large outdoor hearth or cooking pit filled with fire-cracked rock. Most of the artifact debris worthy of piece-plotting was found between Feature 5 and the areas of fallen daub along the western limit of the excavation.

Three areas of the Unit C4 dooryard had been disturbed by intrusive features dug down from Household Unit C3. These were Features 2, 6, and 8, all of which will be described in the course of our discussion of Unit C3.

One of the activities of Household C4 was the production of small flat iron ore mirrors. Some of the raw material used was ilmeno-magnetite from the Cacaotepec source (Group IV-B). We know that two mirrors from this source were traded to San Lorenzo, Veracruz (Pires-Ferreira 1975: Table 17). Evidently San Lorenzo reciprocated with gifts of Xochiltepec White vessels, nine sherds of which were found in Unit C4. One sherd believed, on the basis of neutron activation, to be Calzadas Carved from San Lorenzo, Veracruz, was also found in the dooryard (Hector Neff, pers. comm.). Presumably the Calzadas Carved vessel arrived bearing some desirable commodity, since San José Mogote already had plenty of its own carved gray pottery. It would be interesting to know exactly what product San José Mogote received in exchange for its gifts of iron ore mirrors: cacao? rubber? pearly mussels from Gulf Coast rivers?

In addition to pottery from the Gulf Coast, Household C4 also received vessels of Paloma Negative, a pottery type from the Basin of Mexico (Flannery and Marcus 1994: Fig. 12.159). San José Mogote may have reciprocated with gifts of Delfina Fine Gray vessels (Flannery and Marcus 1994:259-62).

Radiocarbon Date[1]

One 1960s charcoal sample from Unit C4 yielded a conventional date of 2930 ± 120 B.P., or roughly 980 b.c. (SI-465). The calibrated two-sigma range would be 1430-820 B.C.

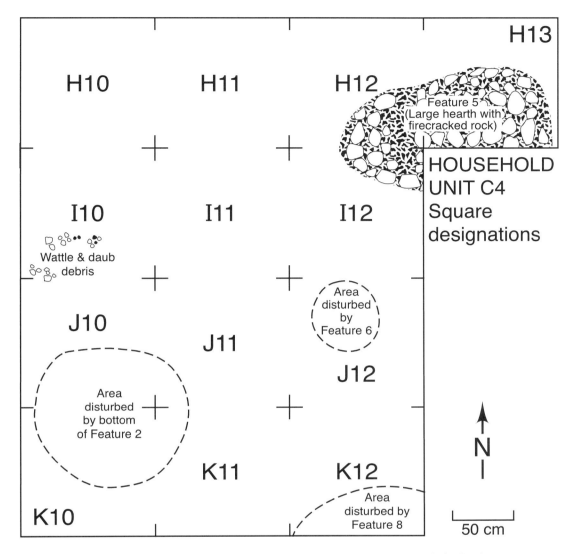

Figure 14.1. Plan of Household Unit C4, showing square designations and major landmarks.

Daub

This unit produced dozens of daub fragments. Impressions of the canes indicated that their diameters ranged from 0.6 cm to 1.8 cm. The house had been plastered on the outside with a layer of whitewashed clay 3-5 mm thick. In the Munsell system, its surface color was "pink" (7.5 YR 7/4).

Ceramics

Some 4637 sherds were recovered from the dooryard of Household Unit C4; they have been described by Flannery and Marcus (1994: Table 14.1). As mentioned above, we found 12 sherds from interesting trade wares. However, these amounted to only 0.003 of the sherds from the unit.

Chipped Stone

  Chert (89%)
    hammerstone: 1 fragment
    ordinary flake cores: 7 (Fig. 14.2*a*)
    core platform edges: 2 (Fig. 14.2*b, c*)
    bipolar flake cores: 2
    core tool: 1
    flake spokeshave: 1
    flake perforators/gravers: 28 (Fig. 14.2*d-g*)
    denticulate scraper: 1 (Fig. 14.2*h*)
    denticulate core scraper: 1
    denticulate flakes: 4
    endscraper: 1
    sidescraper: 1
    retouched flakes: 4

---

[1]In this volume, uncalibrated dates are given as "b.c.," and dendrocalibrated dates as "B.C." (see Chapter 26, Radiocarbon Dating).

utilized flakes: 29 (Fig. 14.2*i, j*)
flakes, not utilized: 106
Obsidian (6%)
  prismatic blade fragments, utilized: 2 (Fig. 14.2*k, L*)
  prismatic blade fragments, no sign of use: 3
  utilized flake: 1
  flakes, not utilized: 7
Other (5%)
  quartz flakes: 2
  quartz fragments: 2
  ignimbrite flakes: 6
Comment: Pires-Ferreira (1975) determined that two obsidian flakes were from Zinapécuaro and two from Otumba.

Ground Stone

Fragment of subrectangular two-hand mano with airfoil cross-section, gneiss. Estimated width, 9 cm; maximum thickness, 4.5 cm.

Worked Sherds

Small sherd, probably Leandro Gray, smoothly cut into a rectangle 27 mm long × 9 mm wide (Fig. 14.3*a*).

Irregular worked sherd, Leandro Gray, 25 × 23 mm, one side showing part of a perforation that may have been drilled into the vessel from which the sherd came (Fig. 14.3*b*).

Shell

Pearly Freshwater Mussels
  4 fragments, possibly *Barynaias*: (1) 14 × 10 mm × 1 mm; (2) 8 × 9 × 1 mm; (3) 12 × 10 × 1 mm; (4) 15 × 8 × 1 mm
Pacific Marine Bivalves
  fragment of pearl oyster (*Pinctada mazatlanica*), 27 × 15 × 4 mm
Pacific Marine Univalves
  complete horn shell (*Cerithium stercusmuscarum*), 25 mm long (Fig. 14.3*c*)
Unidentified Shell
  2 fragments, 26 × 9 × 1 mm and 15 × 8 × 1 mm

Iron Ore Specimens

Lump of magnetite ore, Group I-B, from Loma Los Sabinos near Zimatlán. Pires-Ferreira (1975: Table 12) also identified lumps from this source at Coyotepec in the Valley of Oaxaca and Etlatongo in the Valley of Nochixtlán.

Partially worked lump of ilmeno-magnetite ore, Group IV-B, from Loma Salinas near San Lorenzo Cacaotepec. As mentioned above, Pires-Ferreira (1975: Table 17) found that this source was the one used for two small flat mirrors traded to San Lorenzo, Veracruz.

Two fragments of iron ore mirrors (not subjected to Mössbauer spectrum analysis).

Mica Specimens

Three pieces from the same sheet of dark brown mica, with a total weight of 1.3 g. One is 27 × 23 × 1.5 mm, cut on at least two sides. Each of the others is 26 × 23 × 1.5 mm.

A single piece of black mica weighing 0.5 g., cut on at least two sides; 20 × 12 × 1 mm.

Shattered piece of gold mica weighing 0.3 g.; 30 × 20 mm, and less than 1 mm thick.

Piece of black mica weighing 0.3 g., and cut on at least three sides; 20 × 13 mm, and less than 1 mm thick.

Figurines

Some 34 figurine fragments were found on the dooryard surface. They have been described and illustrated by Marcus (1998a:145 and Figs. 12.1-12.2), and 7 piece-plotted examples are shown in Figure 14.4. While most fragments came from small solid figurines, there were at least two pieces of large white-slipped hollow dolls.

Stone Ornament

A tubular bead of fine green metamorphic stone was found, 11 mm long and 8 mm in diameter; possibly jadeite(?) (Fig. 14.3*d*).

Bone Ornament?

A shaft of the distal R. femur of a Mexican cottontail (*Sylvilagus cunicularius*) was found, which appears to have been trimmed to form a tubular bone bead, possibly for a necklace.

Animal Bones

Represented in the debris from Household C4 were at least two individual deer (one adult, one juvenile), two individual pocket gophers, a dog, a mud turtle, and a cottontail.
Large Mammals
  white-tailed deer (*Odocoileus virginianus*)
    1 hyoid
    1 L. distal humerus (adult)
    1 L. distal femur, unfused (juvenile)
    1 distal metapodial, unfused (juvenile)
    1 fragment of innominate
    1 rib
    1 vertebra fragment
    1 limb bone splinter
Small Mammals
  domestic dog (*Canis familiaris*)
    1 carbonized canine tooth
    1 maxilla fragment with premolar
    1 maxilla fragment with upper R. molars
    1 tooth root
    1 metapodial
    1 second phalanx

pocket gopher (*Orthogeomys grandis*)
upper L. incisors from two different gophers
1 upper R. incisor
1 lower L. incisor
1 proximal R. humerus
1 right tibia
eastern cottontail (*Sylvilagus floridanus*)
1 R. mandible fragment
1 L. distal humerus
1 R. innominate
Reptiles
mud turtle (*Kinosternon integrum*)
1 marginal carapace scute

Feature 5

Feature 5 was a large outdoor hearth or roasting pit filled with fire-cracked rocks, found in Squares H12 and H13 of the Unit C4 dooryard (Fig. 14.3*e*). It measured roughly 1.75 by 1.0 m, and had been dug 15-20 cm down into the Zone D1 midden. One of the fire-cracked rocks proved to be a fragment of basin-shaped metate 4.7 cm thick. This large outdoor cooking facility is reminiscent of Feature 7 in Household Unit E (Chapter 13) and provides a contrast with Feature 6 in Unit C3 (see below).

Insights from Artifact Plotting

Figures 14.4-14.7 present the distributions of chert cores, perforators/gravers, shell and mica fragments, iron ore specimens, ground stone, worked sherds, figurine fragments, and utilized chert flakes on the Unit C4 dooryard. (Utilized flakes were recorded by square, rather than piece-plotted.) Of particular interest is the contrast between the features and artifact distributions in Unit C4 and Unit C3, the residence stratigraphically above it. There are hints here (and elsewhere on the site) that small, circular, ash-filled hearths (like Feature 6 of Unit C3) tended to appear in women's activity areas, while large, irregularly shaped roasting pits filled with fire-cracked rock (like Feature 5 of Unit C4) tended to appear in men's activity areas. It is necessary to review the artifact distributions for both units to see the full array of supporting data for this dichotomy.

Feature 5 was not an ordinary culinary hearth. No broken charcoal braziers or fire-blackened ollas were found adjacent to it, as was the case with Feature 6. In our entire 13 m² exposure of Unit C4, we recovered only one fragment of the kind of two-hand mano used by women, and it had been discarded far from Feature 5 (Fig. 14.5). We suspect that this roasting pit may have been a man's facility for special cooking events, such as the roasting of a deer or a group of dogs.

Let us now look at the locations of chert cores (Fig. 14.5) and utilized flakes (Fig. 14.6). Four cores had been discarded to the north and west of Feature 5, while another five were scattered across the southern squares of the excavation. All but two of the utilized flakes had been discarded between Feature 5 and the wattle-and-daub concentration in Square I10. Clearly, a lot of cutting activity had been carried out in that part of the dooryard, and some of it may have been related to the preparation of material to be cooked in Feature 5.

When we turn to those items possibly related to shell or mica working (Fig. 14.7), we see two clear concentrations. One group of chert perforators/gravers, shells, and mica stretches west from Feature 5 for a distance of 3 m. Another cluster of perforators/gravers and mussel shell appears in Square K10, and might have been more extensive, had that area not been disturbed by an intrusive pit from Unit C3. What we may be seeing in Figure 14.7 are the "toss zones" from two shell workers, one of whom also worked mica. Some of the utilized flakes seen in Figure 14.6 might have been associated with the northern concentration.

Finally, all four iron ore specimens (including two mirror fragments and a partially worked lump) were scattered across Squares I10-I12, near the northern concentration of perforators/gravers, shell, and mica. This area, stretching west from Feature 5, may have been one where items from multiple craft activities had been discarded.

We suspect that our excavation of Unit C4 exposed a men's work area and an associated outdoor roasting pit. If we are correct, it appears that the man (or men) involved had engaged in the working of shell, iron ore, and mica, as well as other activities producing signs of use on chert flakes. The scarcity of evidence for women's activities in our exposure of C4 provides a contrast with Unit C3 (below).

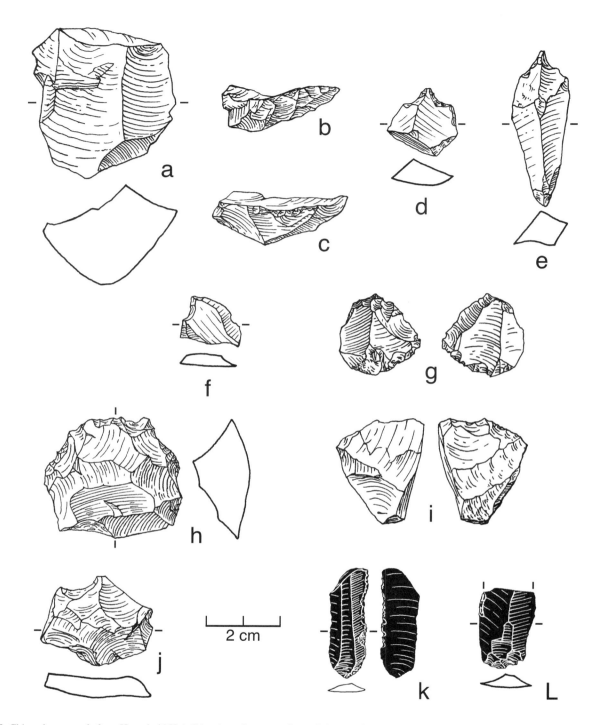

Figure 14.2. Chipped stone tools from Household Unit C4. *a-j* are chert. *a*, ordinary flake core. *b, c*, core platform edges. *d-f*, flake perforators/gravers. *g*, extremely worn perforator/graver. *h*, denticulate scraper. *i, j*, utilized flakes. *k, L*, prismatic obsidian blade fragments, utilized.

Figure 14.3. Items found in Household Unit C4. *a, b,* worked sherds; dashed line in *b* indicates where the vessel had been perforated, perhaps to repair a crack with string. *c,* complete horn shell (*Cerithium stercusmuscarum*) with a smaller shell lodged in its operculum. *d,* tubular jadeite(?) bead. *e,* Feature 5, a large outdoor hearth or roasting pit filled with fire-cracked rock. (Some rocks have been removed to show the depth of the basin.) Scale in cm; white arrow points north.

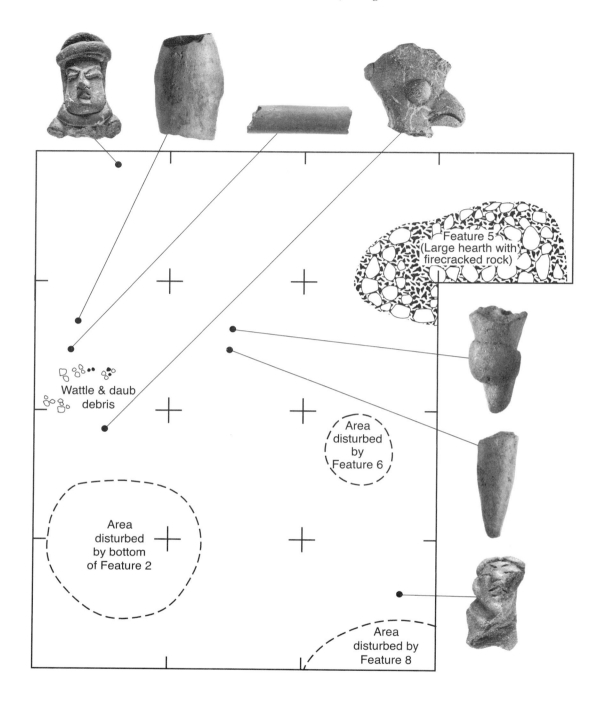

Figure 14.4. Figurine fragments piece-plotted on the dooryard of Household Unit C4.

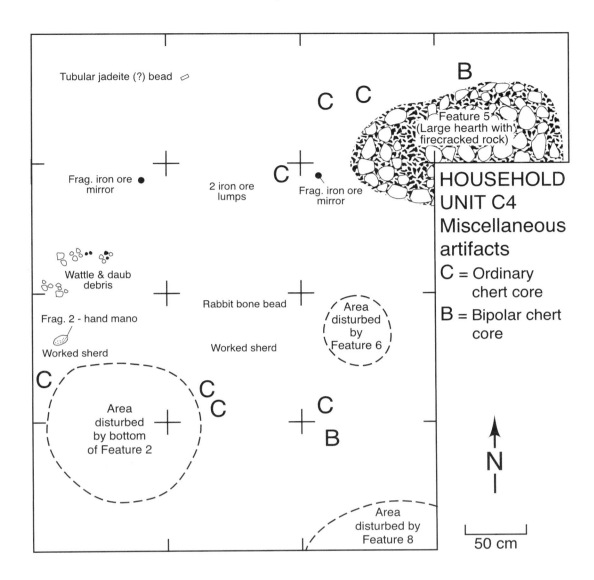

Figure 14.5. Distribution of chert cores and a variety of other materials on the dooryard of Household Unit C4.

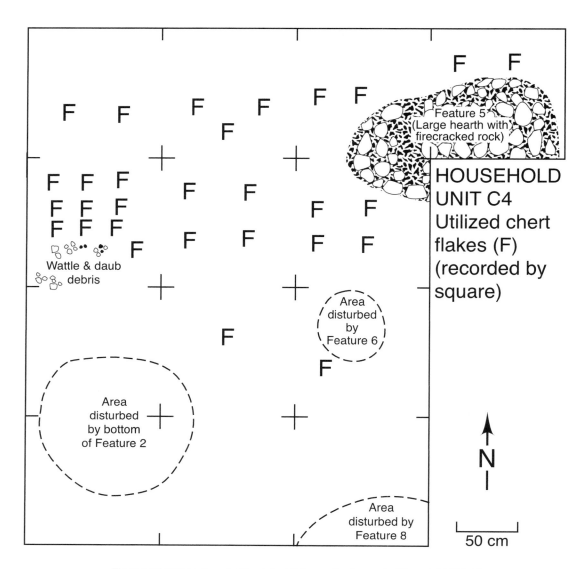

Figure 14.6. Distribution of utilized chert flakes on the dooryard of Household Unit C4.

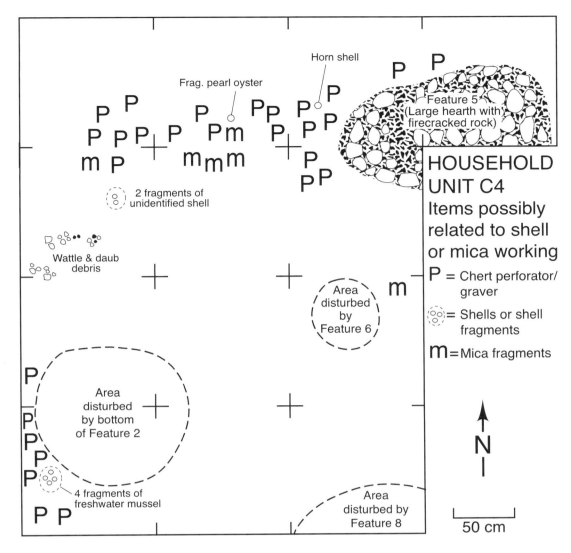

Figure 14.7. Distribution of items possibly related to shell or mica working throughout Household Unit C4.

Household Unit C3

Our exposure of Household Unit C3 revealed an area of wattle-and-daub collapse, presumed to be from the east wall of the house, plus 13 m² of the dooryard to the east. There were four features in the dooryard, two of them utilitarian and two of them almost certainly ritual.

One of the utilitarian facilities was Feature 6, a stone-lined, ash-filled outdoor hearth with a broken charcoal brazier and cooking pots lying nearby (Fig. 14.8). There was also a bell-shaped pit, Feature 2, that had been used as an earth oven. Because of the hearth, brazier, cooking pots, and earth oven, we suspect that this part of the dooryard was a woman's work area. Fragments of metates and manos, Fidencio Coarse jars, and other artifacts

associated with food preparation were more abundant in our exposure of Unit C3 than they had been in our exposure of C4.

The possibility that this part of the dooryard was a woman's activity area gives extra significance to Features 3 and 8 (Fig. 14.8). These were two shallow, lime-plastered, brightly painted basins which we believe were used for the kind of water divination the Zapotec called *quela hueniy niça*. According to sixteenth-century documents and ethnographic data, this kind of divination ritual was performed by women (Marcus 1998a:11-13). The presence of these basins near Features 2 and 6 suggests that such divination was already part of women's ritual during the Formative.

Finally, the large number of figurine fragments (68) in this area reinforces our impression that it was a venue for women's household ritual (Marcus 1998a).

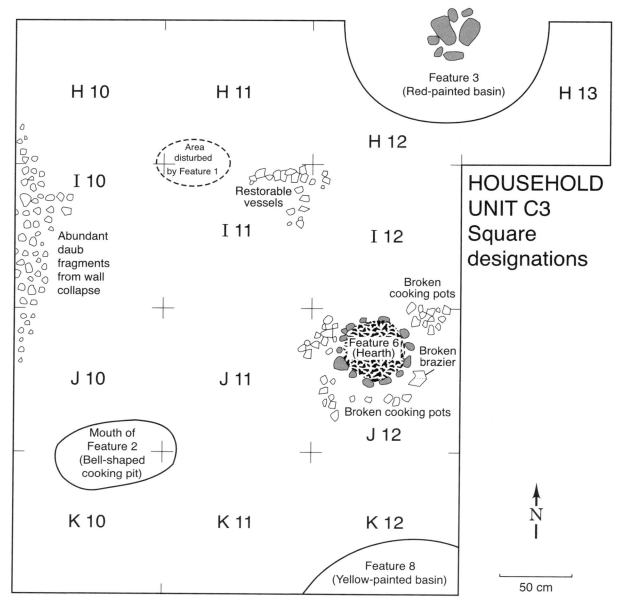

Figure 14.8. Plan of Household Unit C3, showing square designations and notable landmarks.

Radiocarbon Dates

One conventional radiocarbon date on charcoal from the Unit C3 floor came out 3120 ± 120 B.P., or roughly 1170 b.c. (SI-464). The calibrated two-sigma range would be 1650-1030 B.C. (See also the date from Feature 2, below.)

Daub

This unit produced dozens of whitewashed daub fragments, some of which showed that replastering had taken place during the lifetime of the house. The original clay plaster varied from 2 to 5 mm in thickness; in the case of replastered specimens, both layers of plaster averaged 3 mm. In the Munsell system, the color of the surface was "pink" (7.5 YR 7/4). Impressions in the daub indicated that the canes used in construction had diameters ranging from 0.7 to 1.7 cm (Fig. 14.9*a*).

Ceramics

Some 6998 sherds were found on the dooryard of Household Unit C3; they have been described by Flannery and Marcus (1994: Table 14.1). Perhaps because it included an area where cooking was done, Unit C3 produced more Fidencio Coarse sherds (3246) and Lupita Heavy Plain sherds (201) than any other residential exposure in Area A. Evidently food and water storage, boiling in jars, and cooking over charcoal braziers were common activities in the area we exposed.

In addition to abundant utilitarian pottery, the dooryard debris also included a few ceramics from outside the valley. The most common were sherds of Xochiltepec White (13) and La Mina White (10), two probable Gulf Coast wares. Since Household C3 was engaged in making iron ore mirrors for export, it is not surprising that it received gifts of exotic pottery. However, such foreign sherds represented only .003 of the Unit C3 sample.

Chipped Stone
    Chert (94%)
        hammerstones: 2 (Fig. 14.9*b*)
        ordinary flake cores: 23 (Fig. 14.10*a*)
        core face: 1 (Fig. 14.10*b*)
        core made on reworked hammerstone: 1
        core spokeshave: 1
        flake perforators/gravers: 38 (Fig. 14.10*c, d*)
        large retouched flake perforator: 1
        core perforators: 2
        denticulate scraper: 1 (Fig. 14.10*e*)
        denticulate flake: 1
        endscraper: 1 (Fig. 14.10*f*)
        core scraper: 1 (Fig. 14.10*g, h*)
        retouched flakes: 9 (Fig. 14.11*a, b*)
        utilized flakes: 29
        flakes, not utilized: 185
    Obsidian (3%)
        prismatic blade fragments, utilized: 3 (Fig. 14.11*d*)
        prismatic blade fragments, no sign of use: 2
        unilaterally retouched blade segment: 1 (Fig. 14.11*e*)
        pieces used as wedges: 2 (Fig. 14.11*f, g*)
        flakes, not utilized: 3
    Other (2%)
        quartz fragments: 2
        igneous flakes: 2
    Comment: Pires-Ferreira (1975) neutron-activated 8 pieces of obsidian from Household C3. She reported 3 blades from Zinapécuaro, 3 flakes from Otumba, 1 flake from Guadalupe Victoria, and 1 flake from Altotonga.

Ground Stone
    Broken subrectangular one-hand mano with subrectangular cross-section, gneiss. All three surfaces (top, bottom, and end) are very finely ground. This is probably not a mano for grinding maize; it may have been used with the rectangular lipped metate described below. Length, 7+ cm (broken); width, 5.7 cm; thickness, 6 cm (Fig. 14.12*b*).
    Nondescript mano fragment.
    Fragment of lipped metate, ignimbrite; the grinding surface goes down at a 45° angle from the lip toward the central trough. Rim to base, 7.6 cm; base to grinding surface, 1 cm near the center and 4 cm near the edges (Fig. 14.12*a*).
    Fragment of slab metate, ignimbrite, with a slightly concave upper surface. Length, 14+ cm (broken); width, 6+ cm (broken); thickness, 4 cm (Fig. 14.12*c*).

Fragment of basin-shaped metate, 4.5 cm thick at the center of the basin.
Two *canicas* or pecked and ground stone balls, one 21 mm in diameter, the other 18 mm in diameter (Fig. 14.12*d, e*).

Worked Sherds
    Triangular worked sherd of Leandro Gray with excised motif, chipped along the edges, 4 × 3 cm (Fig. 14.13*e*).

Shell
    Ornaments
        fragment of nacreous ornament, shaped like a ring with at least 1 loop for suspension, 9 × 2 × 1 mm (Fig. 14.12*f*)
        fragment of nacreous ornament, shaped like a ring, 9 × 4 × 1 mm (Fig. 14.12*g*)
        small dove shell, *Columbella* (= *Pyrene*) *major*, top removed for suspension; would originally have been ca. 10 mm long
    Pearly Freshwater Mussels
        valve of *Barynaias*, 20 × 15 × 1 mm
        fragment of *Barynaias* (manufacturing waste), 17 × 20 × 1 mm
        fragment of *Barynaias* (manufacturing waste), 22 × 19 × 1 mm, cut on at least 2 sides
        fragment of *Barynaias* (manufacturing waste), 19 × 4 × 1 mm
        unidentified cut fragment of pearly mussel, 15 × 17 × 1 mm
    Pacific Marine Bivalves
        2 fragments of pearl oyster (*Pinctada mazatlanica*), both manufacturing waste: (1) 16 × 11 × 4 mm; (2) 24 × 14 × 4 mm
        fragment of spiny oyster (*Spondylus calcifer*), 57 × 14 × 15 mm, manufacturing waste which includes the hinge (Fig. 14.12*h*)
        2 unidentified fragments of bivalve: (1) 16 × 3 × 2.5 mm; (2) 36 × 17 × 2.5 mm; both manufacturing waste
        fragment of Venus clam (*Chione* sp.), 20 × 16 × 1 mm
    Pacific Marine Univalves
        broken button shell (*Modulus catenulatus*), 18 mm in diameter (Fig. 14.12*i*)
        horn shell (*Cerithidea mazatlanica*), 17 mm long
        horn shell, 23 mm long (Fig. 14.12*j*)
        2 fragments of dove shell: (1) 33 × 14 × 5 mm; (2) 35 × 16 × 4 mm
        unidentified estuary snail

Iron Ore Specimens
    Two lumps of magnetite ore, Group I-A, from near Tenango. Pires-Ferreira (1975: Table 11) describes the Tenango magnetite source as one of the most commonly used at San José Mogote.
    Small, flat, circular mirror, 13 mm in diameter and 2 mm thick (Fig. 14.13*a*).

Mica

Two pieces of black mica, cut on at least two sides, torn on the other, totaling 1.9 g: (1) 40 × 16 × 1.5 mm; (2) 40 × 16 × 1 mm (Fig. 14.3*b*).

Piece of black mica, cut on one side, weight 0.2 g, 19 × 8 × 0.5 mm.

Shattered pieces of mica, totaling 1.3 g; apparently, they came from (1) a piece of white mica roughly 37 × 20 × 1 mm thick, and (2) a piece of black mica 17 × 17 × 2 mm thick.

Shattered pieces of mica, totaling 1.9 g; apparently, they came from (1) a piece of white mica 24 × 28 × 1 mm thick, and (2) a piece of brown mica 18 × 16 × 1 mm thick.

Shattered pieces of mica, totaling 0.8 g; apparently they came from (1) a piece of brown mica measuring 20 × 23 mm and cut on at least four sides; (2) a piece of black mica measuring 16 × 30 mm and cut on one side; and (3) a piece of white mica measuring 30 × 14 mm and cut on one side.

Shattered pieces of mica, totaling 2.2 g; apparently they came from (1) a piece of white mica, 48 × 17 mm, and (2) a piece of black mica, 25 × 17 mm, cut on two sides.

Piece of white mica, cut on one edge, weight 0.1 g, 23 × 17 mm.

Piece of white mica, cut on one edge, weight 0.2 g, 22 × 23 mm.

Figurines

Some 68 figurine fragments, an unusually large number, were found on the dooryard of Household Unit C3. They have been described and illustrated by Marcus (1998a:146-51 and Figs. 12.3-12.10). Included were small solid figurines of women and animals, as well as a number of limbs from large hollow white-slipped dolls.

Several factors probably contributed to the unusually rich collection of figurines from Household Unit C3. First, as mentioned above, the part of the dooryard we excavated seems to have included an area where a number of women's rituals (including water divination) were performed. Second, judging by the amount of imported marine shell on the dooryard and the evidence for craft production of mica and magnetite artifacts, this residence may have belonged to a family of relatively high status, one with important ancestors to consult. Based on the similarity of hairdos on four of the figurines (Marcus 1998a: Fig. 12.3), we suspect that one (or more) of the prominent female ancestors of this family had worn her hair in bangs below a headband.

Pottery Mask

A broken pottery mask (or possible piece of an effigy vessel) was found in Square H11. This mask has been described and illustrated by Flannery and Marcus (1994: Fig. 12.103).

Stone Ornaments

Tubular bead of jadeite(?), 11 mm long × 6 mm in diameter (Fig. 14.13*c*).

Disk bead of jadeite(?), 7 mm in diameter, 3 mm hole drilled in it (Fig. 14.13*d*).

Imported Marine Fish

Unidentified fish vertebra, 1 cm in diameter and 1.4 cm long.

Carbonized Plants

42 cob fragments and 1 kernel of maize (*Zea mays*)
10 seeds of nanche or West Indian cherry (*Malpighia* sp.)
1 cotyledon of black walnut (*Juglans* cf. *major*)

Animal Bones

Represented in the debris from Household C3 were the remains of at least two adult deer, three dogs, two pocket gophers, and traces of jackrabbit, cottontail, and raccoon. There was also one bone of coot, a bird which is a migrant to Oaxaca between December and March. Its habitat was probably the backwaters or marshy areas along the Atoyac River.

Large Mammals
    white-tailed deer (*Odocoileus virginianus*)
        1 L. and 1 R. petrous bone
        2 L. scapulae from 2 different deer
        1 L. distal humerus
        1 L. distal femur
        1 L. calcaneum
        fragments of 2 vertebrae
Small Mammals
    domestic dog (*Canis familiaris*)
        1 R. maxilla fragment
        1 R. premaxilla fragment
        1 upper R. incisor from a second premaxilla
        1 upper R. premolar
        1 upper L. molar
        1 smashed upper L. maxilla, adult dog
        1 smashed R. mandible of a juvenile dog
        1 molar fragment
        1 mandible fragment
        1 lower L. first molar
        1 atlas vertebra
        1 scapula fragment
        1 L. distal humerus
        1 L. distal femur
        1 L. distal tibia
        1 metapodial
        1 R. astragalus
        1 phalanx
        1 fragment of vertebra
    pocket gopher (*Orthogeomys grandis*)
        1 lower incisor
        2 R. proximal ulnae
    jackrabbit (*Lepus mexicanus*)
        1 R. mandible
        1 L. innominate

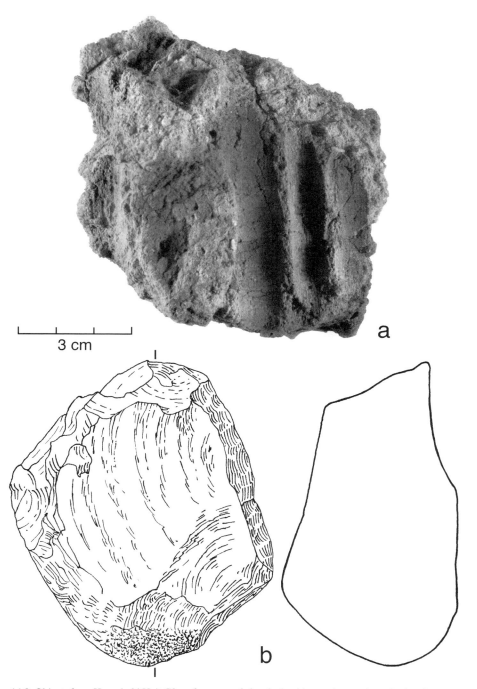

Figure 14.9. Objects from Household Unit C3. *a*, fragment of clay daub with cane impressions. *b*, chert hammerstone.

eastern cottontail (*Sylvilagus floridanus*)
   1 R. distal humerus
raccoon (*Procyon lotor*)
   1 nearly complete R. humerus, burnt
Birds
   coot (*Fulica americana*)
      1 tibiotarsus

Invertebrates
   1 land snail (*Euglandina*)
Unidentified
   about 50 mammal fragments, 20 of them burned

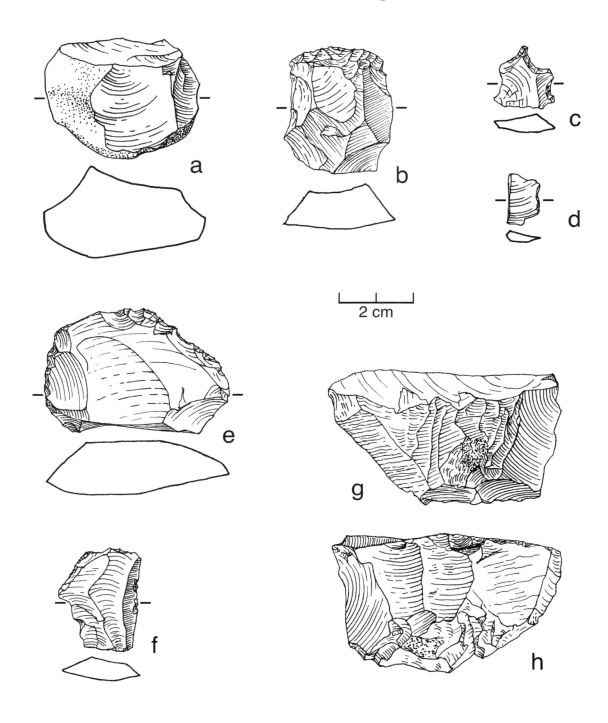

Figure 14.10. Chert artifacts from Household Unit C3. *a*, ordinary flake core. *b*, core face. *c, d*, flake perforators/gravers; *c* is mainly a perforator, *d* is mainly a graver. *e*, denticulate scraper. *f*, endscraper. *g, h*, two views of the same core scraper.

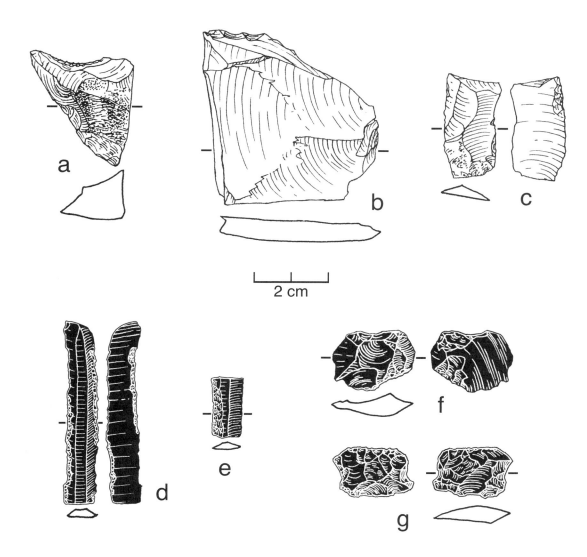

Figure 14.11. Chipped stone artifacts from Household Unit C3. *a-c* are chert. *a, b*, retouched flakes. *c*, utilized bladelike flake, redeposited in Feature 2. *d-g* are obsidian. *d*, prismatic blade fragment, utilized. *e*, unilaterally retouched prismatic blade segment. *f*, flake showing use as a wedge. *g*, fragment of biface (possibly the base of a projectile point), showing use as a wedge.

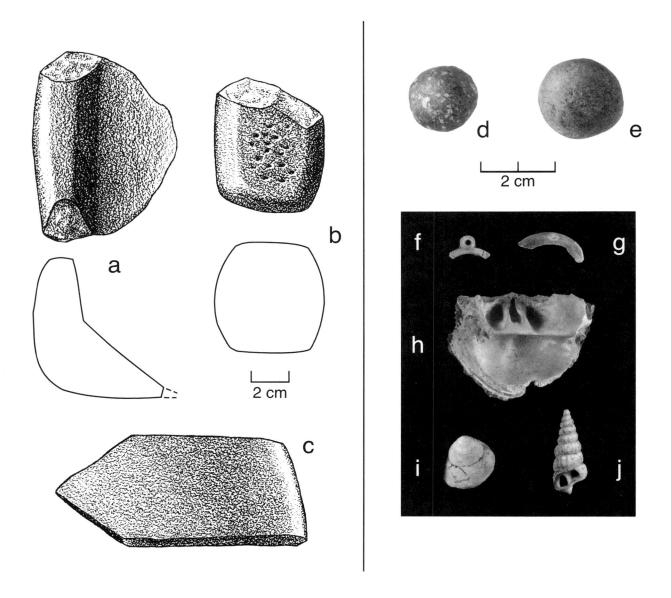

Figure 14.12. Objects from Household Unit C3. *a*, fragment of lipped metate. *b*, broken one-hand mano. *c*, fragment of slab metate. *d, e, canicas* or pecked and ground stone balls. *f*, fragment of shell ring with loop for suspension. *g*, fragment of shell ring. *h*, fragment of *Spondylus* valve. *i*, button shell. *j*, horn shell (*Cerithidea*).

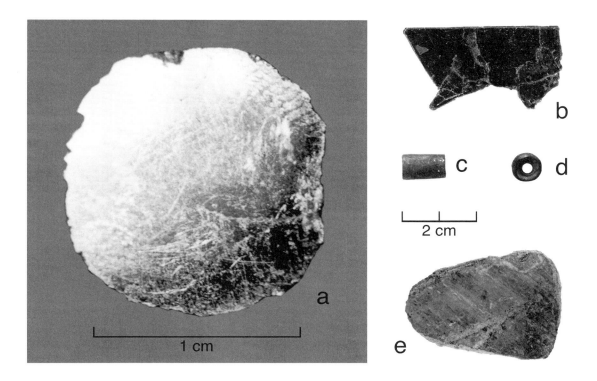

Figure 14.13. Miscellaneous artifacts from Household Unit C3. *a*, flat, circular iron ore mirror from Square H13 (shown many times actual size). *b*, piece of black mica, cut on at least two sides. *c*, tubular bead of jadeite(?). *d*, disk bead of jadeite(?). *e*, triangular worked sherd.

Features in the Dooryard

Feature 2

Feature 2 was a bell-shaped pit, originating at the level of the dooryard of Household Unit C3. The nearby surface of the dooryard had been given a layer of clay, perhaps to strengthen the mouth of the pit. That mouth was only 0.7 m in diameter, but by the time the pit had reached its full depth of 0.65 m, it had expanded to 1.35 m in diameter (Fig. 14.14). As can be seen in the cross-section drawing (Fig. 14.15*a*), Feature 2 had been heated to the point where its clay-lined walls became red and almost as hard as brick. In the bottom of the pit we discovered a layer of charcoal, topped with fire-cracked rocks. In turn, this layer of rocks was topped by white ash. There were identifiable burnt cornstalks in the charcoal layer, suggesting that this was one type of fuel used.

We do not know how Feature 2 was used. It may originally have been created as a storage pit, but in the end it was used as some kind of earth oven. But for what material? Cornstalks do not seem an appropriate fuel for agave hearts, which usually require oak or manzanita wood. The firing of gray or black pottery in a reducing environment is one possibility, but we found no kiln wasters or other evidence for this activity.

Feature 2 may have remained open for some time after the abandonment of Household Unit C3. However, when the time came for Household Unit C2 to be laid out, Feature 2 was filled in and capped with a layer of clay. The sherds and other items swept into it at that time essentially duplicate those found on the dooryard of Unit C3.

Radiocarbon Dates

A burnt cornstalk from Feature 2 yielded a conventional radiocarbon date of 2880 ± 95 B.P., roughly 930 b.c. (Gx-0875). The calibrated two-sigma range would be 1375-825 B.C.

Ceramics

The sherds from Feature 2 have been described by Flannery and Marcus (1994:303).

Figure 14.14. Feature 2, a bell-shaped pit used as an earth oven, during excavation. *Above*, the upper part of the pit has been excavated; the hard-baked wall can be seen as a white streak in the south profile of Square J10. *Below*, the base of the pit has been opened to show the fire-cracked rock. Scale in cm; arrow points north.

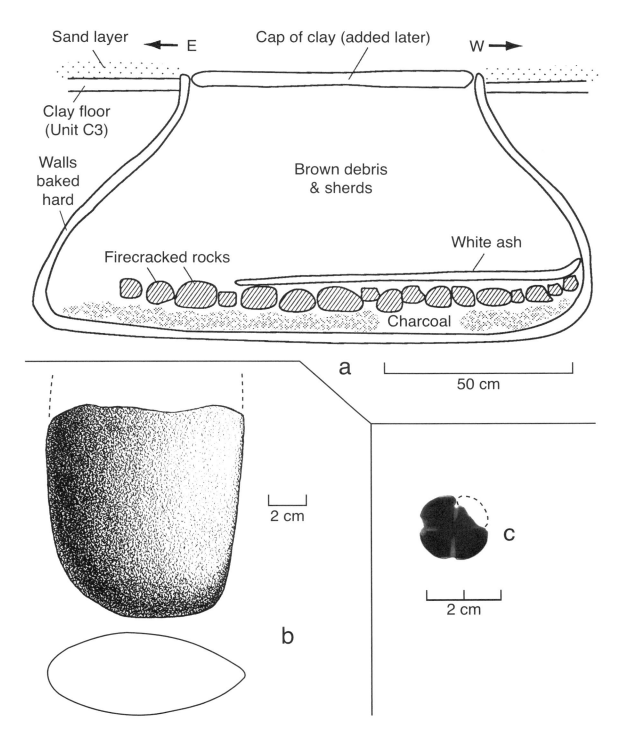

Figure 14.15. Feature 2 and two artifacts redeposited in it. *a*, cross-section of the feature. *b*, fragment of two-hand mano, reused as an oven rock. *c*, broken quatrefoil jadeite(?) plaque, found in the "brown debris" layer.

Figure 14.16. Feature 3, a red-painted basin in Squares H12 and H13. *Above*, view from directly overhead. *Below*, view from the east. Scale in cm; arrow points north. (The basin was cut in half by the nearby arroyo.)

Chipped Stone
  Chert
    1 utilized, bladelike flake (Fig. 14.11*c*)
  Obsidian
    1 flake, not utilized

Ground Stone

In Feature 2 we found a fragmentary subrectangular two-hand mano of quartzite, with two convex grinding surfaces and a lenticular cross-section (Fig. 14.15*b*). This mano had been reused as one of the heated rocks when the pit became an earth oven. Length, 12+ cm (broken); maximum thickness, 5.5 cm; maximum width, 10.6 cm.

Shell
  Fragment of pearly mussel shell, 15 × 10 × 1 mm (manufacturing waste).
  Olivella shell, 15 mm long, top broken off for suspension as an ornament.

Mica
  Piece of white mica, 22 × 11 mm, weighing 0.2 g; cut on one edge.

Stone Ornament
  Quatrefoil jadeite(?) plaque, broken, 19 mm in diameter (Fig. 14.15*c*).

Animal Bones
  1 possible fragment of dog humerus
  5 unidentified splinters, probably from deer long bones

Feature 6

Feature 6 was a well-made stone-lined hearth in Square J12 of the dooryard (Fig. 14.8). It was 50-55 cm in diameter and 10-15 cm in depth, deep enough to disturb the dooryard of Household C4 below it. The fill of the hearth was ash with small pieces of charcoal. As mentioned earlier, sherds from broken cooking pots and charcoal braziers surrounded Feature 6.

This circular, ash-filled hearth appears to us to be a venue for ordinary food preparation by the woman (or women) of the household. It is not surprising that it was created outdoors, since as mentioned earlier, almost none of our wattle-and-daub houses contained anything resembling a permanent hearth.

Feature 3

Feature 3 was a circular area 1.2 m in diameter, recessed 5 cm into the dooryard of Household Unit C3 (Fig. 14.16). It had been clay-plastered, given a coating of lime plaster over that, and then painted red with specular hematite. At the time of its discovery there were some nondescript stones lying in its center, but we believe these represent postoccupational debris.

As discussed previously by Marcus (1998a: Chapter 3), we believe that Feature 3 had been lime-plastered to waterproof it so that it could be used as the kind of ritual basin in which Zapotec women performed *quela hueniy niça*. This was a divination ritual in which kernels of maize were tossed onto the surface of a water-filled basin for the purpose of seeing whether those that floated formed odd-numbered or even-numbered groups (see Chapter 5). Such divination was used to determine the causes of illnesses, to make decisions about future activities, and to resolve other questions requiring supernatural guidance.

Feature 8

Feature 8 was a circular basin about the same size as Feature 3, but only partly exposed by our excavation (Fig. 14.8). It lay roughly 3 m south of Feature 3 and, like the latter, had first been given a layer of clay plaster, then a coating of lime plaster. It differed from Feature 3, however, in that it was painted yellow rather than red. We believe that it, too, was a ritual basin for water divination.

We find it significant that these two ritual basins, Features 3 and 8, were painted with two of the colors commonly attributed to the "four world quarters" of the Zapotec cosmos. We would very much like to know whether the dooryard of Household Unit C3 had originally contained four such basins, each painted a different color. Unfortunately, a nearby arroyo had already removed half of Feature 3 before our arrival, and it was not clear in what direction we would need to expand in order to search for other basins.

Insights from Artifact Plotting

Figures 14.17-14.22 present the distributions of hammerstones, chert cores, metates, manos, perforators/gravers, shell and mica, iron ore specimens, beads, figurines, utilized chert flakes, and other items lying on the dooryard. (Utilized flakes were recorded by square, rather than by piece-plotting.) For various reasons, involving both features and artifact distributions, we believe that our excavation of Unit C3 exposed a woman's work area. Feature 6 appears to be a culinary hearth surrounded by broken cooking pots and charcoal braziers/potstands. Feature 2, while it may have been created originally as a storage pit, ended up as an earth oven with cornstalks for fuel. Mano and metate fragments were more numerous on the Unit C3 dooryard than they had been in Unit C4.

Figures 14.17 and 14.18 document the discard of three items related to chert flake production and use: hammerstones, cores, and utilized flakes. There appear to be at least three concentrations of cores, the largest of which runs east-west between the Feature 6 hearth and the Feature 2 cooking pit. If we are correct in our suspicion that this was part of a woman's work area, it would seem that the women of Unit C3 were involved in primary flake production. They also used and discarded many flakes in the area, but not in Square J11, where so many cores were concentrated (Fig. 14.18).

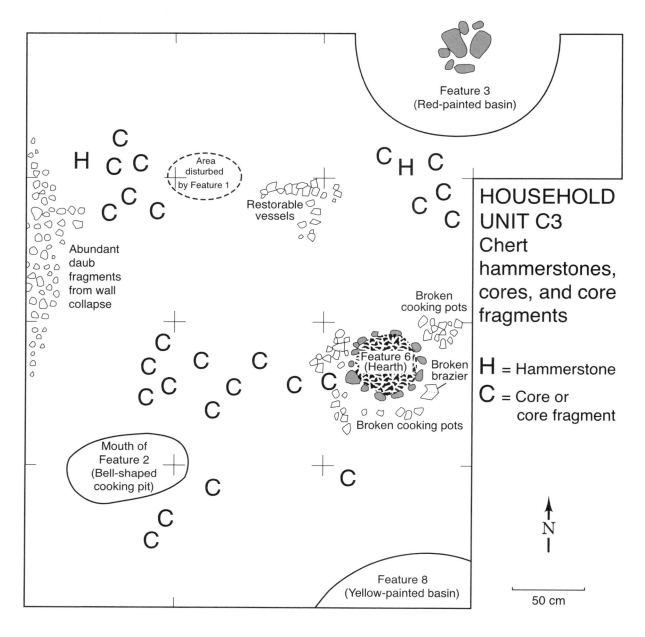

Figure 14.17. Distribution of chert hammerstones, cores, and core fragments on the dooryard of Household Unit C3.

An interesting possibility is raised by the fact that all cores found in Unit C3 were ordinary flake cores. Was this the type most often used by women during primary flake production? Recall that in Unit C4, which we interpret as a man's work area, two of the nine complete cores were bipolar. We pursue this topic more fully in our discussion of Household Unit C1 (below), where ordinary and bipolar cores occurred in different clusters.

Figure 14.19 shows some fragments of manos and metates discarded to the south of Features 2 and 6, and between Feature 3 and the area of wall collapse in Squares H10-I10. (One of the metate fragments was lipped, but does not show the loop handle we have associated with men's ritual metates.)

Figure 14.20 shows items possibly related to shell or mica working. Their abundance in this area suggests that women were involved in ornament or costume making. The largest concentrations of perforators/gravers and shells occur in the northern part of the excavation, between Feature 3 and the area of wall collapse. Two other concentrations (one involving five pieces of mica) lie to the west and southwest of the Feature 6 hearth. Since this residence appears to have belonged to a family of relatively high

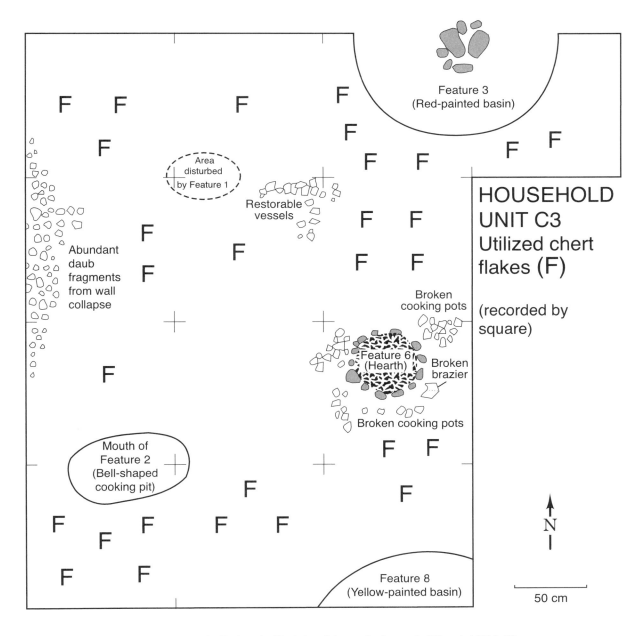

Figure 14.18. Distribution of utilized chert flakes on the dooryard of Household Unit C3.

rank, it would be no surprise to learn that their need for masks, costumes, and ornaments was high. We have already mentioned the high numbers of figurine fragments in this activity area; nine heads are shown in Fig. 14.21.

Finally, Figure 14.22 shows the distribution of items too scattered or too few in number to suggest a pattern. Some may simply be objects lost in the dooryard debris. A complete circular iron ore mirror (Fig. 14.13*a*) was found east of Feature 3; it appears to be a finished ornament that got lost, rather than an item in the process of manufacture. The same is true of the two jadeite(?) beads, both small enough to have been lost on the dooryard. Two lumps of magnetite suggest that the Unit C3 family was collecting and working iron ore, but our excavation did not expose the area where the polishing was done. This might mean that the polishing was not done by women.

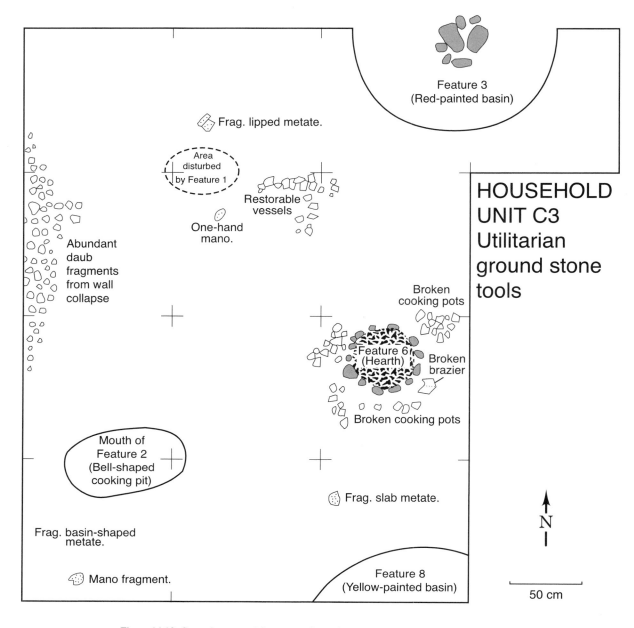

Figure 14.19. Ground stone tool fragments piece-plotted on the dooryard of Household Unit C3.

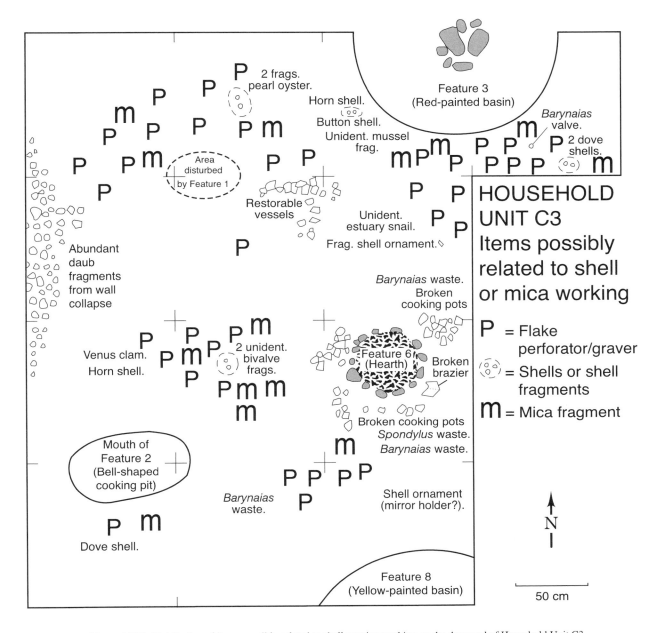

Figure 14.20. Distribution of items possibly related to shell or mica working on the dooryard of Household Unit C3.

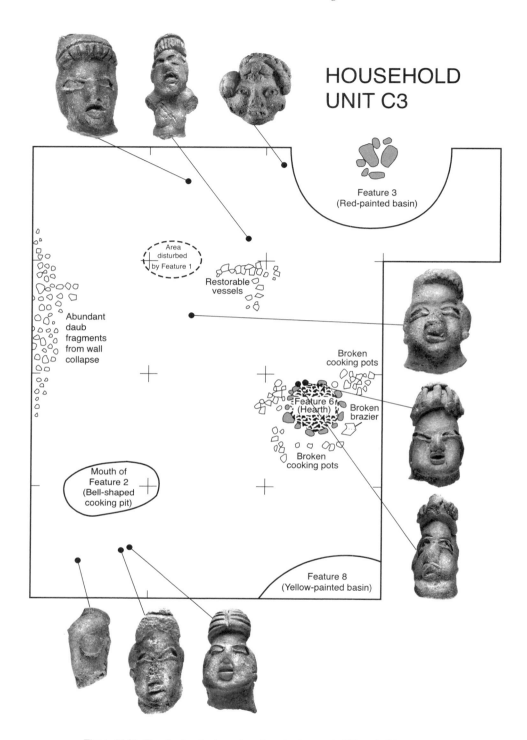

Figure 14.21. Figurine heads piece-plotted on the dooryard of Household Unit C3.

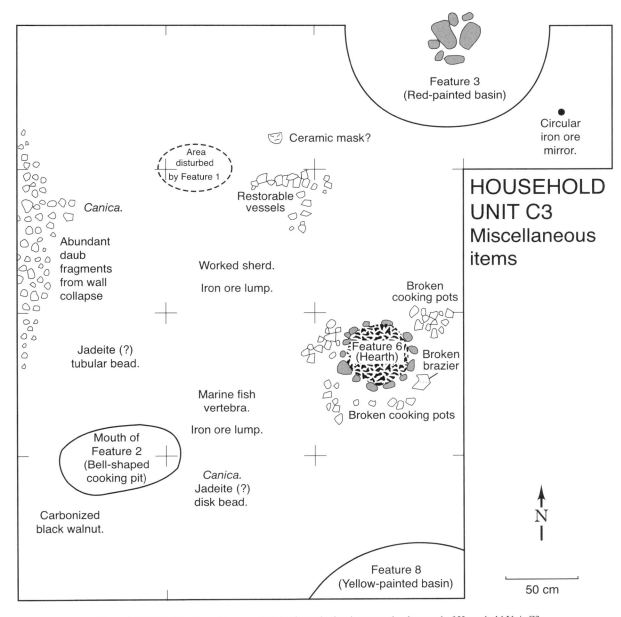

Figure 14.22. Distribution of iron ore, jadeite(?), and other items on the dooryard of Household Unit C3.

Household Unit C2

Our excavation of Household Unit C2 caught parts of two structures, separated by 1.5 m of intervening dooryard (Fig. 14.23). It is likely that both these buildings were part of the same residence, as in the case of House 16/17 in Area B (Chapter 18). Normally, residences in villages of the San José phase were separated by 20-30 m of open space. When buildings were found this close together, one usually appeared to be the main house and the other a kitchen, cook shack, or lean-to.

Both structures were of wattle-and-daub with partial stone foundations. The northern building, which filled almost half the excavated area, seems to have been the most substantial. It was represented by three large postmolds, a line of wall foundation stones, and scattered wattle-and-daub debris. Just inside its south wall was an oval storage pit (Feature 1), which began at the level of the floor and was capped by a clay lid.

The southern building was less substantial and may have been a cook shack or ramada of some kind. We found only one corner of this structure, which had smaller postmolds than its

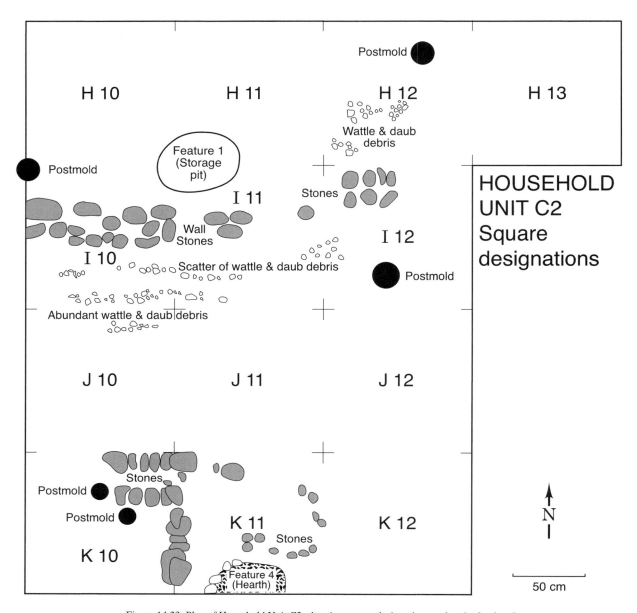

Figure 14.23. Plan of Household Unit C2, showing square designations and major landmarks.

northern counterpart and produced no evidence of fallen daub. It did, however, have an L-shaped stone foundation framing an apparent corner (Fig. 14.24). Just east of this corner was Feature 4, a small outdoor hearth with a partial stone lining, reminiscent of Feature 6 in Unit C3.

Unfortunately, Unit C2 was only the second residence recovered by our Oaxaca project, and although we did piece-plot all significant artifacts, we did not keep the sherds from the northern and southern structures separate, as we later did with House 16/17 of Area B. Had we done so, we suspect that we might have found

more Fidencio Coarse cooking pots and Lupita Heavy Plain charcoal braziers in the less substantial building.

Based on several lines of evidence—the small ash-filled hearth, the potential cook shack, and the number of figurines and ground stone tools discarded near them—we believe that the southern part of the excavation included a woman's work area.

Finally, the massive quantities of daub and burned canes we recovered suggest that the northern structure or "main house" might have been deliberately burned (see Daub below). Unit C2 was unusual in this regard, since most houses of the San José

Figure 14.24. Architectural details of Square K10, Household Unit C2. *Above*, L-shaped arrangement of wall foundation stones, believed to be the northeast corner of a cook shack or ramada. *Below*, closeup of a postmold near the L-shaped wall corner. Scale in cm; arrow points north.

phase showed no evidence of having been burned. While it is possible that Unit C2's position near the eastern periphery of the piedmont spur had left it vulnerable to a raid, its posts had not been burned. It therefore did not meet the criteria established in Chapter 5 for houses burned in raids, and we consider the cause of the fire unknown.

Radiocarbon Date

Our expected date for Unit C2 was roughly 900 b.c. A sample of the carbonized wall canes yielded a conventional date of 2730 ± 120 B.P., or roughly 780 b.c. (SI-463). Adding one standard deviation to 780 would bring it to our expected date of 900 b.c. The calibrated two-sigma range would be 1200-760 B.C.

Daub

The collapse of the northern structure of Household Unit C2 had left behind hundreds of burned daub fragments (Fig. 14.25a). Because of this large quantity of daub, many details of construction were present. One daub fragment had the impressions of a bundle of five canes (diameters 0.7, 0.8, 1.0, 0.8, and 0.8 cm) lashed together with twine. Another impression showed a rope crossing the canes.

The daub itself was 3-4 cm thick except in the gaps between cane bundles, where it could be 7.7 cm thick. The spaces between canes were usually no more than 1.5-2 cm.

Several fragments showed that the house had been plastered and whitewashed at least twice, with the clay plaster varying between 1.5 and 4 mm thick. In the Munsell system, the surface color would be "very pale brown" to "light yellowish brown" (10 YR 7/4 to 6/4).

Ceramics

Some 3993 sherds were recovered from Household Unit C2; they have been described by Flannery and Marcus (1994: Table 14.1). Among the imported vessels were 10 sherds of Xochiltepec White and 6 sherds of La Mina White, both possibly from the Gulf Coast. For some of the other exotic wares, like Delia White, we do not know the provenience.

Chipped Stone
Chert (94%)
hammerstone: 1
cores: 6 (Fig. 14.25b)
core face, possibly utilized: 1 (Fig. 14.25c)
bipolar flake cores, or scaled flakes therefrom: 2 (Fig. 14.25d)
flake spokeshaves: 2
flake perforators/gravers: 44 (Fig. 14.25e-h)
burins: 2 (Fig. 14.26c)
endscraper on small blade: 1 (Fig. 14.26b)
retouched flakes: 6
utilized flakes: 13 (Fig. 14.26a)
flakes, not utilized: 113

Obsidian (4%)
prismatic blade fragments, utilized: 4 (Fig. 14.26d, e)
flake, utilized: 1
flakes, not utilized: 4
Other (1%)
large chipped sandstone disk (a reworked piece of ground stone tool): 1 (Fig. 14.26f)
igneous flakes: 2
Comment: Pires-Ferreira (1975) neutron-activated 6 pieces of obsidian from Unit C2. She reported 1 blade and 2 flakes from Zinapécuaro, and 1 blade and 2 flakes from Otumba.

Ground Stone
Fragment of two-hand mano with airfoil cross-section, quartzite (Fig. 14.27e). Length, 10+ cm (broken); maximum width, 6 cm; maximum thickness, 9 cm.
Fragment of limestone mano, reused as chopper (Fig. 14.27d). Length, 8.2 cm; width, 8.0 cm; thickness, 4.5 cm.
Fragment of basin-shaped metate, 2.4 cm thick at center of basin.
Fragment of rectangular lipped metate (Fig. 14.28a). The fragment is only 22 × 12.5 cm; the original thickness would have been 4 cm; rim to base height, 4.3 cm.
Small fragment of stone bowl, 3 × 2 cm.
Large limestone polishing stone with one flat facet, broken (Fig. 14.27c). Width, 6.9 cm; thickness, 3.8 cm. This stone may have been used for polishing stone bowls.
Pounder made of mica schist (Fig. 14.27a). Maximum diameter, 9.0 cm.
Broken fragment of a spherical limestone pounder (Fig. 14.27b). Maximum diameter, 8.5 cm.

Shell
Ornament
One fragment of ornament made from nacreous shell, presumably pearl oyster (Fig. 14.28b). The original ornament was rectangular, 18 mm wide and 2 mm thick. Its original length is unknown; the broken fragment is 23 mm long. It has two drill holes in it, each 2 mm in diameter.
Pearly Freshwater Mussels
fragment of *Barynaias*, 18 × 8 × 1 mm
fragment of unidentified pearly shell, 19 × 16 × 1 mm
Pacific Marine Bivalves
nearly complete valve of heart shell (*Cardita* sp.), 35 × 16 × 1 mm (Fig. 14.28c)
section of shell margin trimmed off a second *Cardita*, 21 × 6 × 1 mm (manufacturing waste)
beachworn valve of Venus clam (*Pitar* sp.)
Pacific Marine Univalves
none
Unidentified
fragment of drilled shell

Iron Ore Specimens

Two lumps of mixed magnetite/ilmenite ore, Group IV-A, from near Arrazola; the largest is 3 × 3 × 2.5 mm (Fig. 14.28*d*). Pires-Ferreira (1975: Table 16) also found specimens from this source in Household Unit C1 and at the site of Tierras Largas.

Unfinished mirror of magnetite from the Group I-A source near Tenango, one of the most common sources used at San José Mogote (Pires-Ferreira 1975: Table 11).

Mica

Shattered piece of white mica, cut on two edges, weighing 1.1 g; 36 × 25 × 1 mm.

Figurines

Some 23 fragments of small solid figurines were recovered from Household Unit C2 (described and illustrated in Marcus 1998a:151, Figs. 12.11-12.12). Many of the piece-plotted fragments occurred not in the northern building but in the dooryard, near the Feature 4 hearth and the corner of the southern building. This may have been an area for food preparation and other activities associated with women, and may also have served as an area for women's ancestor ritual.

Imported Marine Fish

Two small fish vertebrae were found.

Imported Mammal Products

Two shell plates from a nine-banded armadillo (*Dasypus novemcinctus*). Armadillo shell, likely imported from the Isthmus of Tehuantepec, may have been used for costumes, shell rattles, or containers.

Animal Bones

Large Mammals

white-tailed deer (*Odocoileus virginianus*)

1 antler fragment, burned

Small Mammals

domestic dog (*Canis familiaris*)

1 lower R. canine

1 lower R. first premolar

1 possible limb fragment

2 metapodial fragments

pocket gopher (*Orthogeomys grandis*)

1 upper R. incisor

eastern cottontail (*Sylvilagus floridanus*)

1 skull fragment

1 L. mandible

1 R. proximal radius

1 L. proximal tibia

1 R. distal tibia

raccoon (*Procyon lotor*)

1 R. proximal radius

Human

1 incisor

Features Associated with Household Unit C2

Feature 1

Feature 1 was a subfloor storage pit, just inside the northern building. It originated at the level of the floor and went down only 22 cm (Fig. 14.23). The pit was oval at its mouth (55 cm × 43 cm) and tapered to 28 cm in diameter at its base. Feature 1 was capped by a hard clay lid, possibly to conceal its contents or to prevent anyone from stepping in it. The side walls and floor were blackened, not by burning but by the pit's original contents, which might have consisted of stored raw material for craft activity (iron ore lumps, for example). After the pit fell into disuse, it had been filled in with loose brown earth.

Feature 4

Feature 4 was a small hearth with a partial stone lining, located in the dooryard next to the southern building (Fig. 14.23). Its diameter was 41 cm, and when found it was filled with white and yellow ash. Roughly half of this hearth lay in Square K11, while the rest extended into the unexcavated area to the south. We interpret this feature as a culinary hearth of the type used by women; it resembled Feature 6 in Unit C3.

Insights from Artifact Plotting

Figures 14.29-14.32 present the distributions of manos, metates, pounders, perforators/gravers, shell and mica, utilized chert flakes, and figurine fragments from Household Unit C3. Let us begin with ground stone tools. The largest concentration occurred in Square K12, not far from the Feature 4 hearth, and consisted of a metate fragment, two pounders, and a piece of stone bowl. A limestone polisher showed up in K11 nearby. Several of these discarded tools are likely to have been for food preparation, reinforcing our suspicion that the southern half of the excavated area was devoted to women's activities. Two more fragments of metates or manos showed up in Square J10, just north of our presumed cook shack or ramada (Fig. 14.29).

Five of the six piece-plotted figurines shown in Figure 14.30 also were discarded in our suspected women's activity area. This is one more instance where a scatter of discarded figurine parts appears near a circular, ash-filled, partly or wholly stone-lined culinary hearth (see Unit C3).

A different pattern can be seen in the distribution of items related to shell or mica working (Fig. 14.31). More than two dozen chert perforators/gravers had evidently been discarded in the northern structure or "main house," along with specimens of heart shell, Venus clam, and pearly freshwater mussel. While we cannot be sure whether a man or a woman was responsible for this debris, it appears to have resulted largely from shell working; no mica was found in this building.

Two other scatters of perforators/gravers occurred in Unit C2. One, accompanied by a burin and a broken shell ornament, appeared in the gap between the two buildings (Square J11). The

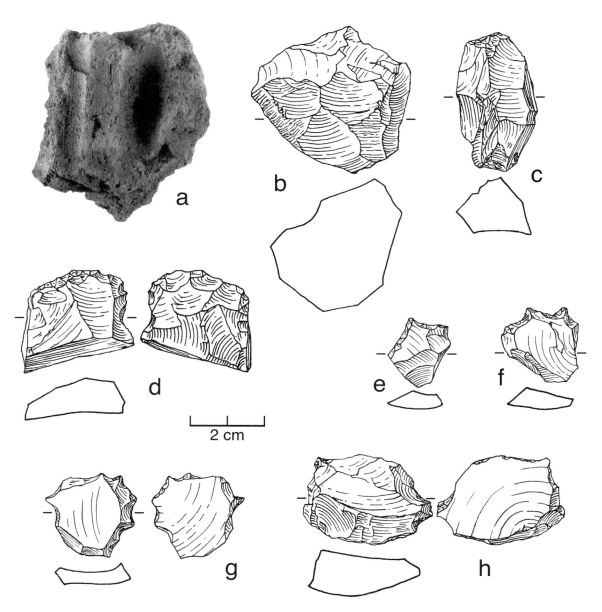

Figure 14.25. Objects from Household Unit C2. *a*, chunk of burned clay daub, showing impression of a large cane or slender wooden pole. *b-h*, chert tools. *b*, ordinary flake core. *c*, core face, possibly utilized. *d*, scaled flake from bipolar core. *e*, flake perforator/graver. *f*, perforator/graver with two nipples. *g*, perforator/graver with three or four nipples. *h*, perforator/graver with two worn-down nipples.

other scatter appeared in our suspected women's work area near the Feature 4 hearth, and included a second burin as well as a bit of mica. Tentatively, it would appear that most shell working took place either in the "main house" or in the dooryard. However, we did not expose much of the southern building.

The distribution of utilized chert flakes (Fig. 14.32), while not tremendously informative, reinforces the pattern seen in perforators/gravers. More than two-thirds of the flakes were scattered around the northern building, where so many perforating or

graving tools had been discarded. A smaller number showed up in our suspected woman's activity area to the south. The most parsimonious explanation is that whatever the activity responsible for the northern scatter of perforators/gravers, it also involved cutting with naturally sharp flakes.

Finally, it appears that the family in Unit C2 collected and worked iron ore, but we did not find the activity area where the work was done.

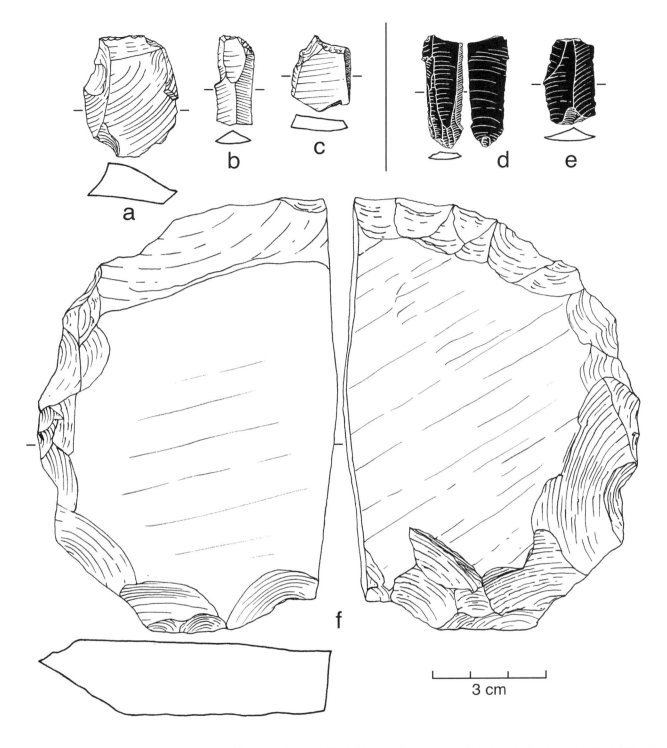

Figure 14.26. Chipped stone tools from Household Unit C2. *a-c* are chert. *a*, utilized flake. *b*, endscraper on small blade. *c*, burin. *d, e*, prismatic obsidian blade fragments, utilized. *f*, large chipped sandstone disk.

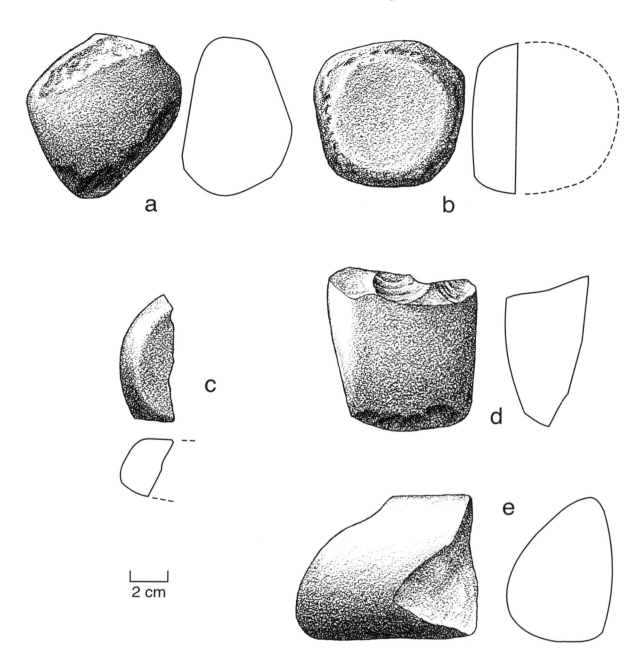

Figure 14.27. Ground stone tools from Household Unit C2. *a*, pounder, mica schist. *b*, fragment of pounder, limestone. *c*, broken polishing stone, limestone. *d*, fragment of mano, reused as a chopper. *e*, fragment of mano with airfoil cross-section.

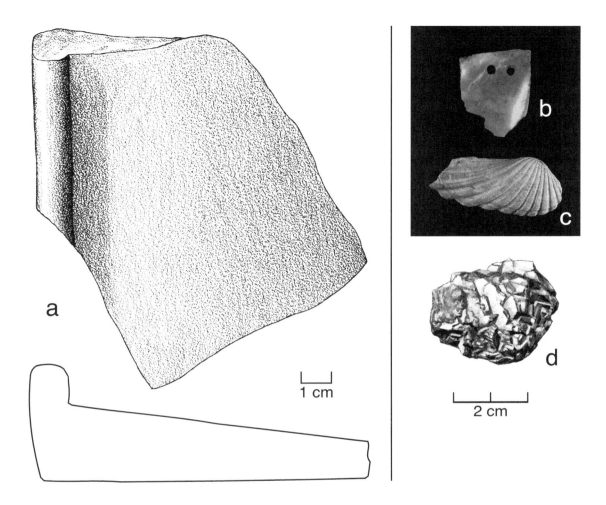

Figure 14.28. Objects from Household Unit C2. *a*, fragment of rectangular lipped metate. *b*, fragment of nacreous shell ornament with two drill holes. *c*, nearly complete valve of heart shell (*Cardita* sp.). *d*, lump of ilmeno-magnetite (painting by J. Klausmeyer).

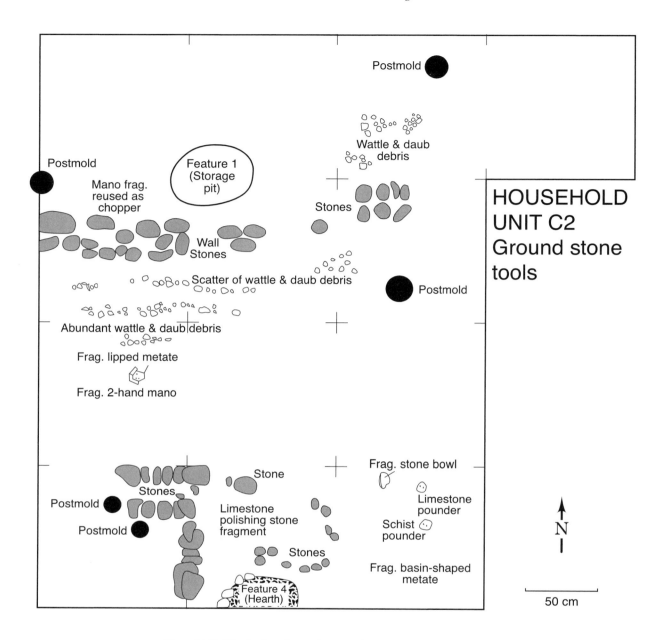

Figure 14.29. Distribution of ground stone tools throughout Household Unit C2.

HOUSEHOLD UNIT C2 : Figurines

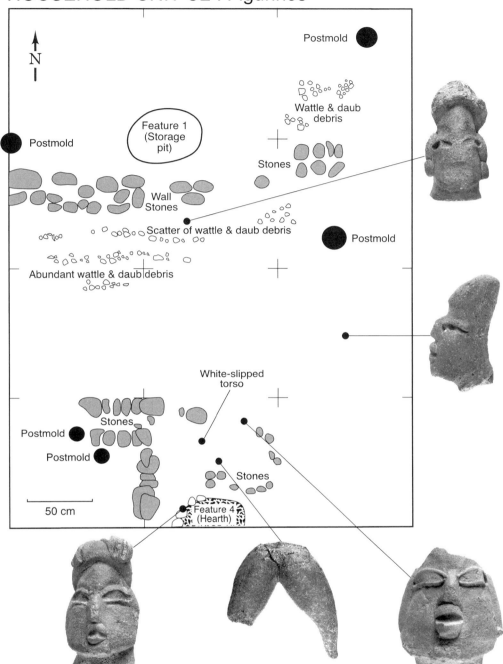

Figure 14.30. Figurine fragments piece-plotted in Household Unit C2.

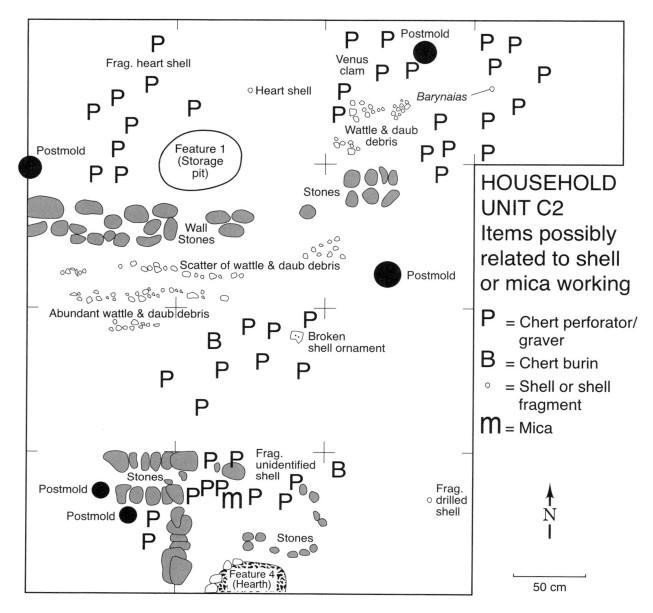

Figure 14.31. Distribution of items possibly related to shell or mica working throughout Household Unit C2.

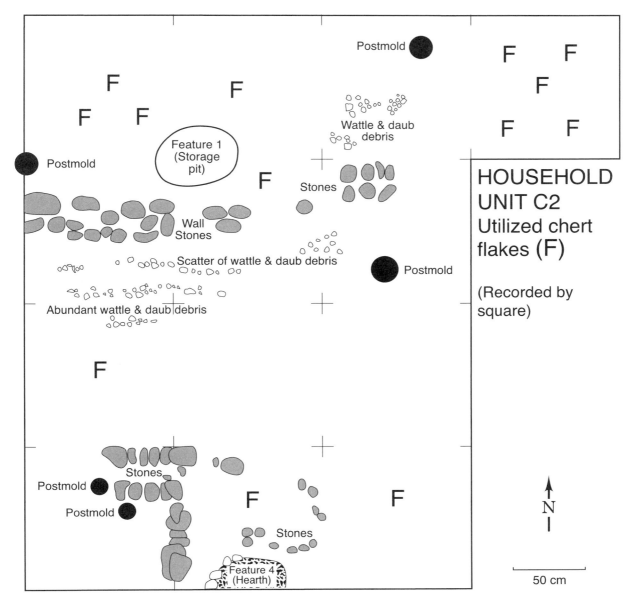

Figure 14.32. Distribution of utilized chert flakes throughout Household Unit C2.

Household Unit C1

Household Unit C1 was the first residence ever excavated by our project. It was found at a time when we were still in the process of discovering what Early Formative houses looked like. As a result, even though we did piece-plot all significant artifacts, the sherds from Unit C1 were not separated into "house floor" versus "dooryard," as was done with later residences. (To be sure, very little dooryard was present in our exposure of Unit C1.)

The northern edge of the house—represented by a postmold, a short line of wall foundation stones, and several areas of wall

collapse (including pieces of daub with pole impressions)—ran east-west through Squares I10-I12 (Fig. 14.33). The southern edge of the house (represented by wattle-and-daub wall collapse) lay about 3 meters to the south, in Squares K10-K12. Between the two lines of wattle-and-daub debris were areas of well-preserved floor, especially in Squares J10-J12. The only exposure of dooryard was a narrow strip running east-west in Squares H10-H12. As a result, we found none of the usual outdoor features such as bell-shaped pits and hearths.

Near the northern limit of our excavation we found another east-west line of wattle-and-daub debris, including a piece bear-

HOUSEHOLD UNIT C1: Square designations

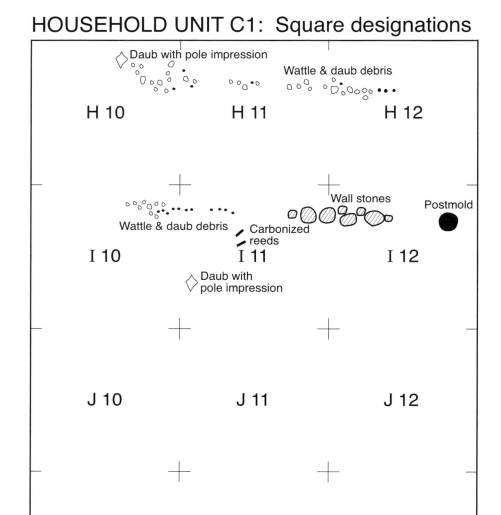

Figure 14.33. Plan of Household Unit C1, showing square designations and major landmarks.

ing a pole impression. This line of debris, roughly 75 cm beyond the northern wall line of the house, may have come from an outbuilding that was part of the same household. Unfortunately, most of this second structure had been carried away by the arroyo.

Radiocarbon Dates

An AMS date from this house came out 2810 ± 40 B.P., or roughly 860 b.c. (Beta-179078). The calibrated two-sigma range would be 1040-850 B.C. A conventional date submitted during the 1960s came out 2640 ± 120 B.P., or roughly 690 b.c. (SI-462). Since our expected date for Unit C1 was ca. 900 b.c., we prefer the newer AMS date.

Daub

One wall of the house had left behind dozens of daub fragments with cane impressions 0.8-1.6 cm in diameter. It was clear from the diversity of diameters that little effort had been made to keep the canes uniform within each bundle. One chunk of daub (Fig. 14.34*a*) bore the impression of two canes and a small wooden pole. The two cane impressions were 1.0 and 1.3 cm in diameter, while the pole was no more than 2.0 cm in diameter, indicating that it was part of the wattle rather than one of the upright posts.

The clay daub was 3-4 cm thick on average except for the gaps between cane bundles, where it reached 7.7 cm. The outside of the house had been coated with whitewashed clay plaster 2-4 mm thick. In the Munsell system, the surface color ranged from "pink" (7.5 YR 7/4) to "light yellowish brown" (10 YR 6/4) to "gray" (10 YR 5/1). One chunk of daub revealed that the house had been replastered at least once.

Ceramics

Some 3473 sherds were recovered from Household Unit C1. They have been described by Flannery and Marcus (1994: Table 14.1). Imported ceramics included 13 sherds of Xochiltepec White and 2 sherds of La Mina White. While distinctive, these sherds represented only .004 of the sample.

Chipped Stone

Chert (87%)
  ordinary flake cores: 6
  bipolar flake cores: 8
  flake spokeshave: 1
  flake perforators/gravers: 15 (Fig. 14.34*d*)
  retouched flakes: 3 (Fig. 14.34*b*)
  utilized flakes: 10 (Fig. 14.34*c*)
  flakes, not utilized: 103
Obsidian (9%)
  fragment of possible bipolar core: 1
  prismatic blade fragments, utilized: 7 (Fig. 14.34*e*)
  prismatic blade fragments, no sign of use: 2
  flake, utilized: 1
  flakes, not utilized: 4
Other (4%)
  igneous flakes: 7
  Comment: Pires-Ferreira (1975) neutron-activated 7 pieces of obsidian from Unit C1. She reported 2 blades from Zinapécuaro, 2 blades from Otumba, a flake and possible bipolar core from Guadalupe Victoria, and a flake from El Chayal.

Ground Stone

Subrectangular two-hand mano with airfoil cross-section, quartzite; one corner broken off (Fig. 14.34*j*). Maximum length, 22 cm; maximum width, 11.3 cm; maximum thickness: 5.7 cm.
Pottery burnishing pebble, chert, with 15 × 10 mm of burnishing surface (Fig. 14.34*i*).

Shell

Ornaments
  Fragment of broken pearl oyster(?) ornament, 27 × 18 mm and 2 mm thick, with a hole 6 mm in diameter drilled in it (Fig 14.34*f*).
  Disk-shaped bead, probably *Spondylus* shell, broken; original diameter 13 mm, thickness 2 mm. There is a hole 2 mm in diameter drilled through the center (Fig. 14.34*g*).
Pearly Freshwater Mussels
  small fragment
Pacific Marine Bivalves
  5 small fragments of cut pearl oyster shell
  small fragment of *Spondylus* shell
Pacific Marine Univalves
  none

Iron Ore Specimens

Lump of magnetite ore, Group I-A, from near Tenango. Pires-Ferreira (1975: Table 11) found this to be one of the most common sources used at San José Mogote.
Lump of mixed magnetite-ilmenite ore, Group IV-A, from near Arrazola. Pires-Ferreira (1975: Table 16) also found items from this source in Household Unit C2 and at the site of Tierras Largas.

Mica

A piece of black mica was found, cut on four sides to form a long slender rectangle, weighing 0. 3 g; 36 × 9 × 1 mm (Fig. 14.34*h*).

Figurines

Some 26 fragments of small solid figurines were found in Household Unit C1. They have been described and illustrated by Marcus (1998a:152 and Figs. 12.13-12.14).

Carbonized Plants

Fragments from at least 9 maize cobs (*Zea mays*) were found.

Animal Bones

The animal bones from Household Unit C1 were limited to remains from two dogs. Our excavation evidently missed most of the bone debris associated with this residence, either because the bones had been discarded outdoors or because food consumption took place in an outbuilding.
Small Mammals
  domestic dog (*Canis familiaris*)
    1 lower R. canine tooth
    1 proximal R. ulna and 1 proximal L. ulna from two different dogs
    1 R. astragalus
    1 eroded metapodial

Insights from Artifact Plotting

Figures 14.35-14.39 present the distributions of chert cores, utilized flakes, perforators/gravers, shell, mica, iron ore, ground stone, and figurine fragments from Unit C1. It is clear that for some household tasks—food preparation, sewing, and mica working, among others—our excavation missed the main activity areas. Some of those areas may in fact have been outdoors, which is why it is important to excavate the dooryard.

An interesting pattern emerges, however, when we look at the distribution of chert cores (Fig. 14.35). Ordinary cores and bipolar cores have different distributions. Four ordinary cores cluster in Square H10 and adjacent I10. Four bipolar cores cluster in Square H12 and adjacent H11. In Squares I12-J12, three bipolar cores were accompanied by a single ordinary core. We tentatively suggest that these clusters may be "drop zones" created either by two knappers with different flake removal techniques, or by one knapper who used different techniques on different occasions.

Recall that in Household Unit C3 (above), we raised the possibility that the ordinary core was the type most often used by women for primary flake production. Might we be seeing gender-based preferences here, with men using bipolar techniques more often, and women choosing multidirectional techniques? Were these techniques simply idiosyncratic preferences, or were they chosen to produce specific types of flakes?

Parry (1987) presents a simpler alternative for the differences between ordinary and bipolar cores. Bipolar flakes, he points out, result from reducing a core by direct percussion while it is resting on an anvil, "usually to produce small flakes for use as expedient tools." He goes on to add that "novice knappers, who have not yet learned the force and striking angles needed to detach flakes," may through their own inexperience produce products that "in some cases resemble bipolar flakes" (Parry 1987:36).

This cautionary note from Parry warns us that the difference between a "drop zone" of ordinary cores and a "drop zone" of bipolar cores may only mean that one knapper used an anvil while the other did not, or that one knapper was a novice.

Unfortunately, the distribution of utilized flakes (which were recorded by square, rather than piece-plotted) adds no further insights to this question. Our small sample of such flakes (Fig. 14.36) does not indicate that they were discarded near the cores from which they were struck.

Let us now turn to the evidence for shell working (Fig. 14.37). The two main concentrations of chert perforators/gravers occur in Squares H10-H11 (8 specimens) and K10-J11 (4 specimens). For what it is worth, the H10-H11 cluster overlaps with a "drop zone" of ordinary cores. No cluster of perforators was found to overlap a "drop zone" of bipolar cores. The H10-H11 cluster apparently lay in the narrow strip of dooryard north of the house. Three perforators/gravers were also found near the limit of the house floor in Squares I11-I12. If the house had been swept not long before abandonment, that event might account for the relative absence of artifacts in the middle of the floor (Squares J10-J12) as well as the greater numbers near the northern and southern walls, where sweeping may have been less thorough.

Shells, mica, perforators/gravers, iron ore lumps, a two-hand mano, and a burnishing pebble were also tossed or swept toward the south wall of the house, primarily in Squares K10-K12 (Figs. 14.37-14.38). In all, our suspicion is that at least part of the artifact distribution we are seeing in Unit C1 reflects housecleaning. Four of six piece-plotted figurines (Fig. 14.39) lay outside the area of house floor.

When we compare what we learned from Unit C1 to what we learned from Units C4-C3, we are again struck by how much information is lost when one does not expose the dooryard accompanying the house. Many men's and women's activities took place outdoors, resulting in features and artifact scatters not found in the house, especially a regularly swept house.

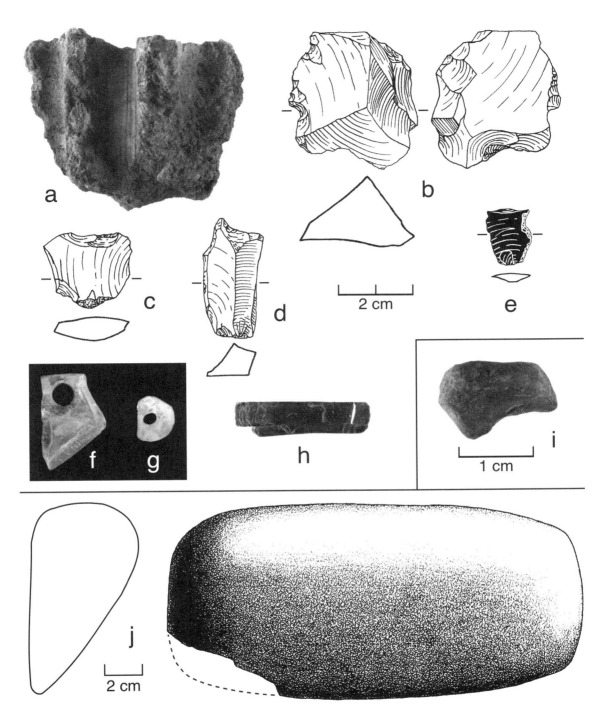

Figure 14.34. Objects from Household Unit C1. *a*, chunk of burned clay daub with cane and pole impressions. *b*, retouched chert flake. *c*, utilized chert flake. *d*, chert perforator/graver. *e*, prismatic obsidian blade fragment, utilized. *f*, fragment of pearl oyster(?) ornament. *g*, broken disk bead, probably *Spondylus* shell. *h*, piece of black mica cut on four sides. *i*, pottery-burnishing pebble, chert. *j*, subrectangular two-hand mano with airfoil cross-section.

HOUSEHOLD UNIT C1:
Chert flake cores (or core fragments)

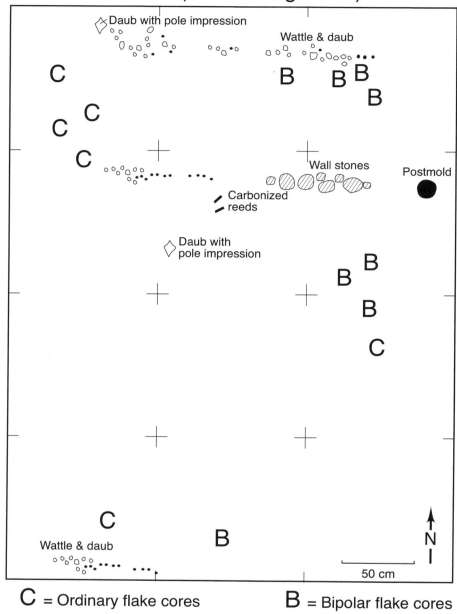

C = Ordinary flake cores   B = Bipolar flake cores

Figure 14.35. Distribution of chert cores and core fragments throughout Household Unit C1.

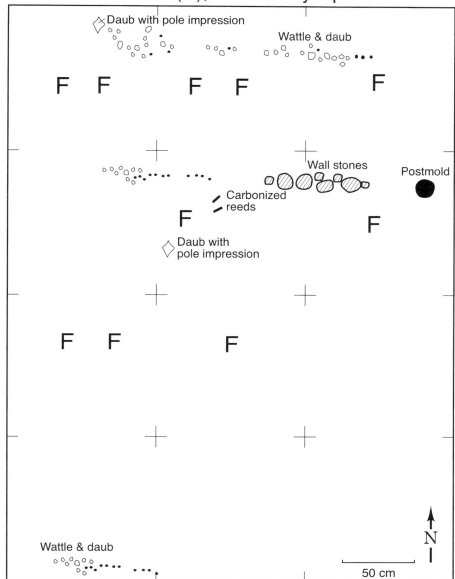

Figure 14.36. Distribution of utilized chert flakes throughout Household Unit C1.

HOUSEHOLD UNIT C1:
Items possibly associated with shell or mica working

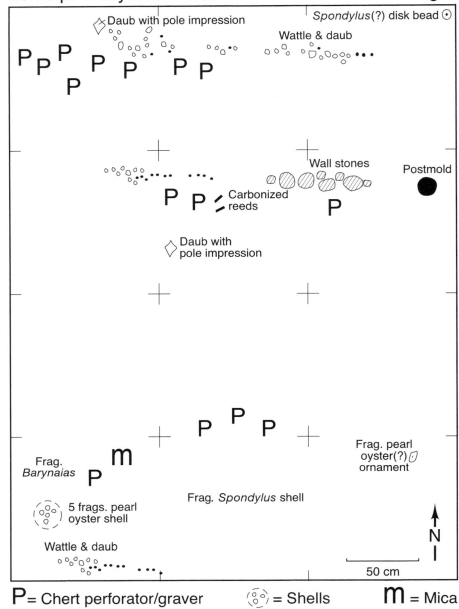

Figure 14.37. Distribution of items possibly associated with shell or mica working throughout Household Unit C1.

HOUSEHOLD UNIT C1: Miscellaneous items

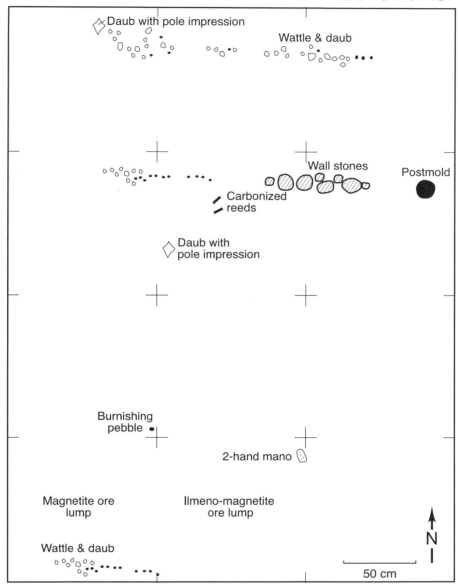

Figure 14.38. Distribution of ground stone and iron ore items in the southern part of Household Unit C1.

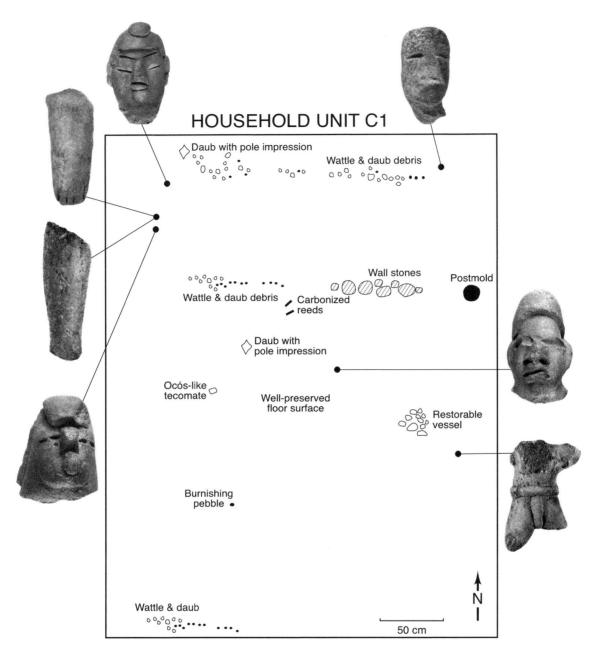

Figure 14.39. Figurine fragments piece-plotted in Household Unit C1.

IV

Chapter 15

An Introduction to Area B

Area B of San José Mogote lies midway between Area C and Mound 1, overlooking the southern slopes of the piedmont spur (Fig. 1.1, Chapter 1). It spans the boundary between the lands of Guadalupe Etla and those of the *agencia* of San José Mogote.

We were drawn to Area B because, like Area C, it had a cut bank left by modern adobe makers. This cut bank had many exposed layers of Formative deposits, and we knew it could be shaved to verticality, producing a Master Profile like the one in Area C. We hoped that the profile would reveal a different neighborhood of houses, one that we could compare and contrast with Areas A and C.

The Area B cut bank was 99.5 m long and ran east-west, actually crossing into Area C near its western limit. In 1969 we began shaving this bank with square-ended shovels, sharpened miners' digging bars, and trowels. We were only able to complete the westernmost 70 m of the Area B profile that season. We drew the stratigraphy and found it rather unexciting, since much of the deposit consisted of arroyo fill and slopewash (Flannery and Marcus 1994: Fig. 4.9). We could see, however, that bedrock was rising as we moved east. Since we knew from past experience that Formative villagers tended to place their houses on high points, we made plans to continue eastward.

In 1974 we completed and drew the easternmost 29.5 m of the Area B profile. This time the results were more interesting. The profile did rise in elevation as it ran east, eventually passing over an area of piedmont spur whose soft bedrock was perfect for the carving out of residential terraces. In the profile we could see house floors in cross-section, as well as pits, hearths, and rain runoff canals.

We selected a 5 m stretch of the eastern Area B profile to investigate. By that point in our project, we had shifted from using 1 × 1 m squares to using 2 × 2 m squares. This allowed us the flexibility to dig by larger squares when we were going though slopewash or construction fill, then divide each 2 × 2 m square into four 1 × 1 m squares whenever we encountered a house. Thus, a square called N1E6 could become four smaller squares named "N1E6-southeast," "N1E6-northwest," and so on.

The Area B excavation was begun by John W. Rick in 1974 and expanded by Marcus in 1978. Since the stratigraphy has already been discussed by Flannery and Marcus (1994:333-34), we will present here only enough data to put the Area B households in context.

The Stratigraphy of Area B

Figure 15.1 shows our chosen 5 m section of the Area B Master Profile, drawn before excavation began. N1E6 and N1E7 were the first 2 × 2 m squares excavated; work eventually expanded westward into Square N1E5.

Bedrock

The soft bedrock of Area B was riddled with postholes, pits, and small canals. One bell-shaped pit, Feature 65, belonged to the Tierras Largas phase. A much larger pit, Feature 58 (shown in Fig. 15.1), appeared to be a San José phase cistern.

Burial 18 was found in a bedrock pit below a house floor during the course of shaving the profile. The floor was assigned

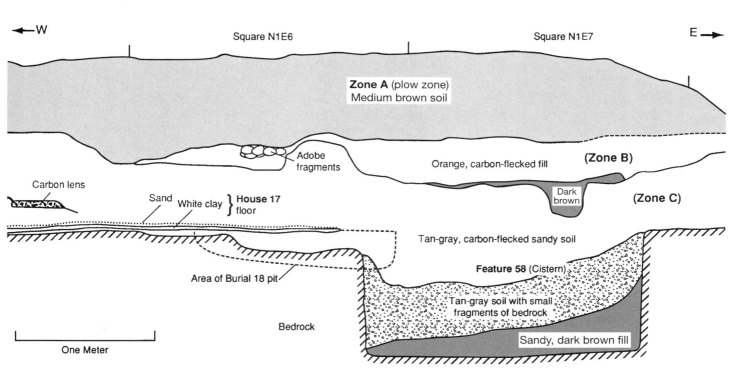

Figure 15.1. A 5 m section of the Area B Master Profile, drawn after it had been shaved to verticality but before excavation had begun. This drawing shows the stratigraphic relationships of Zones A, B, and C, the cross-sectioned floor of House 17, the area of Burial 18, and the Feature 58 cistern.

to House 17; the location of the burial pit is shown by dashed lines in Figure 15.1.

Zone C

Stratigraphic Zone C was a thick layer of tan earth, resulting from the decomposition of wattle-and-daub walls. It was associated with the House 16/17 Complex, our most nearly complete San José phase residence (Chapters 18-19).

Zone B

Stratigraphic Zone B was a layer of orange, carbon-flecked fill whose ceramics dated to the Middle Formative period. Its

contents included a small remnant of House 21, a Guadalupe phase residence (not visible in the Fig. 15.1 profile), as well as adobe fragments from a collapsed Middle Formative building that lay outside the area we excavated.

Zone A

Stratigraphic Zone A was a thick layer of medium brown soil that had been repeatedly plowed. While it contained Guadalupe and Rosario phase pottery, its most notable contents were a series of intrusive Postclassic (Monte Albán V) burials. It also featured occasional Postclassic trash pits, some excavated so deeply into the underlying deposits that they penetrated areas of the House 16/17 Complex.

Chapter 16
A Tierras Largas Phase Feature
from Area B

The profile left by modern adobe makers in Area B was a ragged one. As our workmen shaved that profile to a state of verticality, they discovered that the adobe makers had dug deeply enough to expose bedrock in places. Remembering the palisade postholes we had found in Area C, we decided to clean a two-meter-wide strip of bedrock along the base of the profile. While we did not find a palisade, we did recover a bell-shaped pit of the Tierras Largas phase. Apparently this feature lay in the dooryard of a household unit, but the rest of that unit is partially buried beneath a modern house and could not be explored further.

Feature 65

Feature 65 was a bell-shaped pit, dug into bedrock just south of the Area B Master Profile. It fell in Squares N1E8-N2E8 of the grid of 2 × 2 m squares established for Area B. (The location of those squares can be calculated by consulting Figure 17.4 of Chapter 17.) Owing to destruction by the adobe makers, only the lower 65 cm of the pit had been preserved. Its floor was oval, ranging from 1.1 to 0.86 m in diameter (Fig. 16.1a).

The contents of Feature 65 included three partially restorable pottery vessels, 84 sherds, 31 pieces of chipped stone, a mano, two metates, marine shell, and five complete or fragmentary figurines.

Ceramics

The 84 sherds from Feature 65 have been described by Flannery and Marcus (1994:119-20). Six of the 84 sherds were Atoyac Yellow-white, suggesting that the pit had been filled either (1) very late in the Tierras Largas phase or (2) during the Tierras Largas/San José transition.

Restorable Vessels

The three restorable vessels from the pit were (1) a Tierras Largas Burnished Plain hemispherical bowl, (2) a Matadamas Orange jar, and (3) an Atoyac Yellow-white cylindrical bowl.

Chipped Stone
Chert (87%)
    flake cores: 4
    utilized flakes: 4
    flakes, not utilized: 19
Obsidian (13%)
    utilized flake: 1
    flakes, not utilized: 3

Ground Stone
Fragment of subrectangular two-hand mano with airfoil cross-section, red sandstone (Fig. 16.1b). The fragment is 10.5 cm long, 9.5 cm wide, and averages 5.5 cm thick.

Small fragment of slightly lipped, basin-shaped metate (Fig. 16.1c). The fragment is 13 cm long; its original height was 6 cm, and it is roughly 3 cm thick in the middle of the basin.

Complete rectangular, box-shaped lipped metate with loop handle, ignimbrite, broken but restorable (Fig. 16.2a). The length is 22 cm, and the handle would add 4 cm to this. The width is 14 cm, and the thickness at the lip is 6 cm. This appears to be another example of a metate for some non-utilitarian task, such as grinding powdered tobacco to mix with lime. The loop handle would have made it possible to carry it back and forth between one's home and a ritual

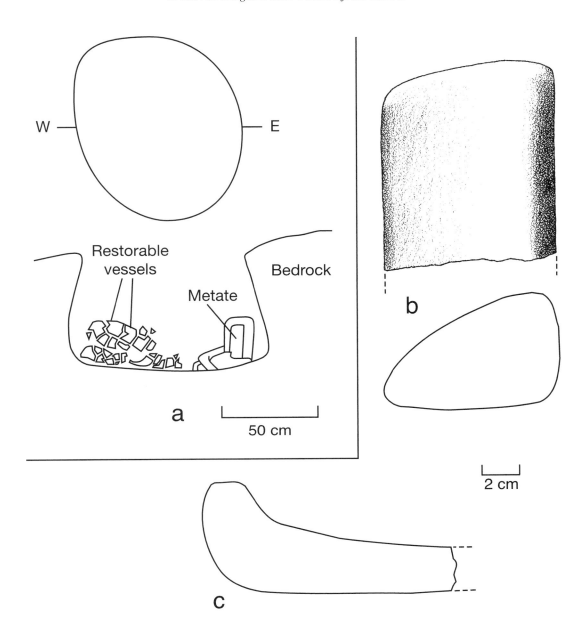

Figure 16.1. Feature 65 and some of the ground stone tools found within it. *a,* plan and cross-section of the feature. *b,* fragment of two-hand mano with airfoil cross-section. *c,* cross-section of slightly lipped basin-shaped metate fragment.

Figure 16.2. Artifacts from Feature 65. *a*, top and side views of rectangular, box-shaped metate with loop handle. *b*, rectangular ornament of *Spondylus* shell. *c*, crude figurine.

venue such as a Men's House, and the metate's boxlike shape would prevent a valuable substance like powdered tobacco from spilling. It is likely that, in contrast to most metates, this was a man's artifact.

Shell

Ornament of carefully trimmed *Spondylus* shell, rectangular, 28 × 15 × 2 mm (Fig. 16.2*b*). The presence of this specimen indicates that the working of imported *Spondylus* shell was underway at that time, although not on the scale seen in the later San José phase.

Figurines

Feature 65 produced one complete figurine (Fig. 16.2*c*) and four fragments. All have been described by Marcus (1998a:86 and Fig. 9.14). Two of the most interesting fragments appear to be from hollow dolls, covered with Atoyac Yellow-white slip. If we are correct, they represent Oaxaca's oldest examples of that type of figurine. The implication would be that white-slipped dolls appeared in Oaxaca as soon as Atoyac Yellow-white slip came in to use—in other words, during the transition from Tierras Largas to San José times.

Chapter 17

Area B: The Earliest Occupation of the Lower Terrace

One of the most interesting discoveries made in Area B was that the practice of architectural terracing goes back at least to the San José phase. Since Caso's work more than 60 years ago, it has been known that the site of Monte Albán was artificially terraced to accommodate thousands of houses. What we had not expected was that 700 years before Monte Albán, the piedmont spur at San José Mogote had been terraced to accommodate Early Formative houses. This terracing took the form of flat dooryard surfaces hacked out of the gently sloping bedrock. The main tools used were celts made of metamorphic rock, which was harder than the volcanic tuff bedrock. Despite their hardness, these celts eventually became blunt from the constant battering (Fig. 17.1b).

Our excavations in Area B exposed parts of two dooryards, referred to simply as the Lower and Upper Terraces. The Lower Terrace was, among other things, the artificially leveled surface on which the House 16/17 Complex had been built (Chapter 18). At its northern limit we discovered an irregular standing face of hacked bedrock, rising like a wall 50-60 cm high (Fig. 17.1a). Nearby lay a number of blunted celts that had evidently been used to convert the bedrock slope into a series of descending steps, each large enough for a residence. At the top of the bedrock face began the flat surface of the Upper Terrace, apparently the dooryard of another house that lay uphill from House 16/17.

In this chapter we discuss the earliest traces of occupation on the Lower Terrace. This terrace had a complex history, which can be discussed in terms of four main stratigraphic units (see Chapter 15). The lowest unit consisted of San José phase postholes, pits, small rain runoff canals, and cisterns, all dug into bedrock. Above that lay the House 16/17 Complex, its dooryard and activity areas, all dating to the Late San José phase and assigned to stratigraphic Zone C.

Postholes and Features in Bedrock

The first occupants of the Lower Terrace had solved their household water problems by digging a large cistern (Feature 58) in bedrock (Fig. 17.2). This cistern was 2 m in diameter and roughly 90 cm deep. It evidently received water from a series of small canals that diverted rain runoff away from the houses. (One San José phase house at the site of Tierras Largas was equipped with a similar diversion canal; see Fig. 17.3.) There was even a small canal running west from Feature 58 to carry away any overflow, should the cistern fill to the brim.

As shown in Figure 17.4, bedrock in the area had also been penetrated by 19 postholes. Their pattern was confusing, since they came down from different depths and belonged to more than one household. Some of the holes appear atypically large, but this is almost certainly because the bedrock was friable in places and crumbled when penetrated.

Feature 58 (The Cistern)

Because the rain runoff entering Feature 58 had sometimes carried sand or soil in suspension, there was a residue of sandy, dark brown earth lying on the floor of the feature. At some point, the cistern outlived its usefulness and was deliberately filled in. A layer of tan-gray soil with fragments of bedrock had resulted from the first stage of this filling-in process. The stony fragments may be debris left by the hacking of bedrock to widen the terrace. San José phase domestic refuse had also been swept into Feature 58. The villagers had taken advantage of the cistern's large size to discard bulky items such as chert cores, manos, and broken metates.

Figure 17.1. Area B provided our oldest evidence for the conversion of a slope into architectural terraces. In *a*, the workman on the left kneels on the Lower Terrace; the workman on the right kneels on the Upper Terrace. Between them is a 50-60 cm high "step" produced by hacking bedrock. At *b* we see a stone celt found above House 17, battered and blunted from long usage in contouring bedrock.

The debris in Feature 58 also included our only remains of the crested guan, a 2 kg bird whose range includes the pine-oak forests of highland Oaxaca, although it is more common in the tropical lowlands. It may have been hunted for its iridescent plumage.

Chipped Stone
    Chert (93%)
        flake cores: 10
        flake spokeshave: 1
        nosed flake tool: 1
        utilized flakes: 9
        flakes, not utilized: 21
    Obsidian (4%)
        prismatic blade fragment: 1

        flake, not utilized: 1
    Other (2%)
        quartz core: 1

Ground Stone
    Subrectangular one-hand mano made on an ignimbrite stream cobble, worked on two faces and two sides. Both ends have also been used for pounding. Length, 11 cm; width, 6.5 cm; thickness, 4.2 cm (Fig. 17.5*a*).
    Fragment of subrectangular two-hand mano with airfoil cross-section, ignimbrite. The fragment is 12 cm long, which may represent half the unbroken length. Width 9.5 cm; thickness, 5 cm (Fig. 17.5*c*).
    Fragment of loaf-shaped two-hand mano with airfoil cross-section, granitic rock. Length, >16 cm (broken); width, 9

Figure 17.2. Postholes, features, and rain runoff canals dug into bedrock in Area B. The workman is cleaning Feature 58, a large San José phase cistern (see also Figure 15.1, Chapter 15).

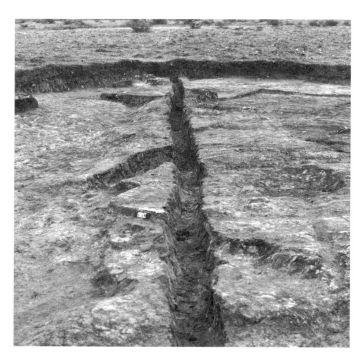

Figure 17.3. Small canal excavated into bedrock at the site of Tierras Largas. This canal likely served to divert rain runoff away from House LSJ-1 (San José phase).

cm; thickness, 5 cm (Fig. 17.5*b*).
Small fragment of slab metate, quartzite. The surviving fragment is 10 × 8.5 × 4 cm (Fig. 17.5*d*).
Broken saddle-shaped metate, ignimbrite. Length, 28.5 cm; width, 20 cm; maximum thickness, ca. 9 cm (Fig. 17.5*e*).

Mica
Thirteen pieces of gold mica totaling 5.7 g, the largest fragment measuring 95 × 41 × 2 mm. Several pieces have at least one trimmed side. It is possible that all these fragments were once part of a single "book."

Figurines
Two fragments of small solid figurines were found in the cistern. They have been described by Marcus (1998a:183).

Animal Bones
Large Mammals
  white-tailed deer (*Odocoileus virginianus*)
    1 fragment of proximal tibia
    1 R. calcaneum
    15 long bone splinters
Small Mammals
  domestic dog (*Canis familiaris*)
    1 atlas

eastern cottontail (*Sylvilagus floridanus*)
    1 L. mandible
    1 L. unfused proximal tibia
    1 L. unfused distal tibia
Birds
  crested guan (*Penelope purpurascens*)
    1 large humerus

Feature 50

Feature 50 was a pit dug into bedrock in Area B, just to the south of the area shown in Figure 17.4. Its function is unknown, and its original dimensions could not be determined because it lay partly below a modern house.

Figurines
Fragments of four small solid figurines had been swept into Feature 50. They have been described in Marcus (1998a:183 and Fig. 13.21, nos. 1 and 2).

Feature 59

Feature 59 was another pit dug into bedrock, just to the south of Squares N1E4/N1E5 (Fig. 17.6*a*). As in the case of Feature 50, its original dimensions could not be determined since it lay partially below a modern house. While Feature 59 was probably created originally as a storage feature, it ended up as a receptacle for trash.

Ground Stone
The distal end of a pestle made from fine-grained metamorphic rock. The surviving fragment is 8-8.5 cm in diameter and 5 cm long (Fig. 17.6*b*).
One basin-shaped metate of pink ignimbrite, incomplete. Length, >35 cm; width, >21 cm; maximum thickness, 10 cm; thickness near center of basin, 6-6.5 cm (Fig. 17.6*c*).

Figurines
Two fragments of small solid figurines were found in Feature 59 (Marcus 1998a:183).

Animal Bones
white-tailed deer (*Odocoileus virginianus*)
    1 vertebra
    1 L. distal tibia

Material from Bedrock Depressions Found While Cleaning the Area B Profile

Mica
A piece of shattered gold mica was found, weighing 0.6 g, originally ca. 33 × 20 mm.

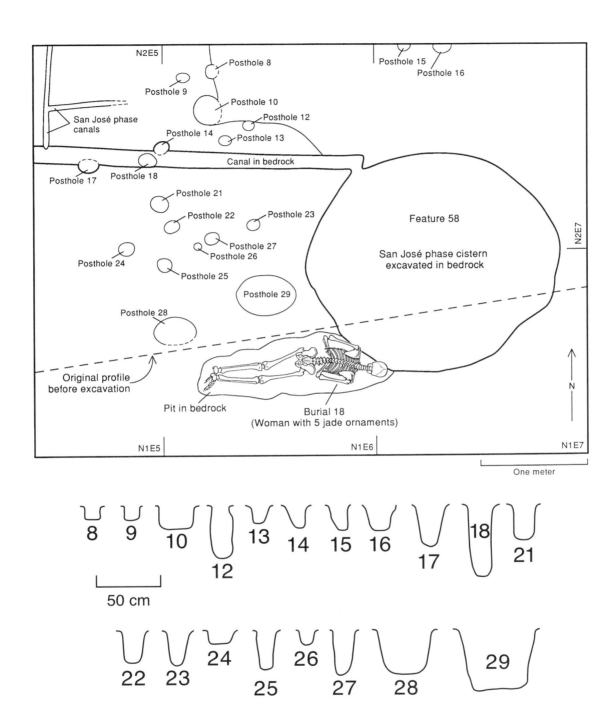

Figure 17.4. Postholes and features in bedrock below Houses 16/17. *Above*, plan view of the area. *Below*, cross-sections of postholes.

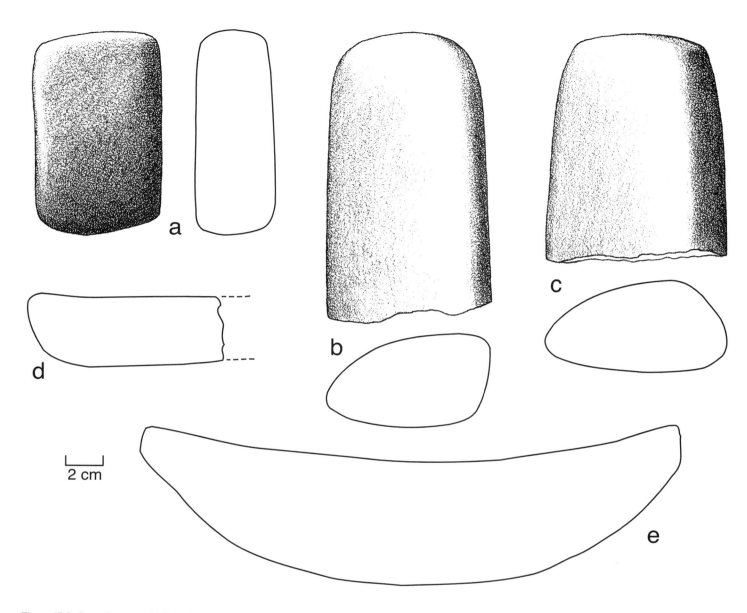

Figure 17.5. Ground stone tools discarded in the Feature 58 cistern. *a*, subrectangular one-hand mano. *b, c,* two-hand manos with airfoil cross-section. *d*, cross-section of slab metate fragment. *e*, cross-section of saddle-shaped metate.

Bone Ornament

 A pendant was found, made from a tusk of collared peccary (*Dicotyles tajacu*) (Fig. 17.7).

Animal Bones
 Small Mammals
  domestic dog (*Canis familiaris*)
   1 L. proximal tibia
   1 L. distal tibia and fibula (fused)
  pocket gopher (*Orthogeomys grandis*)
   1 upper incisor
   1 R. distal humerus

 eastern cottontail (*Sylvilagus floridanus*)
  1 L. mandible
 Mexican cottontail (*Sylvilagus cunicularius*)
  1 R. proximal humerus
  2 R. distal humeri (two individuals)
 unidentified cottontail (*Sylvilagus* sp.)
  1 unfused proximal tibia, immature rabbit
Human
 a few fragments

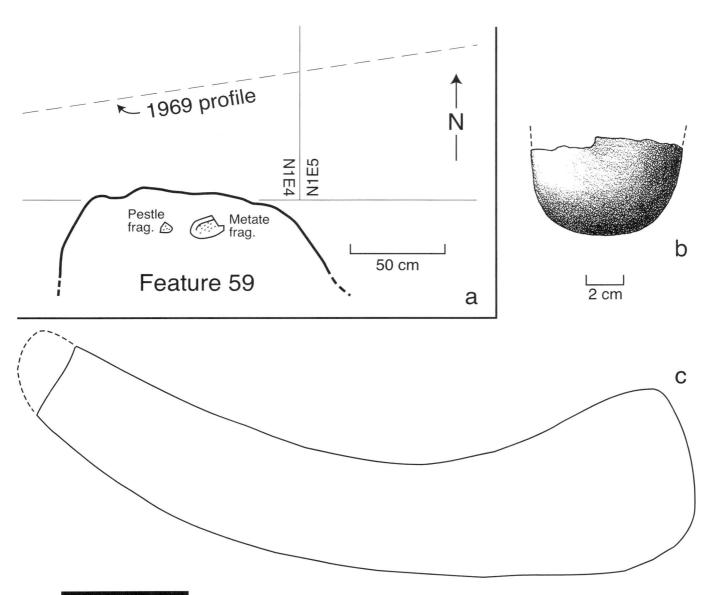

Figure 17.6 (*above*). Feature 59, a pit in bedrock, and its contents. *a*, plan view of the feature. *b*, distal end of pestle. *c*, cross-section of basin-shaped metate.

Figure 17.7 (*left*). Peccary tusk pendant found in a bedrock depression near the 1969 Master Profile, Area B.

Chapter 18

Area B: Houses 16 and 17

Houses 16 and 17 were built on the Lower Terrace during the Late San José phase, stratigraphically above the bedrock features discussed in Chapter 17 (Fig. 18.1). While we referred to both of these buildings as "houses" when we first discovered them, it eventually became clear that only House 17 was a typical wattle-and-daub residence. House 16 turned out to be a lean-to or roofed work area of some kind, perhaps connected to House 17 as shown in our reconstruction drawing (Fig. 18.2). The posts in House 16 were smaller in diameter and fewer in number than those of a typical house, and there was no evidence of daub from collapsing walls.

There were other differences between Houses 16 and 17. House 17 had real walls, with a coating of whitewash almost approaching a slip. House 16, on the other hand, had a number of features usually found outdoors, such as a hearth and an unusual fire pit. One of the craft activities in this household unit was the manufacture of bifaces from heat-treated chert, and more of that work had been carried out in the lean-to than in the house. Other crafts carried out in or around House 16 included basket making and the production of pottery from clay molds.

This residence was one in which representations of Earth/Earthquake motifs were dominant on ceramics (Flannery and Marcus 1994:344-48). The occupants of the House 16/17 Complex also appeared to be of relatively high rank. They had access to more deer meat; sumptuary goods of jadeite(?), *Spondylus,* and pearl oyster; and exotic items like stingray spines and drum otoliths than the average household. They had also received a presumed Cesto White vessel from the Basin of Mexico (Flannery and Marcus 1994:333-41). Beneath the floor of House 17, they had buried a woman with the largest quantity of jadeite(?) found so far in a San José phase context.

House 17

House 17 had a carefully made floor of white clay, covered by the usual layer of sand. Owing to postoccupational erosion, only 3-4 m² of the sand surface was well preserved; fortunately, the clay floor could be traced over a wider area.

In the sections that follow, we divide the material from House 17 into four microstratigraphic units. First, we discuss the material (1) lying directly on the house floor or (2) deliberately cached beneath it. Next we present (3) material from below the floor, which appeared to be associated with an earlier stage of the house. Finally, we present (4) a few items found above the floor which are likely (but not conclusively) associated with House 17.

1. Material Lying Directly on the House 17 Floor

Daub

Daub fragments found during the excavation of House 17 often displayed a nicely smoothed outer surface of whitewashed clay that is not as white as the lime plaster used on public buildings, but whiter than that of the average house. (In the Munsell system, the color would be described as "white," 5YR 8/1, to "pinkish white," 5YR 8/2.) Several fragments, while not preserving the outer surface of the building, bore measurable cane impressions. Modal diameters for these impressions were 12 mm, 10 mm, and 6 mm, and as usual the canes were grouped in bundles.

Ceramics

Some 170 sherds were found in association with House 17. In contrast to House 16 (see below), only 9 of those sherds were from the domestic cooking ware Fidencio Coarse, while 77 were

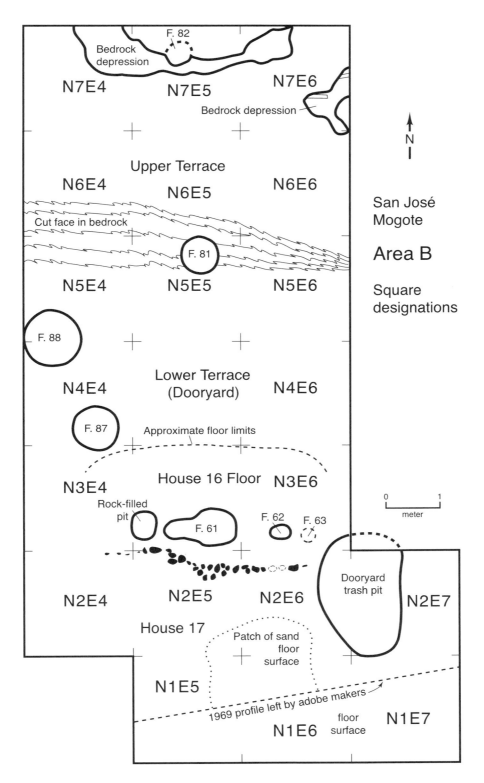

Figure 18.1. Area B, showing square designations and notable landmarks.

HOUSE 17

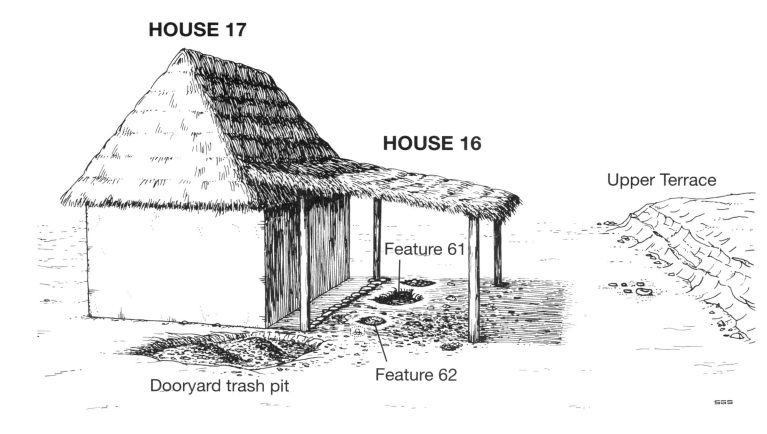

Figure 18.2. Artist's reconstruction of the relationship between Houses 16 and 17. Also shown are the dooryard trash pit and the cut face in bedrock at the limits of the Lower Terrace.

from the serving-bowl ware Atoyac Yellow-white. It thus appears that while meals may have been served in House 17, most of the cooking (and other tasks involving coarse jars) was probably done in House 16, the lean-to (Flannery and Marcus 1994:336).

We did plot one restorable Fidencio Coarse *tecomate*, Vessel 1, in Square N2E6. It was undecorated except for a sloppy red wash. Possibly because House 17 had been swept before abandonment and contained a relatively small sample of sherds, it yielded only one exotic fragment, a Xochiltepec White jar neck.

Chipped Stone

The chipped stone sample from the House 17 floor was smaller (109 items) than the House 16 sample. It contrasted not only with the House 16 sample, but also with the chipped stone collections from Area A. For example, House 17 did not produce a single flake perforator/graver, a tool that had been one of the most common in Area A households (Chapter 14).

Furthermore, even though we know that the family occupying House 16/17 was engaged in making bifaces from heat-treated chert, we found hardly any evidence for that activity on the House 17 floor. The only biface roughout fragment found there

was one that had been reused as a chopper. Parry (1987: Fig. 40) describes House 17 as having "relatively high densities of finished tools," as opposed to debitage. In other words, it was a place where a number of tools were used and left, but not the place where most of them were made.

Chert (86%)
  hammerstones: 3 (Fig. 18.3*a, b*)
  ordinary flake cores: 8
  bipolar cores: 7
  core tool: 1
  flake tool: 1
  flake scraper: 1
  denticulate flake: 1
  biface roughout fragment, reused as a chopper: 1
  large perforator/scraping plane: 1
  retouched flakes: 3
  utilized flakes: 11
  flakes, not utilized: 56
Obsidian (12%)
  prismatic blade fragment, utilized: 1
  prismatic blade fragments, no sign of use: 2

notched blade: 1
graver fragment?: 1
retouched flake: 1
flakes, utilized: 3
flakes, not utilized: 4
Other (2%)
quartz flake: 1
quartzite flake: 1

Ground Stone
Fragment of loaf-shaped two-hand mano with oval cross-section, fine-grained micaceous sandstone. The fragment is 10.5 cm long, 8.5 cm wide, and 3 cm thick (Fig. 18.3*c*).
Fragment of subrectangular two-hand mano with planoconvex cross-section, granite/diorite. The fragment is 13 cm long, 9 cm wide, and 4.2 cm thick (Fig. 18.3*d*).
Oval cobble used as a pigment grinder, with traces of red powder still preserved on its surface. Its dimensions are 5 × 4.5 × 2.5 cm (Fig. 18.4*a*).
Travertine *canica* or pecked and ground stone ball, 2.1 cm in diameter (Fig. 18.4*b*).

The following two items were discarded together in Square N2E6, at the northern limit of the House 17 floor:

Fragment of loaf-shaped two-hand mano with oval cross-section and two convex grinding surfaces, ignimbrite. The fragment is 8 cm long, 9.5 cm wide, and 5 cm thick, and one edge shows that it was used as a hammer after it broke (Fig. 18.3*e*).
Fragment of lightly used slab metate, made of hard metamorphic rock (possibly schist). The original diameter of this metate might have been 25 cm, but it is now broken. Its thickness is about 4 cm. Had this metate been used for a longer period of time, it probably would have become basin-shaped (Fig. 18.3*f*).

Shell
Ornaments
Disk bead, made from an unidentified beachworn shell. The ornament is chipped, but originally was ca. 15 mm in diameter; the hole drilled in the center is 2 mm in diameter (Fig. 18.4*c*).
Pacific Marine Bivalves
Piece trimmed from the hinge of a pearl oyster (*Pinctada mazatlanica*), 10 × 10 × 2 mm.
Unidentified
Two fragments of marine shell, (1) 10 × 10 × 1 mm, (2) 8 × 4 × 1 mm.

Iron Ore Specimen
A lump of magnetite was found, 11 × 8 × 5 mm.

Mica
Piece of dark brown mica, trimmed on at least one edge, weighing 10 g; 38 × 33 mm and 4 mm thick (Fig. 18.4*e*).
Piece of dark brown mica, perhaps cut on as many as two edges, weighing 0.6 g; 36 × 30 mm and 1 mm thick (Fig. 18.4*d*).
Piece of gold mica, originally weighing 0.8 g; this specimen had disintegrated into a mass of paper-thin fragments, none more than 33 × 25 mm.
Piece of brown mica, weighing 0.6 g, 24 × 16 × 1 mm.
Decomposing mass of whitish gold mica, weighing 3.5 g; 55 × 36 × 1 mm.

Figurines
Some 21 fragments of small solid figurines were found in association with House 17. Seventeen fragments were plotted on (or at the level of) the house floor. Two were found just below the level of the floor, and two more were found along the line of wall stones separating Houses 16 and 17. All these fragments have been described and illustrated by Marcus (1998a:171-73, Fig. 13.4), and six of the most interesting are shown in Figure 18.5.

Stone Ornament
One piece of a broken jadeite(?) earspool, coated with red pigment, was found on the floor. Made from dark, mottled green jadeite(?), the earspool had a tubular shaft 16 mm in diameter and flared at one end; its original length would have been greater than 20 mm. In one side of the shaft were two drill holes, each 2.5 mm in diameter, suggesting that other elements had been attached to the ear ornament (Fig. 18.4*g*).

Imported Marine Fish
Complete stingray spine, 9.7 cm long (family Dasyatidae). The spine, which was presumably used for ritual bloodletting, had been partially drilled at the base as if for suspension (Fig. 18.4*f*).

Animal Bones
Large Mammals
white-tailed deer (*Odocoileus virginianus*)
1 antler tine (possibly saved to be made into a tool)
1 other antler fragment
1 R. petrous bone
1 mandible fragment?
1 R. calcaneum
collared peccary (*Dicotyles tajacu*)
1 L. maxilla
1 R. scapula
Small Mammals
domestic dog (*Canis familiaris*)
1 R. mandible
1 permanent tooth (adult)

1 deciduous tooth (puppy)
1 vertebra fragment
1 rib
1 L. second metacarpal
1 R. second metacarpal
1 R. fourth metatarsal
pocket gopher (*Orthogeomys grandis*)
   2 upper incisors
   1 lower incisor
   1 L. distal tibia
   5 limb bone splinters
jackrabbit (*Lepus mexicanus*)
   1 L. radius
   1 metapodial
eastern cottontail (*Sylvilagus floridanus*)
   2 cheek teeth
   1 R. distal humerus
   1 L. tibia
   1 L. calcaneum
Mexican cottontail (*Sylvilagus cunicularius*)
   1 R. proximal radius
   1 R. innominate
   1 R. metatarsal
unidentified cottontails (*Sylvilagus* spp.)
   2 cheek teeth
   1 R. unfused scapula
   1 humerus fragment
Human
   1 skull fragment
   1 tooth
   1 long bone shaft fragment
Unidentified
   32 splinters of mammal long bone

2. Items Deliberately Buried below the House 17 Floor

In Square N1E6 of House 17, two possible woodworking tools had been stored in a small cavity below the floor (Fig. 18.6). These tools do not appear to be preforms for celts, but were made from the same kind of hard metamorphic rock. They showed signs of having been used for the kind of sanding and smoothing that woodworking might require. The way these two artifacts had been stored below the floor suggests that they were special tools, kept where they could always be found when needed.

Rectangular artifact of crystalline metamorphic rock, 16 cm long, 6 cm wide, and 2.5 cm thick. All its surfaces are absolutely flat, made so from repeated smoothing or sanding (Fig. 18.6a).
Rectangular/subrectangular artifact of fine-grained metamorphic rock, 11.2 cm long, 3.5 cm wide, and 4 cm thick. Several of its working surfaces are flat as the result of smoothing or sanding, but the ends are slightly convex as the result of pounding (Fig. 18.6b).

Burial 18

A middle-aged woman had been buried below the floor of House 17, her burial pit extending into bedrock (Fig. 17.4, Chapter 17). This woman, designated Burial 18, was fully extended, face down with her arms folded across her chest. She was accompanied by three jadeite(?) beads and two jadeite(?) earspools (Fig. 18.4h). Two of the beads and one earspool were found in her mouth; the other earspool was found below her right clavicle; the third bead was found under her chest. It is possible that all the ornaments had been placed in her mouth at the time of burial, and that some rolled out into the burial bundle when her jaw muscles decayed.

Dimensions of earspools: length, 14 mm; diameter of shaft, 8 mm; diameter of flared end, 13 mm.
Dimensions of disk beads: average diameter, 10 mm; drill hole in center, 2 mm.

The earth surrounding Burial 18 produced fragments of four small solid figurines (Marcus 1998a:183 and Fig. 13.23). All appeared, however, to have been accidentally included in the fill.

Insights from Artifact Plotting

Figures 18.7-18.11 present the distributions of hammerstones, chert cores, utilized flakes, miscellaneous chert and obsidian tools, ground stone tool fragments, craft items, and ornaments on the floor of House 17. Our overall impression is that our excavation most fully exposed the northeast quadrant of the house, whose east wall evidently ran through the pile of daub fragments between the dooryard trash pit and the best-preserved patch of sand floor surface. The north wall presumably followed the stone threshold running between Houses 16 and 17. Assuming that to be the case, much of the patterning we see may simply reflect the tossing or sweeping of debris toward the north and east walls.

Let us begin with the distribution of tools related to primary chert flake production (Fig. 18.7). Immediately we note some separate clusters of ordinary cores and bipolar cores, like those seen earlier in Household Unit C1 of Area A (Chapter 14). Evidently some flaking was done while holding the core on an anvil (Parry 1987:36), while other flaking resulted from direct percussion. We cannot be sure whether this was done by two different knappers, or by one knapper at different times. One group of bipolar cores had been tossed toward the stone threshold, while another had been discarded near the east wall. Most ordinary cores lay farther from the wall.

We can look next at the distribution of utilized chert flakes (Fig. 18.8) to see if it provides any further insight. Four utilized flakes lay near the stone threshold, possibly as the result of sweeping. The remaining seven were scattered across the floor and do not in general show a close association with the cores from which they were struck.

Figure 18.9 gives the location of piece-plotted retouched tools, too few in number to provide much of a pattern. Once again, our impression is that we are seeing items tossed or swept toward the northeast corner of the house.

The distribution of ground stone tools (Fig. 18.10) reinforces our suspicion that House 17 was not the place where most of the food preparation was carried out. A few small fragments of manos or metates form a line parallel to the stone threshold, perhaps tossed or swept there. At least one showed signs that its last use was as a hammerstone, rather than as a grinding stone. That might have been the case with most of them.

The only ground stone tools definitely remaining where they had last been touched were the two woodworking(?) sanders/ smoothers. Still in perfect condition, they had evidently been cached below the floor in Square N1E6, where they remained even after House 17 had been abandoned. Their storage place might have been further hidden by placing a reed mat over that part of the floor.

Finally, Figure 18.11 gives the location of piece-plotted craft items or imported objects. Since we found little evidence for shell working in the house, the occasional fragments of that material may be from broken ornaments. The jadeite(?) earspool found in Square N1E6, although broken, would originally have been one of the largest and most spectacular known for the San José phase. Like the elegant stingray spine found in the northeast corner of the house, it may well have been one of the sumptuary goods of a person of relatively high rank.

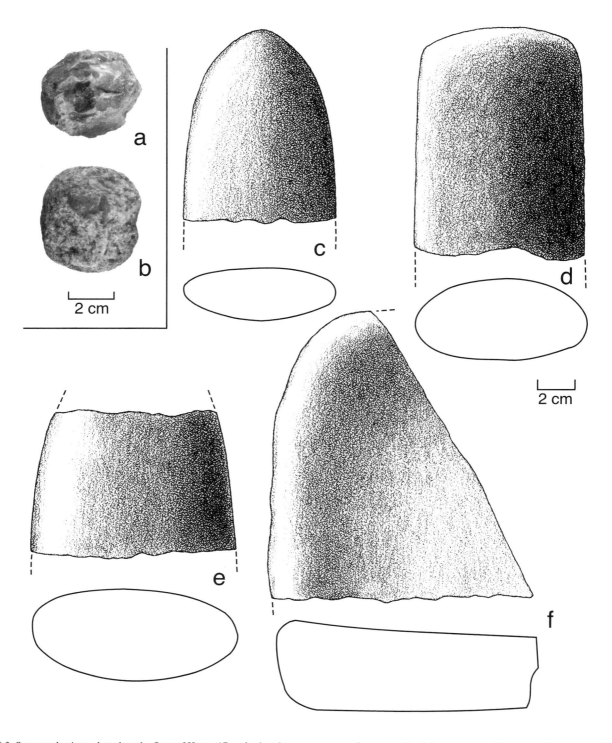

Figure 18.3. Stone tools piece-plotted on the floor of House 17. *a, b,* chert hammerstones. *c,* fragment of loaf-shaped mano. *d,* fragment of subrectangular mano. *e,* fragment of loaf-shaped mano. *f,* fragment of slab metate. *e* and *f* were discarded together in Square N2E6.

Figure 18.4. Artifacts associated with House 17. *a-g* were piece-plotted on the floor. *a*, cobble used as pigment grinder. *b, canica* or pecked and ground stone ball. *c*, disk bead of marine shell. *d, e*, pieces of cut and trimmed dark brown mica. *f,* stingray spine (partly drilled for suspension?). *g*, broken earspool of dark green jadeite(?); two drill holes can be seen on the left edge. *h*, two jadeite(?) earspools and three jadeite(?) disk beads found with Burial 18, below House 17.

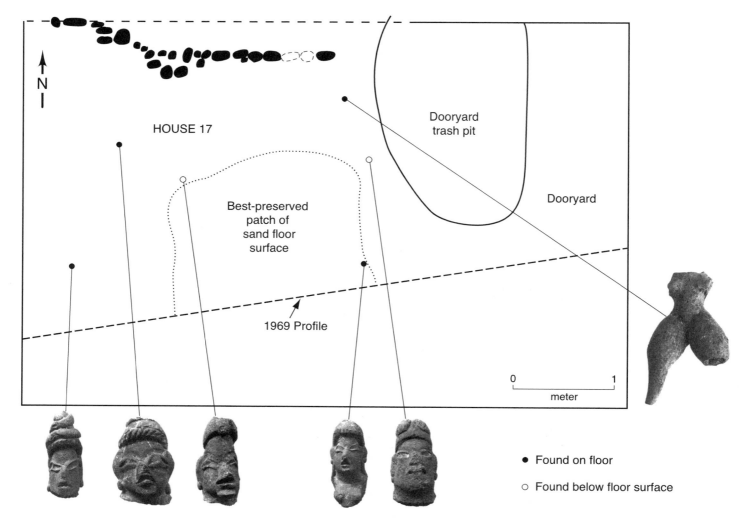

HOUSE 17

Best-preserved
patch of
sand floor
surface

1969 Profile

Dooryard
trash pit

Dooryard

0   1
meter

● Found on floor

○ Found below floor surface

Figure 18.5. Six figurine fragments piece-plotted on (or just below) the floor of House 17.

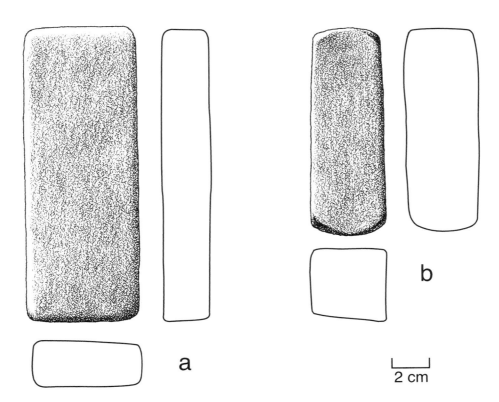

Figure 18.6. Two sanding/smoothing tools, possibly for woodworking, stored in a small cavity below the floor of House 17 (Square N1E6). *a*, made of crystalline metamorphic rock, has six flat surfaces. *b*, made of fine-grained metamorphic rock, has four flat surfaces; its ends are slightly convex as a result of pounding and polishing.

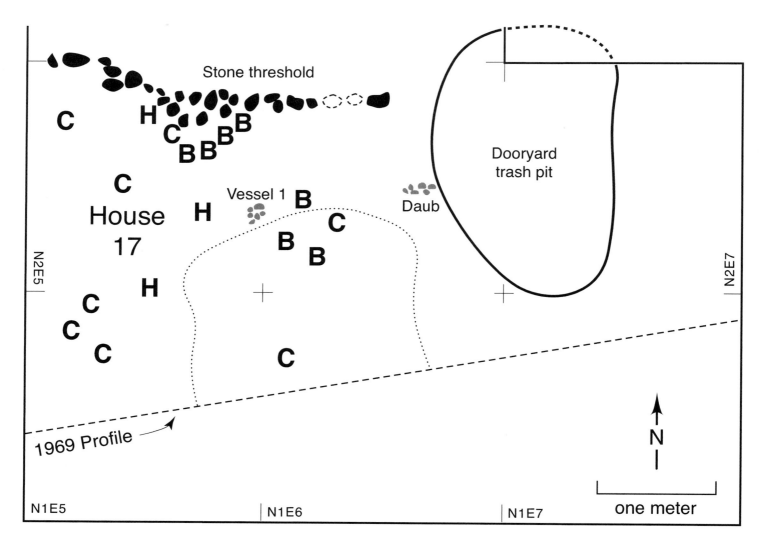

House 17. Chert tools. **H**=Hammerstone. **C**=Ordinary flake core. **B**=Bipolar core. Dotted line encloses best-preserved patch of sand floor surface.

Figure 18.7. Distribution of tools related to primary flake production, found on the floor of House 17.

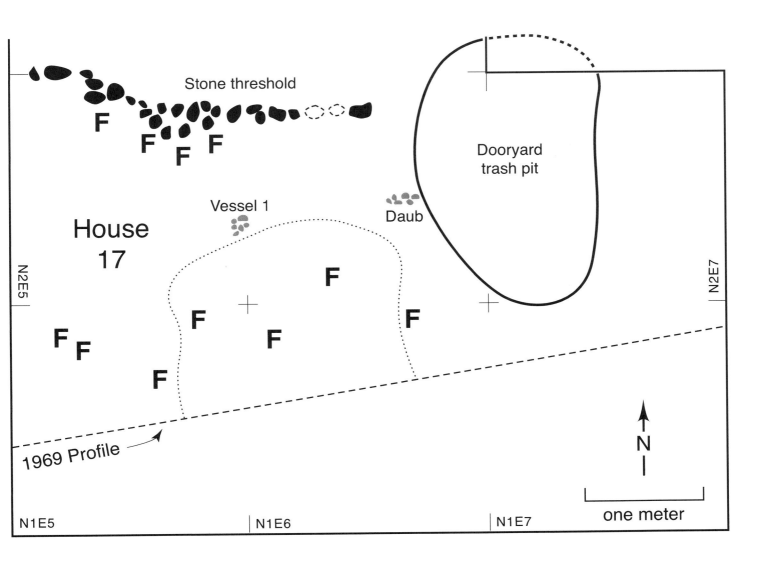

Figure 18.8. Distribution of utilized chert flakes (F) on the floor of House 17.

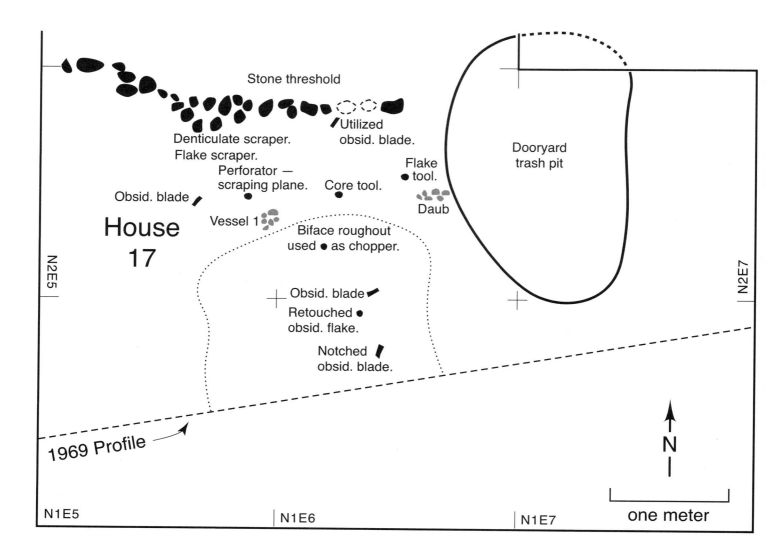

Figure 18.9. Miscellaneous chipped stone tools found on the floor of House 17.

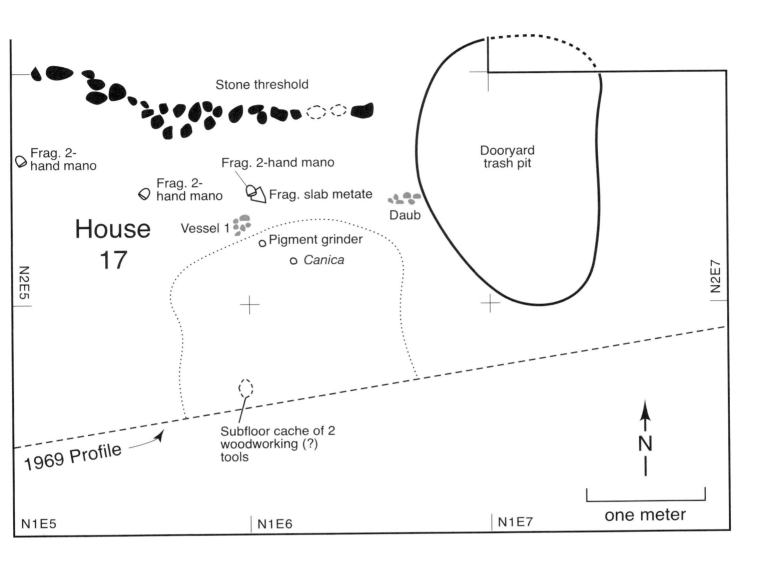

Figure 18.10. Ground stone tools found on (or cached below) the floor of House 17.

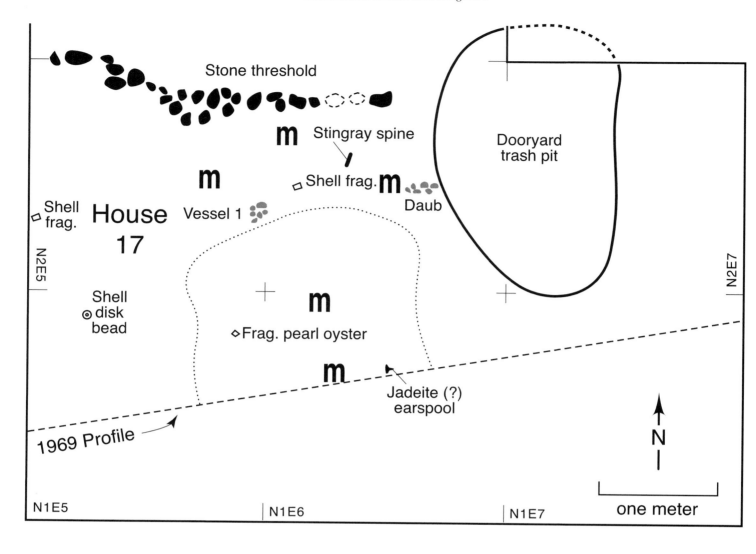

Figure 18.11. Location of craft items or imported objects on the floor of House 17: mica (m), shell, jadeite(?), and a complete stingray spine.

3. Material below the House 17 Floor, Probably from an Earlier Stage of the House

Upon removing the floor of House 17, we encountered a layer of San José phase debris some 15-20 cm thick. It appeared to be refuse left behind from an earlier stage of House 17. Assuming that to be the case, it would seem that during that earlier stage, the occupants of House 17 were involved in shell working (6 chert perforators/gravers, 6 shell items) but not in biface working.

The implied change over time from a less specialized family to a biface-producing family is interesting. It contrasts with the situation in Area A, where perhaps four or five generations of families remained shell workers and iron ore mirror producers

(Chapter 14). Reynolds' multidimensional scaling, reported in Chapter 25, suggests that during the earlier stage of House 17, its activities were more like those of a typical Area C residence.

Chipped Stone
    Chert (86%)
        flake cores: 9
        core tool: 1
        flake perforators/gravers: 6 (Fig. 18.12a)
        flake spokeshave: 1 (Fig. 18.12b)
        retouched flakes: 2
        flakes, utilized: 23
        flakes, not utilized: 101

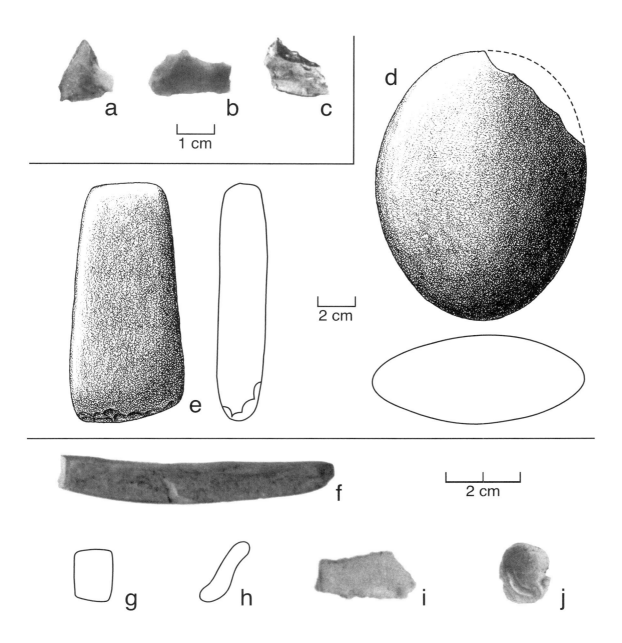

Figure 18.12. Objects from a layer of debris below the floor of House 17, probably belonging to an earlier stage of the same house. *a*, chalcedony perforator/graver. *b*, chalcedony spokeshave. *c*, obsidian perforator/graver. *d*, one-hand mano. *e*, chipped and blunted celt. *f*, deer bone spatula. *g*, shell rectangle. *h*, fragment cut from pearl oyster. *i*, fragment of travertine. *j*, drum otolith.

Obsidian (13%)
  bipolar flake core: 1
  prismatic blade fragments, utilized: 10
  prismatic blade fragments, no sign of use: 2
  perforator: 1 (Fig. 18.12*c*)
  retouched flake: 1
  flake, utilized: 1
  flakes, not utilized: 6

Other (1%)
  quartz fragment: 1
  ignimbrite flake, utilized: 1

Ground Stone
  Ovoid one-hand mano, made on a crystalline igneous(?) cobble; oval cross-section, two convex grinding surfaces. The cobble is 15 × 11 cm and ca. 5 cm thick (Fig. 18.12*d*).

Badly chipped and blunted celt made of fine-grained metamorphic rock. Length, 13 cm; average width, 5.5 cm;
thickness, 2.4 cm. It appears that in its last stage of use,
this celt was used to cut bedrock until it became so blunt
that it was discarded. It was found in Square N1E5, not far
from one of the rain runoff canals underlying House 17,
and might have been used to dig such a canal in bedrock
(Fig. 18.12*e*).

Bone Tools

Spatula made on a shaft fragment from a deer metapodial (possibly even a reworked piece of a broken deer metapodial
awl). The object is 7.3 cm long, 1.2 cm wide, and about 2
mm thick. The working end is rounded (Fig. 18.12*f*).
Worked canine tooth of domestic dog, possibly intended for
an ornament but never drilled.

Shell

Ornaments
rectangle of pearly shell, 14 × 11 mm, not identified (Fig.
18.12*g*)
Pearly Freshwater Mussel?
small fragment, 10 × 8 mm
Pacific Marine Bivalves
fragment cut from pearl oyster (*Pinctada mazatlanica*), 20
× 5 mm (Fig. 18.12*h*)
Unidentified
2 fragments of marine shell: (1) 10 × 15 mm; (2) 10 ×
10 mm
7 fragments from the same unidentified shell, all < 5 × 5
mm in size

Mica

Piece of gold mica weighing 2.4 g, 70 × 44 × 1 mm; cut on
at least one edge, perhaps with a chert graver.

Travertine

Piece of travertine, 25 × 12 mm, probably from the source
at Fábrica San José, 5 km to the east. This was a common
raw material for *canicas* (Fig. 18.12*i*).

Figurines

Two figurine heads (Marcus 1998a:173) were found.

Imported Marine Fish

An otolith of drum (family Sciaenidae), 1.5 cm in diameter
(Fig. 18.12 *j*), was found.

Animal Bones

Large Mammals
white-tailed deer (*Odocoileus virginianus*)
several fragments of vertebrae
10 long bone shaft fragments
Small Mammals

domestic dog (*Canis familiaris*)
2 fragments of maxilla
2 L. mandible fragments from 2 dogs
2 R. mandible fragments from 2 dogs
2 canine teeth
1 L. lower first molar
1 R. distal humerus
1 fragment of radius shaft
1 rib
pocket gopher (*Orthogeomys grandis*)
2 lower incisors
eastern cottontail (*Sylvilagus floridanus*)
1 metapodial
Mexican cottontail (*Sylvilagus cunicularius*)
1 L. mandible
1 lower incisor
unidentified cottontails (*Sylvilagus* spp.)
1 cheek tooth
Reptiles
mud turtle (*Kinosternon integrum*)
1 marginal carapace scute
Birds
coot (*Fulica americana*)
1 L. femur
unidentified bird
1 fragment
Unidentified
57 splinters, mainly from mammal long bones

4. Material above the House 17 Floor

A small amount of additional San José phase debris was
found a short distance above the floor of House 17. It may be
material originally associated with the house, but since it was
not found in direct contact with the floor, we present it as a
separate category.

Chipped Stone

Chert (100%)
flake core: 1
flakes, not utilized: 5

Ground Stone

A blunted and battered celt of dark greenish-black metamorphic rock was found. The original length is difficult to estimate
precisely, but should have been about 11 cm. The width is 5 cm
and the thickness 3 cm. This may be one of the celts used to
hack out the terrace or dig storage pits in bedrock (Fig. 17.1*b*,
Chapter 17).

Animal Bones

domestic dog (*Canis familiaris*)
2 upper incisors
1 L. upper molar

1 fragment of canine tooth
jackrabbit (*Lepus mexicanus*)
1 metapodial
unidentified
2 fragments

House 16

We initially considered this structure to be a house, based on its sand-coated clay floor. However, as work proceeded on House 16 it became clear that it had no wattle-and-daub walls, and was more likely a lean-to or roofed work area attached to House 17. It contained fuel-burning features which probably would have produced too much smoke to be used in an enclosed structure.

Radiocarbon Date
See Feature 62, below.

Daub
Significantly, House 16 produced no daub.

Ceramics

Some 607 sherds were found in association with House 16. In contrast to House 17 (see above), the House 16 sample included 107 sherds of the cooking ware Fidencio Coarse, mostly the remains of jars and *tecomates*. Evidently most of the cooking was carried out in this lean-to or "cook shack." As we pointed out in our pottery volume (Flannery and Marcus 1994:336), this raises the possibility that some high-status household units consisted of several structures, with one reserved for domestic tasks such as cooking. If this was so, the absence or abundance of Fidencio Coarse in any one structure may not be chronologically useful. Rather, it may reflect functional differences between structures.

The family occupying House 16/17 evidently made some of its own pottery, since House 16 produced a baked clay mold of the type appropriate for making cylindrical bowls (see Feature 62B, below). It is likely that such vessels were mostly of Atoyac Yellow-white, since cylinders of that ware outnumbered those of Leandro Gray by almost four to one during the Late San José phase (Flannery and Marcus 1994:337).

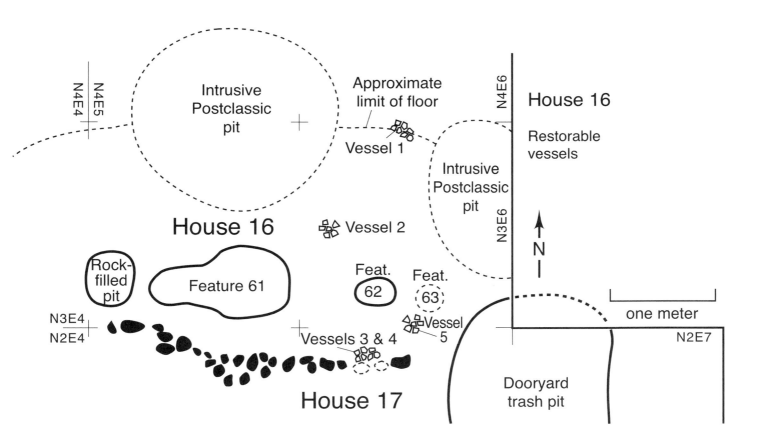

Figure 18.13. Restorable vessels piece-plotted on the floor of House 16. Vessel 6 could not be plotted because its sherds were too widely scattered. Vessel 7 was part of the postoccupational debris in Feature 61.

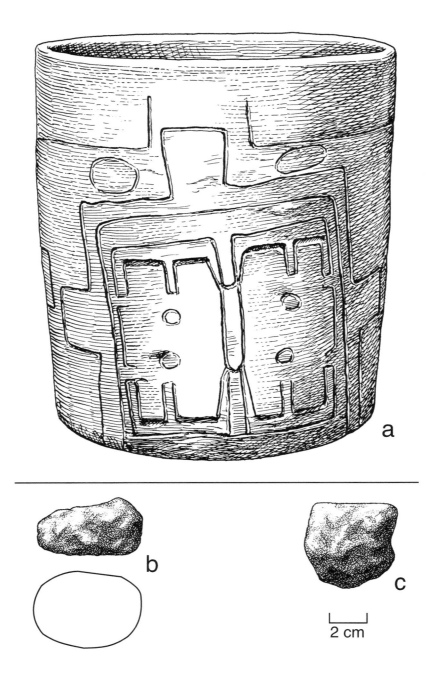

Figure 18.14. Artifacts piece-plotted on the floor of House 16. *a,* Atoyac Yellow-white cylinder with complex incised design of Earth and the four world directions (see Flannery and Marcus 1994: Fig. 12.88). This vessel has now been restored by the Centro Regional de Oaxaca, INAH (drawn from a photo in Fernández 1997). Height: 25 cm. *b, c,* chert hammerstones.

Restorable Vessels

In addition to the sherds mentioned above, six completely or partially restorable vessels were discovered in House 16. They were as follows:

Vessels 1 and 2, although plotted at separate locations within Square N3E6, turned out to be two parts of the same Atoyac Yellow-white cylinder. This vessel was incised with our most iconographically complete version of Earth—the four world quarters in the mouth of a giant feline—and was illustrated in Flannery and Marcus (1994: Fig. 12.88). It has since been restored by the Centro Regional de Oaxaca (INAH); the restoration is shown in Figure 18.14*a*.

Vessel 3, plotted in Square N2E6, was an Atoyac Yellow-white cylinder with three incised lines at the rim and a triple line-break with a freestanding element (Plog's Motif 4).

Vessel 4, plotted in Square N2E6, was an Atoyac Yellow-white cylinder with two incised lines at the rim and a standard double line-break (Plog's Motif 50).

Vessel 5, plotted in Square N2E5, was a Lupita Heavy Plain outleaned-wall bowl.

Vessel 6 was half a vessel, pieced together from 17 sherds scattered over the floor of House 16. It was a foreign piece, a bowl with a sunburst "grater bowl" pattern incised on the interior of the base. The vessel was slipped white over a reddish clay body; neither the clay, nor the slip, nor the design appear to be local. We have assigned Vessel 6 to Cesto White, a common type of the Manantial phase at Tlapacoya-Zohapilco in the Basin of Mexico. Niederberger (1987: Fig. 482) illustrated several bowls with similar designs.

Vessel 7, whose sherds were among the postoccupational debris in Feature 61, was an undecorated Fidencio Coarse jar with the usual sloppy red wash on its neck and shoulders.

As we pointed out in Flannery and Marcus (1994:338), it was typical for the residences of highly ranked San José phase families to contain a variety of foreign wares. The sample from House 16 confirms this pattern. In addition to the probable Cesto White "grater bowl" from the Basin of Mexico, we also recovered two Coatepec White sherds like those found in the Tehuacán region; one possible Madera Brown sherd from Morelos; and five sherds of Xochiltepec White vessels, probably from the Gulf Coast.

We have already given our reasons for dating the House 16/17 Complex to the Late San José phase (Flannery and Marcus 1994:336-39). Part of our reasoning has to do with the predominance of Atoyac Yellow-white over Leandro Gray. There is, however, also synchronic variation involved in that predominance. Because the House 16/17 Complex belonged to a residential ward emphasizing Earth/Earthquake motifs, it might be expected to have more Atoyac Yellow-white, since that ware was so often the medium for those motifs. Indeed, there were remarkably few Sky/Lightning motifs in House 16, even on the gray pottery (ibid.). This finding emphasizes the fact that there is more than just chronological change involved in our various San José phase pottery samples.

Chipped Stone

House 16 produced one of the largest collections of chipped stone from any domestic structure at San José Mogote: 440 items, 409 of which were chert. The reason for both the large size of the collection and the high percentage of chert seems to have been the fact that this roofed work area was the epicenter of biface production for the household (Parry 1987:98-106).

Chert (93%)
    hammerstones: 2 (Fig. 18.14*b, c*)
    ordinary flake cores: 32 (Fig. 18.15*a*)
    bipolar cores: 3 (Fig. 18.15*b*)
    discoidal core: 1 (Fig. 18.15*c*)
    flake perforators/gravers: 3 (Fig. 18.15*d*)
    scrapers: 4
    sidescrapers: 2
    spurred scraper: 1
    denticulate scraper: 1
    denticulate flake: 1
    biface roughouts: 6 (Fig. 18.15*h, i*)
    biface roughout used as chopper: 1
    biface thinning flakes: 3 (Fig. 18.16*a, b*)
    retouched flakes: 5 (Fig. 18.15*e*)
    utilized flakes: 26 (Fig. 18.15*f, g*)
    flakes, not utilized: 318
Obsidian (6%)
    bipolar flake core: 1 (Fig. 18.16*c*)
    prismatic blade fragments, utilized: 7 (Fig. 18.16*d-h*)
    prismatic blade fragment, no sign of use: 1
    utilized flakes: 3
    flakes, not utilized: 15
Other (1%)
    quartz cores: 2 (conjoinable)
    quartz fragment: 1
    ignimbrite core: 1

Ground Stone

Complete one-hand mano, made on an oval limestone cobble; lightly used (on one side only). Dimensions: 10 × 8 cm, 5 cm thick (Fig. 18.16*i*).

Roughly half of a one-hand mano with two convex grinding surfaces, ignimbrite. The fragment is 6 cm thick and 4.5 cm wide (Fig. 18.16*k*).

Tip of a loaf-shaped two-hand mano with oval cross-section and two convex grinding surfaces, ignimbrite. The length of the fragment is 4 cm, the width is 8 cm, and the thickness is 3.5 cm (Fig. 18.16*j*).

Tip of a loaf-shaped two-hand mano with oval cross-section and two convex grinding surfaces, igneous rock. Length of fragment, 6.5 cm; width, 9.5 cm; thickness, 5 cm (Fig. 18.16*L*).

Mano spall.

Fragment of basin-shaped metate, ignimbrite. The fragment is 16 cm long. The basin would have been 7.4 cm high at the outer edge, 6.6 cm thick nearer to the center (Fig. 18.17a).

Possible woodworking tool made of crystalline igneous rock. Now broken, the tool would originally have been 5 cm wide, and has an airfoil cross-section varying in thickness between 1.5 and 3 cm. The flat surfaces are polished from use, while the end shows signs of pounding (Fig. 18.17b).

Elongated rubbing stone made on an ignimbrite(?) stream cobble. Length, 7 cm; width, 4.8 cm; thickness, 2.5 cm (Fig. 18.17c).

Spherical pounder or hammerstone of hard gray sedimentary rock, 5.5 cm in diameter (Fig. 18.17d).

Fragment of celt, dark greenish-black metamorphic rock, reused as a pounder or hammerstone; 5.5 cm wide, 4.5 cm long (Fig. 18.17e).

Bone Tools

A distinctive feature of the bone tool assemblage from House 16 was the number of large needles that appeared appropriate for making baskets, rather than for more delicate sewing. Evidently this roofed work area was considered an appropriate area for basket-making. It would have been shaded, but better lit than the inside of the house itself.

House 16 also produced two possible deer antler pressure flakers—not surprising, since this was a residence where a great deal of chert was retouched.

Scarred antler tine, apparently used as a pressure flaker. Length, >4.8 cm (broken) (Fig. 18.17f).

Badly broken deer antler tine, apparently used as a pressure flaker. Length, >2.3 cm (broken) (Fig. 18.17g).

Distal end of a probable basketry needle, made on a splinter of deer long bone. The cross-section is oval and the tip slightly curved; the object is scratched and worn from long use. Length, >6.5 cm (broken); diameter, 2-3 mm (Fig. 18.17h).

Tip of a needle made from a splinter of deer long bone. The fragment is 3 cm long and appears to have originally been part of a large needle (possibly for basketry). However, it broke and had a new eye drilled only 3 cm from the tip. After being reused in some way, perhaps as a sewing needle, it broke again (Fig. 18.17i).

Two pieces, possibly from the same basketry needle. One piece, 5.2 cm long, has a point. The other, 4.5 cm long, is broken right through the eye. The original needle would have been at least 10 cm long, and had an oval cross-section (4 × 2 mm) (Fig. 18.17j, k).

Midsection of a probable basketry needle, made on a splinter of deer long bone. Length of fragment, 3.2 cm; diameter, 3.5 mm (Fig. 18.17L).

Modified distal femur of a dog, separated from its shaft by a cut made with a chipped stone tool, some 4.5 cm from the distal end. This object could be an artifact in its own right (such as a handle), or it might be the by-product of cutting a bone tube from a dog femur (Fig. 18.17m).

Worked Sherd

Chipped and ground sherd disk, 7.5 cm in diameter, made from a jar body sherd. It has been biconically drilled, leaving a hole slightly off center; the hole starts out 10 mm in diameter on each side and tapers to 5 mm. This object may be a pot lid, in which case the perforation could have been for a knotted cord used as a lifter (Fig. 18.18a).

Shell

Although the House 16/17 family was clearly involved in shell working, little of it seems to have been carried out in the lean-to. House 16 produced only three perforators/gravers, a paltry number compared to the residences in Area A (Chapter 14). The adjacent dooryard produced more evidence for shell working (Chapter 19), either because it was a locus for that craft or because that was where most shell working debris was discarded. A few broken pearl oyster ornaments did show up in House 16.

Ornaments

Curved section from a broken pendant made of pearl oyster (*Pinctada mazatlanica*). The piece is roughly 5 cm long and up to 1.6 cm wide. It was evidently part of an elaborate ornament, incised with a crosshatched design similar to those seen on some Atoyac Yellow-white vessels. Three small holes were begun along one edge, but never completed (Fig. 18.18c).

Fragment of a ring-shaped ornament made of pearl oyster. The inner edge of the ring would have been smooth, while the outer edge was denticulate. The surviving fragment is about 1 cm long, and while its original size is difficult to estimate, it might have been the right size to serve as a holder for a circular magnetite mirror (Fig. 18.18d).

Pearly Freshwater Mussels

Irregular fragment trimmed from the valve of a mussel, possibly *Barynaias*. Length, 23 mm (Fig. 18.18e).

Pacific Marine Bivalves

Piece of pearl oyster valve, 41 × 30 × 2 mm, with a hole drilled along one margin. This could be part of an ornament that broke during manufacture (Fig. 18.18h).

Fragment from the shell of an unidentified bivalve, 32 × 20 mm (Fig. 18.18g).

Pacific Marine Univalve

Gastropod shell 15 mm in diameter, too beachworn to be identified; the central portion is literally worn away (Fig. 18.18f).

Unidentified

A total of 7 fragments of shell too small to be identified, scattered over four different parts of the floor; each fragment is less than 10 mm in diameter.

Iron Ore Specimen

There was a lump of iron ore, 15 × 10 × 10 mm.

Mica Specimens

Irregular piece of gold to whitish-gold mica weighing 0.3 g; 53 × 27 × 1 mm (Fig. 18.18*i*).

Eight fragments of a disintegrated piece of gold to whitish-gold mica weighing 0.5 g; no piece is larger than 20 × 20 mm, and all are paper thin.

Minute fragments of a disintegrated piece of gold mica (unmeasurable).

Piece of black to brownish-black mica weighing 1.2 g, cut on at least two edges; 50 × 33 × 1 mm (Fig. 18.18*j*).

Fragment of dark brown mica weighing 1 g, cut on at least one edge, 17 × 15 × 1 mm.

Lump of mica schist weighing about 5 g. This may be part of the rock formation from which the mica was extracted.

Other Minerals

A lump of Precambrian gneiss containing veins of hematite was found near the northern limit of Square N3E6. This specimen reinforces Payne's (1994) conclusion that such gneiss formations were a primary source of red pigment.

Figurines

Some 33 figurine fragments were associated with the House 16 floor; they have been described by Marcus (1998a:174-76). Most of the fragments are of small solid figurines, but there were also two pieces of hollow white "baby dolls."

An interesting aspect of the collection is that four of the small solid figurine heads have eyes, noses, and mouths modeled in so similar a way that they could all have been made by the same woman (Fig. 18.19; see also Marcus 1998a: Figs. 13.6-13.7). All these heads were found with a few meters of the Feature 62 hearth, believed to be the center of a woman's work area.

Ceramic Mask

Among the wall stones at the south end of House 16, we found the broken ceramic mask shown in Figure 18.18*b*. This was a typical Formative mask, designed to cover only the lower half of the wearer's face. Two holes drilled in the cheeks would have accommodated the cords that held the mask in place.

This mask is made from the same clay body used for Atoyac Yellow-white, but was left unslipped. It appears to represent a human face, not unlike those seen on figurines of the San José phase (Marcus 1998a:176-77). We suspect that such masks were worn during dances or other rituals. This one may have allowed the dancer to impersonate a (generalized) human ancestor.

Stone Ornament

A large jadeite(?) earspool was found. It had a hole drilled in the shaft, suggesting that some other material was suspended from the ornament. Length, 21 mm; diameter of shaft, 18 mm; diameter of flared end, 28 mm; hole drilled in shaft, 3 mm in diameter. This is the largest jadeite(?) earspool known so far from the San José phase, reinforcing our impression that the family occupying House 16/17 was of relatively high rank (Fig. 18.20*a*).

Potential Bone Ornament?

One canine tooth from a dog was found in the southeast quadrant of Square N3E6 (Fig. 18.20*c*). Since it appeared to have been carefully cleaned and polished, we suspect that it may have been set aside as a potential necklace element.

Animal Bones

Many more animal bones were found in House 16, the roofed work area, than in House 17. There were several possible explanations for this distribution, all having to do with discard behavior. One possibility is that a substantial amount of cooking and eating went on around Feature 62, the hearth in Square N3E6 of House 16, with animal bones being tossed north toward the limits of the work area. Another possibility is that some of the bone debris swept out of House 17 was left in House 16 temporarily before being carried off to a midden.

Whatever the case, faunal remains were abundant on the House 16 floor, and fell generally into two groups. The largest and best preserved bones lay in Square N3E6, especially to the north of the Feature 62 hearth. The smaller and more worn bone fragments—essentially the "fine fraction" of the faunal debris—lay near the stone threshold dividing Houses 16 and 17. We describe these two groups of remains separately.

Bones from Square N3E6: The "Large Fraction"

The remains from Square N3E6 were rich in deer and dog. At least two adult deer and one fawn were represented; the dogs included at least two adults and one puppy. Most of the deer bones came from meat-bearing parts of the hind leg, and one proximal tibia had cut marks on its medial surface 2 cm below the articulation, suggesting how the leg had been disarticulated.

At least one of the adult dogs seems to have been born without a first premolar (Fig. 18.20*b*). This congenital abnormality has already been discussed in Chapter 4.

Among the small mammals discarded in Square N3E6 were at least one jackrabbit, four eastern cottontails, and two Mexican cottontails. One first phalanx of jackrabbit had two cut marks near its proximal end, indicating how the foot had been trimmed from the leg. Virtually none of the rabbit bones were burned, suggesting that they had been used in stews rather than roasted.

Large Mammals
    white-tailed deer (*Odocoileus virginianus*)
        fragments of 2 L. ulnae
        fragments of vertebrae
        1 rib
        1 L. innominate (chewed by dogs)
        1 R. innominate
        1 L. distal femur, adult
        1 R. proximal femur, unfused

2 R. proximal tibiae, fused
1 R. proximal tibia, unfused
1 L. distal tibia
Small Mammals
    domestic dog (*Canis familiaris*)
        1 L. frontal bone
        2 occipital regions from 2 different dogs
        1 L. premaxilla
        1 L. maxilla, adult
        1 R. maxilla from a different adult
        fragments of 2 canine teeth
        1 R. mandible, complete, congenitally lacking the P$_1$
        1 R. mandible from a different dog
        2 L. mandibles
        1 R. lower first molar
        several deciduous teeth from a puppy
        1 atlas
        1 axis
        1 L. proximal femur
        1 other L. femur fragment
        2 metapodial fragments
    pocket gopher (*Orthogeomys grandis*)
        1 R. scapula
        1 R. humerus
    jackrabbit (*Lepus mexicanus*)
        1 L. mandible
        1 L. proximal radius
        1 L. distal femur
        1 R. distal femur
        1 metacarpal
        2 first phalanges
    eastern cottontail (*Sylvilagus floridanus*)
        1 R. mandible
        1 L. scapula
        2 R. ulnae, adults
        1 R. proximal femur
        1 L. distal tibia, adult
        2 L. tibiae, unfused (juveniles)
        1 metapodial
    Mexican cottontail (*Sylvilagus cunicularius*)
        1 L. scapula
        1 R. scapula
        1 R. innominate
        1 L. femur, unfused
        1 L. proximal tibia, adult
        1 R. distal tibia, adult
        shaft fragments of 2 tibiae
    unidentified cottontail (*Sylvilagus* sp.)
        1 vertebra
Reptiles
    mud turtle (*Kinosternon integrum*)
        1 carapace scute
Human
    several skull fragments

1 mastoid process
1 R. mandible fragment
1 molar
1 L. fibula
Unidentified
    75 long bone splinters, mostly deer and dog

Bones in or near the House 16/17 Stone Threshold: The "Fine Fraction"

In contrast to the mass of relatively large and well-preserved bones from Square N3E6, the remains from the extreme southern part of House 16 appeared to be smaller bone fragments that had been swept aside over the years, where they gradually worked their way into the sand layer of the floor or the crevices among the threshold stones. Not surprisingly, small mammal remains predominated.

Large Mammals
    white-tailed deer (*Odocoileus virginianus*)
        1 R. astragalus
        1 R. calcaneum
Small Mammals
    domestic dog (*Canis familiaris*)
        1 R. maxilla
        1 adult tooth fragment
        1 deciduous tooth fragment from a puppy
        1 L. second metacarpal
        1 R. second metacarpal
        2 L. innominates, both unfused
        1 R. astragalus
        2 phalanges from adult dogs
    pocket gopher (*Orthogeomys grandis*)
        2 R. premaxillae
        1 lower incisor
    jackrabbit (*Lepus mexicanus*)
        2 metatarsals (burned)
        1 other metapodial fragment
    eastern cottontail (*Sylvilagus floridanus*)
        2 metapodials
    Mexican cottontail (*Sylvilagus cunicularius*)
        1 L. mandible
        1 R. proximal radius
        1 R. innominate
    unidentified cottontails (*Sylvilagus* spp.)
        1 R. scapula, unfused
        1 fragment of humerus
Human
    1 skull fragment
    1 tooth fragment
    1 molar, young individual
    1 clavicle
Unidentified
    36 long bone splinters, mostly mammal

Features in House 16

We found several interesting features in House 16. Feature 61 in Square N3E5 was a keyhole-shaped fire pit, believed to have been used for heat-treating chert in order to prepare it for biface manufacture. Immediately to the west of Feature 61 was a rock-filled pit which was not assigned a feature number, since it was not clear that it was artificial (it may simply have been a natural depression, filled in with stones). In Square N3E6 we found Feature 62, an oval hearth for cooking food, and Feature 63, a subfloor cache of figurines arranged in a ritual scene.

Feature 61

Feature 61, found in the southeast quadrant of Square N3E5, was a keyhole-shaped fire pit whose walls had been reddened by heat. Its main chamber was roughly 80 × 74 cm in size and about 15 cm deep. On its west side was an extension 50 × 32 cm in size, whose purpose may have been to facilitate adding or removing material from the main chamber. This made the total east-west length of the pit roughly 1.32 m.

The contents of Feature 61 were ash and abundant fire-cracked chert nodules. John Rick, the experienced flint knapper who excavated this feature in 1974, immediately identified it as a fire pit for heat-treating chert to make it easier to flake. William J. Parry (1987) concurred, considering such heat-treating appropriate for a family as heavily involved in chert biface production as this one.

A few extraneous artifacts had been redeposited in Feature 61, as follows:

1 utilized chert flake
2 chert flakes, not utilized
1 utilized obsidian flake
1 piece of brown mica with two edges cut, weighing 0.9 g;
   60 × 17 × 1 mm

Feature 62

Feature 62 was an apparent culinary hearth in Square N3E6. The hearth was oval, roughly 40 × 30 × 10-12 cm deep. Its contents were ash and bits of charcoal.

Given the high percentage of Fidencio Coarse pottery in House 16, we suspect that this was an area where a woman (or women) did much of the cooking. (If this was indeed a woman's work area, it is not surprising that the surrounding floor produced four figurine heads similar enough to have been made by the same woman; see above).

An unanswered question is, Who did the heat-treating of chert in nearby Feature 61? Was it the same woman (or women) using the Feature 62 hearth? Or did she share the roofed work area with a man who was a flint knapper and biface maker?

Radiocarbon Date[1]

Charcoal from this hearth yielded a date of 2890 ± 40 B.P., or roughly 940 b.c. (Beta-179079). The calibrated two-sigma range for this date is 1200-940 B.C.

Feature 62B

As discussed by Payne (1994), one of the principal techniques used in forming San José phase pottery was press-molding. This usually consisted of pressing clay over a previously made pot or gourd vessel, but from time to time we found fragments of lightly baked clay molds from which vessels could be produced in quantity. Our most complete example of such a mold came from Feature 62B, a shallow depression adjacent to Feature 62 in House 16. Shown in Figure 18.20*d*, this mold was probably used for making flat-based bowls with vertical walls like those in Atoyac Yellow-white and Leandro Gray. The clay used for the mold resembles that from the La Casahuatera locality near San Lorenzo Cacaotepec (Stolmaker 1973), and is similar to that used for *crema* wares during Monte Albán I. There is a burned hole in the base of the mold which may result from the burning of a wooden handle, one used to speed up the drying of molded vessels by holding them near a fire.

Feature 63

A cache of four figurines was discovered just below the floor of House 16. The location of this cache, designated Feature 63, is given in Figure 18.19. The four figurines were arranged in a scene (Fig. 18.21); three of them lay supine and fully extended, their arms folded across their chests and their heads pointing slightly north of east. This orientation may be significant, since many San José phase villagers were buried fully extended with their heads to the east. The fourth figurine appears to have been seated upright originally, atop the bodies of the three supine figures. However, under the weight of the overburden, it had fallen over. This seated figurine seems to be a man depicted in a position of authority, with his hands on his knees; when discovered, he had a considerable amount of red pigment rubbed into his hair and ear ornaments.

All four figurines in Feature 63 are similar enough to have been made by the same woman. Each wears prominent earspools and a pendant on the chest. These pendants may represent *Spondylus*, pearl oyster, or even magnetite ornaments.

While we cannot read the mind of the person arranging the scene, Feature 63 seems to us to represent the burial of one individual seated in a position of authority, laid to rest atop three companions buried in postures of obeisance. On a modest scale, it brings to mind Grave 26 from the Panamanian site of

---

[1]In this volume, uncalibrated dates are given as "b.c.," and dendrocalibrated dates as "B.C." (see Chapter 26, Radiocarbon Dating).

Sitio Conte (part of a Coclé chiefdom), in which one chiefly individual was buried in a seated position atop a layer of 21 fully extended retainers (see Lothrop 1937: Fig. 31; Marcus and Flannery 1996:100). For a more detailed analysis of Feature 63, see Marcus 1998a:177-81.

Feature 63 reminds us that although figurines may often have been used to create scenes, archaeologists rarely uncover them in that context. Such scenes may have lasted only as long as it took to communicate with one's ancestors—perhaps only a few hours—while the figurines themselves could last thousands of years. Only in those rare cases where the scenes remained undisturbed are we made aware of how much ritual information we may be missing. Even Feature 63 came close to being destroyed: an intrusive post from a later house took off the head of one of the supine figurines.

Rock-Filled Pit

Just to the west of Feature 61 was an oval pit or natural depression 58 by 44 cm in extent (Fig. 18.19). Its contents consisted entirely of nondescript rocks. Rick did not assign a feature number to this pit because he was not convinced that it was of human manufacture.

Insights from Artifact Plotting

Figures 18.22-18.29 show the distribution of chert cores, biface roughouts/preforms, scrapers, utilized flakes, ground stone tools, basketry needles, pressure flakers, perforators/gravers, shell, mica, obsidian, and jadeite(?) on the floor of House 16.

Since we know that the occupants of this lean-to were involved in stone tool manufacture, let us begin with chert cores (Fig. 18.22). Ordinary (multidirectional or unidirectional) cores were scattered throughout House 16. The eastern half of the lean-to had particularly impressive concentrations, probably because the gradual movement of debris was west-to-east, beginning with heat-treating in Feature 61 and ending with discard in the dooryard trash pit. Bipolar and discoidal cores occurred in such low numbers that no pattern is evident.

Items related to chert biface production were also concentrated in the eastern half of the lean-to (Fig. 18.23). Biface roughouts or thinning flakes left on the floor were occasionally used for secondary tasks, such as chopping or cutting.

Scrapers of different types were scattered across the floor (Fig. 18.24); most were generalized or amorphous scrapers made on flakes. Two sidescrapers had been left just west of the Feature 62 hearth.

Utilized chert flakes occurred on several areas of the House 16 floor (Fig. 18.25). At least 14 of them, however, encircled the Feature 62 hearth. This might mean that the woman using the hearth had made the area a "drop zone" for informal cutting activity.

Figure 18.26 gives the locations of ground stone tools piece-plotted in House 16. Most were so fragmentary that their only

utility would have been in a secondary role, such as a pounder or hammerstone. For that reason, items that were clearly hammerstones or pounders have been included in the same drawing. It was impossible for us to guess which hammerstones were used to strike off chert flakes and which were used for other tasks.

Figure 18.27 gives the location of antler tine pressure flakers, basketry needles, a possible woodworking tool, and a modified dog femur. Given the areas where basketry needles were left, we suspect that their user might have been sitting (or kneeling) between Features 61 and 62. As mentioned earlier, this may well have been part of a woman's work area.

Antler tine pressure flakers, however, had been left near the northwestern limits of the lean-to, and may have been used by a different individual, possibly a man. The pressure flakers may have been used to put the final touches on bifaces. Thus, despite the challenge presented by discard behavior, our tool plotting may have revealed a spatial separation of artifacts related to (1) biface production and (2) basket making—two potentially gender-related tasks.

Most of the evidence for shell and mica working was concentrated on the eastern half of the lean-to floor (Fig. 18.28). As we shall see, even more shell had been discarded in the dooryard to the north (Chapter 19). Most mica fragments lay near Features 62 and 63, where so many chert flakes utilized for cutting had been left.

Finally, Figure 18.29 gives the location of utilized obsidian blade fragments, an iron ore lump, and some one-of-a-kind items such as a jadeite(?) earspool. Note that the 7 utilized obsidian blades cluster near the Feature 62 hearth, as did the 14 utilized chert flakes shown in Figure 18.25. This reinforces our impression that a lot of cutting activity had gone on around the hearth.

Material below the House 16 Floor, Possibly Associated

A small amount of material, mostly chipped stone and animal bone, was found stratigraphically below the floor of House 16. We present it here because it might belong to an earlier stage of the roofed work area. Note that, like the material from below House 17, the small sample of chipped stone from below House 16 shows no evidence of the chert biface manufacture which characterized the final stage of the House 16/17 Complex.

Chipped Stone
  Chert (84%)
    bipolar core: 1
    retouched flake: 1
    utilized flakes: 3
    flakes, not utilized: 11
  Obsidian (5%)
    prismatic blade fragment, utilized: 1
  Other (11%)
    quartz flakes: 2

Animal Bones
Large Mammals
white-tailed deer (*Odocoileus virginianus*)
1 petrous bone
Small Mammals
domestic dog (*Canis familiaris*)
1 fragment of canine tooth
1 R. proximal radius
1 L. astragalus
eastern cottontail (*Sylvilagus floridanus*)
1 L. calcaneum
unidentified cottontail (*Sylvilagus* sp.*)*
1 phalanx
Amphibians
toad (probably intrusive)
1 limb bone

Material above the House 16 Floor, Possibly Associated

In Square N3E5 we found a small number of animal bones, too far above the House 16 floor to be considered in direct contact with it. We present that material separately even though, in general, it appears to be more of the same kind of debris found on the floor.

Animal Bones
Large Mammals
white-tailed deer (*Odocoileus virginianus*)
several limb bone splinters
Small Mammals
domestic dog (*Canis familiaris*)
1 R. mandible fragment, adult
1 R. mandible, puppy
1 R. lower first molar, adult
1 deciduous incisor, puppy
1 L. proximal radius
1 rib
1 L. fourth metatarsal
2 other metapodial fragments
eastern cottontail (*Sylvilagus floridanus*)
1 L. innominate
1 R. tibia, unfused
Amphibians
toad (possibly intrusive)
1 fragment of pelvis
1 limb bone
Unidentified
27 limb bone splinters

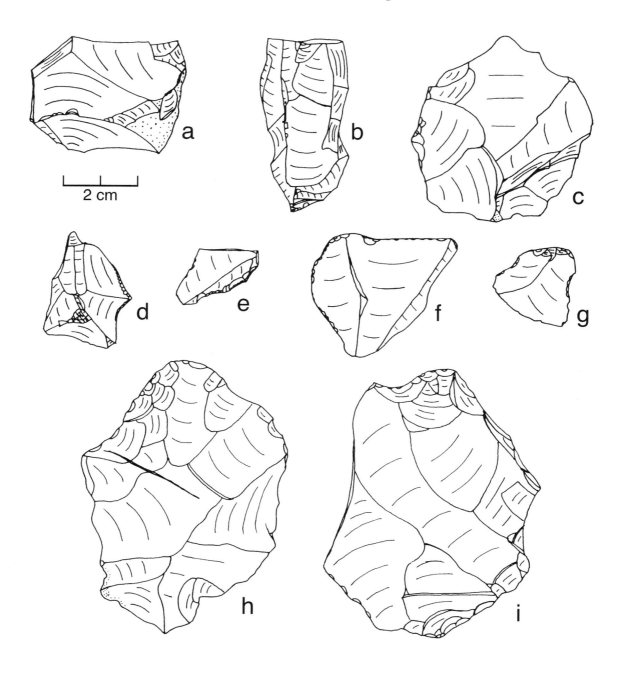

Figure 18.15. Chert tools from the floor of House 16. *a*, flake core. *b*, bipolar core. *c*, discoidal core. *d*, perforator/graver. *e*, retouched flake. *f, g*, utilized flakes. *h, i*, biface roughouts. (After Parry 1987.)

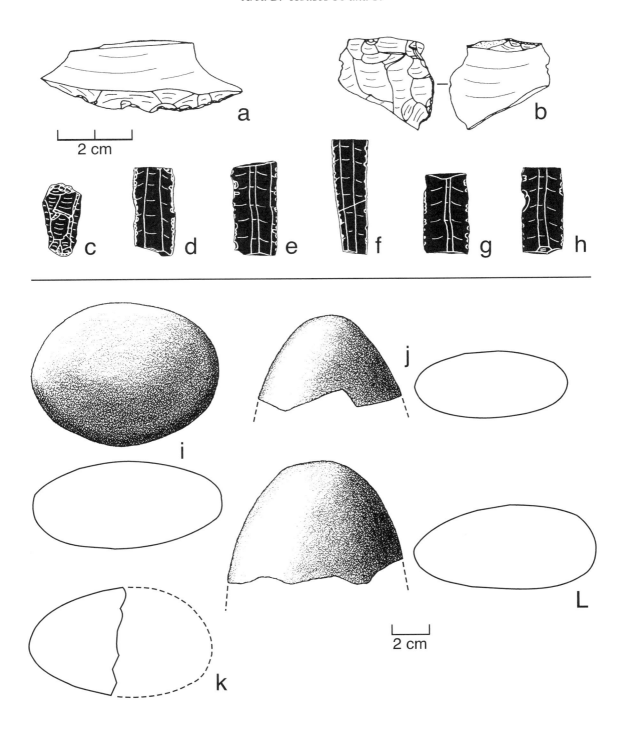

Figure 18.16. Stone tools from the floor of House 16. *a, b* are chert. *a*, overshot biface thinning flake, ventral aspect. *b*, utilized flake that originated as a biface thinning flake. *c-h* are obsidian. *c*, bipolar flake core. *d-h*, utilized prismatic blade fragments. *i*, complete one-hand mano. *j*, tip of two-hand mano, ignimbrite. *k*, cross-section of one-hand mano. *L*, tip of two-hand mano, igneous rock.

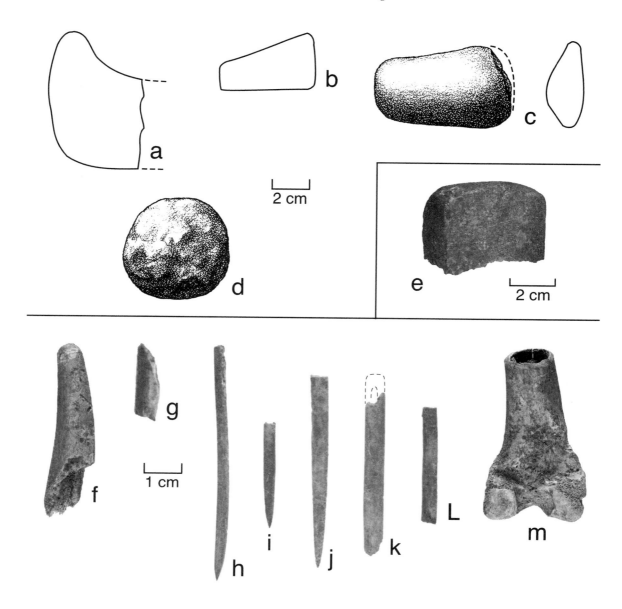

Figure 18.17. Artifacts plotted on the floor of House 16. *a*, cross-section of basin metate fragment. *b*, cross-section of possible woodworking tool. *c*, elongated rubbing stone. *d*, spherical pounder. *e*, fragment of celt reused as pounder. *f*, antler tine pressure flaker. *g*, badly broken antler tine flaker. *h-L*, fragments of probable basketry needles made of deer bone. *j* and *k* appear to be part of the same needle. *i* appears to have been reworked into a sewing needle after it broke. *m*, neatly cut dog femur, possibly a handle for a tool.

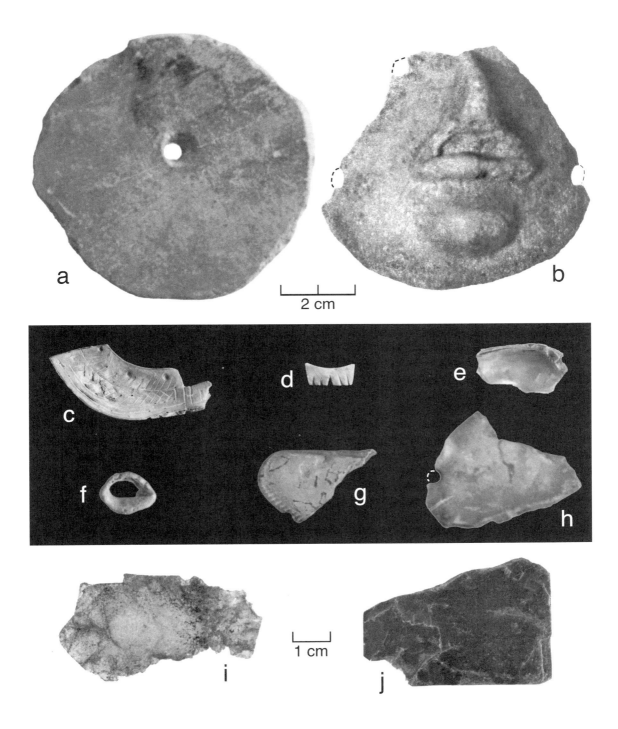

Figure 18.18. Objects plotted on the floor of House 16. *a*, worked sherd, biconically drilled. *b*, broken ceramic mask. *c*, fragment of crosshatched pearl oyster pendant. *d*, piece of denticulate pearl oyster ornament. *e*, fragment of pearly mussel valve. *f*, beachworn gastropod. *g*, fragment of unidentified bivalve. *h*, drilled piece of pearl oyster valve. *i*, piece of whitish-gold mica. *j*, brownish-black mica, cut on at least two edges.

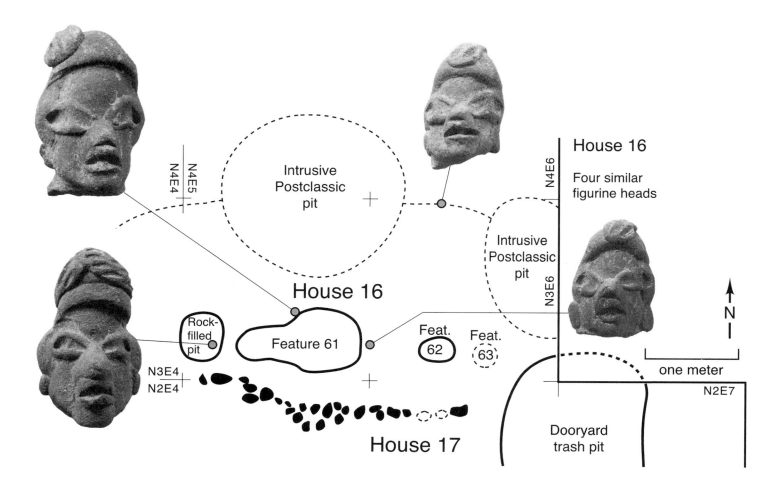

Figure 18.19. Four figurine heads with features so similar that they might all have been made by the same woman. For details, see Marcus (1998a:174 and Figs. 13.6-13.7).

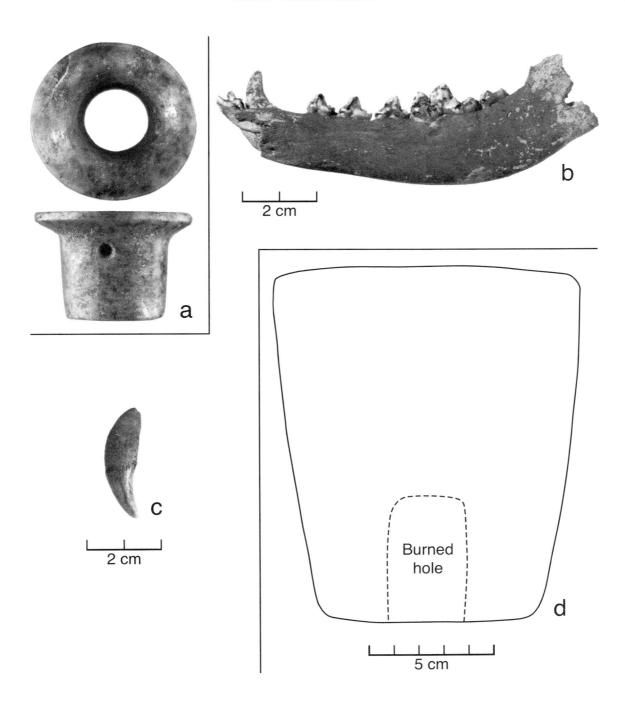

Figure 18.20. Objects from the House 16 floor (*a-c*) and Feature 62B (*d*). *a*, top and side views of jadeite(?) earspool. Diameter of flared end, 28 mm (shown greater than actual size). *b*, right mandible of dog, congenitally missing the P_1. *c*, canine tooth of dog, perhaps saved to be drilled as a necklace element. *d*, lightly baked clay mold from Feature 62B, probably used for forming flat-based bowls with nearly vertical walls.

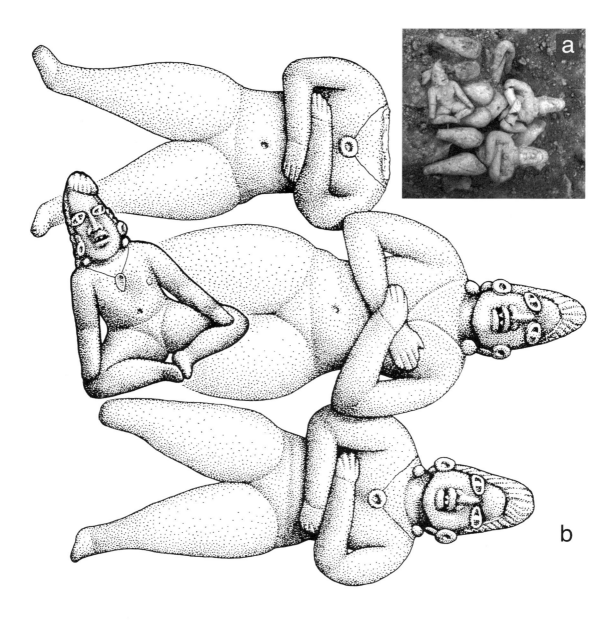

Figure 18.21. Four figurines from Feature 63, arranged in the form of a scene. *a*, photograph of the scene as it came to light below the floor of House 16. *b*, artist's reconstruction of the scene. Height of seated figurine, 6.8 cm.

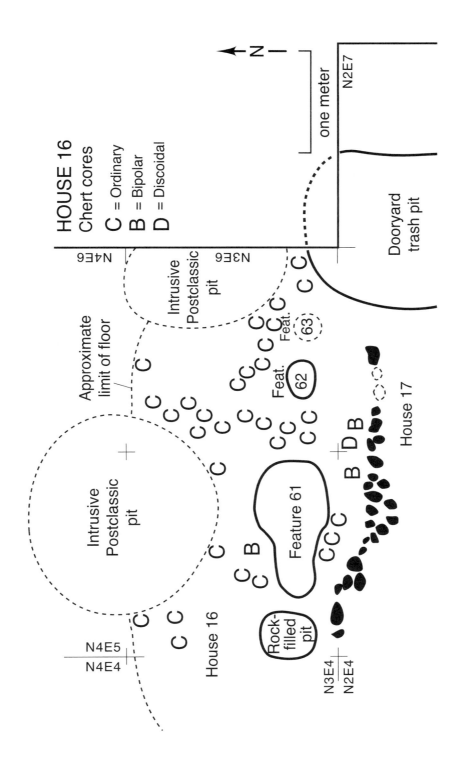

Figure 18.22. The distribution of ordinary, bipolar, and discoidal chert cores on the floor of House 16.

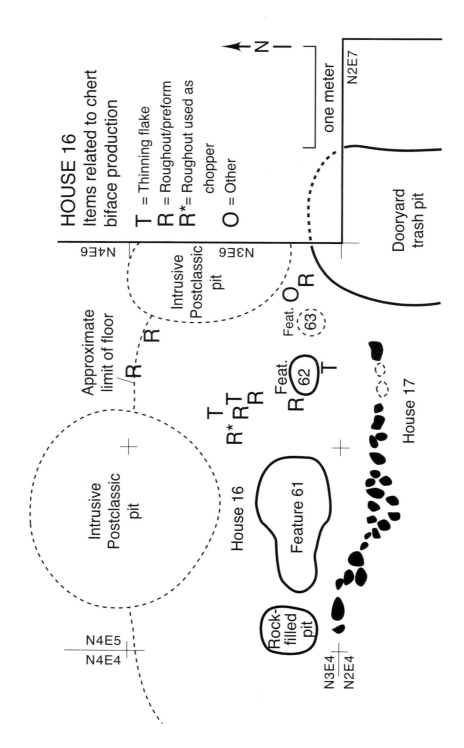

Figure 18.23. Items related to chert biface production, plotted on the floor of House 16.

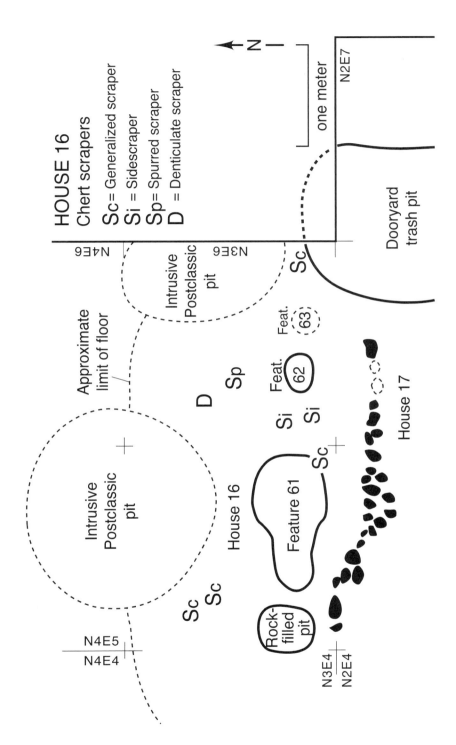

Figure 18.24. Distribution of scrapers of several kinds on the floor of House 16.

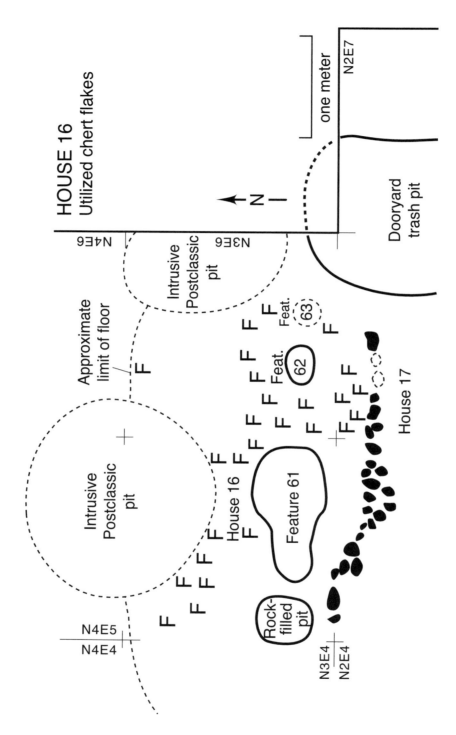

Figure 18.25. Distribution of utilized chert flakes on the floor of House 16. (Although a few were piece-plotted, most were recorded by 1 × 1 m quadrants within squares.) Some utilized flakes had originally been biface-thinning or core-rejuvenation flakes.

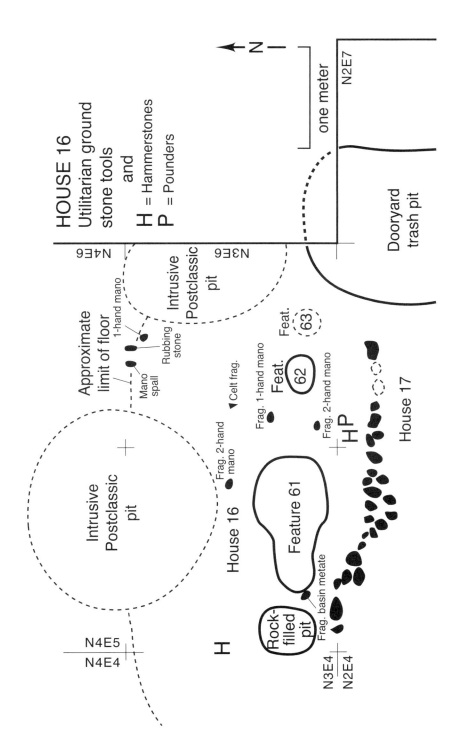

Figure 18.26. Utilitarian ground stone tools, chert hammerstones, and pounders, all plotted on the floor of House 16.

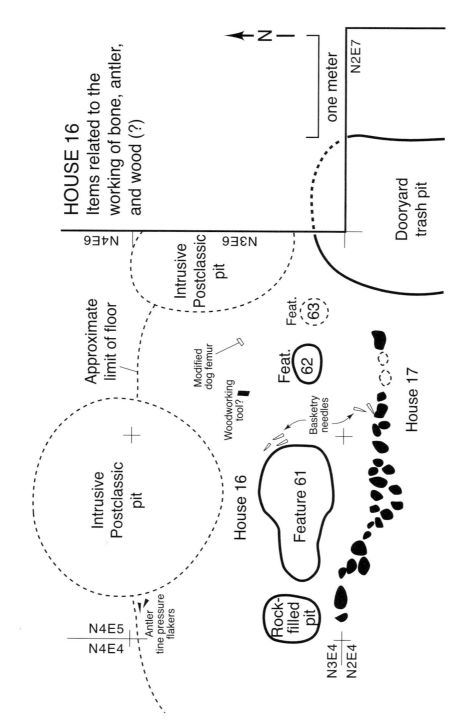

Figure 18.27. Antler tine pressure flakers, basketry needles, and a possible smoother/sander for woodworking, all plotted on the floor of House 16.

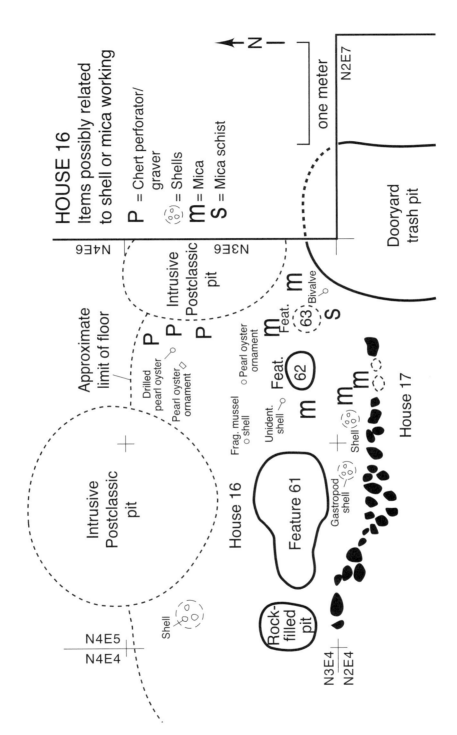

Figure 18.28. Distribution of items possibly related to shell or mica working on the floor of House 16.

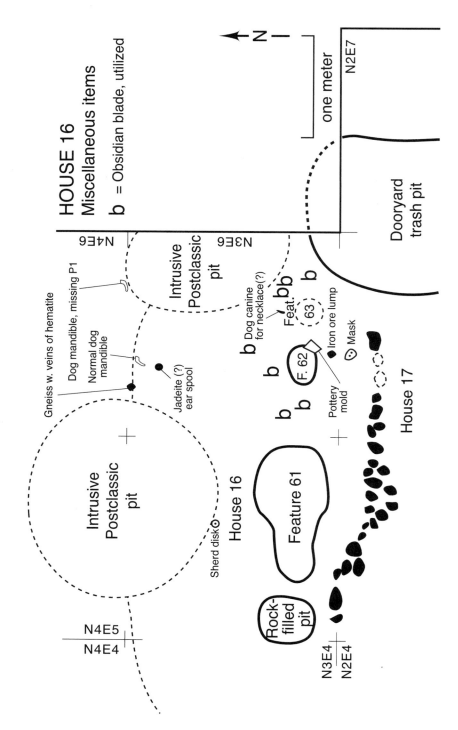

HOUSE 16
Miscellaneous items
b = Obsidian blade, utilized

Figure 18.29. Miscellaneous items piece-plotted on the floor of House 16. Note that all 7 utilized obsidian blades were discarded in the southern half of Square N3E6, a presumed woman's work area.

Chapter 19
Area B: The House 16/17 Dooryard

In Area A, we managed to expose several dooryards with interesting features (see Chapter 14). In the case of the terrace surrounding House 16/17, there was an added dimension: we could see which parts of the dooryard were behind the house, which were to the left as one faced the house, and which were to the right. Our analysis could thus be guided by the model of de la Fuente (1949), who collected native Zapotec terms for the various parts of the dooryard (Fig. 3.2*a*, Chapter 3). Let us begin, however, with the trash pit just east of the residence: a pit probably made necessary by the large number of flakes this biface-making family produced.

The Dooryard Trash Pit

Immediately to the east of House 16/17 was a large irregular trash pit, 2.3 m long north-south, 1.5 m wide east-west, and roughly 25-35 cm deep (Fig. 18.1, Chapter 18). Most of the items in the pit were debris from chert knapping and biface manufacture. Other materials, however, had been tossed in as well.

Chipped Stone
Chert (90%)
hammerstone: 1 (Fig. 19.1*a*)
flake cores: 6
core fragments/chunks: 7
utilized blade: 1
biface fragments: 2 (Fig. 19.1*b, c*)
biface roughout: 1
discoidal biface: 1
utilized flakes: 26
flakes, not utilized: 173 (includes biface thinning flakes; see Fig. 19.1*d, e*)

Obsidian (8%)
bipolar flake core: 1
prismatic blade fragments, utilized: 7 (Fig. 19.1*f*)
biface (projectile point?) tip: 1
wedge: 1
utilized flake: 1
flakes, not utilized: 9
Other (1%)
quartz core: 1
quartz fragment: 1
quartzite flake: 1

Ground Stone
Fragment of pestle, ignimbrite. Diameter, 6 cm; length of fragment, 6 cm (Fig. 19.1*g*).
Stream cobble 6.4 cm long and 4 cm wide, used to grind *barro colorado* (see below) and still covered with that material (Fig. 19.1*h*).

Pottery Pigment
Lump of *barro colorado,* roughly 4 cm in diameter (Fig. 19.1*i*). This brick red, iron-oxide-rich clay occurs in "pods" in the Precambrian gneiss formations of the Valley of Oaxaca (Payne 1994:8, Fig. 2.1). It was ground, probably with cobbles like the one described above, and mixed with water to produce the red wash used on Fidencio Coarse pottery.

Shell
Piece of pearl oyster (*Pinctada mazatlanica*), probably waste from ornament manufacture, 55 × 47 mm (Fig. 19.2*a*).

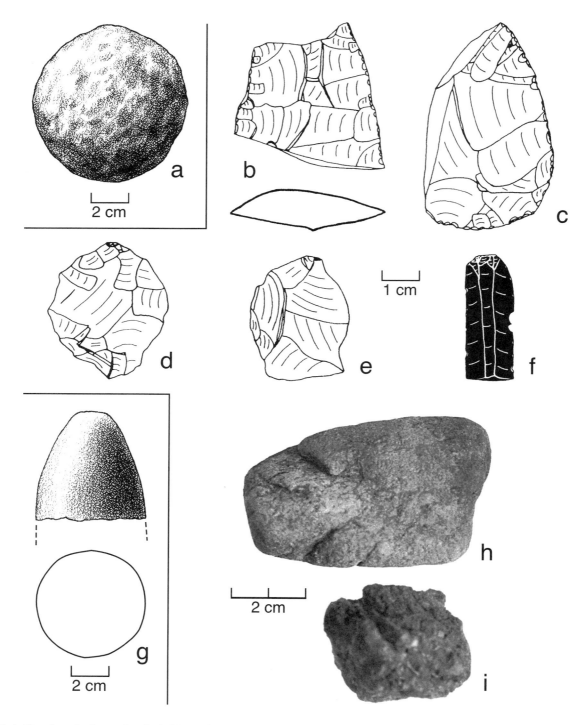

Figure 19.1. Artifacts from the dooryard trash pit, House 16/17 Complex. *a*, hammerstone. *b, c*, fragments of chert bifaces. *d, e*, biface thinning flakes. *f*, utilized prismatic obsidian blade. *g*, pestle fragment. *h*, stream cobble used to grind *barro colorado. i*, lump of *barro colorado.*

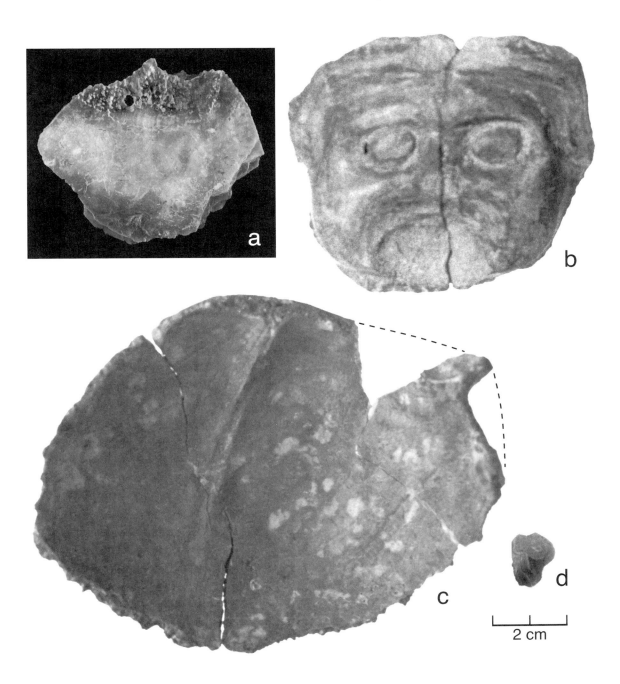

Figure 19.2. Objects from the dooryard trash pit, House 16/17 Complex. *a*, large piece of pearl oyster. *b*, ceramic mask. *c*, shallow saucer made from a human cranium. *d*, drum otolith.

Saucer Made from Human Cranium

One of the most interesting items from the dooryard trash pit was a shallow saucer made from a human cranium. Its original diameter was probably 11.5 cm, but the item was too broken to measure accurately (Fig. 19.2*c*). The source of the cranium is unknown. We do not know whether it was a relic saved from an ancestor, or a trophy made from the skull of an enemy.

This was our oldest example of an artifact made from a human skull, but certainly not the last. A shallow bowl made from a skull accompanied Burial 25 at Tomaltepec, a Monte Albán Ic adult male (Whalen 1981: Plate 41).

Ceramic Mask

One broken mask of burnished Leandro Gray pottery was found in the trash pit. The mask would have covered only the lower half of the face, which is typical of many Formative masks (Fig. 19.2*b*).

Figurines

Seven fragments of small solid figurines were found in the dooryard trash pit. They have been described by Marcus (1998a:173 and Fig. 13.4, nos. 7, 8).

Imported Marine Fish

An otolith from a drum (family Sciaenidae) was found, 15 mm in diameter (Fig. 19.2*d*).

Animal Bones

The animal bones from the dooryard trash pit were similar to the sample from House 16. Included were the remains of at least two deer, two or three dogs, two gophers, two jackrabbits, and three cottontails.

Large Mammals
    white-tailed deer (*Odocoileus virginianus*)
       1 antler tine (large adult male)
       several vertebrae
       1 femur of foetal deer
Small Mammals
    domestic dog (*Canis familiaris*)
       1 R. parietal (adult)
       1 occipital (puppy)
       1 L. mandible (with no congenital tooth loss)
       3 ribs
       3 metacarpals (adult)
       1 metacarpal (puppy)
       1 L. distal tibia
       1 L. distal fibula
       1 calcaneum
       1 phalanx
    pocket gopher (*Orthogeomys grandis*)
       2 L. mandibles
       1 R. proximal humerus
       1 L. proximal femur
       1 L. tibia (unfused)

       1 L. calcaneum
    jackrabbit (*Lepus mexicanus*)
       1 lower incisor
       1 radius fragment
       2 R. innominates
       1 L. distal tibia
       1 metatarsal
       1 phalanx
    eastern cottontail (*Sylvilagus floridanus*)
       2 R. mandibles
       1 L. mandible
       1 R. distal radius
       1 R. ulna
       1 L. innominate
       1 metatarsal
    Mexican cottontail (*Sylvilagus cunicularius*)
       3 metapodials
    unidentified cottontails (*Sylvilagus* spp.)
       1 R. proximal femur
Reptiles
    mud turtle (*Kinosternon integrum*)
       1 plastron scute
Human
    1 mandible fragment
    5 loose teeth
    1 clavicle
    1 radius
    several rib fragments
    1 patella
    several phalanges
Unidentified
    46 long bone fragments, mostly dog, deer, and human

The North Dooryard or Lago'

To the north of House 16, our excavations exposed roughly 24 m² of dooryard. Because we do not believe that the main door of the House 16/17 Complex would have faced north toward the blank bedrock face at the limit of the Lower Terrace, we consider this part of the dooryard to have been the "backyard" of the complex. The squares involved were N5E4, N5E5, N5E6, N4E4, N4E5, and N4E6. Three pits labeled Features 81, 87, and 88 were also found in this area (Fig. 18.1, Chapter 18).

A considerable amount of debris had been discarded in this area to the rear of the house, the *lago'* in the terminology of the Yalálag Zapotec (de la Fuente 1949:38). The debris, which included waste from biface manufacture, resembled that from House 16, and much of it could have originated there.

Chipped Stone

Chert (83%)
    ordinary flake cores: 45 (Fig. 19.3*a*)
    discoidal core: 1
    core tool: 1

flake perforators/gravers: 11
scrapers: 2
sidescraper: 1
biface preforms: 2 (Fig. 19.3*b*)
retouched flakes: 15
utilized flakes: 36
flakes, not utilized: 372
Obsidian (16%)
bipolar flake cores: 4
prismatic blade fragments, utilized: 23 (Fig. 19.3*c, d*)
prismatic blade fragments, no sign of use: 8
prismatic blade fragments, retouched: 2
percussion blade: 1
flake perforator: 1
wedge: 1
retouched flake: 1
utilized flakes: 21
flakes, not utilized: 33
Other (1%)
quartz flakes: 3
quartz fragment: 1

Ground Stone

Fragment of loaf-shaped two-hand mano with airfoil cross-section, possibly sandstone. The fragment is 14 cm long, 9 cm wide, and averages 6 cm thick (Fig. 19.3*e*).

Fragments of three different manos too small to classify; some fire-cracked.

Roughly half of a saddle-shaped metate made from purplish ignimbrite. This metate may once have been 35 cm in diameter; the surviving fragment is 17 cm wide, with an average thickness of 5.5 cm (Fig. 19.3*f*).

Roughly half of a basin-shaped metate, possibly quartzite. The surviving fragment is 30 × 20 cm. The metate would have been 3 cm thick in the middle and 8 cm thick near the rim of the basin (Fig. 19.4).

Fragment of basin-shaped metate, possibly mica schist. The surviving fragment is 32 × 15 cm. The metate would have been up to 11 cm thick near the center, and 18 cm thick near the rim of the basin.

Fragment of metate, possibly quartzite, too small to classify but perhaps basin-shaped.

Fragment of broken and battered celt, dark greenish-black metamorphic rock. The surviving fragment is 6 cm long, 5 cm wide, and 2 cm thick. This celt broke as the result of use on very resistant material, and may have been one of the tools used to hack out the bedrock terrace (Fig. 19.5*a*).

Fragment of broken and battered celt, dark greenish-black metamorphic rock. The surviving fragment is 6 cm long, 6.5 cm wide, and 3.2 cm thick. This is another celt that may have broken in the process of hacking out the bedrock terrace (Fig. 19.5*b*).

Fragment of broken and battered celt, dark greenish-black metamorphic rock. The surviving fragment is 5.7 cm long and 5.0 cm thick. This battered celt, found while cleaning the profile, is another that may have been broken in the process of hacking out the bedrock terrace (Fig. 19.5*c*).

Canica or pecked and ground stone ball, limestone, 2 cm in diameter (Fig. 19.5*d*).

Woodworking Tools?

One of the most interesting discoveries made in the dooryard was a pair of possible woodworking tools like those found cached below the floor of House 17 (Fig. 18.6, Chapter 18). Similar in design to the intact pair of tools stored below the floor, these artifacts may represent an earlier set, one that broke and had to be discarded. One of the possible woodworking tools was found in Square N5E6 of the North Dooryard; the other was found while cleaning the profile not far away.

Fragment of subrectangular smoother/sander with rectangular cross-section, and worn facets on both faces and both edges, made of fine-grained metamorphic rock. The surviving fragment is 3.5 cm long, 6.5 cm wide, and 2.2 cm thick (Fig. 19.5*e*).

Fragment of subrectangular smoother/sander with rectangular cross-section, one flat face and one slightly convex face, made of fine-grained metamorphic rock. The surviving fragment is 4 cm long, 6 cm wide, and 3 cm thick (Fig. 19.5*f*).

Bone Tools

The North Dooryard debris was noteworthy for its high number of bone tools, especially sewing needles; at least five of the latter were found. Recall that at least four basketry needles, but no definite sewing needles, were found in House 16; no needles at all were found in House 17. Bearing in mind the usual caveats about discard behavior, the pattern we see might suggest that most fine sewing was carried out in the sunlit dooryard, while most basket weaving was carried out in the shaded lean-to, and less sewing/weaving was done in the darkened house.

Long awl or pressure flaker made from a long bone shaft of white-tailed deer. This object is 8.8 cm long and has a maximum diameter of 1.9 cm. We are uncertain about its function; although it looks superficially like an awl, its tip is fractured in such a way as to suggest use as a pressure flaker (Fig. 19.6*a*).

Proximal end of a sewing needle with eye, oval in cross-section. The fragment is 24 mm long and 4 mm in diameter (Fig. 19.6*b*).

Distal end of a sewing needle, round in cross-section. The fragment is 22 mm long and 3 mm in diameter, tapering to a point (Fig. 19.6*c*).

Distal end of sewing needle with round cross-section, possibly fire-hardened at the tip. The fragment is 23 mm long and 3 mm in diameter, tapering to a point (Fig. 19.6*d*).

Midsection of sewing needle with round cross-section. The fragment is 22 mm long and 2 mm in diameter (Fig. 19.6*e*).

Midsection of sewing needle with round cross-section. The fragment is 20 mm long and 3 mm in diameter (Fig. 19.6*f*).

Midsection of possible basketry needle with round cross-section. The fragment is 32 mm long and 4 mm in diameter (Fig. 19.6*g*).

Midsection of bone needle with round cross-section. The fragment is 41 mm long and 3 mm in diameter. The needle from which this section came would have been quite long, perhaps too long to have been an ordinary sewing needle; it may have been for basketry (Fig. 19.6*h*).

Midsection of bone needle with oval cross-section. The fragment is 27 mm long and flaring, with the diameter increasing from 3 to 4 mm. Its unusual shape suggests that it may be a basketry needle, rather than a sewing needle (Fig. 19.6*i*).

Fragment cut from the shaft of a long bone (deer?), perhaps a waste product of bone tool manufacture, >54 mm long (broken).

Shell
  Ornament
    Subrectangular pendant of unidentified pearly shell, perforated at one end for suspension. Length, >15 mm (broken); width, 8 mm; diameter of perforation, 1.5 mm (Fig. 19.6*j*).
  Pearly Freshwater Mussels
    Complete valve of *Barynaias* sp., 45 mm long, probably unused raw material.
    Three fragments of freshwater mussel found together, probably manufacturing waste: (1) 10 × 20 mm; (2) 10 × 20 mm; (3) 15 × 25 mm.
    Three fragments of freshwater mussel found together, probably manufacturing waste: (1) 10 × 15 mm; (2) 30 × 20 mm; (3) 10 × 20 mm.
    Shattered fragments of freshwater mussel, probably from a fragment 10 × 15 mm in size.
  Pacific Marine Bivalves
    Fragment of pearl oyster (*Pinctada mazatlanica*) that may have broken while being perforated for suspension; 25 × 20 × 2 mm, with the perforation 5 mm in diameter.
    Three possible fragments of pearl oyster, all manufacturing waste: (1) 10 × 20 × 2 mm; (2) 10 × 20 × 2 mm; (3) 10 × 20 × 2 mm with a drill hole.
    Possible fragment of spiny oyster (*Spondylus calcifer*), probably manufacturing waste, 20 × 35 × 2 mm.
    Complete valve of Venus clam (*Chione* [= *Anomalocardia*] *subrugosa*), evidently unused raw material, 35 × 25 mm (Fig. 19.6 *k*).
  Pacific Marine Univalves
    None.
  Unidentified
    Five fragments of unidentified shell: (1) 8 × 16 mm; (2) 8 × 15 mm; (3) 8 × 8 mm; (4) 10 × 10 mm; (5) 10 × 15 mm.

Iron Ore Specimen
  Fragment of broken magnetite mirror, 5 mm wide and originally >10 mm long (Fig. 19.6*L*).

Mica
  Irregular piece of white mica, cut on at least four edges, weighing 1 g; roughly 34 × 21 × 1 mm (Fig. 19.6*m*).
  Piece of brown mica, 13 × 6 mm and paper thin.
  Piece of gold mica, cut on one edge, weighing 0.1 g; 15 × 8 × 1 mm.
  Piece of gold mica, 8 × 8 mm and paper thin.
  Disintegrating fragments of gold and white mica totaling 0.3 g. The largest gold fragment is 24 × 27 mm, and the largest white fragment is 17 × 5 mm.

Figurines
  Sixteen fragments of small solid figurines were found on the North Dooryard; they have been described by Marcus (1998a:181 and Figs. 13.17-13.18).

Imported Marine Fish
  Two fragments of palatine from grunt (family Pomadasyidae) (Fig. 19.6*n, o*).
  Articulated epihyal and ceratohyal from snapper (family Lutjanidae) (Fig. 19.6*p*).
  Hyomandibular from drum (family Sciaenidae, cf. *Cynoscion* sp.) (Fig. 19.6*q*).
  Vertebral spine from unidentified fish, 15 mm long, broken (Fig. 19.6*r*).
  Dorsal spine from unidentified fish, 20 mm long (Fig. 19.6*s*).
  Fish element, unidentified.

Carbonized Plants
  2 cotyledons of avocado (*Persea* sp.)
  many fragments of pine charcoal (*Pinus* sp.)

Animal Bones
  Hundreds of animal bone fragments were scattered across the North Dooryard, with the densest cluster occurring in Square N5E6 and the second densest in N4E6. Like the faunal collection from House 16, the North Dooryard sample appeared to be the refuse of a family of high rank with access to a wide range of animals. Represented in the collection were the remains of at least two deer, four dogs, three gophers, two jackrabbits, and six cottontails. We also found a few species that may not have been part of the food supply—a lizard, a toad, and several wild mice that may simply have burrowed into the dooryard and died.

Some insights into the way the House 16/17 family was provisioned in the period preceding abandonment were provided by the body parts present from deer and dog (Fig. 19.7). Deer were represented by a left forelimb and part of a left hindlimb, but no feet (carpals, tarsals, or phalanges). This suggests that the carcass may have been trimmed elsewhere, perhaps by a relative or neighbor who provided House 16/17 with some meat-bearing limbs. Dogs, however, were represented by feet, skull fragments, and major limb bones, suggesting that they might have been butchered either in House 16 or its dooryard. (To be sure, the dog meat could have been shared with relatives or neighbors as well.)

Large Mammals
  white-tailed deer (*Odocoileus virginianus*)
    1 antler tine
    2 R. temporal bones
    1 L. temporal bone
    2 R. zygomatic arches
    2 L. mandibles
    1 R. mandible
    1 L. hyoid
    1 L. scapula fragment
    2 L. distal humeri
    1 R. humerus fragment
    1 R. radius
    1 L. radius fragment
    1 L. ulna fragment
    1 L. ulnar carpal
    1 R. intermediate carpal
    1 R. radial carpal
    1 R. distal metacarpal
    1 L. distal metacarpal (just fusing)
    4 conjoining thoracic vertebrae
    1 sacral vertebra
    2 ribs
    1 innominate
    1 femur shaft fragment?
    11 long bone fragments
    2 other fragments (chewed by dogs?)
Small Mammals
  domestic dog (*Canis familiaris*)
    1 R. frontal bone
    1 L. frontal bone
    1 L. parietal bone
    1 L. parietal bone
    1 fragment of temporal bulla
    1 L. basioccipital bone
    3 R. maxillae (adult dogs)
    1 L. maxilla
    1 L. upper third incisor
    2 R. upper incisors
    1 L. upper canine tooth
    1 R. upper canine tooth
    1 L. upper fourth premolar
    1 R. upper fourth premolar
    2 L. mandibles (adult dogs)
    1 L. lower canine tooth
    1 R. lower canine tooth
    2 fragments of other canine teeth
    1 R. lower first molar
    1 atlas (chewed)

    1 L. distal humerus
    1 L. proximal radius
    1 R. proximal radius (unfused, juvenile)
    1 R. proximal radius (fused, adult)
    1 L. radius shaft
    1 L. distal radius (unfused, juvenile)
    2 R. proximal ulnae
    1 L. ulna (unfused, juvenile)
    1 L. second metacarpal
    1 L. femur (chewed)
    2 L. third metatarsals
    2 other fragments of metapodials
    1 second phalanx
    1 other fragment of phalanx
  pocket gopher (*Orthogeomys grandis*)
    3 R. upper incisors
    2 L. upper incisors
    1 R. lower incisor
    other incisor fragments
    1 R. humerus
    1 L. distal ulna
    1 R. distal tibia
  jackrabbit (*Lepus mexicanus*)
    2 L. mandibles
    1 L. second premolar
    1 R. proximal radius
    1 R. distal ulna
    2 metatarsals
    2 other fragments of metatarsal
  eastern cottontail (*Sylvilagus floridanus*)
    3 R. mandibles
    1 L. mandible
    2 R. proximal scapulae
    1 L. proximal scapula
    1 R. distal humerus
    1 R. proximal radius
    3 L. innominates
    1 R. innominate
    2 R. distal tibiae
    2 L. distal tibiae
    2 metatarsals
  Mexican cottontail (*Sylvilagus cunicularius*)
    2 R. mandibles
    1 L. mandible
    2 L. proximal scapulae
    3 R. distal humeri
    1 R. proximal radius
    1 L. proximal radius
    1 L. proximal ulna
    2 metacarpals
    1 R. innominate
    1 R. proximal femur
    1 L. proximal femur
    1 L. tibia shaft

1 R. calcaneum
3 metatarsals (from 2 different rabbits)
unidentified cottontails (*Sylvilagus* spp.)
    1 R. mandible fragment
    1 incisors
    3 cheek teeth
    other fragments of teeth
    1 ulna shaft
    3 rib fragments
    1 R. innominate fragment
    2 metatarsals
    5 other scraps
weasel (*Mustela frenata*)
    1 R. mandible
unidentified small carnivore
    1 incisor

Reptiles
    mud turtle (*Kinosternon integrum*)
        1 coracoid
        1 costal scute
        1 lateral marginal scute, burned

Birds
    Montezuma quail (*Cyrtonyx montezumae*)
        1 tibiotarsus
    coot? (cf. *Fulica* sp.)
        1 tibiotarsus
    band-tailed pigeon (*Columba fasciata*)
        1 ulna
        1 tibiotarsus

unidentified bird
    1 long bone shaft fragment
Human
    1 premolar tooth
    1 fragment of radius?
    1 metacarpal
    3 other scraps
Unidentified
    210 bone splinters, mostly from the long bones of deer and dog

Small Animals That May Have Died in Their Burrows in the Dooryard
    spiny pocket mouse (*Liomys irroratus*)
        1 L. mandible
    unidentified mice of the family Cricetidae
        1 fragment of mandible
        1 humerus
        1 femur
    small lizard (cf. *Sceloporus* sp.)
        1 R. dentary
        1 humerus
        1 tibia
    toad (*Bufo* cf. *marinus*)
        2 scapulae
        1 humerus
        1 radius
        1 fragment of pelvis
        2 vertebrae

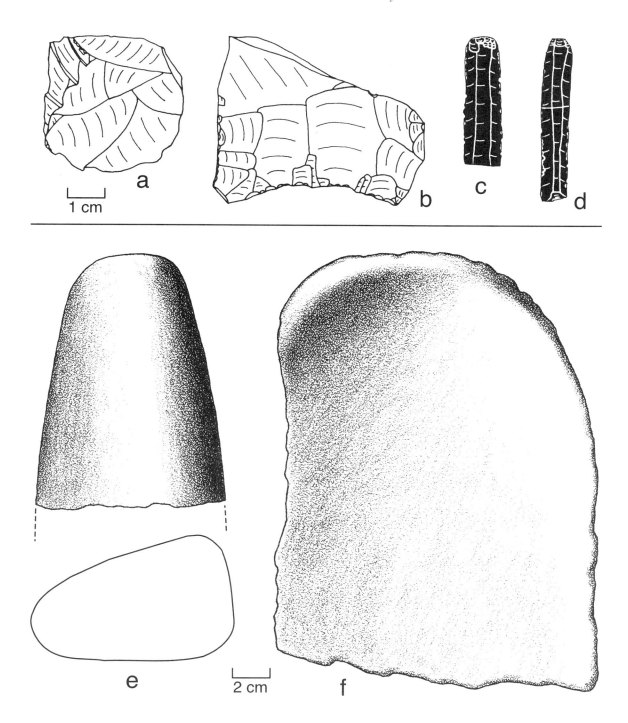

Figure 19.3. Artifacts found on the North Dooryard of the House 16/17 Complex. *a*, chert flake core. *b*, chert biface preform that broke during thinning; designed to be lanceolate, with a concave base. *c, d,* utilized prismatic obsidian blade fragments. *e*, fragment of two-hand mano with airfoil cross-section. *f*, portion of saddle-shaped metate.

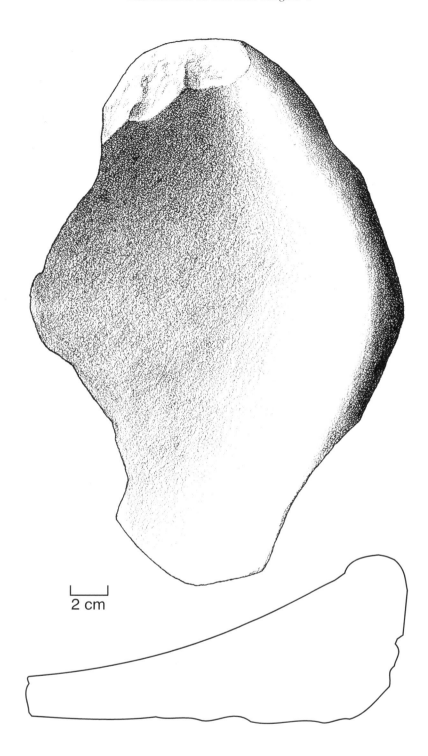

2 cm

Figure 19.4. Portion of basin-shaped metate from the North Dooryard of the House 16/17 Complex; possibly quartzite.

Figure 19.5. Ground stone artifacts from the North Dooryard of the House 16/17 Complex. *a-c*, battered celts, probably worn from hacking bedrock. *d, canica* or pecked and ground stone ball. *e, f,* fragments of subrectangular smoothers/sanders, possibly woodworking tools.

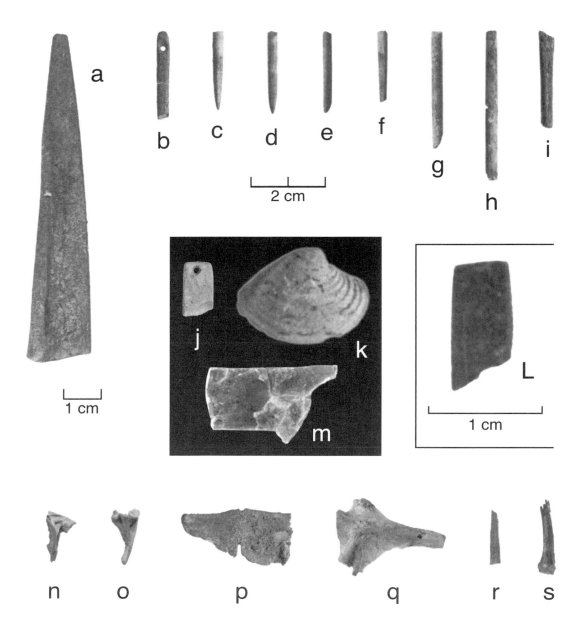

Figure 19.6. Objects from the North Dooryard of the House 16/17 Complex. *a,* long awl or pressure flaker of deer bone. *b,* proximal end of sewing needle with eye. *c, d,* distal ends of sewing needles. *e, f,* midsections of sewing needles. *g-i,* midsections of large needles, possibly for basketry. *j,* pendant of unidentified pearly shell. *k,* unmodified Venus shell. *L,* fragment of magnetite mirror (shown larger than actual size). *m,* piece of white mica cut on at least four edges. *n, o,* two fragments of palatine from grunt. *p,* epihyal and ceratohyal from snapper. *q,* hyomandibular from drum. *r, s,* spines from unidentified fish.

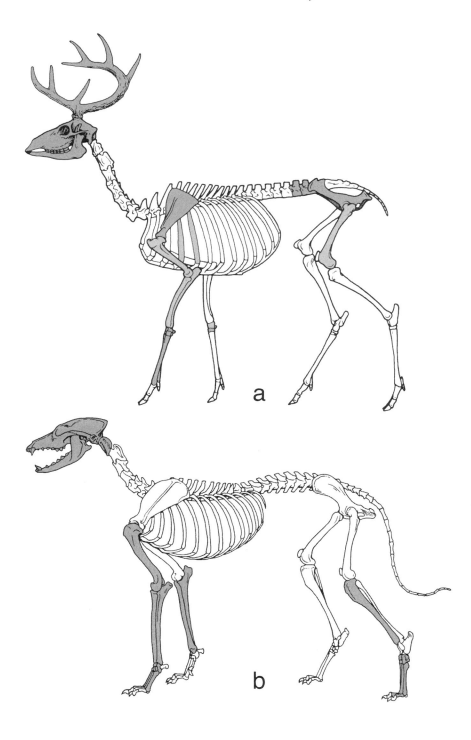

Figure 19.7. Remains of deer (*a*) and dog (*b*) were abundant on the North Dooryard of the House 16/17 Complex. Skeletal elements present are shown as shaded. It would appear that the deer were butchered (and the feet discarded) elsewhere; following this, the carcasses were divided among several households, with House 16/17 receiving most of a left forelimb and part of a left hindquarter. Dogs were represented by skulls, limb bones, and feet, but may also have been shared with other households.

Features in the North Dooryard

Feature 81

Feature 81 was a pit dug into bedrock in Square N5E5, right at the base of the cut bedrock face that marked the northern limit of the Lower Terrace (Fig. 19.8). It was roughly 70-75 cm in diameter. Although it began at the level of the dooryard, only its lower 35-40 cm, which had penetrated bedrock, was well preserved. Whatever its original purpose, this pit had eventually been filled in with refuse such as ash, chert flakes, imported marine fish, and animal bones. Among the faunal remains was a possible specimen of the lesser scaup, a duck which is a common winter visitor to the Mexican highlands.

Chipped Stone
  Chert (100%)
    utilized flake: 1
    flake, not utilized: 1

Figurine
  fragment of small solid figurine (Marcus 1998a:181)

Imported Marine Fish
  basioccipital, genus unknown

Animal Bones
  Small Mammals
    pocket gopher (*Orthogeomys grandis*)
      1 R. lower incisor
    eastern cottontail (*Sylvilagus floridanus*)
      1 R. distal humerus
      1 L. unfused distal radius
      1 L. unfused distal tibia
  Birds
    cf. lesser scaup (*Aythya affinis*)
      1 radius

Feature 87

Feature 87 was a pit excavated into bedrock in Square N4E4, just northwest of House 16; it began at the level of the dooryard (Fig. 19.8). Unfortunately, the upper portion of this pit had been disturbed by an intrusive feature; only the lower 30 cm or so, which had penetrated bedrock, was well preserved. The base of the pit was 80-90 cm in diameter.

There were hints that Feature 87 might have been a small cistern. According to botanist C. Earle Smith, Jr. (pers. comm., 1980), the lower part of the pit contained "a concentration of broken-down wood which looks as though it had been laid down in water." The presence of small aquatic snails in the lower fill also suggests that water may have stood for some time in the pit.

Chipped Stone
  Chert (100%)
    flake core: 1
    flakes, not utilized: 2

Figurine
  fragment of small solid figurine (Marcus 1998a:182)

Plant Remains
  waterlogged wood: roughly 0.5 kg
  waterlogged grass: 50 g

Invertebrate Remains
  small aquatic snails, not identified to genus: 4

Feature 88

Feature 88 was a bell-shaped pit, roughly 1.14 m in basal diameter (Fig. 19.8). It lay in Squares N4E4 and N5E4, a few meters northwest of House 16. Although it began at the level of the dooryard, only its lower 30 cm, which had penetrated bedrock, was well preserved. Originally dug as a storage feature, it ended up as a receptacle for household trash.

Chipped Stone
  Chert (100%)
    endscraper?: 1
    utilized flake: 1
    flakes, not utilized: 12

Shell
  fragment of unidentified pearly freshwater mussel, 20 × 15 × 1 mm
  beachworn turret shell, cf. *Turritella*, 30 mm long

Figurine
  fragment of small solid figurine (Marcus 1998a:182)

Animal Bones
  domestic dog
    1 fragment of R. mandible with permanent first molar still unerupted
  unidentified small mammal
    1 lumbar vertebra

Insights from Artifact Plotting

Figures 19.9-19.15 show the distribution of chert cores, biface roughouts/preforms, obsidian tools, ground stone, bone needles, shell and mica debris, figurine fragments, and miscellaneous small items on the North Dooryard. While most of the pattern is probably the result of discard behavior, there are some interesting cases of clustering.

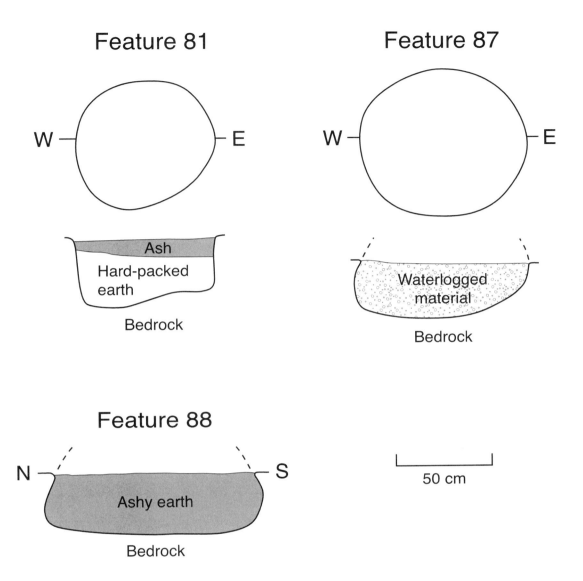

Figure 19.8. Plans and cross-sections of Features 81, 87, and 88, three pits excavated in the North Dooryard of the House 16/17 Complex. For the locations of these pits see Figure 18.1, Chapter 18.

Chert cores, for example, tended to occur in two clusters: one between Feature 88 and the cut bedrock face in Square N5E4, the other in Squares N4E6-N5E6 (Fig. 19.9). No cores were discarded in N4E5 or N5E5. This pattern suggests that an effort was made to keep the pathways between House 16 and Features 81, 87, and 88 clear of bulky debris. No such effort was made in the case of discarded obsidian tools, which are smaller and less conspicuous; they were spread more evenly across the northern part of the dooryard (Fig. 19.10).

Ground stone tools, like cores, are bulky, and their distribution seemed to reflect a similar effort to keep open the pathways to the dooryard pits (Fig. 19.11). The three battered celts found near the southeast corner of N5E4 may have been discarded after the

hacking of bedrock, or the digging of bedrock pits.

The situation is somewhat different with bone needle fragments (Fig. 19.12). As mentioned earlier, while we cannot be sure exactly where the sewing needles were originally used, their virtual restriction to the dooryard may mean that most finer sewing was done outdoors, where the light was better. An awl and two possible basketry needle fragments were discarded near the sewing needles.

Items associated with shell and mica working were small and relatively unobtrusive, and (like obsidian fragments) seemed to be spread more evenly across the dooryard (Fig. 19.13). Nevertheless, even in the case of perforators/gravers and shell fragments, there appears to have been a tendency to discard them

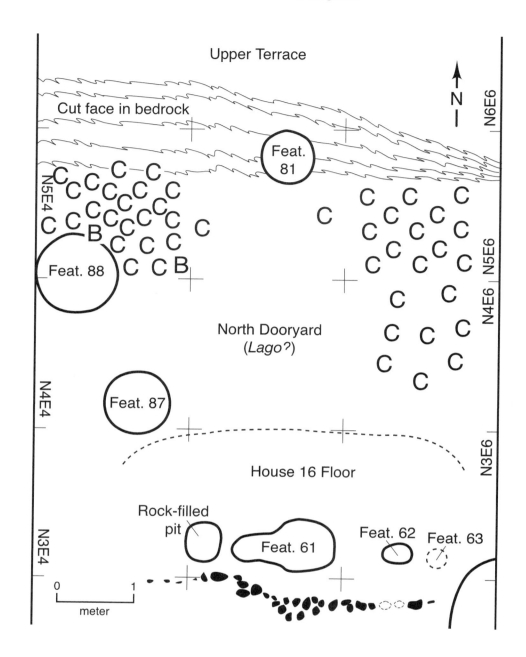

Figure 19.9. As shown by this plan of the North Dooryard of the House 16/17 Complex, discard areas for chert cores (C) and biface preforms (B) were very localized.

to the north of Feature 88, and away from the path leading from House 16 to Feature 81. This suggests that the pits in the North Dooryard may have been visited often during the time the house was occupied.

Given that House 16 included a likely woman's work area and a buried figurine scene, it was not surprising to find a number of figurines scattered around the adjacent dooryard (Fig. 19.14). However, they also tended not to lie in the paths between House 16 and Features 81, 87, and 88.

Miscellaneous small items—marine fish bone, carbonized avocado seeds, and a broken magnetite mirror (Fig. 19.15)—present a discard pattern not unlike that of shell fragments.

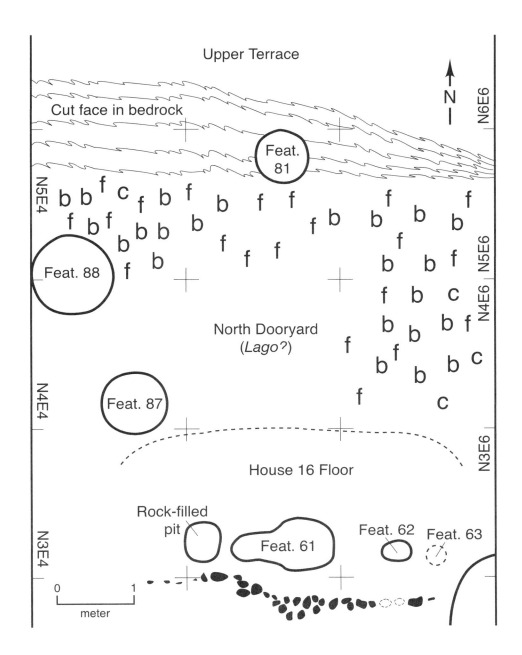

Figure 19.10. Distribution of three categories of obsidian tools on the North Dooryard of the House 16/17 Complex: c = bipolar flake cores, b = utilized prismatic blade fragments, f = utilized flakes.

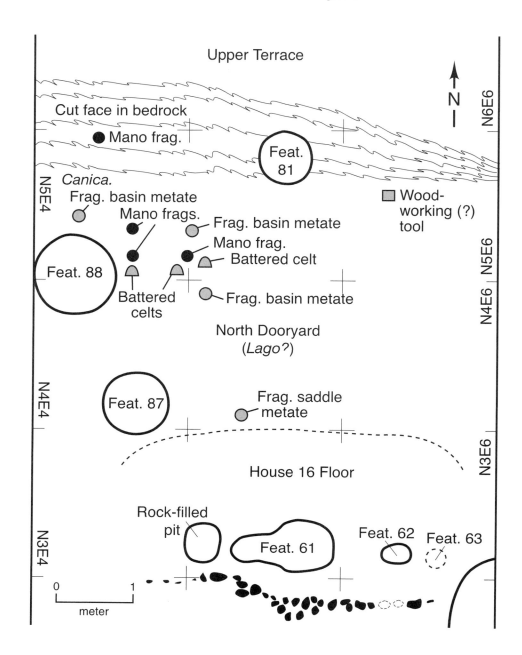

Figure 19.11. Ground stone tools plotted on the North Dooryard of the House 16/17 Complex.

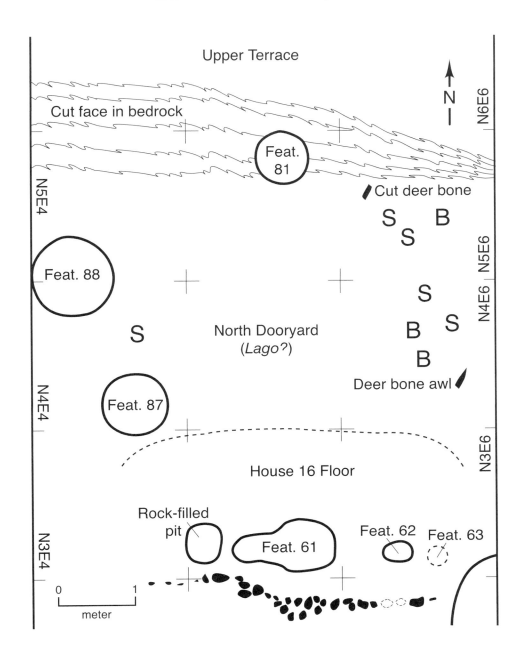

Figure 19.12. Distribution of bone tools on the North Dooryard of the House 16/17 Complex: S = probable sewing needles, B = probable basketry needles.

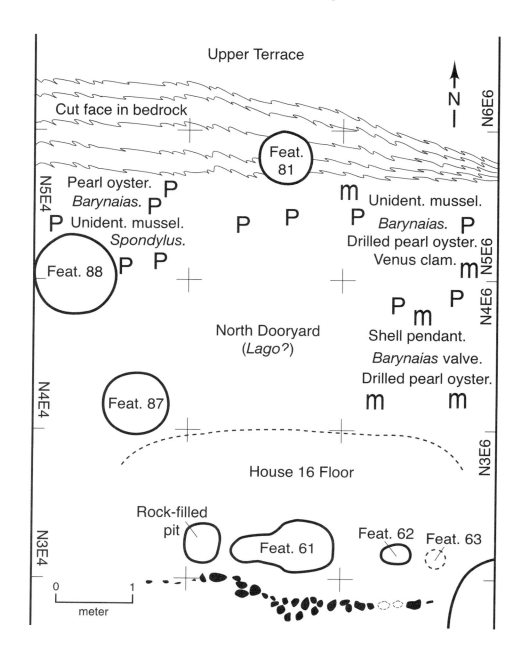

Figure 19.13. Distribution of items possibly associated with shell or mica working on the North Dooryard of the House 16/17 Complex, given by square, since many of the smaller items were recovered in the screen: P = chert perforator/graver, m = mica.

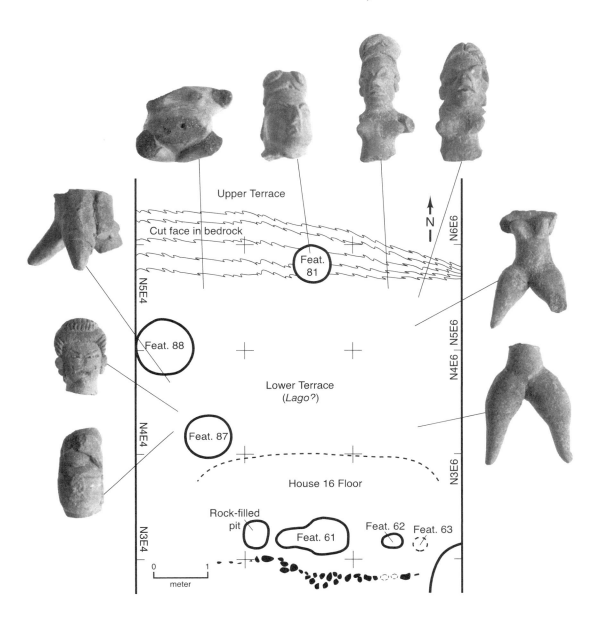

Figure 19.14. Figurine fragments plotted on the North Dooryard of the House 16/17 Complex.

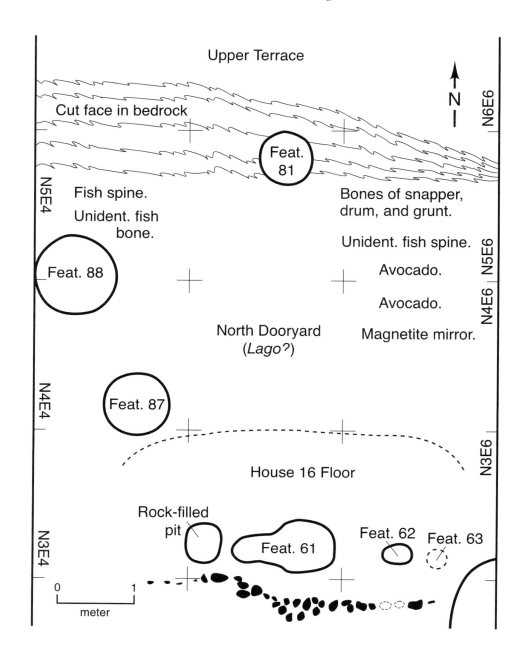

Figure 19.15. Miscellaneous items found on the North Dooryard of the House 16/17 Complex: imported marine fish, carbonized avocados, and a broken magnetite mirror.

The West Dooryard or Zio'

To the west of House 16/17, in Squares N2E4 and N3E4, we managed to excavate 8 m² of the *zio'*, or lateral dooryard, flanking the west side of the house. While our sample from this area was limited, we could see differences between the north and west parts of the dooryard. For example, the West Dooryard had no refuse from biface manufacture, and it had many fewer animal bones per square meter than the North Dooryard. It also lacked the shell and mica debris found in the latter.

Chipped Stone
  Chert (80%)
    flake cores: 4
    flake perforators/gravers: 2
    drill: 1
    sidescraper/graver: 1
    scraper fragment: 1
    denticulate scraper: 1
    denticulate unifacial chopping tool: 1
    retouched flake: 1
    utilized flakes: 9
    flakes, not utilized: 82
  Obsidian (18%)
    bipolar flake core: 1
    prismatic blade fragments, utilized: 3
    burin: 1 (on blade)
    wedges: 4 (2 on blade fragments)
    utilized flakes: 6
    flakes, not utilized: 8
  Other (2%)
    quartz flakes: 2

Ground Stone
  Fragment of subrectangular two-hand mano with lenticular cross-section, coarse metamorphic rock. The upper grinding surface is convex, while the lower surface is nearly flat. The fragment is 16 cm long, 11 cm wide, and 6 cm thick (Fig. 19.16*a*).
  Fragment of subrectangular two-hand mano with oval or lenticular cross-section, crystalline metamorphic rock. Both grinding surfaces are convex. The fragment is 14 cm long, 8 cm wide, and 4.5 cm thick (Fig. 19.16*b*).

Bone Tools
  Distal end of a broken deer bone awl, very worn, with a flat cross-section. The length of the fragment is 55 mm (Fig. 19.16*c*).
  Fragment of the worked and polished ulna from an unidentified bird about the size of a duck. The length of the fragment is 58 mm.

Mica
  Fragment of brown mica, cut on two edges weighing 0.2 g; 15 × 15 mm and paper thin.

Figurines
  Two fragments of small solid figurines were found in the West Dooryard (Marcus 1998a:183 and Fig. 13.18).

Carbonized Plants
  Multiple fragments of pine charcoal (*Pinus* sp.).
  A few fragments of legume charcoal (cf. *Prosopis* sp., *Acacia* sp.).

Animal Bones
  Large Mammals
    white-tailed deer (*Odocoileus virginianus*)
      1 L. astragalus (broken, chewed, burned, and eroded)
  Small mammals
    domestic dog (*Canis familiaris*)
      1 broken premolar
      1 L. distal humerus
      1 R. femur shaft
    pocket gopher (*Orthogeomys grandis*)
      1 cheek tooth
    jackrabbit (*Lepus mexicanus*)
      1 R. lower incisor
      1 metapodial
    eastern cottontail (*Sylvilagus floridanus*)
      1 L. scapula
      1 R. ulna
    Mexican cottontail (*Sylvilagus cunicularius*)
      1 L. mandible
      1 R. ulna
    unidentified cottontails (*Sylvilagus* spp.)
      1 metapodial
  Birds
    1 R. proximal fibula, family Cracidae (cf. *Crax* sp. or *Penelope* sp.)
    1 unidentifiable radius fragment

Small Animals That May Have Burrowed into the Dooryard and Died
  1 L. mandible of white-footed mouse (*Peromyscus* sp.)
  1 R. femur and 1 L. tibia of unidentified mouse
  1 dentary and 1 R. tibia of small lizard (cf. *Sceloporus* sp.)
  2 long bones of toad (*Bufo* cf. *marinus*)

The East Dooryard or Zio'

Our excavations exposed very little of the dooryard east of House 16/17, and that exposure was further reduced by the presence of the dooryard trash pit described above. Essentially, our sample comes from the extreme north of Square N1E7 and the eastern half of Square N2E7.

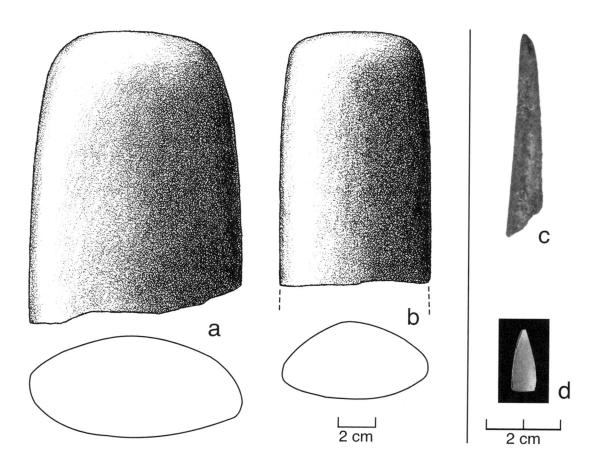

Figure 19.16. Artifacts from the East and West Dooryards of the House 16/17 Complex. *a, b,* fragments of two-hand manos with lenticular or oval cross-sections, West Dooryard. *c,* distal end of deer bone awl, West Dooryard. *d,* triangular shell plaque (possibly an inlay), East Dooryard.

Chipped Stone
  Chert (100%)
    core rejuvenation flake: 1
    flake perforator?: 1
    utilized flakes: 2

Shell
  Ornament
    Complete shell plaque, probably of pearl oyster; triangular
      in shape, 23 mm long, with a maximum width of 9 mm
      (Fig. 19.16*d*). Like many such plaques, this may have
      been a shell inlay for a wooden mask.
  Pearly Freshwater Mussel
    a few scraps
  Unidentified
    beachworn marine shell

Mica
  piece of gold mica weighing 0.4 g; 31 × 23 mm and paper
    thin

Animal Bones
  Small Mammals
    domestic dog (*Canis familiaris*)
      1 L. mandible (with full complement of premolars)
    jackrabbit (*Lepus mexicanus*)
      1 radius fragment
      1 L. distal tibia
    eastern cottontail (*Sylvilagus floridanus*)
      1 R. distal radius
      1 R. ulna
      1 L. innominate
    unidentified cottontails (*Sylvilagus* spp.)
      1 R. proximal femur

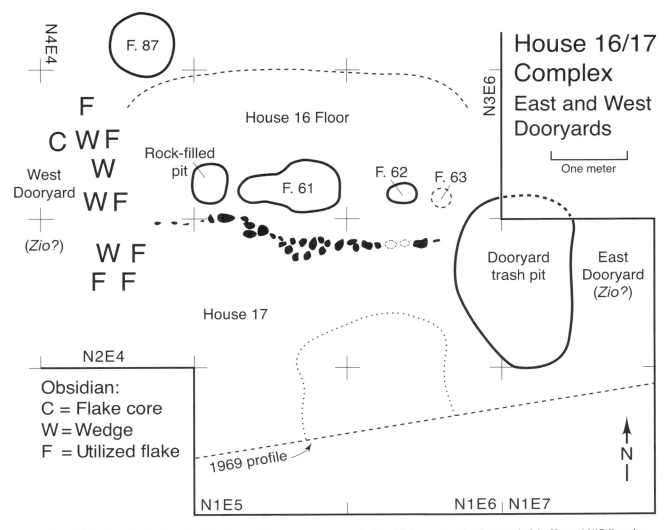

Figure 19.17. The distribution of obsidian bipolar flake cores, wedges, and utilized flakes on the West Dooryard of the House 16/17 Complex.

Human
2 teeth
1 clavicle fragment
fragments of rib
Unidentified
11 long bone splinters, mostly deer and human

Insights from Artifact Plotting

Our exposures of the West and East Dooryards were small, giving them limited utility in terms of analyzing artifact distributions. Figures 19.17 and 19.18 give the locations of obsidian tools, ground stone tools, and shell ornaments.

An unusual number of obsidian artifacts showed up in the West Dooryard (Fig. 19.17). Especially interesting was the fact that

four of the obsidian pieces, according to William J. Parry (pers. comm., 1987), had been used as wedges. We have no explanation for such a high frequency of wedges in a relatively small area. Given everything else we know about House 16, however, we wonder if thin obsidian wedges might have been used to split canes or reeds into strips for making mats or baskets. This possibility is raised by the fact that a bone awl of the type used in basket making was found in the same area (Fig. 19.16c).

Activity Areas in the House 16/17 Complex: An Overview

Having examined each component of the House 16/17 Complex in detail, let us now step back and take a broader look at the whole Lower Terrace of Area B (Fig. 19.19). Our "coarser grained" look at the entire household unit builds on Parry's at-

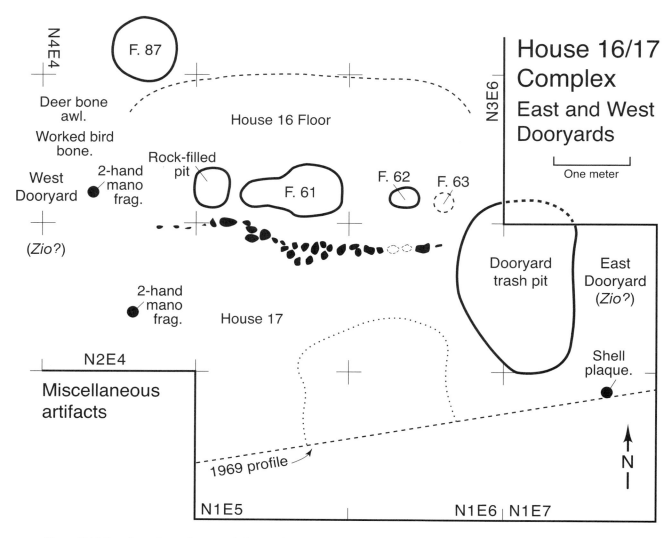

Figure 19.18. Locations of ground stone tools, bone tools, and shell ornaments on the East and West Dooryards of the House 16/17 Complex.

tempt to reconstruct areas of tool manufacture, use, and discard, based on chipped stone debris (Parry 1987:41). Like Parry, we begin with the caveat that no activity was restricted to a single area; it is simply the *dominant activity* for each area that is shown in Figure 19.19.

It seemed to Parry that House 17 was an area where chert tools were used (and sometimes left), but not where they were usually made. Most chert tool manufacture took place in House 16, the lean-to on the north side of House 17. A great deal of waste from biface manufacture was discarded in an area stretching east from House 16 past the dooryard trash pit. To be sure, other chert debris

was carried to the North Dooryard and dumped near the base of the cut bedrock face. However, the householders were careful not to let this debris impede traffic to and from the three pits they had dug in the dooryard (Features 81, 87, and 88).

We should add that the House 16 lean-to was also used for cooking, figurine-based ancestor ritual, heat-treating of chert, and basket making. Finer sewing may have been done in the dooryard to the north. The same areas at the base of the cut bedrock face that had been used for chert discard were also used for the waste from shell working.

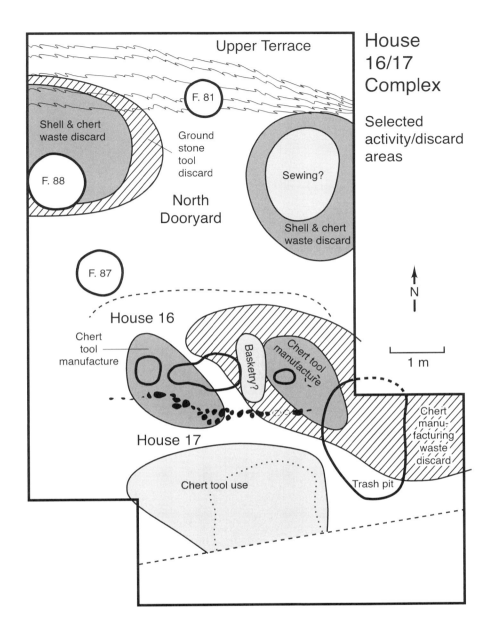

Figure 19.19. Overall patterns of tool manufacture, use, and discard in the House 16/17 Complex, as suggested by artifact plotting. No activity was completely restricted to one area; what are shown are the main areas for each activity. Chert activity areas follow Parry (1987: Figure 41).

Cooking does not seem to have taken place in House 17. The occupants evidently prepared their meals in the House 16 lean-to, and discarded food remains (such as animal bones and avocado seeds) in the dooryard north of the house. We suspect that periodically, the house and dooryard were swept and the accumulated debris taken to a midden somewhere.

We learned a lot about San José phase use of space from the House 16/17 Complex because our exposure (more than 50 m²) amounted to a transect containing a house, a lean-to, outdoor features, and part of a dooryard. It was also the case that by the time we excavated Area B, we had seen enough residences to be able to distinguish their components and analyze them separately. In the case of the House 16/17 Complex, piece-plotting was an invaluable tool—not at the "micro" level of the individual square, but at the "macro" level of the whole 50 m² exposure. We could see areas where tools were made, areas where tools were used and left, and areas where debris was discarded. At such a scale, discard behavior is not a pattern-destroying enemy; it is a pattern-building, behavior-revealing ally.

Chapter 20

Area B: The Upper Terrace

As mentioned earlier, the Upper Terrace of Area B was 50-60 cm higher than the Lower Terrace. It began at the cut face in bedrock near Feature 81 and ran north beyond the limits of our excavation. We ran out of time before we reached the house for whose construction the Upper Terrace had been leveled. However, our excavation exposed more than 20 m² of its dooryard.

The oldest evidence of occupation found on the Upper Terrace was domestic refuse swept into some natural depressions in bedrock, as well as into Feature 82, a deliberate pit (Fig. 18.1, Chapter 18). Stratigraphically above the filled-in depressions, we found a stratum of hard-packed earth and household debris that appeared to be the dooryard of a residence. All materials found on or beneath this dooryard dated to the San José phase.

Because our sample of sherds from the Upper Terrace was not closely tied to a house, we did not include it in our volume on Early Formative ceramics (Flannery and Marcus 1994). It seemed better to wait for a future opportunity to excavate the Upper Terrace in its entirety. At that point, we will be in a better position to divide the sherd sample into (1) ceramics associated with a house, and (2) sherds scattered across the dooryard. We did record a restorable Atoyac Yellow-white bowl, called Vessel 1, which we found inverted on the Upper Terrace.

The Earliest Occupation: Features and Natural Depressions in Bedrock

No postholes were found among the natural bedrock depressions in the area we excavated, which suggests that that part of the terrace was always an outdoor area rather than part of a house. In the debris swept into the depressions, we found further evidence that San José phase cooking was often done in portable braziers using prepared pine charcoal. We recovered large quantities of such charcoal, along with sherds from Lupita Heavy Plain braziers.

Feature 82

Feature 82 was a cylindrical pit in Square N7E5 (Fig. 20.1a); its base had penetrated a natural bedrock depression that ran east-west for more than 4 m. The pit was 45 cm in diameter; its original depth, while greater than 30 cm, could not be determined. Like the nearby depression, it had eventually been filled with household trash.

Ceramics
Roughly half of a Lupita Heavy Plain charcoal brazier was found.

Chipped Stone
Chert (33%)
flakes, not utilized: 2
Obsidian (67%)
prismatic blade fragment, utilized: 1
flakes, not utilized: 3

Mica
Irregular piece of gold mica, roughly 65 × 30 × 2 mm (Fig. 20.1b).
Piece of brownish-gold mica, cut on at least one side and perhaps as many as three sides, weighing 3.5 g; 65 × 38 × 2 mm.

Feature 82

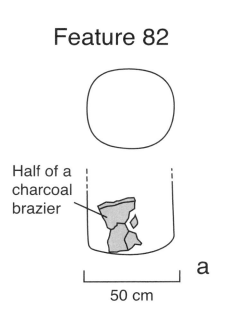

Half of a charcoal brazier

50 cm

a

b

Figure 20.1. Feature 82 and its contents. *a*, plan and cross-section of the feature. *b*, piece of gold mica from Feature 82.

2 cm

Carbonized Plants
   Nearly 1 kg of prepared pine charcoal (*Pinus* sp.).

Animal Bones
   domestic dog (*Canis familiaris*)
      1 deciduous canine tooth from a puppy
      1 L. proximal ulna (chewed)
   raccoon (*Procyon lotor*)
      1 fragment of L. humerus
   human
      1 phalanx
   unidentified
      8 fragments

Irregular Bedrock Depression Running East-West through Squares N7E4-N7E6

A large, ragged natural depression in the ignimbrite bedrock of the Upper Terrace had become a convenient place for the occupants to sweep their trash, especially animal bones.

Chipped Stone
   Chert (85%)
      flake denticulate: 1
      retouched flake: 1
      utilized flakes: 3
      flakes, not utilized: 6
   Obsidian (15%)
      bipolar core: 1
      wedge made on a prismatic blade fragment: 1

Kiln Waster?
   A possible kiln waster of Leandro Gray ware was found in the bedrock depression. This discovery suggests that a nearby household, possibly even one on the Upper Terrace, was engaged in producing that important, carved-incised San José phase pottery type. Leandro Gray was a ware produced under conditions of reduced-oxygen firing, perhaps even smudging. Pine charcoal, of which 1 kg was found in Feature 82, might have been a suitable fuel for such smudging.

Mica
   A piece of gold mica was found, weighing 0.1 g; 8 × 6 mm and paper thin.

Figurines
   Some 18 fragments of small solid figurines were found on the Upper Terrace, mostly in the bedrock depression. These have been described by Marcus (1998a:184).

Bone Ornament
   A canine tooth of a dog, drilled for suspension, was found.

Animal Bones
   We recovered a large sample of faunal remains from the bedrock depression. Represented were at least two individual deer, one adult and one young; at least two Mexican cottontails and two to three eastern cottontails; and at least two dogs, one adult and one puppy. The deer were represented mainly by meat-bearing bones. The dogs, on the other hand, were represented almost entirely by less desirable portions such as teeth and paws,

suggesting that the more desirable parts of the carcass had been taken elsewhere.

Large Mammals
    white-tailed deer (*Odocoileus virginianus*)
        1 R. mandibular ramus
        2 fragments of thoracic vertebrae
        1 R. proximal radius
        1 rib fragment
        1 L. proximal femur
        1 R. proximal tibia
        1 L. proximal tibia
        1 unfused distal metapodial
        1 fragment of long bone
Small Mammals
    domestic dog (*Canis familiaris*)
        1 L. maxilla fragment
        1 R. upper third incisor
        1 R. upper canine
        1 L. upper canine
        1 L. upper first premolar
        1 R. upper fourth premolar
        1 L. mandible fragment
        1 R. mandible fragment
        1 L. lower third incisor
        1 R. lower second premolar
        1 L. lower third premolar
        1 fragment of another premolar
        1 deciduous incisor from a puppy
        1 L. second metacarpal (chewed)
        1 R. fourth metatarsal
        1 distal metapodial
        1 L. distal phalanx
    pocket gopher (*Orthogeomys grandis*)
        1 R. upper incisor
        1 R. lower incisor
    jackrabbit (*Lepus mexicanus*)
        1 R. calcaneum (burned)
    eastern cottontail (*Sylvilagus floridanus*)
        1 L. mandible fragment
        1 L. lower incisor
        1 L. proximal humerus
        1 L. distal humerus
        1 R. humerus
        1 L. distal radius
        1 R. distal radius
        1 R. innominate
        1 R. tibia (burned)
        1 R. tibia (unburned)
        1 R. tibia shaft
        1 L. distal tibia
    Mexican cottontail (*Sylvilagus cunicularius*)
        2 R. mandibles
        1 R. incisor
        1 R. innominate

        1 R. proximal tibia
        1 L. proximal tibia
        1 R. shaft of tibia
        1 L. distal tibia
        1 L. calcaneum (burned)
        1 metacarpal
    unidentified cottontails (*Sylvilagus* spp.)
        1 R. skull fragment
        1 rib
        1 phalanx (unburned)
        2 phalanges (burned)
    gray fox (*Urocyon cinereoargenteus*)
        1 R. proximal humerus
    small rodents
        1 R. humerus, family Cricetidae
Reptiles
    mud turtle (*Kinosternon integrum*)
        1 L. anal plate of plastron
Birds
    Montezuma quail (*Cyrtonyx montezumae*)
        1 L. coracoid
    unidentified duck
        1 R. tibia fragment
Human
    1 skull fragment
    1 rib
    1 fibula
    1 long bone shaft fragment
Unidentified
    70 fragments (4 of them burned)

Bedrock Depression in Square N7E6, East of Feature 82

A smaller natural bedrock depression in Square N7E6 of the Upper Terrace had been filled with ash. Flotation yielded the following carbonized plants.

Carbonized Plants
    1 cotyledon of avocado (*Persea* sp.)
    several fragments of prepared pine charcoal (*Pinus* sp.)

*Some Conclusions about the Earliest Occupation
of the Upper Terrace*

Even though we did not find the earliest house for whose construction the Upper Terrace had been leveled, we can draw certain inferences from the debris in Feature 82 and the bedrock depressions: (1) the family involved had ready access to such desirable game as white-tailed deer; (2) they worked mica; (3) they may have reduce-fired their own Leandro Gray pottery; (4) they cooked with prepared pine charcoal, and may even have used that same fuel for firing ceramics; and (5) like the earliest occupants of the Lower Terrace, they do not seem to have been involved in chert biface manufacture.

The Second Occupation: The Upper Terrace Dooryard

Overlying the bedrock depressions of the Upper Terrace, we found a hard-packed layer of earth that appeared to be the dooryard of a San José phase house. Nearly 100 items of chipped stone were lying on or trampled into it. We found clusters of broken manos and metates discarded at several places on the dooryard. Much of the chipped stone was concentrated in Square N7E6, and included no evidence for biface manufacture. Judging by the manufacturing waste, the family occupying the Upper Terrace seemed more interested in shell working.

Chipped Stone
> Chert (82%)
>> flake cores: 17
>> sidescraper: 1
>> large denticulate scraper/chopper: 1
>> denticulate flake: 1
>> utilized flakes: 11
>> flakes, not utilized: 46
> Obsidian (17%)
>> prismatic blade fragments, utilized: 9
>> wedge: 1
>> drill: 1
>> utilized flakes: 5
> Other (1%)
>> quartz flake: 1

Ground Stone from Square N7E4
> Fragment of loaf-shaped two-hand mano with triangular cross-section, made of what appears to be metamorphic rock. The fragment is 14 cm long, each of its three grinding facets are 7-8 cm wide, and its maximum thickness is 6.5-7.0 cm (Fig. 20.2*a*).
> Three mano spalls.

The following items were all discarded together in Square N7E4:
> Fragment of loaf-shaped two-hand mano with planoconvex cross-section, volcanic(?) rock. The fragment is 12 cm long, 9.5 cm wide, and 7 cm thick (Fig. 20.2*b*).
> Fragment of basin-shaped metate, quartzite. The fragment is 12.5 × 12 cm, and its maximum thickness near the edge is 5.5 cm. Nearer to the center it narrows to 4.5 cm thick (Fig. 20.2*c*).
> Fragment of saddle-shaped metate. The fragment is 8 × 7 cm and 4.2 cm thick (Fig. 20.2*d*).

Ground Stone from Square N6E6
The following items were discarded together in the southeast corner of Square N6E6:
> Fragment of loaf-shaped two-hand mano with airfoil cross-section, ignimbrite. The fragment is 6 cm long, 10 cm wide, and has an average thickness of 4.5 cm (Fig. 20.3*a*).

Fragment of slab metate, quartz conglomerate. The fragment is 17 × 10 cm in area and 4-5 cm thick (Fig. 20.3*b*).

Worked Sherd
> Chipped and ground disk made from a jar body sherd, 9 cm in diameter and 8 mm thick. The type is either Fidencio Coarse or Lupita Heavy Plain. This object may be a pot lid (Fig. 20.3*c*).

Shell
> Ornaments
>> Complete plaque made from pearl oyster (*Pinctada mazatlanica*), shaped like a truncated triangle, 40 mm long, 20 mm wide at the base (Fig. 20.4*a*).
>> Subrectangular plaque made from unidentified pearly shell, 14 × 13 mm in area.
>> Complete disk made from pearl oyster, 18 mm in diameter (Fig. 20.4*b*).
>> Fragment of pearl oyster(?) ornament, possibly a magnetite mirror holder. Originally ring-shaped, the ornament has a smooth interior edge, while the outer edge is carved like a Maya "eccentric flint." The piece is 20 mm long and 8 mm wide (Fig. 20.4*c*).
>> Complete *Olivella* shell, drilled at one end for suspension and truncated by a cut on the opposite end; 35 mm long, 16 mm in diameter (Fig. 20.4*d*). Olive shells like this appear on anthropomorphic urns of the Classic period, where they are depicted as "tinklers" sewn to the edges of garments or to a cloth tie (see Caso and Bernal 1952: Figs. 2, 63, 72, and 346).
> Pearly Freshwater Mussel
>> Fragment of *Barynaias*(?), 15 × 20 × 1 mm, cut on one edge; manufacturing waste.
>> Fragment of mussel valve, 8 × 15 × 1 mm; manufacturing waste.
>> Fragment of mussel valve, 25 × 25 × 1 mm; manufacturing waste.
> Pacific Marine Bivalves
>> Piece of *Pinctada mazatlanica*, 25 × 30 × 2 mm, cut on one edge; manufacturing waste.
>> Piece of pearl oyster, 15 × 25 × 2 mm; manufacturing waste.
>> Piece of pearl oyster, 25 × 12 × 2 mm; manufacturing waste.
>> Piece trimmed from pearl oyster valve, cut on three edges, 10 × 10 × 2 mm; manufacturing waste.
> Pacific Marine Univalves
>> Complete *Olivella* shell, unused raw material; only 15 mm long.
> Unidentified
>> Three fragments of unidentifiable shell, all smaller than 10 × 10 mm.

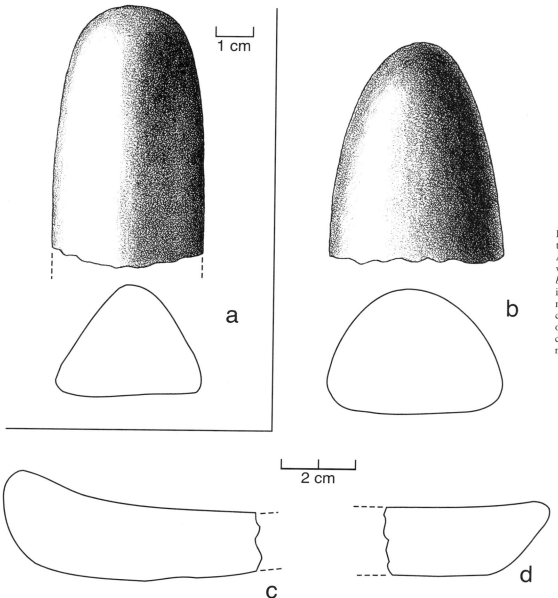

Figure 20.2. Ground stone tools from the Upper Terrace, Area B. *a*, two-hand mano with triangular cross-section. *b-d* were all discarded together in Square N7E4. *b*, two-hand mano with planoconvex cross-section. *c*, cross-section of basin-shaped metate. *d*, cross-section of saddle-shaped metate.

Iron Ore Specimens

  Fragment of broken magnetite mirror, weighing 0.8 g. Dimensions, 15 × 8 mm. Highly polished obverse, roughly smoothed reverse; strongly magnetic (Fig. 20.4*e*).

  Lump of ilmeno-magnetite, weighing 25.1 g. Dimensions, 23 × 20 × 16 mm (Fig. 20.4*f*).

Mica

  Mass of crushed mica, consisting of (1) one piece of brown mica, cut on one or two edges, 32 × 15 mm and paper thin; and (2) three pieces of gold mica, measuring 23 × 14 mm, 26 × 15 mm, and 14 × 7 mm, all paper thin. Total weight, 0.7 g.

  Shattered piece of gold mica, weighing 1.4 g and originally 36 × 19 mm in area; cut on one edge.

Imported Marine Fish

  Broken pectoral spine from an unidentified fish; the fragment is 17 mm long (Fig. 20.4*g*).

  Supracleithrum from an unidentified fish.

  Fragment of fish, unidentified.

Carbonized Plants

  Many fragments of pine charcoal (*Pinus* sp.).

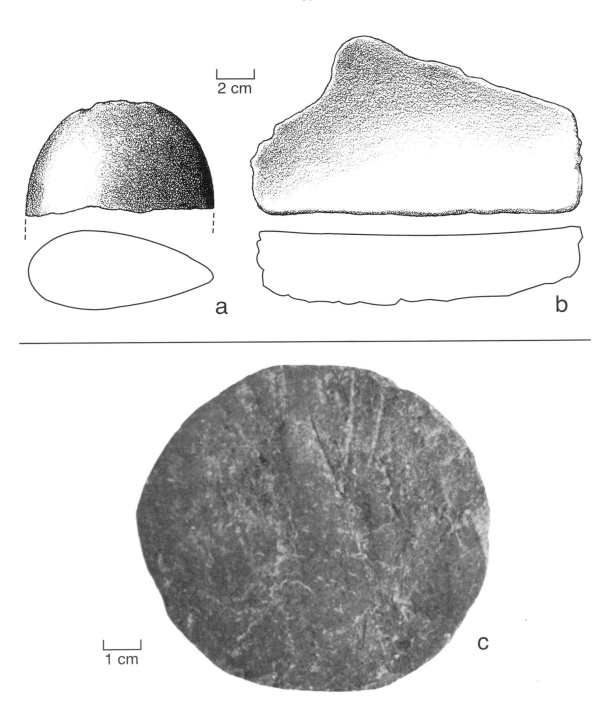

Figure 20.3. Artifacts from the Upper Terrace, Area B. *a*, fragment of two-hand mano with airfoil cross-section. *b*, fragment of slab metate. *c*, chipped and ground sherd disk, probably a pot lid.

Figure 20.4. Objects from the Upper Terrace, Area B. *a*, triangular pearl oyster plaque. *b*, pearl oyster disk. *c*, fragment of pearl oyster(?) ring with eccentric carved edge. *d*, olive shell drilled at one end for suspension. *e*, fragment of broken magnetite mirror; maximum length, 15 mm (shown larger than actual size). *f*, lump of ilmeno-magnetite. *g*, broken pectoral spine from unidentified marine fish.

Animal Bones
  domestic dog (*Canis familiaris*)
    1 R. proximal fourth metatarsal
  toad (*Bufo* cf. *marinus*), possibly intrusive
    1 humerus
    1 femur
    1 tibia/fibula
    several metatarsals
  human
    1 rib
  unidentified
    5 fragments

Insights from Artifact Plotting

Figures 20.5-20.8 show the distribution of chert cores, utilized flakes, ground stone tools, shell, mica, iron ore, marine fish parts, and other items on the Upper Terrace. The scatter of cores and utilized flakes (Fig. 20.5) suggests that the dooryard surface between the two natural bedrock depressions was seen as a convenient discard area.

Discarded fragments of utilitarian ground stone fell into two clusters (Fig. 20.6). The larger cluster, in Square N7E4, had three mano spalls and two fragments of recognizable mano types. The smaller cluster, in the southeast quadrant of Square N6E6, had pieces of one mano and one metate. All the fragments were too small to have been of use as anything but expedient hammerstones. Our impression is that these items were there as the result of general housecleaning.

Fragments of shell and mica were localized in Squares N7E5-N7E6 (Fig. 20.7). Several of the shell plaques looked complete and still usable, but perhaps they were inlays from a mask that had broken or worn out. Once inlays had been glued to another object, it may have been considered easier to make new ones than to pry them off for reuse.

Miscellaneous small items (Fig. 20.8) were scattered through the same discard area as chert cores and utilized flakes. Only the worked sherd (which may have been a pot lid) and the drilled dog canine appeared reusable. The rest of the items looked like housecleaning debris from a relatively well-to-do household.

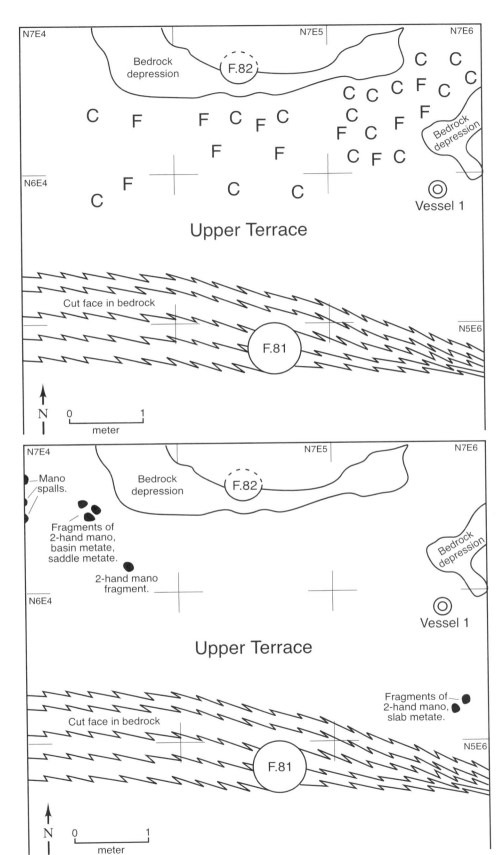

Figure 20.5. Distribution of chert flake cores (C) and utilized flakes (F) on the Upper Terrace Dooryard, Area B.

Figure 20.6. Utilitarian ground stone tools plotted on the Upper Terrace Dooryard, Area B.

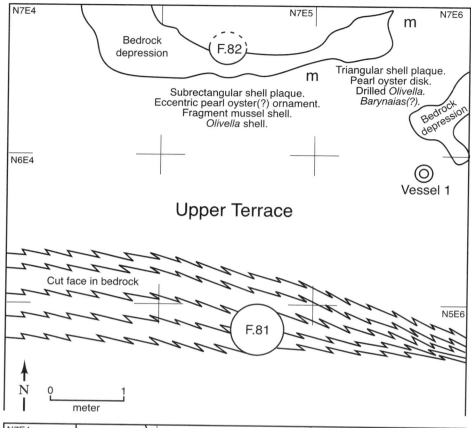

Figure 20.7. Distribution of major shell and mica (m) items on the Upper Terrace Dooryard, Area B.

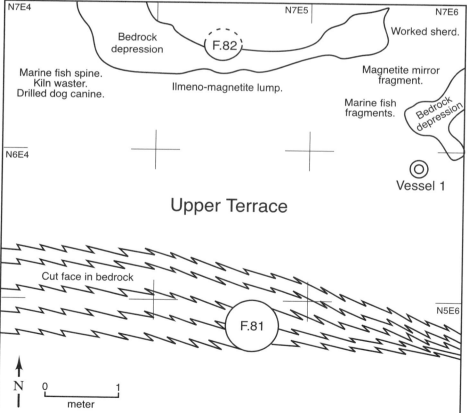

Figure 20.8. Distribution of miscellaneous objects (iron ore, marine fish, kiln wasters, worked sherds, and teeth) on the Upper Terrace Dooryard, Area B.

Chapter 21

A Guadalupe Phase House from Area B

Sometime after the abandonment of House 16/17, the Lower Terrace was deliberately covered with earthen fill to the top of the cut bedrock face. Some of this earth moving may have been related to the construction of public buildings to the north and west. For example, Structure 8, a large temple platform of the Guadalupe phase, was built not far away in Area C. This public construction left little room for ordinary Guadalupe phase residences in Area C.

In Area B, however, a Guadalupe phase house was built stratigraphically above the layer of earthen fill covering the Lower Terrace. This residence, designated House 21, was later damaged by intrusive Postclassic burials. As a result, we were able to recover only a few square meters of what might originally have been a 15-20 m² house. The surviving remnant occupied parts of Squares N5E4 and N6E4.

House 21

House 21 proved interesting because it had three superimposed floors: the original floor, plus two later resurfacings. We numbered these floors from the top down, in the order in which they were found; this made Floor 1 the uppermost and most recent, Floor 2 the second, and Floor 3 the lowest and oldest. We piece-plotted artifacts on all three floors (Figs. 21.2-21.4). Floor 3 had the most debris, apparently because many small artifacts had become buried in the sand layer atop the original floor, and remained there when the second floor was laid over them.

In our account below we describe the floors in chronological order, beginning with Floor 3.

Floor 3 (Oldest)

Chipped Stone
    Chert (77%)
        flake core: 1
        flake graver: 1
        flake graver/scraper: 1
        scraper: 1
        denticulate flake: 1
        utilized flakes: 5
        flakes, not utilized: 10
    Obsidian (19%)
        flake graver?: 1
        utilized flake: 1
        flakes, not utilized: 3
    Other (4%)
        ignimbrite core: 1

Bone Tool
    A fragment of a bone needle was found. It was burned, about 10 mm long, and 3 mm in diameter. This appears to be a sewing needle, but since the proximal end is missing, we cannot determine whether or not it had an eye (Fig. 21.1a).

Shell
    We recovered a fragment from the valve of a pearly freshwater mussel (possibly *Barynaias*), 10 × 8 × 1 mm. This appears to be a piece of raw material, not a fragment of ornament.

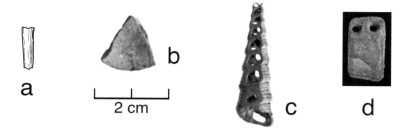

Figure 21.1 (*left*). Objects associated with House 21. *a*, bone needle fragment from Floor 3. *b*, fragment of beachworn bivalve from Floor 2. *c*, carved horn shell from Floor 2. *d*, rectangular pearl oyster ornament with two drill holes, found below House 21.

House 21, Floor 3 (Oldest)

Figure 21.2. Objects plotted on Floor 3 of House 21: C = chert core, U = utilized chert flake, F = chert flake, not utilized. The dashed line indicates the abrupt southern limit of the best preserved sand floor surface. To the north, the limits are less well defined. Guadalupe phase.

Animal Bones
   Large Mammals
      white-tailed deer (*Odocoileus virginianus*)
         1 rib fragment
   Small Mammals
      domestic dog (*Canis familiaris*)
         1 fragment of L. upper fourth premolar
         1 R. lower second molar
         1 metapodial
      pocket gopher (*Orthogeomys grandis*)
         1 incisor

         1 R. maxilla
         1 fragment of L. maxilla
      jackrabbit?
         1 fragment of L radius
      Mexican cottontail (*Sylvilagus cunicularius*)
         1 L. proximal scapula
   Human
      1 incisor
   Unidentified
      12 splinters, mostly mammal

House 21, Floor 2 (Second)

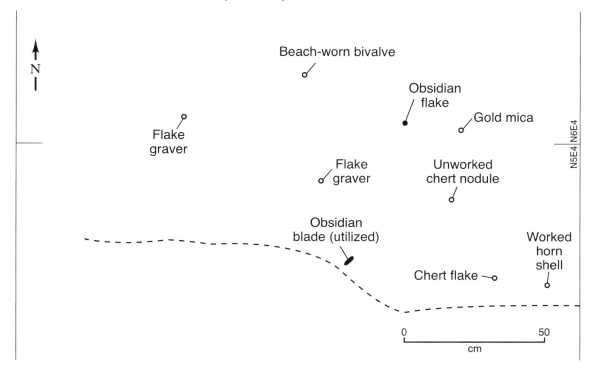

Figure 21.3. Objects plotted on Floor 2 of House 21. The dashed line indicates the abrupt southern limit of the best preserved sand floor surface. Guadalupe phase.

Floor 2 (Second)

Chipped Stone
 Chert (67%)
  unworked nodule: 1
  flake gravers: 2
  flake, not utilized: 1
 Obsidian (33%)
  prismatic blade fragment, utilized: 1
  flake, not utilized: 1

Shell
Pacific Marine Bivalves
 Fragment of beachworn shell, possibly a marsh clam; 10
  × 15 mm (Fig. 21.1*b*).
Pacific Marine Univalves
 Modified horn shell, probably *Cerithidium,* 35 mm long.
  It has been shaved on both sides so that the internal
  chambers are visible (Fig. 21.1*c*).

Mica
 Shattered piece of gold mica trimmed on one side, originally
  30 × 19 × 1 mm; weight, 0.1 g.

Floor 1 (Most Recent)

Daub
 Chunk of burnt daub with three cane impressions, 3.5 cm
  thick, with no surviving outer surface. Diameters of the
  cane impressions are 15 mm, 13 mm, and 12 mm.

Chipped Stone
 1 obsidian flake, not utilized

Material Found Just below House 21, Possibly Associated

Ground Stone
 Fragment of mano, metamorphic rock, too small for shape
  to be determined.

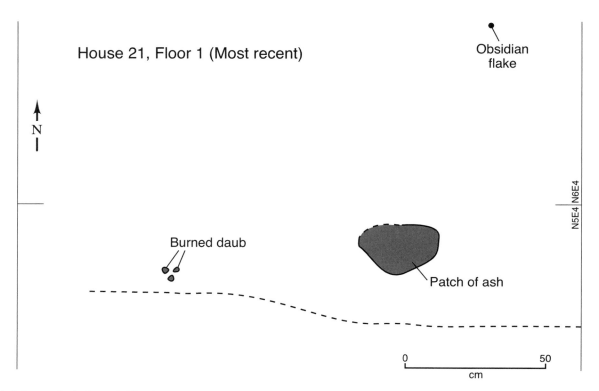

Figure 21.4. Only a patch of ash, an obsidian flake, and a few chunks of daub could be plotted on Floor 1 of House 21; possibly the house had been swept not long before abandonment. The dashed line indicates the abrupt southern limit of the best preserved sand floor surface. Guadalupe phase.

Shell
   Ornament
      Subrectangular pendant, pearl oyster, with two holes drilled
        at the upper end; 20 × 10 × 2 mm (Fig. 21.1*d*).
   Pacific Marine Bivalves
      Fragment of conch or spiny oyster, 20 × 10 × 2 mm.
   Unidentified
      Five fragments of shell, possibly manufacturing waste,
        ranging in size from 15 × 10 to 10 × 10 mm.

Animal Bones
   Large Mammals
      white-tailed deer (*Odocoileus virginianus*)
        1 L. distal femur
   Small Mammals
      pocket gopher (*Orthogeomys grandis*)
        1 R. upper incisor
      eastern cottontail (*Sylvilagus floridanus*)
        1 L. distal tibia
   Unidentified
      8 splinters, mostly mammal

The History of House 21: Insights from Artifact Plotting

The surviving remnant of House 21 was so small that we cannot even be sure which quadrant of the house we recovered. The items left on Floor 3 suggest that the original occupants had a chipped stone tool assemblage like that of many San José phase families: scrapers, flake gravers, denticulate flakes, and utilized flakes of chert and obsidian. They sewed with bone needles, worked some shell, but showed no evidence of biface working (Fig. 21.2).

After the laying down of Floor 2, the occupants of the house continued to work marine shell and mica with small flake gravers (Fig. 21.3). Floor 1, belonging to the final stage of occupation, was unfortunately the least informative, perhaps because it had been swept not long before abandonment. A patch of ash in Square N5E4 might have spilled from one of the culinary charcoal braziers popular during the Guadalupe phase (Fig. 21.4).

V

Chapter 22

A San José Phase House on Mound 1

Mound 1 of San José Mogote, the tallest and most pyramidal of all the mounds at the site, is actually a natural hill whose circumference and height were increased by prehistoric construction (Fig. 22.1). We estimate the original hill to have been at least 70 m in diameter and 12 m high. When we began to excavate, we found more than 3 m of cultural overburden on parts of the hilltop. Since that overburden had been reduced by building collapse and erosion, the height of Mound 1 in ancient times would have been even more impressive.

Early Formative Use of the Mound

We found no evidence that the hilltop had been used during Espiridión or Tierras Largas times. Its first two buildings dated to the San José phase. One of those buildings was House 13, an ordinary wattle-and-daub residence, built directly on sterile soil near the top of the hill (see below). The other building was evidently more elaborate, but is known only from its eroded floor and fallen pieces of its walls. All signs indicate that the structure was a small, lime-plastered public building like Structure 7 in Area C (Flannery and Marcus 1994:357-62). It is likely that it was a Men's House built on the summit of the hill by the occupants of Area A, which lay along the east side of Mound 1. If that is the case, it suggests that the Area C and Area A residential wards maintained separate Men's Houses—not unexpected behavior for a society with multiple descent groups.

Below the level of the fallen lime-plastered daub (and presumably below the building's floor, although the latter was badly eroded) we found an unusual ritual offering: the skull of an immature spider monkey (*Ateles geoffreyoi*), coated with red ochre and bearing traces of the building's lime plaster (Marcus 1998a: Fig. 8.37). In the debris near the collapsed building we

found San José phase sherds; a lump of unworked iron ore; a fragment of a weakly magnetic iron ore mirror; pieces of pearl oyster, *Spondylus* shell, and conch; probable fish-spine bloodletting tools; and other items typical of the San José phase household debris in Area A.

The place chosen for the lime-plastered building lies near the center of the hilltop, and may in fact have been its original high point. From the San José phase onward, until late in the Rosario phase, that spot remained the scene of ritual activity. Continuing construction there resulted in seven superimposed layers of wall stubs and earthen fill. The earliest layer—the one containing the collapsed lime-plastered San José phase building, with its spider monkey offering—has been designated stratigraphic Zone F.

House 13

As mentioned above, House 13 was built on sterile soil. It lay on the eastern summit of Mound 1, only 60 m west of our excavations in Area A. Only its southern half could be excavated, since its northern half was covered by the foundations of Structure 14, a stone masonry public building whose earliest construction stage dated to the Rosario phase (Fig. 22.2). House 13 fell within the same grid of 2 × 2 m squares we used for Structure 14. To excavate House 13, however, we divided the squares into the 1 × 1 m quadrants more appropriate for investigating a house (Fig. 22.3).

House 13 would have been roughly 3 × 5 m in area, with its doorway on the west (Fig. 22.4). This doorway, presumed to be in the middle of one of the long sides, was framed with stones. We also recovered nine postmolds that had penetrated the sterile soil of Mound 1.

Figure 22.1. Aerial oblique photo of Mound 1 at San José Mogote, showing the location of House 13 relative to Structures 14, 19, 21, and 22. Areas A (to the east) and C (to the west) are also visible. (Photograph courtesy of Tonny Zwollo.)

In contrast to House 2 of Area C (see Chapter 9), at least five of House 13's postmolds (nos. 2, 3, 4, 6, and 9) were found along the outer margins of the floor, suggesting that many posts in the wattle-and-daub walls were weight-bearing. A few postmolds (nos. 5, 7, and 8) occurred farther inside the house; we do not know whether they were from substitute posts added when the originals deteriorated, or from posts providing extra support for the south end of the roof. All postmolds were relatively small

(15-16 cm in diameter) and one (no. 2) contained a stone wedge, presumably added when the post became loose. One post (no. 1) helped frame the doorway.

To the south of House 13, our excavation exposed a small area of dooryard associated with the residence. At least part of the dooryard contained a household midden with abundant chunks of burnt daub. House 13, therefore, resembled several of the Area C residences in having its midden to the south of the house

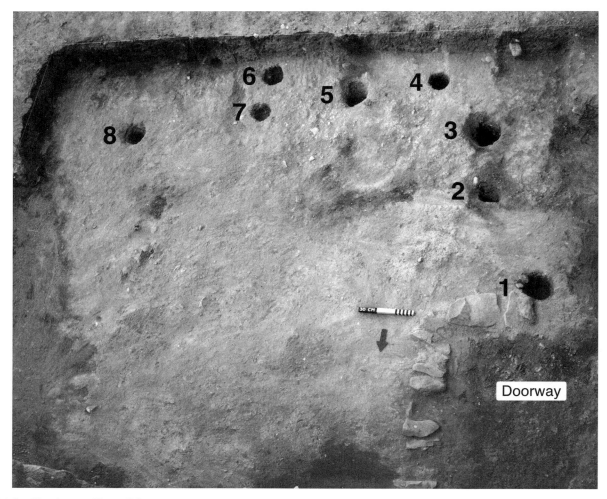

Figure 22.2. Looking down on House 13 from a vantage point atop the south wall of Structure 14. In this view, north is at the bottom of the photo, as the black arrow indicates; the painted scale is 30 cm long. Excavated postmolds have been numbered. (At this stage of the excavation, Postmold 9 had not yet been discovered.)

itself, perhaps because of the prevailing wind. Whether the daub was from House 13 or some other building is not clear; none of House 13's posts appeared to have been burned.

Because of its location, we will describe House 13 in the context of other residences on Mound 1. It should be said, however, that a case could be made for considering this house part of Area A. The occupants of House 13 seem to have been producers of *Spondylus* and freshwater mussel ornaments, and consumers of pearl oyster ornaments. There were six fragments of iron ore in and around the house. Similar raw materials and manufacturing waste characterized Household Units C4-C1 in Area A. It is significant that Reynolds' multidimensional scaling (Chapter 25) groups House 13 with the Area A residences.

The craft item in highest frequency in House 13 was mica, numerous small fragments of which were piece-plotted. These fragments appeared to be debris from the cutting of mica sheets, perhaps to make inlays for decorating costumes or masks.

Unresolved in our minds is the question of whether House 13 represented a residence in its own right, or was one of the outbuildings of a multistructure residence. Assuming that it was a household in its own right, its construction and floor debris suggest that it was the home of a family of modest status (Flannery and Marcus 1994:329-32). House 13 was not well made. Its daub was roughly the same buff color as Tierras Largas Burnished Plain, having been given an outer coating of slightly finer clay but no whitewash. Daub fragments reveal that its corners were slightly rounded rather than nicely squared, another trait seen in the houses of lower-ranked families. House 13 yielded less deer bone than the usual whitewashed house with well-made square corners. A small bone needle for sewing was found, but there was no evidence of the longer basketry needles found in more elaborate residences like House 16/17 of Area B. There was also no jadeite lying directly on the floor, although a small fragment was found not far above the floor (see below).

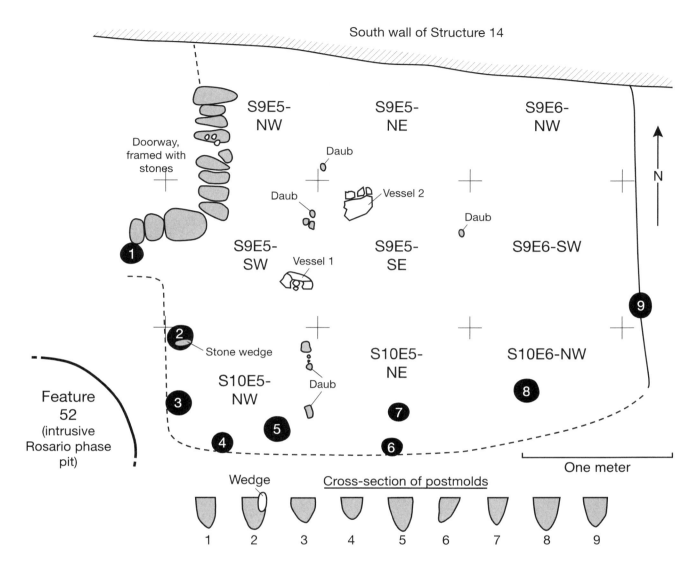

Figure 22.3. Plan of House 13, showing major landmarks, postmolds and their cross-sections, and the designations of the 1 × 1 m quadrants of each 2 × 2 m square. In this plan, north is at the top.

We should make clear that we found no evidence to indicate that House 13 was part of a multistructure residence. We raise that possibility only because it seems to us, intuitively, that the summit of Mound 1, with its apparent San José phase public building, should have been the venue for a more impressive residence than House 13. To be sure, there might have been such a residence nearby. Unfortunately, the area around House 13 was so disturbed by Rosario phase constructions that we had no opportunity to search for additional San José phase houses.

The House 13 Floor

Radiocarbon Date[1]

No radiocarbon date is available for House 13. A San José phase AMS date is available from an ash layer found not far to the west, but that ash is believed to antedate House 13. The ash layer covered the sterile soil one meter below Monument 3, a carved stone used as the threshold for a corridor between two public buildings (Flannery and Marcus 2003: Fig. 4).

The ash layer (which was discovered while excavating below Monument 3 in order to establish its stratigraphic context) was associated with Early San José phase sherds, while House 13 is considered Late San José phase (see below). Small bits of charcoal from the ash gave a date of 2960 ± 40 B.P., or roughly 1010 b.c. (Beta-176907). The calibrated two-sigma range would be 1300-1030 B.C. Our expected date for House 13, on the other hand, would be closer to 900-850 b.c.

---

[1]In this volume, uncalibrated dates are given as "b.c.," and dendrocalibrated dates as "B.C." (see Chapter 26, Radiocarbon Dating).

Figure 22.4. Artist's reconstruction of House 13, as it might have looked from the west during occupation.

Daub

Scattered chunks of daub were found on the floor, and the midden in the dooryard yielded more fragments. As mentioned earlier, the daub was not whitewashed.

Ceramics

Some 353 sherds were associated with House 13. That total includes both the sherds from the house floor, and the much smaller number that came from the dooryard to the south. The collection has been described by Flannery and Marcus (1994:331-32).

The pottery from House 13 reinforces our impression that the family occupying this house was of only modest rank, since the ceramics were less elaborately decorated than collections from the houses of more highly ranked families. The variety of double-line-break motifs on Atoyac Yellow-white bowls was limited, consisting mainly of Plog's Motifs 23 and 54 (Flannery and Marcus 1994: Figs. 12.19-12.20). Designs on Leandro Gray vessels were also limited, with only one case of Pyne's Motif 1 (Lightning) and two cases of her Motif 16. The presence of the Lightning motif, however, strengthens our suspicion that House

13 was related to Area A, whose pottery also featured Sky or Lightning motifs.

Several vessel forms suggest a relatively late San José phase date for House 13. Included were a Leandro Gray bowl with a slightly everted rim; an Atoyac Yellow-white bowl with an everted rim; a Lupita Heavy Plain brazier with a basketry-impressed (rather than mat-impressed) floor; and a restorable Atoyac Yellow-white composite silhouette bowl with exterior incising (designated Vessel 3). All those attributes went on to become more common in the subsequent Guadalupe phase.

Vessel 3 was actually found in the midden area of the dooryard. Plotted on the floor of the house were fragments of restorable Vessel 1 (a Leandro Gray outleaned-wall bowl) and restorable Vessel 2 (an Atoyac Yellow-white effigy vessel of some kind; Fig. 22.3).

In addition, the presence of Delia White and Coatepec White-rimmed Black sherds in House 13 strengthens our impression that the house dated to late in the San José phase. The scarcity of San José Red-on-White leads us to the same conclusion.

While House 13 had most of the pottery types seen in San José phase times, it yielded only a few sherds of such luxury wares as Delfina Fine Gray, Xochiltepec White, and Delia White. This scarcity would be in keeping with a family of modest status. We did find one sherd of an imported ware, but it could not be securely identified.

Chipped Stone
 Chert (87%)
  nodule: 1
  hammerstone: 1
  flake cores: 16
  core, secondarily utilized: 1
  core tool: 1
  scraper/spokeshave: 1 (Fig. 22.5*a*)
  flake perforators /gravers: 18 (Fig. 22.5*b-f*)
  flake perforators/drills: 4
  burins?: 4
  denticulate scraper: 1 (Fig. 22.5*g*)
  denticulate flake: 1
  wedge: 1
  backed flake, utilized: 1
  retouched flakes: 2
  utilized flakes: 23
  flakes, not utilized: 143
 Obsidian (12%)
  prismatic blade fragments, utilized: 6
  prismatic blade fragment, no sign of use: 1
  truncated prismatic blade, utilized: 1
  wedge: 1
  utilized flakes: 2
  flakes, not utilized: 18 (includes bipolar flake from blade, Fig. 22.5*h*)
  microflake: 1
 Other (1%)
  quartz fragments: 3

Ground Stone
 Planoconvex one-hand mano of crystalline metamorphic rock, broken; one end may have been used as a pounder (Fig. 22.5*i*). Length, 5.5+ cm (broken); width, 7 cm; thickness, 4 cm.
 One-hand mano with oval cross-section, made on a small ignimbrite cobble, broken (Fig. 22.5*j*). Original length, possibly 7 cm (surviving fragment 4 cm long); width, 5 cm; thickness, 4 cm.
 Small fragment of mano, 3 × 2.3 × 0.5 cm.
 Spall from an unidentified ground stone tool.
 Oval rubbing stone made of sandstone, 6 × 5 × 4 cm (Fig. 22.5*k*).

Raw Material
 Fragment of Fábrica San José travertine, a common raw material for *canicas* or pecked and ground stone balls, 30 × 30 × 6 mm.

Bone Tool
 Distal end of a needle made from a deer(?) bone splinter. The surviving fragment is 19 mm long and 3 mm in diameter (Fig. 22.6*a*).

Worked Sherds
 Broken sherd disk, chipped and ground from a Fidencio Coarse jar body sherd; originally 9 cm in diameter and 1.2 cm thick.
 Worked Fidencio Coarse jar body sherd, 7 cm in diameter and 0.7 cm thick. A hole 6 mm in diameter was begun in the center, but never finished; the intent was to produce a hole by biconical drilling.

Shell
 It appeared from the refuse in House 13 that its occupants were producers of artifacts from *Spondylus* shell and pearly freshwater mussel, since manufacturing waste from those mollusks was present. On the other hand, only one possible ornament of pearl oyster was found, and there was no manufacturing waste from that species. No gastropods were found in House 13.
 Ornaments
  Fragment of pearl oyster(?) ornament, 10 × 7 mm; 2 mm thick.
 Pearly Freshwater Mussels
  Fragment from the margin of a freshwater mussel, worked, possibly *Barynaias* (Fig. 22.6 *b*); 31 × 5 × 1 mm.
  Three pieces of freshwater mussel, each about 5 × 5 mm; manufacturing waste.
  Piece of freshwater mussel, 8 × 8 × 1 mm.
  Fragment of freshwater mussel, possibly *Barynaias*; 11 × 9 × 1 mm.
 Pacific Marine Bivalves
  Two fragments of *Spondylus* shell, possibly debris from shellworking; one is 18 × 11 × 5 mm, the other 22 × 7 × 5 mm.
 Pacific Marine Univalves
  None.
 Unidentified
  Two fragments of shell, one 5 × 7 × 1 mm, the other 5 × 5 × 1 mm.

Iron Ore Specimens
 Unworked lump of magnetite weighing 5.8 g; 25 × 10 × 5 mm.
 Unworked lump of ilmeno-magnetite weighing 3.6 g; 24 × 10 × 5 mm.

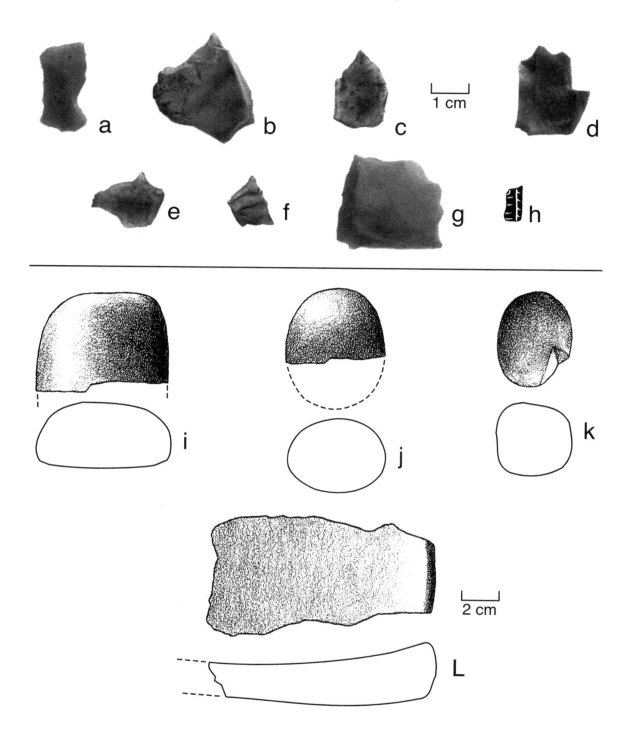

Figure 22.5. Stone tools from House 13 or its dooryard. *a-g* are of chert or chalcedony. *a*, scraper/spokeshave. *b-f*, perforators/gravers. *g*, denticulate scraper. *h*, bipolar flake from obsidian blade. *i*, planoconvex one-hand mano. *j*, oval one-hand mano. *k*, rubbing stone. *L*, fragment of saddle-shaped metate. (*a-k* are from the house floor; *L* is from the dooryard.)

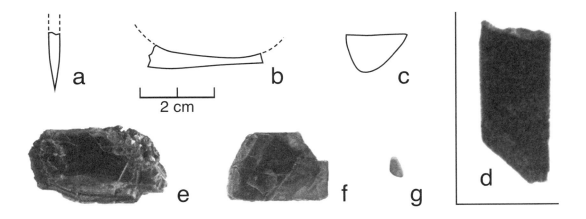

Figure 22.6. Items found in House 13, or in its dooryard, or just above its floor debris. *a*, distal end of bone needle. *b*, fragment from margin of freshwater mussel. *c*, fragment from broken pearl oyster(?) ornament. *d*, fragment of magnetite mirror; maximum length, 14 mm (shown larger than actual size). *e*, chunk of brown mica. *f*, piece of brown mica, cut on four edges. *g*, small fragment of jadeite(?) ornament. *a* and *b* were found on the house floor; *c* was found in the dooryard; *d-g* were found just above the floor debris, and therefore not conclusively associated with House 13.

Unworked lump of ilmeno-magnetite weighing 2.4 g; 12 × 10 × 5 mm.

Unworked lump of magnetite weighing 1.5 g; 25 × 8 × 4 mm.

Unworked lump of magnetite weighing 1.3 g; 18 × 8 × 4 mm.

Unworked lump of magnetite weighing 0.2 g; 15 × 8 × 2 mm.

Just above the floor debris of House 13, and not conclusively associated with it, we found a fragment of magnetite mirror weighing 0.9 g (Fig. 22.6*d*); 14 × 6 × 3 mm. This fragment reminds us of the magnetite ornament found with Burial 24-1 at Tomaltepec (Whalen 1981: Plate 25). Burial 24-1 was a young woman, buried in the same grave as Burial 24-2, an adult male who is presumed to be her husband.

Mica

Fragment of white mica, 4 × 4 × 1 mm.

Three fragments of brown mica: (1) 13 × 10 × 1 mm; (2) 10 × 5 × 1 mm; (3) 18 × 14 × 1 mm.

Fragment of brown mica cut on one edge, 20 × 16 × 1 mm.

Fragment of gold mica cut on two edges, 25 × 8 × 1 mm.

Fragment of gold mica cut on two edges, 10 × 6 × 1 mm.

Two fragments of gold mica, one 9 × 6 × 1 mm, the other 10 × 5 × 1 mm.

Shattered flakes of light gold mica from a piece originally 15 × 8 × 1 mm.

Fragment of gold mica cut on at least two edges, 20 × 12 × 1 mm.

Shattered flakes of gold mica from a piece originally 10 × 7 × 1 mm.

Fragment of brown mica cut on two edges, 10 × 10 × 1 mm.

Just above the floor debris of House 13, and not conclusively associated with it, we found two pieces of brown mica totaling 8.4 g: (1) a chunk, 35 × 20 × 5 mm; and (2) a piece cut on four edges, 27 × 18 × 1 mm (Fig. 22.6*e, f*).

Figurines

Some 14 figurine fragments were associated with House 13. They have been described by Marcus (1998a:160-61 and Fig. 12.23). While 13 were fragments of small solid figurines, one was a piece of arm from a large hollow doll, obviously locally made because it was slipped with Atoyac Yellow-white engobe (Fig. 22.7).

Stone Ornament

Just above the floor debris of House 13, and not conclusively associated with it, we found a 0.3 g fragment from a broken polished jadeite(?) ornament, 6 × 4 × 2 mm (Fig. 22.6*g*).

Animal Bones

Large Mammals
white-tailed deer (*Odocoileus virginianus*)
a few possible limb bone splinters
Small Mammals
domestic dog (*Canis familiaris*)
2 chips from adult teeth
1 deciduous incisor from a puppy
1 metapodial

eastern cottontail (*Sylvilagus floridanus*)
    1 R. and 1 L. premaxilla
    1 unfused proximal L. tibia
    1 metatarsal
Mexican cottontail (*Sylvilagus cunicularius*)
    1 complete L. mandible
    1 R. radius
    1 distal L. tibia, burned
unidentified small mammals
    1 calcaneum
    3 other fragments
Birds
    1 ulna fragment (unidentified)
    1 third phalanx (unidentified)
Human
    2 skull fragments from a child
    1 rib

The House 13 Dooryard

Owing to disturbance caused by public construction during the Rosario phase, only a small part of the dooryard remained intact.

Chipped Stone
Chert (95%)
    flake cores: 3
    flake perforators/gravers: 3
    steep sidescraper: 1
    utilized flake: 1
    flakes, not utilized: 10
Obsidian (0%)
    none
Other (5%)
    quartz core: 1

Ground Stone
Fragment of saddle-shaped metate, made of conglomerate (Fig. 22.5*L*). The surviving piece is 12 × 6 cm and averages 2.7 cm thick.

Shell
Fragment of broken pearl oyster(?) ornament (Fig. 22.6*c*), 10 × 10 × 2 mm.

Mica
Shattered piece of white mica, originally 15 × 15 × 1 mm.

Figurines
Five fragments of small solid figurines were found outside the immediate floor area of House 13; three of these were in the dooryard just south of the house. They have been described by Marcus (1998a:160-61).

Animal Bone
Small Mammals
    Mexican cottontail (*Sylvilagus cunicularius*)
        1 R. tibia
Reptiles
    1 vertebra from an unidentified lizard

Insights from Artifact Plotting

Figures 22.8-22.10 present the distributions of chert cores and utilized flakes, obsidian blades, ground stone, iron ore, chert perforators, gravers and drills, and items of shell and mica found in or near House 13. For the most part, what the distributions suggest is a tendency for discarded items to end up (1) outside the door or (2) in the southeast quadrant of the house.

Cores and utilized flakes exemplify this pattern (Fig. 22.8). Five flake cores were found in the doorway or just to the south of it. Ten of the remaining eleven cores were found in the southeast corner of the house or just outside it. The distribution of utilized flakes was similar. Seven were found in the doorway, and eleven of the remaining sixteen lay near the south or east walls of the house. Perhaps the sweeping of the house had begun at the center, and gradually moved the debris toward the corners.

Ground stone tool fragments also tended to be concentrated in the southeast corner of the house (Fig. 22.9, *top*). By the time they were discarded, most were too small to serve as anything but expedient pounders. As for small items such as obsidian blades and iron ore lumps (Fig. 22.9, *bottom*), it appears that most ended up outside the floor area.

The categories of items most widely scattered over the house floor were those associated with shell and mica working (Fig. 22.10). It is possible that one or more episodes of shell working took place after the house had been swept for the last time.

One group of ten or eleven perforators/gravers encircled a spot near the center of Square S9E5. Another group of drills, perforators, and possible burins encircled postmold no. 8. These areas could be "drop zones" that were simply not swept before House 13 was abandoned. We cannot tell whether they represent the work spaces of two individuals, or two episodes of craft activity by the same individual. Pearly freshwater mussel and *Spondylus* shell would seem to have been the main raw materials worked, although we also found six scatters of mica near the south wall of the house (or just beyond it). The high frequency of perforators/gravers, drills, and burins was, as mentioned earlier, reminiscent of Household Units C4-C1 in nearby Area A.

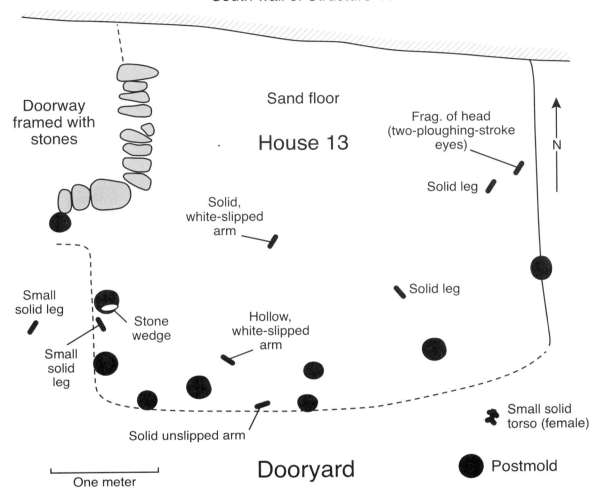

South wall of Structure 14

Doorway framed with stones

Sand floor

House 13

Frag. of head (two-ploughing-stroke eyes)

Solid leg

Solid, white-slipped arm

N

Solid leg

Small solid leg

Stone wedge

Small solid leg

Hollow, white-slipped arm

Small solid torso (female)

Solid unslipped arm

Postmold

One meter

Dooryard

Figure 22.7. Nine figurine fragments plotted in and around House 13.

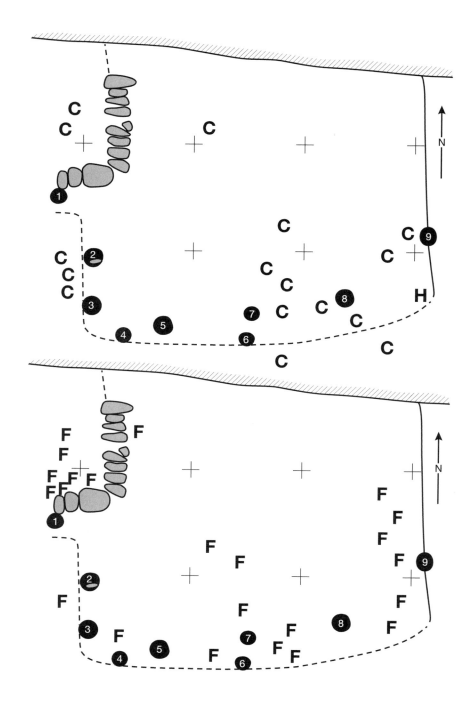

Figure 22.8. Distribution of chert hammerstones (H), flake cores (C), and utilized flakes (F) in and around House 13.

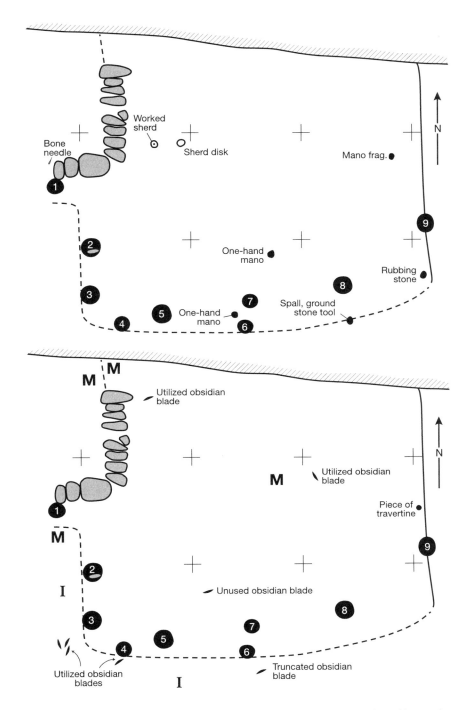

Figure 22.9. Plans of House 13, showing the distribution of ground stone, obsidian blades, needles, worked sherds, and lumps of magnetite (M) or ilmeno-magnetite (I).

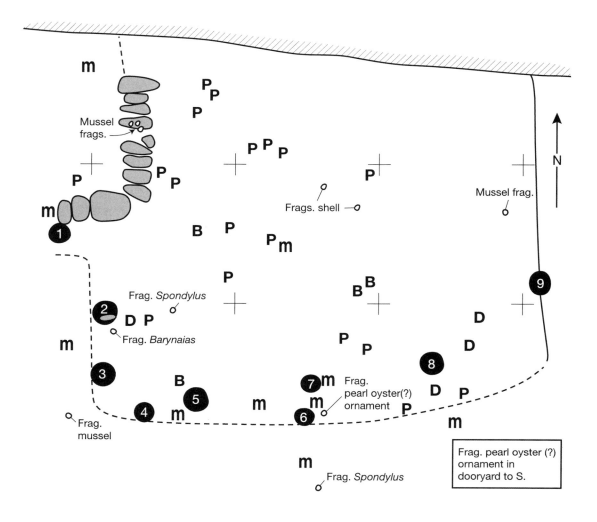

Figure 22.10. The distribution of items possibly associated with shell and mica working in and around House 13: P = flake perforator/graver, D = flake perforator/drill, B = possible burin, m = mica. Shell fragments are individually labeled.

Chapter 23

Rosario Phase Residences on Mound 1

In Chapter 22 we mentioned stratigraphic Zone F atop Mound 1, which included a collapsed Men's House of the San José phase. During the Middle Formative Guadalupe and Rosario phases, a number of intrusive burials and offerings were placed in the fill of Zone F. Many of these burials were secondary interments, incomplete skeletons moved to the summit of Mound 1 after a period of burial elsewhere. Such burials might belong to individuals from highly ranked families of the Guadalupe and Rosario phases, whose relatives chose to have them reburied atop Mound 1.

Eventually, community leaders of the Rosario phase decided to build a drylaid stone masonry building above Zone F. This building, designated Structure 19B, was the first construction stage of what was to become a larger platform for public buildings (Fig. 23.1). In stratigraphic terms, the layer of earthen fill enclosed by the masonry walls of Structure 19B has been designated Zone E. The sherds in the Zone E fill date Structure 19B to the Rosario phase.

A Brief History of Structure 19

Structure 19, the stone masonry platform for which Structure 19B was only the first stage, had a very long and complex history. It will be discussed in detail in a later volume, *Excavations at San José Mogote 2: The Cognitive Archaeology*. In this chapter we give only a brief summary of the structure's building phases, in order to set the stage for the Rosario phase residences above it.

1. Structure 19B, built relatively early in the Rosario phase, was a masonry platform 17 m on a side and oriented 8° north of east. Its fill, as mentioned earlier, constituted stratigraphic Zone E.

2. Atop Structure 19B the Rosario community placed Structure 28, an adobe building 1.5 m high and measuring 14.2 by 13.4 m. It supported a massive wattle-and-daub temple whose floor was recessed into the surface of Structure 28. Structure 28 and its thick layer of earthen fill were assigned to stratigraphic Zone D.

3. When the walls of the Structure 19B platform began to buckle outward under the weight of Structure 28, the builders surrounded it with a still larger stone masonry platform, whose outer walls were buttressed with massive, sloping piles of stones (Flannery and Marcus 1990: Fig. 2.12). This larger construction, measuring 25.5 by 20.0 m, has been designated Structure 19A. It was oriented true east-west, a change in orientation from Structure 19B.

4. Finally, later in the Rosario phase, the stone masonry platform was enlarged for the final time, coming to measure 28.5 by 21.7 m. This stage—the first one we discovered, and hence the first numbered—has been designated Structure 19. Charcoal from the fill of this final enlargement of the platform has been dated to 2560 ± 180 B.P., or 610 b.c. (Beta-179876).[1] The calibrated two-sigma range for this date would be 1110-350 B.C.

5. Late in its history, the Structure 28 temple was deliberately burned in a fire so intense that the sand in its adobe walls and puddled adobe floor was converted to masses of vitrified cinders (Marcus and Flannery 1996: Fig. 135). Charcoal from a fallen roof beam dates this conflagration to 2550 ± 60 B.P., or 600 b.c. (Beta-177624). The calibrated two-sigma range for this date would be 820-500 B.C. The temple was never rebuilt after this

---

[1]In this volume, uncalibrated dates are given as "b.c.," and dendrocalibrated dates as "B.C." (see Chapter 26, Radiocarbon Dating).

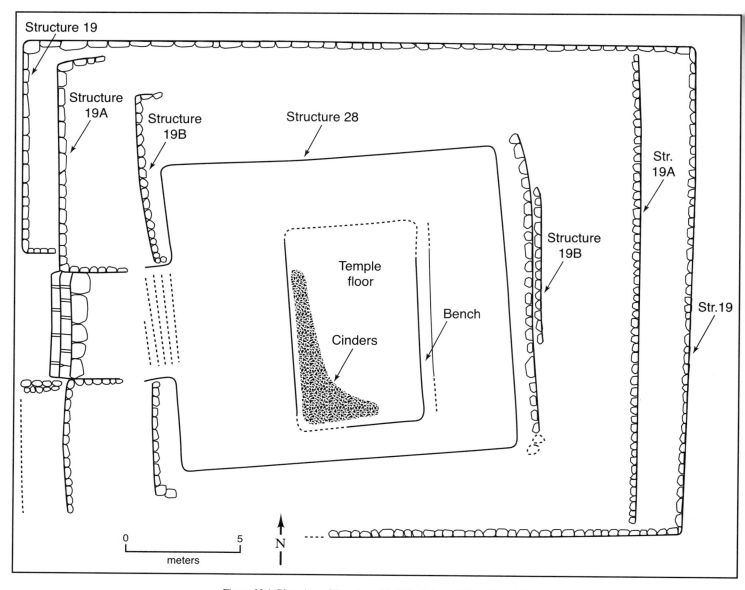

Figure 23.1. Plan view of Structures 28, 19B, 19A, and 19 on Mound 1.

destruction, which was presumably the outcome of a raid by a rival village. Instead, the focus of Rosario ritual activity shifted to Structure 37, a new temple built not far to the north (Flannery and Marcus 2003:11802).

6. Once Structure 37 had become the main Rosario phase temple, the function of the Structure 28/Structure 19 locality changed from ritual to residential. The ruins of the burned temple were covered with basketloads of earth, until the area was level enough to build on. In spite of this leveling, the mound of overburden above Structure 19 was now so steep that it needed a retaining wall on its eastern side to keep it from eroding. Its western side did not have as steep a dropoff, since the old Structure 19 stairway had been left uncovered to provide access to the summit.

7. Once the area had been leveled and the retaining wall established, two new buildings were erected. One was a unique circular platform, Structure 31 (Marcus and Flannery 1996: Fig. 138), which will be discussed in a future volume. The second building was an adobe residence, Structure 27. The stratum containing Structures 27 and 31 was designated stratigraphic Zone C.

8. What follows is a description of Structure 27. Square designations refer to the grid of 2 × 2 m squares established above Structure 19 (Fig. 23.2), which were used for all stratigraphic levels from the surface (Zone A) down to Zone F (Fig. 23.3). Depths refer to a datum established on the highest point of the mound of overburden. (There was a geodesic benchmark there when we arrived.)

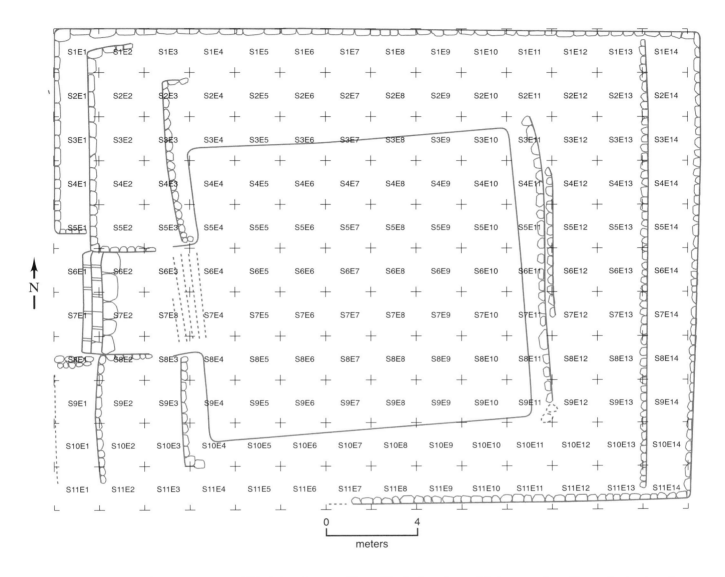

Figure 23.2. The grid of 2 × 2 m squares established above Structure 19, providing horizontal control during excavation of the overburden above it.

Structure 27, Zone C

At its thickest, Zone C extended from 1.4 m to 1.7 m below datum. The matrix of Zone C was buff to yellowish-buff earth, a product of the postoccupational breakdown of its adobe walls. Running along the eastern limits of Zone C was the retaining wall mentioned above. This retaining wall, which protected Structure 27 from erosion up until its abandonment, was best preserved in Squares S6E10-S8E11 (Fig. 23.4).

Owing to postoccupational collapse and leveling, only the south side of Structure 27 could be mapped. This building remnant occupied Squares S9E6-S9E9. The remains consisted of the adobe foundations of an outer wall, plus the stub of a north-south internal wall which created the two spaces we called Room 1 and Room 2 (Fig. 23.5). Room 1 (on the west) was 2.6 m wide. Room 2 (on the east) was 3 m wide. Patches of hard, burnished clay floor were associated with each room; we recorded the sherds, chipped stone, shell, and other artifacts lying on these floor surfaces.

Unfortunately, too little of Structure 27 was preserved to allow us to suggest a function for each room. The artifact sample from the floor suggested that the building was a residence rather than a public building. Given its lofty position above Structure 28, we suspect that this might once have been the residence of an important family.

Figure 23.3. Work beginning on the first 2 × 2 m squares laid out on the mound of overburden above Structure 19. The crew is exposing stratigraphic Zone A, which will be discussed in a later volume. (View from the north-northeast.)

Room 1

Ceramics

The ceramics we list below represent the total screened sample from the floor of Room 1. They clearly date Structure 27 to the Rosario phase. We do not, however, consider this collection a "pure" sample of the ceramics used in a Rosario phase household. It contains too many small, redeposited sherds from earlier time periods to constitute such a sample. This is a familiar problem at multicomponent sites with long chronological sequences. The digging of pits for burials and features (or even to obtain clay for adobe making) inevitably brings older sherds to the surface, where they become mixed with those of the household.

Data from nearby sites like Fábrica San José (Drennan 1976a) do not suggest that earlier pottery types such as Matadamas Orange, Avelina Red-on-Buff, or Tierras Largas Burnished Plain survived into the Rosario phase (see Appendix A). The following collection of ceramics, therefore, should be seen as including not only Rosario phase types like Socorro Fine Gray, Josefina Fine Gray, Guadalupe Burnished Brown, and Fidencio Coarse, but also small redeposited sherds of the Guadalupe, San José, and Tierras Largas phases.

In this and all subsequent lists of Rosario phase ceramics, we follow Drennan (1976a:21-45) with regard to pottery types,

vessel shapes, and attributes of Socorro Fine Gray bowls such as rim forms, rim eccentricities, and decoration.

Socorro Fine Gray
    bowls with outleaned/outcurved walls, rims: 17
    bowls with outleaned/outcurved walls, bases: 4
    composite silhouette bowls, plain: 3
    composite silhouette bowls with negative painting: 3
    composite silhouette bowl with zoned toning: 1
    composite silhouette bowl, incised, with negative painting: 2
    oval bowl with pinched-in sides: 3
    globular jar, rim: 1
    undecorated body sherds: 31
Josefina Fine Gray
    outleaned-wall bowl, rim: 1
    incurved rim bowl, rim: 1
    composite silhouette bowl, plain: 1
    composite silhouette bowl, incised: 1
    tecomate rims: 2
    undecorated body sherds: 8
Guadalupe Burnished Brown
    large outleaned-wall bowls, rims: 12
    large outleaned-wall bowls, bases: 4
    undecorated body sherds: 36

Figure 23.4. This retaining wall of adobes (reinforced with stones) protected the eastern limits of Zone C from erosion.

Fidencio Coarse
    jar rims: 9
    undecorated body sherds: 140
Lupita Heavy Plain
    bowls with outleaned walls, rims: 28
    bowls with outleaned walls, bases: 2
    undecorated Suchilquitongo tripod dish, foot: 1
    undecorated Suchilquitongo tripod dish, rim: 1
    tecomate rims: 2
    rims too small to diagnose: 3
    undecorated body sherds: 118
Atoyac Yellow-white
    outleaned-wall bowls, plain rims: 11
    outleaned-wall bowl, double-line-break incised: 1
    outleaned-wall bowl, plain beveled rim: 1
    cylinders, plain rims: 2
    cylinders, incised rims: 2
    undecorated body sherds: 48
Leandro Gray
    cylinder rims, plain: 4
    outleaned-wall bowls, plain rims: 4

jar with vertical neck: 1
    rims, too small to diagnose: 6
    undecorated body sherds: 58
Delfina Fine Gray
    cylinder rim, incised: 1
    cylinder bases, plain: 2
Delia White
    beakers: 4
    undecorated body sherds: 2
Xochiltepec White
    outleaned-wall bowl: 1
Matadamas Orange
    jar rim: 1
    hemispherical bowls, rims: 3
    tecomate: 1
    undecorated body sherd: 1
Avelina Red-on-Buff
    hemispherical bowl rims: 3
Tierras Largas Burnished Plain
    jar rim: 1
    outleaned-wall bowls, rims: 2
    tecomate rim: 1
    undecorated body sherds: 43
San José Black-and-White
    cylinder rim, incised: 1
    jar with vertical neck: 1
San José Red-on-White
    outleaned-wall bowls, rims: 2
Unclassifiable
    rim sherd: 1
    body sherds: 50

Attributes of Socorro Fine Gray Outleaned/Outcurved-Wall Bowls
    Rim Form 1, no eccentricity, no decoration: 5
    Rim Form 2, no eccentricity, no decoration: 7
    Rim Form 3, no eccentricity, no decoration: 1
    Rim Form 4, Eccentricity 3, no decoration: 1
    Rim Form 5, no eccentricity, no decoration: 1
    Rim Form 7, horizontal band of zoned toning: 1
    Rim Form 8, no eccentricity, no decoration: 1

Chipped Stone
    Chert (61%)
        flake cores: 4
        flake perforator: 1
        flake spokeshave: 1
        utilized flakes: 5
        flakes, not utilized: 55
    Obsidian (7%)
        prismatic blade fragment, utilized: 1
        prismatic blade fragment, no sign of use: 1
        flakes, not utilized: 6

Figure 23.5. Two views of Structure 27. *Above*, view from the northeast, with Tomás Cruz serving as scale. *Below*, view from the southeast. Note that Zone C has been excavated all the way to the edge of the mound of overburden.

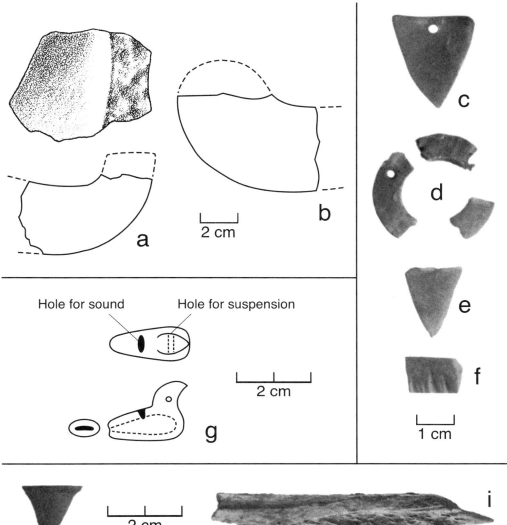

Hole for sound   Hole for suspension

Figure 23.6. Objects recovered from Structure 27 or its dooryard. *a, b*, fragments of lipped metates, Room 1. *c*, triangular pendant of pearl oyster(?), Room 1. *d*, fragments from (perhaps two) ring-shaped pendants of pearl oyster(?), Room 1. *e*, triangular piece of pearl oyster waste, Room 1. *f*, fragment of waste from *Spondylus* shell, Room 1. *g*, bird effigy whistle, Room 1. *h*, fragment of burnished pottery earspool, Room 2. *i*, perforator made from a long bone splinter, dooryard; the point is at the right end in the photograph. Rosario phase.

Other (31%)
 quartz cores: 3
 quartz flakes: 31
 Comment: The high number of quartz flakes is a puzzling feature of this house. Quartz is a poor raw material, and this house clearly had access to higher quality Matadamas chalcedony.

Ground Stone
 Small fragment of lipped metate, ignimbrite; thickness 3.8 cm (Fig. 23.6*a*).
 Small fragment of lipped metate, ignimbrite; thickness 4.8 cm (Fig. 23.6*b*).

Shell
Ornaments
 Triangular pendant of pearl oyster(?), perforated at one end. The ornament is 25 × 20 mm, and 1.5 mm thick; the perforation is 3 mm in diameter (Fig. 23.6*c*).
 Four fragments from (perhaps two) different ring-shaped pearl oyster(?) pendants, each of which would have been about 30 mm in diameter when complete. One ring would have been about 6 mm wide, the other about 7 mm wide. One surviving perforation for suspension is 2 mm in diameter (Fig. 23.6*d*).
Pacific Marine Bivalves
 Triangular piece of pearl oyster (*Pinctada mazatlanica*), apparently manufacturing waste trimmed off during ornament production; 20 × 10 × 1 mm (Fig. 23.6*e*).

Fragment from the orange-colored margin of a large *Spondylus* shell, apparently manufacturing waste trimmed off during ornament production; 15 × 10 × 2 mm (Fig. 23.6*f*).

Comment: No pearly freshwater mussels or Pacific marine gastropods were found in or near Structure 27.

Ceramic Whistle

A small whistle in the shape of a bird, apparently made from Socorro Fine Gray pottery, was found in Room 1. The instrument is 20 mm long and 16 mm high, and produces the shrill sound of a referee's whistle. It is perforated for suspension, presumably so that it could be worn around the owner's neck (Fig. 23.6*g*). Ethnohistoric references (e.g., Cárdenas Valencia 1639 [1937]:15-16) indicate that high-pitched whistles were frequently used by Mesoamerican societies to direct warriors in combat. Like the whistles used during loud sporting events, their shrill notes could be heard above the noise of the fray (Marcus and Flannery 1996:133-34).

Animal Bones

Human
    1 tooth
    1 phalanx
Unidentified
    15 splinters, mostly from the long bones of deer or humans

Room 2

Ceramics

The pottery from Room 2 constitutes the total screened sample from the room. Like the ceramics from Room 1, however, it contains not only Rosario phase types from the period during which Structure 27 was occupied, but also small, redeposited sherds from earlier periods.

Socorro Fine Gray
    bowls with outleaned/outcurved walls, rims: 25
    bowl with outleaned/outcurved walls, base: 1
    composite silhouette bowl with negative painting: 1
    composite silhouette bowl with zoned toning: 1
    composite silhouette bowl, incised: 1
    composite silhouette bowls, incised, with negative painting: 2
    tecomate, incised: 1
    tecomate, plain: 1
    bird effigy fragment: 1
    undecorated body sherds: 25
Josefina Fine Gray
    outleaned-wall bowls, rims: 3
    undecorated body sherds: 7
Guadalupe Burnished Brown
    large outleaned-wall bowls, rims: 4
    undecorated body sherds: 30

Fidencio Coarse
    jar rims: 4
    undecorated body sherds: 128
Lupita Heavy Plain
    bowls with outleaned walls, rims: 12
    bowl with outleaned wall, base: 1
    charcoal braziers, rims: 3
    charcoal brazier, base: 1
    undecorated body sherds: 134
Atoyac Yellow-white
    outleaned-wall bowls, plain rims: 15
    outleaned-wall bowl, double-line-break incised: 1
    outleaned-wall bowl, plain beveled rim: 1
    cylinders, plain rims: 9
    cylinder, incised rim: 1
    outleaned-wall bowl, base: 1
    cylinder bases, incised: 2
    cylinder body sherd, hachured Earth motif: 1
    bowl with bolstered rim: 1
    jar with vertical neck: 1
    outleaned-wall bowl, incised: 1
    undecorated body sherds: 63
Leandro Gray
    cylinder rims, plain: 5
    outleaned-wall bowl, plain rim: 1
    cylinder rims, incised: 2
    outleaned-wall bowl rim, double-line-break incised: 1
    outleaned-wall bowl rim, pennant incised?: 1
    outleaned-wall bowl, base: 1
    cylinder body sherds, incised Lightning motifs: 2
    rims, too small to diagnose: 2
    undecorated body sherds: 82
Delfina Fine Gray
    undecorated body sherd: 1
Delia White
    cylinders: 2
Xochiltepec White
    cylinder: 1
    undecorated body sherds: 3
Matadamas Orange
    jar rim: 1
    hemispherical bowls, rims: 3
    undecorated body sherds: 5
Avelina Red-on-Buff
    hemispherical bowls, rims: 4
    undecorated body sherds: 2
Tierras Largas Burnished Plain
    jar rim: 1
    hemispherical bowls, rims: 4
    tecomate body sherd with rocker stamping: 1
    rims, too small to diagnose: 2
    undecorated body sherds: 61
San José Black-and-White
    cylinder rim, plain: 1
    undecorated body sherds: 2

Unclassified
    rim sherds: 3
    body sherds: 64

Attributes of Socorro Fine Gray Outleaned/Outcurved Wall Bowls
    Rim Form 1, no eccentricity, no decoration: 3
    Rim Form 2, no eccentricity, no decoration: 11
    Rim Form 2, Motif h in negative painting: 2
    Rim Form 2, Motif d in fine-line incising: 1
    Rim Form 2, Motif g in wide-line incising: 1
    Rim Form 3, Motif h in negative painting: 1
    Rim Form 3, Eccentricity 3, Motif g(?) in negative painting: 1
    Rim Form 3, Motif i in wide-line incising: 1
    Rim Form 4, no eccentricity, no decoration: 1
    Rim Form 5, Eccentricity 3, Motif l in wide-line incising: 1
    Rim Form 7, Motif g in wide-line incising: 1
    Rim Form 7, Eccentricity 7, unclassified motif in fine-line incising: 1

Chipped Stone
    Chert (88%)
        flake cores: 4
        flake perforators: 9
        flake denticulate: 1
        retouched flake: 1
        utilized flakes: 5
        flakes, not utilized: 100
    Obsidian (7%)
        prismatic blade fragment, utilized: 1
        utilized flake: 1
        flakes, not utilized: 8
    Other (4%)
        quartz flakes: 6

Bone Tools
    Broken tubular bead, apparently made from the long bone of a bird. Length, 20 mm; diameter, 4 mm.

Shell
    Fragment of pearl oyster (*Pinctada mazatlanica*), apparently manufacturing waste. Area, 12 × 11 mm; 3 mm thick.

Ceramic Earspool
    A fragment of a burnished pottery earspool was found in Room 2. It appears to belong to the "napkin ring" type, which is common in Middle Formative sites elsewhere in Mesoamerica, but rare in the Valley of Oaxaca. The fragment is 15 × 15 mm in size (Fig. 23.6*h*).

Ceramic Mask
    Small fragment of a mask made from unslipped plain ware, with one perforation for a cord that could be pushed through from the outside.

Animal Bones
    Small Mammals
        domestic dog (*Canis familiaris*)
            1 R. upper cheek tooth
            1 R. second metacarpal
        eastern cottontail (*Sylvilagus floridanus*)
            1 L. frontal bone
            1 L. distal humerus
            1 R. distal tibia
        Mexican cottontail (*Sylvilagus cunicularius*)
            1 L. distal humerus
        raccoon (*Procyon lotor*)
            1 L. distal humerus
        unidentified small rodent
            1 humerus
    Human
        1 skull fragment
    Unidentified
        15 splinters of mammal long bone
    Comment: The sample from Structure 27 was small, and the scarcity of deer bone (while possibly the result of sampling error) is interesting. Since we found no real midden areas in Zone C, it could simply mean that most food refuse was periodically removed from the summit of the mound.

The Structure 27 Dooryard

We found several patches of stamped earth surface near the remains of Structure 27. On the assumption that these patches were part of a dooryard surrounding the house, we saved the bone tool listed below, which was found on one of them. Unfortunately, owing to the deteriorated condition of the earthen surface, we cannot consider the tool securely associated.

Bone Tool
    A perforator was found, made on a splinter of large mammal bone, 7.5 cm long (Fig. 23.6*i*).

The Zone B Residence

Following their abandonment, Structures 27 and 31 suffered considerable destruction. Part of this destruction may have been the result of erosion, but even more of it probably resulted from deliberate leveling by the creators of stratigraphic Zone B, the stratum that overlay Zone C.

Zone B was a thick layer, running from 40-50 cm below datum to 135 cm below datum. As in the case of Zone C, the matrix of Zone B was buff or yellowish-buff earth, resulting from the collapse and erosion of adobe walls. Much of this collapse probably took place during the hiatus in occupation that followed the Rosario phase (see Chapter 24).

The principal architectural remains in Zone B belonged to a Rosario phase elite residence, consisting of a central patio flanked on the north, south, and west by blocks of adobe-walled rooms. It is likely that there had also been rooms to the east of the patio,

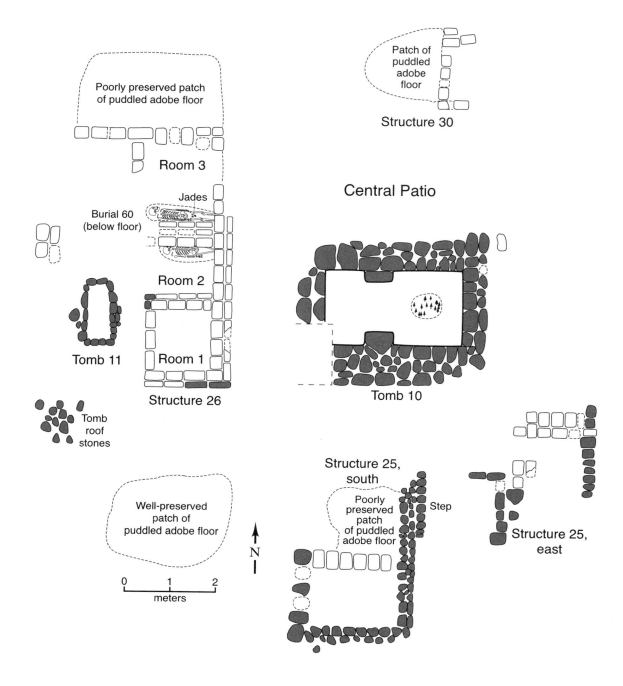

Figure 23.7. Plan of the Zone B Residence, showing the relationship of Structures 25, 26, and 30.

but that was the area most damaged by postoccupational erosion. The builders evidently knew in advance that erosion would be a problem, since they had built retaining walls along the eastern margins of Zone B.

We excavated Zone B over the course of two field seasons. The north, south, and west room blocks of the residence had become so detached from one another through erosion that each was given its own structure number in the field. Only when the whole of Zone B had been excavated did it become clear that we were dealing with a single, poorly preserved residence that must once have covered roughly 200 m². Because its fragmentary room blocks were excavated separately, the building is a composite of our Structures 25, 26, and 30. For simplicity it can be referred to as "the Zone B Residence."

We would reconstruct the Zone B Residence as a rectangular building 14-15 m on a side. In the center was an open 8 × 8 m patio, under whose floor we found a two-chambered stone masonry tomb (Fig. 23.7). To the west of the patio lay Structure 26, our best-preserved block of three rooms, built mainly of rectangular adobes, but with room corners occasionally reinforced with stones. The highest adobes preserved in Rooms 2 and 3 appeared at 90-110 cm below datum, while the wall foundations went down to a depth of 135 cm. Room 1, however, was a small, well-made storage room that continued down to 200-210 cm below datum—more than a meter below the floors of the neighboring rooms (see below). No lime plaster was found anywhere in the building, the outer walls having simply been plastered with clay. The floor was made of puddled adobe.

To the south of the central patio lay Structure 25, our second-best-preserved room block. It consisted of the stone and adobe foundations for at least one complete room (called Structure 25-south) and parts of others (called Structure 25-east). A low step accompanied the eastern entrance to Structure 25-south, indicating that not all floors in the room block were on the same level.

Finally, to the north of the central patio we found Structure 30, which consisted of a single adobe wall stub and an associated patch of puddled adobe floor. Weathered adobe debris lying nearby indicated that much of this room block eroded away after the Zone B Residence had been abandoned.

Given its size and prominent location atop the mound of Structure 19 overburden—at that time the highest point on the site—we suspect that the Zone B Residence belonged to an elite family, perhaps the most highly ranked Rosario phase family living at San José Mogote. It is therefore worth considering what this residence does, and does not, share with Structure 7 of Site SMT-11b at San Martín Tilcajete (Spencer and Redmond 2001:221-22). Structure 7, which dates to Monte Albán Ic, is at the moment our earliest example of a Zapotec "palace."

Similarities with Tilcajete's Structure 7

1. Both buildings had walls of rectangular adobes above stone foundations.

2. Both buildings consisted of rooms arranged around a central patio. (Structure 7 of Tilcajete had 8 relatively large rooms; we do not know how many rooms the Zone B Residence had).

3. Although most rooms were rectangular, both buildings had evidence of L-shaped rooms.

4. Both buildings used steps to adjust for the fact that not all room floors were on the same level.

Differences

1. Structure 7 of Tilcajete had more formal and impressive stone masonry wall foundations, often many courses high.

2. Structure 7 was somewhat larger, measuring 16 m on a side; we reconstruct the Zone B Residence as 14-15 m on a side.

3. Structure 7 had a slightly larger patio, measuring perhaps 10 m across instead of 8 m.

4. The Zone B Residence had a stone masonry tomb under its central patio, a feature of many later Zapotec palaces. The lack of a comparable tomb in Structure 7, however, may not be significant. The Tilcajete palace was deliberately burned in a raid (Spencer and Redmond 2001), so its primary resident may have been killed or taken captive before he could order the construction of his tomb.

5. Finally—and, we believe, significantly—Structure 7 appears to have been built by corvée labor, while the Zone B Residence does not. Structures 25/26/30 were all built of adobes that were similar in color, 40 cm × 20 cm in size, and 10 cm thick. The Tilcajete palace contained adobes of at least three different sizes, colors, and soil proveniences, suggesting that different labor groups had participated in its construction. This would seem to confirm a useful rule of thumb, proposed originally by William T. Sanders (1974), that palaces are more likely than chiefly residences to have been built by corvée labor.

Let us now look at the Zone B Residence, room block by room block.

Structure 26

Room 1

Room 1 was a 1.4 × 1.2 m storage unit; it was unlike any other Rosario phase room we have recovered, since it continued down for more than a meter below the floor of the adjacent rooms in its block (Figs. 23.8-23.10). This semi-subterranean room reflects a new strategy for storage, one that may be transitional between the bell-shaped pits of the Guadalupe phase and the above-ground storage rooms of the Monte Albán I era. Whatever the history of uses to which Room 1 was put, its final use seems to have been for the storage of five pottery vessels (including an effigy incense burner), all complete, though cracked by the weight of the overburden.

Figure 23.8. The excavation of Zone B. At this stage, work is just beginning on Room 1 of Structure 26, an unusually deep storage room (foreground). In the background, five workmen extend the excavation of Zone B to the very edge of the mound of overburden. (View from the northwest.)

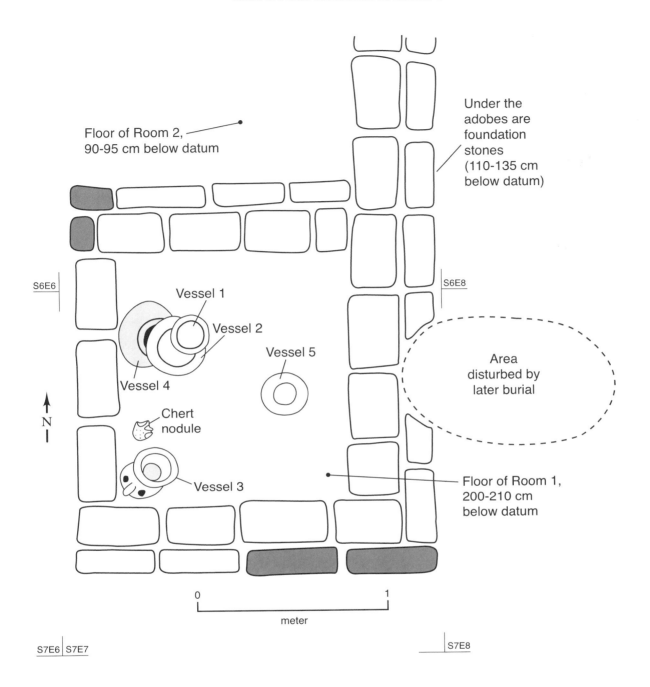

Floor of Room 2,
90-95 cm below datum

Under the
adobes are
foundation
stones
(110-135 cm
below datum)

S6E6

Vessel 1

Vessel 2

Vessel 5

Vessel 4

S6E8

Area
disturbed by
later burial

Chert
nodule

N

Vessel 3

Floor of Room 1,
200-210 cm
below datum

0   1

meter

S7E6 | S7E7

S7E8

Figure 23.9. Plan of Room 1, Structure 26, showing square designations and locations of Vessels 1-5. White rectangles are adobes (some set horizontally, some set on edge). Shaded rectangles are stones.

Figure 23.10. The excavation of Structure 26. *a*, Alejandro Mendoza begins work on Room 1 (background) while Armando Jiménez excavates Room 2 (foreground). This view is from the north. *b*, Room 1 seen from the southwest following excavation. The wooden scale is one meter long, and the black arrow points north.

Radiocarbon Date

A piece of charcoal from Room 1 dated to 2590 ± 40 B.P., or 640 b.c. (Beta-179877). The calibrated two-sigma range would be 820-770 B.C.

Whole Vessels (Fig. 23.11)

Vessel 1: deep plainware bowl with flat base and flaring wall

Vessel 2: Guadalupe Burnished Brown outleaned-wall bowl

Vessel 3: white-slipped effigy incense burner

Vessel 4: Fidencio Coarse jar filled with ash and tiny burned human bone fragments, possibly from a cremation

Vessel 5: white-slipped plate (or possibly a lid for Vessel 3)

Sherds in Room Fill (Diagnostics Only)

Socorro Fine Gray
  bowls with outleaned/outcurved walls, rims: 8
  bowl with outleaned/outcurved wall, base: 1
  composite silhouette bowls, plain: 3
  composite silhouette bowl, negative painting: 1
  composite silhouette bowl, incising and zoned toning: 1
  rims, too small to diagnose: 5
Josefina Fine Gray
  composite silhouette bowl, plain rim: 1
  body sherd: 1
Guadalupe Burnished Brown
  bowls with outleaned/outcurved walls, rims: 2
Fidencio Coarse
  jar rims: 2
  jar shoulder with neat jabs: 1
  jar shoulder with zoned punctation: 1
Lupita Heavy Plain
  bowls with outleaned/outcurved walls, rims: 2
Atoyac Yellow-white
  cylinder, plain rim: 1
  cylinder, incised rim: 1
  outleaned-wall bowls, plain rims: 5
  outleaned-wall bowl, base: 1
Leandro Gray
  cylinders, plain rims: 2
  cylinder, fine incised hachure, red pigment: 1
  cylinder, plain base: 1
Other
  redeposited sherds of San José and Tierras Largas phase types: 6

Attributes of Socorro Fine Gray Outleaned/Outcurved-Wall Bowls

Rim Form 2, no eccentricity, no decoration: 3
Rim Form 2, Motif c in negative painting: 1
Rim Form 2, Motif d in zoned toning and fine-line incising: 1
Rim Form 4, no eccentricity, no decoration: 1

Figure 23.11. Five pottery vessels found stored in Room 1, Structure 26. (1) Deep plainware bowl. (2) Guadalupe Burnished Brown bowl. (3) White-slipped effigy incense burner. (4) Fidencio Coarse jar (filled with ash and burned human bone from a possible cremation). (5) White-slipped plate (possibly a lid for Vessel 3).

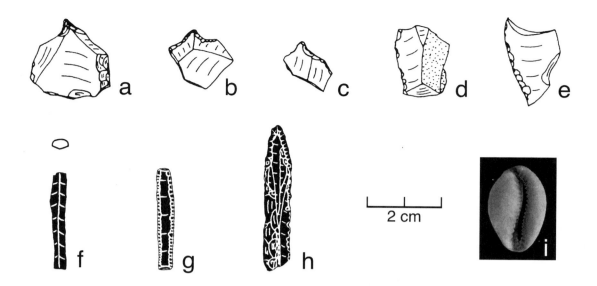

Figure 23.12. Objects found in Room 1, Structure 26. *a-e* are chert: *a-c*, flake perforator; *d, e*, utilized flakes. *f-h* are obsidian: *f, g*, both sides (and cross-section) of delicately pressure-flaked lancet fragment; *h*, perforator/drill made on a crested blade. *i*, cowrie shell.

Rim Form 4, Eccentricity 3, Motif g in zoned toning and
   fine-line incising: 1
Rim Form 12, no eccentricity, no decoration: 1

Chipped Stone
   Chert (75%)
      very large nodule of raw material: 1
      ordinary flake cores: 4
      discoidal core: 1
      flake perforators: 3 (Fig. 23.12*a-c*)
      retouched flakes: 3
      utilized flakes: 9 (Fig. 23.12*d, e*)
      flakes, not utilized: 107
   Obsidian (8%)
      lancet fragment of green obsidian, delicately pressure-
         flaked: 1 (Fig. 23.12*f, g*)
      perforator/drill of black obsidian: 1 (Fig. 23.12*h*)
      utilized flakes: 6
      flakes, not utilized: 6
   Other (16%)
      quartz flakes: 23
      igneous flakes: 5
Comment: The pressure-flaked obsidian lancet, made from a
   green obsidian blade, has been illustrated previously by
   Parry (1987: Fig. 52*c*). It appears to have been part of a
   bloodletting tool like those found elsewhere in and around
   the Zone B Residence (see below). Parry has concluded
   that such lancets were an important component of Rosario
   phase elite ritual paraphernalia.

The number of quartz flakes in this room is surprising, since much better raw material was available at the Matadamas chert quarry only 5 km away.

Bone Tool
   The tip of a needle made from a splinter of deer(?) long bone was found. The size suggests a sewing needle. Fragment, 10 mm long.

Shell
   Pacific Marine Bivalves
      fragment of pearl oyster (*Pinctada mazatlanica*), 10 × 4
         × 1 mm
      fragment of trimmed shell, unidentified oyster, 20 × 15
         × 1 mm
   Pacific Marine Univalves
      broken cowrie shell (*Cypraea* sp.), 23 × 15 mm (Fig.
         23.12 *i*)
   Unidentified
      manufacturing waste, 25 × 5 × 2 mm

Animal Bones
   The faunal remains from Room 1 consisted mainly of fine debris, such as might have been left behind despite periodic removal of the larger bone fragments. Such debris might, in fact, represent refuse accidentally swept into the lower part of the storage unit during housecleaning.

Large Mammals
  white-tailed deer (*Odocoileus virginianus*)
    1 incisor tooth
Small Mammals
  domestic dog (*Canis familiaris*)
    1 L. proximal third metacarpal
    1 unfused epiphysis of L. proximal femur
    1 L. proximal fourth metatarsal
  jackrabbit (*Lepus mexicanus*)
    1 R. zygomatic arch
  eastern cottontail (*Sylvilagus floridanus*)
    1 R. proximal femur, unfused
  unidentified cottontail (*Sylvilagus* sp.)
    1 R. distal humerus
Birds
  mourning dove (*Zenaidura macroura*)
    1 coracoid
Reptiles
  1 limb bone from an unidentified lizard
Human
  18 small fragments, mostly teeth and limb bone splinters
Unidentified
  65 splinters, mostly from deer, dog, and human

Room 2

Room 2 of Structure 26 was L-shaped, running north-south for 1.1 m. It flanked Room 1 on both the north and west, and probably provided access to that storage unit (Fig. 23.13).

Ceramics
  Socorro Fine Gray
    bowls with outleaned/outcurved walls, rims: 4
    composite silhouette bowls, plain: 2
    globular jar, rim: 1
  Fidencio Coarse
    jar rims: 2
  Lupita Heavy Plain
    brazier/potstand, rim: 1
  Atoyac Yellow-white
    cylinder, rim with incising: 1
    outleaned-wall bowls, plain rims: 2
    outleaned-wall bowl, incised rim: 1
  Leandro Gray
    cylinder, plain rim: 1
    outleaned-wall bowl, incised rim: 1
  Other
    redeposited sherds of San José and Tierras Largas phase
      types: 10

Attributes of Socorro Fine Gray Outleaned/Outcurved-Wall Bowls
  Rim Form 1, no eccentricity, no decoration: 2
  Rim Form 2, no eccentricity, no decoration: 1
  Rim Form 6, no eccentricity, no decoration: 1

Chipped Stone
  Chert (79%)
    flake core: 1
    flake perforators: 2
    flake spokeshaves: 2
    utilized flakes: 4
    flakes, not utilized: 29
  Obsidian (10 %)
    prismatic blade fragment, utilized: 1
    utilized flakes: 3
    flake, not utilized: 1
  Other (10 %)
    quartz flakes: 5

Shell
  Pacific Marine Univalves
    battered fragment of horn shell (cf. *Cerithium* sp.)
  Unidentified
    fragment of large shell, possibly a conch, 15 × 5 × 5 mm

Animal Bones
  Large Mammals
    white-tailed deer (*Odocoileus virginianus*)
      1 antler fragment, adult deer
      1 L. mandible, juvenile deer
  Small Mammals
    pocket gopher (*Orthogeomys grandis*)
      1 cheek tooth
  Unidentified
    11 splinters, most probably from deer long bone

Tomb 11

Below the floor of Room 2 and less than a meter west of Room 1, we found Tomb 11 (Fig. 23.13). This was a single-chambered stone masonry crypt some 70 cm deep. It measured 1.3 m by 50 cm at the top of its walls, but narrowed to 1.1 m by 43 cm as it descended. Its floor was made of gneiss flagstones (Fig. 23.14*a*).

Tomb 11 had been reopened and its contents removed, probably at the time the Zone B Residence was abandoned. A pile of roof stones, evidently removed at that time, lay two meters to the south of the tomb (Fig. 23.7). In addition to small bits of human bone, two items (described below) were found in the fill of the tomb. There is no guarantee that either item accompanied the original burial, although the obsidian lancet was lying directly on the flagstone floor.

Obsidian Lancet

The midsection of a lancet chipped from smoky gray obsidian was found on the floor of the tomb. The fragment is 25 mm long and tapers from 9 mm to 5 mm in diameter (Fig. 23.14*b*). The original artifact may have been at least 10 cm in length. This appears to be our second example of an obsidian bloodletting

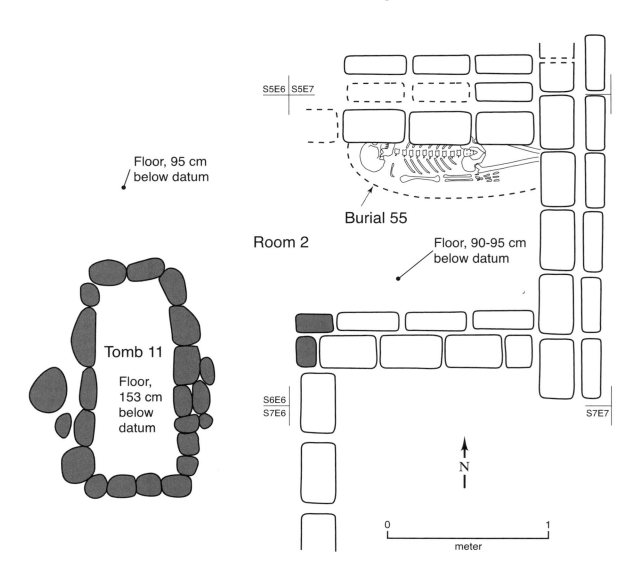

Figure 23.13. Plan of Room 2, Structure 26, showing square designations, Burial 55, and Tomb 11. White rectangles are adobes (some set horizontally, some set on edge). Shaded objects are stones.

tool associated with the Zone B Residence. It was previously illustrated by Parry (1987: Fig. 52*d*).

Dog Mandible

The left mandible of a dog was found in the fill of the tomb.

Burial 55

Burial 55 was the complete skeleton of a young woman between 16 and 20 years of age (Hodges 1989: Appendix 1). She lay fully extended, face up, head to the west, partially below the wall separating Rooms 2 and 3 (Fig. 23.13).

The fact that her body lay beneath three of the basal adobes of the wall suggested that she might have been incorporated into the building as a dedicatory offering. Burial 55 was not accompanied by any artifacts. In her pelvic area, however, we found the poorly preserved remains of what may have been a late-term foetus.

2 cm

Figure 23.14. Tomb 11 and its contents. *a*, Tomb 11 seen from the north, with its floor of gneiss flagstones uncovered. *b*, midsection of an obsidian lancet or bloodletting tool, found on the flagstone floor.

Room 3

Judging from its wall stubs, Room 3 of Structure 26 was 1.8 by 1.6 m in area (Fig. 23.15). We found no artifacts on the eroded floor. Below the floor, however, we found Burial 60, the fully extended skeleton of a woman laid out east-west, parallel to the south wall of the room (Figs. 23.15-23.17).

Ceramics
  Socorro Fine Gray
    bowls with outleaned/outcurved walls, rims: 2
    composite silhouette bowl, plain rim: 1
    hemispherical bowl, deep parallel grooved lines: 1
    globular jar, rim: 1
  Fidencio Coarse
    jar rims: 2
  Lupita Heavy Plain
    braziers/potstands, rims: 2
  Atoyac Yellow-white
    outleaned-wall bowl, incised rim: 1
    body sherd: 1
  Leandro Gray
    cylinder, plain rim: 1
  Other
    redeposited Matadamas Orange bowl rim: 1

Attributes of Socorro Fine Gray Outleaned/Outcurved-Wall Bowls
    Rim Form 3, Motif h in fine-line incising: 1
    Rim Form 2, Motif c in negative painting: 1

Figurine
    A typical Rosario phase torso was found.

Burial 60

Burial 60 was the skeleton of a woman 25-35 years of age (Hodges 1989: Appendix 1). She had been buried fully extended, face up, head to the west, under the floor of Room 3.

There were signs that this woman was someone of relatively high rank. Her skull displayed the tabular erect deformation sometimes given to elite children early in life (Fig. 23.17*a*), and

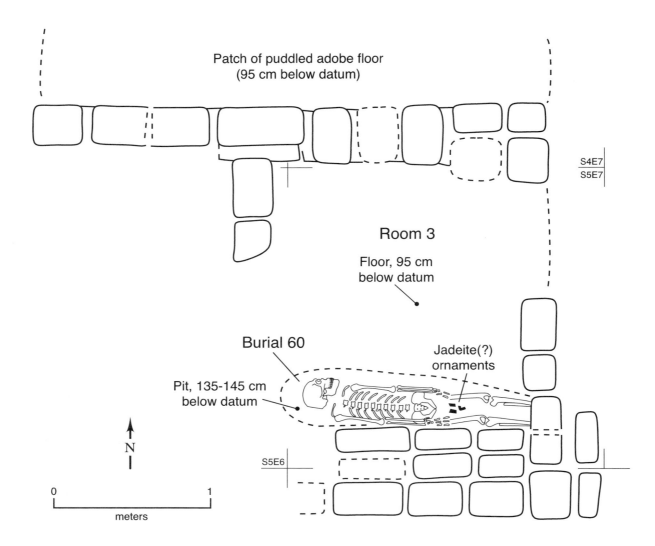

Figure 23.15. Plan of Room 3, Structure 26, showing square designations and Burial 60. White rectangles are adobes (some set horizontally, some set on edge).

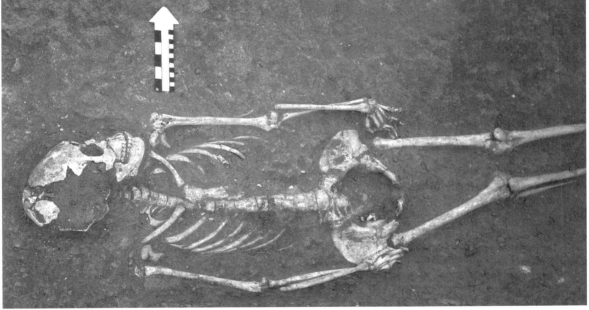

Figure 23.16. Details of Room 3, Structure 26. *Above*, view from the north-northeast, showing Squares S5E6 and S5E7, adobe foundations of the northern wall, and the puddled adobe floor to the north (refer to Figure 23.15). *Below*, Burial 60, a woman 25-35 years of age, laid to rest beneath the floor of Room 3.

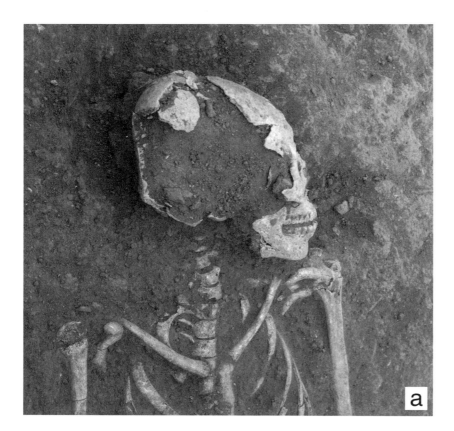

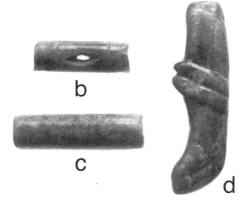

Figure 23.17. Details of Burial 60. *a*, closeup of cranium showing tabular erect deformation. *b, c*, tubular beads of jadeite(?), one of which has had two oval slivers removed. *d*, jadeite(?) ornament in the shape of a hockey stick. (Length of *d*, 53 mm.)

she had received an offering of three jadeite(?) ornaments, placed between her thighs (see below).

Jadeite(?) Ornaments

Tubular bead, 25 mm long, 8 mm in diameter. It had been carved on both sides, leaving oval openings, each greater than 4 mm long (Fig. 23.17*b*).

Tubular bead, 35 mm long, 9 mm in diameter (Fig. 23.17*c*).

Unusual ornament, shaped like a hockey stick with two cords or straps wrapped around it (Fig. 23.17*d*).

In addition to these ornaments, we found two slivers of jadeite(?) that appear to have come from the oval openings in the 25 mm-long tubular bead. The fact that these slivers were saved to be included with Burial 60 suggests that jadeite was a prized commodity. It even raises the possibility that when an elite patron presented an artisan with jadeite to be worked, he or she expected that everything—including the trimmed-off waste—would be returned. Such control of luxury resources, whose possession was socially restricted, was not uncommon in rank societies.

Structure 25-South

All that remained of Structure 25-south were the partial stone and adobe foundations for two rooms, the southern one measuring 2.0 by 1.3 m (Fig. 23.18). The partially preserved northern room was entered by way of a stair step on the east. This room had retained a patch of its puddled adobe floor (Fig. 23.19), and all the artifacts listed below were lying on that patch.

Ceramics (Diagnostics Only)

Socorro Fine Gray
bowls with outleaned/outcurved walls, rims: 8
composite silhouette bowls, plain rims: 2
composite silhouette bowl, negative painting: 1
cylinder, incised parallel lines: 1
globular jar, rim: 1
Guadalupe Burnished Brown
outleaned-wall bowl, rim: 1
Lupita Heavy Plain
braziers/potstands, rims: 2
Atoyac Yellow-white
cylinder, plain rim: 1
cylinder, excised rim: 1
outleaned-wall bowls, plain rims: 2
outleaned-wall bowl, incised rim: 1
Leandro Gray
cylinders, plain rims: 2
Delia White
beaker rim: 1
Other
redeposited sherds of San José and Tierras Largas phase types: 25

Attributes of Socorro Fine Gray Outleaned/Outcurved-Wall Bowls

Rim Form 2, too small to show eccentricity or decoration: 4
Rim Form 2, decorated with negative painting: 1
Rim Form 3, Motif i done in fine-line incising: 2

Chipped Stone

Chert (70%)
flake cores: 2
flake perforator: 1
retouched flakes: 3
utilized flakes: 16
flakes, not utilized: 9
Obsidian (16%)
prismatic blade fragments, utilized: 2
wedge: 1
flakes, not utilized: 4
Other (14%)
quartz flakes: 6

Ground Stone

Roughly one-third of a basin-shaped metate, recrystallized metamorphic rock, probably schist; extremely worn. Width, 28 cm; thickness (base to grinding surface), 2.5 cm (Fig. 23.20).

Shell

Ornaments
piece of a pearl oyster(?) artifact, 15 × 7 × 1.5 mm, cut on several edges
Pearly Freshwater Mussels
piece of unidentified mussel, 11 × 10 × 1 mm
Pacific Marine Bivalves
piece of *Spondylus* shell, 15 × 10 × 2 mm

Mica

Three fragments of white mica, weighing about 0.1 g. The largest fragment is 15 × 12 mm and paper thin; the other two pieces seem to be flakes from the larger fragment.

Animal Bones

Small Mammals
eastern cottontail (*Sylvilagus floridanus*)
1 R. proximal femur
1 other limb fragment
Human
1 tooth
1 fragment of pelvis
Unidentified
6 splinters, one of them burned

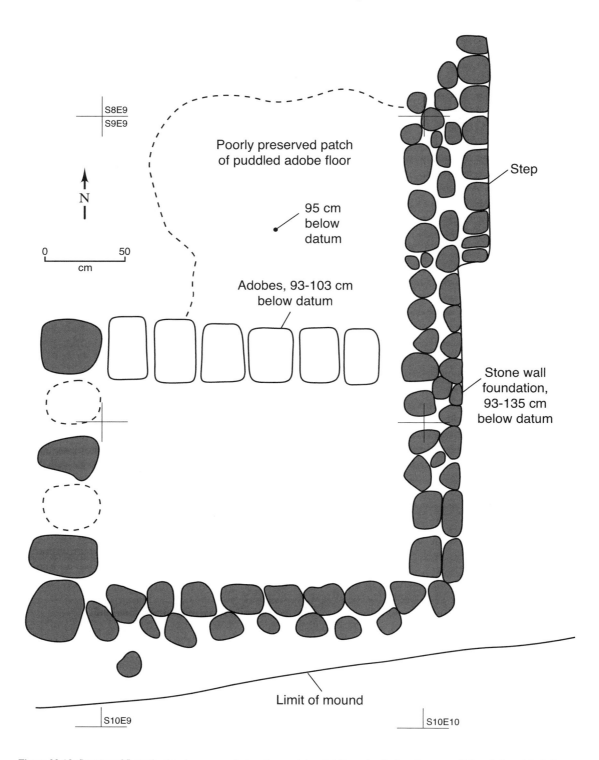

S8E9
S9E9

Poorly preserved patch
of puddled adobe floor

N

95 cm
below
datum

0   50
    cm

Adobes, 93-103 cm
below datum

Step

Stone wall
foundation,
93-135 cm
below datum

Limit of mound

S10E9   S10E10

Figure 23.18. Structure 25-south, showing square designations, adobes (white rectangles), and stone wall foundations (shaded).

Figure 23.19. In this view from the northeast, a workman cleans the adobe wall foundation of Structure 25-south. In the lower left corner of the photo one can see some of the stones in the foundations of the east wall. All the artifacts from this room block came from the patch of puddled adobe floor in the foreground.

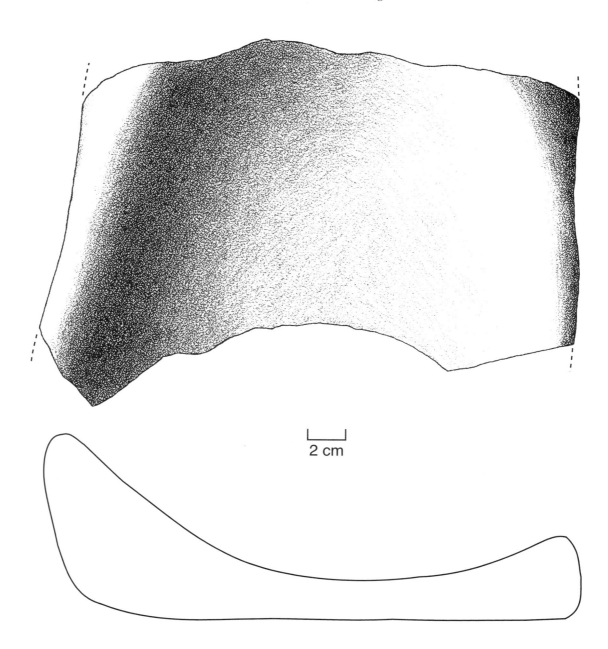

Figure 23.20. Portion of basin-shaped metate found on the floor of Structure 25-south.

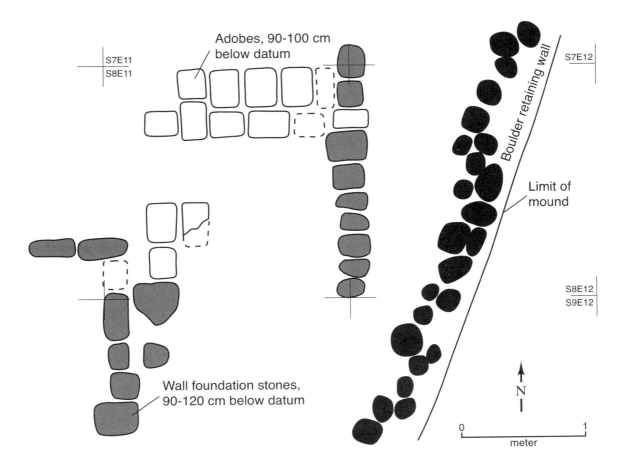

Figure 23.21. Plan of Structure 25-east, showing square designations, adobes (white rectangles), wall foundation stones (shaded), and a boulder retaining wall (black).

Structure 25-East

All that remained of Structure 25-east were the partial wall foundations of two rooms, lying just east of Structure 25-south (Fig. 23.21). The only artifacts found in association with these rooms were sherds, pieces of chipped stone, and a figurine head.

Ceramics (Diagnostics Only)
    Socorro Fine Gray
        bowls with outleaned/outcurved walls, rims: 2
        composite silhouette bowl, negative painting: 1
        bowl, basal sherd: 1
        globular jar, rim: 1
    Lupita Heavy Plain
        brazier/potstand, rim: 1
    Atoyac Yellow-white
        outleaned-wall bowl, incised rim: 1
        outleaned-wall bowls, bases: 2

Other
    redeposited sherds of Guadalupe, San José, and Tierras
        Largas phase types: 18

Attributes of Socorro Fine Gray Outleaned/Outcurved-Wall Bowls
    Rim Form 2, unknown motif in negative painting: 1
    Rim Form 3, Eccentricity 1, Motif a in fine-line incising: 1

Chipped Stone
    Chert (86%)
        flake core: 1
        utilized flakes: 2
        flakes, not utilized: 3
    Obsidian (14%)
        utilized flake: 1

Figurine
    One figurine head of a type common in the Guadalupe phase was found.

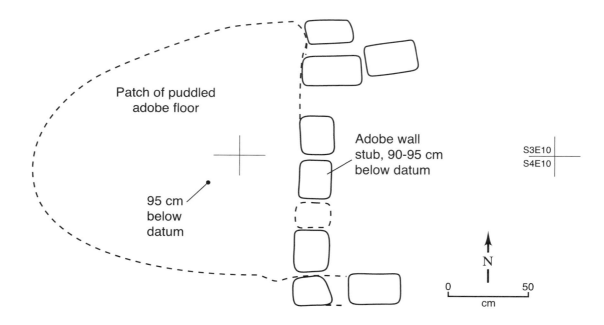

Figure 23.22. Plan of Structure 30, showing square designations and surviving adobes (white rectangles). This appeared to be only a remnant of a badly destroyed room block.

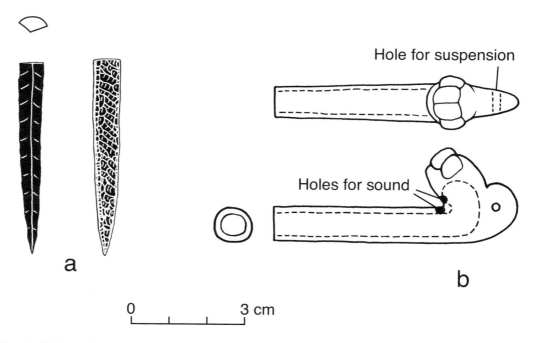

Figure 23.23. Artifacts found below adobe debris on isolated floor patches, Zone B Residence. *a*, both sides (and cross-section) of a broken lancet, made on a green obsidian blade; found in Square S7E10. *b*, two views (and cross-section) of a ceramic whistle in the shape of a jaguar's or puma's paw; found in Square S8E10.

Structure 30

The only remaining trace of the room block on the north side of the central patio was one adobe wall stub and a patch of puddled adobe floor. These remains were designated Structure 30 (Fig. 23.22). The only artifacts found on the floor were sherds.

Ceramics (Diagnostics Only)
　Socorro Fine Gray
　　bowl with outleaned wall, small rim with both incising and zoned toning: 1
　　composite silhouette bowl, plain rim: 1
　　composite silhouette bowl, plain base: 1
　　composite silhouette bowls, rims with negative painting: 2
　　composite silhouette bowl, rim with excising?: 1
　Josefina Fine Gray
　　body sherd, incised: 1
　Guadalupe Burnished Brown
　　outleaned-wall bowl, rim: 1
　Fidencio Coarse
　　jar rim: 1
　　tecomate rim: 1
　　body sherd with sloppy jabs: 1
　Lupita Heavy Plain
　　outleaned-wall bowls, rims: 2
　　brazier/potstand, annular base: 1
　Atoyac Yellow-white
　　cylinder, incised rim: 1
　Leandro Gray
　　cylinders, plain rims: 2
　　cylinder, plain base: 1

Isolated Patches of Floor

Isolated patches of puddled adobe floor were found in the gaps between Structures 26, 25-south, 25-east, and 30. Such patches were numerous enough to indicate that all the Zone B room blocks had once been part of a single building. Many of the floor patches bore fragments of fallen adobes.

Several interesting items were found below the adobe debris on isolated patches of floor near Structures 25 and 26. Although they cannot be assigned to a specific room, their position below the fallen adobes suggests that they were in the Zone B Residence when its walls collapsed.

Obsidian Lancet

The point of a pressure-flaked lancet of green obsidian was found in Square S7E10, just west of Structure 25-east. The fragment is 54 mm long and tapers from 7 mm in diameter to a needlelike point; when complete, the lancet may have been more than 10 cm long (Fig. 23.23a). This would appear to be the third Rosario phase bloodletting tool associated with the Zone B Residence.

Effigy Whistle

A whistle in the shape of a jaguar's or puma's paw, made of Socorro Fine Gray pottery and perforated for suspension, was found in Square S8E10, just east of Structure 25-south. The total length of the artifact is 64 mm, and the tubular part is 10 mm in diameter. The feline's toes were carefully modeled, and the foot projects out in such a way that the tubular part could serve as the animal's leg (Fig. 23.23b). The perforation would have allowed this whistle to be worn around the neck, like the bird effigy whistle found with Structure 27. Like the latter, it might have served to direct men in situations with high background noise, such as armed combat.

Cottontail Bone

The right innominate of a Mexican cottontail (*Sylvilagus cunicularius*) was found in Square S7E8, just east of Structure 26.

The Central Patio

The Zone B Residence is, for the moment at least, Oaxaca's oldest known example of an extended family house with adobe rooms arranged around a central patio. While the 8 × 8 m patio provides a Middle Formative precursor for the internal patios in later Zapotec palaces, it should be noted that its surface was puddled adobe, not lime plaster or genuine stucco.

Tomb 10

We discovered a two-chambered tomb below the floor of the central patio in the Zone B Residence (Fig. 23.24). Such central tomb placement was to become a feature of many later Zapotec palaces, as was the division of the tomb into a main chamber and a smaller antechamber.

Tomb 10 was 3 m long and 1.7 m wide. It was built of stone masonry, with a floor of flagstones (Fig. 23.25). Two 27-cm-long walls divided it into a main chamber (1.65 m long) and an antechamber (0.86 m long). The doorway between the two chambers was 1.15 m wide. The walls and floor of the tomb had been given two layers of plaster: first tan clay, then a more fugitive white lime plaster which survived only in protected areas like the corners of the tomb (Fig. 23.26a). In the main chamber there were four localized ash deposits on the tomb floor, as well as a circular deposit of powdered red ochre 60 cm in diameter (Fig. 23.27).

Like Tomb 11 (see above), Tomb 10 had been reopened and its contents removed, probably at the time the Zone B Residence was abandoned. While the intent of those reopening the tomb was presumably to carry away the occupant and his or her offerings, a few items were overlooked because they lay buried beneath the deposit of red ochre in the main chamber. When we screened this ochre deposit we discovered one human patella, which had been hidden by the red powder. This patella—plus a worn molar, a worn premolar, and two tiny fragments of human bone—were

Figure 23.24. Having completed the excavation of stratigraphic Zone B out to the limit of the mound of overburden, the workmen are now shaving horizontally to make sure no postmolds or subfloor features have been missed. It was during this careful shaving that Tomb 10 (foreground) came to light, below the patio of the Zone B Residence.

all that remained of the tomb's occupant. We also discovered the following offering of obsidian artifacts in the red ochre.

Offering of Obsidian (Fig. 23.28)

11 side-notched atlatl points of green obsidian

1 obsidian blade segment, utilized

2 obsidian flakes

Comment: According to an analysis by Parry (1987:119-22), all 11 atlatl points were made from three large green obsidian blades. Those blades had been broken into 12 segments, 11 of which were retouched into projectile points ranging in length from 25 to 30 mm. The twelfth segment was evidently considered too small to make into a point, but was included in the offering and shows edge wear consistent with use of some kind.

Several of the atlatl points retained so much of the shape of the original blade segment that they could be conjoined (Parry 1987:122). For example, in Figure 23.28, the bases of the two points on the left in the top row conjoin; so do the bases of the two points in the middle of the second row.

While the age and sex of the tomb's occupant cannot be determined, the size of the patella and the wear on the teeth suggest an adult individual. We would not be surprised to learn that the occupant of Tomb 10 was a highly ranked adult male, whose role in raiding and community defense was symbolized by the offering of 11 atlatl points. At any rate, the occupant was evidently so important a person that when his (or her) family abandoned the residence, they took the skeletal remains with them.

Mano Reused in Wall of Tomb

One of the stones used in the masonry construction of Tomb 10 was a discarded mano. While its context is secondary, we describe it here because it could be Rosario phase in date.

Complete subrectangular two-hand mano with triangular cross-section, made of recrystallized metamorphic rock. Length, 16 cm; width, 9.6 cm; maximum thickness, 4.8 cm (Fig. 23.26*b*).

Sherd Collections from Tomb (Diagnostics Only)

While the association of Tomb 10 with Structures 25/26/30 was clear from the stratigraphy, we saved every sherd found in

Area disturbed by intrusive feature

Figure 23.25. Tomb 10 at the end of the excavation. With his whisk broom, Tomás Cruz indicates the spot on the flagstone floor where 11 projectile points were found in a deposit of red ochre. (View from the northeast.)

Figure 23.26. Details of Tomb 10. *a*, closeup of the northeast corner of the tomb, showing traces of lime plaster on the tan clay. *b*, subrectangular mano reused as a stone in the wall of the tomb.

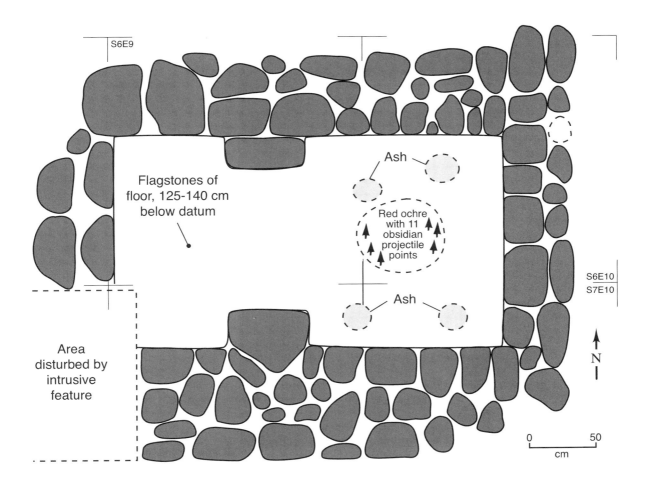

Figure 23.27. Plan of Tomb 10, showing square designations and various features found on the floor.

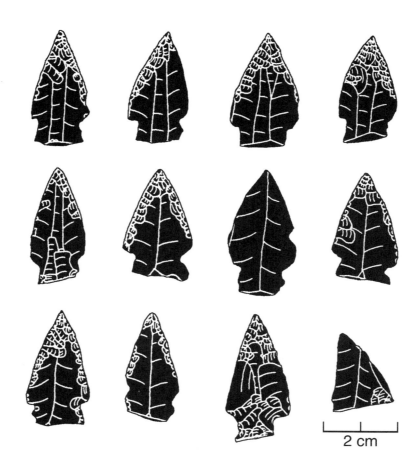

2 cm

Figure 23.28. Eleven projectile points made from segments of three large green obsidian blades, plus a utilized leftover segment from one of the blades (lower right). Several of the points conjoin (see Parry 1987: Figure 47). All these points were found in a deposit of red ochre on the floor of Tomb 10 (see Figure 23.27).

the course of its excavation. In part, this was done in the hope of establishing the moment at which the contents of the tomb had been removed. We know that all the following collections are from secondary (if not tertiary) contexts, but we present them for the sake of completeness.

1. *Sherds Found beneath the Floor of the Tomb*
    Socorro Fine Gray
        body sherd: 1
    Josefina Fine Gray
        body sherds: 2
    Guadalupe Burnished Brown
        outleaned-wall bowl rim: 1
    Lupita Heavy Plain
        braziers/potstands, rims: 2
    Atoyac Yellow-white
        cylinder, plain rim: 1
    Clementina Fine Red-on-Buff
        body sherd: 1

2. *Sherds Trapped in Tomb Construction.* These sherds were found among the wall stones and floor stones of Tomb 10, imbedded in such a way as to indicate that they were incorporated during its construction.

    Socorro Fine Gray
        outleaned-wall bowl, Rim Form 2, Eccentricity 3, Motif c in fine-line incising: 1
        composite silhouette bowl, plain rim: 1
        composite silhouette bowl, negative painting: 1
        bowls with slightly everted rim: 2
    Josefina Fine Gray
        cylinder rim: 1
    Guadalupe Burnished Brown
        outleaned-wall bowl, plain rim: 1
        outleaned-wall bowl, bolstered rim: 1
    Lupita Heavy Plain
        braziers/potstands, rims: 5

Atoyac Yellow-white
  cylinder, plain rim: 1
  hemispherical bowl, plain rim: 1
Leandro Gray
  body sherds: 4
Other
  redeposited sherds of San José and Tierras Largas
    phase types: 8

3. *Sherds from the Fill above the Flagstone Floor.* These
   sherds were in fill which postdated the reopening of the
   tomb and the removal of its contents.

Socorro Fine Gray
  outleaned-wall bowl, Rim Form 3, Eccentricity 3: 1
  outleaned-wall bowl, Rim Form 3, Eccentricity 4: 1
  composite silhouette bowls, plain rims: 2
  composite silhouette bowl, base: 1
  bottle with vertical neck, plain rim: 1
  rims, too small to diagnose: 6
Josefina Fine Gray
  body sherd: 1
Guadalupe Burnished Brown
  outleaned-wall bowls, rims: 2
  bowl with incurved rim: 1
  mat-impressed bowl base: 1
Fidencio Coarse
  body sherd with neat jabs: 1
Lupita Heavy Plain
  brazier/potstand, rim: 1
  brazier/potstand, mat-impressed floor: 1
Other
  redeposited sherds of the Guadalupe, San José, and
    Tierras Largas phases: 20
Comment: The sherd samples indicate that Tomb 10, as
  expected, was built during the Rosario phase. It also
  appears to have been reopened and cleaned out during

that phase. While the Socorro Fine Gray bottle listed
above could indicate a Late Rosario phase date for the
cleaning out of the tomb, not a single sherd attributable to Monte Albán Ia (for example, Caso, Bernal,
and Acosta's Types G15, G16, G17, C4, etc.) can be
associated with the Zone B Residence.

The Retaining Wall

By the time the Zone B Residence was built, the mound of
overburden above Structure 19 was even taller (and its summit
even smaller) than it had been during the occupation of Zone C.
We estimate that no more than 220-270 m² of level area would
have been available to the builders of Structures 25/26/30. We
cannot be more precise than that because we know that the summit was reduced by erosion prior to our arrival.

Like the occupants of Zone C, the builders of the Zone B
Residence attempted to prevent erosion by building a revetment
or retaining wall along the margins of the summit (Fig. 23.21).
The longest unbroken stretch of wall, composed of irregular
fieldstones or small boulders, ran for about 14 m along the curving eastern edge of the summit, from Square S3E12 to Square
S10E12. The wall, up to 80 cm wide in places, first appeared at
1.1 m below datum and continued down to 1.35 m below datum.
The placement of this wall suggests that in Zone B, as in Zone
C, the east side of the summit was considered the most likely to
erode. Evidently the stairway on the west gave that side of the
summit a less precipitous slope.

There was a shorter stretch of revetment stones along the
southern margin of the summit in Square S10E8. This line of
boulders, only 1.9 m long, lay barely 40 cm from Structure 25-
south. The proximity of this room block to the dropoff from the
summit underscores the space limitations that the builders of the
Zone B Residence faced. The remains of Structure 25-east, for
example, lay only 80 cm from the dropoff on the east side. Only
on the west, where Room 3 of Structure 26 lay 2.3 m from the
dropoff, did the builders apparently see no need for revetment.

Chapter 24
Mound 1: Epilogue

The Zone B Residence was the last Rosario phase house built on the Structure 19 overburden and, we believe, the last built on Mound 1. To be sure, it may not have been the last Rosario phase house built at San José Mogote.

At the end of the Rosario phase, there was a substantial movement of population from the Etla region to the summit of Monte Albán. Our colleagues on the Settlement Pattern Project (Kowalewski et al. 1989) have determined that half the Rosario phase villages whose occupations failed to continue into Monte Albán Ia can be found in the southern Etla subvalley.

Our excavations between 1966 and 1980 suggest that as much as 95% of San José Mogote's population may have left at the end of the Rosario phase, presumably to play a leading role in the founding of Monte Albán. We suspect that most other communities in the southern Etla region who joined in the move to Monte Albán had been subordinate villages within the San José Mogote chiefdom. The southern Etla subvalley may have contributed 2000 of Monte Albán's earliest inhabitants, easily the lion's share.

It is tempting to speculate that Tombs 10 and 11 were cleaned out because the occupants of the Zone B Residence reopened them, bundled up the human remains and most of the offerings, and took it all with them when they left for Monte Albán. This will remain speculation unless, and until, DNA can be extracted from the teeth or patella in Tomb 10 and matched to an elite secondary burial somewhere on Monte Albán.

VI

Chapter 25

A Multidimensional Scaling of San José Phase Houses and Their Contents

by Robert G. Reynolds

In preparation for this volume I conducted a multidimensional scaling of 18 San José phase houses, household units, or dooryards and their contents. The purposes of the study were twofold. On the one hand, we wanted to see which houses were most alike in terms of the items associated with them; we were especially interested in seeing to what extent houses from the same "neighborhood" would be similar. This was accomplished using a Q-mode analysis. Second, we wanted to see which items co-occurred, either because (1) they were regularly used together, or (2) they were used by the same families. This was accomplished using an R-mode analysis, which looks at the underlying dimensions of co-occurrence.

We selected the San José phase for this study because it had provided the largest sample of residences from the study area. Eighteen houses or household units of the San José phase appeared to have produced useful samples of artifacts, shell, mica, or other materials for analysis. From among the classes of items associated with these houses, we chose 20 for our study. We tried to choose a broad spectrum of items, so that food processing, craft production, ritual, interregional exchange, and the expression of social status would all be reflected in the sample.

The Sample of Residences

The 18 residential proveniences used in the study are listed in Table 25.1. Included were Houses 6, 5, 2, 9, 1, 10, 4, 7, and 14 from Area C (House 14 and its adjacent midden were combined to increase the inventory); Household Units C4, C3, C2, and C1 from Area A; Houses 17 and 16 from Area B; the North Dooryard adjacent to House 16; materials from the earlier stage of House 17, found just below it; and House 13 on Mound 1.

The Sample of Household Items

The 20 household items chosen for the study are also given in Table 25.1. For the purposes of analysis each item was given an abbreviated label, which I list below. These labels will be used to reference the items in all of the tables and figures that follow.

chert cores of all types (CORES)
chert perforators/gravers (PERFGR)
biface preforms/roughouts (BIFPRE)
prismatic obsidian blades (OBSID)
two-hand manos or fragments thereof (MANOS)
celts or fragments thereof (CELTS)
bone awls or *piscadores* (BONEAWL)
sewing needles (SEWNEED)
basketry needles (BASKNEED)
pearly freshwater mussels (MUSSEL)
pearl oyster (PEARLOY)
Spondylus shell (SPONDYL)
horn shells (HORNSHL)
mica fragments (MICA)
iron ore mirrors (IRONMIR)
iron ore lumps (IRONLUM)
stone "cutting boards" (CUTBORD)
canicas or pecked/ground stone balls (CANICA)
ornaments of jadeite(?) (JADEORN)
marine fish parts (FISH)

In determining how many items there were in each residence, there were a number of issues to be resolved. If three pieces of mica could be glued together to form one, did they count as one

446

Table 25.1 The Frequency of 20 Representative Items in 18 San José Phase Houses/Dooryards

Provenience	CORES	PERFGR	BIFPRE	OBSID	MANOS	CELTS	BONEAWL	SEWNEED	BASKNEED
House 6	4	—	—	3	—	—	—	1	—
House 5	1	—	—	2	—	—	—	—	—
House 2	14	10	—	11	1	2	2	1	1
House 9	23	—	—	—	2	2	—	—	—
House 1	5	3	—	1	1	—	—	—	—
House 10	4	1	—	2	—	—	—	1	1
House 4	23	18	—	36	2	1	1	—	—
House 7	2	—	—	1	—	1	—	1	—
H14/Midden	6	—	—	1	1	—	—	1	—
H. Unit C4	11	28	—	5	1	—	—	—	—
H. Unit C3	25	38	—	6	—	—	—	—	—
H. Unit C2	9	44	—	4	2	—	—	—	—
H. Unit C1	14	15	—	9	1	—	—	—	—
House 17	15	—	1	4	3	—	—	—	—
SubH.17	9	6	—	12	—	1	—	—	4
House 16	36	3	7	8	2	1	—	—	3
N.Door/H16	46	11	2	33	1	3	1	5	—
House 13	17	18	—	8	—	—	—	1	—

(continued)

Provenience	MUSSEL	PEARLOY	SPONDYL	HORNSHL	MICA	IRONMIR	IRONLUM	CUTBORD	CANICA	JADEORN	FISH
House 6	—	2	—	—	—	—	—	1	—	—	—
House 5	—	1	1	—	—	—	1	1	—	—	—
House 2	8	9	—	2	3	—	—	—	—	3	3
House 9	11	2	—	—	4	—	—	—	—	3	2
House 1	—	1	—	—	2	—	—	—	—	—	—
House 10	—	—	—	—	—	—	—	—	—	—	—
House 4	3	33	—	3	5	—	—	—	—	1	5
House 7	—	1	—	—	1	—	—	—	—	—	—
H14/Midden	2	2	1	1	1	—	1	—	—	—	—
H. Unit C4	4	1	—	1	6	2	2	—	2	1	1
H. Unit C3	5	2	1	2	14	1	2	—	—	2	2
H. Unit C2	2	1	—	—	1	—	2	—	—	—	—
H. Unit C1	1	6	2	—	5	—	2	—	1	—	—
House 17	—	1	—	—	1	—	1	—	—	—	—
SubH.17	1	1	—	—	5	—	—	—	—	—	—
House 16	1	3	—	—	5	1	1	—	1	1	—
N.Door/H16	8	4	1	—	6	1	—	—	—	—	6
House 13	6	1	2	—	15	1	6	—	—	1	—

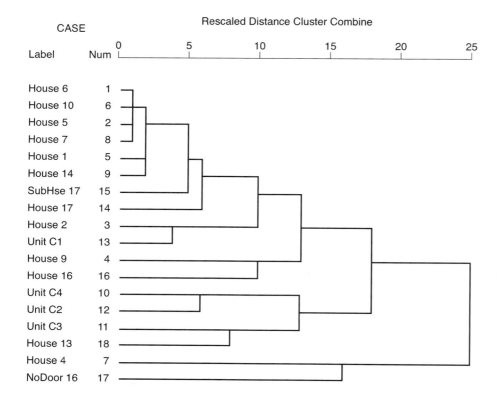

Figure 25.1. Dendrogram showing similarity distances of 18 San José phase houses/dooryards, based on the distributions of 20 items. All but two labels are self-explanatory. SubHse17 refers to the earlier version of House 17 (Chapter 18). NoDoor16 refers to the dooryard immediately north of House 16 (Chapter 19).

fragment or three? If a jade bead was found just above the floor, was it closely associated enough to be included with that house or not? In such matters I relied on the assessments of Flannery and Marcus, who had witnessed all of the archaeological contexts and handled all of the items. The numbers I used represent their best judgment regarding each object.

Preliminary Dendrograms

Before starting a complex multidimensional scaling, it is often useful to undertake a simpler preliminary analysis, to see whether the data contain any obvious clustering that would warrant a scaling approach. I chose to do a hierarchical cluster analysis, because the data consist of counts. The distance metric used was "city block," and the clustering method was "farthest neighbor." The results were displayed as dendrograms, because we expected to see different levels of association among houses or items.

Figure 25.1 presents a dendrogram generated by hierarchical cluster analysis of the 18 residential proveniences to be used in our Q-mode scaling. The dendrogram reveals that clustering is indeed present in the data. Let us consider what kinds of relationships some of the clusters might reveal.

First of all, Houses 6, 10, 5, and 7 of Area C are clustered at the first stage, and Houses 1 and 14 of Area C are evidently the most closely related to that cluster, since they are added at the next stage of the dendrogram. This pattern makes sense intuitively since (1) all these houses were found in the same residential

ward, and (2) none could be extensively exposed, reducing the likelihood of finding something unique in them.

It is interesting that SubHse17, the probable earlier stage of House 17, is the next most closely linked residence to the Area C cluster mentioned above. This supports the conclusion (advanced in Chapter 18) that before the occupants of House 16/17 began to specialize in biface production, their activities were more like those of a typical Area C house. Note that House 16, the lean-to where most of the biface production took place, is quite far removed from SubHse17 at this stage of the dendrogram, not combining with it until several stages later.

In Chapter 22, it was suggested that one might consider House 13 to belong to Area A. That possibility is supported by House 13's clustering with Household Units C3, C4, and C2 at stage 3 of the dendrogram.

Finally, it is interesting that Houses 2, 9, and 4 do not cluster closely with the remaining Area C houses. These were the three most extensively excavated houses in that residential ward, and each had unusual contents that set it apart. For example, House 4 had high quantities of obsidian blades and pearl oyster fragments; House 9 was strangely lacking in obsidian blades, but had high quantities of mussel shell. It may be that the greater the exposure of any given house, the greater the likelihood of finding something atypical. (However, the Area A household units all clustered in spite of their more extensive exposures.)

Figure 25.2 presents a dendrogram generated by a hierarchical cluster analysis of the 20 household items to be used in our R-

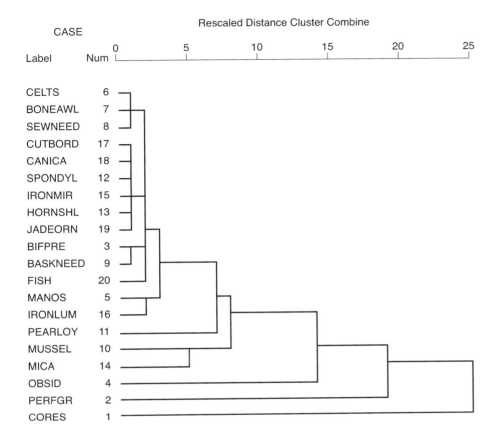

Figure 25.2. Dendrogram showing similarity distances of 20 items, based on their frequencies in 18 San José phase houses/dooryards.

mode scaling. The same clustering approach used for the Q-mode analysis was employed. One of the most prominent clusters to emerge consists of jadeite(?) ornaments, horn shells, iron ore mirrors, *Spondylus* shells, *canicas*, and "cutting boards." It is not clear whether these items cluster because they frequently occurred in houses with a lot of craft activity, because they were often associated with highly ranked families, or both.

A second cluster, which is linked to the first cluster at the next stage of the dendrogram, consists of celts, bone awls, and sewing needles. We suspect that the underlying link for these three items may be the fact that they all co-occurred in House 4, House 9, and the dooryard north of House 16.

A third initial cluster, consisting of biface preforms and basketry needles, may result from the relatively high numbers of those items in House 16 and its dooryard. A similar cluster involving fragments of pearl oyster, pearly freshwater mussel, and mica probably results from their frequent co-occurrence in craft debris.

Finally, we note that chert cores, perforators/gravers, and obsidian blades all come out at the apex of the dendrogram. This very likely reflects that fact that most residences contained all three of these items.

While clearly demonstrating a tendency for the data to be clustered, the dendrogram leaves us unsatisfied. We cannot

be sure if two or more items cluster because they were used together in the same activity, or because they result from two or more activities carried out by the same family. The R-mode multidimensional scaling analysis was performed to shed further light on the situation.

The Multidimensional Scaling Program

Multidimensional scaling has enjoyed significant upgrading over the last 15 years, making it worth looking back at some of the earlier efforts of the Oaxaca project.

When I carried out my Q-mode and R-mode multidimensional scaling analyses of the living floors in Guilá Naquitz Cave (Reynolds 1986), we were using the Guttman-Lingoes SSA-1 program, one of the earliest scaling programs. The Q-mode analysis, which searched for the most similar 1 × 1 m squares on each floor, used a chi-square partition distance metric. Partitions were based on the occurrences of variables in four categories (seasonal plants, the cactus/agave group, animal bones, and chert debitage). Several of these categories grouped variables, since the raw counts in each square were often low. For the R-mode analysis, which compared items rather than squares, we used Pearson's *r* correlations for the variables.

Stimulus Number	Stimulus Name	Dimension 1	Dimension 2	Dimension 3	Dimension 4
1	House 6	1.4535	-.2618	.2882	-.1167
2	House 5	1.6795	-.1008	.3461	-.1439
3	House 2	-.1777	-.2064	.4167	.2007
4	House 9	.4214	-.8679	-.9300	.7877
5	House 1	1.3317	.0195	.1017	-.0756
6	House 10	1.4677	-.1256	.1863	-.0431
7	House 4	-2.7467	-1.0840	2.3494	.3261
8	House 7	1.6575	-.1102	.2172	-.0233
9	House 14	1.3969	-.2429	.0821	.1249
10	Unit C4	-.3895	1.5279	-.0586	-.0952
11	Unit C3	-1.9117	1.8486	-.8034	.3266
12	Unit C2	-.9998	2.8282	.1730	-.5144
13	Unit C1	-.1693	.2972	.2389	-.1552
14	House 17	.7751	-.6399	-.3587	.0154
15	SubHse 17	.4934	-.2197	.3256	-.4598
16	House 16	-.7295	-1.3879	-1.3373	.0238
17	NoDoor 16	-2.9826	-1.9131	-.7282	-.7822
18	House 13	-.5701	.6385	-.5092	.6043

Figure 25.3. Q-mode stimulus coordinate matrix for 18 San José phase houses/dooryards, carried to four dimensions. For this matrix, Kruskal's Stress is .02137 and the squared correlation (RSQ) is .99814, which means that 99.8% of the variance has been explained.

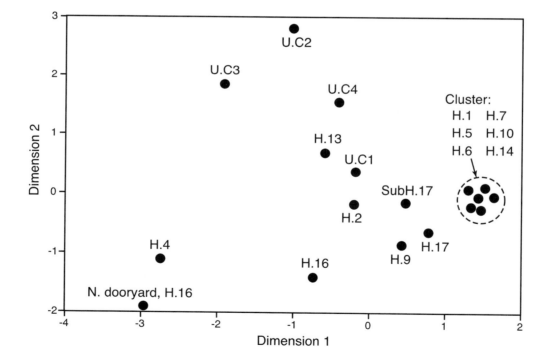

Figure 25.4. Q-mode scatterplot of San José phase houses/dooryards, plotted in two dimensions. (Although the Q-mode analysis had been carried to four dimensions at this time, only dimensions 1 and 2 were used in this scatterplot.) It appears that dimension 1 isolates a cluster of Area C houses (nos. 1, 5, 6, 7, 10, and 14), while dimension 2 pulls House 13 and all the Area A household units (C1-C4) toward the top of the scatterplot. This reinforces the integrity of residential wards A and C.

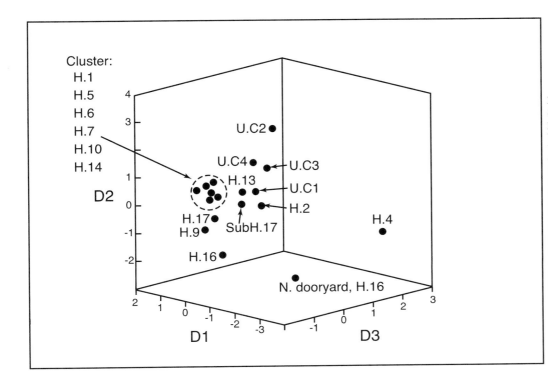

Figure 25.5. Q-mode scatterplot of San José phase houses/dooryards, plotted in three dimensions. (Although the Q-mode analysis had been carried to four dimensions at this time, only dimensions 1, 2, and 3 were used in this scatterplot.) In this diagram, just as in the two-dimensional version, the integrity of Areas A and C is preserved by the first two dimensions. Dimension 3 isolates House 4, and dimension 4 (not shown) isolates House 9, suggesting that those houses are atypical in some way. The earlier version of House 17 ("SubH.17") is more like Houses 2 and 13 than it is like the later, biface-producing version ("H.17").

A number of updated programs, which allow more combinations of approaches as well as better visualization of the results, have now become available. For my study of San José phase houses, I used SPSS Version 12.0, a program that can be used for multidimensional scaling in both the Q- and R-modes. For the details of the program, I direct the reader to the user's guide (SPSS 2003).

The SPSS Q-mode analysis (which compared our 18 residential units) used a Euclidean distance measure between units. The data were viewed as ordinal in nature, since a count for any variable within a house reflects the occurrence of a piece that can be small or large. Viewing the counts as ordinal prevents bias based upon the size or completeness of the object. Ties between data points were broken optimally.

The R-mode analysis (which compared objects of 20 kinds) also used a Euclidean distance measure between objects. In this case, however, the data were standardized as Z-scores and the results treated as interval data. The relative size of a piece was less of an issue in the R-mode analysis, since we were just looking for the co-occurrence of items.

In both analyses, S-stress statistics were used to control convergence. In each case, an optimally scaled data matrix was produced, accompanied by statistics designed to tell us how much of the variance had been explained. Included were Young's S-Stress Formula 1, Kruskal's Stress Formula 1, and the RSQ (R-squared) statistic. RSQ values reflect the proportion of variance (disparities) in the scaled data in the partition (row, matrix, or entire data set) that is accounted for by their corresponding distances.

In determining how many dimensions were necessary to achieve an optimal matrix, we were guided by the stress statistics. At a certain point in each analysis, adding another dimension did not produce either a reduction in stress or a significant improvement in the RSQ statistic.

At no point in either the Q- or R-mode analysis was it necessary to go beyond six dimensions. By then, the RSQ statistic typically showed that we had explained more than 97% of the variance. One unsolved problem with carrying a study to six dimensions, of course, is that there is no way to illustrate that many dimensions graphically. Thus, although we present stimulus coordinate matrices carried to four or six dimensions, our scatterplots are limited to three dimensions (see below). As we will see later in this chapter, the SPSS multidimensional scaling program explained more of the variance in houses and items—using fewer dimensions—than a corresponding factor analysis performed on the same data set.

Which Houses/Household Units Are Most Alike? The Q-Mode Analysis

Figure 25.3 presents the Q-mode stimulus coordinate matrix for our 18 San José phase houses, household units, or dooryards, carried to four dimensions. It was not necessary to go beyond four dimensions, since at that point 99.8% of the variance had been explained.

I tried various ways of depicting the Q-mode results graphically. Figure 25.4 is a scatterplot using the first two of the four dimensions to which the analysis had been carried. Examination

				Dimension			
Stimulus Number	Stimulus Name	1	2	3	4	5	6
1	Cores	.7731	.6707	-.7462	-.3463	.5806	-.2384
2	Perfgr	-1.9983	-1.0112	-.3061	-.6727	.8684	.5428
3	Bifpre	.9632	1.9586	.5511	-1.6601	-.0352	-.1336
4	Obsid	1.0018	-.8517	.3119	.3436	1.3300	-.4678
5	Manos	1.2419	-.3735	.0827	-2.0949	-.5128	.1954
6	Celts	1.9659	.7852	-.5041	.6766	-.0987	.1089
7	Boneawl	1.5951	-.5997	-.4229	.6383	-1.1663	-.0978
8	Sewneed	1.0418	.6135	.2829	1.5679	.5929	.0723
9	Baskneed	1.6645	1.3169	.0147	-.6497	.1389	-.0392
10	Mussel	-.0816	-.2874	-1.3885	1.0452	-.7399	-.2901
11	Pearloy	.8734	-1.9902	.9973	-.5034	-.0209	-.8415
12	Spondyl	-1.8408	1.0291	1.0378	1.2676	.3870	-1.0970
13	Hornshl	-.7815	-2.4190	.2505	-.5445	.0623	-.1200
14	Mica	-1.5738	.1902	-.8702	-.2092	.1929	-.7741
15	Ironmir	-1.8207	.3339	-.9083	.5643	.6487	1.0349
16	Ironlum	-2.6804	.6538	-.1362	-.4712	-.2098	-1.0475
17	Cutbord	-.5101	.5840	3.3557	.8045	-1.2977	.7519
18	Canica	-.9926	.3717	-.2171	.0004	.6229	1.9224
19	Jadeorn	-.3982	-.1197	-1.1268	-.2595	-1.8483	-.0416
20	Fish	1.5576	-.8552	-.2584	.5031	.5052	.5600

Figure 25.6. R-mode stimulus coordinate matrix for 20 categories of objects found in San José phase houses, carried to six dimensions. For this matrix, Kruskal's Stress is .04448 and the squared correlation (RSQ) is .97030, which means that 97% of the variance has been explained.

of both the coordinate matrix (Fig. 25.3) and the scatterplot (Fig. 25.4) allows us to see what has been accomplished. Dimension 1 extracted a cluster of six Area C houses. These houses—nos. 1, 5, 6, 7, 10, and 14—all scored high on this dimension and shared two important characteristics. As mentioned earlier, they all belonged to the same residential ward, and had all been exposed on a modest scale. They were, in effect, the "generic residences" of Area C.

Dimension 2 accomplished something different: House 13 and Household Units C1-C4 all scored high on this dimension, which pulled them toward the top of the scatterplot. Units C1-C4 all belonged to the same residential ward, Area A. Dimension 2 tells us that House 13 was similar enough to be considered part of that ward, a possibility suggested in Chapter 22.

It is significant that dimensions 1 and 2 each succeeded so well in identifying residences from the same neighborhood. Note, also, that they were able to do this regardless of whether the bulk of the archaeological exposure consisted of a house floor, a dooryard, or some combination of the two.

There are several other interesting aspects of Figure 25.4. SubHse17, the earlier stage of House 17, came out as close to House 2 and the Area C cluster as it did to the later stage of

House 17. This reinforces the notion (advanced in Chapter 18) that before the House 17 family began specializing in biface production, their activities were more like those of typical Area C families.

We also note that Houses 2, 4, and 9 of Area C are "outliers": neither closely similar to each other, nor to the other residences in their ward. They all scored low or negative on dimension 1, the one on which six other Area C houses scored high. Houses 2, 4, and 9 were the most extensively excavated houses in Area C, and it may be that the greater exposure revealed something about each that set it apart from the Area C cluster. (In the case of House 9, for example, its striking lack of perforators/gravers may be one of the reasons it came out near House 17, and far from the other Area C houses.)

If dimensions 1 and 2 of our Q-mode analysis seem focused on residential wards, dimensions 3 and 4 seem focused on the "outliers" mentioned above. Dimension 3 isolates House 4 as somehow different, while House 9 scores its highest positive value on dimension 4. Unfortunately, there is no easy way to display all four dimensions graphically.

In Figure 25.5, however, we present a three-dimensional scatterplot featuring dimensions 1, 2, and 3. This scatterplot

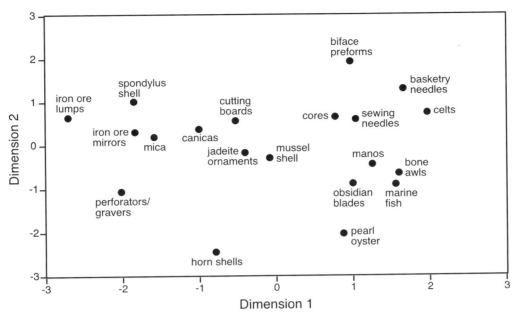

Figure 25.7. R-mode scatterplot of objects from San José phase houses, plotted in two dimensions. (Although the R-mode analysis had been carried to six dimensions at this time, only dimensions 1 and 2 were used in this scatterplot.) Some potentially interesting groupings include (1) biface preforms, needles for sewing and basketry, chert cores, and celts at upper right, and (2) a circle of items possibly related to making ornaments (horn shell, pearl oyster, obsidian blades, mussel shell, jadeite[?] ornaments, and perforators/gravers) in the lower half of the scatterplot. Also, iron ore lumps lie near iron ore mirrors at far left.

reinforces many of the patterns seen in Figure 25.4, the two-dimensional plot. Houses 1, 5, 6, 7, 10, and 14 of Area C still cluster tightly. House 13 and Household Units C1–C4 of Area A are still grouped together. Houses 2, 4, and 9 still stand out as different from the other Area C houses. The earlier stage of House 17 remains more similar to houses from other wards than to the later stage of House 17.

What the three-dimensional scatterplot adds is a closer relationship between House 16 and the dooryard just to its north. While the North Dooryard is still somewhat of an outlier, it is closer to House 16 than to any other residential unit. Neither is positively associated with any of the four dimensions, but their negative scores are similar to each other.

In sum, Q-mode analysis indicates that during the San José phase, one can see specialization on two levels. Families within each residential ward seem to have shared a number of activities, leading their houses to cluster. The iron ore mirror production seen in all residences of Area A would be an example. Such neighborhood differences showed up immediately with dimensions 1 and 2.

At the same time, even within each ward, there seem to have been families with a unique or uncommon specialty that set them apart. Chert biface production, basket making, and woodworking (although woodworking tools were not included in our sample) might be examples of such specialties. In our study, the less common specialties associated with individual households did not come into focus until we had reached dimensions 3 and 4.

As suggested earlier, the more square meters of a house you expose, the greater the likelihood that you will find evidence for a unique or uncommon activity. In retrospect, we wish that San José phase families had not bothered to sweep their houses; it would have increased our sample of items.

Associations among Household Items: The R-Mode Analysis

Figure 25.6 presents the R-mode stimulus coordinate matrix for the 20 household items we have chosen, carried to six dimensions. It proved necessary to carry the R-mode analysis to six dimensions in order to reach the point where 97% of the variance had been explained.

Our expectations for the R-mode analysis, of course, were different from those of the preceding Q-mode analysis. We knew that there could be several alternative reasons why any two items, A and B, would co-occur within household units in our sample. It might happen because items A and B were used together, or it might happen simply because the same family engaged in two activities, one using A, the other, B. In the latter case, the co-occurrence would be coincidental. We therefore had to employ large doses of common sense.

Figure 25.7 is a scatterplot based on the first two dimensions of our scaling. A few of the pairs (or groupings) of items seem intuitively reasonable. For example, it makes sense that iron ore mirrors and iron ore lumps would be associated, since residences

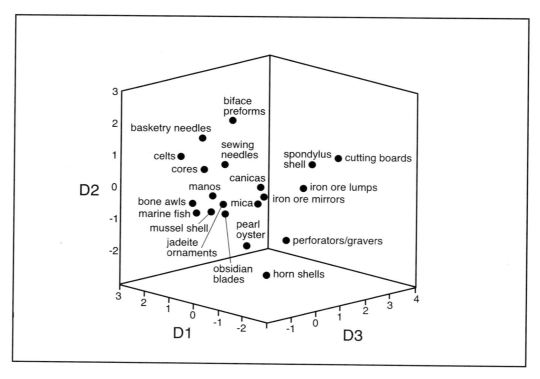

Figure 25.8. R-mode scatterplot of objects from San José phase houses, plotted in three dimensions. (Although the R-mode analysis had been carried to six dimensions at this time, only dimensions 1, 2, and 3 were used in this scatterplot.) Potentially interesting groupings include (1) *Spondylus* shell and cutting boards; (2) cores, celts, needles for sewing and basketry, and biface preforms, at upper left; (3) a group of items possibly related to making ornaments (perforators/gravers, pearl oyster, and horn shell) at lower right; and (4) a group of items imported into the valley (obsidian blades, jadeite[?] ornaments, mussel shell, and marine fish) at lower left. Iron ore lumps and mirrors are still scoring very negative on dimension 1 and mildly positive on dimension 2, but now the mirrors lie close to mica and *canicas*.

polishing the former would be likely to accumulate the latter. The grouping of biface preforms, needles for sewing and basketry, chert cores, and celts also makes sense, since they all co-occurred in the House 16/North Dooryard complex.

The loose grouping of horn shells, pearl oyster, mussel shell, obsidian blades, perforators/gravers, and jadeite(?) ornaments is less easily interpreted. Many of those items, however, are tools or raw materials for making ornaments, and might tend to be dropped or discarded together.

Let us turn now to Figure 25.8, a scatterplot based on dimensions 1, 2, and 3, to see if any further insights are forthcoming. Some of the associations we saw in the two-dimensional scatterplot are repeated here. Iron ore lumps and iron ore mirrors still have negative scores on dimension 1 and mildly positive scores on dimension 2, but in the three-dimensional plot, the mirrors are joined by mica and *canicas*. We are intrigued by the grouping of *Spondylus* shells and "cutting boards" because it might mean that the former were trimmed on the latter. The association of perforators/gravers, pearl oyster, and horn shell (hinted at already in Fig. 25.7) makes intuitive sense, because it groups two types of marine shell with the chert tools used to convert them into ornaments.

Figure 25.8 also presents us with an interesting grouping of chert cores, celts, needles for sewing and basketry, and biface preforms. All of these items were well represented in the House 16/North Dooryard complex (Chapters 18-19). We therefore suspect that their co-occurrence in that residential unit is the underlying reason for their grouping in the scatterplot.

Figure 25.8 also shows a grouping of items, all of which had to be imported into the Valley of Oaxaca: obsidian blades, jadeite(?) ornaments, pearly freshwater mussels, and marine fish parts. One possible reason for this grouping is that houses receiving high numbers of obsidian blades also tended to have more than their share of other imports. In this regard, House 4 and the House 16/North Dooryard complex come to mind. While we suspect that families of higher rank probably received more imports, it is also the case that the excavators exposed the aforementioned houses more extensively, increasing the likelihood of recovering imports.

We should point out that some items failed to provide us with much information, either at the two-dimensional or three-dimensional level. Two-hand manos were among them. The problem may be that most specimens were only broken fragments of old manos, too small to serve their original function.

Factor Analysis

I also subjected the data in Table 25.1 to corresponding Q- and R-mode factor analyses. Both factor analyses used principal components analysis as their extraction method. My purposes in conducting the factor analyses were (1) to check on the appropriateness of viewing the raw data as ordinal (rather than interval or ratio) and (2) to determine whether factor analysis would have worked better than multidimensional scaling if the raw data were assumed to be interval in nature.

The Q-mode version of the factor analysis needed five factors to explain 95% of the variance, and did not reach the 98.5% level until eight factors had been extracted. The R-mode version of the factor analysis required eight factors just to explain 91.9% of the variance, and did not reach the 95% level until ten factors had been extracted. We therefore concluded that multidimensional scaling using an ordinal interpretation of the data was, in fact, the best approach for our purposes. It explained more of the variation, using fewer dimensions, than a corresponding factor analysis. We feel that this was because factor analysis exploited the precise variation in the data, assuming that each measure was made using the same units. However, the size and complexity of the items that made up the counts worked against this assumption, and is probably one of the reasons why multidimensional scaling worked better in this case, even though it made fewer assumptions about the data.

Conclusions

Of the two types of multidimensional scaling we applied to the San José phase data set, the Q-mode analysis was easier to interpret than the R-mode analysis. Perhaps the most striking success of the Q-mode analysis was that it confirmed the integrity of the residential wards.

All the household units of Area A, plus nearby House 13, emerged as similar to each other. Six of the Area C houses also came out in a tight cluster, separate from Area A. This reinforces a number of previous models for San José Mogote, for example: (1) there was craft specialization by ward in the San José phase, and (2) families within each ward shared enough activities with their kinsmen or neighbors to make their ward appear distinct

and corporate. Parry's (1987:27) conclusion that families within a ward "did cooperate in procurement or exchange of local raw materials, but did not cooperate with households in different residential wards" thus fits well with our results. So does the evidence that each ward's iconography emphasized its occupants' common descent from a specific "celestial spirit" (Marcus and Flannery 1996:95-96).

Other suspicions about village organization are reinforced by our Q-mode multidimensional scaling. One is the idea that even within a relatively homogeneous ward, there might be individual families who performed a unique or atypical activity. Biface manufacture is one example. (Celt manufacture—evidence for which came from an Area C midden rather than a house—might have been another.) This would constitute specialization at the household level. Candidates for household specialization would include House 4, House 9, and the House 16/17/North Dooryard complex; but since these were among the most extensively excavated residences, we cannot be sure how much of their coordinate distances from other houses reflects greater exposure, and how much reflects uniqueness.

Finally, our Q-mode analysis suggests that a family could acquire a new craft specialty over time, as House 17 apparently did between its first and second stages.

As for the R-mode analysis, it clearly detected co-occurrences among items. Our interpretive problem was that we could not always tell whether the reasons for co-occurrence were *functional* (e.g., someone working pearl oyster with chert perforators/gravers) or *coincidental* (e.g., one spouse making biface preforms while the other wove baskets using bone needles). Both types of co-occurrence are of interest; it is frustrating not to be able to distinguish them.

Of all the groupings observed in the R-mode scatterplots, we suspect that the co-occurrence of imports (obsidian blades, jadeite[?] ornaments, mussel shells, and marine fish) is most likely to reflect the differential success of some families in interregional exchange. We suspect that the groupings of (1) iron ore mirrors with iron ore lumps and (2) perforators/gravers with pearl oyster and horn shell may well be functional. "Cutting boards" might have been used when trimming shell, although our sample of occurrences is small. And sadly, even after a six-dimension R-mode analysis, we still don't know the function of *canicas*.

Chapter 26

Radiocarbon Dating

During the course of our excavation we collected scores of charcoal samples, more than we could afford to submit for radiocarbon dating. Our samples ran from hundred-gram chunks of carbonized post to tiny, half-gram corn kernels.

In the 1960s and 1970s, of course, it was only the larger samples that could be analyzed. In that era of conventional radiocarbon dating, laboratories wanted at least 25 grams of charcoal, and even then the standard deviation for your date might be 150 years or more. Years "B.P." (before the present) were calculated using the 5568-year half-life for ^{14}C, even after physicists had learned that the true half-life was closer to 5730 years. To convert your Formative dates to "B.C.," you subtracted 1950 from "B.P.," even when the year was 1970.

Our first dates from San José Mogote were supplied by the Smithsonian Institution and the University of Michigan, whose radiocarbon laboratories no longer exist. We submitted our largest charcoal samples and still got large standard deviations. However, Dr. Richard Crane of the University of Michigan radiocarbon lab gave us invaluable advice. "Never run all your radiocarbon samples," he said. "Twenty years from now, radiocarbon dating will be even more accurate, and you'll be sorry if you don't have any samples left." Then he added, "Don't throw away the samples that are too small by today's standards. Someday there will be a way to run them."

His words were prophetic, because today we have AMS (Accelerator Mass Spectrometric) dating, which can produce dates from samples as small as a sesame seed. We also have dendrocalibration, which gets us closer to "real time" as opposed to "radiocarbon time."

In preparation for the writing of this volume we secured two new grants, allowing us to run 20 AMS dates from San José Mogote. Most were run on charcoal samples considered too small in the 1960s, yet the AMS method produced standard deviations as low as 40 years. We are indebted to the Office of the Vice President for Research, University of Michigan, and the Foundation for the Advancement of Mesoamerican Studies Inc. (Crystal River, FL) for supplying funds for these new dates. All AMS dates were run by Beta Analytic of Miami, Florida, who also provided us with the most up-to-date dendrocalibration. To increase our sample, we also had 14 of our previous ^{14}C dates dendrocalibrated to INTCAL98 standards (Stuiver et al. 1998).

The Future of Formative Chronology

Although many Mesoamerican archaeologists are now receiving dendrocalibrated dates, the absolute chronology of Formative Mesoamerica is still largely based on subtracting 1950 from radiocarbon years B.P. The reason is that calibrated Formative dates (B.C.) are often a century or more older than uncalibrated dates (b.c.). Mixing the two kinds of dates confuses our efforts to compare regions with similar pottery styles.

Consider, for example, the San José phase of the Valley of Oaxaca and the San Lorenzo phase of southern Veracruz. In Coe and Diehl's (1980a, 1980b) report on San Lorenzo, which uses uncalibrated, conventional radiocarbon dates, the San Lorenzo phase falls between 1150 and 900 b.c. Our uncalibrated dates assign the San José phase to 1150–850 b.c.—roughly the same period—which is just what the shared ceramic style suggests. Suppose, however, that we were to use only our dendrocalibrated AMS dates for the San José phase. In this case the San José phase would fall between 1350/1300 B.C. and 1000/950 B.C., making it appear that carved-incised gray ware bowls with Lightning motifs

456

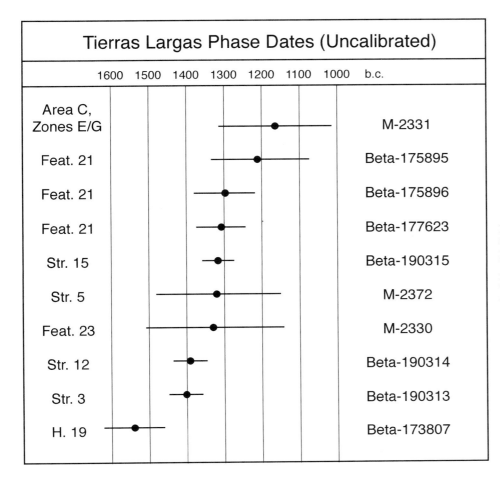

Figure 26.1. Uncalibrated versions of radiocarbon dates relevant to the Tierras Largas phase. The black dots are dates b.c., derived by subtracting 1950 from the conventional radiocarbon age (B.P.). The horizontal lines give the one-sigma range to either side of the black dot. (Data from Table 26.1.)

began two centuries earlier in Oaxaca than in Veracruz. In point of fact, we consider such vessels to have appeared simultaneously in both regions, and the traded vessels mentioned earlier in this volume make that likely.

In this chapter we will present two absolute chronologies: *uncalibrated* and *calibrated*. We present our uncalibrated chronology first, because that is still the one on which most Meso-american Formative sequences are based. We realize, however, that as excavation of Formative sites proceeds, and more and more dates are dendrocalibrated, there will come a time when it seems anachronistic to cling to our "b.c." dates. In preparation for that day, we provide an alternative chronology based on calibrated dates.

The Espiridión Complex

No charcoal samples are available for the Espiridión Complex.

The Tierras Largas Phase

Table 26.1 presents 9 dates for the Tierras Largas phase, and one date (M-2331) that is believed to lie at the Tierras Largas/San José phase transition. Some of the dates have already been discussed in Chapter 7. We have augmented them with four dates from Tierras Largas phase Men's Houses in Area C. These Men's Houses will be discussed in detail in a future volume, *Excavations at San José Mogote 2: The Cognitive Archaeology.*

Let us first consider the uncalibrated versions of our Tierras Largas phase dates, those produced by subtracting 1950 from the "B.P." date. These "b.c." dates are presented graphically in Figure 26.1, arranged in order from oldest (at the bottom) to youngest (at the top).

In previous publications (e.g. Flannery and Marcus 1994:376) we estimated that the Tierras Largas phase had begun by 1400 or 1350 b.c. and lasted until 1200 or 1150 b.c. Our new dates suggest that the phase may have begun by 1500 b.c.—earlier than expected—but had indeed ended by 1150 b.c.

We have already discussed House 19, Feature 23, and the Feature 21 palisade in Chapter 7. As for the four charcoal samples from Men's Houses, we note that the uncalibrated dates do a good job of reflecting their stratigraphic relationships.

Structure 3 (1400 b.c.) was the earliest of the Men's Houses in the Control Section of the Area C Master Profile. Structure 6 (undated) was the next built. Structure 5 (1320 b.c.) was built after Structure 6, but before Structure 15. Structure 15 was built

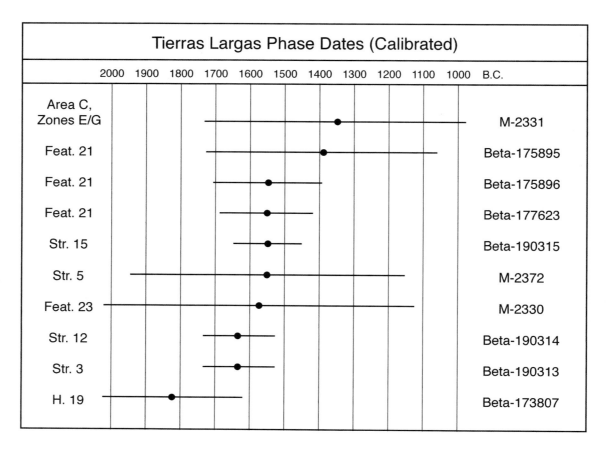

Figure 26.2. Dendrocalibrated versions of radiocarbon dates relevant to the Tierras Largas phase. The horizontal lines give the two-sigma range in years B.C. The black dots indicate the midpoint of the two-sigma range (not the intercept, use of which is discouraged by radiocarbon experts).

Table 26.1. Radiocarbon Dates for the Tierras Largas Phase

Provenience	Conventional ¹⁴C Yrs B.P.	B.P. Date Minus 1950	Calibrated 2σ Range	Laboratory No.
House 19 (Area C)	3490 ± 80	1540 b.c.	2020-1620 B.C.	Beta-173807
Feature 21 (Palisade)				
Post 5	3260 ± 60	1310 b.c.	1680-1410 B.C.	Beta-177623
Post 4	3250 ± 80	1300 b.c.	1700-1390 B.C	Beta-175896
Post 3	3160 ± 130	1210 b.c.	1720-1060 B.C.	Beta-175895
Feature 23 (Area C)	3280 ± 180	1330 b.c.	2010-1110 B.C.	M-2330
Men's Houses (Area C)				
Structure 3	3350 ± 40	1400 b.c.	1730-1520 B.C.	Beta-190313
Structure 12	3340 ± 40	1390 b.c.	1720-1520 B.C.	Beta-190314
Structure 5	3270 ± 160	1320 b.c.	1940-1140 B.C.	M-2372
Structure 15	3270 ± 40	1320 b.c.	1630-1440 B.C.	Beta-190315
Area C, interface of Zones E/G	3120 ± 150	1170 b.c.	1720-970 B.C	M-2331

last, with its lime-filled pit (Feature 55) literally intruding into the floor of Structure 6. Structure 15 also produced a date of 1320 b.c., but was not stratigraphically contemporaneous with Structure 5. (Given the large standard deviation of the Structure 5 date, it could lie anywhere between 1400 and 1320 b.c.)

In the Threshing Floor Sector of Area C, there was another stratigraphic sequence of Men's Houses. Structure 12 (1390 b.c.) was the first built; Structure 11 (undated) was built later on almost the same spot (see Fig. 7.13 of Chapter 7). Unfortunately, we lack the stratigraphic information necessary to interdigitate the Men's Houses of the Threshing Floor Sector with those of the Control Section.

The occupants of San José Mogote, of course, continued to build lime-plastered Men's Houses well into the San José phase. Structure 7 of Area C would be a San José phase example (Flannery and Marcus 1994:357-62). So would the badly destroyed Men's House in Zone F below Structure 19 on Mound 1 (Chapter 22). Generally speaking, we could argue that such Men's Houses were built for at least 300 years, between 1400 and 1000 b.c.

Finally, as discussed in Chapter 7, we believe that the M-2331 date (1170 b.c.) falls near the Tierras Largas phase/San José phase transition.

Calibrating the Tierras Largas Phase Dates

Figure 26.2 gives, in graphic form, the calibrated two-sigma ranges for our 10 Tierras Largas phase dates. One of the first things we notice is the dramatic difference between (1) a conventional radiocarbon date with a 160-year standard deviation (e.g., Structure 5), and (2) an AMS date with a 40-year standard deviation (e.g., Structure 15). The results argue forcefully for paying the higher price and getting an AMS date.

What do the calibrated dates tell us about the "real age" of the Tierras Largas phase? With 95% probability, they tell us that House 19 was built between 2020 and 1620 B.C. The Men's Houses of Area C were most likely built between 1730 and 1440 B.C. Two of the palisade posts from Feature 21 were hewn between 1700/1680 B.C. and 1410/1390 B.C. The third palisade post was undoubtedly hewn during the same period, but its two-sigma range is too long to be helpful. The range midpoints for all three posts fall between 1545 and 1390 B.C.

Calibration gives us a somewhat different perspective on date M-2331, charcoal from the interface of Zones E and G in Square S33A of Area C. Zone G belonged to the Tierras Largas phase, Zone E to Early San José. From which zone did the charcoal come? Its uncalibrated date (1170 b.c.) lay near the presumed transition from one phase to another.

Interestingly, its huge calibrated two-sigma range reveals that M-2331 could belong to either phase. The charcoal could either be from Zone G, or be a piece of a burnt post intrusive from Zone E. Its midpoint, 1345 B.C., may provide us with the calibrated version of the Tierras Largas/San José transition. That means that in "real time," the Tierras Largas phase might have

begun by 1800 B.C. and ended by 1350/1300 B.C. It may, in other words, have been 450-500 years long.

The San José Phase

Table 26.2 presents 15 radiocarbon dates from San José phase proveniences, and one date (M-2331) that we believe falls at the transition from the Tierras Largas phase to the San José phase. We have grouped the dates by residential ward where appropriate.

In previous publications (e.g. Flannery and Marcus 1994:384) we suggested that the San José phase probably began between 1200 and 1150 b.c. and lasted until 900 or 850 b.c. None of our new dates from Beta Analytic change that estimate, since all of them fall between 1010 and 860 b.c. Our two oldest dates (M-2331 and SI-464) have large standard deviations, but their midpoints fall between 1200 and 1150 b.c.

Two of the Smithsonian dates (SI-462 and SI-463) appear too young, although both fall within two standard deviations of 900 b.c. Both these charcoal samples were small by the standards of conventional radiocarbon dating. Sample Beta-179078 was also small, but this did not present a problem, since it was AMS-dated. It came out much closer to its expected date than SI-462, and with a smaller standard deviation. We have decided to rely on Beta-179078, and therefore did not bother to have SI-462 dendrocalibrated.

In Figure 26.2 we present, in graphic form, all these uncalibrated San José phase dates. We have grouped the dates into Early, Middle, and Late stages of the San José phase, based on our assessments of the associated ceramics and the actual stratigraphic sequence for each residential ward. It will be immediately apparent that the radiocarbon dates are not precise enough to reinforce the division of the San José phase into Early, Middle, and Late stages. This is particularly true of the dates with standard deviations of 120 years or more. Trying to subdivide a 300-year phase using dates with two-sigma ranges of 240 years is an exercise in futility. In such cases, the ceramic horizon markers are more useful tools for subdivision.

Calibrating the San José Phase Dates

Figure 26.4 gives, in graphic form, the calibrated two-sigma ranges of 15 of our San José phase dates. One of the first things we notice is that dendrocalibration has adjusted some of the dates whose radiocarbon ages were in conflict with their stratigraphic positions.

The dates from Household Units C1 and C2 are the most improved. Before calibration, Unit C1 dated to 860 b.c. while Unit C2 dated to 780 b.c., making C1 "older" than C2, even though it lay stratigraphically *above* the latter (Fig. 26.3). After calibration, the midpoint of Unit C2's range is 980 B.C., while Unit C1's is 945 B.C., supporting their stratigraphic relationship (Fig. 26.4).

Less improved are the dates from levels D2 and D1 of the Zone D Midden in Area A. Level D2 still appears younger than

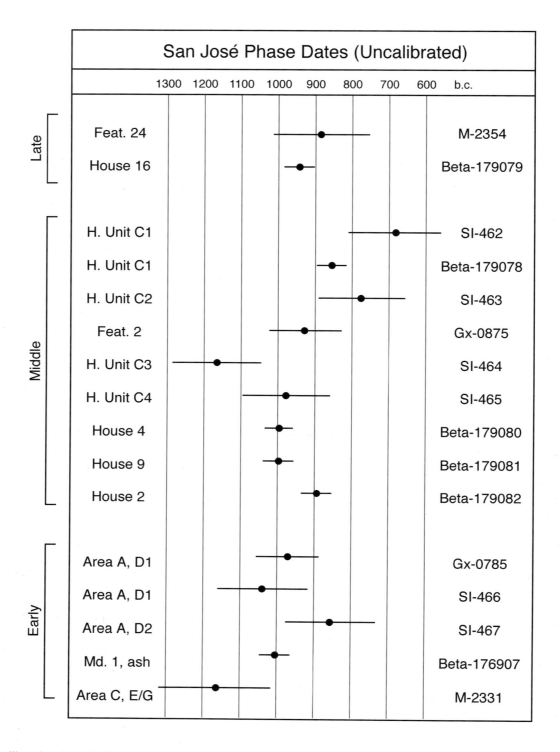

Figure 26.3. Uncalibrated versions of radiocarbon dates relevant to the San José phase. The black dots are dates b.c., derived by subtracting 1950 from the conventional radiocarbon age (B.P.). The horizontal lines give the one-sigma range to either side of the black dot. (Data from Table 26.2).

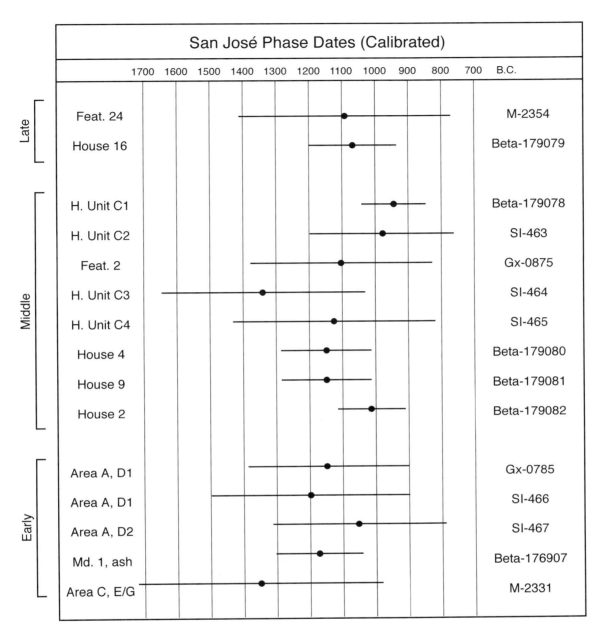

Figure 26.4. Dendrocalibrated versions of radiocarbon dates relevant to the San José phase. The horizontal lines give the two-sigma range in years B.C. The black dots indicate the midpoint of the two-sigma range (not the intercept, use of which is discouraged by radiocarbon experts).

Table 26.2. Radiocarbon Dates for the San José Phase

Provenience	Conventional ^{14}C Yrs B.P.	B.P. Date Minus 1950	Calibrated 2σ Range	Laboratory No.
Area C, interface of Zones E/G	3120 ± 150	1170 b.c.	1720-970 B.C.	M-2331
Mound 1, ash layer below Monument 3	2960 ± 40	1010 b.c.	1300-1030 B.C.	Beta-176907
Area A Midden				
Zone D2	2810 ± 120	860 b.c.	1310-790 B.C.	SI-467
Zone D1	2990 ± 120	1040 b.c.	1500-900 B.C.	SI-466
Zone D1	2925 ± 85	975 b.c.	1390-900 B.C.	Gx-0785
Area C Houses				
House 2	2850 ± 40	900 b.c.	1120-910 B.C.	Beta-179082
House 9	2950 ± 40	1000 b.c.	1290-1020 B.C.	Beta-179081
House 4	2950 ± 40	1000 b.c.	1290-1020 B.C.	Beta-179080
Area A Houses				
Unit C4	2930 ± 120	980 b.c.	1430-820 B.C.	SI-465
Unit C3	3120 ± 120	1170 b.c.	1650-1030 B.C.	SI-464
Feature 2	2880 ± 95	930 b.c.	1375-825 B.C.	Gx-0875
Unit C2	2730 ± 120	780 b.c.	1200-760 B.C.	SI-463
Unit C1	2810 ± 40	860 b.c.	1040-850 B.C.	Beta-179078
Unit C1	2640 ± 120	690 b.c.	n.a.	SI-462
Area B Houses				
House 16 (Feature 62)	2890 ± 40	940 b.c.	1200-940 B.C.	Beta-179079
Feature 24 (Area B/C conn. trench)	2840 ± 150	890 b.c.	1410-780 B.C.	M-2354

D1, though not by as many years. We are reassured that the differences in age are no greater than one might expect in a midden full of prepared charcoal from old trees. "Old charcoal" could also account for the date from Household Unit C3 being so much older than that from Unit C4.

As for the age of the San José phase in "real time," Figure 26.4 suggests that the phase probably began by 1350/1300 B.C. and had ended by 1000/950 B.C. It may, in other words, have been 350-400 years long.

Like their uncalibrated counterparts, the calibrated dates in Figure 26.4 are still not precise enough to match our division into Early, Middle, and Late subphases. By spreading the dates out over a longer span of time, however, calibration makes it easier to see which dates provide a plausible sequence, and which probably reflect charcoal from the inner rings of old trees.

Our best guess is that San José phase activity was underway in Area C before 1300 B.C. By the twelfth century B.C. the Zone D Midden in Area A was accumulating, and a Men's House had been built atop Mound 1. The associated pottery places these events in the Early San José phase.

During the Middle San José phase, Houses 9 and 4 were built in Area C, and Household Units C4 and C3 were occupied in Area A. Four dates suggest that these events took place during the second half of the twelfth century B.C. We suspect that date SI-464 was run on prepared charcoal from an old tree. We have no explanation for Beta-179082, but are reassured by the fact that its two-sigma range at least overlaps with the dates from Houses 9 and 4.

While the pottery associated with Household Units C2 and C1 would place them in our Middle San José phase, their calibrated dates of 980-945 B.C. are what we would expect for the Late San José phase.

The calibrated dates from House 16 and Feature 24—both assigned to the Late San José phase on the basis of the associated pottery—seem too early, although their two-sigma ranges at least overlap with the date from Household Unit C1. Once again, we are reminded of the futility of trying to subdivide a 350-400 year phase using dates whose two-sigma ranges are sometimes greater than 250 years.

The Guadalupe Phase

In previous publications, we have assigned the Guadalupe phase to the period 850-700 b.c. (uncalibrated). We have also explained that the diagnostic pottery of the Guadalupe phase is most typical of the Etla subvalley:

> The farther one moves south and east from the Etla region, however, the less one sees these diagnostics; in the southern Valle Grande and the eastern Tlacolula subvalley, the pottery of 850-700 [b.c.] is sufficiently different to make the use of the term "Guadalupe phase" a bit inappropriate.... [T]his regional diversity tells us that dynamic changes were underway, with competing centers arising in different areas of the valley. [Marcus and Flannery 1996:111]

Unfortunately, our excavations at San José Mogote provided only one new Guadalupe phase radiocarbon date. The problem is that during the Guadalupe phase, much of the piedmont spur was converted from residential space to "public" or "ceremonial" space, and the Guadalupe phase public buildings we found did not produce charcoal samples. To increase our sample of Guadalupe phase residences, we would have needed to excavate to the north and east, perhaps even east of the railroad tracks on the San José Mogote/San Sebastián Etla border.

We did recover one charcoal sample associated with Late Guadalupe phase pottery. While digging below Monument 3, the carved stone threshold for the corridor between Structure 14 and 19 on Mound 1, we encountered an extensive charcoal layer (Flannery and Marcus 2003: Fig. 4). This layer provided the following AMS date:

> Beta-179879:
>> 2670 B.P. ± 40
>> 720 b.c. (uncalibrated)
>> dendrocalibrated 2σ range: 900-790 B.C.

Beta-179879 supports an ending date for the Guadalupe phase of about 700 b.c. To support a starting date of 850 b.c., we can turn to a previous date, M-2102. This conventional radiocarbon date came from a carbonized pine post in stratigraphic Zone F3, Area A, Barrio del Rosario Huitzo. That burnt post, set into sterile soil and incorporated into the fill of a temple platform called Structure 4, can be seen in a previous publication (Flannery and Marcus 1994: Fig. 4.8). We believe this post to have been put in place at the transition from the San José phase to the Guadalupe phase. A piece large enough to be identifiable as *Pinus* sp. gave the following conventional date:

> M-2102:
>> 2800 B.P. ± 150
>> 850 b.c. (uncalibrated)
>> dendrocalibrated 2σ range: 1390-760 B.C.

Needless to say, securing a larger sample of Guadalupe phase dates from good, sealed stratigraphic contexts should be a future priority. Our other charcoal samples from Huitzo came mostly from fill, rather than house floors or *in situ* carbonized posts, and we consider most of the results less than optimal.

The Rosario Phase

With the Rosario phase, our chronology is back on firmer ground. All Rosario ^{14}C dates from San José Mogote were run in recent years by Beta Analytic. Most are AMS dates with small standard deviations, and all have been dendrocalibrated.

Table 26.3 presents 8 dates from San José Mogote and 2 from Household Unit R-2 at Fábrica San José (Drennan 1976a: Table 1). During the occupation of Unit R-2, Fábrica San José would have been a satellite village in the chiefdom centered at San José Mogote.

In previous publications (e.g., Marcus and Flannery 1996:121), we have estimated that the Rosario phase began by 700 b.c. and ended by 500 b.c. All 10 dates in Table 26.3 support those previous estimates. The two earliest dates, 730 b.c. and 720 b.c., are within one standard deviation of our proposed starting date. The youngest date, 510 b.c., could hardly be closer to our proposed ending date. These results are particularly pleasing in light of the fact that many of our Rosario samples came from temples or temple platforms, rather than house floors or sealed features. Samples from fill always run the risk of being redeposited pieces of earlier charcoal.

Many of the proveniences listed in Table 26.3 have been discussed in Chapters 22 and 23. All of the Rosario public buildings will be described in detail in a future volume. In order to make Table 26.3 more useful, however, we will provide the following brief notes on the samples it lists.

Feature 47 (described in Chapter 11) was a Rosario phase roasting pit with evidence of ritual cannibalism.

Structures 19, 28, 26, and 37 were all located on Mound 1. Structure 19 (described in Chapter 22) was a large Rosario phase stone masonry platform. Sample Beta-179876 was a conventional date run on charcoal from the final construction stage of this platform (Square S2E14).

Structure 28 (also described in Chapter 22) was a Rosario phase temple built atop Structure 19. Sample Beta-177624 was an AMS date run on charcoal from a roof beam that fell when Structure 28 was burned (Flannery and Marcus 2003:11802).

Structure 37 was a more recent Rosario phase temple, built not far to the north after Structure 28 burned (Flannery and Marcus 2003:11802). Sample Beta-177626 was charcoal from a burnt post in Structure 37 (ibid.).

Structure 26 (described in Chapter 23) was part of a Rosario phase elite residence, built above the ruins of Structure 28. Sample Beta-179877 was charcoal from Room 1 of Structure 28. Table 26.3 suggests that the entire period from the completion of Structure 19 to the building of Structures 37 and 26 fell within the Middle Rosario phase, 640-590 b.c.

The Structure 28 temple sat atop the Structure 19 masonry platform. The Structure 37 temple sat above the first stage of another stone masonry platform, Structure 14. Between Structures 14 and 19 ran a narrow corridor for which Monument 3 (Flannery and Marcus 2003: Fig. 3b) served as a carved stone threshold. Monument 3 (discussed in Chapter 5) depicts a sacrificed prisoner with his hieroglyph name.

After this monument and the buildings flanking it fell into disuse, a soil horizon (complete with humic layer) formed on the erosional debris that gradually covered up the carved stone. At some point two well-made stone-lined hearths, Features 18 and 19, were created in the old soil horizon (Flannery and Marcus 2003:11803). A *terminus ante quem* for Monument 3 is provided by AMS dates Beta-173808, Beta-175897, and Beta-175898, which were run on charcoal from these hearths. Of these three dates, the one that most closely fits our expectations is the 560 b.c. date from Feature 18. The 630 b.c. date from Feature 19 is older than expected, but perhaps only by a standard deviation. On the other hand, we consider the 730 b.c. date from Feature 19 too old. Since some of the fuel in the hearth appeared to be

Table 26.3. Radiocarbon Dates for the Rosario Phase

Provenience	Conventional ^{14}C Yrs B.P.	B.P. Date Minus 1950	Calibrated 2σ Range	Laboratory No.
Feature 47 (Area C)	2640 ± 40	690 b.c.	840-790 B.C.	Beta-179878
Structure 19, fill (Mound 1)	2560 ± 180	610 b.c.	1110-350 B.C.	Beta-179876
Structure 28, roof beam (Mound 1)	2550 ± 60	600 b.c.	820-500 B.C.	Beta-177624
Structure 26, Room 1 (Mound 1)	2590 ± 40	640 b.c.	820-770 B.C.	Beta-179877
Structure 37, post (Mound 1)	2540 ± 90	590 b.c.	840-400 B.C.	Beta-177626
Feature 19, above Monument 3	2680 ± 40	730 b.c.	900-800 B.C.	Beta-175897
Feature 19, above Monument 3	2580 ± 40	630 b.c.	820-760 B.C. or 620-590 B.C.	Beta-175898
Feature 18, above Monument 3	2510 ± 40	560 b.c.	790-500 B.C.	Beta-173808
Fábrica San José Unit R-2, Feat. 51	2460 ± 80	510 b.c.	800-390 B.C.	Tx-1699
Fábrica San José Unit R-2, H 9 (A)	2670 ± 60	720 b.c.	920-780 B.C.	Tx-1700

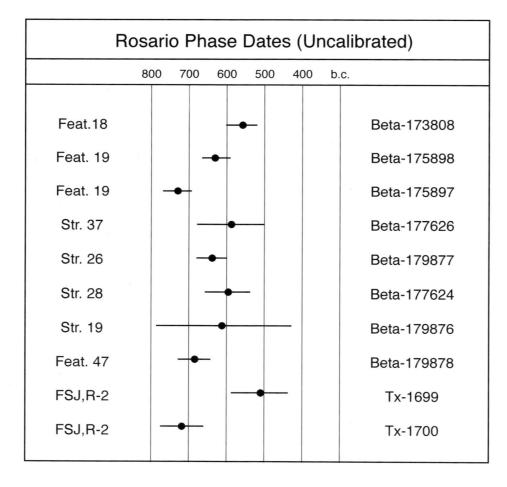

Figure 26.5. Uncalibrated versions of radiocarbon dates relevant to the Rosario phase. The black dots are dates b.c., derived by subtracting 1950 from the conventional radiocarbon age (B.P.). The horizontal lines give the one-sigma range to either side of the black dot. (Data from Table 26.3.)

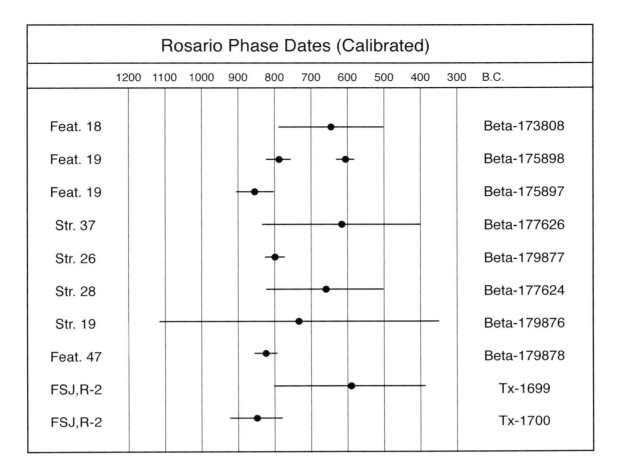

Figure 26.6. Dendrocalibrated versions of radiocarbon dates relevant to the Rosario phase. The horizontal lines give the two-sigma range in years B.C. The black dots indicate the midpoint of the two-sigma range (not the intercept). Note that Beta-175898 has two possible calibrations.

prepared charcoal, it is possible that Beta-175897 dated one of the inner rings of an old tree.

Finally, the two dates from Fábrica San José both come from Household Unit R-2 of the Rosario phase. Sample Tx-1700 comes from the floor of the house itself, while Tx-1699 comes from Feature 51, a basin-shaped hearth (Drennan 1976a: Fig. 66). Drennan (op. cit.:118-19) notes that the floor of the house also had small circular areas of ash, reflecting the use of charcoal braziers. As suggested above, the prepared charcoal used in braziers often came from large pines with many rings, spanning the life of the tree. That may explain why these two dates from the same house cover the entire Rosario phase (720-510 b.c.).

Figure 26.3 presents, in graphic form, our uncalibrated Rosario dates. To the extent possible, we have preserved the stratigraphic relationships of the proveniences from which they came (e.g., Structure 26 was built above Structure 28, which in turn was built above Structure 19; see above). However, just as our San José phase dates were too imprecise to reinforce a division into early, middle, and late subphases, our Rosario dates are too imprecise to duplicate the stratigraphy of Mound 1. (For example, Structure 28 was stratigraphically older than Structure 26, but the ¹⁴C dates do not reflect this.)

In all honesty, we would have been astonished if the dates had closely matched the stratigraphy. In the first place, upright posts, roof beams, and charcoal prepared from large pine trees all present problems of differing tree ring ages, as discussed above. Second, one cannot expect ¹⁴C dates with standard deviations of 40-180 years to monitor architectural changes that may have taken only 20-30 years to make. We count ourselves lucky that our dates clustered as well as they did.

Calibrating the Rosario Phase Dates

Figure 26.6 gives, in graphic form, the calibrated two-sigma ranges of our 10 Rosario phase dates. If for the moment we set aside the largest standard deviations, it would appear that the events of the Rosario phase took place mostly between 900 and 600 B.C.

During the ninth century B.C., someone was roasted and eaten in Feature 47 of San José Mogote. During the eighth century, construction began on the public buildings of Mound 1. Sometime between 800 and 650 B.C. in "real time," the Structure 28 temple was built atop Structure 19, functioned for awhile, then was destroyed by fire. Not long after that, Structure 37 was built atop Structure 14.

It seems likely that Monument 3 was carved—and installed as the threshold of a corridor running between Structures 14 and 19—sometime during the seventh century B.C. By the end of that century it had fallen into disuse and was slowly covered up with the products of erosion.

Structure 27 and the Zone B Residence were built above the ruins of the Structure 28 temple, also probably during the seventh century. The Structure 26 date (Beta-179877) seems too early in light of its stratigraphic position. It could be charcoal from an inner ring of an old tree, or simply Early Rosario charcoal, redeposited in a Late Rosario storage room.

Finally two hearths, Features 18 and 19, were created on the old soil surface above Monument 3. The Feature 18 date, whose range midpoint is 645 B.C., seems just about right. And calibration gives us a different perspective on the Feature 19 dates, especially Beta-175898.

Because of the twists and turns of the dendrocalibration curve, some conventional B.P. dates wind up intercepting it in two places. Beta-175898 is such a date: its calibrated two-sigma range can be either 820–760 B.C. or 620–590 B.C. We do not know which of these ranges provides the best date, but obviously the younger range overlaps more strongly with the Feature 18 date.

It is revealing that Beta-173808 and Beta-175898 show better concordance *after* calibration than they did *before*. It also reinforces our suspicion that Beta-175897, the other date from Feature 19, was charcoal from the inner ring of an old tree, and therefore provided too old a date. Our best guess is that Features 18 and 19 were created at the end of the Rosario phase, perhaps even after the abandonment of San José Mogote had begun.

What We Learned by Dendrocalibrating

We have now looked at calibrated and uncalibrated versions of 38 radiocarbon dates from San José Mogote. We knew in advance that the calibrated dates would make the site older, so that did not come as a surprise. What surprised and pleased us was that calibration sometimes adjusted problematic dates so that they no longer appeared to be too old, too young, or out of stratigraphic order relative to other dates.

From the standpoint of social evolution, the most significant contribution made by dendrocalibration was to alter our perception of the *tempo of change*. Whether we intend it or not, phases based on stylistic change in ceramics often give the impression of being about the same length. Even when we have added conventional "b.c." dates to them, we find ourselves saying that our Formative phases are "about 200–300 years long."

Dendrocalibration not only makes each date older, it spreads the phases out until we can see that some are longer or shorter than we realized.

The Tierras Largas phase was a time of egalitarian life in politically autonomous villages. Differences in status were achieved rather than inherited; leaders were self-selected, fully initiated, successful entrepreneurs. Calibrated dates now suggest that San José Mogote may have remained in this phase of social organization for half a millennium, from 1800 to 1300 B.C.

The length of the Tierras Largas phase makes the eventual transition to hereditary rank seem all the more sudden. Yes, villagers of the Early San José phase continued to build Men's Houses well into the twelfth century B.C. By that time, however, they were also deforming the heads of children from highly ranked families and using sumptuary goods like iron ore mirrors, jadeite(?) earspools, and stingray spines. By the tenth century B.C., Men's Houses had been replaced by massive public buildings of planoconvex adobes and drylaid stone masonry.

The San José phase was a period when the supremacy of San José Mogote seems to have been unchallenged. The subsequent Guadalupe phase seems to have been one in which San José Mogote's regional influence "cycled down," with rivals like Huitzo and Tilcajete on the rise. Calibration now shows that these phases were of unequal length. The San José phase may have been a 350–400 year period of unchallenged dominance. Guadalupe may have witnessed only 200–250 years of retrenchment. The San José phase "peak," in other words, was longer than the Guadalupe phase "trough" (Marcus 1992b, 1998b).

During the Rosario phase, San José Mogote seems to have become revitalized and dominant again, although it may now have controlled only the Etla subvalley. The new Rosario "peak" may have lasted for 300 years, from 900 to 600 B.C. In the end, however, San José Mogote gathered its population and that of its dependencies, and seized the summit of Monte Albán.

Thus, the fact that we found more remains of the Tierras Largas, San José, and Rosario phases than of the Guadalupe phase is only partly attributable to changes in use of the piedmont spur. Guadalupe was also the shortest phase.

Some Afterthoughts

We are not advocating a wholesale rush to a calibrated Formative chronology. Large numbers of Formative sites still have only "b.c." dates, and as stated earlier, it would be confusing to intermix them with "B.C." dates. We do think, however, that dendrocalibration did more than make our phases older. By bringing us closer to their real ages, it reminded us that social evolution has its own "punctuated equilibrium" of stasis, gradual change, and rapid change, and that our interpretations are affected by whether the peaks were longer or shorter than the troughs.

Chapter 27

The Household Archaeology of San José Mogote: Its Potential Theoretical Contributions

We have now compared and contrasted the Formative houses of San José Mogote. We do not need to summarize the site's household activities in this chapter, since we have done that already in Chapters 4 and 5. It would also be premature to attempt a definitive "paleoethnography" of San José Mogote before bringing out our volumes on its cognitive and mortuary archaeology. A much more complete picture of village society will emerge once cosmology, religion, ideology, iconography, and the social *personae* encoded in burials have been added to our data on subsistence, exchange, and household crafts.

The household archaeology of San José Mogote has, however, already produced data relevant to the testing, confirmation, or rejection of a number of models for the origin and evolution of village society. Rather than presenting a traditional summary and conclusions, therefore, we will use this chapter to address those potential contributions.

The Origins of Sedentary Life in the Mexican Highlands

Early Formative occupation at San José Mogote began prior to 1500 b.c.[1] The place chosen for settlement was a piedmont spur near a bend in the Atoyac River. There was evidently much less soil on the spur at that time than there is now. Many parts of the site seem to have been exposed (or nearly exposed) bedrock, into which the earliest house floors, postholes, and storage pits were excavated.

Even in Area C, the part of the site that has produced the earliest houses, there is no evidence of Late Archaic occupation. Unlike the Levant or the Pacific coast of Peru, Oaxaca seems not to have been a region where sedentary life began before the appearance of pottery. While there had been open-air base camps in the Archaic, like Gheo-Shih (Flannery and Spores 1983:23-25), none of them seem to have developed into permanent villages.

This discontinuity between Archaic and Formative settlement lends support to an earlier model, one in which the decision to settle in permanent, year-round villages was not made until maize was capable of producing 200-250 kg per hectare (Flannery 1973). This is the minimum yield that today's Zapotec farmers require before they clear mesquite from the alluvium to make way for corn (Kirkby 1974). Maize is estimated to have reached that threshold between 2000 and 1500 b.c. (Kirkby 1973: Fig. 48).

By the Tierras Largas phase, large storage pits were associated with individual residences at both San José Mogote and Tierras Largas. This reinforces the possibility that *privatization of storage* may have been a key turning point in social evolution (Flannery 1972, 2002). Once families were no longer obligated to pool harvests, or share them with their less productive neighbors, the stage was set for economic inequality.

Because so many early features had been preserved in its bedrock, San José Mogote also provides us with a model for the origins of irrigation. We suspect that the first canals were dug to divert rain runoff away from houses. This move may have been followed by the notion that runoff could be diverted into cisterns (Chapter 17). The logical next step was creating small canals to

---

[1]In this volume, uncalibrated dates are given as "b.c.," and dendrocalibrated dates as "B.C." (see Chapter 26, Radiocarbon Dating).

divert water onto cornfields, providing another potential source of economic inequality.

The Origin of War

San José Mogote has also provided a test for Kelly's (2000) model of the origin of war. As discussed in detail in Chapter 5, Kelly's cross-cultural study suggests that raiding becomes more likely once societies have grown large enough to be divided into equivalent segments, such as patrilineal, matrilineal, or ancestor-based cognatic descent groups. The Tierras Largas phase seems to fit Kelly's model, since it has produced evidence for (1) Men's Houses of the type used by segmented societies; (2) burned residences; and (3) wooden palisades. By the Early San José phase, we believe we have iconographic evidence for ancestor-based descent groups (Marcus 1989).

Bride Exchange and Marriage Payments

One other correlate of segmentary society emerges from the study by Kelly (2000:48). The same corporate mentality that makes murders or insults into group offenses—requiring group retaliation—also makes intersegmental marriage into a group contract, requiring marriage payments. In Chapter 9, we consider Burial 1 of Area C (Fig. 9.30) to be evidence that there was intergroup bride exchange. If marriage payments began in the Tierras Largas phase, along with our other evidence for segmentary society, they might be reflected in the archaeological data. For example, some proportion of the shell ornaments that began showing up in Tierras Largas times may relate to bridewealth. If so, it would explain the increasing interest in shell "valuables" at a time when all other signs point to a society without hereditary rank.

Models of Hunting, Sharing, and Cooking

Tierras Largas and San José phase data also provide support for models concerned with the ways early societies procured and prepared foods. On the basis of features discovered in Areas A and B, we have concluded that women did much of the cooking for their nuclear families by boiling food in pots over small circular hearths or portable charcoal braziers. We believe that men, on the other hand, sometimes used large outdoor roasting pits to prepare feasts for their extended families or groups of neighbors. Such large meals, cooked over heated rocks, most likely consisted of deer or dog meat. Our data thus tend to support Speth's (2000) pueblo model, in which most boiling was done by women and most roasting by men.

Data from Houses 4 and 16/17 at San José Mogote, and Feature 99 at the site of Tierras Largas, suggest that certain kinds of meat were shared among families. Some houses appear to have received entire limbs from deer that had been butchered elsewhere. In other cases, up to five (or more) dogs appear to have been butchered for a feast. Thus, while the storage of a

family's maize seems to have been a "privatized" activity for each residence, meat was more widely distributed. Evidence that deer hunting may even have been a communal activity has been discussed in Chapter 4.

This pattern seems to support the model for early men's and women's food procurement advanced by Hawkes (1990, 1997) and O'Connell et al. (2002). According to their model, early women concentrated on low-risk foods (especially plants) for the provisioning of their immediate family, while men concentrated on high-risk/high-return foods (especially larger game), the sharing of which could be used to build alliances. While this model was generated from hunter-gatherer data, aspects of this behavior may have lasted into the early village period.

Deliberate Village Growth

Many changes accompanied San José Mogote's transition from a society based on achieved status to one based on ascribed status. Not the least of these was the growth of the village to 70 hectares, an increase so great that it cannot be explained through normal population growth; it had to have involved immigration from outlying areas.

While there were probably several reasons for this growth, at least two are suggested by a comparison of the Tierras Largas and San José phases. First of all, the San José phase village expanded well beyond the defensive palisades of the Tierras Largas phase, and we found little evidence that any San José phase houses had been deliberately burned. These facts suggest that one motivation behind the size increase may have been an attempt to become so large as to be safe from raids. By deliberately encouraging the occupants of smaller and more vulnerable hamlets to move in, the leaders of San José Mogote created a larger and more easily defended chiefly center.

A second motivation for growth can be seen in the escalation of craft activity between the Tierras Largas and San José phases. There can be little doubt that this happened under the patronage of an emerging elite. The leaders of San José Mogote became the conduit through which many raw materials and craft goods entered and exited the valley; for example, they negotiated for prismatic obsidian blades from the Central Mexican Highlands, then pooled and distributed them to their followers (Chapter 4). Iron ore mirrors, produced under their aegis, were dispatched to the elites of other regions. It was in the interest of the leaders of San José Mogote to attract as many craft specialists as they could. The more artisans they had as clients, the greater the prestige of the chiefly patrons, both inside and outside the valley.

It would not surprise us, for example, to learn that Area A of San José Mogote was a residential ward of recent immigrants to the village. In contrast to the western part of the site, Area A was not founded until Early San José times (Chapter 13). Once established, however, it became a ward specializing in iron ore mirror production for perhaps three centuries.

We suspect that at least some of the iron ore lumps from which mirrors were made had been collected as tribute from subordinate villages below San José Mogote. This possibility is suggested by the unworked ore lumps found at smaller villages along the presumed route between San José Mogote and some of its main ore sources (Chapter 5). If our suspicions are correct, it suggests that some craft specialties were overseen by an elite with the power to enforce tribute.

Finally, our excavations revealed an unexpected by-product of village growth: in order to pack as many houses as possible onto the piedmont spur, its slopes had to be converted into occupational terraces (Chapter 17). Not only were areas of sloping bedrock hacked into terraces, the latter were sometimes given bedrock cisterns and drainage canals. We were excited to find that three features considered typical of Monte Albán—terracing, drains, and subterranean water storage—were already present at San José Mogote by Early Formative times.

The Integrative Role of Ritual

It would appear that in Oaxaca, craft specialization by residential ward was present as early as there were leaders to foment it. San José phase society, however, was probably only a chiefdom of two administrative tiers, one without the strong centralized authority of more complex chiefdoms. It has been argued by Rappaport (1979) and others that societies without strongly centralized authority tend to rely heavily on ritual as a means of social integration.

That ritual may take several forms. At the level of the household, descent group, or residential ward, we may see a continuation of integrative rituals that were already important in egalitarian or "autonomous village" societies. At the regional level, however, we see new rituals aimed at (1) establishing the chief's authority over outlying communities, or (2) promoting his success in the endless competition with rival chiefs. Evidence from the San José phase supports such a model.

While we intend to deal with ritual more extensively in a future volume, some general points can be mentioned here. At the individual level, men and women in Formative society seem to have performed gender-specific rituals. The woman's ritual province was her home, where she performed rituals of divination and addressed recent ancestors through the medium of small handmade figurines (Marcus 1998a). Men's ritual was focused on the Men's House, a building so small that its use must have been restricted to a subset of the men: those individuals who had passed through multiple levels of initiation. In such houses, we suspect, fully initiated men met, planned raids, conducted certain rituals out of the view of women, and ingested ritual plants (Marcus 1999).

It appears that by the Early San José phase, if not before, each residential ward maintained its own Men's House. Residents of a ward shared venison, chert, certain other raw materials, and sometimes a craft or two. Figurines, masks, and costume parts suggest that there were songs, dances, and ritual impersonation of ancestors, animals, and grotesque beings. Feasting on dogs and deer may have accompanied some rituals.

Exotic raw materials, such as mollusk shell, mica, iron ore, feathers, armadillo shell, and more, circulated through houses of the San José phase. Some items were used for personal ornamentation, some for costumes, and some undoubtedly as indicators of hereditary rank, although we cannot always determine an item's function.

As time went on, some families (like the one occupying House 16/17 of Area B) adopted new craft specialties (Chapter 18). The chert biface found in House 4 of Area C suggests that other families received some of House 16/17's craft products. While many craft goods circulated, perhaps in exchange for venison, dog meat, or some other item, a few were more restricted. Our house-to-house evidence suggests that prismatic blades, iron ore mirrors, and earspools of jadeite(?) became increasingly associated with elite families.

Regarding the raw materials for ritual and prestige items, we find yet another model to be supported by data from the San José and Guadalupe phases. Spencer (1990), citing ethnographic data, argues that a chief's sphere of control over resources tends to have a radius of one day's walk from his village (see also Marcus 1983b:462-63). This would seem to have been true during the San José phase, a time when the two most frequently used sources of iron ore for mirrors lay a day's walk from San José Mogote (Chapter 5). During the Guadalupe phase, however, rival chiefly centers arose at Huitzo in the north and Tilcajete in the south, potentially reducing access to those sources. Mirror production at San José Mogote ceased at this time, although it continued in other parts of Mexico.

One model no longer supported by data from San José Mogote is the idea that evolutionary changes of the San José phase can somehow be linked to the influence of powerful neighbors, such as the Olmec of the Gulf Coast. This model, proposed more than 30 years ago by Flannery (1968), has not stood the test of time. It has been replaced by a new model adapted from the work of biologist Sewall Wright. In this model, the most favorable conditions for rapid social evolution occur when competing societies are "adaptively autonomous but still periodically in contact" (Flannery and Marcus 2000:32).

While referring the reader to Flannery and Marcus (2000) for details, we can summarize here a few of the discoveries that caused us to give up on Flannery's 1968 model. First, it turns out that the art style of the San José phase resembles that of the Basin of Mexico more closely than it does that of the Gulf Coast. This is especially true of the incised white ceramics and their Earth motifs, which find counterparts at Tlapacoya and Tlatilco, but not in the San Lorenzo phase.

Second, the public architecture of the San José phase cannot be Olmec-inspired; among other things, it includes planoconvex adobes and lime plaster, neither of which is known from the San Lorenzo phase (see below).

Third, most of the emergent novelty in the San José phase is clearly of local origin. The production of small flat magnetite mirrors is so far unique to San José Mogote. What San Lorenzo seemed to favor was multidrilled iron ore beads (Coe and Diehl

1980a:242), none of which have been found in Oaxaca. San José Mogote's extensive use of mica further distinguishes it from San Lorenzo—and the list of differences goes on.

Today we would see emerging rank societies in the Basin of Mexico, Morelos, Puebla, Veracruz, and Chiapas as strongly adapted to their respective regions, but sufficiently in contact to cause relevant innovations to spread rapidly among them. It was almost certainly this competition among chiefly families—rather than the inordinate influence of any one society—that encouraged the flamboyant behavior we see in the Early Formative.

From Men's House to Temple

In Mesoamerica, the transition from one form of society to another was usually accompanied by changes in public buildings and the use of ritual space. This subject will be addressed more fully in our future volume on the cognitive archaeology of San José Mogote.

The oldest public buildings to appear in Oaxaca were Men's Houses. These small one-room buildings appeared early in the Tierras Largas phase and lasted until midway through the San José phase, a period of some 300-400 years in "real" time (Chapter 26).

As mentioned above, Men's Houses are most typical of segmentary societies run by a subset of adult men who have passed through multiple hurdles on their way to achieved high status. Since Areas A and C seem to have maintained separate Men's Houses during the Early San José phase, we believe that each such house was built by one segment of society, perhaps an ancestor-based descent group occupying a specific residential ward. During Tierras Largas times, it appears that some senior men were buried in a seated or tightly flexed position near the Men's House; Burial 29 (Marcus and Flannery 1996: Fig. 75) would be one example.

Even after making the transition to a society based on hereditary rank, the villagers of San José Mogote continued for awhile to build Men's Houses. With the gradual extension of a chief's authority beyond his own village, however, new types of ritual buildings became necessary. Soon there arose a need for public buildings that would emphasize San José Mogote's authority over the subordinate villages in its hinterland.

Structures 1 and 2 in Area A were platforms for newer and larger public buildings with regional significance. Built stratigraphically above the ruins of Household Unit C1, these large stone masonry platforms are shown in a previous publication (Flannery and Marcus 1994: Figs. 18.7-18.11). The stones used to build their sloping walls and stairways were, in some cases, brought from subordinate communities on both sides of the Atoyac River.

Some workers had brought volcanic tuff, quarried from outcrops nearby. Others had made round adobes, using the broken-off bases of large jars as molds. Basketloads of earthen fill had been brought from areas of black alluvial soil, red piedmont soil, and gray-green soil from stony ridges. Most significantly,

the limestone and travertine came from known quarries on the lands of other communities. It would appear, therefore, that the leaders of San José Mogote could now call on the manpower of other villages for public construction; autonomy had been lost. [Marcus and Flannery 1996:11]

Structures 1 and 2, dating to the Late San José phase, are relevant to Carneiro's (1991:168-69) model for the difference between "simple rank society" and "chiefdom." While both types of society have hereditary inequality, it is only when nearby villages lose their autonomy and come under the authority of one leader that we can say an actual chiefdom has been created. We may never determine exactly when rank became hereditary at San José Mogote, but we can say that by the Late San José phase, the leaders of that site could demand travertine blocks from Fábrica San José and limestone blocks from Rancho Matadamas.

One other discovery of cultural-historical significance has to do with the origin of the adobe brick. It appears that, at least in Oaxaca, adobes were created as a rapid way to build retaining walls within the fill of Late San José phase public buildings. Our first adobes, found in the San José and Guadalupe phases, were circular and planoconvex. By Rosario times, they had given way to the rectangular adobes that characterized Oaxaca architecture for the remainder of prehistory.

Some Principles of Chiefly Society

Over the years a number of authors, drawing on the ethnographic record, have suggested sets of principles by which chiefly societies operate. Several of those principles are supported by excavations at San José Mogote and neighboring Formative villages.

For example, clues to the different treatment of highly ranked people can be seen in the mortuary data, which will be covered in detail in a future volume. In Chapter 1, we referred to a San José phase cemetery at Tomaltepec where Whalen (1981:48-58 and Appendix III) found the remains of nearly 80 individuals. A group of six tightly flexed adult men stood out as different, receiving two-thirds of the stone slab grave covers, 88% of the jadeite(?) beads, and 50% of the pottery vessels with Lightning motifs. They were also four times as likely to have had the bones of secondary burials added to their graves, raising intriguing questions about whether ancestors, prematurely deceased heirs, or multiple wives might have been added to the burials of highly ranked men.

In the Guadalupe and Rosario phases, there are hints that hypogamous marriages were used to strengthen relations between San José Mogote and its satellite villages. As mentioned in Chapter 1, the richest Guadalupe phase burials at Fábrica San José (which was a provider of salt and travertine to San José Mogote) were women (Drennan 1976a). Burial 39, for example, may have been an elite woman sent from San José Mogote to marry a community leader at Fábrica San José (Marcus and Flannery 1996:114-15). The same can be said of Burial 54, a Rosario phase woman buried in a richly furnished grave at Fábrica San José.

Her cranial deformation resembles that of elite women buried at San José Mogote (Marcus and Flannery 1996:132-35).

Based on what we know about the later Zapotec, our guess would be that male community leaders tended to have more than one wife; that some of those wives came from other communities; and that the first-born son of the most highly ranked wife inherited his father's position of leadership. All these principles would be typical of chiefdoms in the ethnographic record.

As we mentioned in Chapter 4, Carneiro (2003) stresses the fact that "war leader" is one of the most important of a chief's multiple roles. By the Rosario phase, that role may have become associated with a specific set of artifacts. The occupant of Tomb 10 in the patio of the Zone B Residence, Mound 1, had been supplied with 11 atlatl points made from large obsidian blades (Chapter 23). Effigy whistles, suitable for directing warriors in combat, were also associated with Rosario elite residences on Mound 1.

Yet another ethnography-based model for the chiefdom involves the taking of captives for sacrifice, torture, ritual cannibalism, or conversion into slaves (Redmond 1994). Here, once again, the Rosario phase contributes supporting data. The captive depicted on Monument 3, with his heart removed, had clearly been sacrificed. The fact that his hieroglyphic name was added to the monument underscores a principle of chiefly warfare revealed by Buck (1949): killing one rival chief, whose name is widely known, makes the battle more memorable than the killing of 50 anonymous warriors.

As for the other ritual uses to which captives might have been put, there are further hints in our Rosario phase data. At least one woman found with the Zone B Residence on Mound 1 may have been sacrificed and incorporated into an adobe wall (Chapter 23). And one unfortunate individual—perhaps a captive, although that cannot be proven—had been cooked in Feature 47 of Area C (Chapter 11).

The San José Mogote Chiefdom as a Precursor to the Monte Albán State

Excavations at San José Mogote have also contributed to a new view of the culture history of the Valley of Oaxaca. As recently as 1966, it was considered plausible that the founders of Monte Albán had come from outside the valley. Monte Negro in the Tilantongo Valley, a mountaintop site with Monte Albán Ic-style pottery, was frequently mentioned as the place from which the founders might have come (Paddock 1966:90).

Today we know that the founders of Monte Albán came from within the Valley of Oaxaca, and that most of them (perhaps as many as 2000) came from the chiefdom headed by San José Mogote. We also have an idea *why* they came. As mentioned in Chapter 5, chiefly warfare was intense during the Rosario phase, and by Monte Albán Ia the defensible hilltop had become the key variable at the top of the settlement "decision tree" for the Etla subvalley (Fig. 5.20b). Monte Albán, of course, would have been the ultimate defensible hilltop location for an Etla-based chiefdom whose significant rivals lived at places like Tilcajete (Spencer and Redmond 2001).

In an earlier essay (Flannery and Marcus 1983:74) we pointed out that the Rosario-phase ceramic style, public architecture, and hieroglyphs of San José Mogote make it a logical precursor for Monte Albán Ia. As described in Appendix A, many attributes of Socorro Fine Gray pottery carry over into the burnished gray ware of early Monte Albán I. Structure 19 at San José Mogote, with its large orthostats and limestone block stairway, anticipates the architecture of Building L in the Main Plaza at Monte Albán. The hieroglyph on Monument 3 at San José Mogote, already Zapotec in style, continued to be used in later writing at Monte Albán.

When one combines our discoveries at San José Mogote with those reported recently from Tilcajete (Spencer and Redmond 2001), Monte Negro (Balkansky et al. 2000, 2004), and the Valley of Huamelulpan (Balkansky 1998), a model for the origins of urbanism and the state begins to take shape. Several cases of early urbanism in highland Oaxaca seem to have involved the deliberate relocation of valley-floor populations to defensible mountaintops, a process the ancient Greeks called *synoikism* (Demand 1990). In some cases, this relocation gave the new mountaintop centers the strategic advantage they needed to crush their rivals and create valley-wide states.

At this writing, it appears that the former San José Mogote chiefdom—now transformed into Monte Albán, and joined by its allies—warred repeatedly with Tilcajete until it finally overthrew its lord (and burned his palace) around 20 b.c. And it also now seems clear that Monte Negro had nothing to do with the founding of Monte Albán. Rather, Monte Negro represents a Tilantongo Valley polity that relocated to a mountaintop in order to avoid being taken over by its expansionist neighbor, Monte Albán. In other words, the emerging threat of Monte Albán may have set off a chain reaction of defensive urbanization.

Particularly exciting are the new data emerging from the Huamelulpan Valley, where a process analogous to the founding of Monte Albán seems to have taken place. Santa Cruz Tayata—the paramount village of the area's largest Middle Formative chiefdom—apparently relocated to the top of a mountain nearby, creating the urban center of Huamelulpan (Balkansky 1998).

Having two parallel cases, one at Monte Albán and the other at Huamelulpan, energizes our search for regularities in the origins of urbanism and the state. It leads us to hope that one day there will be half a dozen chiefly centers whose household archaeology is reported in as much detail as we have provided here. To be sure, the work is onerous and the cost of publication high. However, it will be worth the effort if it uncovers meaningful similarities and differences in Formative behavior, freed from all of the usual background noise.

Appendix A
Middle Formative Pottery

Throughout this volume we have referred to the pottery recovered in Formative houses, features, and dooryards. In the case of Espiridión, Tierras Largas, and San José phase houses, there was no need to list that pottery in detail, since it has already been described in our monograph on Early Formative ceramics of the Valley of Oaxaca (Flannery and Marcus 1994).

Unfortunately, our monograph on the Middle Formative ceramics of the valley is not yet finished. For that reason, we have presented lists of all the pottery from the Rosario phase residences described in Chapter 23. Those lists include pottery types whose full descriptions will not be published until our Middle Formative monograph is complete. As a result, we have designed this appendix to give the reader brief synopses of Guadalupe and Rosario phase pottery types, pending full publication.

The Guadalupe Phase

The six main pottery types of the Guadalupe phase were Fidencio Coarse, Lupita Heavy Plain, Atoyac Yellow-white, Socorro Fine Gray, Josefina Fine Gray, and Guadalupe Burnished Brown. The first three types were already present in the San José phase, and are described in our monograph on Early Formative ceramics. The last three types made their first appearance in the Guadalupe phase. Socorro Fine Gray was a waxy, highly burnished gray ware, which rapidly replaced Leandro Gray. Josefina Fine Gray, somewhat less abundant, had a burnished gray slip that did not bond well to its whitish clay body. Guadalupe Burnished Brown was a bay to medium-brown utilitarian ware that increased over time, relative to Lupita Heavy Plain.

Atoyac Yellow-white reached its peak in the Guadalupe phase; outleaned-wall bowls were particularly common in this ware.

Plastic decoration on the shoulders of Fidencio Coarse jars also reached its greatest diversity at this time (Drennan 1976a: Fig. 27). Luxury white wares like Delia White and Coatepec White were a minor part of the Guadalupe assemblage.

Socorro Fine Gray and Josefina Fine Gray were used mainly for bowls that appeared to be the size appropriate for individual servings. Particularly typical of the Guadalupe phase were composite silhouette bowls in both these gray wares. A distinctive incised motif of the phase was the "diamond-in-a-box" (Drennan 1976a: Fig. 25*b*).

The Rosario Phase

During the Rosario phase, Socorro Fine Gray replaced Atoyac Yellow-white as the dominant bowl ware. While composite silhouette bowls continued to be popular, there was an explosion of bowls with flat bases and outleaned or outcurved walls. Three distinct forms of decoration occurred on these bowls. One was a form of "negative" or "resist" painting which appears white against the natural gray of the sherd. The second, called "zoned toning," used the subtle contrast between matte and burnished areas to create a pattern. The third was a side-to-side stretching out of the earlier "diamond-in-a-box" motif, giving the impression of a diamond-shaped blank space between two naval pennants (Flannery and Marcus 1990: Fig. 2.17*a-d*).

Equally typical of the Rosario phase were a wide range of rim profiles and rim eccentricities on outleaned-wall bowls in Socorro Fine Gray. Drennan (1976a:37-43) defined twelve different rim profiles, each of which could be combined with one of seven different rim eccentricities; in addition, such rims could be decorated with any one of nine motifs done in incising, zoned toning, or negative painting. Since these rim attributes turned out to have chronological significance, we have listed them in our Rosario phase sherd lists (Chapter 23).

Of the rim profiles defined by Drennan, four (nos. 6, 7, 8, and 12) were restricted to the Rosario phase, while the other eight lasted into Early Monte Albán I (= Ia). Of his seven rim eccentricities, five (nos. 2, 3, 4, 6, and 7) were restricted to the Rosario phase, while the other two lasted into Monte Albán Ia. Incised naval pennants, zoned toning, and negative white-on-gray painting were restricted to the Rosario phase. During Monte Albán Ia they were replaced by the incised motifs that Caso, Bernal, and Acosta (1967) referred to as G15, G16, and G17.

Another innovation of the Rosario phase was a shallow dish with solid tripod supports. We have called this "the Suchilquitongo tripod dish," after a site in the Etla subvalley where they were particularly abundant.[1] Such dishes could occur in Lupita Heavy Plain or Guadalupe Burnished Brown, and as in the case of the gray bowls mentioned above, their attributes changed over time. During the Rosario phase, tripod dishes were without paint or plastic decoration. However, they lasted into Monte Albán Ia times, at which point their rims often came to be painted red. The red could be weak red (Caso, Bernal, and Acosta's Type C2) or bright garnet (Caso, Bernal, and Acosta's Type C4). During Monte Albán Ia, many Suchilquitongo tripod dishes were also given a fillet band of plastic decoration.

The Monte Albán Ia Phase

It should be clear from the preceding discussion that many Monte Albán Ia pottery types were elaborations of Rosario phase antecedents. Fidencio Coarse jars of the Rosario phase, with their drab maroon or brick-red wash, became a lighter buff, and their wash gradually became a clearer red, until they were transformed into the Type C2 jars of Monte Albán Ia. Guadalupe Burnished Brown, one of the most common utilitarian wares of the Rosario phase, evolved into several of the *café* types of Monte Albán Ia, including Caso, Bernal, and Acosta's K3 and K8. Socorro Fine Gray was clearly the direct ancestor of the Monte Albán Ia burnished gray Types G3, G5, G15, G16, and G17. What disappeared in Monte Albán Ia were four of the gray bowl rim forms, five of the rim eccentricities, and all of the pennant incising, zoned toning, and negative white-on-gray (Drennan 1976a:56).

Drennan's Multidimensional Scaling

The best advice we can give to anyone planning to excavate a Middle Formative site in the Valley of Oaxaca is to take advantage of Drennan's (1976a, 1976b) multidimensional scaling, which used dozens of attributes of Socorro Fine Gray, Fidencio Coarse, Guadalupe Burnished Brown, and Atoyac Yellow-white pottery to seriate ceramic collections. Note, however, that Drennan's method is intended for use on samples from good excavated contexts, such as house floors. Because the method depends on the changing percentages of one attribute to another, it is not intended for use on mound fill samples or surface collections, where there is no guarantee that all the sherds are actually contemporaneous. For many of the same reasons, picking up a single sherd and saying "this is Rosario" or "this is Monte Albán Ia" can be a mistake. It is the changing frequencies of types and attributes, rather than simple presence/absence, that allow you to see where you are in the sequence.

---

[1]Drennan (1976a) refers to these vessels as "Suchilquitongo footed plates," which we consider a synonym.

Appendix B

Resumen en español

El sitio de San José Mogote se encuentra en una loma – en realidad una península de la zona piemontesa – cerca del Río Atoyac, en el municipio de Guadalupe Etla, Oaxaca. Rodeado al este, al oeste y al sur por terrenos fértiles de aluvión, parece haber sido (1) el lugar en donde comenzó la vida aldeana en el Valle de Oaxaca y (2) el centro sociopolítico más poderoso del Valle de Oaxaca durante los siglos anteriores a la fundación de Monte Albán.

En el capítulo 1 se discuten el descubrimiento de San José Mogote y sus primeras cinco épocas de ocupación: Espiridión (antes de 1500 a.C.), Tierras Largas (1500-1150 a.C.), San José (1150-850 a.C.), Guadalupe (850-700 a.C.) y Rosario (700-500 a.C.).

Poco se sabe de la época Espiridión, cuyos restos se encuentran enterrados a grandes profundidades. Durante la época Tierras Largas, la sociedad parece haber sido "igualitaria", o sea, una sociedad en la que cualquier diferencia de prestigio entre individuos era adquerida durante la vida y no heredada de los padres. San José Mogote era la aldea más grande entre las 19 que se conocen en el valle (tenía una superficie de al menos 7 hectáreas y quizás más). Tenía casas de bajareque, pequeños edificios públicos del tipo "Casa de Varones" y una palizada defensiva.

Durante la época San José aparecieron las primeras señales de jerarquía social, es decir, era una sociedad donde las diferencias de prestigio eran hereditarias. El pueblo creció enormemente (hasta 70 ha) y mostraba diferencias sociales en el acceso a muchos materiales: espejos de mineral de hierro; ornamentos de jade, concha madreperla, y ostra espinosa (*Spondylus*); navajas prismáticas de obsidiana; mica; y cerámica de otras regiones de

Mesoamérica. La gente de alto rango acostumbraba la deformación tabular del cráneo y ser enterrada en posición sedente o sumamente flexionada. Construyeron grandes plataformas de mampostería de piedras y adobes redondos para elevar sus templos. La diversidad de materias primas sugiere que San José Mogote ya dominaba otras aldeas, las cuales tenían la obligación de aportar materiales para la construcción.

Durante la época Guadalupe, se observa que San José Mogote tuvo dificultad para mantener su dominio sobre las aldeas subordinadas, a causa de la naciente competencia entre nuevos centros señoriales rivales. Dos de dichos rivales fueron Huitzo (al noroeste) y San Martín Tilcajete (al sur). Aunque San José Mogote todavía abarcaba 60-70 ha (por mucho la mayor comunidad de las 45 en el valle), ya no controlaba tanto territorio. Parece, por ejemplo, haber perdido el acceso a los mejores yacimientos de mineral de hierro para la elaboración de espejos.

Durante la época Rosario, San José Mogote recuperó un poco de su poder político. Se extendió sobre más de 60-65 ha y creemos que contaba con alrededor de 1,000 habitantes. Se hallaba en la cúspide de una pirámide jerárquica de 18-23 aldeas en el subvalle de Etla; era el centro señorial de una "jefatura máxima" o "jefatura compleja" de tres niveles de administración. Sus jefes vivieron en casas grandes con paredes de adobes cuadrangulares, y sus sacerdotes estuvieron a cargo de impresionantes templos erigidos sobre grandes plataformas de mampostería de piedra y barro.

Sin embargo, San José Mogote solamente controlaba la tercera parte del valle. El centro señorial de Tilcajete dominaba al menos 10-12 aldeas en el Valle Grande, y Yegüih dominaba otras 10-12 en el subvalle de Tlacolula. El conflicto entre jefaturas rivales fue tan feroz que existía una "tierra de nadie" (o zona de exclusión) de 80 km² entre San José Mogote, Tilcajete y Yegüih (Figura 1.7).

A fines de la época Rosario, unos 2,000 habitantes de San José Mogote y sus aldeas subordinadas abandonaron el fondo del subvalle de Etla para establecerse en la cima de Monte Albán, un cerro que se encontraba precisamente en "tierra de nadie". Aprovecharon su posición elevada y fácilmente defendible para iniciar una guerra que, después de varios siglos, llegó a ganar Monte Albán, unificando todo el valle y creando un estado zapoteco.

El medio ambiente

El capítulo 2 presenta un resumen del clima y el medio ambiente del Valle de Oaxaca. Las tres zonas fisiográficas principales son (1) el fondo plano y aluvial del valle, (2) la zona piemontesa que tiene una pendiente que va de suave a empinada, a menudo cortada por barrancas fluviales y (3) la zona de alta montaña. En estas tres zonas, los zapotecos históricos practicaron cuando menos seis tipos diferentes de agricultura: la pluvial, la agricultura en aluvión permanentemente húmedo, la de irrigación con pozos de poca profundidad, la de irrigación con canales, la de inundaciones y la de terrazas en las laderas. El clima es templado y semiárido, con 550 mm de precipitación anual que se concentran principalmente entre mayo y septiembre.

El Río Atoyac y su afluente, el Río Salado, crearon un valle en forma de *Y*, el cual cuenta con tres subvalles: Etla en el norte, Tlacolula en el este y el Valle Grande (o subvalle de Zimatlán) en el sur. San José Mogote se encuentra en el centro del subvalle de Etla – el subvalle más alto, más estrecho y mas frío, pero también el que posee 40% de la "tierra de clase I" del todo el valle (5,117 ha de un total de 12,740).

Casi todas las primeras aldeas del Formativo fueron establecidas en las estribaciones de la zona piemontesa, pequeñas penínsulas que se extienden dentro de la llanura aluvial del Río Atoyac – lomas bajas, libres de inundaciones, rodeadas por tierra de clase I –. Como el subvalle de Etla tenía tantas localidades de este tipo – con posibilidades para la realización de multiples tipos de agricultura – rápidamente se convirtió en la zona más poblada del valle.

Las residencias del Formativo

El capítulo 3 examina las casas de bajareque del Formativo y las técnicas empleadas en su excavación. Las casas tradicionales de la gente zapoteca nos sirvieron como referencia. Las casas prehistóricas eran desde 3 × 5 m hasta 4 × 7 m, con postes de pino, muros de carrizo y barro, y techos de juncos o paja. Los pisos eran de barro apisonado, con una capa delgada de arena encima de ellos para conformar una superficie seca.

Alrededor de cada casa se encontraba un solar o zona de trabajo al aire libre, a veces con un diámetro de entre 30 a 40 m. En estos solares se encontraban elementos de diversos tipos que nunca aparecen dentro de la casa: hogares, hornos, pozos de almacenamiento y elementos para ritos. El etnólogo Julio de la Fuente, quien estudió las residencias tradicionales zapotecas en Yalálag, recopiló las palabras indígenas correspondientes a cada parte de un solar. Nuestra experiencia en San José Mogote nos ha convencido de que el arqueólogo que analiza solamente la casa, soslayando el estudio del solar, pierde la mitad de la historia de una residencia. Las casas se barrieron innumerables veces durante su funcionamiento; en contraste, en los solares es mucho más factible encontrar áreas de actividad intactas.

Las casas de San José Mogote se excavaron siguiendo un retícula con unidades de 1× 1 m, utilizando cribas corrientes y finas. Se ubicaron los artefactos tridimensionalmente ("piece plotting").

Actividades domésticas

En los capítulos 4 y 5 se discuten todas las actividades domésticas de las cuales hay evidencias en las casas, los solares y los basureros de San José Mogote. La lista comienza con la agricultura y la recolección de plantas silvestres, ampliamente documentadas en las muestras de plantas carbonizadas. Continúa con la caza de animales salvajes y la crianza de perro domesticado (se ilustran algunos cambios genéticos que se manifiestan los perros del Formativo.) Se presentan también evidencias del almacenamiento de la cosecha, la preparación de las comidas familiares y los banquetes.

Entre las actividades artesanales de San José Mogote se encuentran la alfarería; la elaboración de artefactos de pedernal; la fabricación y uso de metates, manos, morteros y otras piedras para moler; la fabricación y utilización de hachas y aplanadoras para tallar madera y la producción de artefactos de obsidiana importada. Un tipo especial de metate, con forma de caja portátil, tal vez servía para moler plantas rituales como el tabaco (Figura 4.20).

La lista de actividades sigue con el empleo de agujas pequeñas para coser y de agujas grandes para el trabajo de la cestería. Usaron piedras ásperas para afilar agujas. Se hicieron tapas de ollas usando tiestos perforados. La sal comestible para el consumo de los habitantes de San José Mogote era preparada en la aldea subordinada de Fábrica San José, donde había manantiales de agua salada.

Los artesanos de San José Mogote importaban conchas madreperla, ostras espinosas (*Spondylus*) y almejas de agua dulce para fabricar ornamentos, utilizando grabadores-perforadores de pedernal. Principalmente en un solo barrio, el Área A (ver abajo), se dedicaban al pulido y bruñido de pequeños espejos de mineral de hierro destinados a la exportación. Aprovecharon los abundantes yacimientos de magnetita, hematita y mica de distintos colores existentes en la zona piemontesa del Valle de Oaxaca.

Entre las actividades rituales identificadas a través de los restos arqueológicos, se encuentran los cantos, las danzas, el uso de máscaras y disfraces, y la invocación a los antepasados. Cientos de figurillas – encontradas principalmente en áreas de actividad femenina (y nunca en las "Casas de Varones") – parecen haber sido usadas en escenarios rituales como el Elemento 63 (ver abajo): en dichos escenarios, estas figurillas representaban antepasados recientes, quienes eran invocados por las mujeres de la familia, para pedirles servicios y favores, probablemente en casos de enfermedad, mala suerte o mala cosecha. Varias de las figurillas representan individuos bailando disfrazados, orando o cantando.

El autosacrificio con sangradores; la adivinación utilizando cuencos llenos de agua y pintados de diversos colores; el uso de tambores de carapazón de tortuga; y la circulación de plumas y pieles de animales exóticos también desempeñaron su rol en la vida ritual (capítulo 5).

Casi desde la fundación de San José Mogote, se registraron incursiones bélicas de pequeños grupos de guerreros. El Área C de San José Mogote tenía una palizada defensiva de postes de pino; además, varias casas o templos del pueblo fueron incendiados durante las épocas Tierras Largas y Rosario. Así empezó una tradición muy larga en Oaxaca: la de las guerras entre comunidades. En el capítulo 5 se discuten los criterios arqueológicos para distinguir si una casa se quemó accidentalmente o como resultado de una incursión.

El Área C

El Área C (capítulos 6 a 11) se encuentra en el margen oeste de la loma. De esta parte, los vecinos de Guadalupe Etla habían extraído grandes volúmenes de arcilla para elaborar adobes. Fue posible convertir su excavación en un perfil de 99 m de largo en sentido norte-sur, el cual reveló la presencia de una serie de casas del Formativo. Las residencias, los elementos y los edificios públicos más antiguos del sitio se encontraron en esta área.

La Casa 20, ubicada en la capa estratigráfica H, es la más antigua de todas. Pertenece a la época Espiridión, contemporánea a la época Purrón en el Valle de Tehuacán (capítulo 7).

La Casa 19, ubicada en la capa G2, pertenece a la fase Tierras Largas Temprano; su fechamiento radiocarbónico es 1540 a.C. (sin calibración). La casa parece haber sido totalmente quemada, posiblemente durante una incursión bélica. Otra evidencia de los conflictos entre aldeas nos la ofreció el Elemento 21, una sección de palizada defensiva que consistió en una doble línea de postes de madera. En total, encontramos los restos de tres palizadas de la época Tierras Largas. Varios de los postes estaban carbonizados, y proporcionaron fechas radiocarbónicas de aproximadamente 1300 a.C. (sin calibración).

La Casa 18, varios basureros, y una serie de pozos troncocónicos de la época Tierras Largas fueron descubiertos en las capas G y F del Área C.

En las capas E y D salieron a la luz varias casas de la época San José. En orden estratigráfico aparecieron la Casa 15 (San José Temprano), y las Casas 6, 5, 2, 3, 11, 9, 1, 10 y 4 (San José Medio). Las Casas 2, 9 y 4 fueron especialmente interesantes.

La Casa 2 tenía las impresiones de un petate en el piso y varios depósitos de ceniza con restos carbonizados de maíz, chile, calabaza, tuna, biznaga y hierbas como el chipil, el quintonil y el epazote. En el piso de la casa apareció abundante evidencia de la fabricación de ornamentos de almeja de agua dulce, importada de los ríos del Golfo de México.

En la Casa 9 (1000 a.C. sin calibración) aparecieron varios objetos y elementos asociados a la alfarería. El Elemento 38 era un pequeño pozo de depósito bajo el piso. Estaba lleno de ceniza blanca y fina, del tipo que usan los alfareros zapotecos cuando hacen cerámica moldeada; una capa delgada de ceniza evita que la nueva vasija se pegue al molde. En el piso de la casa se encontraron dos bolas de arcilla para cerámica y varios trozos de hematita que, una vez molida, habrían servido para preparar un engobe rojo.

La Casa 4 parece haber estado en funcionamiento durante muchos años, pues tenía tres pisos: el piso original y dos reparaciones. Los ocupantes habían acumulado mucha más obsidiana de lo normal y trabajaban abundante madreperla. Entre las abundantes figurillas apareció una miniatura en forma de taburete de cuatro patas, posiblemente un símbolo de alto rango. En varias sociedades de jefatura de Centroamérica, los acompañantes del jefe llevaban un taburete de ese tipo adondequiera que el jefe viajaba, asegurando que, cuando se sentaba, su cabeza estaría en una posición más alta que la de sus subordinados. Sospechamos que el taburete en miniatura se usaba con una figura sedente que representaba un antepasado de alto rango.

Más arriba, en la capa C de este mismo barrio, se encontraron dos casas de la época San José Tardío: las Casas 7 y 14 (capítulo 10).

Durante la época Guadalupe, el Área C fue escenario de la construcción de varias plataformas para templos del Formativo Medio. Un interesante elemento de la época Rosario fue el 47, un gran horno subterráneo (capítulo 11). Entre el carbón y las piedras quemadas del interior, se encontraron restos de un individuo que aparentemente fue cocido durante un ritual de canibalismo.

El Área A

El Área A (capítulos 12-14), en el extremo este de la loma, contenía los restos de un barrio de artesanos especializados en la manufactura de espejos de mineral de hierro. Un reconocimiento superficial del Área A reveló una concentración en una hectárea de 500 trozos de mineral de hierro, entre ellos magnetita, ilmenomagnetita y hematita. Esta cifra equivale al 99% de todo el mineral de hierro arqueológico hallado en el valle.

Cuatro unidades domésticas (C1-C4) excavadas en el Área A se dedicaban al pulido y el bruñido de pequeños espejos de mineral de hierro, usando como abrasivo polvo de hematita. También trabajaron almejas de agua dulce, ostras espinosas y mica, utilizando grabadores-perforadores de pedernal para cortar y perforar esta materia prima.

En los solares de varias unidades domésticas se encontraron elementos que casi nunca aparecieron dentro de las casas. El solar de la Unidad C4 reveló un área de actividad, probablemente de hombre(s), la cual contenía un horno grande quizás para ofrecer banquetes. El solar de la Unidad C3 contaba con un área de actividad de mujer(es); contenía un hogar doméstico y dos cuencos rituales para el *tiniyaaya niça*, un ritual zapoteco de adivinación con agua (Figura 5.15).

El Área B

El Área B (capítulos 15-21) se encuentra en el margen sur de la loma. Allí los aldeanos de la época San José habían convirtido una pendiente natural en una serie de terrazas artificiales para acomodar sus casas. Las terrazas se crearon cortando la roca madre con hachas de piedra metamórfica. Algunas casas constaban de pequeños canales de desagüe e incluso con cisternas en la roca madre. Esto significa que tres de las características de la ciudad de Monte Albán – terrazas residenciales, desagües y depósitos subterráneos de agua – existían en San José Mogote 500 años antes de la fundación de Monte Albán.

La unidad doméstica más extensivamente investigada en el Área B fue la Casa 16/17, la cual consistía en dos estructuras. La Casa 17 era una residencia bien construida de esquinas perfectamente escuadradas y un grueso lechado de cal sobre las paredes de bajareque. La "Casa 16" era en realidad un cobertizo o área de trabajo techada, probablemente agregada a la Casa 17 como se muestra en la Figura 18.2. Este cobertizo contenía un hogar para calentar el pedernal, haciéndolo más maleable. Este tratamiento era necesario porque los ocupantes se dedicaban a la manufactura de lanzas bifaciales de pedernal y calcedonia. Se encontraron lascas de todas las etapas de trabajo en la "Casa 16", en el solar al norte de la casa y descartadas en un gran foso de basura aledaño a la casa.

Otras artesanías de la Casa 16/17 eran la cestería, que se hacía con largas agujas de hueso; la manufactura de ornamentos de madreperla y la producción de alfarería moldeada. Cuidadosamente escondidas bajo el piso de la Casa 17, se encontraron dos instrumentos de piedra que pueden haber sido usados para alisar la madera.

La Casa 16/17 perteneció aparentemente a una familia de alto rango. Una mujer enterrada bajo el piso tenía dos orejeras y tres cuentas de jade. Otra orejera de jade, más grande y elegante, fue encontrada en la "Casa 16". La residencia también contenía máscaras de cerámica, una espina de mantarraya y vasijas importadas de la Cuenca de México, la Costa del Golfo y el Valle de Tehuacán. El consumo de venado aparentemente fue mayor en comparación a la mayoría de las casas de esta época.

Bajo el piso de la "Casa 16", aparentemente en un área de actividad de mujer(es), se encontraron cuatros figurillas enterradas en forma de una escena ritual (Figura 18.21). Tres de las figurillas se encontraron extendidas, con los brazos cruzados sobre el pecho en una posición de subordinación. La cuarta figurilla estaba en posición de autoridad, sedente encima de las otras tres, con las manos sobre las rodillas. Esta escena (Elemento 63) nos recuerda que muchas figurillas servían para formar escenas que propiciaban la comunicación ritual con los antepasados. Sin embargo, pocas figurillas quedaron en su lugar original, negando a los arqueólogos muchos datos.

Bajo el piso de la Casa 17 se encontraron los restos de otra casa, casi seguramente una etapa más antigua de la misma. Es interesante que esta etapa previa carecía de evidencias de producción de lanzas bifaciales; aparentemente esta especialidad artesanal se originó en la etapa final de la Casa 17.

El Montículo 1

El punto geográfico más prominente de San José Mogote fue el Montículo 1, una colina natural modificada que dominaba el resto de la aldea. La colina original parece haber tenido un diámetro de 70 m y una altura de 12 m. La población prehistórica aumentó la altura otros 3 m al levantar varias construcciones, principalmente edificios públicos.

En el extremo este de la cima apareció una residencia de la época San José, la Casa 13 (capítulo 22). Era de bajareque y medía aproximadamente 3 × 5 m. Su hechura era relativamente pobre, con pilotes delgados y sin lechada de cal como recubrimiento. El inventario de artefactos asociados a esta casa incluye agujas de hueso para coser, numerosos vestigios de mica y seis pedazos de mineral de hierro. Los ocupantes fueron modestos productores de ornamentos de ostra espinosa (*Spondylus*) y almeja de agua dulce, una artesanía también documentada en el Área A. (Un estudio de escalamiento multidimensional realizado por Robert Reynolds [capítulo 25] indica que, según su inventario, la Casa 13 puede considerarse como parte del Área A.)

La mayoría de las construcciones localizadas en la cima del Montículo 1 eran edificios públicos; la primera fue una "Casa de Varones" de la época San José. Durante la época Rosario, se construyeron grandes plataformas de mampostería de piedra y barro (Estructuras 14 y 19) y un importante templo sobre una plataforma de adobes y relleno (Estructura 28). La información sobre estos edificios públicos de la época Rosario será presentada en un futuro volumen sobre la cosmología, religión e iconografía de San José Mogote.

En los últimos días de su historia, el templo de la Estructura 28 había sido escenario de un fuerte incendio que lo destruyó, dejando muchas vigas carbonizadas y miles de fragmentos de recubrimiento de barro vitrificado. Según una muestra de carbón tomada de una de dichas vigas, esto ocurrió alrededor de 600 a.C. (sin calibración). Lo más probable es que el incendio haya sido el resultado de una incursión bélica ordenada por un jefe rival.

Después de la destrucción de este templo principal, los líderes de San José Mogote levantaron uno nuevo (Estructura 37) hacia el norte. Sobre las ruinas de la Estructura 28, erigieron una serie de residencias para familias de alto rango. La primera de ellas fue la Estructura 27, desafortunadamente dañada por la erosión después de su abandono. La segunda residencia de la elite nos permitió conocer mejor su planta original, aunque la erosión la había dividido en tres partes, denominadas Estructuras 25, 26, y 30. Parece que originalmente consistió en una serie de cuartos alrededor de un patio interior (capítulo 23).

El complejo habitacional del lado oeste, llamado Estructura 26, era el más completo; sus muros eran de adobes cuadrangulares sobre cimientos de piedras levemente trabajadas. En su esquina sureste apareció el Cuarto 1, una unidad de almacenamiento de 1.7 m², hundido más de un metro bajo el nivel del patio. Abandonadas en el Cuarto 1, había cinco vasijas que tal vez fueron usadas para agasajar huéspedes o ejecutar ciertos ritos. La vasija más interesante es un incensario antromorfo que representa la primera etapa de una larga tradición zapoteca: el incensario efigie usado para comunicarse con los antepasados nobles, el cual envía una columna de incienso hacia las nubes, lugar en donde se suponía que moraban estos seres (Figura 23.11).

Aplanado bajo una de las paredes del Cuarto 2 de la misma Estructura 26, se encontró el esqueleto de una mujer adulta, al parecer incorporado al edificio como ofrenda sacrificial. Bajo el piso del Cuarto 3, se encontró el entierro de una mujer de alto rango, con deformación craneal tabular y una ofrenda compuesta por tres ornamentos de jade.

Abajo del patio interior de la residencia, formada por Estucturas 25, 26 y 30, salió a la luz la tumba más grande de la época Rosario. Con 3 m de largo y casi 2 m de ancho, era de mampostería de piedra y presentó dos secciones: una cámara principal y una antecámara más pequeña. Su piso era de lajas de esquisto. Denominada Tumba 10, representa el primer ejemplo que conocemos de otra larga tradición zapoteca: la tumba de dos cámaras, enterrada bajo el patio de una residencia de elite.

La Tumba 10 parece haber sido vaciada a fines de la época Rosario, un momento en el cual San José Mogote se abandonó casi totalmente (ver abajo). Casi todos los huesos humanos y las ofrendas fueron removidos y llevados por los residentes cuando abandonaron el lugar. Pasaron por alto algunas cosas pequeñas debido a que estaban escondidas en un depósito de ocre rojo. Dentro del ocre aparecieron la rótula de un esqueleto y una ofrenda de 11 puntas de átlatl hechas de obsidiana negra-verdosa.

Otros objetos interesantes que estaban asociados a las residencias de elite eran sangradores de obsidiana (algunos tallados en forma de espina de mantarraya) y silbatos-efigie de cerámica gris. Los silbatos, que emiten un sonido muy agudo (como el silbato de un árbitro) estaban perforados para llevarse suspendidos en el cuello. En Mesoamérica, fueron utilizados silbatos estridentes de este tipo para dirigir a los guerreros en combate. La combinación de finos sangradores, puntas de átlatl y silbatos nos hace sospechar que el jefe que vivió en el complejo Estructura 25/26/30 era un líder, tanto en las actividades de carácter ritual como en la protección militar de la comunidad.

El abandono de San José Mogote y la fundación de Monte Albán

A fines de la época Rosario, la población del Valle de Oaxaca se encontraba dividida en tres sociedades de jefatura de tamaño desigual: (1) una entidad mayor en el subvalle de Etla (2,000 personas), encabezada por San José Mogote, (2) una entidad en el Valle Grande (700-1,000 personas), encabezada por San Martín Tilcajete y (3) una entidad en el subvalle de Tlacolula (700-1,000 personas), encabezada por Yegüih. Estas tres entidades se hallaban separadas por una "tierra de nadie" (o zona de exclusión) de 80 km², cuyo punto de referencia más prominente era el cerro que hoy día se conoce como Monte Albán.

Alrededor de 500 a.C. (sin calibración), San José Mogote – la comunidad más grande del valle durante más de 800 años – perdió posiblemente el 95% de su población. No fue San José Mogote la única aldea en perder población; según nuestros colegas del proyecto "Patrones de Asentamiento del Valle de Oaxaca", la mitad de las aldeas de la época Rosario cuya ocupación *no* continuó en el siguiente período puede encontrarse en la parte sur del subvalle de Etla, o sea, en la parte controlada por los jefes de San José Mogote (capítulo 24).

Simultáneamente, se produjo una rápida oleada poblacional hacia la antigua "tierra de nadie", sobre todo hacia la cima de Monte Albán. En otras palabras, San José Mogote y sus aldeas subordinadas contribuyeron al menos con 2,000 personas para la fundación de la nueva ciudad de Monte Albán.

Cansados de las incursiones de sus rivales, los jefes de San José Mogote buscaron un cerro que se elevaba 400 m sobre el fondo del valle, donde empezaron a construir 3 km de muros defensivos. Utilizaron esta nueva base para iniciar una campaña bélica contra sus rivales. La guerra duró varios siglos, teniendo como desenlace la destrucción de Tilcajete aproximadamente en 20 a.C., según nuestros colegas Charles Spencer y Elsa Redmond (capítulo 27).

Estudios especiales

El capítulo 25 presenta un análisis escalamiento multidimensional realizado por Robert Reynolds. Utilizando 20 variables (clases de objetos), comparó las 18 casas más extensivamente excavadas pertenecientes a la época San José. Su estudio confirmó la semejanza de actividades dentro de cada barrio de la aldea. Por ejemplo, seis de las casas del Área C (Casas 1, 5, 6, 7, 10 y 14) formaban un grupo aparte; y todas las del Área A (C1-C4), en combinación con la Casa 13 del Montículo 1, formaban otro grupo. Varias casas – por ejemplo, las Casas 2, 4, 9 y 16/17 – resultaron estar estadísticamente aisladas por sus artesanías especiales. Se puede concluir que, aunque cada barrio de San José Mogote mostró cierta uniformidad en términos de actividades, dentro de cada barrio había ciertas familias que desempeñaban una especialidad única.

En el capítulo 26 se presentan dos cronologías del Formativo (*con* y *sin* calibración). La cronología sin calibración facilita las comparaciones con otras regiones de Mesoamérica, donde la mayoría de las fechas radiocarbónicas son del tipo tradicional. La cronología calibrada (la cual produce épocas más largas) nos prepara para una arqueología del futuro, la cual tendría más fechas calibradas.

Conclusiones

No es posible presentar una interpretación definitiva sobre San José Mogote en tanto no sean publicados los futuros volúmenes sobre cosmología, religión, ritual, y costumbres funerarias. Sin embargo, la arqueología de las unidades domésticas ha producido datos que nos permiten evaluar varias teorías y modelos sobre la vida aldeana.

En el Medio Oriente y la costa del Perú, la vida en aldeas empezó antes de la agricultura. En Oaxaca fue todo lo contrario. Después de milenios de agricultura primitiva, las mazorcas de maíz finalmente alcanzaron un tamaño que permitía cosechas de entre 200 y 250 kg por hectárea, así como una vida sedentaria. Entre el 2000 y el 1500 a.C., las primeras aldeas aparecieron junto al Río Atoyac. Sus casas de bajareque eran del tamaño correspondiente a una familia nuclear, cada una con pozos de depósito suficientes para almacenar 1,000 kg de maíz por familia.

La teoría de Raymond Kelly predice que, una vez que una sociedad aldeana ha crecida al punto de estar organizada en segmentos (linajes o grupos de familias con descendencia común), es posible que participe en incursiones bélicas de vez en cuando. Esta teoría parece ser confirmada por las palizadas defensivas y las casas quemadas de la época Tierras Largas, además de la presencia de "Casas de Varones", variables todas que reflejan una sociedad segmentada y con conflictos.

Alrededor del 1150 a.C., San José Mogote alcanzó rápidamente unas 70 hectáreas y empezó a manifestar las características propias de una sociedad de jefatura. Su crecimiento se debe, con toda probabilidad, a los intentos de los jefes de San José Mogote de concentrar a toda la gente posible en una aldea grande, tanto para fortalecerse contra sus vecinos, como para tener muchos artesanos bajo su control. Durante la época San José, aumentó dramáticamente la importación de obsidiana, concha madreperla, ostra espinosa (*Spondylus*) y almeja de agua dulce; la exportación de espejos de mineral de hierro; y el uso de materias primas del valle como la mica, el ocre y la hematita.

Varias artesanías de la época San José presentan datos que fortalecen modelos teóricos aplicados con frecuencia a la economía de sociedades de jefatura. Se ha propuesto, por ejemplo, que en jefaturas "simples" (las de sólo dos niveles de administración), la distancia entre la residencia del jefe y el límite de su control sobre los recursos locales es normalmente el viaje de un día. A este propósito, los yacimientos de mineral de hierro más importantes para la fabricación de espejos se encontraban a 27 km al norte y 33 km al sur de San José Mogote – el viaje de un día en ambos casos –. Pedazos de mineral de hierro detectados en la superficie de pequeñas aldeas en el camino entre San José Mogote y los yacimientos, sugieren que algunas comunidades subordinadas entregaron magnetita al centro señorial en calidad de tributo.

Durante la época Guadalupe, dos centros señoriales rivales – Huitzo en el norte y Tilcajete en el sur – parecen haber limitado el acceso a los yacimientos de mineral de hierro, con lo cual se terminó la producción de espejos en San José Mogote. Como fue mencionado previamente, Guadalupe fue una época durante la cual San José Mogote tuvo que luchar por mantener el control sobre sus aldeas subordinadas. Una aldea que se mantuvo subordinada fue Fábrica San José. La existencia de lujosos entierros de mujeres en Fábrica San José sugiere que *la hipogamía* – la costumbre de enviar mujeres de alto rango desde San José Mogote hasta Fábrica San José para casarse con los líderes locales – reforzó la dominación del centro señorial.

Durante la época Rosario, San José Mogote recuperó mucho de su poder político; sin embargo, tuvo que luchar constantemente con sociedades rivales en otras partes del valle. Su arquitectura, su cerámica y sus jeroglifos muestran que la sociedad Rosario se estaba convirtiendo en el verdedero antecesor de la sociedad Monte Albán I.

Durante la época Rosario, San José Mogote parece haber sido la cabeza de una jefatura "máxima", o sea, una de tres niveles de administración: (1) un centro señorial de 60-65 ha con varios templos de mampostería de piedra y con una elite ocupando una residencia con patio interior y paredes de adobes; (2) aldeas de 3-5 ha con un solo templo y con un subjefe ocupando una residencia de bajareque y (3) aldeas de 1 ha, sin edificios públicos y miembros de la elite.

Es importante señalar al lector que San José Mogote no tenía la capacidad para convertirse en un estado arcaico. El estado arcaico zapoteco únicamente pudo formarse después de que San José Mogote y sus aldeas subordinadas – un mínimo de 2,000 personas – se apoderaran de la cima de Monte Albán, y después de varios siglos de crecimiento demográfico, alianzas políticas, agricultura intensiva y guerra, lograran derrotar a todos sus rivales y unificar el Valle de Oaxaca. Fue precisamente esta incorporación de tres o cuatro sociedades rivales – contra su voluntad – la que finalmente generó una entidad política mucho mayor que cualquier sociedad de jefatura, o sea, el estado zapoteco encabezado por Monte Albán.

References Cited

Agrinier, Pierre
1989 Mirador-Plumajillo, Chiapas y sus relaciones con cuatro sitios del horizonte olmeca en Veracruz, Chiapas y la costa de Guatemala. *Arqueología* 2:19-36. Mexico.

Ahern, Emily M.
1973 *The Cult of the Dead in a Chinese Village*. Stanford: Stanford University Press.

Anderson, David G.
1994 *The Savannah River Chiefdoms*. Tuscaloosa: University of Alabama Press.

Balkansky, Andrew K.
1998 Urbanism and early state formation in the Huamelulpan Valley of southern Mexico. *Latin American Antiquity* 9:37-67.

Balkansky, Andrew K., S. A. Kowalewski, V. Pérez Rodríguez, T. J. Pluckhahn, C. A. Smith, L. R. Stiver, D. Beliaev, J. F. Chamblee, V. Heredia Espinoza, and R. Santos Pérez
2000 Archaeological survey in the Mixteca Alta of Oaxaca, Mexico. *Journal of Field Archaeology* 27:365-389.

Balkansky, Andrew K., Verónica Pérez Rodríguez, and Stephen A. Kowalewski
2004 Monte Negro and the urban revolution in Oaxaca, Mexico. *Latin American Antiquity* 15:33-60.

Barth, Fredrik
1987 *Cosmologies in the Making: A Generative Approach to Cultural Variation in Inner New Guinea*. Cambridge: Cambridge University Press.

Benz, Bruce F.
2001 Archaeological evidence of teosinte domestication from Guilá Naquitz, Oaxaca. *Proceedings of the National Academy of Sciences* 98(4):2104-2106.

Binford, Lewis R.
1983 *In Pursuit of the Past*. New York: Thames and Hudson.

Blake, Michael, J. E. Clark, B. Voorhies, G. Michaels, M. W. Love, M. E. Pye, A. A. Demarest, and B. Arroyo
1995 Radiocarbon chronology for the Late Archaic and Formative Periods on the Pacific Coast of southern Mesoamerica. *Ancient Mesoamerica* 6:161-183.

Blanton, Richard E.
1978 *Monte Albán: Settlement Patterns at the Ancient Zapotec Capital*. New York: Academic Press.

Borhegyi, Stephan F. de
1961 Shark teeth, stingray spines, and shark fishing in ancient Mexico and Central America. *Southwestern Journal of Anthropology* 17(3):273-296.

Buck, Peter H.
1949 *The Coming of the Maori*. Wellington, New Zealand: Whitcombe and Tombs.

Canseco, Alonso de
1580[1905] Relación de Tlacolula y Mitla hecha en los días 12 y 23 de agosto respectivamente. In *Papeles de Nueva España*, Segunda Serie, Geografía y Estadística, Vol. 4, edited by Francisco del Paso y Troncoso, pp. 144-154. Madrid: Est. Tipográfico "Sucesores de Rivadeneyra."

Cárdenas Valencia, Francisco de
1639[1937] Relación historial eclesiástica de la provincia de Yucatán de la Nueva España, escrita el año de 1639. *Biblioteca Histórica Mexicana de Obras Inéditas*, vol. 3. Mexico: Antigua Librería Robredo de Jose Porrúa e Hijos.

Carneiro, Robert L.
1981 The chiefdom: precursor of the state. In *The Transition to Statehood in the New World*, edited by Grant D. Jones and Robert R. Kautz, pp. 37-69. Cambridge: Cambridge University Press.
1987 Further reflections on resource concentration and its role in the rise of the state. In *Studies in the Neolithic and Urban Revolutions: The V. Gordon Childe Colloquium, Mexico, 1986*, edited by L. Manzanilla, pp. 245-260. BAR International Series 349.
1991 The nature of the chiefdom as revealed by evidence from the Cauca Valley of Colombia. In *Profiles in Cultural Evolution: Papers from a Conference in Honor of Elman R. Service*, edited by A. T. Rambo and K. Gillogly, pp. 167-190. Anthropological Papers no. 85, Museum of Anthropology, University of Michigan. Ann Arbor.
2003 *Evolutionism in Cultural Anthropology: A Critical History.* Boulder, CO: Westview Press.

Caso, Alfonso and Ignacio Bernal
1952 *Urnas de Oaxaca.* Memorias del Instituto de Antropología e Historia, no. 2. Mexico.

Caso, Alfonso, Ignacio Bernal, and Jorge R. Acosta
1967 *La Cerámica de Monte Albán.* Memorias del Instituto de Antropología e Historia, no. 13. Mexico.

Clark, J. E.
1991 The beginnings of Mesoamerica: *Apologia* for the Soconusco Early Formative. In *The Formation of Complex Society in Southeastern Mesoamerica*, edited by W. R. Fowler, pp. 13-26. Boca Raton: CRC Press.

Coe, Michael D. and Richard A. Diehl
1980a *In the Land of the Olmec*, vol. 1: *The Archaeology of San Lorenzo Tenochtitlán.* Austin: University of Texas Press.
1980b *In the Land of the Olmec*, vol. 2: *The People of the River.* Austin: University of Texas Press.

Coe, Michael D. and Kent V. Flannery
1967 *Early Cultures and Human Ecology in South Coastal Guatemala.* Smithsonian Contributions to Anthropology, vol. 3. Washington, D.C.

Córdova, Juan de
1578[1942] *Vocabulario en Lengua Zapoteca.* Mexico: Pedro Charte y Antonio Ricardo.

Covarrubias, Miguel
1946 *Mexico South: The Isthmus of Tehuantepec.* New York: Alfred Knopf.

Davidson, Janet M.
1987 *The Prehistory of New Zealand.* Auckland, NZ: Longman Paul.

de la Fuente, Julio
1949 *Yalálag: Una Villa Zapoteca Serrana.* Museo Nacional de Antropología. Serie Científica 1. México, D.F.

Demand, Nancy H.
1990 *Urban Relocation in Archaic and Classical Greece: Flight and Consolidation.* Norman: University of Oklahoma Press.

Drennan, Robert D.
1976a *Fábrica San José and Middle Formative Society in the Valley of Oaxaca.* Prehistory and Human Ecology of the Valley of Oaxaca, vol. 4, edited by Kent V. Flannery. Memoirs no. 8, Museum of Anthropology, University of Michigan. Ann Arbor.
1976b A refinement of chronological seriation using nonmetric multidimensional scaling. *American Antiquity* 41(3):290-302.

Drucker, Philip, Robert F. Heizer, and Robert J. Squier
1959 *Excavations at La Venta, Tabasco, 1955.* Smithsonian Institution Bureau of American Ethnology, Bulletin 170. Washington, D.C.: U.S. Government Printing Office.

Espíndola, Nicolas de
1580[1905] Relación de Chichicapa y su partido. In *Papeles de Nueva España*, Segunda Serie, Geografía y Estadística, vol. 4, edited by Francisco del Paso y Troncoso, pp. 115-143. Madrid: Est. Tipográfico "Sucesores de Rivadeneyra."

Evans, B. J.
1975 Appendix II: Mössbauer spectroscopy. In *Formative Mesoamerican Exchange Networks, with special reference to the Valley of Oaxaca*, by Jane Pires-Ferreira, pp. 87-101. Memoirs no. 7, Museum of Anthropology, University of Michigan. Ann Arbor.

Felger, Richard Stephen and Mary Beck Moser
1985 *People of the Desert and the Sea: Ethnobotany of the Seri Indians.* Tucson: University of Arizona Press.

Fernández Dávila, Enrique
1997 San José Mogote, Etla. *Arqueología Mexicana* V(26):18-23.

Flannery, Kent V.
1967 Vertebrate fauna and hunting patterns. In *The Prehistory of the Tehuacán Valley*, vol. 1: *Environment and Subsistence*, edited by Douglas S. Byers, pp. 132-177. Austin: University of Texas Press.
1968 The Olmec and the Valley of Oaxaca: A model for inter-regional interaction in Formative times. In *Dumbarton Oaks Conference on the Olmec*, edited by Elizabeth P. Benson, pp. 79-110. Washington, D.C.: Dumbarton Oaks.
1972 The cultural evolution of civilizations. *Annual Review of Ecology and Systematics* 3:399-426.
1976a Empirical determination of site catchments in Oaxaca and Tehuacán. In *The Early Mesoamerican Village*, edited by Kent V. Flannery, pp. 103-117. New York: Academic Press.
1976b Contextual analysis of ritual paraphernalia from Formative Oaxaca. In *The Early Mesoamerican Village*, edited by Kent V. Flannery, pp. 333-345. New York: Academic Press.
1983 Precolumbian farming in the valleys of Oaxaca, Nochixtlán, Tehuacán, and Cuicatlán: a comparative study. In *The Cloud People: Divergent Evolution of the Zapotec and Mixtec Civilizations*, edited by Kent V. Flannery and Joyce Marcus, pp. 323-339. New York: Academic Press.

1986a Ground-stone artifacts. In *Guilá Naquitz: Archaic Foraging and Early Agriculture in Oaxaca, Mexico*, edited by Kent V. Flannery, pp. 147-156. Orlando: Academic Press.
1986b Food procurement area and preceramic diet at Guilá Naquitz. In *Guilá Naquitz: Archaic Foraging and Early Agriculture in Oaxaca, Mexico*, edited by Kent V. Flannery, pp. 303-317. Orlando: Academic Press.
1986c Artifacts of wood and related materials. In *Guilá Naquitz: Archaic Foraging and Early Agriculture in Oaxaca, Mexico*, edited by Kent V. Flannery, pp. 163-168. Orlando: Academic Press.

Flannery, Kent V. (editor)
1976 *The Early Mesoamerican Village*. New York: Academic Press.
1986 *Guilá Naquitz: Archaic Foraging and Early Agriculture in Oaxaca, Mexico*. Orlando: Academic Press.

Flannery, Kent V. and Joyce Marcus
1976a Evolution of the public building in Formative Oaxaca. In *Cultural Change and Continuity*, edited by Charles E. Cleland, pp. 205-221. New York: Academic Press.
1976b Formative Oaxaca and the Zapotec cosmos. *American Scientist* 64:374-383.
1990 Borrón, y cuenta nueva: setting Oaxaca's archaeological record straight. In *Debating Oaxaca Archaeology*, edited by Joyce Marcus, pp 17-69. Anthropological Papers no. 84, Museum of Anthropology, University of Michigan. Ann Arbor.
1994 *Early Formative Pottery of the Valley of Oaxaca*. Memoirs no. 27, Museum of Anthropology, University of Michigan. Ann Arbor.
2000 Formative Mexican chiefdoms and the myth of the "mother culture." *Journal of Anthropological Archaeology* 19:1-37.
2003 The origin of war: new ^{14}C dates from ancient Mexico. *Proceedings of the National Academy of Sciences* 100(20):11801-11805.

Flannery, Kent V. and Joyce Marcus (editors)
1983 *The Cloud People: Divergent Evolution of the Zapotec and Mixtec Civilizations*. New York: Academic Press.

Flannery, Kent V., Chris L. Moser, and Silvia Maranca
1986 The excavation of Guilá Naquitz. In *Guilá Naquitz: Archaic Foraging and Early Agriculture in Oaxaca, Mexico*, edited by Kent V. Flannery, pp. 65-95. Orlando: Academic Press.

Flannery, Kent V. and C. Earle Smith, Jr.
1983 Monte Albán IV foodstuffs in Guilá Naquitz Cave. In *The Cloud People: Divergent Evolution of the Zapotec and Mixtec Civilizations*, edited by Kent V. Flannery and Joyce Marcus, p. 206. New York: Academic Press.

Flannery, Kent V. and Ronald Spores
1983 Excavated sites of the Oaxaca Preceramic. In *The Cloud People: Divergent Evolution of the Zapotec and Mixtec Civilizations*, edited by Kent V. Flannery and Joyce Marcus, pp. 20-26. New York: Academic Press.

Flannery, Kent V. and Jane Wheeler
1986a Animal food remains from Preceramic Guilá Naquitz. In *Guilá Naquitz: Archaic Foraging and Early Agriculture in Oaxaca, Mexico*, edited by Kent V. Flannery, pp. 285-295. Orlando: Academic Press.
1986b Comparing the Preceramic and modern microfauna. In *Guilá Naquitz: Archaic Foraging and Early Agriculture in Oaxaca, Mexico*, edited by Kent V. Flannery, pp. 239-246. Orlando: Academic Press.
n.d. Faunal remains from Cueva Blanca (unpublished manuscript).

Ford, Richard I.
1976 Appendix XIII: Carbonized plant remains. In *Fábrica San José and Middle Formative Society in the Valley of Oaxaca*, by Robert D. Drennan, pp. 261-268. Memoirs no. 8, Museum of Anthropology, University of Michigan. Ann Arbor.

Fox, Aileen
1976 *Prehistoric Maori Fortifications in the North Island of New Zealand*. Auckland, NZ: Longman Paul.

Garfinkel, Yosef
2003 *Dancing at the Dawn of Agriculture*. Austin: University of Texas Press.

Gilmore, Melvin R.
1934 The Arikara method of preparing a dog for a feast. *Papers of the Michigan Academy of Science, Arts and Letters* 19:37-38.

Goldman, Irving
1963 *The Cubeo Indians of the Northwest Amazon*. Urbana, IL: University of Illinois Press.

Gordus, A. A., W. C. Fink, M. E. Hill, J. C. Purdy, and T. R. Wilcox
1967 Identification of the geologic origins of archaeological artifacts: an automated method of Na and Mn neutron activation analysis. *Archaeometry* 10:87-96.

Grove, David C.
1974 *San Pablo, Nexpa, and the Early Formative Archaeology of Morelos, Mexico*. Vanderbilt University Publications in Anthropology, no. 12. Nashville, Tennessee.
1984 *Chalcatzingo: Excavations on the Olmec Frontier*. London: Thames and Hudson.

Hall, D. W., G. A. Haswell, and T. A. Oxley
1956 *Underground Storage of Grain*. British Colonial Office, Pest Information Laboratory, Department of Scientific and Industrial Research. London: H. M. Stationery Office.

Harris, Edward C.
1975 The stratigraphic sequence: a question of time. *World Archaeology* 7:109-121.
1979 *Principles of Archaeological Stratigraphy*. New York: Academic Press.

Hawkes, Kristen
1990 Why do men hunt? Benefits for risky choices. In *Risk and Uncertainty in Tribal and Peasant Economies*, edited by Elizabeth Cashdan, pp. 145-166. Boulder: Westview Press.

Hawkes, Kristen, James F. O'Connell, and N. G. Blurton-Jones
1997 Hadza women's time allocation, offspring provisioning, and the evolution of post-menopausal lifespans. *Current Anthropology* 38:551-578.

Hodges, Denise C.

1989 *Agricultural Intensification and Prehistoric Health in the Valley of Oaxaca, Mexico.* Memoirs no. 22, Museum of Anthropology, University of Michigan. Ann Arbor.

Hole, Frank
1986 Chipped-stone tools. In *Guilá Naquitz: Archaic Foraging and Early Agriculture in Oaxaca, Mexico,* edited by Kent V. Flannery, pp. 97-139. Orlando: Academic Press.

Hole, Frank, Kent V. Flannery, and James A. Neely
1969 *Prehistory and Human Ecology of the Deh Luran Plain.* Memoirs no. 1, Museum of Anthropology, University of Michigan. Ann Arbor.

Kaplan, Lawrence and Thomas F. Lynch
1999 *Phaseolus* (Fabaceae) in archaeology: AMS radiocarbon dates and their significance for pre-colombian agriculture. *Economic Botany* 53(2):261-272.

Keeley, Lawrence H.
1996 *War Before Civilization.* New York: Oxford University Press.

Keen, Angeline Myra
1958 *Sea Shells of Tropical West America.* Stanford: Stanford University Press.

Kelly, Raymond C.
2000 *Warless Societies and the Origin of War.* Ann Arbor: The University of Michigan Press.

King, Mary Elizabeth
1986 Preceramic cordage and basketry from Guilá Naquitz. In *Guilá Naquitz: Archaic Foraging and Early Agriculture in Oaxaca, Mexico,* edited by Kent V. Flannery, pp. 157-161. Orlando: Academic Press.

Kirkby, Anne V. T.
1973 *The Use of Land and Water Resources in the Past and Present Valley of Oaxaca, Mexico.* Prehistory and Human Ecology of the Valley of Oaxaca, vol. 1, edited by Kent V. Flannery. Memoirs no. 5, Museum of Anthropology, University of Michigan. Ann Arbor.
1974 Individual and community responses to rainfall variability in Oaxaca, Mexico. In *Natural Hazards: Local, Regional, and Global,* edited by Gilbert F. White, pp. 119-128. New York: Oxford University Press.

Kirkby, Michael J., Anne V. Whyte, and Kent V. Flannery
1986 The physical environment of the Guilá Naquitz cave group. In *Guilá Naquitz: Archaic Foraging and Early Agriculture in Oaxaca, Mexico,* edited by Kent V. Flannery, pp. 43-61. Orlando: Academic Press.

Kopytoff, Igor
1971 Ancestors as elders in Africa. *Africa* 41(2):129-141.

Kowalewski, Stephen A., Gary M. Feinman, Laura Finsten, Richard E. Blanton, and Linda M. Nicholas
1989 *Monte Albán's Hinterland, Part II: The Prehispanic Settlement Patterns in Tlacolula, Etla, and Ocotlán, the Valley of Oaxaca, Mexico.* Memoirs no. 23, Museum of Anthropology, University of Michigan. Ann Arbor.

Lambert, Wayne
1972 *Petrographic Study of Thin Sections L-3346 (Atoyac Gris Fine Ceramic Type, Tlapacoya) and L-3345 (Delfina Fine Gray Ceramic Type, Oaxaca).* Report sent jointly to Christine Niederberger and Kent V. Flannery.

LeBlanc, Steven A. with Katherine E. Register
2003 *Constant Battles: The Myth of the Noble Savage.* New York: St. Martin's Press.

Lees, Susan
1973 *Sociopolitical Aspects of Canal Irrigation in the Valley of Oaxaca, Mexico.* Prehistory and Human Ecology of the Valley of Oaxaca, vol. 2, edited by Kent V. Flannery. Memoirs no. 6, Museum of Anthropology, University of Michigan. Ann Arbor.

Leopold, Aldo Starker
1959 *Wildlife of Mexico: The Game Birds and Mammals.* Berkeley: University of California Press.

Lesure, Richard G.
1999 Figurines as representations and products at Paso de la Amada, Mexico. *Cambridge Archaeological Journal* 9(2):209-220.

Lingoes, James C.
1973 *The Guttman-Lingoes Nonmetric Program Series.* Ann Arbor: Mathesis Press.

Lorenzo, José Luis
1958 Un sitio precerámico en Yanhuitlán, Oaxaca. *Instituto Nacional de Antropología e Historia, Dirección Prehistoria, Publicación* 6. México, D.F.
1960 Aspectos físicos del Valle de Oaxaca. *Revista Mexicana de Estudios Antropológicos* 16:49-63.

Lothrop, Samuel K.
1937 *Coclé. Part 1: An Archaeological Study of Central Panama.* Peabody Museum of Archaeology and Ethnology Memoirs, no. 7. Cambridge, MA: Harvard University.

Lowe, Gareth W.
1959 *Archaeological Exploration of the Upper Grijalva River, Chiapas, Mexico.* Papers of the New World Archaeological Foundation, no. 2. Provo: Brigham Young University.

Lowry, R. B., G. C. Robinson, and J. R. Miller
1966 Hereditary ectodermal dysplasia. Symptoms, inheritance patterns, differential diagnosis, management. *Clinical Pediatrics* 5(7):395-402. Philadelphia.

McIntosh, Roderick J. and Susan Keech McIntosh
1979 Terracotta statuettes from Mali. *African Arts* 12(2):51-91.

MacNeish, Richard S.
1954 An early archaeological site near Pánuco, Veracruz. *Transactions of the American Philosophical Society* 44 (5):539-641. Philadelphia.

MacNeish, Richard S., Melvin Fowler, Angel García Cook, Frederick Peterson, Antoinette Nelken-Terner, and James A. Neely
1972 *The Prehistory of the Tehuacán Valley,* vol. 5: *Excavations and Reconnaissance.* Austin: University of Texas Press.

MacNeish, Richard S., Antoinette Nelken-Terner, and Irmgard W. Johnson
1967   *The Prehistory of the Tehuacán Valley,* vol. 2: *Nonceramic Artifacts.* Austin: University of Texas Press.

MacNeish, Richard S., Frederick A. Peterson, and Kent V. Flannery
1970   *The Prehistory of the Tehuacán Valley,* vol. 3: *Ceramics.* Austin: University of Texas Press.

Marcus, Joyce
1983a   The Espiridión complex and the origins of the Oaxacan Formative. In *The Cloud People: Divergent Evolution of the Zapotec and Mixtec Civilizations,* edited by Kent V. Flannery and Joyce Marcus, pp. 42-43. New York: Academic Press.
1983b   Lowland Maya archaeology at the crossroads. *American Antiquity* 48:454-488.
1989   Zapotec chiefdoms and the nature of Formative religions. In *Regional Perspectives on the Olmec,* edited by Robert J. Sharer and David C. Grove, pp. 148-197. School of American Research Advanced Seminar. Cambridge: Cambridge University Press.
1992a   *Mesoamerican Writing Systems.* Princeton, NJ: Princeton University Press.
1992b   Dynamic cycles of Mesoamerican states. *National Geographic Research & Exploration* 8:392-411.
1993   Ancient Maya political organization. In *Lowland Maya Civilization in the Eighth Century A.D.,* edited by Jeremy A. Sabloff and John Henderson, pp. 111-183. Washington, D.C.: Dumbarton Oaks.
1998a   *Women's Ritual in Formative Oaxaca: Figurine-making, Divination, Death and the Ancestors.* Memoirs no. 33, Museum of Anthropology, University of Michigan. Ann Arbor.
1998b   The peaks and valleys of ancient states: an extension of the dynamic model. In *Archaic States,* edited by Gary M. Feinman and Joyce Marcus, pp. 59-94. School of American Research Advanced Seminar. Santa Fe, NM: SAR Press.
1999   Men's and women's ritual in Formative Oaxaca. In *Social Patterns in Pre-Classic Mesoamerica,* edited by David C. Grove and Rosemary A. Joyce, pp. 67-96. Washington, D.C.: Dumbarton Oaks.

Marcus, Joyce and Kent V. Flannery
1994   Ancient Zapotec ritual and religion: an application of the direct historical approach. In *The Ancient Mind,* edited by Colin Renfrew and Ezra B. W. Zubrow, pp. 55-74. Cambridge: Cambridge University Press.
1996   *Zapotec Civilization: How Urban Society Evolved in Mexico's Oaxaca Valley.* New York: Thames and Hudson.

Messer, Ellen
1978   *Zapotec Plant Knowledge: Classification, Uses, and Communication About Plants in Mitla, Oaxaca, Mexico.* Prehistory and Human Ecology of the Valley of Oaxaca, vol. 5, part 2. Memoirs no. 10, Museum of Anthropology, University of Michigan. Ann Arbor.

Mudar, Karen
n.d.   A discussion of the stingless honeybee and the hairless dog in Mesoamerica. Unpublished manuscript.

Munsell Color Company
1954   *Munsell Soil Color Charts.* Baltimore: Munsell Color Co.

Newell, William H.
1976   Good and bad ancestors. In *Ancestors,* edited by William H. Newell, pp. 17-29. The Hague and Paris: Mouton.

Nicholas, Linda M.
1989   Land use in prehispanic Oaxaca. In *Monte Albán's Hinterland, Part II: The Prehispanic Settlement Patterns in Tlacolula, Etla, and Ocotlán, the Valley of Oaxaca, Mexico,* by Stephen Kowalewski et al., vol. 1, pp. 449-505. Memoirs no. 23, Museum of Anthropology, University of Michigan. Ann Arbor.

Niederberger, Christine
1987   *Paléopaysages et Archéologie Pré-urbaine du Bassin de Mexique.* Etudes Mésoamericaines 11, Mexico.

O'Connell, James F., K. Hawkes, K. Lupo, and N. G. Blurton-Jones
2002   Male strategies and Plio-Pleistocene archaeology. *Journal of Human Evolution* 43:831-872.

Paddock, John
1966   Oaxaca in ancient Mesoamerica. In *Ancient Oaxaca,* edited by John Paddock, pp. 83-242. Stanford: Stanford University Press.

Parry, William
1987   *Chipped Stone Tools in Formative Oaxaca, Mexico: Their Procurement, Production and Use.* Memoirs no. 20, Museum of Anthropology, University of Michigan. Ann Arbor.

Payne, William O.
1994   The raw materials and pottery-making techniques of Early Formative Oaxaca: an introduction. In *Early Formative Pottery of the Valley of Oaxaca,* by Kent V. Flannery and Joyce Marcus, pp. 7-20. Memoirs no. 27, Museum of Anthropology, University of Michigan. Ann Arbor.

Piperno, Dolores and Kent V. Flannery
2001   The earliest archaeological maize (*Zea mays* L.) from highland Mexico: new accelerator mass spectrometry dates and their implications. *Proceedings of the National Academy of Sciences* 98(4):2101-2103.

Pires-Ferreira, Jane W.
1975   *Formative Mesoamerican Exchange Networks, with Special Reference to the Valley of Oaxaca.* Memoirs no. 7, Museum of Anthropology, University of Michigan. Ann Arbor.

Plog, Stephen
1976   Measurement of prehistoric interaction between communities. In *The Early Mesoamerican Village,* edited by Kent V. Flannery, pp. 255-272. New York: Academic Press.
n.d.   *The Measurement of Prehistoric Human Interaction.* Undergraduate honors thesis in the Department of Anthropology, University of Michigan, Ann Arbor.

Pyne, Nanette
1976   The fire-serpent and were-jaguar in Formative Oaxaca: a contingency table analysis. In *The Early Mesoamerican Village,* edited by Kent V. Flannery, pp. 272-280. New York: Academic Press.

Ramírez Urrea, Susana
1993 *Hacienda Blanca: Una Aldea a través del tiempo en el Valle de Etla, Oaxaca.* Tesis de la Escuela de Antropología, Universidad de Guadalajara, Mexico.

Rappaport, Roy A.
1979 *Ecology, Meaning, and Religion.* Richmond, CA: North Atlantic Books.

Redmond, Elsa M.
1994 *Tribal and Chiefly Warfare in South America.* Studies in Latin American Ethnohistory & Archaeology, vol. 5, edited by Joyce Marcus. Memoirs no. 28, Museum of Anthropology, University of Michigan. Ann Arbor.

Renfrew, Colin, J. E. Dixon, and J. R. Cann
1966 Obsidian and early culture contact in the Near East. *Proceedings of the Prehistoric Society* 32:30-72.

Reyment, Richard and K. G. Jöreskog
1996 *Applied Factor Analysis in the Natural Sciences.* Cambridge: Cambridge University Press.

Reynolds, Robert G.
1986 An adaptive computer model for the evolution of plant collecting and early agriculture in the eastern Valley of Oaxaca. In *Guilá Naquitz: Archaic Foraging and Early Agriculture in Oaxaca, Mexico*, edited by Kent V. Flannery, pp. 439-500. Orlando: Academic Press.
2000 The impact of raiding on settlement patterns in the northern Valley of Oaxaca: an approach using decision trees. In *Dynamics in Human and Primate Societies: Agent-Based Modeling of Social and Spatial Processes*, edited by Timothy A. Kohler and George J. Gumerman, pp. 251-274. Oxford: Santa Fe Institute.

Sanders, William T.
1974 Chiefdom to state: political evolution at Kaminaljuyu, Guatemala. In *Reconstructing Complex Societies: An Archaeological Colloquium*, edited by Charlotte B. Moore, Supplement to the Bulletin of the American Schools of Oriental Research 20:97-116. Cambridge, MA.

Schmieder, Oscar
1930 *The Settlements of the Tzapotec and Mije Indians, State of Oaxaca, Mexico.* University of California Publications in Geography, vol. 4, pp. 1-184. Berkeley.

Schwartz, Marion
1997 *A History of Dogs in the Early Americas.* New Haven: Yale University Press.

Serra Puche, MariCarmen
1993 *Daily Life: Formative Period in the Basin of Mexico.* Cuernavaca: Floresta Ediciones.

Shepard, Anna
1963 Beginnings of ceramic industrialization: an example from the Oaxaca Valley. *Notes From a Ceramic Laboratory,* no. 2. Washington, D.C.: Carnegie Institution of Washington.

Smith, Bruce
1997 The initial domestication of *Cucurbita pepo* in the Americas 10,000 years ago. *Science* 276:932-934.
2001 Documenting plant domestication: the consilience of biological and archaeological approaches. *Proceedings of the National Academy of Sciences* 98(4):1324-1326.

Smith, C. Earle, Jr.
1978 *The Vegetational History of the Oaxaca Valley.* Prehistory and Human Ecology of the Valley of Oaxaca, vol. 5, part 1. Memoirs no. 10, Museum of Anthropology, University of Michigan. Ann Arbor.

Smith, D. W.
1970 Recognisable patterns in human malformation. *Major Problems in Clinical Pediatrics* 7:176-180.

Smith, Judith E.
1981 Appendix IX: formative botanical remains at Tomaltepec. In *Excavations at Santo Domingo Tomaltepec: Evolution of a Formative Community in the Valley of Oaxaca, Mexico*, by Michael E. Whalen, pp. 186-194. Memoirs no. 12, Museum of Anthropology, University of Michigan. Ann Arbor.

Spence, Michael W., Jerome B. Kimberlin, and Garman Harbottle
1984 State-controlled procurement and the obsidian workshops of Teotihuacan, Mexico. In *Prehistoric Quarries and Lithic Production*, edited by Jonathon E. Ericson and Barbara A. Purdy, pp. 97-105. Cambridge: Cambridge University Press.

Spencer, Charles S.
1990 On the tempo and mode of state formation: neoevolutionism reconsidered. *Journal of Anthropological Archaeology* 9:1-30.
2003 War and early state formation in Oaxaca, Mexico. *Proceedings of the National Academy of Sciences* 100(20):11185-11187.

Spencer, Charles S. and Elsa M. Redmond
2001 Multilevel selection and political evolution in the Valley of Oaxaca, 500-100 B.C. *Journal of Anthropological Archaeology* 20:195-229.
2003 Militarism, resistance, and early state development in Oaxaca, Mexico. *Social Evolution & History* 2(1):25-70.

Speth, John D.
2000 Boiling vs. baking and roasting: a taphonomic approach to the recognition of cooking techniques in small mammals. In *Animal Bones, Human Societies*, edited by Peter Rowley-Conwy, pp. 89-105. Oxford (UK): Oxbow Books.

Spores, Ronald and Kent V. Flannery
1983 Sixteenth-century kinship and social organization. In *The Cloud People: Divergent Evolution of the Zapotec and Mixtec Civilizations*, edited by Kent V. Flannery and Joyce Marcus, pp. 339-342. New York: Academic Press.

SPSS
2003 *SPSS Base 12.0 User's Guide.* Chicago: SPSS Inc.

Stolmaker, Charlotte
1973 *Cultural, Social and Economic Change in Santa María Atzompa.* Ph.D. dissertation, University of California at Los Angeles. Ann Arbor: University Microfilms.

Stuiver, Minze, P. J. Reimer, E. Bard, J. W. Beck, G. S. Burr, K. A. Hughen, B. Kromer, G. McCormac, J. van der Plicht, and M. Spurk
1998   INTCAL98 radiocarbon age calibration, 24,000-0 cal BP. *Radiocarbon* 40(3):1041-1083.

Tolstoy, Paul and André Guénette
1965   Le placement de Tlatilco dans le cadre du Pré-classique du Bassin de Mexico. *Journal de la Société des Américanistes* LIV:47-91.

Tolstoy, Paul and Louise I. Paradis
1970   Early and Middle Preclassic culture in the Basin of Mexico. *Science* 167:344-351.

Vaillant, George C.
1935a *Excavations at El Arbolillo.* Anthropological Papers of the American Museum of Natural History, vol. 35, part 2. New York.
1935b *Early Cultures of the Valley of Mexico: Results of the Stratigraphical Project of the American Museum of Natural History in the Valley of Mexico, 1928-1933.* Anthropological Papers of the American Museum of Natural History, vol. 35, part 3. New York.

Vogt, Evon Z.
1969   *Zinacantan: A Maya Community in the Highlands of Chiapas.* Cambridge: Belknap Press of Harvard University Press.

Wauchope, Robert
1938   *Modern Maya Houses: A Study of their Archaeological Significance.* Carnegie Institution of Washington, Publication 502. Washington, D.C.

Weaver, Muriel Porter
1967   *Tlapacoya Pottery in the Museum Collection.* Indian Notes and Monographs, Miscellaneous Series no. 56. New York: Museum of the American Indian.
1972   *The Aztecs, Maya and their Predecessors.* New York: Seminar Press.

Wendorf, Fred
1968   Site 117: a Nubian Final Paleolithic graveyard near Jebel Sahaba, Sudan. In *Prehistory of Nubia,* vol. 2, edited by Fred Wendorf, pp. 954-995. Dallas: Southern Methodist University.

Whalen, Michael
1981   *Excavations at Santo Domingo Tomaltepec: Evolution of a Formative Community in the Valley of Oaxaca, Mexico.* Prehistory and Human Ecology of the Valley of Oaxaca, vol. 4. Memoirs no. 12., Museum of Anthropology, University of Michigan. Ann Arbor.
1986   Sources of the Guilá Naquitz chipped stone. In *Guilá Naquitz: Archaic Foraging and Early Agriculture in Oaxaca, Mexico,* edited by Kent V. Flannery, pp. 141-146. New York: Academic Press.

White, Christine D., Michael W. Spence, F. J. Longstaffe, and K. R. Law
2000   Testing the nature of Teotihuacán imperialism at Kaminaljuyú using phosphate oxygen-isotope ratios. *Journal of Anthropological Research* 56:535-558.

Whitecotton, Joseph
1977   *The Zapotecs: Princes, Priests, and Peasants.* Norman: University of Oklahoma Press.

Williams, Howel and Robert F. Heizer
1965   Geological notes on the ruins of Mitla and other Oaxacan sites, Mexico. *Contributions of the University of California Archaeological Research Facility* 1:41-54.

Winter, Marcus C.
1972   *Tierras Largas: A Formative Community in the Valley of Oaxaca.* Unpublished dissertation, University of Arizona, Tucson.

Wright, Henry T.
1984   Prestate political formations. In *On the Evolution of Complex Societies: Essays in Honor of Harry Hoijer,* edited by Timothy K. Earle, pp. 41-77. Malibu: Undena Press.

Wright, Norman P.
1960   *El Enigma del Xoloitzcuintli.* México, D.F.: Instituto Nacional de Antropología e Historia.

Zárate, Bartolomé de
1581[1905] Relación de Guaxilotitlán. In *Papeles de Nueva España, Segunda Serie, Geografía y Estadística,* vol. 4, edited by Francisco del Paso y Troncoso, pp. 196-205. Madrid: Est. Tipográfico "Sucesores de Rivadeneyra."

Index